National Strategies for Regional Integration
South and East Asian Case Studies

Edited by

Joseph Francois, Pradumna B. Rana,
and Ganeshan Wignaraja

Asian Development Bank

A Co-publication of the Asian Development Bank and Anthem Press

Anthem Press
www.anthempress.com

Asian Development Bank
www.adb.org

This edition first published in 2011 by

ANTHEM PRESS
75-76 Blackfriars Road,
London SE1 8HA, UK
or PO Box 9779, London SW19 7ZG, UK
and 244 Madison Ave. #116, New York, NY
10016, USA

and
Asian Development Bank
6 ADB Avenue, Mandaluyong City, 1550
Metro Manila, Philippines

British Library Cataloguing in Publication Data
A catalogue record for this book is available from the British Library.

Library of Congress Cataloging in Publication Data
A catalog record for this book has been requested.

ISBN-13: 978 0 85728 993 3 (Pbk)
ISBN-10: 0 85728 993 4 (Pbk)

Foreword

Asia, a pivotal region in the world economy, is at an important cross-road in its development path. Having successfully integrated into the global economy over the last five decades through outward-oriented development strategies, the region has embarked on a process of closer regional cooperation and integration. Several factors—the spread of production networks, improvements in infrastructure, falling trade barriers, and technological progress—have spurred the process. One key challenge for an interdependent Asia remains how to strengthen and spread the benefits of the process of regional cooperation and integration. An essential element is effective national strategies for regional cooperation and integration.

The way Asian economies develop and implement effective approaches to regional cooperation and integration is insufficiently understood. Using a set of country cases based on a similar framework, the study examines how each country's integration with its neighbors and more distant regional economies might be improved. Five of these cases are from South Asia (India, Pakistan, Bangladesh, Nepal, and Sri Lanka) and three are from East Asia (the People's Republic of China, Thailand, and Singapore). The country cases illustrate the diversity of Asian development experience and offer lessons for other countries and regions interested in developing national strategies to foster regional integration.

The study indicates four important lessons: (i) integrate with a large neighboring economy, (ii) emphasize market orientation in regional strategy, (iii) tailor the policy mix to fit national circumstances, and (iv) involve the private sector in developing regional strategy.

Jong Wha Lee
Head, Office of Regional Economic Integration
Asian Development Bank

Acknowledgments

National Strategies for Regional Integration: South and East Asian Case Studies is a knowledge product of the Office of Regional Economic Integration (OREI) of the Asian Development Bank (ADB). It was prepared by a team of experts led by Ganeshan Wignaraja (Principal Economist, OREI); Joseph Francois (Principal Consultant); and Pradumna B. Rana (former Senior Advisor, OREI and presently Senior Fellow at Nanyang Technological University).

The book, financed by ADB's technical assistance funding program under Regional Technical Assistance 6282 (Study on Economic Cooperation between East Asia and South Asia), was prepared by Sharad Bhandari.

The editors received support from many individuals in ADB. Rosechin Olfindo and Genevieve De Guzman provided excellent research assistance as well as organizational support for the project. Special thanks are due to Muriel Ordoñez, Annette Pelkmans-Balaoing, Hugh Finlay, Erin Prelypchan, Wilhelmina Paz, Ma. Rosario Razon, and Ma. Liza Cruz. We are most grateful to them all.

Useful suggestions were provided by participants at an inception workshop in ADB headquarters on 1–2 June 2006, a finalization workshop in Singapore on 27–28 November 2006, a seminar at ADB headquarters on 5 June 2007, and a seminar in New Delhi on 10 March 2008.

The opinions expressed in the book are those of the authors and do not represent the views of ADB.

Contributors

Suthiphand Chirathivat is Associate Professor at the Department of Economics, Chulalongkorn University in Bangkok, Thailand.

Joseph Francois is Professor at the Department of Economics, Johannes Kepler University Linz, Austria, and the principal consultant for the study.

Ejaz Ghani is Senior Research Economist at the Pakistan Institute of Development Economics in Islamabad, Pakistan.

Binod Karmacharya is Regional Cooperation Advisor of the Asian Development Bank's (ADB) Nepal Resident Mission in Kathmandu, Nepal.

Nagesh Kumar is the Director-General of Research and Information System for Developing Countries in New Delhi, India.

Nephil Maskay is Deputy Director of the Nepal Rastra Bank in Kathmandu, Nepal.

Ramkishen Rajan is Associate Professor at the School of Public Policy, George Mason University in Virginia, USA.

Pradumna B. Rana is Senior Fellow at the Division of Economics, School of Humanities and Social Sciences, Nanyang Technological University in Singapore.

Mohammed Ali Rashid is Associate Professor at the Economics Department, North South University in Dhaka, Bangladesh.

Chayodom Sabhasri is Associate Professor at the Department of Economics and the Director of Economics Research Centre, Chulalongkorn University in Bangkok, Thailand.

Pooja Sharma is a consultant at ADB.

Shandre Mugan Thangavelu is Associate Professor at the Department of Economics and Director of the Singapore Centre for Applied and Policy Economics, National University of Singapore.

Nadeem Ul Haque is Division Chief for the Asian region at the International Monetary Fund Institute. He was formerly the Vice-Chancellor of the Pakistan Institute of Development Economics in Islamabad, Pakistan.

Dushni Weerakoon is Deputy Director and Fellow at the Institute of Policy Studies in Colombo, Sri Lanka.

Ganeshan Wignaraja is Principal Economist at the Office of Regional Economic Integration, ADB, and the team leader of the study.

Zhang Yunling is Professor and Director of the Institute of Asia-Pacific Studies, Chinese Academy of Social Sciences in Beijing, People's Republic of China.

Contents

Illustrations

Tables

Figures

Appendix Tables

Boxes

Introduction, Findings, and Policies

Ganeshan Wignaraja, Joseph Francois, and Pradumna B. Rana

Setting and Purpose of Study

East and South Asia include some of the world's most dynamic open economies as well as several least developed countries. This study examines the diverse experience of regional integration of a sample of South and East Asian economies. Using a set of country cases based on a similar framework, the study addresses an important policy question: how can each country's integration with its neighbors and more distant regional economies be improved? Of the eight country studies, five are from South Asia (India, Pakistan, Bangladesh, Nepal, and Sri Lanka) and three are from East Asia (the People's Republic of China [PRC], Thailand, and Singapore). The country cases—which differ by per capita income, economic growth rate, country size, and location—provide fascinating insights into the relationship between regional economic performance and strategies for regional integration at country level. The study also offers lessons for other countries and subregions which are interested in developing national strategies to foster pan-Asian integration. As the next section shows, relations between South and East Asian economies have evolved considerably since pre-colonial times. The country cases focus on the period since 1990, as this period marks the beginning of strengthening integration between South and East Asian economies. The global economic crisis is expected to have a temporary, short-term negative impact on the process of South Asia-East Asia integration. Once global economic recovery commences, the pace of South Asia-East Asia integration is expected to pick up.

It is noteworthy that during the five decades prior to the 1990s, South and East Asian economies were relatively isolated from one another in terms of economic relations and there was little talk of pan-Asian integration. There was little bilateral trade and investment flows in goods or services. Furthermore, the only trade agreement that covered the two subregions was the Bangkok Agreement (now called the Asia-Pacific Trade Agreement [APTA]) signed in 1975 (that covered Bangladesh, PRC, India, Lao People's Democratic Republic [Lao PDR], Republic of Korea, and Sri Lanka). This relative isolation is associated with poor connectivity, barriers to regional trade and investment, and a lack of political signals to foster South Asia–East Asia integration.

Today, South Asia is experiencing a new economic era. The subregion's economies have witnessed rapid economic growth in the wake of the economic reforms of the 1980s and 1990s. In recent years, the importance of regional integration for South Asia's future growth has been increasingly recognized. The South Asian Association for Regional Cooperation (SAARC) was established in 1985. The emergence of India as a global economic powerhouse, as well as the acceleration of economic growth in the rest of South Asia has generated increasing support for regional integration. There is also a more favorable regional trade and investment regime in South Asia with liberalization of foreign direct investment (FDI) regulations, implementation of the South Asia Free Trade Agreement (SAFTA), increased bilateral FTAs, and market-friendly economic policies.

With the stalling of the global trade talks under the World Trade Organization (WTO), the progress in regionalism in other regions of the world, and the regionalization of global production networks, there is now heightened interest in pursuing deeper regional integration across Asia (Asian Development Bank [ADB] 2008). In this regard, India's Look East Policy states its policy intent for closer economic relations with East Asia and discussions are under way on an ASEAN+6 FTA (Association of Southeast Asian Nations involving East Asia, India, Australia, and New Zealand). An ASEAN+6 FTA could eventually be expanded to cover other South Asian countries. Model-based studies suggest that an FTA involving East and South Asian economies can result in economic benefits for all members and limited loses for non-members.[1]

Other countries in South Asia (such as Pakistan and Sri Lanka) are also now initiating FTA discussions with different East Asian countries and several (Bangladesh, Bhutan, Nepal, and Sri Lanka) are members of the Bay of Bengal Initiative for Multi-Sectoral Technical and Economic Cooperation (BIMSTEC). Despite these promising signs, however, studies suggest that the level of integration in South Asia remains low, with a host of challenges, including underinvestment in infrastructure, variable logistics effi-

---

[1]   Using a computable general equilibrium model, Francois and Wignaraja (2008) estimate that the global welfare gains from an ASEAN+3 (Association of Southeast Asian Nations plus People's Republic of China, Japan, and Republic of Korea) and South Free Trade Agreement (FTA) are $260.1 billion. This compares with $213.4 billion for an ASEAN+3 FTA. The negative impact on the rest of the world from the two scenarios is estimated to be only $3 billion and $9.3 billion, respectively. Furthermore, using a gravity model, Rodriguez-Delgado (2007) finds that the formation of South Asia Free Trade Agreemnet (SAFTA) would generate higher trade flows in the region. Such trade flows would be higher if SAFTA extended toward other groups such as ASEAN.

ciency, cumbersome bureaucratic regulations, high trade barriers, and low levels of firm-level technological capability.[2] Complementarities between South Asian countries are also limited and hence South Asia should adopt a two-track approach: integration within itself, and better integration with East Asia (and the rest of the world).[3] The twin tracks will complement and supplement each other ensuring a higher chance of success.

While there is growing policy interest in pan-Asian economic integration schemes, there has been only limited systematic study at country-level of actual patterns, determinants, and policy suggestions. Most of the literature on Asian regionalism focuses either on South Asia or East Asia separately. Furthermore, there are few country-level studies on strategies to deal with pan-Asian integration in a holistic manner. The few exceptions include studies focused on the relations of Asia's largest economies with subregional groupings. Accordingly, there is a need for a set of country case studies on South Asia–East Asia integration. Such a study would provide comparison of different options for regional integration.

The study addresses two related sets of questions.

- What is the extent of integration between a given economy and its immediate neighbors as well as more distant regional economies?
- What strategies should countries pursue to improve integration with neighbors and distant regional economies?

The remainder of the book consists of country chapters on a mix of South and East Asian economics—India, Pakistan, Bangladesh, Nepal, Sri Lanka, the PRC, Thailand, and Singapore. These chapters provide a country perspective on Asian integration (current and prospective). This includes the most populous (the PRC and India), the most modern and open (Singapore), and a set of countries spanning a range of incomes and size across Asia—Thailand, Pakistan, Bangladesh, Nepal, and Sri Lanka (see Appendix Table A1.1 for country profiles). The case studies also encompass different levels of industrial development—the PRC, Singapore, and Thailand have the largest industrial sectors. With such diversity, the country chapters provide important, local insight into regional themes. These chapters provide a more direct and local set of case studies, examining (i) the direction of goods and services trade, (ii) national policies on trade and investment, (iii) infrastructure and logistics, (iv) the role of geography, (v) institutions, and

---

[2]   There is growing literature on the achievements, challenges, and prospects of South Asian integration. For a recent selection see the papers in Ahmed and Ghani (2007 ed.), Chandra and Kumar (2008), De and Bhattacharyay (2007), and Wilson and Otsuki (2007), and Wignaraja (2008).

[3]   See Rana and Dowling (2009).

(vi) the regional focus of the countries covered. There is also a chapter which examines micro-level factors which affect export performance in the PRC.

The impact of the global economic crisis notwithstanding, South Asia is in the process of transformation. Rapid growth since liberalization in the 1980s and 1990s has transformed South Asia into a booming, outward-oriented region. However, many challenges still remain: (i) lack of competitiveness in some sectors of manufacturing, (ii) infrastructure bottlenecks, (iii) residual bureaucratic impediments to private sector development, (iv) macroeconomic imbalances, and (v) political tensions. All these factors and others have contributed to low intra-regional trade activity. Compared to other regions, intra-regional trade shares in South Asia are relatively low.[4] In this volume, the majority of country studies are devoted to South Asia in light of the fact that there are few comprehensive studies on regional integration strategies for South Asia, and that the region still has some way to go to reach levels of economic integration and cooperation enjoyed by its East Asian neighbors. The remaining country studies in the book are devoted to East Asia (PRC, Thailand, Singapore), which may offer lessons for South Asia.

A historical overview of South Asia's relations and integration with East Asia, findings and policies from the country cases, and lessons from country experiences and the Association of Southeast Asian Nations (ASEAN) are provided below.

South Asia's Relations and Integration with East Asia

South Asia has a long history of economic and political relations and cultural and religious exchanges with East Asia which date back to the pre-Christian era. Three distinct periods can be distinguished: the precolonial years, the colonial period, and the postcolonial period.

Precolonial Years

The first millennium of the Christian era was a period of rapid growth for India and China. Trade ties between these two countries also increased and the expansion of trade links between these countries widened localized networks into regional ones.[5] Exports from India comprised mainly

---

[4]   Intra-regional trade shares in SAARC have risen from 3.8% to 6.7% between 1997 and 2007. In contrast, intra-regional trade shares for ASEAN were 23.7% in 1997 and 26.8% in 2007; for ASEAN + PRC, Japan, and Korea, shares were 36.5% in 1997 and rose to 43.3% in 2007. *Source:* Asia Regional Integration Center (ARIC) database, July 2008.

[5]   For a comprehensive discussion, see Shankar (2004).

rice, sugar, and textiles, while imports were more varied and included Indonesian spices, various kinds of woods, Chinese silk, gold, and nonprecious metals such as tin, copper, and vermillion. India and China were in contact with each other through a network of land and sea routes. Land routes started off as localized networks and were gradually linked into a long-distance trading channel known as the Silk Road. There were two major maritime ports in the east coast of India, namely, the port of Coromandel (near present-day Chennai) and Bengal. There is evidence of extensive trade with Burma and Thailand. The opening of the straits of Malacca in the 5th century enabled direct contact with the north-western edge of the Java Sea region where intraregional trade was strong and led to the establishment of the Srivijaya Empire (present-day Indonesia). This, together with the emergence of the Chola Empire in South India and the Sung Dynasty in China in the 10th and 11th centuries as large, unified, and prosperous regional powers, provided an additional fillip to regional economic trade and exchange. Strategically located on the great maritime route connecting China and the West, Southeast Asia also provided a staging ground for merchants from the East and the West. Various strategic allowances were also made. Rajendra I of the Chola dynasty conducted a naval expedition to Srivijaya to protect trade with China. Rajendrachola Deva I named the island of Singapore (Singapura) in the 10th century AD. Hence, during the precolonial period, in addition to being the dominant region of the world, Asia was one of the most integrated regions of the world.

Together with land and seaborne commerce, traders, missionaries, priests, adventurers, and fortune seekers moved from South Asia to Southeast Asia. The Sanskrit language, Hinduism, and Buddhism were like old wine lacing East Asia's culture. Names from the Sanskrit language and various Hindu-Buddhist cults were adopted in East Asia. The common people too were influenced by the stories of the Ramayana, and various deities became popular.

The Colonial Period (the 18th and 19th centuries)

During the colonial period, Europeans (Portuguese, Spanish, Dutch, British, French, and Americans) were able to take control of international trade of Asia, thereby diverting the profits from this trade to Europe. This distorted center–periphery relations and made Europe stronger while the Asian empires and kingdoms became weaker. Economic links between South Asia and East Asia also weakened as South Asian soldiers were used to quash rebellions in other parts of Asia such as China (the Opium War) and Malaya.

The Postcolonial Period (1950s onward)

Under India's first prime minister, Jawaharlal Nehru, India started to re-engage with East Asia. The Asian Relations Conference held in New Delhi in 1947 served as one of the earliest attempts to form a pan-Asian identity. Forming a common cause with other Asian leaders on decolonization, Western imperialism, equality, and developing-world solidarity, Nehru helped to forge the Bandung Spirit of 1955 which led to the nonaligned movement. This phase of India's engagement with East Asia, however, ended with India's border war with China in 1962, and preoccupation with Pakistan. India turned inward and adopted the Soviet model of development.

India started to enhance its links with East Asia only in 1992 when it launched its Look East Policy in the aftermath of the Cold War and the start of its economic liberalization policies. Under the Congress Government of Manmohan Singh, the Look East policy has been reenergized with renewed focus on India's place in the global economy. Other South Asian countries have also followed suit. Look East policies in South Asia have sought to establish trade and investment links with the dynamic ASEAN and now the East Asian countries. India's engagement with ASEAN began as a sectoral dialogue partnership in 1992, which was upgraded into a full dialogue partnership in 1995 and membership in the ASEAN Regional Forum in 1996. The first summit-level interaction began in November 2002. A Long-Term Vision 2020 paper for the ASEAN–India partnership was prepared and is being implemented. Since 1995, India has also participated in the East Asia Summits that bring together the heads of states and governments of ASEAN+3 plus Australia, New Zealand, and India. At the Summit in Singapore last year, it was decided to revive the 3,000-year old Nalanda University in India as a pan-Asian center of excellence. The recent observer status given to the PRC and Japan in SAARC also portends well for South Asia–East Asia economic relations. At the 2006 Asia–Europe Finance Ministers' meeting, a decision was made to expand membership to include India, Mongolia, Pakistan, and the ASEAN Secretariat from the Asian side, and Romania and Bulgaria from the European side.

More recently, as in other parts of the world, there has been a proliferation of FTAs between South Asia and East Asia (Figure 1.1). As of February 2009, there were five FTAs concluded, eight under negotiation and at least another seven have been proposed. This contrasts with only one FTA in 1976. The most significant of the concluded FTAs so far is the India–Singapore Comprehensive Economic Cooperation Agreement (CECA) which was signed in June 2005. The CECA, which took effect in August 2005, covers trade not only in goods but also services, investments, and cooperation in technology, education, air services, and human resources. The others include the Asia–Pacific Trade Agreement administered by the United Nations Economic and

Figure 1.1 Number of FTAs Between South Asia and East Asian Countries

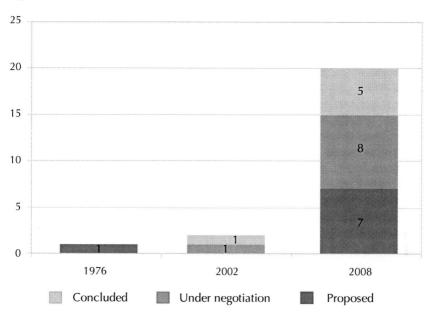

Notes: Concluded = signed and/or under implementation; Under negotiation = Framework Agreement signed and FTA is under negotiation; Proposed = under study.

FTA = free trade agreement.

Source: ADB FTA Database (www.aric.adb.org), as of February 2009.

Social Commission for Asia and the Pacific (UNESCAP) (involving various South Asian countries as well as the PRC, the Republic of Korea, and the Lao PDR) and two bilateral FTAs involving Pakistan. In addition, eight FTA agreements are under negotiation between South and East Asian countries. These are the ASEAN–India[6], India–Thailand, BIMSTEC, PRC–Pakistan, India–Republic of Korea, Malaysia–Pakistan, Pakistan–Singapore, and Pakistan–Indonesia FTAs. Another eight FTAs have been proposed—including between the PRC and India, Japan and India, Malaysia and India, Pakistan and the Philippines, Pakistan and Thailand, and Singapore and Sri Lanka.

Numerous infrastructure projects also serve to tie South Asia closer to East Asia. South Asian countries are participating in UNESCAP's Asian Highway Network and the Trans-Asian Railway Network. Discussions are also proceeding on reopening the World War II-era Stillwell Road linking Assam state with the PRC's Yunnan Province through Myanmar. This

---

[6] Talks were concluded in August 2008 and the agreement to be signed by the end of 2008.

follows the reopening of a direct overland trade route along the Nathu La pass on the border between Sikkim and the Tibet Autonomous Region in July 2006 after 44 years.

It is useful to attempt to summarize the extent of integration in the subregions. Tables 1.1a and 1.1b provide data on the value of merchandise trade of the sample countries with both South Asia and East Asia for 1975, 1990, and 2007. Also provided is the sample countries trade with both subregions as a share of world trade for 2007. Some general points emerge from the table: (i) although from a low base, the value of trade of South Asian countries with other South Asian countries, which more than doubled between 1975 and 1990, increased more than tenfold between 1990 and 2007; (ii) from a higher base, the value of South Asian countries trade with East Asian countries grew even faster during the two subperiods; (iii) the giant Indian and the PRC economies are key drivers in interregional trade flows; (iv) from a high base, the value and increase of the East Asian countries trade with other East Asian countries is much larger than its growing trade with South Asia; (v) East Asian economies rely more than South Asian countries on regional markets than extraregional markets.

At the time of writing, recent developments in 2008—the terrorist attacks in Mumbai and the onset of the global financial crisis—seemed to cast a shadow over growing South Asia-East Asia economic relations. These events are likely to exert a damping effect on the pace of South Asia-East Asia economic relations in the short term. For instance, there may be reduced demand for goods and inputs produced in production networks spanning South and East Asia. Faced with a credit crunch, multinationals may reduce foreign investment in projects involving activity in both subregions. Pressures from powerful industrial lobbies may result in some protectionist measures being imposed. In the medium term, however, there are grounds for optimism and a return to pre-2008 levels of integration activity across South and East Asia. These include: (i) the Obama Administration engaging in intense diplomatic efforts to reduce tensions between India and Pakistan, (ii) a global recovery which is expected to start sometime in 2010, and (iii) growing regional markets in South and East Asia, led by PRC and India, which offer opportunities to take up slack demand and capacity.

As the economic dynamism of the South Asian and East Asian regions continues, relations and integration between South Asia and East Asia are bound to increase further. What distinguishes the present engagement with East Asia from the previous one during the precolonial period is that it is operating on multiple fronts: South Asia's historical, cultural, and ideological links are being complemented by growing economic interdependence, including movement of capital and human resources and a growing number of free trade agreements and security relationships.

Table 1.1a Value of Merchandise Trade with East Asia and South Asia, $ Mn

	Trade with South Asia			Trade with East Asia		
	1975	1990	2007	1975	1990	2007
Bangladesh	118	318	3,275	106	1,742	9,471
India	270	584	10,031	1,240	7,525	114,466
Nepal	n.a.	95	2,550	n.a.	351	767
Pakistan	168	344	2,175	615	3,595	16,473
Sri Lanka	106	254	4,039	344	1,426	5,442
PRC	247*	1,162	50,608	5,738*	66,547	881,885
Singapore	217	2,705	18,979	4,844	53,871	328,842
Thailand	111	961	6,460	2,287	27,372	163,091

*Available data for the PRC = 1978.

PRC = People's Republic of China, n.a. = not available, $ Mn = millions of US dollars.

East Asia includes 10 ASEAN countries, Japan; Republic of Korea; People's Republic of China; Hong Kong, China; and Taipei,China. South Asia includes Bangladesh, Bhutan, India, Maldives, Nepal, Pakistan and Sri Lanka.

Source: International Monetary Fund, *Direction of Trade Statistics* (October 2008).

Table 1.1b Share in Country's Trade with World, %

Country	Trade with South Asia		Trade with East Asia	
	1990	2007	1990	2007
Bangladesh	6.0	9.4	32.7	27.3
India	1.4	2.5	18.0	28.7
Nepal	11.9	59.8	44.0	18.0
Pakistan	2.7	3.7	27.7	27.8
Sri Lanka	5.6	18.9	31.5	25.5
PRC[a]	1.0	2.3	57.1	40.6
Singapore	2.4	3.4	47.4	58.5
Thailand	1.7	2.2	48.5	55.5

[a] Available data for the PRC = 1978.

PRC = People's Republic of China, % = percent.

East Asia includes 10 ASEAN countries, Japan, Republic of Korea, People's Republic of China, Hong Kong, China and Taipei,China. South Asia includes Bangladesh, Bhutan, India, Maldives, Nepal, Pakistan and Sri Lanka.

Source: International Monetary Fund, *Direction of Trade Statistics* (October 2008).

Findings and Policies from the Country Cases

The eight country cases from South Asia and East Asia in this book provide insights on regional integration, determinants, and policies from a national perspective. Particular focus has been given in the country case studies to infrastructure initiatives, customs modernization and logistics improvement, foreign investment policies, trade liberalization, reduction of service barriers, measures to improve export competitiveness, and public–private sector partnerships. These are likely to be the key ingredients of successful national strategies for regional integration.[7] The main findings are summarized below.[8]

South Asia Cases

India

Kumar and Sharma note that South Asia's largest and most dynamic economy, India, has long pursued the development of economic relations with South Asia and East Asia. India has significant potential to play the role of a regional hub in South Asia that also connects the region with East Asia (and Central Asia). In 1990/91 and 2004–2005, the share of Indian exports to South Asia has grown from 2.9% to 5.2% and that to East Asia from 19.7% to 26.7%. India's export growth is being led by sectors including health care and information technology (IT) services, pharmaceuticals, and automobiles. Foreign direct investment (FDI) inflows into India from East Asia (14% of FDI total inflows) are significant, and India has also emerged as an outward investor in East Asia (12% of FDI outflows). Although India's FDI outflows to South Asia are growing, such flows are still relatively small. Policies adopted which help improve economic relations with East and South Asian economies include (i) a phased and calibrated liberalization of the trade policy regime; (ii) the adoption of the Look East policy in 1991 to strengthen economic relationships with ASEAN and East Asian countries (where India became a full dialogue partner of ASEAN in 1996 and a framework agreement was signed in 2003); (iii) a liberalized FDI policy (1991 Industrial Policy and 2006 FDI Policy) which has been accompanied by increasing FDI inflows; (iv) liberalization of policy governing outward FDI (Indian enterprises are now permitted to invest with automatic approval abroad up to 100%); (v) new legislation on special economic zones in 2005 to systematically promote exports (including relaxation of rules pertaining to industrial licensing and small scale industry reservation); (vi) priority given to infrastructure

---

[7]   Schiff and Winters (2003), Wignaraja (2003), ADB (2008) and Francois, Rana and Wignaraja eds. (2009).

[8]   Data in this section draws on the country chapters in this volume.

development, including the adoption of an integrated corridor approach, corporatization of management, model concession agreement for public–private partnership in national highway development, and establishment of independent regulatory authorities; and (vii) signing of trade and transit agreements with Bangladesh, Nepal, and Bhutan (currently linked with India through its rail network), as well as provision of transit facilities to its Nepal trade links (Radhikapur and Phulbari) to trade and transit through Bangladesh.

Kumar and Sharma make several recommendations to improve India's economic relations with East Asia and South Asia which include (i) providing better information to exporters (Indian food exporters face problems with Japan's import regulations and face frequent changes in rules and regulations in Southeast Asia); (ii) addressing physical infrastructure bottlenecks and delays at land border customs stations with Bangladesh and Nepal; (iii) enhancing supply capabilities in Bangladesh and Nepal by encouraging Indian investments on their export platforms (e.g., $3 billion investment of Tata Group in Bangladesh); (iv) providing education and training could be areas for greater cooperation and increased trade flows with South Asian and East Asian nations; (v) exploiting synergies in services through regional economic integration in East and South Asia; (vi) adopting a coordinated approach in addressing issues related to sanitary and phytosanitary (SPS) measures, as well as technical barriers to trade (TBTs), in East and South Asia with the aim of reaching mutual recognition agreements; and (vii) developing a common transport policy for South Asia.

Pakistan

As ul Haque and Ghani argue, Pakistan is presently emphasizing a policy of improving economic ties with East and South Asian countries. Economic relations with neighboring South Asia are limited for historical and political reasons. For instance, South Asia accounts for 4.5% of Pakistan's exports and 2.7% of imports. Those with East Asia are more significant—34.5% of Pakistan's imports, 14% of exports, and 2.3% of FDI inflows. The PRC is Pakistan's biggest trading partner in East Asia. Several policy initiatives underpin the economic ties between Pakistan and East Asia: (i) the Strategic Vision East Asia policy to help stimulate ties with Southeast Asia; (ii) an investment policy that opened up all economic sectors to FDI and allowed full foreign ownership (leading to intensive investment in Japanese joint ventures and independent power producer projects); (iii) elimination of state enterprise control over imports and exports of certain products; (iv) conversion of Saindak Project into an export processing zone (EPZ) allowed Pakistan's entry into the world market for metal exports; (v) private sector involvement in economic activities at Port Qasim (Pakistan's second deep seaport) and establishment of a modern terminal complex at Lahore airport to improve port efficiency; and (vi) construction of a new international airport in Sialkot to be a hub for the leather and surgical goods industries.

Many policies are suggested by ul Haque and Ghani to bolster economic relations between Pakistan and East Asia, including (i) conclusion of an FTA with the PRC to widen the Silk Road between the two countries, reducing Pakistan's production costs; (ii) attainment of full dialogue partnership with ASEAN, which could strengthen Pakistan's overall economic relationship with ASEAN, establish joint ventures, and attract more investments; (iii) improvements to transport logistics to enhance Pakistan's export competitiveness, including the widening of the Karachi–Lahore highway and the promotion of rail transport for containers moving between Karachi and Lahore; (iv) a coherent regulatory framework for goods and services that promotes competition; (v) strengthening of the Monopoly Control Authority's enforcement capacity; (vi) upgrading of telecommunications infrastructure; and (vii) enhancing business services and technological support for the development of small and medium-sized enterprises (SMEs). Policies to improve ties with South Asia include implementation of the South Asian Free Trade Agreement (SAFTA) which came into force in July 2006, investments in infrastructure (especially road and rail links), streamlining of bureaucratic controls governing regional trade, and improving political relations with India.

Bangladesh

Ali Rashid argues that since economic liberalization, Bangladesh has established significant economic relations with East Asia, which is the source of 83% of FDI inflows and around 40% of imports. However, Bangladesh's share of exports to East Asia (6.8%) and South Asia (1.6%) remains small as a result of a narrow export base, few complementarities with other countries in the region, and inadequate infrastructure. Bangladesh's trade with South Asia may be understated because of significant illegal imports from India. Some policies that have contributed to Bangladesh's external orientation toward East and South Asia include (i) memberships in SAFTA, BIMSTEC, and APTA; (ii) improvement of operation and security of Chittagong Port (part of $31 million financed by ADB); (iii) simplification and improvement of customs procedures including processing of customs declaration and payment through the Automated System for Customs Data (ASYCUDA) system; and (iv) bilateral investment treaties signed with most East and Southeast Asian countries. Continuation of policy reforms, improvements to the investment climate, and liberalization of policies toward services imports will steadily increase integration with East Asia.

Additional measures are suggested by Ali Rashid to improve economic relations with South Asia: (i) improvement of the Dhaka–Chittagong corridor, especially the Chittagong Port facilities (Bangladesh's principal transport corridor, which provides potential subregional linkages to the northeastern states of India as well as to West Bengal, Bhutan, and Nepal); (ii) signing of a transit agreement between India and Bangladesh (to facilitate the Bangladesh–Nepal corridor via the Phulbari–Banglabandha transit route); (iii) development of an electronic monitoring system and risk-management and post-clearance audit procedures for customs clearance facilitation; (iv) implementation of SAFTA and removal of nontariff and paratariff barriers to intraregional trade; (v) promotion of investment cooperation under SAFTA to enhance Bangladesh's export supply capability; and (vi) upgrades to metrology testing and standards infrastructure, bringing them to international levels.

Nepal

Karmacharya and Maskay suggest that Nepal has particularly close economic ties with neighboring India owing to its landlocked, mountainous nature, and narrow economic base. Much of Nepal's trade transits through Indian ports. Accordingly, a high concentration of Nepal's trade is with India (67.2% of exports and 57.4% of imports, according to official estimates that fail to account for illegal trade). Indian inward investment in Nepal is also significant. Other South Asian economies account for less than 1% of Nepal's total trade. East Asian economies are an important source of Nepal's imports (25.8%) but exports to East Asia are small (less than 5%). Some policy actions that aim to improve economic relations with East and South Asian economies are (i) development of an air cargo complex to facilitate cargo movement; (ii) adoption of the Customs Reform and Modernization Action Plan and facilitation measures, including systematic customs clearance procedures (at the border points of Birgunj, Biratnagar, and Bairahawa) and automated customs data software; and (iii) the establishment of the One Window Committee and Investment Promotion Board, as well as broad investment incentives and tax concessions.

According to Karmacharya and Maskay, measures needed to enhance economic relations with East and South Asia include (i) promoting Nepal as a transit route between India and the PRC (including amendments to the India–Nepal Transit Treaty) and as an air corridor for countries in SAARC and ASEAN+3; (ii) implementing a comprehensive strategy to attract FDIs, including strengthening of the Investment Promotion Board and One Window Committee; (iii) amending the Industrial Enterprises and Foreign Investment Acts; (iv) establishing an EPZ and external investment agency; (v) enacting effective economic diplomacy to create investment links and enhance investments from SAARC and ASEAN+3; (vi) promoting potential services sectors for FDI, including hydropower (improving production and enhancing transmission links with India) and offshore service center for regional countries; and (vii) establishing an electronic data interchange and a road-based inland clearance depot in Birgunj.

Sri Lanka

Weerakoon argues that Sri Lanka—the earliest economy in South Asia to adopt economic reforms—has notable economic relations with East Asia, which accounts for 55% of FDI inflows and absorbs 10% of Sri Lanka's exports. Meanwhile, Sri Lanka's economic relations with South Asian economies have been growing. For instance, Sri Lanka's exports to South Asia rose fivefold to 10% between 1998 and 2005, largely because of expanding India–Sri Lanka trade. Inward investment from India to Sri Lanka has also increased, with India accounting for 6.2% of FDI inflows to Sri Lanka. Closer ties with East and South Asian economies can be attributed to the following policy factors: (i) the implementation of an Indo–Sri Lanka Free Trade Agreement, which has encouraged exports and inward investment from India; (ii) a liberal export-oriented FDI regime which has attracted some investment in the services sector; (iii) the adoption of customs reforms and trade facilitation measures such as the introduction of ASYCUDA, electronic data systems, and the Sri Lanka Automated Cargo Clearance System; (iv) the development of the Southern Highway, which has improved road access from production centers to ports; and (v) private sector participation in terminal operations to improve efficiency at Sri Lanka ports including Colombo, Sri Lanka's key link to international sea routes.

Weerakoon makes some recommendations to strengthen economic relations with East and South Asia, including (i) promoting a more strategic FDI partnership with the PRC and Malaysia; (ii) implementing new ports projects, particularly completion of a new South Harbor (in 2009) and construction of a new port in Hambantota (funded by the PRC); (iii) restructuring the Sri Lanka Ports Authority to unbundle port management and improve the efficiency of port operations; (iv) undertaking a proposed 4-hectare offshore shopping complex and airport-related business process outsourcing (BPO) zone as an investment opportunity for Indian entrepreneurs; (v) implementing further structural reforms to address domestic export supply constraints and fully benefit from the enhanced market access opportunities provided by regional agreements; and (vi) continuing deregulation of barriers to inward investment in services and exports.

East Asian Cases

The PRC

According to Zhang, the PRC—the region's largest and fastest growing economy—has successfully forged close economic relations with the rest of East Asia since liberalization. East Asia now accounts for half of the PRC's foreign trade and more than 60% of its FDI inflows. Forty percent of the PRC's considerable FDI outflows also go to other East Asian countries. Policy reforms, accession to the World Trade Organization (WTO), the PRC's emphasis on FTAs with regional partners, the Government's FDI promotion strategy, and infrastructure investments are all associated with this regional orientation. More recently, the PRC has witnessed growing economic relations with South Asia. For instance, its total trade with South Asia has increased tenfold since 2000 to reach $50.8 billion in 2007 (equivalent to 2.3% of total trade). Furthermore, the PRC's cumulative FDI outflows to South Asia are small (amounting to $33 million in 2003–2005) but have grown steadily. With the emergence of India, trade and services between the PRC and India lie at the forefront of the PRC's economic relations with South Asia. There is considerable potential for large-scale FDI and financial flows to South Asia given the PRC's significant foreign exchange reserves. Three noteworthy policy imperatives in the PRC underlie growing economic relations between the PRC and South Asian economies: (i) new efforts at trade diplomacy to improve economic relations with South Asian economies, such as the signing of an FTA with Pakistan in 2005 and a feasibility study of a PRC–India FTA; (ii) the adoption of an invest-abroad strategy to support overseas investments by PRC firms; and (iii) large investments in coastal harbors such as Shanghai, Ningbo, and Guangzhou to reduce transactions costs on sea freight. The size and sustained rapid growth of the PRC's economy can help the country play a pivotal role in strengthening economic relations between East Asia and South Asia. In this regard, closer economic ties between the PRC and India could enable India to act as a gateway to South Asia.

The following measures are suggested by Zhang to strengthen such economies ties: (i) a comprehensive economic cooperation package under the likely PRC–India FTA; (ii) the development of an energy corridor between the PRC and Pakistan; (iii) closer engagement of the PRC in SAARC, building on its initial status as an observer; (iv) continued modernization of the PRC's seaports that are closest to South Asia; and (v) improvements to the Karakoram Highway, which links the PRC's western and southern regions with Pakistan, as well as reconstruction of the Stilwell Road which could link the PRC and India.

Thailand

Through an outward-oriented strategy led by FDI, Thailand has experienced impressive economic growth and increasing economic ties with East Asia according to Chirathivat and Sabhasri. The share of Thailand's exports destined for East Asia increased from 43.5% to 47.1% between 2000 and 2007. Meanwhile, exports to South Asia are small but have increased (2.7% of exports in 2007). Interestingly, there is also evidence of FDI inflows from South Asia (mainly India) into Thailand amounting to $37.1 million in 1998–2005. Indian investment into Thailand has taken place in IT services, motor vehicles, steel, gems, and jewelry. The direction of Thailand's trade and investment links has been influenced by several aspects of its export-oriented FDI-led strategy, including (i) longstanding membership in ASEAN Free Trade Agreement (AFTA) and negotiations for a Thailand–India FTA (with an early harvest program), (ii) liberalization of investment regulations and investment promotion by the Thai Board of Investment, (iii) liberalization of regulations governing the services sector, (iv) development of EPZs, and (v) upgrading of the main seaport at Laem Chabang. There is growing recognition in multinational and regional policy circles that Thailand can build on its early achievements and become a corridor linking its Asian neighbors with one another.

Suggestions made by Chirathivat and Sabhasri in this vein are: (i) greater focus by the Thai Board of Investment on attracting FDI inflows from the PRC and India, including provision of detailed information on cost conditions and market opportunities; (ii) emphasis on lowering logistics costs and improving logistics systems to world class levels; (iii) development of transport corridors linking Thailand with East Asia and South Asia including the Asian Highway; and (iv) improvement in the competition policy framework (including revision of the 1999 Competition Policy Law).

Singapore

As a high-income city-state, this economy occupies a strategic location in Asia, according to Thangavelu and Rajan. Its geographic location, outward-oriented business-friendly policies, world-class logistics and infrastructure, membership in AFTA, and high level of educational attainment have made Singapore a natural hub for strong economic relations with East Asia (which accounted for 53% of the city-state's total exports in 2005). Economic relations with South Asia are growing from a small base—Singapore's export share to South Asia amounted to 3.5% in 2005, of which India alone made up 2.6%. Likewise, the bulk of Singaporean FDI in South Asia goes to India (1.1% of total FDI outflows in 2000–2003). Singapore's investments in India encompass a wide spectrum of activities, notably infrastructure, logistics services, banking, pharmaceuticals, and telecommunications.

Thangavelu and Rajan argue that Singapore could further strengthen its economic relationships with East Asia through (i) harmonizing the rules of origin in existing FTAs with those under negotiation; (ii) strengthening its competition policy framework; (iii) emphasizing intellectual property rights protection through comprehensive legislation and surveillance mechanisms; (iv) enhancing support for the development of Singaporean SMEs as independent exporters and overseas investors; and (v) upgrading human capital and training, particularly for the services sector. Additional measures are also required to support the growth of economic relations with South Asia, particularly India: (i) economic diplomacy to promote the East Asia Summit process and lobbying for inclusion of India and other South Asian economies in the Asia-Pacific Economic Cooperation (APEC) forum, (ii) expansion of Singapore's FTA strategy to cover more South Asian economies, and (iii) facilitation of Singaporean investment in South Asian economies.

Lessons from Country Cases and ASEAN

It is increasingly recognized that the process of "regionalism is too complex and sui generis to generate universal operational rules."[9] Nonetheless, rules of thumb or lessons of experience can be drawn from the analysis of the case studies of South and East Asian countries that might be relevant to the development of regional integration strategy in most circumstances. Four lessons can be distinguished as follows.

- **Integrate with a large neighboring economy.** Not all partners are equal. Integration into dynamic production networks of a large open neighboring economy can bring numerous externalities to a given economy and its enterprises.
- **Emphasize market orientation in regional strategy.** Emphasis on markets for resource allocation and promotion of greater competition on domestic markets encourages efficiency. Where market imperfections arise, however, intervention may be required.

---

[9]   Schiff and Winters (2003) p. 25.

- **Tailor policy mix to national circumstances.** There is no one-size-fits-all strategy. Key ingredients of regional strategy—investment in infrastructure, improvement of logistics, open trade and investment policies, measures to improve export competitiveness, and public–private sector partnerships—need to be modified and sequenced to suit individual country needs and priorities.
- **Involve the private sector in developing regional strategy.** The behavior of foreign and domestic firms influences the formation and deepening of regional production networks in different industries. Accordingly, close involvement of the private sector in discussions of regional strategy and FTA negotiations is critical.

ASEAN is one of Asia's oldest regional groups. Its rich experience offers broad lessons on developing a dynamic regional organization among members as well as broader international cooperative frameworks. Five lessons from ASEAN are noteworthy: (i) Establish a clear charter and long-term implementation strategies; (ii) Strengthen institutional structures; (iii) Narrow development gaps among members; (iv) Move towards FTA consolidation; and (v) Ensure that dispute settlement mechanisms are pragmatic (see Box 1.1).

Box 1.1 Lessons from ASEAN: A Success Story of Regional Integration*

ASEAN's establishment in 1967 in Bangkok marked the first step in Southeast Asia's move toward regional integration. Since then, it has matured into an example of successful regional integration in the developing world. It is comprised of 10 members (Brunei, Cambodia, Indonesia, Lao PDR, Malaysia, Myanmar, Philippines, Singapore, Thailand, and Viet Nam) and covers more than 567 million people or nearly one tenth of the world's population. From its inception, members have consistently pursued integration initiatives with the view of creating a free trade area of goods, services, people, and investments. Its collective objectives are embodied in three pillars, namely: (i) ASEAN Security Community; (ii) ASEAN Economic Community; and (iii) ASEAN Sociocultural Community.

Embarking on the ASEAN Economic Community (AEC 2015) has led to impressive economic growth for Southeast Asian members, as well as a reduction in poverty and higher living standards for the region. In particular, its five founding members (Indonesia, Malaysia, Philippines, Singapore, and Thailand) have benefited from vibrant economic growth, earning the reputation of being the production and manufacturing locus of "Factory Asia". The experience

---

of ASEAN integration may offer lessons for South Asia and elsewhere in the developing world. These include:

- **Establish a Clear Charter and Long-Term Implementation Strategies.** The establishment of an ASEAN Community funded on the aforementioned three pillars and the ambitious move from an AEC 2020 pledge to an AEC 2015 reflects the degree of commitment that ASEAN member countries have in achieving a prosperous regional community. The blueprint for AEC 2015 is to nurture a policy environment that is conducive to business yet is flexible enough to adjust to a shifting global economic landscape. It aims to accelerate regional integration through priority sectors with the goal of establishing a single market and production base in the region that is fully integrated and competitive with the global economy. From this blueprint are the core building blocks, such as the ASEAN Free Trade Area (AFTA), the ASEAN Investment Area (AIA), and the ASEAN Framework Agreement on Services (AFAS).

- **Strengthen Institutional Structures.** Deeper integration cannot be achieved without institutions that have the clout and human resources to enforce policies and mechanisms. ASEAN started out as a relatively loose institutional body, but has moved toward a more rule-based, structured system. It also presently keeps a permanent secretariat staffed by nearly 100 full-time personnel, which is comparable to the human resources of other regional organizations in the developing world. This support network is key in establishing and setting policies, coordinating and implementing, and enforcing present and future agreements and protocols for the organization.

- **Narrow the Development Gap among Members.** ASEAN countries are diverse in terms of their economic development. ASEAN includes Singapore, an industrialized, advanced economy, along with less developed, newer members such as Cambodia, Lao PDR, Myanmar, and Viet Nam (CLMV). To address this development divide, resources such as financial and technical assistance, capacity building, and technology transfer are devoted to these low-income countries to ensure their full participation in the integration process and to prevent them from falling into the " low cost labor trap" by helping them climb the value product ladder. For low-income countries, phased elimination of exclusions also allows for flexibility and safeguards less developed members. This progressive sequencing of trade liberalization is also met with supportive measures that address supply-side constraints, competitiveness, and trade capacity. In 2001, ASEAN launched the IAI (Initiative for ASEAN Integration) as an assistance platform for CLMV and its more economically advanced neighbors. The four key areas for which hundreds of projects have been launched have been infrastructure, human resource development, information and communications technology, and regional economic integration. In addition, ASEAN formed the ASEAN Development Fund in 2005[a], which pools financial resources from members for technical assistance activities under the three pillars, with the aim to narrow development gap among members so that ASEAN can accelerate and deepen its own economic integration process. Finally, managed development assistance from multilateral intitutions and donor countries help CLMV countries strengthen the fundamental underpinnings of their economic systems.

- **Move toward FTA Consolidation.** Escalating market processes and the rise of multinational production networks in East Asia have led to an increase in intra-regional trade activity, with ASEAN increasingly exporting to itself.[b] With the recent proliferation of Free Trade Agreements (FTAs), ASEAN policy makers recognize that these agreements are assuming greater importance as trade policy instruments. If designed in line with World Trade Organization principles, FTAs can achieve dynamic gains by generating greater trade and foreign direct investment (FDI) among members through liberalization and facilitation of trade. Because these key production networks and manufacturing chains are rooted in member countries, ASEAN is touted as the natural "hub" for formal region-wide economic integration (e.g., in an ASEAN+3 or ASEAN+6 agreement). A prospective East Asia-wide FTA will most likely have ASEAN as its core grouping. In light of its critical role as the lynchpin of economic integration, ASEAN is moving toward harmonizing its provisions, especially as the ASEAN "plus" level to ensure a seamless shift toward broader regional agreements in the future.

- **Ensure that Dispute Settlement Mechanisms are Pragmatic.** Trade disputes are likely to increase with deeper integration so a workable and effective dispute settlement mechanism is important. ASEAN is now in the process of depoliticizing the process with the establishment of an independent appellate body to handle appeals and disputes much like the World Trade Organization's proceedings on disputes. Investment in human resources with legal expertise to form such an institutional body for its regional trade matters is key.

* Hew (2008)

[a] The total contribution from each member country is about US$700,000; the bulk of contributions are used for the operations of the ASEAN Secretariat and the remaining are deposited in the ASEAN Development Fund (ADF). In 2002, the ADF was around US$2 million. Source: ADB staff estimates and ASEAN Secretariat (2008).

[b] Intra-regional trade shares for ASEAN were 23.7% in 1997 and 26.8% in 2007. Source: Asia Regional Integration Center (March 2009), International Monetary Fund, *Direction of Trade Statistics* (December 2008).

References

Asian Development Bank (ADB). 2008. *Emerging Asian Regionalism: A Partnership for Shared Prosperity.* Manila: ADB.

Ahmed, S., and E. Ghani, eds. 2007. *South Asia: Growth and Regional Integration,* Delhi: Macmillan India Ltd.

Chandra, R., and R. Kumar. 2008. South Asian Integration Prospects and Lessons from East Asia. *ICRIER Working Paper* 202. New Delhi: Indian Council for Research on International Economic Relations (ICRIER).

De, P., and B. N. Bhattacharyay. 2007. Prospects of India–Bangladesh Economic Cooperation: Implications for South Asian Regional Cooperation. *ADB Institute Discussion Paper* 78. Tokyo: ADB Institute.

Francois, J. F., and G. Wignaraja. 2008. Pan-Asian Integration: Economic Implications of Integration Scenarios. *Global Economy Journal,* Vol. 8, Issue 3, pp. 1–46.

Francois, J. F., P. B. Rana, and G. Wignaraja, eds. 2009. *Pan-Asian Integration: Linking East Asia with South Asia,* Basingstoke (UK): Palgrave Macmillan. Introduction, Findings, and Policies.

Hew, D. 2008. Conclusion: Towards an ASEAN Economic Community by 2015. In *Brick by Brick: The Building of an ASEAN Economic Community,* edited by Wei-Yen and D. Hew. Singapore: Institute of Southeast Asian Studies.

Kumar, N., K. Kesavapany, and Y. Chaocheng. 2007. *Asia's New Regionalism and Global Role: Agenda for the East Asia Summit.* New Delhi: Research and Information System for Developing Countries (RIS) and Singapore: Institute of Southeast Asian Studies (ISEAS).

Rana, P. B., and M. J. Dowling. 2009. Economic Integration in South Asia and Lessons from East Asia. In *Pan-Asian Integration: Linking East Asia with South Asia,* edited by J. F. Francois, P. B. Rana, and G. Wignaraja. Basingstoke (UK): Palgrave Macmillan.

Rodriguez-Delgado, J. D. 2007. SAFTA: Living in a World of Regional Trade Agreements. *IMF Working Paper* WP/07/23.

Schiff, M., and L. A. Winters. 2003. *Regional Integration and Development.* Washington, DC: World Bank.

Shankar, V. 2004. Towards an Asian Economic Community: Exploring the Past. In *Towards and Asian Economic Community: Vision of a New Asia,* edited by N. Kumar. New Delhi: RIS and Singapore: ISEAS.

Wignaraja, G. 2003. Competitiveness Analysis and Strategy. In *Competitiveness Strategy in Developing Countries,* edited by G. Wignaraja. London: Routledge.

_____. 2008. Ownership, Technology and Buyers: Explaining Exporting in China and Sri Lanka. *Transnational Corporations*, Vol. 17, No. 2, pp. 1–16.

Wilson, J., and T. Otsuki. 2007. Regional Integration in South Asia: What Role for Trade Facilitation? *World Bank Policy Research Working Paper* 4423. Washington, DC: World Bank.

Table A1.1 Country Profiles, 2007

Country	GDP per capita (constant 2000 US$)	GDP Growth Rate (%), 2000–2007	Population, total (Mn)	Openness (trade % of GDP)	Manufacturing, value added (% of GDP)	Poverty Headcount Ratio (PPP, at US$1/day)
Bangladesh	439.4	5.8	158.6	50.8	17.9	41.3 (2000)
India	685.6	7.6	1,123.3	45.8	16.4	34.3 (2004)
Nepal	242.5	3.1	28.1	41.0	7.7	24.1 (2004)
Pakistan	660.5	5.5	162.4	36.2	19.5	17.0 (2002)
Sri Lanka	1,143.6	4.9	19.9	68.8	18.5	5.6 (2002)
PRC	1,791.3	10.2	1,320.0	72.0 (2006)	33.5 (2005)	9.9 (2004)
Singapore	28,964.2	5.3	4.6	433.0	25.5	–
Thailand	2,712.7	5.0	63.8	132.5	34.5	2.0 (2002)

– = no data, PRC = People's Republic of China, GDP = gross domestic product, Mn = million, PPP = purchasing power parity, $ = US dollar.

GDP growth rate based on compounded annual growth rate = $(FV/PV)^{1/n} - 1$. Openness indicates exports and imports of goods and services as a % of GDP (current $). Poverty headcount ratio based on 2005 data for the years in parentheses.

Source: World Bank, *World Development Indicators*. Accessed March 2009.

India

Nagesh Kumar and Pooja Sharma

Introduction

India's recent economic performance has attracted widespread attention. With an average annual rate of growth of 8% sustained over the past few years and a robust outlook for the future, India is emerging as a driver for growth in Asia. Economic reforms undertaken since 1991 have deepened India's economic integration with the world economy, and trade and international investments now occupy a far more important place in the economy than ever. India has also taken a keen interest in regional economic integration with South Asia and East Asia. It is an active member of the South Asian Association for Regional Cooperation (SAARC) and the Bay of Bengal Initiative for Multi-Sectoral Technical and Economic Cooperation (BIMSTEC), among other initiatives for regional integration in South Asia. It has also adopted a Look East Policy to guide its foreign economic relationships and deepen engagement with the Association for South East Asian Nations (ASEAN) and East Asian countries, and has articulated a vision of broader pan-Asian economic integration.

This paper briefly overviews the macroeconomic performance of the Indian economy and the emerging patterns of its global economic integration. It also discusses India's approach to regional economic integration in South Asia and East Asia. Its sections (i) provides an overview of the macroeconomic performance of the Indian economy, the economic outlook, and global economic integration against the background of reforms undertaken since 1991; (ii) deals with inbound and outbound foreign direct investment (FDI) flows with special reference to South and East Asian countries; (iii) examines the emerging trends and patterns in merchandise trade and preferential trading arrangements; (iv) provides a brief overview of the recent reforms undertaken in transport infrastructure and trade administration, including trade facilitation–related issues; (v) discusses the trends and patterns in India's services trade; and (vi) concludes with a few suggestions for policy.

Economic Structure and External Orientation

India's economic performance and its approach to international economic integration have undergone a significant, albeit gradual, reorientation since the early 1990s. With the adoption of economic reforms in 1991, international trade policy has evolved from conventional passive adherence to the multilateral liberalization process to a more assertive multitrack involvement. This new approach is characterized by keener participation in multilateral trade talks through the formation of strategic alliances with other developing countries, and simultaneous pursuit of regional, subregional, interregional, and bilateral economic arrangements. The motivations for strengthening regional trade arrangements are multifaceted and range from political and strategic considerations to economic and commercial imperatives, in the face of increasing regionalism in Europe and the Americas.

Macroeconomic Performance and Structure

India's economic growth performance has progressively accelerated over the past five decades. In the first 30 years since independence, India's growth rate averaged 3.5% per year, a rate that was christened the Hindu rate of growth. Since 1980, however, there has been a marked acceleration in growth and the average annual real gross domestic product (GDP) growth over the 1980s, 1990s, and first 3 years of the new millennium was close to 6%. There has been a further acceleration in the growth trajectory since 2003 with the Indian economy registering an average growth rate of 8.5% over the past 4 years (Figure 2.1).

Furthermore, as the growth rate of population has declined over time from 2.3% to 1.6%, per capita GDP has been rising much faster than before. The average rate of per capita income growth therefore has moved up from only 1.2% during the first three decades in the post-Independence period to nearly 4% during the 1990s and 6.8% in the last few years (Figure 2.2). With these rates of growth, the economy in terms of GDP in current prices is projected to be around $850 billion in 2006 with a per capita GDP of $750 (International Monetary Fund [IMF] 2006).

Another important aspect of India's recent growth has been the decline in the volatility in GDP growth from the pre-1980s period (Kelkar 2004). The economy has been remarkably resilient to external and internal shocks, as demonstrated over the past decade, without much disruption, of the effects of the East Asian crisis, a slowdown in the world economy toward the end of the 1990s, and oil price shocks since. The robust growth has been accompanied so far by relative price stability. In a developing country such as India, inflationary pressures could have severe consequences for the poor, apart from their adverse impacts on economic competitiveness.

Figure 2.1 India's GDP Growth Rates, 1950/51–2006/07

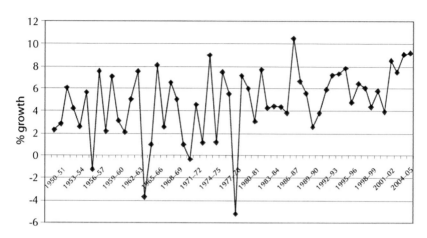

GDP = gross domestic product, % = percent.

Source: Authors based on data available from National Accounts, Central Statistical Organisation, available at http://mospi.nic.in.

There was a steady decline in inflation rate (measured in terms of the growth in consumer price index), which was around 4–5% until recently. India has also achieved relative stability in the real exchange rates, under a managed float regime for its currency.

The potential for India to sustain its rapid growth is widely annotated. The Goldman Sachs BRIC studies note that "India has the potential to show the fastest growth over the next 30 and 50 years" (Wilson and Purushothaman 2003). They estimated per capita growth rate to be above 5% (or over 6.5% in GDP) over the next 30 years. Another study projects India's growth rate to 2025 at 7% "with more upside potential than downside risk" (Rodrik and Subramaniam 2004). In sustaining high growth rates, India will also benefit from the demographic transition that would witness a rising proportion of working-age population in the coming years. In contrast, the proportion of working-age population in many developed countries such as Japan and in emerging economies such as the People's Republic of China (PRC) would be declining.

The Indian economy has witnessed a major structural shift from agriculture, which accounted for 40% of GDP in 1980/81, to services, which were responsible for over 53% of GDP in 2005/06. The share of agriculture recently has dropped below 20%. Rising growth rates of service sectors means that services account for an even higher proportion of GDP. Nonetheless, there are some concerns regarding the resulting imbalances in the structures of GDP and the employment. For instance, while the services sector contributes well over half the GDP, agriculture continues to

**Figure 2.2 Average GDP and Per Capita GDP Growth
in Different Subperiods**

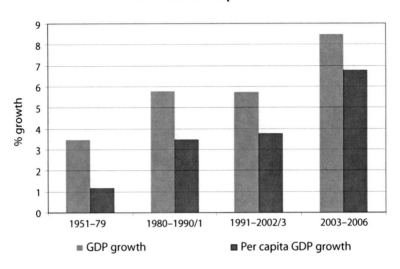

GDP = gross domestic product, % = percent.

Source: Authors based on data available from National Accounts, Central Statistical Organisation, available at http://mospi.nic.in.

account for the bulk of the labor force (Figure 2.3). This also implies that the sharp deceleration in agricultural performance since the second half of the 1990s (Figure 2.4) would have a considerable impact on poverty incidence. In manufacturing, growth is marked by lack of uniformity and stability across subsectors and across periods. Growth decelerated during the second half of the 1990s, although it has again picked up in recent years. There is likewise little evidence of corresponding growth in manufacturing employment. Regions and states also show widening divergence, with states better endowed with physical infrastructure and human capital growing faster than poor and stagnating states such as Uttar Pradesh and Bihar.

Economic growth has been led by services, which emerged as the dominant activity in the Indian economy during the mid-1980s, replacing agriculture. From the mid-1990s, growth in services has exceeded the growth performance of the industrial sector. It has been suggested that the share of services in India's GDP has moved beyond the predicted average based on cross-country experience (Gordon and Gupta 2003). While the rate of growth in agriculture and industry decelerated during the latter part of the 1990s, services continued to surge. A number of factors have contributed to the growth performance in services, including higher domestic consumer

Figure 2.3 Structure of the Indian Economy, 2005–2006

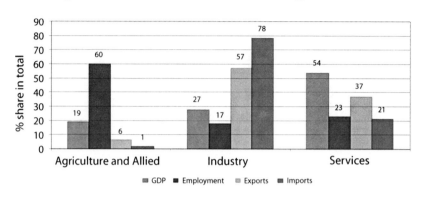

Note: GDP and trade data correspond to 2005–2006 but employment to 1999/2000.

GDP = gross domestic product, % = percent.

Sources: Authors based on data available from Central Statistical Organisation, 2006; Reserve Bank of India, 2006; Planning Commission, 2001.

and business demand for services, greater use of outsourcing, and rising exports. Supply-side factors, including policy reforms and technological advances and innovations, also played important roles.[1]

Reforms in India's industrial policy, initiated in the 1980s, contributed to the acceleration in industrial growth. After a period of relative stagnation from the mid-1960s to the beginning of the 1980s, the annual average rate of growth of the manufacturing sector increased to 6.6% in the 1980s and further to 8% between 1992/93 and 1996/97. Unit labor costs in organized manufacturing in India declined during the period 1974–1998 as labor productivity grew much faster than wages (Nagaraj 2004). Nonetheless, industrial performance during the 1990s could still be considered uneven, given the marked deceleration in investments and output growth during the latter part of the 1990s. In fact, compared to services, the improvement in India's industrial performance since 1991 is not significant, especially when compared to growth recorded in most other industrializing Asian economies (Balakrishnan and Babu 2003, Nagaraj 2003). However, in the more recent period, industrial growth did manage to pick up to a rate of 8.6% in 2004/05 from 7.6% in 2003/04 and to 9.0% in 2005/06. In the first quarter of 2006/07, industrial output has grown 9.7%.

Agriculture and allied activities remain India's biggest employers, accounting for approximately 59% of aggregate employment and serving

---

[1]   See Gordon and Gupta (2003).

Figure 2.4 India's GDP Growth by Sector, 1990/91–2005/06

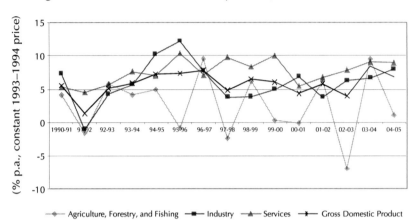

Source: Authors based on data available from National Accounts, Central Statistical Organisation, various years, available at http://mospi.nic.in.

as a significant motor of overall economic growth via rural demand. However, agriculture only contributed approximately 18% of GDP during 2005/06, so that its relative importance has declined on the production side. The gap in labor productivity between agriculture and nonagricultural activities also widened, despite an increase in agricultural labor productivity during the 1990s. Overall growth targets and equity concerns are therefore being undermined by the poor performance of the agricultural sector.

Poverty alleviation is one of the most important challenges facing Indian policy makers. Despite the ongoing academic debate on the measurements and consistency of poverty estimates, the fact is, the proportion of the population below the poverty line has dropped. Going by the poverty headcount ratio, the population under poverty line declined from about 44% in 1983 to 26% in 1999/2000, a period covered by the 55th round of National Sample Survey (NSS) survey.[2] Notwithstanding such a reduction in the proportion of the people below the poverty line, India still has about

---

[2] At the same time, it has been argued that there has been a methodological problem associated with the estimation of poverty in the 55th round (1999/2000) of National Sample Survey. A recent study (Sen and Himanshu 2004) has shown that during 1993/94 to 1999/2000 the poverty ratio fell at most by 3%, and that the number of poor may have increased over this period. However, it has been argued that the current Indian poverty line is a starvation line based on minimum calorie intake, which understates poverty measured by a more holistic criterion of overall minimum needs (Guruswamy and Abraham 2006).

250 million people who are considered poor. This poses a major policy challenge. In recent years, for instance, the crisis in agriculture, where the bulk of the poor are employed, has manifested itself in increasing numbers of farmer suicides. There has also been a marked increase in inequality in the 1990s in terms of strong divergence across states and an increase in rural–urban disparities (Deaton and Dreze 2002).

External Orientation

The rapid progress made in the external orientation of the Indian economy since the early 1990s is evident in both the outcome based, *ex post* measures of openness as well as *ex ante* policy indicators of openness. India's merchandise trade–GDP ratio rose rapidly from less than 15.9% in 1991/92 to approximately 34.1% in 2005/06, more than doubling in a span of 15 years. The corresponding increase in India's trade-GDP ratio is much sharper if one includes services trade, which records an increase from 19.3% to 47.5% (Figure 2.5). India's share in world exports of commercial services rose noticeably from 0.6% in 1990 to 2.8% in 2005, making India the 10th largest exporter in services during 2005. However, India's corresponding achievements are much more modest in international merchandise trade, where India's share in world exports rose from 0.5% to 0.9%.

Indian trade policy has undergone a major transformation since the early 1990s. Import tariffs have become the main form of border protection after the elimination of quantitative restrictions in April 2001, which

Figure 2.5 Trade Openness of the Indian Economy, 1980–2005

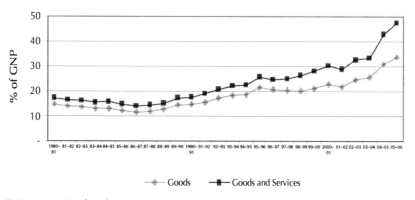

GNP = gross national product, % = percent.

Sources: Central Statistical Organisation; Rerserve Bank of India, various issues, available at http://mospi.nic.in and www.rbi.org.in.

had been maintained on balance of payments grounds. The peak rate of customs duties has been steadily reduced from 150% in 1991/92 to 20% in 2004/05 and further dropped to 12.5% on nonagricultural products during 2006/07. The simple average bound tariff as per India's Uruguay Round commitments was 50.6%. However, the simple average applied most favored nation (MFN) tariff rate fell from 35.3% in 1997/98 to 32.3% in 2001/02 and further to 18.3% during 2005 (World Trade Organization [WTO] 2002 and 2006). Since a number of exemptions are allowed from the standard rates of customs duty, this average also tends to be an overestimate. Although these exemptions detract from the transparency of the Indian import tariff system, India makes relatively little use of nontransparent tariff instruments such as specific and compound duties and tariff-rate quotas. The dispersion in tariff rates also dropped during the 1990s. Exports restrictions have been relaxed and the Government introduced new legislation on special economic zones (SEZs) in 2005 to promote exports systematically. An important, explicitly stated objective of Indian trade policy has been to reduce the average level of Indian tariff rates and align the tariff structure with those prevailing in the ASEAN economies. This objective has been reaffirmed in official central government budget statements since the mid-1990s.

The rationalization in the Indian tariff structure has been phased in over a considerable period of time to allow adjustments by industry and for other sources of tax revenues to develop to compensate for losses in trade tax revenues. It has been argued that a phased and calibrated liberalization of trade policy regime as adopted by India has produced more positive outcomes compared to more dramatic, across-the-board liberalization efforts undertaken by African and Latin American countries. In those other regions, hasty liberalization led to widespread deindustrialization and marginalization of the countries in the international division of labor (Research and Information Systems for Developing Countries [RIS] 2007).

Recent Initiatives in Regional Economic Integration

India has actively participated in regional economic integration schemes since the mid-1970s. India is a founding member of the 1975 Bangkok Agreement, which consists of Bangladesh, Republic of Korea, Lao People's Democratic Republic (Lao PDR), Sri Lanka, and the PRC (in 2001). India has also been an active member of the Asian Clearing Union since its inception in the mid-1970s. India has been participating in SAARC since it was formed in 1985. In recent years, especially over the past decade, India's efforts toward regional economic integration have acquired considerable momentum as summarized below.

Within the South Asia subregion, India has concluded two free trade agreements (FTAs): the India–Sri Lanka FTA (signed in 1998 and effective from 2000) and the South Asian Free Trade Agreement (SAFTA) (signed in 2004 and effective from 2006). Aside from these recent, and broader initiatives, India has longstanding arrangements in the subcontinent, including bilateral treaties of trade and transit and FTAs with Bhutan and Nepal, and exchange of trade preferences with South Asian countries under four rounds of talks with the South Asian Preferential Trade Agreement (SAPTA) since 1995. A preferential trade agreement (PTA) was also signed between India and Afghanistan in March 2003. India does not have an independent trade agreement with Pakistan but has granted Pakistan MFN status since 1996. Pakistan does not accord India the same status and maintains a positive list of 773 importable items from India as per Pakistan's 2005/06 Trade Policy. India has a separate trade agreement with Bangladesh that focuses on economic and technical cooperation, as well as ongoing negotiations with Bangladesh toward an FTA. The initial evidence on the India–Sri Lanka FTA, which was signed in 1998 and has been in operation since 2000, appears positive with respect to increasing trade and investment flows (RIS 2004a, Kelegama 2006, Mukherjee 2006) and is now moving toward a further deepening within the framework of comprehensive economic partnership to cover trade in goods and services, as well as investment and economic cooperation.

India's regional economic integration initiatives outside the South Asian subregion since 1991 have been driven by the Look East Policy, which aims to strengthen economic relationships with the East Asian countries. The policy was initially geared primarily to improve political, strategic, and economic relationships with ASEAN but has since been extended to reinforce economic relationships with the PRC, the Republic of Korea, and Japan. Market forces and development and security concerns in India's northeast, as well as the PRC's growing influence in Southeast Asia, have contributed to India's increased focus in the region. While the PRC and India are strategic competitors in Asia, there is also cooperation between the two countries to address their common energy security and other regional concerns. As part of the Look East Policy, India became a sectoral dialogue partner of ASEAN in 1992 and a full dialogue partner in 1996. In November 2002, the India–ASEAN partnership was upgraded to a summit-level dialogue, leading to the conclusion of the Framework Agreement on Comprehensive Economic Cooperation in 2003, which also incorporates a provision for a possible FTA.[3] The India–ASEAN FTA currently under negotiation is expected to be implemented in a phased manner in 2007. In addition, India signed a Comprehensive Economic Cooperation Agreement (CECA) with Singapore in 2005 and a bilateral Free Trade Framework Agreement Early Harvest Scheme with Thailand under which

---

[3]   See Research and Information Systems for Developing Countries (RIS) (2004b).

preferential concessions have been exchanged since 2004. India is also a part of BIMSTEC, which combines seven South and Southeast Asian countries that signed a framework agreement in 2004 toward the realization of an FTA. India also has a program of subregional cooperation called the Mekong–Ganga Cooperation (MGC)—combining Cambodia, the Lao PDR, Myanmar, Thailand, Viet Nam, and India—which focuses on infrastructure development.

In recent years India has strived to strengthen its economic links with the PRC, Japan, and Republic of Korea. Joint study groups were set up with each of these countries to examine the feasibility of free-trade or economic partnership arrangements. A comprehensive economic cooperation arrangement with the Republic of Korea is currently under negotiation, while talks with Japan on a comprehensive economic cooperation arrangement are to be launched shortly. India and the PRC are also examining the possibility of negotiating a PTA. India's efforts toward economic integration with the East Asian countries are evidenced by the fact that these countries have surpassed North America and the European Union (EU) as India's largest trading partners.[4]

India sees growing engagement with East Asian countries as a building bloc toward a broader Asian grouping. The vision is that of an Asian Economic Community (AEC) that will be an "arc of advantage" for peace and shared prosperity, gradually bringing together different subregions of Asia.[5] The formation of an Asian Economic Community could thus be viewed as the culmination of India's Look East Policy. India also participated in the first East Asia Summit, launched as a forum for dialogue on regional cooperation in Asia, along with the PRC, Japan, the Republic of Korea, Australia, and New Zealand.

Outside Asia, India has also instituted mechanisms for greater cooperation with its historical trading partners. India is negotiating a PTA with the Gulf Cooperation Council (GCC), has signed a framework PTA with MERCOSUR (Argentina, Brazil, Paraguay, and Uruguay) and negotiated PTAs with Chile and the South African Customs Union (SACU). India is also a part of the India–Brazil–South Africa (IBSA) Trilateral Commission, formed in 2004, which is contemplating a SACU–India–MERCOSUR (SIM) Comprehensive Economic Cooperation Arrangement.[6] India also signed a cooperation agreement with the EU in 1994 and in 2004 a proposal was endorsed to upgrade relations with the EU to the level of a strategic part-

---

[4] See Asher and Sen (2005) and Kumar (2005b) for more detailed analyses of India–East Asia economic integration.

[5] See Indian Prime Minister Manmohan Singh's speech at the Third ASEAN (Association of Southeast Asian Nations)–India Business Summit, 21 October 2004. Also see RIS (2003a).

[6] See RIS (2006c) for a discussion of the India–Brazil–South Africa (IBSA) grouping.

nership. India and the EU are currently examining the feasibility of an FTA. India and the United States (US) signed the terms of reference of a commercial dialogue in 2003 and initiated the India–US Trade Policy Forum to strengthen bilateral trade and investment relationship in 2005.

Foreign Direct Investment with Special Reference to East and South Asia

After following a somewhat restrictive policy toward FDI, India has been liberalizing its policy regime considerably since 1991. This liberalization has been accompanied by increasing inflows of FDI. Liberalization has also been accompanied by changes in the sectoral composition, sources, and entry modes of FDI. The increasing recognition of India's locational advantages in knowledge-based industries has also led to increasing investments by multinationals in software development and increased the numbers of global research and development (R&D) centers being set up in India to exploit these advantages. Indian enterprises have also emerged as outward investors and have been involved in a growing number of acquisitions and greenfield investment projects abroad. In this section, India's FDI policy is summarized, as well as emerging trends and patterns in FDI flows.

Foreign Direct Investment Policy Regime

After pursuing a restrictive policy toward FDI over four decades with varying degrees of selectivity, India changed tack in 1990s and embarked on a broader process of reforms designed to increase its integration with the global economy (Kumar 2005a). The 1991 New Industrial Policy (NIP) marked a major departure with respect to FDI policy, with the abolition of the industrial licensing system except where required on strategic or environmental grounds. The NIP also created a system of automatic clearance of FDI proposals fulfilling various conditions, such as the ownership levels of 50%, 51%, 74%, and 100% foreign equity. Furthermore, new sectors were opened up to foreign ownership, such as mining, banking, insurance, telecommunications, construction, and management of ports, harbors, roads and highways, airlines, and defense equipment. Foreign ownership up to 100% is permitted in most manufacturing sectors—in some sectors, even on an automatic basis—except for defense equipment, where it is limited to 26%, and for items reserved for production by small-scale industries, where it is limited to 24%. The dividend balancing and the related export obligation conditions on foreign investors, which applied to 22 consumer goods industries, were withdrawn in 2000.

In April 2006, the Government published the updated Foreign Direct Investment Policy after reviewing and rationalizing the policy and associated procedures. The rationalization involved (i) curtailing the multiple approvals required from the Government and other regulatory agencies; (ii) extending the automatic approval to more sectors; and (ii) opening up new sectors to FDI, including single brand retailing. As a result, India's foreign investment policy has become increasingly liberal, simplified, and transparent. FDI is now permitted in almost all sectors of the economy, with the exception of those sectors included on a negative list.

Alongside the liberalization of policy dealing with inward FDI, the policy governing outward FDI has also been liberalized since 1991. The Guidelines for Indian Joint Ventures and Wholly Owned Subsidiaries Abroad as amended in October 1992, May 1999, and July 2002 provide for the automatic approval of outward FDI proposals up to a certain limit that has been expanded progressively from $2 million in 1992 to $100 million in July 2002. In January 2004, the limit of $100 million was removed and Indian enterprises are now permitted to invest abroad up to 100% of their net worth on an automatic basis. India has also entered into 65 double taxation avoidance treaties, which provide relief through exemptions and tax credits for taxes paid in other countries.

Investment Incentives and Tax Competition

A number of fiscal and financial incentives are provided for investments in priority sectors—such as infrastructure, export-led activities, and underdeveloped regions—which are also available to foreign investors. From March 2000, a host of fiscal and other incentives have been accorded to developers and units established in SEZs. The SEZ Act was enacted in 2005, outlining the incentives that are applicable to national and foreign developers in these zones. Some restrictions that are applicable to foreign investments located elsewhere in the country, including limits on equity participation in sectors reserved for the Small Scale Industry, have been dispensed with for foreign units in the SEZs. The SEZ Act provides for a range of incentives, including tax holidays; exemptions from customs duties and central government excise on equipment, components, and raw materials; and relaxation of rules pertaining to industrial licensing, small scale industry reservation, and the application of environmental and labor laws. In addition, state governments may provide additional incentives to units located in their jurisdictions such as exemptions and/or concessions from state-level taxes, tax deferments, and flexibility in the application of labor laws. In fact, since 1991 interstate competition to attract FDI has been increasing with additional incentives such as capital grants and other direct financial support, including project-specific infrastructure. The leading determinant of investors' decisions, however, was availability of good quality infrastructure (Oman 2000).

Investor Protection and Ownership Restrictions

In general, after entry into the Indian market, foreign firms are accorded national treatment and protected against nationalization and expropriation and permitted to freely repatriate investments and returns on investments. The differential treatment is limited to restrictions on equity participation in specific sectors and in the applicable corporate tax rates.[7] There are also some procedural requirements defined for a foreign entity entering through the joint venture route, or for those setting up another company in the same sector. The Indian legal framework is comprehensive in nature and applicable to all enterprises operating in its territory, which includes legislation governing companies, taxation, factories, labor, competition, dispute settlement, money laundering, consumer protection, and environment protection. Despite the existence of adequate institutional structures, the settlement of legal disputes in India is highly time consuming. Since April 2006, the Government has concluded Bilateral Investment Promotion and Protection Agreements (BIPAs) with 58 countries, of which 49 have been ratified. More agreements are in the process of being finalized or negotiated with other countries.

Disputes between foreign investors and the Government can be referred to the national judicial, arbitral or administrative bodies, or for international conciliation under the Conciliation Rules of the United Nations Commission on International Trade Law, should they not be settled through amicable negotiations within a period of 6 months.[8] Disputes between contracting parties to the BIPA are to be submitted directly to an arbitral tribunal in the absence of amicable resolution.[9] India has also joined the World Bank's Multilateral Investment Guarantee Agency, which provides political risk cover to foreign investors.

Export Processing and Special Economic Zones

India's policy on SEZs was introduced in April 2000, and the SEZ Act (2005) and SEZ Rules (2006) were made formally effective in February 2006. An SEZ can be set up jointly or independently by private and/or public entities, state governments, and state government agencies. Since

---

[7] The rate of corporate tax applicable to Indian and foreign company varies. While corporate income tax on domestic companies is levied at 35% plus a surcharge of 5%, the corresponding rate for foreign companies is 40% with a surcharge of 5%.

[8] If conciliation proceedings do not result in an agreement, then the dispute may be referred for arbitration at the International Centre for the Settlement of Investment Disputes, to the Additional Facility for the Administration of Conciliation, Arbitration and Fact-Finding Proceedings, or to an ad hoc arbitral tribunal in accordance with the Arbitration Rules of the United Nations Commission on International Trade Law, 1976.

[9] Refer to the Indian model text of such a bilateral agreement at www.finmin.nic.in.

2000, eight export processing zones (EPZs) have been converted into SEZs, three new SEZs commenced operations, and 42 more had been approved as of March 2005. As of 31 March 2005, there were eight SEZs functional in India, with a total investment of 18,309 million rupees (Rs) and employment of 100,000, contributing around 5% of total merchandise exports during 2004/05. As per the latest available reports, the total number of operational SEZs has jumped to 28 (Times of India [ToI] 2006). The policy on SEZs has generated significant interest among state-level governments and ministries including commerce and industry, agriculture, and communications. The only exception has been the Ministry of Finance, which has voiced concerns over the public finance implications of the growing number of agreements being entered into by various subnational governments and SEZ developers.[10]

Patterns in Foriegn Direct Investment Inflows

FDI inflows to India grew gradually from $97 million during 1990/91 to a record level of $7.8 billion during 2005/06.[11] The cumulative flows of inward FDI amounted to $39 billion between August 1991 and April 2006. FDI inflows into India have moved increasingly toward services, especially telecommunications, financial, and nonfinancial services, including information technology (IT) support.

Despite the significant increase in foreign investment flows, India remains inconspicuous as a host country from a cross-country perspective. India's shares of global and developing-country FDI inflows were around 0.8% and 2.3%, respectively, during 2004. India has been unable

---

[10]   This is reflected in the recent debate that arose on the limit of 150 as the total number of special economic zones (SEZs). The debate was led by the Ministry of Commerce and Industry, supported by several state governments, who supported relaxation of the limit, with some opposition from the Ministry of Finance due to adverse public finance implications (The Times of India [ToI] 2006). The limit of 150 was relaxed in a recent meeting of an empowered group of ministers, and any review of SEZ rules can now occur only once at least 75 SEZs are operational.

[11]   Until recently, official measurements of foreign direct investment (FDI) inflows consisted only of foreign equity interest in an enterprise. But Indian statistics on FDI have undergone revisions to enhance the comprehensiveness of the FDI data and better align it with international practices. Since 2000/01, two sets of official FDI statistics are provided. The first estimate covers equity capital only and the second additionally includes reinvested earnings and other capital such as intercorporate debt transactions. The process of improving the comparability of Indian FDI data, however, remains an ongoing effort, and is being accomplished by steadily (subject to data availability) extending coverage of FDI to include additional subheads of reinvested earnings and other capital. The official redefinition has resulted in a significant increase in annual estimated FDI inflows representing an average increase of 48.2% between 2000/01 and 2005/06.

to exploit the potential for export-oriented FDI flows in manufacturing, unlike East Asian countries. Multinational investments in Indian manufacturing are largely aimed at serving the local market, in contrast to the large export-oriented investment flows in the PRC. The share of multinational enterprises in India's exports is marginal at less than 10% compared to the corresponding share of 55% in the PRC. However, some multinationals—such as Hyundai, Ford, and Toyota—have recently begun to use India for export-platform production (Kumar 2005a). India is also involved in the globalization of IT services and business process outsourcing. Various official agencies have expressed a sense of urgency in needing to attract more FDI, especially in the development of infrastructure, manufacturing, and labor-intensive sectors (Ministry of Commerce and Industry [MoC&I] 2006, Ministry of Finance [MoF] 2006).

During 2004/05, FDI inflows to India were equivalent to approximately 2% of gross fixed capital expenditure, based on the older definition of FDI, and 3.1% based on the revised definition, an increase from 0.2% in 1992/93. The stock of FDI rose from less than $2 billion in April 1991 to $38.9 billion in March 2006, representing 5% of GDP in 2005/06. FDI inflows increased steadily between 1992/93 and 1997/98. This was followed by a volatile period with a decline in the absolute value of inflows during the final 2 years of the 1990s as well as during the period 2002–2004 with some growth in the intervening years. There has been a recovery in FDI inflows since 2004/05 (Figure 2.6). India's importance in global FDI flows has also shown a marked improvement during the last few years. India's rose from 0.4% in 2001 to 0.8% in 2004, while those hosted by developing countries rose from 1.5% in 2001 to 2.3% in 2004.

Studies have found macroeconomic fundamentals and performance, especially growth in industrial value-added, to be an important driver of FDI inflows in India (Kumar 2005a). Hence, the recent recovery of Indian industry from recession is likely to have favorable effect on FDI inflows in the coming years.

The US is the single largest source of FDI inflows into India after Mauritius, contributing 15.6% of total FDI inflows between August 1991 and April 2006 (Table 2.1)[12]. The US is followed by Japan (6.4%), the Netherlands (6.2%), and the United Kingdom (6%). The other important sources of Indian FDI inflows are Germany, Singapore, the Republic of Korea, and

---

[12] In the remainder of this report, country groupings are defined as follows: (i) East Asia 1: ASEAN, People's Republic of China (PRC), Japan, and Republic of Korea; (ii) East Asia 2: ASEAN; PRC; Hong Kong, China; Japan; Republic of Korea; and Taipei,China; (iii) South Asia: Bangladesh, India, Nepal, Pakistan, and Sri Lanka; (iv) South Asian Association for Regional Cooperation (SAARC): Bangladesh, Bhutan, India, Maldives, Nepal, Pakistan, and Sri Lanka.

Figure 2.6 Growth in FDI Inflows in India, 1990/91–2005/06

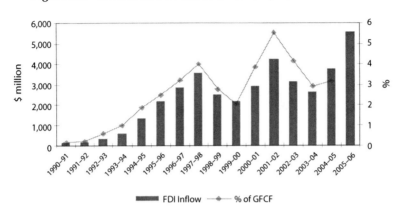

FDI = foreign direct investment, GDP = gross domestic product, GFCF = gross fixed capital formation, % = percent.

Note: The FDI inflow data consisting of equity capital only as comparable data of total FDI is not available for the period prior to 2000/01 but FDI inflows as % of GDP is based on the revised FDI data from 2000/01 onwards.

Source: Authors based on data available from Secretariat for Industrial Assistance (SIA) and National Accounts Statistics (NAS), various issues, available at http://dipp.nic.in and http://mospi.nic.in.

Malaysia. The EU countries accounted for 24% of FDI inflows and the East Asian countries accounted for 24% of FDI inflows during the period 1991–2006. South Asian countries are not important sources of India's FDI inflows, although in recent years Sri Lankan firms have increasingly invested in India. Mauritius contributed the largest share at 37% of actual FDI inflows into India during 1991–2006. These are in fact investments from other sources routed via Mauritius because of the special tax treatment offered to transitional capital in that country.[13] Interestingly, the India–Singapore CECA includes provisions for Mauritius-like tax treatment to Singapore.

The cumulative investments from East Asia are approximately $4.6 billion, representing 14% of cumulative FDI stocks in India in April 2006. Of the East Asian countries, Japan, the Republic of Korea, and Singapore are ranked among the top 10 investing countries in India. Hong Kong, China; Indonesia; Malaysia; Philippines; and Thailand have also important invest-

---

[13] The emergence of Mauritius as the largest source of FDI can be explained by the Double Taxation Avoidance Agreement between Mauritius and India, which allows foreign investors to minimize their tax liabilities. According to the Agreement, corporate profits are taxable in the country of residence of the shareholder and not in the country of residence of the company. As Mauritius is virtually a tax heaven, a company resident in Mauritius escapes tax liability.

Table 2.1 Relative Importance of East Asia and South Asia in India's Cumulative FDI Flows

Region	Actual Inbound August 1991–April 2006		Approved Outbound April 1996–January 2006	
	$ million	% share in total	$ million	% share in total
East Asia	4,642.2	14.1	1,838.1	12.4
ASEAN+3	4,249.3	12.9	1,256.8	8.4
ASEAN	1,366.1	4.1	1,093.9	7.4
PRC	2.9	0.0	154.7	1.0
Japan	2,126.1	6.4	6.2	0.0
Korea, Republic of	754.4	2.3	2.0	0.0
SAARC	18.5	0.1	264.9	1.8
South Asia	14.8	0.0	241.4	1.6
Others				
Mauritius	12,235.3	37.1	1,144.0	7.7
US	5,132.7	15.6	2,410.4	16.2
EU (15)	7,856.0	23.8	1,605.4	10.8
World	32,966.4	100.0	14,878.2	100.0

ASEAN = Association of Southeast Asian Nations, EU = European Union, FDI = foreign direct investment, PRC = People's Republic of China, SAARC = South Asian Association for Regional Cooperation, US = United States, % = percent.

Source: Authors based on data available from *SIA Newsletter*, available at http://dipp.nic.in; Ministry of Finance (http://finmin.nic.in).

ment interests in India. To evaluate changes in the direction of FDI inflows, the source country distribution of FDI stocks as of December 2000 and April 2006 is compared. Singapore has clearly improved its position among the important investing countries in India. Despite the increasing amounts of FDI from Hong Kong, China, the territory has instead lost in ranking. Japan and the Republic of Korea continue to be important sources of FDI, while firms from the PRC have yet to invest significantly in India.

The cumulative inflows of FDI between 1991 and 2006 were concentrated in few high-growth sectors, including electrical equipment, telecommunications, transportation equipment, chemicals, and services. Electrical equipment, including computer software and electronics, was the largest recipient, accounting for over 17% of the cumulative FDI inflows during the same period. This is followed by telecommunications, including cellular and basic telephone services and radio paging, with its contribution of 11.3% of total FDI inflows. The transport equipment industry, including motor vehicles, and the services sector (financial and nonfinancial services) each accounted for over 9% of FDI inflows. Unlike the PRC, very little of the total FDI inflows in India have augmented exports of labor-intensive manufactured products, such as textiles and garments, which accounted for only 1.3% of total FDI inflows during 1991–2006.

Between 2000 and 2006, some changes are discernible in the composition of FDI inflows.[14] The share of services doubled, from 12% to 24.3% in the cumulative FDI flows between the same period.[15] While the biggest gainer was the electrical and electronics equipment industry, the next two subsectors that increased in relative importance were services (telecommunications, financial, and nonfinancial services). Fuels, consisting of power and oil, and transport equipment also witnessed an increase in their recorded shares (Figure 2.7).

FDI from the major East Asian countries appears to be concentrated in a few industries (Table 2.2). Between 2000 and 2003, approximately 63.8% of Japanese FDIs in India was allocated to the transport equipment industry.[16] Similarly, over the same period 72.5% of FDIs from the Republic of Korea was concentrated in electrical equipment, including electronics, followed by transport equipment (9.6%). Investments from Singapore

Figure 2.7 Composition of FDI Inflows into India

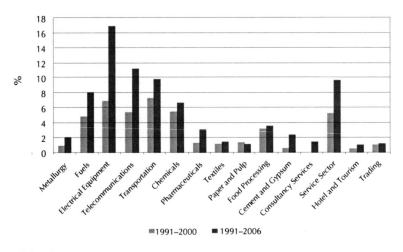

■ 1991–2000   ■ 1991–2006

FDI = foreign direct investment, % = percent.

Source: Secretariat for Industrial Assistance (SIA). *SIA Newsletter*, various issues, available at http://dipp.nic.in.

---

14 Over this period, there was a sharp decline in the share of stocks classified as miscellaneous industries.

15 Services are defined to include telecommunications, consulting, financial and nonfinancial services, hotels, tourism, and trading.

16 Data on sector-wise FDI inflows from different countries and regions is only available for January 2000 to December 2003.

Table 2.2 Share of Top Five Sectors Attracting FDI Inflows from Major Region, Jan 2000–Dec 2003

Sector	United States		Japan		ASEAN		Singapore		Korea, Republic of	
	$ million	% Share	$ million	% Share	$ million	% Share	$ million	% Share	$ million	% Share
Electrical	452.4	30.58	66.8	7.02	53.7	15.07	53.2	22.86	60.7	72.49
Transport	147.5	9.95	602.6	63.82	NA	–	NA	–	8.2	9.62
Telecom	NA	–	NA	–	19.2	5.13	NA	–	NA	–
Services (Financial and nonfinancial)	168.8	11.46	36.4	3.84	20.7	6.06	20.1	9.04	NA	–
Hotel and tourism	NA	–	NA	–	19.2	5.57	13	5.84	NA	–
Trading activities	NA	–	NA	–	21.9	6.48	NA	–	NA	–
Drugs and pharmaceuticals	68.8	4.72	NA	–	NA	–	NA	–	NA	–
Textiles	NA	–	NA	–	NA	–	NA	–	1.2	1.40
Food processing	NA	–	NA	–	NA	–	6.9	2.95	NA	–
Rubber goods	NA	–	18.2	1.88	NA	–	NA	–	NA	–
Power and oil	61.8	4.23			NA	–	NA	–	1.2	1.34
Miscellaneous industrial	NA	–	15.5	1.62	NA	–	5.9	2.57	1.9	2.22
Total of Above	**899.3**	**60.94**	**739.5**	**78.18**	**134.7**	**38.31**	**99.1**	**43.26**	**73.2**	**87.11**

ASEAN = Association of Southeast Asian Nations, $ Mn = millions of US dollars, NA = not available, – = no available data, % = percent.

Source: *SIA Newsletter*, Annual Issue 2003, Ministry of Commerce and Industry, 2006.

were, however, more evenly distributed with the electrical equipment sector, attracting the biggest share of 22.7% of aggregate FDI inflows from Singapore.

Outward Investment

There has been a significant increase in outbound FDIs from India in recent years, increasing from $0.2 billion in 1996/97 to $2.1 billion in 2005/06, and representing 0.4% of total GDP (Figure 2.8). The stock of India's outbound FDIs rose from $0.6 billion in 1995/96 to $7 billion in 2004/05. It has been suggested that India's inbound FDI flows are being rapidly matched by outbound FDI flows, with a record number and value of outbound Indian mergers and acquisitions occurring in 2006 (Business Line 2006, PricewaterhouseCoopers 2006). Indian investments abroad are aimed at acquiring niche technologies and customer bases in addition to resource-seeking investments. FDI is spread across sectors such as IT, pharmaceuticals, electronics, chemicals, steel, engineering, automobiles, and

**Figure 2.8 Annual Flows of Foreign Direct Investment in India,
1999–2005**

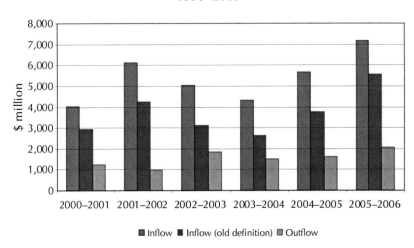

Sources: *SIA Newsletters*, available at http://dipp.nic.in; Ministry of Finance (www.finmin.nic.in)

energy. Outward investments from India to certain markets such as the United Kingdom (UK) have already exceeded the inward FDIs from these markets. Thus, the net flows of FDIs in India are extremely modest, especially for a high-growth developing economy.

The major destinations for India's outbound investment stocks are the US, Mauritius, Russia, Sudan, and UK. However, East Asian and South Asian economies are becoming increasingly important destinations as well. Investments in the PRC, Indonesia, and Singapore are on the rise, while Bangladesh; Hong Kong, China; Malaysia; Nepal; and Sri Lanka have been likewise important regional destinations for some time. There are a number of important investment proposals made in South Asian countries, but have been pending for the lack of approvals by the host countries. These include a major proposal involving $3 billion in Bangladesh by India's Tata Group in gas-based steel, fertilizer, and power plants. This proposal has triggered extensive negotiations between the Tata Group and the Government of Bangladesh. A number of Indian companies such as Mahindra & Mahindra, Tata Motors, and Dabur have intended to invest in Pakistan but have not received an encouraging response.

Manufacturing accounted for nearly 57.7% of India's cumulative FDI outflows, followed by nonfinancial services (32.6%), trading (4.7%), financial services (1%), and others (4%) between 1999/2000 and 2005/06. The major sectors attracting Indian investments abroad include pharmaceuticals, IT, electronics, chemicals, steel, engineering, automobiles, and energy-related acquisitions. Foreign investments by Indian IT companies are motivated by the need to sustain their edge in the sector by acquiring new technology and diversifying into more advanced services and to obtain access to customer bases in destination markets. India's FDI outflows have been driven by the need to secure energy needs and make acquire a larger stake in international knowledge-based industries, such as IT, pharmaceuticals, and biotechnology.

The US is the most important destination of India's outbound FDI and may be used as an illustration to understand India's outbound investments. According to the Federation of Indian Chambers of Commerce and Industry-Ernst & Young (2006), the software and business process outsourcing (BPO) sector accounted for the largest share (58%) in Indian FDIs in the US during the period 2004–2006. Health care (comprising pharmaceuticals, biotechnology, and healthcare services) accounted for 17%, while the remaining 25% was in other sectors such as telecommunications textiles, automotives, and financial services. While the software and BPO sector accounted for more than half of the investments in the US in terms of number of deals, its share in terms of value of investments was 36%, implying that the sector witnessed a large number of smaller investments. A similar situation was found in the healthcare sector. The share of other sectors in value terms was double its share in terms of volume. The biggest deals (worth $400 million) were struck in the telecommunications sector.

Regional economic arrangements have contributed positively to India's investments in Asia (Kumar 2001a, RIS 2004a). The India–Nepal bilateral FTA encouraged some Indian companies to shift their production facilities to Nepal to serve the North Indian market and provide exports to third countries. In January 1999, Indian companies were running 72 of 214 foreign ventures in Nepal, accounting for 53% of the capital of all foreign ventures. Similarly, the India–Sri Lanka FTA has stimulated the restructuring of industry in both India and Sri Lanka in order to exploit efficiency gains. Indian companies have made export-oriented investments in Sri Lanka's rubber and plantation industries, making India that country's third largest source of FDI.

Merchandise Trade with East Asia and South Asia

Trade Performance and Patterns

India's merchandise trade grew at an annual average rate of 23% between 2002 and 2006. In addition to the high growth performance, India's merchandise trade since the early 1990s has diversified considerably both in terms of commodity and country composition of trade. From a regional perspective, East Asia is currently India's dominant trading partner, followed by the EU, North America, Middle East, Africa, and other South

Asian countries. India has therefore increased its integration and interdependence with other Asian economies relative to its other trading partners (Table 2.3). In particular, significant shifts occurred between 1990/91 and 2004/05, which strengthened East Asia's position—especially the PRC's—at the expense of Europe's.

Country-wise, three of the top five markets for Indian exports are East Asian: the PRC; Singapore; and Hong Kong, China. While the US continues to be the dominant destination for India's exports, exports to the PRC have recorded the highest growth rate, becoming the third most important market for India's exports following the US and the United Arab Emirates. Exports to the PRC are concentrated in raw materials—ores, slag, and ash account for more than 50% of Indian exports to the PRC. On the imports side, the PRC became the biggest source of Indian imports during 2004/05, closely followed by the US. The United Arab Emirates is the next most significant country in India's merchandise trade, ranking second as a market for exports and fourth as a source of imports. In South Asia, Bangladesh and Sri Lanka are important markets for Indian exports. India's trade

Table 2.3 Relative Importance of East Asia and South Asia in India's Merchandise Trade

Region	Exports						Imports					
	Value ($ Million)		Share in total exports (%)		Growth (% p.a.)		Value ($ Million)		Share in total imports (%)		Growth (% p.a.)	
	1990/91	2004/05	1990/91	2004/05	1990–2004		1990/91	2004/05	1990/91	2004/05	1990–2004	
East Asia	3,568	20,739	19.7	25.8	17.0		4,483	27,538	18.6	25.2	17.0	
ASEAN	932	8,103	5.1	10.1	19.7		1,722	11,398	7.2	10.4	19.6	
SAARC	533	4,345	2.9	5.4	17.9		131	934	0.5	0.9	20.6	
South Asia	525	4,213	2.9	5.2	17.8		85	862	0.4	0.8	20.0	
N. America	2,830	14,087	15.6	17.5	–		3,235	7,592	13.4	7.0	–	
US	2,673	13,269	14.7	16.5	16.2		2,923	6,832	12.1	6.3	10.4	
Europe	8,456	19,796	46.6	24.6	–		9,731	26,857	40.4	24.6	–	
EU (15)	4,989	16,771	27.5	20.8	10.0		7,067	18,321	29.4	16.8	9.7	
Middle East	1,044	12,536	5.8	15.6	20.7		3,433	8,661	14.3	7.9	18.3	
Africa	468	5,381	2.6	6.7	20.3		573	3,836	2.4	3.5	18.7	
LAC	95	2,105	0.5	2.6	29.4		546	2,018	2.3	1.8	28.5	
World	18,145	80,525	100.0	100.0	14.8		24,073	109,152	100.0	100.0	16.0	

ASEAN = Association of Southeast Asian Nations, EU = European Union, LAC = Latin American Countries, p.a. = per annum, SAARC = South Asian Association for Regional Cooperation, – = no available data.

Notes: The share in case of 2004/05 imports adds up to around 70% only because the origin of approximately 30% of imports is not reported. These imports are mainly petroleum imports.

Source: India Trades, Centre for Monitoring Indian Economy.

with South Asian countries tends to be underestimated because of substantial proportion of trade is conducted informally. A sizeable proportion of India–Pakistan trade is conducted through third countries such as Dubai and Singapore because India does not have MFN status in Pakistan.[17]

Overall trade statistics for East Asia mask important subregional changes that have occurred in India's trading relationship with the region. The PRC has been the strongest relative gainer in India's East Asian trade, while Japan has suffered a sizeable decline in its relative position. Within East Asia, Japan's share declined by 33 percentage points, while the PRC's share increased by 25 percentage points between 1990/91 and 2004/05 (Appendix Table A2.4). Apart from the PRC, Hong Kong, China; Indonesia; and Singapore gained, while Malaysia and Taipei,China declined in relative importance. Within South Asia, Sri Lanka increased its relative position considerably, especially on the imports side, as did Nepal. Bangladesh lost ground, especially on the exports side. While the relative position of Pakistan improved in India's exports markets within South Asia, Pakistan lost position as a source of Indian imports from within the subcontinent.

Manufactured products, which contribute more than 75% of the total merchandise exports, have witnessed considerable changes in the relative importance of different products. The share of products such as chemicals, mineral fuels, iron and steel, electrical equipment, auto parts, and pharmaceutical products has increased, while the share of India's traditional exports such as marine products, textiles, and clothing has declined. Compared to India's top global exports, exports of ores, cotton, and plastic products rank higher among India's exports to East Asia relative to overall international exports. Between 1990/91 and 2004/05, the importance of gems and jewelry, mineral oils and products, iron and steel, organic chemicals, and plastic increased, while the share of cotton, fish, and ores declined in India's exports to East Asia. India's exports to South Asia are more concentrated; mineral oils and products, automobiles and parts, and cereals alone account for approximately 46% of exports to the region. Over time, the importance of automobile and parts declined considerably, while the share of mineral oils and products, cereals, iron and steel, organic chemicals, and electrical equipment increased. Appendix Table A2.5a lists India's top 10 2-digit exports and imports from the East Asian and South Asian economies.

The major commodity groups in India's international imports include fuels, gems and jewelry, electrical machinery, iron and steel, vegetable oils, ships, aircraft, and fertilizers. Although there is considerable overlap among the top few commodity groups in India's global and East Asian

---

[17]   See RIS (2002) for more details.

imports, there are important differences in the relative importance of these groups. For instance, East Asia is a much more important source for India's imports of various types of electrical equipment, vegetable oils, electronic goods, wood products, automotive equipment, and manmade fibers. The composition of India's imports from South Asia varies more widely than India's global or East Asian imports. Imports from South Asia are dominated by agricultural products and nondurable consumer goods such as vegetable oils, tea and coffee, sugar and sugar confectionery, edible fruits and nuts, vegetables, cotton, and beverages. Copper, iron and steel, plastic products, cosmetics, and toiletries also form important groups of imports from South Asia.

So far, India's economic integration with other Asian economies has been largely market-driven (ADB 2002). However, the India–Sri Lanka FTA appeared to increase trade flows among the two countries in recent years. Nonetheless, the statistics above underscore the growing importance of the East Asian economies in India's international trade, suggesting favorable implications for formal regional trade arrangements. East Asia is currently the most buoyant geographic region in terms of international flows of goods and investments and is highly integrated with the global production networks. Policy-driven integration with this region could help strengthen India's foothold in the international division of labor, especially in manufacturing where the growing segmentation of production processes presents considerable opportunities.

Import Protection

During the 1980s, despite reforms undertaken elsewhere in the economy, customs tariff rates increased, with the import-weighted average duty rising from 38% to 87% (between 1980/81 and 1989/90). On the eve of reforms, the peak rate of effective customs rate was as high as 355% (Figure 2.9). Beginning in 1991, rationalization was pursued, leading to a simpler tariff structure and lower overall tariffs. The peak rate of customs duty on non-agricultural products imports dropped sharply from 355% to 20% between 1990 and 2005, and again to 12.5% in 2006–2007.[18] As a result, the simple applied average tariff rate came down to 29.1% in 2004 (WTO 2006). In addition to lower tariff rates, procedures were also rationalized and simplified. Reforms included (i) pruning of notifications, (ii) elimination of large numbers of end-use exemptions, (iii) unification of rates for similar items, and (iv) merging of basic and auxiliary rates during the reform period. The

---

[18] The peak rate was reduced continuously from the 1990s, except when a surcharge was imposed in 1998. During 2001, the 10% surcharge on customs duties was abolished and the peak customs tariff was brought down from 38.5% to 35%.

Figure 2.9 Peak Customs Tariff Rates

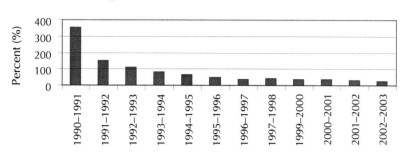

Sources: Economic Survey, 2001–2002 and Union Government Budget Statements.

number of tariff slabs has been cut, with *ad valorem* rates getting reduced to four categories of 5%, 15%, 25%, and 35% in 2001. This has resulted in a significant decline in effective peak rates of protection and reduction in the dispersion in tariff rates.

Significant policy initiatives were also taken for the tariffication of non-tariff measures. Prior to the 1990s, India's trade policy regime was highly complicated. Imports were regulated by both quantitative restrictions (QRs) and high tariff levels. India started dismantling QRs progressively in the 1990s as a part of its trade reform process. Significantly, of over 10,000 tariff lines on imports, 6,161 tariff lines were liberalized simultaneously on 1 April 1996. Import restrictions on 488 tariff lines were removed in 1996, 391 (at 8-digit level) in 1997, 894 in 1998, and 714 in 1999. As part of India's WTO commitment, the dismantling of the restrictions on the remaining 715 items was completed on 31 March 2001. However, as allowed for under Article XX and XXI of the General Agreement on Tariffs and Trade (GATT), QRs are still being maintained on about 5% of the tariff lines (538 items) on health, safety, and moral grounds. With the progressive liberalization of QRs on imports, the share of tariff lines freed for imports increased from 61% in 1996 to around 95% in 2001.

As tariffs and quantitative restrictions declined, India emerged as the biggest initiator of antidumping cases at the end of the 1990s, initiating 448 investigations between 1995 and 2006. The first antidumping investigation in India was initiated in 1992. The number of initiations gradually increased to 81 in 2002 but declined subsequently to 21 in 2004 and 28 in 2005 (WTO 2006). In terms of product category distribution, the largest number of cases has been filed regarding chemicals, petrochemicals, steel, other metals, fibers, and yarns. The countries and/or customs territories against which cases have been filed are the PRC, the EU-25 countries, the Republic of Korea, and Taipei,China (Table 2.4). The EU,

Table 2.4 Regional Distribution of Antidumping Cases, 1992/93–2004/05

Region/country	Investigations initiated
East Asia	224
China, People's Republic of	80
Taipei,China	30
Korea, Republic of	29
Japan	22
Singapore	19
Indonesia	15
Thailand	15
Malaysia	7
Hong Kong, China	6
Philippines	1
South Asia	3
Nepal	2
Bangladesh	1
Others	175
European Union (25)	71
United States	22
Total	402

Source: Annual Report 2004–05, Directorate General of Anti-Dumping and Allied Duties, Ministry of Commerce and Industry.

Indonesia, South Africa, and US filed a total of 124 antidumping cases against India.

Export Promotion

India has a long history of export promotion policies, which have been an integral part of its foreign trade policy. An array of instruments and agencies is involved in applying export promotion policies, which include concessional export credit, export insurance and guarantees, exemption and/or remission of import duties, other indirect taxes levied on inputs used in exports, export and marketing assistance, and other incentives offered to export-oriented enterprises and units located in special economic zones (SEZs). Appendix Table A2.6 lists the main instruments used for export promotion. The major changes in the export promotion policy that have occurred since the early 1990s include the elimination of direct

(Cash Compensatory Support) export subsidy in 1991/92, the phase out of the income tax benefits for export profits in 2003/04 under one of the sections of the Income Tax Act, and introduction of the 2005 SEZ Act and 2006 SEZ Rules. According to Panagariya (1999), despite the long history of export subsidies in India, the break in export growth is observed only after substantial import liberalization and real exchange rate depreciation, suggesting that the administration of the system of export incentives was of little importance in promoting export growth and diversification.

Regional Agreements

India's current regional arrangements have become increasingly broad in scope and currently range from the standard preferential trade in goods agreement, such as the Bangkok Agreement (now called the Asia Pacific Trade Agreement [APTA]), SAFTA, India–Sri Lanka FTA, and India–Thailand FTA, to more comprehensive integration arrangements covering trade in goods, services, and investments, such as the India–Singapore CECA (Table 2.5 and Appendix Table A2.7). Agreements such as SAFTA and BIM-STEC also involve cooperation in trade facilitation measures and cooperation in regional transport and communications infrastructure. The recent set of agreements has been negotiated on a negative-list approach rather than the positive-list approach which was employed in the initial rounds of the SAFTA.

In general, India's sensitive list includes agricultural goods, textiles, apparel, chemicals, leather, and items reserved for small-scale industries. In implementing its bilateral FTAs, India has been encountering problems related to trade deflection, particularly in goods such as vegetable oil, acrylic yarn, zinc oxide, and copper twine under the India–Nepal Trade Agreement (which allows duty-free imports from Nepal in India on a non-reciprocal basis) and goods such as copper products under the India–Sri Lanka FTA. In the case of the India–Nepal trade agreement, this concern led to a backtracking in the liberalization process, with India reintroducing rules of origin criteria in 2002 after having dispensed with them under the 1996 India–Nepal Trade and Transit Agreement. Physical quotas on imports of certain items have also been imposed (Taneja 2006). In the case of India–Sri Lanka FTA, a surge in imports of vegetable oils and pepper resulted in lobbying pressures to restrict such imports despite the imposition of a voluntary cap on vanaspati oil exports by Sri Lanka. India subsequently restricted vanaspati oil imports by allowing only the National Agricultural Cooperative Marketing Federation, a state trading enterprise, to import duty-free vanaspati from Sri Lanka. The importance of SAFTA in terms of trade liberalization is undermined by the presence of more effective overlapping bilateral arrangements in the region. The success of

Table 2.5 Profile of India's Major Free Trade Agreements in Force

Agreement	Approach	Coverage	Tariff liberalization modality/program	Rules of origin	Sensitive products
South Asian Free Trade Agreement	Negative list (NL); Special and differential treatment (SDT)	Goods but also covers harmonization of standards (HS) and customs procedures and classification, removal of barriers to investments, cooperation in transport and communications, and simplification of procedures for business visas.	10-year time frame; Full implementation by 2013 (2016) for non-LDC (LDC) members; Existing tariffs to be reduced to 20 (30) % in 2 (3) years of implementation and thereafter to 0–5% over next 5 (8) years for non-LDC (LDC) members.	40 (30) % value addition for non-LDC (LDC) members and change in tariff classification at HS 4-digit level.	Member-specific sensitive lists, which are to be reviewed every 4 years.India has 865 (744) items on its revised NL for non-LDC (LDC) members.
India–Sri Lanka Free Trade Agreement	NL; SDT	Goods only so far	8-year time frame (2000–08); Phase out of tariffs by over 3 (8)-year period by India (Sri Lanka); Duty-free access on some items in first year; on others margins of preference (25%, 35%, and 50%) in first year; Some items subject to tariff rate quotas (TRQs).	Foreign content no more than 65% of f.o.b.; and Product-to-go transformation at HS 4-digit level and final processing must occur in exporting member; Some products allowed to enter India only through specific ports.	Country-specific sensitive lists: 419 items on India's NL and 1,180 on Sri Lanka's NL.
India–Thailand Early Harvest Scheme	82 items	Goods only		Local value content of 40% of f.o.b.; change in classification at HS 4-digit level; final processing in originating	
India–Singapore CECA	Multiple lists for goods in case of India; NL for goods in case of Singapore.	Goods, services, investment, MRA on standards and technical regulation SPS, cooperation in customs, education, science & technology, air services, intellectual property	4-year time frame; 4-lists in case of India: EHP or duty-free access on specified goods in first year (506 items), list of goods with phased duty elimination based on margin of preference (2202); list of goods with phased duty reduction (2407), and negative list (6551); positive list in services	Multiple criteria and product specific rules: Foreign content no more than 65% of f.o.b.; product to go transformation at HS 4-digit level; certain operations to be performed in originating country.	India-specific NL only at HS 8-digit level in goods

CECA = Comprehensive Economic Cooperation Agreement, EHP = Early Harvest Programme, f.o.b. = free on board, LDC = least-developed country, MRA = mutual recognition agreement, SPS = sanitary and phytosanitary.

Source: Based on texts of agreements, available at http://commerce.nic.in.

Box 2.1 The India–Singapore CECA

India–Singapore Comprehensive Economic Cooperation Agreement (CECA), which came into force on 1 August 2005, is the first such agreement signed by India and could provide useful lessons for future arrangements. The agreement is an integrated package comprising trade in goods and services, as well as the movement of natural persons and investments. It also includes a mutual recognition agreement (MRA) and, provisions for cooperation in science and technology, education, air services, e-commerce, intellectual property protection, media, and dispute settlement. Trade in goods includes exchange of tariff concessions at the HS 8-digit level. A working group on customs cooperation has been established. The MRAs on Standards and Technical Regulations, Sanitary, and Phytosanitary measures provide for recognition of standards and technical regulations on goods. India is to open investments on a positive-list basis (including food products, textiles and apparel, beverages, leather, goods, paper products, chemical products, electronics, motor vehicles, infrastructure, etc.). The existing Double Tax Avoidance Agreement (DTAA) was amended to provide for sharing of information, improved tax treatment, and (Mauritius-like) concessional capital gains tax. Singapore has made commitments on a negative-list basis by opening all manufacturing sectors, save for six. In services, the agreement allows for preferential access in a number of services under the Economic Integration Agreement in Services (EIAS). Visa restrictions are to be relaxed for professionals in over 127 categories and Singapore has agreed to recognize the degrees issued by specified universities and technical education boards of both countries for issuance of multientry visas.

Source: Dr. Ruud Salyasevi, TA team member (personal communication).

SAFTA would, therefore, most likely hinge on the progress in trade facilitation, customs harmonization, and cooperation in regional transport- and trade-related infrastructure, in addition to other challenges such as Pakistan granting MFN status to India.

In general, the rules of origin (ROO) employed in India's trade agreements consist of multiple criteria. The change in tariff classification criteria is generally adopted at the tariff heading (Harmonized System Code [HS] 4-digit) level, but in the India–ASEAN FTA, which is in the final stages of negotiation, the transformation is restricted to the tariff subheading (HS 6-digit) level. In addition, the ROO requires minimum value-added of 35–40%. The ROO also provides for a detailed list of nonqualifying operations as well as some product-specific restrictions.

Among India's trade policy initiatives, the emphasis on closer economic ties with ASEAN has been most emphatic since the early 1990s. However, despite the importance of this issue, negotiations for an ASEAN–India FTA have been arduous. India conceded to a less restrictive FTA with ASEAN than with other trade partners. For instance, in contrast to the general practice of requiring change in tariff classification at the product-heading level, India agreed to a less restrictive classification change of the product's tariff subheading. India also reduced the list of sensitive items from 1,414 to 854 and again to 560. However, disagreement continues on the list of these excluded products. As a result, the January 2007 deadline to implement the ASEAN–India FTA has not been met. The framework agreement, which was signed in October 2004, included provisions for an early harvest program of initial tariff cuts but was likewise dropped.

Government Revenue Role of Tariffs

The importance of import tariffs as a source of government revenue has declined considerably since the early 1990s and is expected to continue to drop. The share of tariffs in total tax revenues peaked at 35.8% during 1989/90, when it was the central government's second-most important source of gross tax revenue after excise duties, which had a share of 44.4%. By the end of 2005/06, customs collections were relegated to fourth place among the important sources of central government receipts from direct and indirect taxes, accounting for around 14% of gross tax receipts. While excise duties remain the most important source of tax revenues, corporate tax and personal income tax collections exceed customs duty collections. The tax on services, which was introduced in 1994 based on a positive-list approach, has also been rapidly gaining in importance, partly offsetting the declining role of trade tariffs in government revenue.

Transport and Trade Administration

Infrastructure is arguably the biggest challenge to India's development process. Despite concerted efforts to promote investments in infrastructure through policy initiatives, fiscal and financial incentives, and public–private partnership ventures, progress has been far from satisfactory. The high-density rail and road corridors are already saturated in terms of capacity, and accelerated economic growth is only going to increase congestion on these routes in the future. Progress in international trade logistics has also lagged far behind growth in international trade. While some unprecedented measures have recently been initiated to enhance capacity—such as the introduction of private participation and competition in the movement of container trains—demand for infrastructure continues to outpace supply. In view of the high priority accorded to infrastructure development, a special infrastructure committee headed by the prime minister was set up in 2004 to fast-track and monitor progress in the sector. The main policy initiatives include an integrated corridor approach, institutionalization of public–private partnerships, corporatization of management, and the establishment of independent regulatory authorities with corresponding legislation.

Brief Overview and Recent Developments in Trade-Related Transport

The major rail and road transport corridors in India consist of the quadrilateral joining the four metropolitan cities (Delhi in the north, Chennai in the south, Mumbai in the west, and Kolkata in the east) and the diagonals, which link those cities with India's most important ports. The Delhi–Mumbai corridor is one of India's most important high-density corridors, and rail and road capacities are fully stretched on this route. Port congestion has also persisted because of delayed evacuation of cargo from ports on account of poor road and rail connectivity. Other corridors run north–south (Srinagar to Kanyakumari) and east–west (Silchar to Porbandar).

Roads

India has an extensive road network of 3.3 million kilometers (km), which carry about 65% of the freight and 80% of passenger traffic. However, highways and expressways, which constitute about 2% of all roads, carry 40% of road traffic. The National Highway Development Project (NHDP) is the major initiative currently being implemented to improve India's road network. Phases I and II of NHDP was launched in 1999 and Phase III in 2005 to upgrade and widen 10,000 km of high-density national highway corridors. National Highways Authority of India is also responsible for ensuring road connectivity to ports. For all road development projects, 100% FDI is automatically permitted. The high priority accorded to the sector is reflected in the application of various incentives, such as tax exemptions for a period of 10 years, and in the terms of the Model Concession Agreement for public-private partnerships in national highway development.

Railways

Indian Railways is a central government monopoly that owns, operates, and regulates the extensive railway network.[19] The railways network can be broadly divided into the following segments: (i) high-density corridors,

---

[19]   In 2005, the Indian railway network consisted of 63,465 route-kilometers (km) of which 47,749 was broad gauge (1,676 mm) and rest mostly meter gauge, with only 4,153 route-km narrow gauge.

consisting of the quadrilateral joining the four metropolitan cities (Delhi, Mumbai, Kolkata, and Chennai) and the diagonals; (ii) connecting lines that feed the high-density corridors (these handle mostly mineral traffic and the growth is dependent on products and emerging market conditions); (iii) alternative routes, which include some recently converted meter-gauge to broad-gauge connections that could provide relief to the high-density corridors; and (iv) low-density lines, which consist of both broad and meter gauges and have uneconomic traffic density with little prospects of traffic growth.[20] The high-density eastern and western routes are saturated in terms of line capacity utilization. The average goods train speed was 23.3 kilometers per hour (km/hr) on broad gauge and 16.9 km/hr on meter gauge. Indian Railways carries mainly bulk cargo, but it has also initiated the provision of multi-modal services with the establishment of the Container Corporation of India Limited (CONCOR) in 1988. CONCOR currently provides the only means by which shippers may obtain containerized freight transportation by rail in India, although this will change soon. Many of CONCOR'S services have road as well as rail transport legs. CONCOR'S volume of business handled has grown rapidly from 109,000 20-foot equivalent units (TEUs) in 1990 to 1.9 million TEUs in 2005.

The Government's railway strategy paper proposed the corporatization of the railways, and although the railway ministry opposed this measure at the time, important noncore activities have been corporatized. CONCOR used to monopolize the movement of container traffic by rail. In January 2006, the Government said it would allow private firms to run container trains for domestic and trade-related traffic. Since then, 12 operators have obtained licenses to run container trains; at least four of these operators have foreign partners. The railway budget statement in February 2006 announced plans for initiating multimodal high-axle[21] loads through computerized control on the western and eastern routes. The Government has also indicated that it planned to develop separate corridors for freight traffic to meet transport needs between India's four main metropolitan cities. To begin with, the Government announced that the work on the New Delhi–Mumbai (western) and New Delhi–Howrah (eastern) projects would commence soon with Japanese aid.

Seaports

The total volume of cargo handled at Indian ports was 573 million tons (Mt) in 2005/06. India has 12 major ports, six each on the east and west

---

20   Ministry of Shipping, Road Transport and Highways, 2006.
21   25-ton-axle-load wagons capable of hauling load up to 80 tons.

Box 2.2 Recent Developments in Indian Infrastructure

Roads. In January 2005, the Committee on Infrastructure adopted an action plan to develop the national highway network, consisting of (i) widening the golden quadrilateral (network linking the four metropolitan cities in India, i.e., Delhi–Mumbai–Chennai–Kolkata), north–south (connecting Srinagar to Kanyakumari), and east–west (connecting Silchar to Porbandar) highway corridors to four lanes. Widening the golden quadrilateral is near completion, and the same work on the other two corridors is expected to be completed by 2009; (ii) widening to four lanes some 10,000 km of high-density national highways (NHDP-III), connecting state capitals through build–operate–transfer (BOT) schemes; (iii) building 20,000 km (NHDP-IV) of two-lane highways for balanced and equitable distribution of road improvements nationwide; (iv) widening to six lanes some 6,500 km (NHDP-V) of the golden quadrilateral and certain other stretches through public–private partnerships and BOT schemes to be completed by 2012; (v) building 1,000 km of expressway (NHDP-VI); (vi) other highway projects (NHDP-VII) such as development of ring roads and bypasses; and (vii) Accelerated North-East Development Program for India's northeast. On the immediate agenda is widening to six lanes some 6,500 km of four-lane highways on the golden quadrilateral and other high-density stretches through public–private partnerships.

Railways. In January 2006, the Government permitted the private sector to operate container freight trains for domestic and export–import traffic. The Government has said it would develop dedicated rail links for freight connecting the four metro-politan cities. Work on the New Delhi–Mumbai and New Delhi–Kolkata Corridors is to commence soon with Japanese financial aid. Work on the New Delhi Dedi-cated Freight Corridor (DFC) inaugurated in October 2006 and the independent line for movement of goods is expected to be complete within 5 years.

Seaports. The major projects underway include dredging the Palk Strait in southern India to facilitate maritime trade and the National Maritime Development Program to modernize and expand port capacity. In addition, the government has instructed each major port to prepare a perspective plan for 20 years and an action plan for 7 years, to be submitted by November 2006. A committee has also finalized the plan for improving rail and road connectivity to major ports within 3 years. A comprehensive National Maritime Policy is also being formulated.

Airports. Greenfield international airports at Bangalore and Hyderabad are under construction. Modernization and expansion of Delhi and Mumbai airports has been awarded through public–private partnerships. A similar plan is under consideration for the Chennai and Kolkata airports. A model concession agreement is being developed to standardize and simplify the participation of private partners in airport modernization and expansion.

NHDP = National Highway Development Project.

Source: Based on information available at www.infrastructure.gov.in and media reports.

coasts and 187 minor and intermediate ports along a 7,517-km coastline.[22] Major ports handle nearly 75% of total traffic. Roughly 95% of India's international trade by volume and 70% by value is carried by sea (TOI 2006). Cargo handled by major ports grew 9.5% per year over the last 3 years. Containerized cargo has grown at the rate of 14% per year over the last 5 years. During 2004/05, 4.5 million TEUs were handled at Indian ports, registering a growth of 12%, but the level of containerization remained at 48.2% (CONCOR 2006). Despite recent growth, India's largest container port, the Jawaharlal Nehru Port Trust (JNPT), handled roughly 2.37 million TEUs in 2004/05 compared to 6.43 million TEUs in Dubai and 21.93 million TEUs in Hong Kong, China during the same period. To attract investments in port construction and modernization, the Government has automatically allowed 100% FDI in port development projects. Investment incentives, such as 100% income tax exemptions, are also available for the first 10 years. Several foreign players, including Maersk, P&O Ports, Dubai Ports International, and PSA Singapore, have invested in Indian ports. Private port operation has contributed to improvements. While the turnaround time achieved by port authorities at the JNPT is 1.16 days, it is 0.79 days at a private container terminal. A container terminal is also being set up near the Kochi port, which is to be developed on a build–operate–transfer (BOT) basis.

Indian ports are currently expanding capacity, upgrading infrastructure, and improving efficiency. To facilitate the process, each port is in the process of preparing a 20-year perspective plan and a 7-year action plan. Projects for improving road and rail connectivity to ports are also ongoing or soon to be sanctioned (Appendix Table A2.8). Recent developments at Indian seaports involve Indian ports establishing integrated SEZs and offering other services that will increase value adding. These include ports like Dighi in Maharashtra, Mundra in Gujarat, Cochin Port, and another 11 major ports drawing up plans for SEZs. These zones are expected to evolve into industrial clusters. The move is driven by the tax incentives offered to SEZs, savings in transactions costs, and easy export–import procedures.

Airports

India has 125 airports of which 11 are designated for international service. In 2004/05, Indian airports handled 60 million passengers and 1.3 Mt of cargo. The key air cargo routes are between India and Europe and the US, India and Singapore, and India and the PRC (MoCA 2006). While cargo

---

[22]   The major ports are Kolkata, Haldia, Paradip, Vishakapatnam, Ennore, Chennai, Tuticorin, Cochin, New Mangalore, Mormugao, Mumbai, Jawaharlal Nehru Port Trust (JNPT), and Kandla.

carried by the international carrier Air India accounts for less than 1% of total cargo exported by weight, it accounts for 35% of the total value of exports. Air India accounts for 97% of the country's total tourists arrivals.

Currently, all airports are owned and operated by the Airports Authority of India (AAI). However, the privatization of the Delhi and Mumbai airports is in progress. New international airports in Bangalore and Hyderabad are being developed by private consortia. Five more greenfield airports will be developed through public–private partnerships, and modernization of the Kolkata and Chennai airports will be initiated. Development of 35 non-metropolitan airports, along with airports in northeast India, has been initiated. The AAI Act has been amended to provide legal support for airport privatization. The Government is preparing a comprehensive civil aviation policy and contemplating setting up an independent Airports Economic Regulatory Authority and the associated legislation. Indian private airlines (Jet, Sahara, Kingfisher, Deccan, and Spicejet) account for around 60% of domestic passenger traffic and some have now started international operations. Air India and Indian Airlines are government-owned international and domestic carriers, respectively. One hundred percent FDI is permissible for existing airports, but Foreign Investment Promotion Board (FIPB) approval is required for FDI beyond 74%. Automatic 100% FDI is permissible for greenfield airports, and foreigners may own 49% of domestic airlines as long as they are not foreign airlines. Nonresident Indians may own 100% of the shares in a domestic airline.

Customs and Trade Facilitation

India has made concerted efforts, especially over the last few years, to simplify, streamline, and automate customs administration. In 1998, the Central Board of Excise and Customs (CBEC)[23] issued a Vision Strategy that aims to facilitate trade through the increased use of IT and by fostering an environment to elicit voluntary compliance. Since 2004, the CBEC has implemented several measures based on the recommendations of the

---

[23] The Central Board of Excise and Customs (CBEC) under the Ministry of Finance is the nodal agency for formulating relevant policy and for administering the associated legislation, rules, and regulations through 35 commissionerates across India. The main CBEC website (www.cbec.gov.in) provides comprehensive information related to customs legislation, rules, regulations, and tariff rates along with information and notifications of changes in such rules and regulations. Another departmental website (www.icegate.gov.in) maintains the Customs Electronic Data Interchange System (ICES) and provides access to the Customs E-commerce Gateway (ICEGATE), providing electronic filing and clearance services to exporters and importers. Along with reforms in tax policy, the CBEC has also implemented a series of administrative reforms based on the recommendations of several expert committees.

Working Group on Trade Facilitations (2004) and the Task Force on Indirect Taxes (2002). The so-called Business Process Re-engineering (BPR) system will involve the setting up of nationwide networks, databases, national data centers, data warehousing facilities, disaster recovery sites, and online tracking of status, and will introduce risk management systems as well as e-payment of customs duties.[24]

The Customs electronic data interchange (EDI) system (ICES) was established in 1995 and is currently running in 34 locations, covering 90% of international trade in terms of volume. During 2004/05, 94% of import documents and 92% of export documentation was processed electronically at the automated locations. The customs e-commerce gateway facility for remote assessment of customs documents (i.e., bills of entry and shipping bills) has also helped reduce export and import documentation requirements. Taxpayers are able to track the status of their customs documents online through special enquiry counters, touch-screen kiosks, and mobile phone short message service (SMS). CBEC also introduced public key infrastructure (PKI) technology, which is also known as a digital signature. The Licensed Certifying Authority (iCert) provides PKI to its clients. In 2005, CBEC set up a risk management system to allow computerized post-clearance audit through introduction of an Accredited Client Programme (ACP) under which clients who are assessed as highly compliant would be assured facilitation. On the export side, consignments below a specified value have been exempted from examination procedures.[25]

A survey based study by Divaakar et al (2006) provides a discussion of the major problems faced by Indian exporters in selected destinations. The survey suggests the US to be the destination where Indian exporters face the highest number of problems, followed by the EU and the Middle East. Far fewer problems are encountered in India's trade with Japan and Southeast Asia, although Indian exports of food face the most problems in Japan. Exporters were also least familiar with Japan's import requirements and other contractual obligations. The biggest problems faced by Indian exporters to Southeast Asia are centered on the frequent changes in rules, regulations, and documentation requirements. While the major problems encountered in the US are related to security, Advanced Cargo Declaration, and Customs-Trade Partnership Against Terrorism (C-TPAT), those in the EU include poor harmonization of rules and procedures and health and phyto-

---

[24] These include the Tax Reform Committee (headed by R. J. Chelliah) 1993, the Advisory Group on Tax Policy and Tax Administration for the Tenth Plan (headed by P. Shome) 1998, the Task Force on Direct and Indirect Taxes (headed by V. L. Kelkar) 2002, and the Working Group on Trade Facilitation (headed by Jayanta Roy) 2004.

[25] Please refer to Chaturvedi (2006), Taneja (2004b), and Sengupta and Bhagbati (2003) for details of various trade facilitation measures introduced in India since 1998.

sanitary issues. The major problems in the PRC were related to language, nontransparency, and poor banking controls on titles to goods. India's trade with Bangladesh and Nepal faces many problems related to physical infrastructure bottlenecks and procedural delays at land border crossings.

Trade Finance

India allows free buying and selling of foreign exchange for current account purposes, as stipulated in the 1999 Foreign Exchange Management Act. Since 2002, authorized foreign exchange dealers are permitted to approve trade credits up to $20 million per import transaction for import of all items permissible under the Foreign Trade Policy (except gold) with a maturity period of less than 3 years.[26] Trade credits exceeding $20 million per import transaction require prior approval of the Reserve Bank of India (RBI).

Box 2.3 Trade Financing Procedures

The term "trade credit" for imports is used to refer to credit extended for imports directly by the overseas supplier, bank, and financial institution for an original maturity period of less than 3 years. Such trade credit includes supplier's credit, where credit for imports into India is extended by the overseas supplier for a period of more than 6 months but less than 3 years; and buyer's credit, under which loans for imports into India are arranged by the importer from a bank or financial institution outside India for a maturity period of less than 3 years. In the mechanism of supplier's credit, the importer company opens a letter of credit from a bank in India, under the usance terms, and the supplier company gets its bills discounted from a foreign office or correspondent of the letter of credit opening bank in India. In the buyer's credit case, the foreign lender raises a loan account in the name of the buyer on the strength of a guarantee, letter of undertaking, or a letter of comfort from the importer's bank in India. All exporters are required to furnish a declaration to the Reserve Bank of India in the prescribed form the export value of goods and services. For exporters, both pre-shipment and post-shipment credits are available in both rupee and dollar denominations. An application for pre-shipment advance is accompanied with confirmed export order or contract, letter of credit, or an undertaking from the merchant exporter, in case goods are to be supplied to a merchant exporter or trading house. Other documents to be supplied for application of credit include the copies of exporter's code, a valid registration-cum-membership certificate, income tax assessment documents, and export credit insurance policy.

[26] Since April 2004, credits up to $20 million per import transaction with a maturity period exceeding 1 year but less than 3 years would be permitted only for import of capital goods. Guidelines covering such credit with a maturity period up to 1 year remain unchanged.

Export credit in foreign currency has increased substantially during the past 5 years. Post-shipment finance is provided against shipping documents or duty drawback claims. Both pre-shipment and post-shipment export credits are made available at concessional terms. RBI sets the ceiling rates for export credit but banks are free to charge lower rates of interest in accordance with their cost of funds, margin requirements and risk perceptions, etc. At present, the upper limit on interest rates on export credit is set as the benchmark prime lending rate less 2.5 percentage points.

A report issued by the Working Group to Review Export Credit highlighted the problems persistently faced by small and medium-sized exporters such as procedural delays in obtaining financing, an inability to optimally utilize special schemes such as the gold card scheme, and their relative inability to take advantage of liberal interest rates on export credit.

Other Issues

Although some progress has been made in the recent past, India continues to suffer from substantial trade transactions costs. For instance, a typical import shipment could take as long as 4–6 days at airports and 6–8 days at seaports in 2004 compared to the international norm of 12 hours (Roy 2004). Some information on India's trade transaction–related problems is summarized in Table 2.6.

India has signed various trade and transit agreements with Bangladesh, Bhutan, and Nepal, all of which are all currently linked to India through its rail network. An additional rail connection with Bhutan is under consideration. India provides port facilities at Kolkata and Haldia and 15 transit routes to and from Kolkata/Haldia for Nepal's trade with third countries. Nepal has also been offered transit facilities at the Mumbai and Kandla ports. India also provides Nepal rail links (through Radhikapur and

Table 2.6 Typical Cargo Handling Times

Transaction	India	International norm
Air freight	Delhi airport	
Exports	2.5 days	Less than 12 hours
Imports	8 days	Less than 12 hours
Containerized sea freight	Mumbai	
Ship waiting time	3–5 days	Less than 6 hours
Export waiting time	3–5 days	Less than 18 hours
Import dwell time	7–14 days	Less than 24 hours

Source: Roy (2004).

Phulbari) for its trade and transit through Bangladesh. India has offered to build a broad-gauge rail link to move containerized traffic from the inland clearance depot terminal at Birgunj in Nepal. India has been seeking transit facilities for its northeastern states through Bangladesh. As for trade with Pakistan, goods are often shipped through a third country such as the United Arab Emirates.

In East Asia, India has road links with Myanmar and the PRC.[27] To increase trade in India's northeast region, the Government has asked Myanmar to open the port of Akyab on the Bay of Bengal to Indian goods. Rail links with neighboring East Asian countries are nonexistent. Of India's main liner trades, the Far East route is the most dynamic, with the last 4 years witnessing a near doubling in the volume of container movement, especially to the PRC and the Republic of Korea. According to a survey by APL, many of the dedicated direct call services listed for the Far East are shuttles to and/or from Southeast Asia, and only one of the 13 strings operating into the Bay of Bengal, for instance, goes beyond Singapore or Malaysia range to East Asia (*Hindu Business Line* 2005).

Services

The most striking aspect of India's economic performance since the early 1990s has been the rapid rise in services.[28] In contrast with traditional merchandise exports such as food and textiles, services has recorded the strongest and most sustained growth rate, averaging a little over 8% per annum since 1992/93. Exports registered one of the fastest growth rates in the world, averaging 20% per annum between 1990/91 and 2005/06, tripling India's share in world exports from 0.6% in 1990 to 1.8% in 2004, and to 2.8% in 2005. While India's position as one of the leading exporters

---

[27] India recently established a road link with the PRC. The Himalayan Nathu La route between Indian state of Sikkim and the Tibet Autonomous Region on the India–PRC border was reopened on 6 July 2006, having been closed since the 1962 border war between India and the PRC. The route was reopened a few days after the first train service was commenced between the eastern PRC and the Tibet Autonomous Region. Trade across the pass would be duty-free, with India allowed to export 29 items and the PRC 15 items. Trade would begin every year on 1 June and continue until 30 September, after which the area becomes impassable because of poor weather. A trade market has been established near the pass on the Indian side of the border. The other facilities include customs, immigration, a bank, and a telecommunications center.

[28] There is a difference in classification practices of different official agencies, which leads to variations in figures for service sector contribution to gross domestic product (GDP). The Reserve Bank of India's (RBI) definition of services includes construction as part of the service sector. In national accounts, construction is covered under industry, which makes services appear smaller.

Table 2.7 Some Information Related to Customs Reforms, December 2006

Subject of Enquiry	Response	Details
Single Admin. Document (SAD)	No	No plans at present to introduce
Harmonized Code (HS)	Yes	8-digit code
Electronic Data Processing Systems	Yes	ICES (Indian Customs Electronic Data Interchange System)
Electronic Data Interchange	Yes	Most of ship's inward manifests submitted electronically by shipping line to customs
Direct trader input	Yes	Some
Internet input	Yes	Most import shipments for which declarations are input through internet
Green channel		Replaced by risk management system
Risk management	Yes	Not applicable
Electronic banking	Yes	Duty and taxes paid through electronic transfer from consignee's bank, few (<5%)
Electronic signature	Yes	Yes, Customs officials can approve declaration using electronic signature rather than physical signature but introduced recently
Private-bonded warehouses	Partial	Import cargo can be moved directly to private warehouse, only after assessment (classification, value confirmation, etc.) but before payment of duties, and stored under customs bond for subsequent clearance
Bonded factories	Partial	Manufacturers (not located in a free trade zone) can receive imported inputs without paying duties but after customs assessment, and store, process, and export the product without paying taxes.

Source: Based on conversations with customs officials.

of IT services is well acknowledged, Indian health services exports are also gradually but steadily gaining ground. The major concerns related to India's service sector are related to the lack of commensurate growth in service sector employment and the sustainability of growth. While the share of services in GDP rose by 7.3 percentage points between 1987/88 and 1999/2000, its share in employment rose by only 3.6 percentage points. The IT sector employs approximately 1.3 million workers out of a total workforce of 397 million. The turnover of workers in this sector is high indicating excess demand, as reflected in rising wages.

Trade in Services

India's total exports of services increased from $4.6 billion in 1990/91 to $60.6 billion during 2005/06 (Table 2.8). The share of services in total exports of goods and services rose from 20% to 37% over the same period. Export growth accelerated considerably in 1997/98, rising from 9% during 1990/97 to 27.5% between 1998 and 2006. Services trade expansion is being led by exports of IT and BPO services, which contributed 38.9% to total services exports during 2005/06. In 2000, India was the world's leading exporter of IT services, ahead of Ireland and the US (Centre D'Etudes Prospectives et D'Informations Internationales [CEPII] 2003). India accounts for 65% of the global industry in offshore IT and 46% of global BPO (National Association of Software and Services Companies [NASSCOM]-McKinsey 2006).

The increased importance of IT exports is reflected in the transformation of the structure of India's services exports since 1990. While the share of travel and transportation in total services exports declined from 53.6% in 1990/91 to 33.3%, the share of miscellaneous services, including IT services, rose from 43.6% to 74.6%. Within miscellaneous services, the share of software exports increased from 22.3% in 1993/94 to 52.2% in 2005/06. More disaggregated data, which is available up to 2001/02, shows that software services contributed approximately 50%, management services contributed approximately 6.3%, and communications services contributed approximately 6.5% to the total receipts from miscellaneous services exports. On the import side, the relative importance of miscellaneous services and travel increased while the share of transportation declined over time. Within miscellaneous services, financial management services accounted for 21.4% and software services accounted for 6.2% of payments for miscellaneous services imports during 2001/02.

India's software services exports amounted to $23.6 billion during 2005/06, representing 14.5% of total export earnings and 38.9% of services exports. India's exports of IT and BPO services are heavily concentrated in two English-speaking countries consisting of the US and the UK, which respectively accounted for 66.5% and 14% of total Indian IT exports during 2004/2005.[29] Exports of IT services to the PRC, Japan,

---

[29] The information on the direction of India's services trade is extremely limited. Partner region-wise/country-wise statistics are available only for a limited number of services, including software, tourism, and flow of students. Even for these sectors, the official country statistics are available mainly on the exports of such services, while partner country data is utilized to examine the import flows. The US and Indian data on offshoring show significant differences, attributable to definitional and methodological differences and incompleteness of the US data (US Government Accountability Office 2005).

Table 2.8 India's Trade in Services, 1990/91–2005/06

	Exports				Imports			
	1990/91	1998/99	2005/06	Growth 1990/91–2005/06 (% p.a.)	1990/91	1998/99	2005/06	Growth 1990/91–2005/06 (% p.a.)
Total ($ million)	4,551	13,186	60,610	20.1	3,571	11,021	38,345	19.3
Share in Total (%)								
Travel	32.0	22.7	12.9	12.8	11.0	15.8	16.7	23.3
Transportation	21.6	14.6	10.4	14.5	30.6	24.3	19.3	17.0
Insurance	2.4	1.7	1.7	19.2	2.5	1.0	2.6	22.3
GNIE*	0.3	4.5	0.5	71.2	4.8	2.9	1.3	12.7
Miscellaneous	43.6	56.5	74.6	na	51.1	55.9	60.2	na
Of which: Software	27.1	19.9	38.9	43.5	22.4	–	–	25.6

*Relates to receipts and payments on government account not included elsewhere as well as receipts and payments on account of maintenance of embassies and diplomatic missions and offices of international institutions.

GNIE = government not included elsewhere, na = not available, p.a. = per annum, $ = US dollar, % = percent, – = no data available.

Source: India's Overall Balance of Payments and Invisibles in India's Balance of Payments, Reserve Bank of India, available at www.rbi.org.in.

Republic of Korea, and Singapore together represented 4.6% of total IT exports during 2004/05. However, top Indian IT firms are diversifying by not only establishing offices in the PRC to serve that market, but also attracting Japanese outsourcing business by employing local PRC and Japanese workers with relevant language skills (NASSCOM-McKinsey 2006).[30]

The success of Indian IT exports since the early 1990s is evident from the international trade statistics and large volumes of discussion on the subject. While the international exports of computer and information services grew at an annual average rate of growth of 23% per annum between 1995 and 2003, India's IT exports grew 38.2% between 1995/96 and 2003/04 (CEPII 2003, RBI 2006). According to Langhammer (2002), Indian IT exports appear to be the only success story, and in that sense an outlier, in the overall developing country performance in service-sector exports. The success of India's IT services industry is attributable to a number of factors, including changes in IT policy since the mid-1980s

---

[30] The location of Indian firms in the northeast PRC city of Dalian reflects the interest in the Japanese market as Dalian is home to a large population of Japanese-speaking Chinese (ToI 2006).

and a proactive policy stance after 1991, including the establishment of software technology parks, an educational policy bias toward higher education, private expansion of engineering education and software training, public sector R&D establishments, opportune events such as General Electric's technology partnership with India beginning 1991, the Y2K (Year 2000) crisis, and contributions from the Indian diasporas (*The Economist* 2006, Srinivasan 2005, Kapur 2002, Kumar 2001b, Saxenia 2002). However, India is facing increasing competition from South Africa, the PRC, and Eastern Europe, along with a potential shortage of skilled workers with relevant language skills.

The other services sectors on which more detailed information is available are tourism and educational services (Table 2.9). South Asia is an important source of tourists and students in India. While East Asia is almost an equally important source of international students, its importance in tourist inflows in India is much less significant. Nepal and Malaysia were the two most important source countries for students, each accounting for around 10% of total student inflows. Bangladesh, Sri Lanka, Thailand, and Viet Nam are likewise important contributors to the pool of foreign students. Sri Lanka and Nepal are also important sources of tourist arrivals in India. Among the East Asian countries, Japan, Republic of Korea, Malaysia, and Singapore are the four countries ranked among the top 15 tourist markets for India. During the 1990s, the Republic of Korea was the fastest-growing tourism market for India after the US.

In terms of outflows on the services account, approximately 90% of Indian students studying abroad are in Australia, Europe, and the US. However, recent media reports have highlighted the rapid rise in the importance of the PRC as a destination for medical education (Box 2.1). The PRC; Hong Kong, China; Malaysia; Singapore; and Thailand are among the important destinations for India's outbound travel. India has become the largest source of tourists for Sri Lanka, and is one of the most important sources for Malaysia, Singapore, and Thailand.

India is also emerging as an important exporter of health services, given its cost competitiveness and the availability of the latest technology and able practitioners. India is already an important exporter of health services to Bangladesh, Bhutan, and Nepal. According to one estimate, about 50,000 patients come from Bangladesh, spending more than $1 million per year on specialized treatments (Rahman 2001). Indian health service providers such as Apollo Hospitals also operate hospitals in Bangladesh, Sri Lanka, and other Asian countries.

A number of East Asian enterprises—especially from the PRC, Malaysia, Singapore, and Thailand—are participating in construction and infrastructure

Table 2.9 Relative Importance of South Asia and East Asia in India's Trade in Selected Services

Region	Credits						Debits			
	Tourist Arrivals into India		International Students in India		IT Services		Tourist		Indian students abroad	
	% share	No.	% share	No.	% share	$ Mn	% share	No.	% share	No.
	2004	2004	2002/03	2002/03	2004/05	2004/05	2003	2003	2001/02	2001/02
East Asia	11.64	402,339	18.78	1,453	7.21	1,277	56.5	2,271,809	1.0	881
ASEAN	5.94	205,374	17.61	1,363	–	–	19.0	76,442	0.8	682
Malaysia	2.44	84,390	10.18	788	–	–	3.6	145,442	0.6	497
Singapore	1.76	60,710	0.13	10	1.69	300	7.7	309,446	–	–
Japan	2.80	96,851	0.66	51	2.82	500	1.2	47,520	0.2	199
South Asia	20.97	725,106	20.25	1,567	–	–	6.6	265,265	0	–
Bangladesh	13.81	477,446	4.81	372	–	–	2.1	84,704	0	0
Nepal	1.49	51,534	10.35	801	–	–	2.2	86,578	0	0
Sri Lanka	3.72	128,711	5.05	391	–	–	2.3	90,603	0	–
Others										
US	15.27	528,120	–	–	66.47	11,769	6.8	272,161	76.0	66,836
UK	16.08	555,907	0.70	54	14.00	2,478	4.9	199,000	6.8	6,016
Australia	–	–	–	–	0.79	139	1.1	45,597	10.8	9,539
World	100.00	3,457,477	100.00	7,738	100.00	17,705	100.0	4,024,363	100.0	87,987

ASEAN = Association of Southeast Asian Nations, IT = information technology, UK = United Kingdom, US = United States, $ Mn = millions of US dollars, – = no data available, % = percent.

Sources: Tourism Statistics of India, 2004; NASSCOM, 2006; Ministry of Human Resource Development.

development in India, such as highways, ports, communication projects, and real estate.

Role of Services

An important contribution of India's trade in services has been its impact on trade balance and balance of payments. While India has run a persistent deficit in merchandise trade, there has been a consistent surplus on its services trade account. This surplus has grown rapidly since the 1990s. Surplus on services trade account rose from 10% of the merchandise trade deficit to 43% in 2005/06. Current transfers by migrants were $24.3 billion during 2005/06 compared to $2.5 billion in 1990/91. Remittances represented over 3% of GDP during 2005/06 and almost a quarter of India's total merchandise exports. The regional sources of remittance inflows into India witnessed a shift during the 1990s. While the oil boom in the Middle East boosted remittances during the 1980s, remittance flows from Australia,

Box 2.4 India–PRC Trade in Education

In the last few years, increasing number of Indian students have been travelling to the PRC for medical studies, seeing high-quality education at a lower cost. Simple admission procedures, increasing importance of English as the medium of instruction, and modern facilities have added to the attractiveness of the PRC as a destination for medical studies. Some PRC universities have tried to align the courses with the Medical Council of India requirements to enable students to qualify the screening tests on return, unlike some Indian students who studied in Russia and other Eastern Europe countries. It is estimated that of the 5,000 Indian students in PRC universities, 2,000 are from the Indian state of Andhra Pradesh (Business Line 2006). Indian students also value the cultural affinities with the PRC. Despite the focus on Western medicine, students are also introduced to traditional Chinese medicine.

Europe and the US, rose during the 1990s.[31] The Middle East and North America each contribute approximately 35% of total inflows, followed by Europe with a share of 20% with the rest of world contributing 10% (Government of India 2002).

The Indian software services industry is unusually export-oriented, especially by general Indian standards. Exports earnings represented more than 77% of total revenue for industry during 2005/06. There are important qualitative differences in the domestic and export markets (Arora et al 2000, Kumar 2001b). While the export market is dominated by services exports, especially customized software development, the domestic market has a greater proportion of revenues from the sale of software packages and products. Also, in comparison to the export markets, Indian firms provide a wider range of services, including higher-end design, in the domestic market. Projects executed for the domestic market are larger and more challenging than export projects. The direct employment in the Indian IT and IT-enabled service sector is estimated to have grown from

---

[31] Three phases in labor migration may be distinguished in recent Indian history. The first phase, from the early 1950s to the early 1970s, involved the movement of persons with technical skills and professional expertise to Canada, United Kingdom, and US, and, to a much smaller extent, Australia and Western Europe. Migration to the US was dominated by highly skilled workers, with a more balanced mix of migrants to the United Kingdom. The second phase, beginning after the first oil shock in 1973, involved movement of low- and medium-skilled workers to the Middle East and was characterized by strong home bias and return migration. Since the early 1990s, a third wave has emerged involving the migration of highly skilled workers to industrial countries (Reserve Bank of India 2003).

284,000 in 1999/2000 to 1,287,000 during 2005/06 (NASSCOM 2006). The sector is estimated to have contributed an additional 3 million indirect and induced jobs.[32]

It has been suggested that services have not only directly contributed to economic and trade growth but they have also helped spur growth in manufacturing and thereby overall exports. Banga and Goldar (2004) find that although service inputs contributed little to the growth in registered manufacturing during the 1980s, this contribution increased substantially (approximately 25% of output growth) in the 1990s. This analysis also suggests that trade reforms also contributed to increase the use of services in the manufacturing sector. Static input–output analysis suggests that agricultural production became more industry- and services-intensive, whereas industrial production became less agriculture intensive and more service intensive. Services themselves became more service-intensive, especially during the 1980s and 1990s (Hansda 2001). Thus, services have strong linkages with the rest of the economy.

Regulatory Regime in Service Sectors

The policy reforms initiated in the services sector since the early 1990s have been wide ranging and phased-in with significant variations in progress across subsectors. The telecommunications sector has been at the forefront of opening up activities to domestic private-sector and foreign investment, corporatizing government providers, establishing and strengthening an independent regulator, and changing associated legislation. Private-sector entry was also permitted in power generation, civil aviation, and oil and gas exploration during the early 1990s. Private investment in insurance was allowed at the end of the 1990s. Insurance also acquired an independent regulator in 2000 and the Government is currently contemplating setting up regulatory authorities for civil aviation, petroleum, and railways.

The improvement in railways' performance and the turnaround of recent policies—such as opening of container traffic for private operations and the inauguration of a separate freight corridor between Mumbai and Delhi—are unprecedented and valuable measures in relaxing the infrastructure constraint on India's growth and development. However, there remain items

---

[32] Indirect employment may be generated in telecommunications, power, construction, facility management, information technology, transportation, catering, and other services. Induced employment is used to refer to employment generated through consumption expenditure of employees on food, clothing, utilities, recreation, health, and other services.

on the reform agenda that need to be addressed, such as improvements to the regulatory framework, strengthening of standard-setting bodies, pricing reforms, and strengthening of institutional structures.

Domestic deregulation and liberalization in general, and telecommunications reforms in particular, were key to the observed growth in services, especially IT and IT services during the 1990s (Gordon and Gupta 2003, Murthy 2004). According to Gordon and Gupta, during the same period of derogation in the 1990s, the communications subsector grew rapidly, and the share of private sector in services increased.

As mentioned earlier, health services exports, through health tourism, telemedicine, and medical transcription, are emerging as important export activities for India. These exports are hampered not only by infrastructure constraints such as poor transport and insufficient low-cost accommodation but also by the absence of an accreditation system for hospitals and laboratories, a quality assurance system, a transparent regulatory regime, and insurance coverage.

Higher education is likewise in dire need of reform, and major investments are likewise required in the setting up of universities, professional colleges, and nursing schools. The estimated $3 billion spent by Indian students annually for financing education abroad (*Indian Express* 2006) partly represents missed opportunities for domestic educational service providers. Political interference, a decline in public financial support, haphazard and uneven privatization, deterioration in standards, and exit by the elite in favor of foreign education have steered the Indian higher education system into disarray (Kapur and Mehta 2004, Kapur and Khilnani 2006). India needs a long-term education policy, together with new legislation, and a domestic regulatory framework with a more effective registration, certification, and rating system. The success of India's IT, IT-enabled services, and BPO exports are underpinned by the relative abundance of skilled workers at relatively low costs. However, according to NASSCOM reports, there is likely to be a shortage of qualified personnel, a phenomenon that is expected to drive up wages and hurt the cost competitiveness of Indian exports.

Trade and Foreign Direct Investment Restrictions in Services

Unilateral service sector liberalization by India has been most successful in Mode 3, although some restrictions remain (Table 2.10). The Government is planning to set up a high-level group in the Planning Commission (similar to the Committee on Infrastructure) to look into all aspects of the services sector and develop a road map for strengthening and sustaining performance (ToI 2006).

Table 2.10 FDI Restrictions in Services

Activity	FDI restrictions
Air transport	Restricted to 49% foreign equity participation (100% for NRI investments but not automatic) in domestic air transport services; No direct or indirect participation by foreign airlines; FDI in airports up to 100% but FDI beyond 74% requires FIPB approval
Railways	FDI not permitted
Ports and harbors	Up to 100% FDI permitted on automatic route for construction and maintenance
Roads and highways	FDI up to 100% through the automatic approval route for construction and maintenance of roads, highways, vehicular bridges, tunnels, and toll roads
Mass rapid transit	FDI up to 100% approved automatically, including for associated real estate development in all metropolitan cities
Banking	Foreign investment cap of 74% from all sources (FDI+FII) on automatic route
Nonbanking financial services	FDI/NRI investment allowed in specified activities subject to minimum capitalization norms and compliance with RBI guidelines
Insurance	FDI cap of 26% under automatic route; licensing by Insurance Regulatory and Development Authority
Telecommunications	Foreign investment cap 74% (including FDI, FII, NRI, FCCBs, ADRs, GDRs, etc.) in basic, cellular, paging, and value-added. ISPs with gateways subject to license and security requirements.
Trading	100% FDI permitted in wholesale cash and carry trading, trading in exports; 51% FDI in single brand retailing; 100% FDI in trading of items sourced from SSI and test marketing allowed but through FIPB route; Not permitted in retail.
Travel, hotels, and restaurants	No restrictions
Information technology services	No explicit restrictions
Health services	No explicit restrictions
Educational services	No restrictions on higher and technical education
Legal services	Foreign lawyers not allowed to practice in India (Mode 4)

ADR = American Depositary Receipt, FCCB = Foreign Currency Convertible Bond, FDI = foreign direct investment, FII = foreign institutional investment, FIPB = Foreign Investment Promotion Board, GDR = Global Depositary Receipts, ISP = internet service provider, NRI = Non-Resident Indians, RBI = Reserve Bank of India, SSI = small-scale industry, % = percent.

Source: Based on FDI Policy 2006.

The General Agreement on Trade in Services and Regional Commitments

India had scheduled only nine sectors in the last round of WTO negotiations in services. However, India's position has since changed considerably and the Government has adopted a much more proactive stance. This

Box 2.5 Foreign Direct Investment (FDI) in Retailing

At present, India does not permit FDI in multibrand retail trade although it is allowed in single-brand retail, franchising, wholesale trade as well as logistics and back-end support. The Indian organized retail sector is transforming rapidly, and most leading Indian business houses have announced major investments. International retail chains including Wal-Mart, Carrefour, and Tesco have displayed keen interest in gaining a foothold in the Indian retail market. The major concern holding back the decision to allow full-fledged FDI in retail is employment constraints. Despite some recent improvements, the bulk of the workforce is trained for the agriculture and informal sectors. Major traders' associations, some political parties, and other industry organizations have been lobbying somewhat effectively against FDI in retail under the present circumstances. According to a KSA Technopak report, unorganized retailing currently accounts for 95% of the total retail trade sector and retailing provides employment and income to an estimated 54 million people working in 12 million small shops. This makes retail activity the second largest employer next to agriculture. In a country such as India, inadequate social security implies that open employment is limited, and that retail acts as a kind of social security net for the unemployed.

change in approach is driven by a number of factors, including high export potential in services and increasing protectionist rhetoric and trade barriers against Indian service providers in markets of export interest. Under the bilateral request-offer approach, it has submitted a revised offer on services in August 2005 (WTO 2006), which was a significant improvement on its initial offer. India has offered to undertake extensive commitments in a number of new services, including architectural and integrated engineering services; veterinary services; environmental services; construction and related engineering services; tourism; educational services; life insurance; services auxiliary to insurance; and recreational, cultural, sporting, and air transport services. New commitments have been offered in cross-border supply, and improvements were made in existing commitments in engineering services, computer and related services, research and development services, basic telecommunication services, value-added telecommunications, construction and related engineering services, banking services, asset management services, and other nonbanking financial services. India had already made a substantial initial offer in Mode 4, and has participated in the complementary multilateral negotiations, being an active member of four of the 17 multilateral sectoral groups that have made requests under this approach (Appendix Table A2.8). India is the coordinator of Mode 1/2 and Mode 4, and a cosponsor of various requests

Box 2.6 Services Success in India: Information Technology (IT)

There is an ongoing debate regarding the factors that led to India's success in the software and IT-enabled services sector. While some observers have argued that India's success has been an outcome of the free play of market forces and benign state neglect (Arora et al. 2000), Kumar and Joseph (2005) argue that India's IT software and business process outsourcing success is primarily because of cumulative government investments to create a supply of qualified workers and to provide the corresponding institutional infrastructure. The system of higher education in engineering and technical discipline, the creation of an institutional infrastructure for science and technology, and the initiation of policies for technology development all helped provide India with a comparative advantage in the IT services sector. Specific policy initiatives directed at the sector emerged with the announcement of the Computer Policy of November 1984, followed by an explicit Computer Software, Development, and Training Policy in 1986. Policy effort came to be focused on software development, and consisted of (i) removal of entry barriers against foreign companies, (ii) removal of restrictions on foreign technology transfers, (iii) participation by the private sector in policy making, (iv) provision for financing software development through equity and venture capital, (v) measures to make available faster and cheaper data communications facilities, and (vi) reductions to and rationalization of taxes, duties, and tariffs. The Government has also permitted private investments in IT training since the early 1980s. Up until the early 1990s, "body-shopping" or on-site provision of programming services, mainly in the United States, was the primary mode of delivery. However, comprehensive reforms in the telecommunications sector since the mid-1980s and the notable institutional intervention in the form of establishment of software technology parks—beginning with Bangalore, Pune, and Bhubaneswar in 1990—helped in the growth of offshore services delivery. Other occurrences, such as the Y2K (Year 2000) crisis, also helped to project globally India's comparative advantage in software service solutions. The role played by the Indian diasporas in outsourcing and offshoring activities to India and in influencing key domestic policy making, such as telecommunications reforms, also needs to be underscored.

in computer and related services, as well as in architecture, engineering, and integrated engineering services. On the other hand, India has received requests in 14 sectors and MFN exemptions for audiovisual services. India has indicated that it can meet requests substantially in sectors such as construction and maritime transport services, and partially in energy and telecommunication services. India would face difficulties, however, in meeting requests in distribution, legal, and audiovisual services. Energy, telecommunication, audiovisual, express delivery, and distribution services are sensitive sectors for India.

Policy Implications

Region-Specific Orientation

The discussion above shows that India's merchandise trade is substantially oriented toward East Asia and South Asia, which together accounted for 32% of India's exports and 24% of imports during 2005/06. Since the early 1990s, East Asia has emerged as India's predominant trading partner, contributing approximately 25% of India's trade. In recent years, trade with East Asia has grown at an even faster pace. Scrutiny of India's preferential trade arrangements additionally reveals that India's policy-driven integration efforts are also biased in favor of regional or bilateral agreements with trading partners in East Asia and South Asia. Only around five[33] out of around 21 of India's officially listed engagements in regional trade agreements (RTAs) are with partners outside East Asia and South Asia. All of its free trade or regional integration agreements under implementation are confined to these two regions. India already has an RTA within South Asia (SAFTA), which has been effective since July 2006, and a framework agreement with ASEAN, which is in the final stages of negotiations. It is also negotiating and discussing trade agreements with the PRC, Japan, and the Republic of Korea. India tends to view these arrangements as building blocks of a broader Asian Economic Community (AEC).[34]

Regional economic integration, apart from being considered as an effective means of spreading the dynamism of Indian economy to the region, is also seen as a source of overall welfare gains. For instance, an RIS study conducted in a computable general equilibrium framework estimated that the economic integration among Japan, ASEAN, the PRC, India, and the Republic of Korea (JACIK) had the potential to generate welfare gains in the order of $210 billion, representing 3% of GDP of the participating economies. These findings have been corroborated by another study conducted at ADB.[35] The East Asia Summit (EAS), in which all the JACIK

---

[33]   These include Framework FTAs with the Gulf Cooperation Council; preferential trade arrangements with South African Customs Union (SACU), MERCOSUR (Argentina, Brazil, Paraguay, and Uruguay), and Chile; and a Comprehensive Economic Cooperation Agreement with Mauritius.

[34]   See among other statements, the Prime Minister Dr Manmohan Singh's inaugural address at the ADB Annual Meeting, Hyderabad, May 2006.

[35]   See Brooks, Roland-Holst and Zhai (2005).

countries participate along with Australia and New Zealand, provides an important forum for launching a broader scheme for regional economic integration which can be broadened further to an Asian Economic Community. Recently, Japan has proposed a Track-II study on the relevance of a Comprehensive Economic Partnership of East Asia, which would combine ASEAN+6 (all EAS countries).

Comparative and Competitive Advantages

A number of differences can be discerned in India's growth path since the 1990s vis-à-vis the other major regional countries. India's economic and export growth is being led by services, especially information technology-enabled services (ITeS) and increasingly health services, which have dominated India's export growth in recent years. The pharmaceuticals and biotechnology industries have also emerged as important driving forces for growth. However, India is lagging behind in merchandise exports, as seen in its inability to achieve meaningful increases in its market share in the exports of agriculture and other traditional goods such as textiles and apparel.

According to RIS (2003a), the technological capabilities of East Asian and South Asian countries are highly complementary in nature. For instance, Japan has established its leadership as a source of technology in a number of industries, including semiconductors, automobiles, industrial automation, electronics, and some chemicals. The Republic of Korea has consolidated its strengths in automotives, consumer electronics, semiconductors, and shipbuilding. The PRC has established expertise in consumer electronics and light engineering, while India has achieved prominence in pharmaceuticals, auto parts, and other industries. There are patterns of complementarity within industries as well. In IT, for example, East Asia has established a lead in hardware capacity, while India and the Philippines have software capabilities. Regional investments are particularly beneficial in infrastructure, logistics, food processing technologies, IT, and hardware, and could also help India move up the value chain in textiles and apparel, leather goods, gems and jewelry, and agricultural products (RIS 2003b). Emerging trends suggest that education and training could be another area for greater cooperation and increased flows between South and East Asia.

Foreign Direct Investment Policy and Regional Production Networks

The liberalization of India's FDI policy regime, as well as growing economic integration with East Asia, has facilitated increasing integration of India with East Asian production networks aiming to exploit complementary strengths. East Asian companies have in fact, begun to exploit India's strengths in R&D, software, and design by locating their global R&D centers in India. For instance, Samsung's R&D center in India recently announced successful development of a hybrid mobile phone that works across Global System for Mobile and Code division multiple access environments. The PRC's Huawei Technologies, like many others, employs hundreds of engineers working on chip design or embedded software development in Bangalore. Hyundai uses its Indian operations as a global sourcing base for compact cars. Toyota is sourcing engines from its Indian plant for Southeast Asian markets. Furthermore, these production networks not only include those belonging to Japanese or Korean companies but also those being developed by Indian enterprises. For instance, Singapore-based NatSteel, Thailand-based Millennium Steel, and Daewoo Trucks have become linked with the production chain of Tata Motors with its acquisition by the latter. The production chain between Daewoo and Tata is being integrated with the former using Tata Motors' expertise in light commercial vehicles and vice versa. Several Indian companies have also begun to rationalize and take advantage of cheaper manufacturing costs for hardware in the PRC and other East Asian countries. The trend is likely to be more entrenched as the emerging free trade arrangements between India and East Asian countries come into effect.

Merchandise Trade Policy

Although East Asia, especially the PRC, has emerged as India's largest trading partner, the trade structure needs to be more broad based. India's exports to the PRC, for instance, are dominated by raw materials such as iron ore. India's trade surpluses with Bangladesh and Nepal have put a strain on bilateral trading relationships and consequently retarded the expansion of trade and investments. There is therefore a need to enhance the supply capabilities of these countries by encouraging Indian investments in their export platforms. Emerging regional trading arrangements are likely to facilitate such investments, as in the case of India–Sri Lanka FTA. Indian investments such as the $3 billion that the Tata Group place into Bangladesh could represent a new trend that would help build these supply capabilities.

Services Trade Policy

Regional investments have proven to be crucial in generating business-related tourism and travel services trade. India's bilateral integration agreement with Singapore goes beyond their offers at the WTO, and includes provisions for liberalizing trade in services, most of important of which pertains to the free movement of persons. This is particularly important given the graying populations of countries such as Japan and the Republic of Korea on one hand, and India's demographic advantage on the other hand. In the face of the slow progress in the multilateral liberalization process, especially in Mode 4, regional agreements could prove to be a more effective vehicle in achieving greater liberalization. Such agreements would also act as useful inputs for negotiations at the multilateral level.

Besides ITeS and software development and health services, where India has some strengths, India is a booming market for many East and South Asian countries for tourism, construction, and transport services. India is already the largest source of tourists in Sri Lanka and is one of the biggest sources of tourists in Malaysia, Singapore, and Thailand. Malaysian, Singaporean, and Thai companies are also active in Indian infrastructure development and construction markets. There is therefore ample room for exploiting synergies in services through regional economic integration.

Customs Procedures and Trade Facilitation

A substantial proportion of India's trade with the South Asian countries is conducted unofficially due partly to high transactions costs through formal trading channels.[36] High transaction costs also accounts for significant amounts of missing trade between South Asian and East Asian countries. In South Asia, the inadequacy of transport infrastructure, facilities at land customs stations (warehousing, parking, quarantine, weighing, and scanning equipment); problems related to motor vehicle regulations; and lack of harmonization of documentation, procedures, risk management systems, and e-connectivity impose major constraints on trade and transit. The attempts to harmonize customs legislations and procedures under the SAARC framework have not yet resulted in much progress.

In general, merchandise trade and investment initiatives have been at the forefront of regional integration. However, in the case of South Asia and East Asia, there is a strong case for according priority to greater cooperation in customs and transport sectors. Member states could evolve a mechanism for sharing information and harmonization of each country's customs procedures with the relevant WTO provision (articles V, VIII, and X of General Agreement on Tariffs and Trade [GATT] 1994).[37] This infor-

---

[36] The total informal trade in the South Asian region was estimated at $3 billion, which was almost double the formal trade in the region for the corresponding year (Taneja 2004a).

[37] The main objective of Article X is to ensure publication of all information related to trade laws and regulations. Article VIII deals with issues related to fee and charges and trade documentation and other requirements. Article V covers freedom of transit documentation, authorized trade and securities, and guarantees for transit trade. However, issues related to sanitary and phytosanitary standards are not covered in the WTO negotiations on trade facilitation.

mation could be used to develop an integrated and common approach to fast-track implementation of trade facilitation measures in member states and in the articulation of common positions with respect to commitments at the WTO. South Asian and East Asian countries should also adopt a coordinated approach in addressing issues related to sanitary and phytos-anitary standards and technical barriers to trade, with the aim of reaching mutual recognition agreements, especially for products where trade is of mutual interest.

Transport and Infrastructure Initiatives

India is currently seeking large amounts of investments in infrastructure, and has taken steps to provide opportunities for alternatives forms of fund-ing mechanism. The aim is to foster public–private partnerships such as BOT, toll-based, and annuity-based structures. Greater exchange of infor-mation, transfer of technical know-how, and sharing of resources among South and East Asian countries could help foster the development of an integrated regional infrastructure. In the case of South Asia, RIS (2004a) recommends the development of a common transport policy.

There also exists tremendous potential for cooperation among South and East Asian economies for investments in regional public goods. Trade and transport infrastructure—including road and rail links, harmonization of road and rail networks, harmonization of transport rules and regulations, improvements to and decongestion at seaports, creation of warehouses, addition of parking facilities at borders, and improvements in logistical support—could significantly contribute to higher output, trade, and effi-ciency growth in South Asia and some East Asian countries.

East and South Asian countries are major holders of foreign exchange reserves, with their combined holdings exceeding $2 trillion. However, because of lack of a regional framework for monetary and financial coop-eration, these resources are invested in instruments such as US treasury bonds rather than regional development. There is a need for financial cooperation in Asia so as to mobilize some of these resources toward infra-structure development, for instance, or toward adjustment assistance for Asian countries grappling with global imbalances. Financial cooperation is therefore an important element in the scheme of East–South Asian eco-nomic integration.

References

Asian Development Bank (ADB). 2002. Preferential Trade Agreements in Asia and the Pacific. In *Asian Development Outlook*. New York: Oxford University Press.

Asher, M. G., and R. Sen. 2005. India-East Asia Integration: A Win-Win for Asia. *Research and Information Systems for Developing Countries (RIS) Discussion Paper* 91. New Delhi: RIS.

Arora, A., V. S. Arunachalam, J. Asundi, and R. Fernandes. 2000. The Indian Software Services Industry. *Heinz School Working Paper* 99-19. Available: http://ssrn.com/abstract=198968

Balakrishnan, P., and S. Babu. 2003. Growth and Distribution in Indian Industry in the 1990s. *Economic and Political Weekly* 20 (September).

Banga, Rashmi, and B. N. Goldar. 2004. Contribution of Services to Output Growth Productivity in Indian Manufacturing: Pre and Post Reform. *Indian Council for Research on International Economic Relations (ICRIER) Working Paper* 139 (August). New Delhi: ICRIER.

Baysan, Tercan, Arvind Panagariya, and Nihal Pitigala. 2006. Preferential Trading in South Asia. *World Bank Policy Research Working Paper* 3813 (January). Washington, DC: World Bank.

Brooks, D., D. Roland-Holst, and F. Zhai. 2005. *Growth, Trade and Integration: Long-term Scenarios of Developing Asia*. Manila: ADB.

Central Statistical Organisation (CSO). 2006. *Press Note*, Press Information Bureau, May 31. Available: http://mospi.nic.in.

Centre D'Etudes Prospectives et D'Informations Internationales (CEPII). 2003. India Bets on Technology Niches. *La Lettre Du No. 221* (March).

Chaturvedi, Sachin. 2006. An Evaluation of the Need and Cost of Selected Trade Facilitation Measures in India: Implications for the WTO Negotiations. *ARTNeT Working Paper Series* 4 (March).

Confederation of Indian Industries (CII). 2006. *Going Global: Indian Multinationals*. India Brand Equity Foundation, New Delhi: CII.

Container Corporation of India Limited (CONCOR). 2006. *Annual Report 2004-05*. Available: www.concorindia.com/

Deaton, A., and J. Dreze. 2002. Poverty and Inequality in India: A Re-examination. *Economic and Political Weekly*. September 7.

Divaakar, S. V., P. Agarwal, and R. K. S. Bhatia. 2006. Trade Facilitation Problems of Indian Exporters: A Survey. In *India and the Doha Work Programs: Opportunities and Challenges*, Veena Jha. New Delhi: United Nations Conference on Trade and Development (UNCTAD) and MacMillan India.

The Economist. 2006. Virtual Champions: India's IT Star are Still Rising Fast. *Now for the Hard Part: A Survey of Business in India*, June 23.

Export-Import Bank of India. 2003. Transaction Costs of Indian Exports: A Review. *Working Paper No. 4*. EXIM Bank of India.

Federation of Indian Chambers of Commerce and Industry (FICCI)-Ernst & Young. 2006. *Report on Direct Investments in the US of America by Indian Enterprises.* Available: www.ey.com

Fugazza, M., and D. Vanzetti. 2006. A South-South Survival Strategy: The Potential for Trade among Developing Countries. *Policy Issues in International Trade and Commodities Study Series* 33. UNCTAD/ITCD/TAB/22. Geneva.

Gordon, J., and P. Gupta. 2003. Understanding India's Services Revolution. International Monetary Fund (IMF) Paper prepared for the IMF-National Council for Applied Economic Research Conference, *A Tale of Two Giants: India's and China's Experience with Reform,* 14–16 November, New Delhi.

Government of India. 2002. *Report of the High Level Committee on the Indian Diaspora.* Available: http://indiandiaspora.nic.in/

Guruswamy, M., and R. J. Abraham. 2006. Redefining Poverty: A New Poverty Line for India. *Centre for Policy Alternatives.* February.

Hansda, Sanjay. 2001. Sustainability of Services Led Growth: An Input-Output Analysis of Indian Economy. *RBI Occasional Working Paper* 22: 1–3. Reserve Bank of India (RBI).

The Hindu Business Line. 2003. ASEAN Ties: India Must Look to the East with Greater Vision. December 31.

_____. 2005. Liner Trade: Loads of Opportunity. December 5.

_____. 2006. Growth, Reforms Set to Boost M&A Activity. August 26.

International Monetary Fund (IMF). 2006. *World Economic Outlook 2006,* April. Washington, DC: IMF.

Kapur, D. 2002. The Causes and Consequences of India's IT Boom. *India Review* 1(2): 91–110.

Kapur, D., and P. B. Mehta. 2004. Indian Higher Education Reform: From Half-Baked Socialism to Half-Baked Capitalism. CID Working Paper 108 (September). Center for International Development (CID), Harvard University.

Kapur, D., and S. Khilnani. 2006. Primary Concerns. *Hindustan Times.* New Delhi, April.

Kelegama, S. 2006. India–Sri Lanka Bilateral Free Trade Agreement. Paper presented at the RIS Seminar on India–Sri Lanka FTA: Trends and Prospects, 20 April, New Delhi.

Kelkar, V. 2004. India: On the Growth Turnpike. 2004 Narayanan Oration, Australia National University, April. Available: http://rspas.anu.edu.au/papas/narayanan/2004oration.pdf

Kumar, N. 2001a. Foreign Direct Investment, Regional Economic Integration and Industrial Restructuring in Asia: Trends, Patterns and Prospects. *RIS Occasional Paper* No. 62. July.

_____. 2001b. Indian Software Industry Development: International and National Perspective. *Economic and Political Weekly* 36, 10 November.

_____. 2002. Toward an Asian Economic Community: Relevance of India. *RIS Discussion Paper* 34. New Delhi: RIS.

_____. 2005a. Liberalization, Foreign Direct Investment Flows and Economic Development: The Indian Experience in the 1990s. *Economic and Political Weekly*. 2 April.

_____. 2005b. Toward a Broader Asian Community: Agenda for the East Asia Summit. RIS Discussion Paper #100. New Delhi.

_____. 2006. Reforms, Global Integration and Economic Development. *Public Policy Research*, June–August: 152–160. London.

Kumar, N., and K. J. Joseph. 2005. Export of Software and Business Process Outsourcing from Developing Countries: Lessons from the Indian Experience. *Asia-Pacific Trade and Investment Review* 1(1): 91–110 (April).

Langhammer, R. 2002. Developing Countries as Exporters of Services: What Trade Statistics Suggest. *Journal of Economic Integration* 17(2): 297-310 (June).

Mahendra Dev, S. 2000. Poverty, Income Distribution, Employment Under Reforms. In *Indian Economy Under Reforms: An Assessment of Economic and Social Impact*, edited by Nagesh Kumar. New Delhi: Bookwell.

Mattoo, A., and A. Subramaniam. 2003. India and the Multilateral Trading System Post-Doha: Defensive or Proactive? In *India and the WTO*, edited by A. Mattoo and R. Stern. Washington, DC: World Bank and Oxford University Press.

Ministry of Commerce and Industry. 2006. *Foreign Direct Investment Policy 2006*. Department of Industrial Policy and Promotion, April.

Ministry of Finance. 2002a. *Economic Survey 2001–02*. Ministry of Finance, Government of India.

_____. 2002b. *Report of the Task Force on Indirect Taxes*. Ministry of Finance, Government of India, October.

_____. 2004. *Report of the Working Group on Trade Facilitation*. Central Board of Excise and Customs, Ministry of Finance, Government of India, October.

_____. 2006. *Annual Report 2005–06*. Ministry of Finance, Government of India.

Mukherjee, I. N. 2006. India–Sri-Lanka FTA. Paper presented at the RIS Seminar on India–Sri Lanka FTA: Trends and Prospects, 20 April, New Delhi.

Murthy, N. R. 2004. The Impact of Economic Reforms on Industry in India: A Case Study of the Software Industry. In *India's Emerging Economy: Performance and Prospects in the 1990s and Beyond*, edited by K. Basu. Cambridge, MA: MIT Press.

Nagaraj, R. 2003. Industrial Policy and Performance since 1980s: Which Way Now? *Economic and Political Weekly*, 30 August.

_____. 2004. Labor Policy: Does India Face a Wage Problem? Note prepared for Conference on Anti-poverty and Social Policy in India, MacArthur Research Network on Inequality and Economic Policy, 2–4 January, Rajasthan.

Naidu, G. V. K. 2004. Whither the Look East Policy: India and Southeast Asia. *Strategic Analysis* 28(2): 331–46.

National Association of Software and Services Companies (NASSCOM). 2006. *Indian IT Industry-Fact Sheet*. Available: www.nasscom.in.

NASSCOM-McKinsey. 2006. Extending India's Leadership of the Global IT and BPO Industries. *NASSCOM-McKinsey Report 2005*.

Oman, C. 2000. *Policy Competition for Foreign Direct Investment*. Development Centre Studies, OECD: Paris.

Panagariya, A. 1999. Evaluating the Case for Export Subsidies. Mimeo, University of Maryland.

Planning Commission. 2001. *Report of the Task Force on Employment Opportunities*. New Delhi: Government of India.

PricewaterhouseCoopers. 2006. India: Record M&A Activity to Continue. *Asia-Pacific M&A Bulletin*.

Rahman, M. 2001. Bangladesh-India Bilateral Trade: An Investigation into Trade in Services. Paper prepared under the SANEI Study Program, Centre for Policy Dialogue, Dhaka. April.

Research and Information Systems for Developing Countries (RIS). 2002. *South Asia Development and Cooperation Report 2001–02,* New Delhi: RIS.

_____. 2003a. Toward an Asian Economic Community. *Policy Brief #1.* New Delhi: RIS.

_____. 2003b. Initiative for Closer Economic Cooperation with Neighboring Countries in South Asia. *RIS Policy Brief #2.* New Delhi: RIS.

_____. 2004a. *South Asia Development and Cooperation Report 2004.* New Delhi: RIS.

_____. 2004b. *ASEAN-India Vision 2020: Working Together for a Shared Prosperity.* New Delhi: RIS.

_____. 2006a. *Toward an Employment-Oriented Export Strategy: Some Explorations.* New Delhi: RIS.

_____. 2006b. Regionalism with an Asian Face: Agenda for East Asia Summit. *RIS Policy Brief # 28.* New Delhi, RIS.

_____. 2006c. India-Brazil-South Africa Economic Cooperation: Toward a Comprehensive Economic Partnership. *RIS Policy Brief #26.* New Delhi, RIS.

_____. 2007. *World Trade and Development Report 2007.* New Delhi: Oxford University Press for RIS.

Reserve Bank of India (RBI). 2003, Invisibles in India's Balance of Payments. *RBI Bulletin,* May.

_____. 2006. India's Balance of Payments. *Reserve Bank Bulletin*. Available: www.rbi.org.in.

Rodrik, D., and A. Subramaniam. 2004. Why India Can Grow at 7 Per Cent a Year or More: Projections and Reflections. *Economic and Political Weekly*. April 17.

Roy, J. 2004. Trade Facilitation in India: Current Situation and the Road Ahead. Paper presented at the EU/World Bank/Boao Forum for Asia Workshop on Trade Facilitation in East Asia, 3–5 November 2004, Shanghai.

Saxenia, A. L. 2002. Bangalore: The Silicon Valley of Asia? In *Economic Policy Reforms and the Indian Economy*, edited by Anne O. Krueger. Chicago: University of Chicago Press.

Sen, A., and Himanshu. 2004. Poverty and Inequality in India. *Economic and Political Weekly*. 18 September.

Sengupta, N., and M. Bhagabati. 2003. *A Study of Trade Facilitation Measures: From WTO Perspective*. Madras Institute of Development Studies, Chennai. August.

Srinivasan, T. N. 2006. *Information-Technology-Enabled Services and India's Growth Prospects*. Brookings Trade Forum 2005, Yale University.

Sundaram, K., and S. D. Tendulkar. 2003. Poverty Has Declined in the 1990s: A Resolution of Comparability Problems in NSS Consumer Expenditure Data. *Economic and Political Weekly*. January 25: 327–337.

Taneja, N. 2004a. Informal Trade in the SAARC Region. *Economic and Political Weekly*. 18 December.

_____. 2004b. Trade Facilitation in the WTO: Implications for India. *ICRIER Working Paper* 128, April.

_____. 2006. India-Pakistan Trade. *ICRIER Working Paper* 182.

The Times of India. 2006. *Tax Sops Push Ports to Anchor SEZ Plans*, Business Times, 11 July.

Tata Statistical Services. 2006. Statistical Outline of India on CDROM 2006.

United Nations Conference on Trade and Development (UNCTAD). 2005. *World Investment Report 2005*. New York: United Nations.

US Government Accountability Office. 2005. US and India Data on Offshoring Show Significant Differences. *Report to Congressional Committees*. October.

Wilson, D., and R. Purushothaman. 2003. Dreaming with BRICs: The Path to 2050. *Global Economics Paper* No. 99. Goldman Sachs.

World Bank. 2000. Trade Blocs. *Policy Research Report*. Washington, DC.

World Trade Organization (WTO). 2002. *India Trade Policy Review 2002*, October, Geneva: WTO.

_____. 2006a. India: Trade Profiles, Statistics Database. Available: http://stat.wto.org/CountryProfile/WSDBCountryPFView.aspx.

_____. 2006b. Trade Picks Up in Mid-2005 but 2006 Picture is Uncertain. *2006 Press Releases*, Press/437. Geneva.

Appendix Tables

Table A2.1 Indian Economic Indicators

Basic Indicators	1990/91	2005/06	Transport sector	2006
Population (Mn)	839	1,107	**Road network (March 2006)**	
GDP (Rs. billion 1993/94 prices)	6,929	15,293[a]	Total length ('000 km)	3,340
NNP per capita (Rs. 1993/94 prices)	7,321	12,416[a]	Expressway	0.2
GDP growth rate (% per annum)	5.6	8.4[b]	National Highways	66.59
Merchandise trade to GDP ratio	14.8	33.8	Single/intermediate lane (%)	35
Goods and services trade to GDP ratio	17.5	47.5	Double lane	55
			Four or more lanes	10
Structure of GDP (% share)	1990/91	2005/06	State highways ('000 km)	128
Agriculture and allied	31.27	18.97	Major district roads	470
Industry	27.64	27.39	Rural and other roads	2,650
Manufacturing	17.14	15.89	Paved length ('000 km)	1,363
Services	41.1	53.64	Paved roads of 2-lane roads (%)	34
			Paved roads of 4-lane roads (%)	1
International trade ($ Mn)			**Ports**	
Merchandise exports	18,145	102,725	Number of major ports (2004/05)	12
Services exports	4,551	60,610	Traffic handled (Mn tons)	568.96
Software	na[c]	23,600	Major ports	423.53
Merchandise imports	24,073	142,416	Non-major ports	145.43
Oil imports	6,028	43,963	Containerized cargo	4.5
Services imports	3,571	38,345	(million TEUs)	
Trade policy			**Railways**	
Applied MFN Tariff (2004)			Total network (route-km)	63,465
All goods		29.1	Broad gauge	47,749
Agricultural goods		37.4	Meter gauge	12,662
Nonagricultural goods (%)		27.9	Narrow gauge	3,054
			Electrified (route-km)	17,320
Employment (1999/2000 in Mn)		397.0	Originating traffic (2004/05)	
Agriculture and allied		237.56	Freight (Mn tons)	602.1
Industry		69.18	Passenger (Mn)	5378
Manufacturing		48.01		
Services		90.28	**Civil aviation**	
			Traffic handled (2004/05)	
			Passengers (Mn)	59.28
			Cargo ('000 tons)	1,280.7

GDP = gross domestic product, km = kilometer, MFN = most-favored nation, Mn = million, na = no data available, NNP = net national product, Rs = rupees, TEU = 20-foot equivalent unit, $ = US dollar, % = percent.

[a] Data corresponds to 2004/05; [b] Based on new series with base year as 1999/2000; [c] $164 million according to TSS Software Corporation, 2006.

Sources: National Accounts Statistics, Central Statistical Organization, available at http://mospi.nic.in; Handbook of Statistics on Indian Economy, Reserve Bank of India and RBI Bulletin, available at www.rbi.org.in; World Trade Organization, 2006; Planning Commission, 2001; National Highway Authority of India, available at www.nhai.org; Economic Survey 2005–06; Container Corporation of India, 2006.

Table A2.2 India's Foreign Direct Investment Policy Regime

Type of Policy/Measure	Details
A. Inbound FDI	
Sectors prohibited	Retail trading (except single-brand retailing); atomic energy; and lotteries, gambling, and betting.
Approval regime	Two approval routes: automatic (RBI) and prior approval (FIPB, MoF).
	1. Prior approval required when greater than 24% foreign equity is proposed for manufacture of items reserved for small-scale businesses.
	2. Prior approval required if investor has an existing interest in the same activity, if acquisition involves shares in existing Indian company in financial services, and where Securities and Exchange Board of India (Substantial Acquisition of Shares and Takeovers) 1997 applies.
	3. Prior approval requirements for sectors subject to equity limits and other conditions on notified list of activities (revised periodically).
	4. Automatic approval up to 100% on those not covered under numbers 1–3 above and those on the prohibited list above (subject to sectoral rules/regulations).
	5. Automatic approval for FDI up to 100% in manufacturing in special economic zone (SEZ) units, except in arms and ammunition, explosives, atomic substances, narcotics and hazardous chemicals, distillation and brewing of alcohol, and cigarettes. No cap on FDI for small-scale industry units in SEZs.
	6. 100% FDI allowed for SEZ township development on a case-by-case basis, and for franchisees for basic telephone services in SEZ.
Fiscal, financial, and other incentives	Those applicable to SEZs/EPZs/EOUs/STPs.
	1. SEZ developer: Exemptions from sector-specific enactments; income tax exemption for any block of 10 years in the first 15 years; duty-free imports/domestic procurement of goods; exemptions from services tax/central sales tax; exemptions of infrastructure capital fund from income tax; individual investments also eligible for income tax exemptions; permission for generation, transmission and distribution of power in SEZs; permission to transfer infrastructure facilities for O&M; authorization to provide and maintain services such as water, electricity, security, restaurants, and recreation facilities on commercial principles; full freedom in allocation of space to approved units on commercial basis.
	2. SEZ units: 100% income-tax exemptions for first 5 years and 50% for 2 years thereafter; exemption from licensing or

continued on next page

Table A2.2 (continued)

Type of Policy/Measure	Details
	approval for imports/domestic procurement; duty-free imports/domestic procurement of goods; duty-free imports/locally procured goods may be utilized over 5 years; domestic sales on payment of customs duty; domestic sales exempt from special additional duty; exemptions from services tax; exemptions of central sales tax on goods from DTA; exemptions from public hearings under Environment Impact Assessment Notification; offshore banking units in SEZs allowed 100% income tax exemptions for 3 years and 50% for next 2 years; permission to subcontract part of production or production-process through units in DTA or through other EOU/SEZ unit; permission to also subcontract part of production process abroad; agriculture/horticulture SEZ units allowed to provide inputs and equipment to contract farmers in DTA.
Other incentives	State governments may provide additional incentives such as state governments could declare the SEZ a public utility and apply the Essential Services Maintenance Act to restrict application of labor laws; state governments may also allow exemptions from state-level taxes such as sales tax, value-added tax (VAT), octroi, turnover tax, etc.
B. Outbound FDI	
Approval regime	Governed by Foreign Exchange Management (Transfer or Issue of any Foreign Security) Regulations, 2000.
	Indian corporation allowed to freely make overseas investments up to 200% (relaxed from an earlier limit of 25%, which was raised to 100% in 2004) of their net worth either through joint ventures or wholly-owned subsidiaries; monetary ceiling (of $100 million) on overseas investment lifted along with some other restrictions.
C. Others	
International agreements	Bilateral Investment Promotion and Protection Agreements (BIPAs)
	Double taxation avoidance agreements.

DTA = Domestic Tariff Area, EDU = export-oriented utility, EP2 = export processing zone, FDI = foreign direct investment, FIPB = Foreign Investment Promotion Board, MDF = Ministry of Finance, O&M = operations and maintenance, RBI = Reserve Bank of India, STP = Software Technology Park.

Source: Based on Foreign Direct Investment Policy, April 2006, Ministry of Commerce and Industry, Government of India.

**Table A2.3 Number of Foreign Companies in India,
Arranged by Country of Origin**

Country	Number of companies	
	1998	2004
United Kingdom	185	307
United States	200	383
Japan	87	130
France	30	67
Germany	42	91
Italy	18	33
Canada	14	29
Hong Kong, China	33	81
Pakistan	5	5
Bangladesh	6	7
Netherlands	24	52
Switzerland	12	31
Sweden	10	19
Australia	27	42
Belgium	4	23
Thailand	3	12
Nepal	5	–
United Arab Emirates	–	14
Singapore	–	168
Korea, Republic of	–	23
Malaysia	–	22
Others	150	211
Total	**871**	**1,750**

– = no data available.

Source: Indiastat and SIA Newsletter 2000, 2003, annual issues, Ministry of Commerce and Industry.

Table A2.4 Relative Importance of Individual Countries in India's Trade with East Asia

Region	Exports					Imports				
	Value ($ Million)		Share in total exports (%)		Growth (% p.a.)	Value ($ Million)		Share in total imports (%)		Growth (% p.a.)
	1990/91	2004/05	1990/91	2004/05	1990–2004	1990/91	2004/05	1990/91	2004/05	1990–2004
East Asia	**3,568.00**	**20,739.50**	**100.0**	**100.0**	**17.00**	**4,483.81**	**27,538.40**	**86.2**	**89.8**	**17.01**
ASEAN	932.00	8,103.02	31.3	39.1	19.74	1,722.48	11,397.90	33.7	41.4	19.59
Brunei Darussalam	0.68	4.87	0.0	0.0	52.18	0.00	0.54	0.0	0.0	59.20
Cambodia	0.14	17.07	0.0	0.1	142.73	0.67	0.24	0.0	0.0	23.64
Indonesia	107.2	1,295.34	3.9	6.2	31.86	80.49	2,536.05	2.1	9.2	35.50
Lao PDR	0.03	2.53	0.0	0.0	114.80	80.49	2,536.05	2.1	9.2	35.50
Malaysia	149.84	1,042.98	5.4	5.0	17.39	534.14	2,245.99	13.9	8.2	17.13
Myanmar	1.74	109.71	0.1	0.5	44.66	84.83	398.47	2.2	1.4	17.83
Philippines	28.12	395.09	1.0	1.9	29.46	4.54	181.88	0.1	0.7	40.88
Singapore	315.33	3,824.22	11.4	18.4	22.93	398.04	2,584.14	10.4	9.4	16.60
Thailand	244.25	879.39	8.9	4.2	11.38	56.7	833.46	1.5	3.0	27.94
Viet Nam	17.03	531.82	0.6	2.6	33.45	55.58	81.08	1.4	0.3	52.09
PRC	18.09	5,343.87	0.7	25.8	62.00	31.12	6,767.64	0.8	24.6	71.01
Hong Kong, China	354.44	3,659.61	12.8	17.6	30.25	141	1,711.09	3.7	6.2	23.54
Taipei,China	144.42	618.26	5.2	3.0	14.48	390.21	1,091.62	10.2	4.0	10.45
Korea, Rep. of	175.57	995.81	6.4	4.8	17.03	297.6	3,428.67	7.7	12.5	21.97
Japan	1,202.24	2,018.92	43.6	9.7	4.86	1,687.4	3,141.43	43.9	11.4	6.47
SAARC	**529.49**	**4,345.44**	**100.0**	**100.0**	**17.9**	**131.41**	**933.62**	**100.0**	**100.0**	**20.6**
South Asia	**521.6**	**4,213.29**	**98.5**	**97.0**	**17.8**	**130.41**	**862.02**	**99.2**	**92.3**	**20.0**
Bangladesh	302.9	1,606.26	57.2	37.0	16.2	17.44	59.24	13.3	6.3	23.5
Bhutan	2.18	84.56	0.4	1.9	105.3	0.81	70.99	0.6	7.6	78.4
Nepal	47.85	742.89	9.0	17.1	25.9	45.4	345.74	34.5	37.0	21.0
Maldives	5.71	47.59	1.1	1.1	27.4	0.19	0.61	0.1	0.1	78.8
Pakistan	40.83	509.17	7.7	11.7	26.4	47.07	92.72	35.8	9.9	31.9
Sri Lanka	130.02	1,354.97	24.6	31.2	19.4	20.5	364.32	15.6	39.0	29.3

ASEAN = Association of Southeast Asian Nations, Lao PDR = Lao People's Democratic Republic, p.a. = per annum, PRC = People's Republic of China, SAARC = South Asian Association for Regional Cooperation, $ = US dollar, % = percent.

Source: IMF Direction of Trade Statistics.

Table A2.5a Structure of India's Exports to East Asia and South Asia, Share of Top 10 Commodities

HS Code	World % Share			East Asia			South Asia		
	1990/91	1998/99	2004/05	1990/91	1998/99	2004/05	1990/91	1998/99	2004/05
71	8.1	17.9	17.9	13.9	28.6	20.0	–	–	–
27	0.0	0.4	8.6	0.0	0.1	11.9	0.0	0.0	22.8
72	1.6	2.0	5.1	2.2	2.2	6.6	1.9	4.5	3.6
62	12.5	9.4	4.6	3.2	1.9	0.8	0.2	1.3	1.3
26	5.2	1.4	4.4	18.7	6.0	15.9	–	–	–
29	1.2	3.5	4.3	2.0	5.3	5.8	0.2	1.5	0.8
84	3.4	2.9	3.9	3.7	2.6	3.0	5.4	6.1	3.8
61	3.7	3.8	3.1	–	–	–	0.1	0.3	0.4
87	2.4	2.1	2.9	1.6	0.4	0.6	34.1	16.3	16.9
73	1.9	1.9	2.7	2.0	1.2	0.7	0.8	4.3	2.0
39	0.4	1.0	2.5	0.2	0.4	3.2	0.5	2.6	2.7
52	8.4	6.1	2.6	11.3	8.9	2.8	11.5	14.1	5.4
03	4.2	3.1	1.6	11.0	9.9	2.3	2.5	1.0	0.3
10	1.5	4.5	2.5	0.0	0.7	0.7	0.1	1.0	5.9
30	2.1	2.2	2.4	1.6	2.4	0.9	6.0	6.5	3.8
07	–	–	–	–	–	–	7.2	6.9	2.6
85	1.3	2.4	2.5	1.8	4.0	2.0	1.4	3.0	2.4
27	29.2	18.9	31.5	5.6	8.1	6.0	1.0	0.2	0.2
71	9.7	21.2	18.9	0.5	1.8	5.4	1.7	0.2	0.3
84	9.1	9.4	8.5	11.1	15.7	17.2	0.0	0.6	3.0
85	4.2	4.7	8.0	10.1	9.7	19.4	0.0	0.2	3.9
72	4.5	2.5	3.0	6.3	3.3	3.1	7.1	3.3	9.1
15	0.9	4.5	2.3	4.3	7.3	7.1	3.7	8.6	4.1
90	2.5	2.2	1.8	3.5	2.5	2.3	0.0	0.0	0.2
89	1.0	0.5	1.6	1.7	0.9	2.8	0.0	0.0	0.0
28	0.8	3.0	1.5	1.0	1.8	1.0	0.0	7.7	3.9
39	2.5	1.7	1.5	4.1	3.5	2.8	0.5	1.0	5.6
88	1.4	0.4	1.5	0.1	1.0	0.3	0.0	0.0	0.0
26	0.5	0.5	0.9	0.3	0.3	0.8	1.0	0.0	0.1
31	1.6	1.9	0.8	0.2	0.3	0.0	0.0	1.4	0.8
44	1.2	0.9	0.8	6.2	2.9	2.2	0.8	2.2	1.7
87	1.3	0.7	0.7	6.2	2.9	2.0	0.0	0.1	0.0
73	1.6	1.1	0.8	2.7	1.8	1.4	0.3	0.5	1.3
40	0.8	0.7	0.6	2.6	1.5	1.3	0.7	1.2	1.4
54	0.6	0.3	0.4	2.8	0.7	1.2	1.3	2.3	1.9
50	0.3	0.2	0.3	1.6	0.8	1.2	0.0	0.0	0.0
74	2.0	0.9	0.5	2.3	1.8	0.6	1.5	0.6	15.0
09	0.0	0.2	0.1	0.1	0.2	0.2	5.8	4.8	5.4
33	0.2	0.1	0.1	0.2	0.1	0.2	0.3	5.3	3.6
17	0.0	0.6	0.3	0.1	0.1	0.1	0.0	6.4	3.5
08	0.6	0.8	0.6	0.8	1.0	0.3	19.0	9.9	3.4

– = no data available.

Source: IndiaTrades, Centre for Monitoring Indian Economy.

Table A2.5b Description of Commodity Codes Corresponding to Table A2.5(a)

HS Code	Commodity description
3	Fish, crustaceans, mollusks, and other aquatic invertebrates
7	Edible vegetables and certain roots and tubers
8	Edible fruit and nuts; peel or citrus fruit or melons
9	Coffee, tea, mate, and spices
10	Cereals
15	Animal or vegetable fats and oils and their cleavage products
17	Sugars and sugar confectionery
26	Ores, slag, and ash
27	Mineral fuels, mineral oils, and products or their distillation
28	Inorganic chemicals
29	Organic chemicals
30	Pharmaceutical products
31	Fertilizers
33	Essential oils and resinoids; perfumery, cosmetic or toilet preparations
39	Plastics and articles thereof
40	Rubber and articles thereof
44	Wood and articles of wood; wood charcoal
50	Silk
52	Cotton
54	Manmade filaments
61	Articles of apparel and clothing accessories, knitted or crocheted
62	Articles of apparel and clothing accessories, not knitted or crocheted
71	Natural or cultured pearls, precious or semi-precious stones, precious metals, etc.
72	Iron and steel
73	Articles of iron or steel
74	Copper and articles thereof
84	Nuclear reactors, boilers, machinery and mechanical appliances; parts thereof
85	Electrical machinery and equipment and parts thereof
87	Vehicles other than railway or tramway rolling stock, and parts and accessories thereof
88	Aircraft, spacecraft, and parts thereof
89	Ships, boats, and floating structures
90	Optical, photographic, cinematographic, measuring, checking, precision, medical or surgical instruments and apparatus; parts thereof

Source: India Trades, Centre for Monitoring Indian Economy.

Table A2.6 Some Major Instruments of Export Promotion

Instruments	Description	Main agencies involved
Export finance (in domestic and foreign currency; pre- and post-shipment)	Banks required to meet a minimum target of 12% of net credit as export credit; concessional interest rates for export finance	Reserve Bank of India, Export-Import Bank of India, other commercial banks
Export insurance and guarantee	Credit risk insurance cover against non-realization of export proceeds, guarantees to financial institutions against export credit, insurance of goods	Export Credit Guarantee Corporation of India Limited, commercial banks, General Insurance Corporation of India, private sector
Export promotion and marketing assistance	Organization of fairs and exhibitions, buyer-seller meetings, product promotion, technology promotion, packaging, market surveys, information dissemination	Indian Trade Promotion Organization, Indian Institute of Packaging, Indian Institute of Foreign Trade
Duty exemption/remission schemes[a]	Duty-free imports of inputs used in exports; post-export replenishment/remission of duty paid on inputs	Director General of Foreign Trade; Central Board of Excise and Customs
Export Promotion Capital Goods Scheme	Duty concessions on imports of capital goods used for exports	Director General of Foreign Trade
Assistance to States for Infrastructure Development of Exports (ASIDE)	Allocation of funds to states for developing export-related infrastructure	Ministry of Commerce and Industry, State Governments
Market access and development assistance (MAI, MDA)	Financial assistance for focus products and markets (current focus markets: the Commonwealth of Independent States, Africa, Latin America); duty credit scrips	Government of India, Export Promotion Councils, Industry and Trade Associations, State Government agencies, Indian Commercial Missions abroad
Units undertaking to export entire production (EOUs/STPs/EHTPs/BTPs)	Duty-free capital goods imports, excise and central sales tax exemptions, income tax exemptions, exemption from industrial licensing, 100% FDI on automatic route, 100% retention of export earnings in EEFC account	Director General of Foreign Trade, state governments
Special economic zones	(see Table A2.1)	Government of India, state governments

BTP = Bio-Technology Park, EEFC = Exchange Earner's Foreign Currency, EHTP = Electronic Hardware Technology Park, EOU = export-oriented unit, FDI = foreign direct investment, STP = Software Technology Park, % = percent.

[a] At present there are two broad types of duty exemption schemes: the first type, which consists of Advance Authorization Scheme (AAS) and Duty Free Import Authorization Scheme (DFCIA), provides for exemption from payment of customs duty. The second type enables post-export remission/replenishment of duty on inputs used in the exported products and consists of two specific schemes, namely Duty Free Replenishment Certificate (DFRC), Duty Entitlement Passbook Scheme (DEPB), and Duty Drawback Scheme (DBK).

Source: Based on the Foreign Trade Policy, 2002–2009, Ministry of Commerce and Industry. Available: http://commerce.nic.in

Table A2.7 India's Current Engagements in Trade Agreements

Agreement	Description	Membership	Status
Agreements Under Implementation			
Multilateral			
Global System of Trade Preferences (GSTP)	Agreement to establish GSTP	Algeria, Argentina, Bangladesh, Benin, Bolivia, Brazil, Cameroon, Chile, Colombia, Cuba, Ecuador, Egypt, Ghana, Guinea, Guyana, India, Indonesia, Iran, Iraq, Libya, Malaysia, Mexico, Morocco, Mozambique, Myanmar, Nicaragua, Nigeria, Pakistan, Peru, Philippines, Republic of Korea, Romania, Singapore, Sri Lanka, Sudan Thailand, Trinidad and Tobago, Tunisia, Tanzania, Venezuela, Viet Nam, Yugoslavia, Zimbabwe	Signed April 1988 (1st round), enforced April 1989 June 2004 (3rd round launched)
		Regional/Subregional	
South Asia Free Trade Agreement	South Asian Free Trade Area	Non-Least Developed Country (LDC) members: India, Pakistan, Sri Lanka LDC members: Bangladesh, Bhutan, Maldives, Nepal	Signed January 2004 Enforced July 2006
Asia-Pacific Trade Agreement (formerly known as the Bangkok Agreement)	Preferential Trade Agreement	Bangladesh, India, Republic of Korea, Sri Lanka (2000)	Signed July 1975 (1st round), enforced June 1976, 1990 (2nd round), July 2004 (3rd round), September 2006 (New agreement enforced)
Bilateral			
India–Sri Lanka FTA	India–Sri Lanka Free Trade Agreement	India, Sri Lanka	Signed December 1998, Enforced March 2000, Current Negotiations on Comprehensive Economic Partnership Agreement (CEPA)

continued on next page

Table A2.7 (continued)

Agreement	Description	Membership	Status
India–Bhutan Trade Agreement and FTA	Bilateral treaty with Bhutan with no negative list	India, Bhutan	Since 1949
India–Nepal Bilateral Treaties of Trade and Transit	Bilateral non-reciprocal FTA with Nepal with elimination of rules of origin in 1996 subject to a negative list. Reintroduction of rules of origin in 2002 and quotas on free entry of some goods	India, Nepal	Since 1960, modified 1971, 1978, 1996, 2002
India–Thailand	Early Harvest Scheme	India, Thailand	Signed October 2003, Early Harvest Scheme enforced September 2004
India–Singapore Comprehensive Economic Cooperation Agreement (CECA)	India–Singapore CECA covers trade in goods, services and investment	India, Singapore	Signed June 2005, enforced August 2005
India–Afghanistan PTA	India–Afghanistan Preferential Trade Agreement	India, Afghanistan	Signed March 2003
TRIPARTITE	Tripartite Agreement on Preferential Trade	Egypt, India, Yugoslavia	Enforced April 1968
Framework Agreements			
India–ASEAN Comprehensive Economic Cooperation (CEC)	Framework Agreement on CEC between ASEAN and India	India, ASEAN countries	Signed October 2003

continued on next page

Table A2.7 (continued)

Agreement	Description	Membership	Status
India–Thailand FTA	Framework Agreement for FTA between India and Thailand	India, Thailand	Signed October 2003, Early Harvest Scheme (on 82 common items operational since September 2004)
India–Sri Lanka CEPA	Framework Agreement on India–Sri Lanka Comprehensive Economic Partnership	India, Sri Lanka	Signed 2004
India–Gulf Cooperation Council (GCC) FTA	Framework Agreement on FTA between India and GCC	India, Bahrain, Kuwait, Oman, Qatar, Saudi Arabia, United Arab Emirates	
India–Chile PTA	Framework Agreement on PTA between India and Chile	India, Chile	Signed January 2005
India–MERCOSUR PTA	Framework Agreement on PTA between India and MERCOSUR	India, Argentina, Brazil, Paraguay, Uruguay, Venezuela	Signed 2004
Bay of Bengal Initiative for Multi-Sectoral Technical and Economic Cooperation (BIMSTEC)	Framework Agreement of BIMSTEC	Bangladesh, Bhutan, India, Nepal, Sri Lanka, Myanmar, Thailand	Signed February 2004
Agreements Under Discussion/Negotiation			
India–Japan Joint Study Group (JSG)	JSG to explore Comprehensive Economic Cooperation Agreement	India, Japan	JSG set up in June 2005

continued on next page

Table A2.7 (continued)

Agreement	Description	Membership	Status
India–PRC JSG	JSG to explore greater cooperation	India, the PRC	JSG set up 2004
India–Korea JSG	JSG to study feasibility of CEPA	India, the Republic of Korea	Agreement to set up JSG signed October 2004
India–Malaysia JSG	JSG to explore CECA	India, Malaysia	Agreement to set up JSG signed December 2004
India–Indonesia JSG	JSG to explore CECA	India, Indonesia	MoU to set up JSG signed November 2005
India–Mauritius JSG	JSG to explore Comprehensive Economic Cooperation Partnership Agreement (CECPA) between India and Mauritius	India, Mauritius	JSG constituted November 2003
India–SACU PTA	PTA to be signed	India, South Africa, Lesotho, Swaziland, Botswana, Namibia	Draft framework agreement finalized September 2004

ASEAN = Association of Southeast Asian Nations, FTA = free trade agreement, PRC = People's Republic of China, PTA = preferential trade agreement, SACU = South African Customs Union.

Source: Based on list of trade agreements and text of agreements available at http://commerce.nic.in/india_rta_main.htm.

Table A2.8 India's Multilateral Requests and Offers in Services

Sector/Mode	Requesting Members
Maritime transport services	Australia; Canada; European Community (EC); Hong Kong, China; Iceland; Japan; Republic of Korea; Mexico; New Zealand; Norway; Panama; Separate Customs Territory of Taipei,China, Penghu, Kinmen, Matsu; and Switzerland.
Computer and related services	Australia; Canada; Chile; EC; Hong Kong, China; India; Japan; Republic of Korea; Mexico; New Zealand; Norway; Pakistan; Peru; Separate Customs Territory of Taipei,China, Penghu, Kinmen, Matsu; Singapore; and United States (US).
Telecommunications	Australia; Canada; EC; Hong Kong, China; Japan; Republic of Korea; Norway; Separate Customs Territory of Taipei,China, Penghu, Kinmen, Matsu; Singapore; and US.
Postal and courier services, including express delivery	EC, Japan, New Zealand, US.
Mode 4	Argentina, Brazil, Chile, Colombia, Egypt, India, Mexico, Pakistan, Peru, Thailand.
Environmental services	Australia; Canada; EC; Japan; Republic of Korea; Norway; Separate Customs Territory of Taipei,China, Penghu, Kinmen, Matsu; Switzerland; and US.
Distribution services	Chile; EC; Japan; Republic of Korea; Mexico; Separate Customs Territory of Taipei,China, Penghu, Kinmen, Matsu; Singapore; and US.
Audiovisual services	Hong Kong, China; Japan; Mexico; Separate Customs Territory of Taipei,China, Penghu, Kinmen, Matsu; Singapore; and US. No collective request to least developed countries.
Energy services	Australia; Canada; Chile; EC; Japan; Norway; Republic of Korea; Saudi Arabia; Separate Customs Territory of Taipei,China, Penghu, Kinmen, Matsu; Singapore; and US.
Private education Services	New Zealand
Construction services	Australia; Canada; EC; Japan; Republic of Korea, Malaysia; Mexico; New Zealand; Norway; Separate Customs Territory of Taipei,China, Penghu, Kinmen, Matsu; Singapore; Turkey; and US.
Architecture, engineering, and integrated engineering services	Australia, Canada, Chile, EC, Japan, Republic of Korea, Mexico, New Zealand, Norway, Switzerland, and US.
Financial services	Australia; Canada; EC; Ecuador; Hong Kong, China; Japan, Republic of Korea; Norway; Separate Customs Territory of Taipei,China, Penghu, Kinmen, Matsu; and US.
Cross-border supply	Chile; Hong Kong, China; India; Mexico; New Zealand; Pakistan; Singapore; Separate Customs Territory of Taipei,China, Penghu, Kinmen, Matsu; Switzerland; and Thailand.
Logistics services	Australia; Canada; Chile; Djibouti; EC; Hong Kong, China; Iceland; Japan; Republic of Korea; Liechtenstein; Mauritius; New Zealand; Norway; Panama; Peru; Separate Customs Territory of Taipei,China, Penghu, Kinmen, Matsu; Singapore; and Switzerland.

Source: http://commerce.nic.in/wto_service.htm

Pakistan

Nadeem Ul Haque and Ejaz Ghani[1]

Economic Structure and External Orientation

Pakistan, like many other developing economies, is actively pursuing a policy of enhancing regional economic cooperation. Of particular interest to Pakistan are the South and East Asian economies. Pakistan is a signatory to the South Asian Free Trade Area (SAFTA), which came into force in July 2006. Pakistan developed its Strategic Vision East Asia initiative in 2003, which aims to stimulate trade and investment ties with South and East Asia. These ties are currently weak but have considerable potential for growth.

In view of the growing trend toward regionalism, it is imperative for Pakistan to solidify its economic relations especially with the South Asian and East Asian countries. The South Asian developing economies are opening up with a view to accelerating their economic growth through greater trade and investment. Against this backdrop, this country paper provides a comprehensive review of economic structure in Pakistan with particular emphasis on trade, investment, and potential for regional cooperation. The rest of this chapter reviews the economic structure and external orientation of Pakistan's economy. This paper (i) discusses Pakistan's foreign direct investment (FDI) regime and policies; (ii) discusses and analyses merchandise trade policies with emphasis on East and South Asia; (iii) highlights infrastructure and trade administration issues; (iv) describes the service sector trade; and (v) concludes the discussion and spells out some policy implications.

External Orientation

Like many other developing countries, Pakistan has benefited from a strong and sustained growth in the world economy in the last decades. Exports during the first 9 months of 2006 were up by 18.6%—rising from $10.18 billion in 2005 to $12.07 billion. Like exports, Pakistan's

---

[1]   The authors are thankful to Mr. Tariq Mahmood, Mr. Karim Khan, Ms. Naseem Akhtar, and M. Afsar Khan for their valuable research assistance.

imports are also highly concentrated in few items: machinery, petroleum and petroleum products, chemicals, transport equipment, edible oil, iron, steel, fertilizer, and tea. These eight categories of imports accounted for 72.5% of total imports during 2005/06. Among these categories, machinery, petroleum and petroleum products, and chemicals accounted for 53.4% of total imports. Pakistan's imports are sourced from a few countries: more than 40% of total imports originate from only seven countries: United States (US), Japan, Kuwait, Saudi Arabia, Germany, the United Kingdom (UK), and Malaysia.

Pakistan's exports are highly concentrated on few items: cotton, leather, rice, synthetic textiles, and sporting goods. These five categories of exports accounted for 74.5% of total exports during the first 9 months of 2006 with cotton alone contributing 58.4%, followed by leather (6.1%), rice (6.9%), and synthetic textiles (1.2%). Pakistan also exports to only a few countries: US; Germany; Japan; UK; Hong Kong, China; Dubai; and Saudi Arabia account for 50% of its exports. The US is the single largest export market for Pakistan, accounting for 27% of its exports, followed by UK; Dubai; Germany; and Hong Kong, China.

Pakistan Recent Trade Initiatives

Given the proliferation of regional agreements and bilateral trade agreements in the region, the Government of Pakistan has likewise initiated a series of preferential trade negotiations, which are at various stages of completion. Pakistan's first free trade agreement (FTA), signed with Sri Lanka, took effect in June 2005 (Appendix Table A3.5). As a result of this agreement, the exports of fruits, vegetables, footwear, engineering products, sanitary goods, chemicals, leather, rice, and some textiles enjoy duty concessions in the Sri Lankan market. A full-fledged FTA with the People's Republic of China (PRC) is also under discussion; an Early Harvest Program has already been effective since January 2006, where Pakistani exports such as leather articles, some textile items, marble, sports goods, fruits, vegetables, and mineral products will have reduced duties in the PRC and all these items were exportable duty-free by January 2008 (Appendix Table A3.2). FTA negotiations with Malaysia are likewise proceeding at a rapid pace, with an early harvest program becoming effective since January 2006 (Appendix Table A3.3). As a result, Malaysia has allowed the export of Pakistani items such as fruits, vegetables, some textile items, and jewelry at concessional rates of duty. Negotiations are expected to conclude in the near future. The SAFTA among the seven South Asian countries has been signed by all members and became operational on 1 January 2006 (Appendix Table A3.4). FTA negotiations with Singapore and the Gulf Cooperation Council (GCC) were expected to conclude by the end of 2006. Bilateral negotiations are underway with

Thailand, while multilateral negotiations are taking place in the context of the Organization of Islamic Countries (OIC), and the Group of Developing Eight countries (D-8). Furthermore, a joint consultative study group for a potential preferential trade agreement (PTA) with the Association of South East Asian Nations (ASEAN) has also been agreed.

Pakistan's Economic Structure

Pakistan's growth in gross domestic product (GDP) was unstable in the 1990s, ranging from 1% in 1997 to an impressive 8.6% in 2005 (Table 3.1). Per capita income growth, on the other hand, averaged 3% during 1990–1992, declined during 1993–2001, and accelerated from 2003. In fact, per capita income grew by an average rate of 13.9% per annum during the 4 years from 2003.

The sharp rise in growth is mirrored in the reduction in poverty incidence. The poverty headcount ratio, measured as less than $1 per day, has fallen from 48% of population in 1990 to 28.1% in 2005. The percentage of the population living below the poverty line is provisionally estimated at 25.4% in 2005, down from 32.1% in 2001. This suggests a decline of 6.7 percentage points in the last 4 years. More importantly, rural poverty has declined more than urban poverty. Provisional estimates show that rural poverty has declined 7 percentage points from 39.0% in 2001 to 31.8% in 2005, while urban poverty fell 5.5 percentage points from 22.7% during the same period. Not surprisingly, unit labor cost increased from 50 Pakistan rupees (PRs) in 1990 to PRs190 in 2005.

The trade openness index, measured as the ratio of exports to GDP, has not shown any marked changes during the 1990s. This could be partly because of the insufficiency of foreign exchange reserves, prompting the Government to resort to frequent currency devaluations and consequently causing imports to fall. Exports also remained low as a result of supply bottlenecks and external demand conditions.

Table 3.1 Key Economic Indicators

Year	Per Capita Income Growth (%)	GDP (%)	Openness (% of GDP)	Poverty Headcount Ratio ($2/day, % of population)	Poverty Headcount Ratio ($1/day, % of population)	Unit Labor Cost (PRs per day)	Per Capita Income (PRs)
1990–1995	1.8	4.7	16.5	28.2	13.7	67.5	25,281.7
1996–2000	0.8	3.4	16.0	25.8	4.0	115.4	26,960.6
2001–2005	2.6	5.2	17.2	0.0	13.5	146.1	29,128.0

GDP = gross domestic product, PRs = Pakistan rupees, $ = US dollar, % = percent.

Source: Pakistan Economic Survey, various issues.

The manufacturing and agricultural sectors, which accounted for almost 62% of GDP in 1969/70, saw their shares decline to almost 48% in 2005/06. Correspondingly, the contribution of services has risen over the years. In 2005, services sectors were responsible for two thirds of real GDP growth (Figure 3.1).

Figure 3.1 Contribution to Real GDP Growth, 2005/06

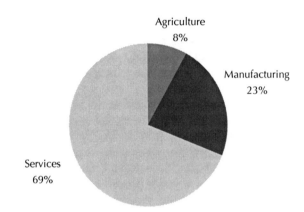

GDP = gross domestic product, % = percent.

Source: Pakistan Economic Survey 2005/06.

Like many other developing countries, Pakistan is a highly regulated economy. While donor-supported program loans have reduced government planning and nationalization, while simultaneously opening some sectors and encouraging privatization, the Government maintains a large role in the domestic market,[2] keeps in place an incentive regime based on protection and subsidies, and practices excessive regulation.[3]

Policy has, therefore, determined the structure of the economy, trade, and entrepreneurship. Mercantilism has characterized Pakistan's industrial and trade policy, stifling domestic commerce (Haque 2006). The result is that very few serious service-sector industries have emerged. Whatever entrepreneurship has prospered has been influenced more by policy than by market demand.

While the economy has opened, as evidenced by low average tariff rates, sectors such as engineering goods remain protected by policy. Other

---

[2] A most important example of a quasi-public-sector enterprise is an armed forces–owned corporate entity.

[3] For example, the Government still dominates agricultural procurement and licenses agricultural markets.

sectors such as construction, retail, entertainment, and leisure remain underdeveloped because of policy neglect and regulatory failures. Several markets in the country such as cement, sugar, and flour are not competitive because the incumbents are able to use the regulatory and pricing regimes to their advantage. The major constraint to new investment and trade in Pakistan may be the uncompetitive market structures (Haque 2006).

Foreign Direct Investment Regime

Foreign Direct Investment

For decades, South Asian countries have been far behind East Asian countries in attracting foreign direct investments (FDIs), as the governments of South Asia were reluctant to open up their markets to foreign companies. Although Pakistan was no exception, the Government in the last few years has pushed through aggressive economic reforms, which have increased FDIs. The Government is also working to attract large-scale FDIs by allowing foreign investors to hold unlimited equity stakes.

In the first 10 months of 2006, FDIs in Pakistan reached $3.0 billion. As seen in Table 3.2, about 75.0% of total FDI originates from six countries: United Arab Emirates, US, Saudi Arabia, Switzerland, UK, and Netherlands. Telecommunications; energy (comprising oil, gas, and power); financial services; trade; construction; chemicals; food; and personal services have been the major recipients of FDIs, accounting for almost 94.0% or $2.1 billion.

Table 3.2 Foreign Direct Investments: Top Sources and Sectoral Destination

Top Investors	Value ($ Mn) (% share)	Top FDI Sectors	Value ($ Mn) (% share)
United Arab Emirates	1,284.6 (42.5%)	Telecommunications	1,000 (77.85%)
United States	419.1 (13.9%)	Energy	304 (72.54%)
Saudi Arabia	273.7 (9.06%)	Financial services	265.5 (97.00%)
Switzerland	161.5 (5.34%)	Trade	81.9 (50.71%)
United Kingdom	151.4 (5.0%)	Construction	54.4 (35.93%)
Netherlands	87.1 (2.9%)	Food	52.7 (60.50%)

FDI = foreign direct investment, $ Mn = millions of US dollars, % = percent.

Source: State Bank of Pakistan.

Over the years, the major sectors for FDIs included power, chemicals, pharmaceutical and fertilizers, mining, oil and gas, and finance. The main concern regarding the recent FDI surge is that most of investment is in telecommunications. There is clearly a need to attract more investments in manufacturing. East Asia's share in Pakistan's FDIs has remained fairly low. Table 3.4 shows FDIs from East Asia during 1990–2005. Its share has remained almost below 15% since 1990. It was only in 1998/99 that East Asia's share exceeded 15%. In the region, Hong Kong, China is the biggest source of FDIs, followed by Singapore and Malaysia.

The share of FDIs to members of South Asian Association for Regional Cooperation (SAARC) is increasing though it is still a small recipient of FDIs relative to members of ASEAN. India and Pakistan took a major share (about 90% during 1997–2004) of FDIs in SAARC. Although the shares of other countries in SAARC are small, they are growing quickly (Table 3.3).

Japan is among the top 10 investors in Pakistan (Table 3.4), amounting to around $30 million annually. The big surge of investment observed in 1995/96 came primarily from intensive investment in independent power producers (IPPs). In 1998/99, big projects such as the Engro-Asahi polyvinyl chloride plant and the Daihatsu Assembly plant pushed up the total volume of investment. Japanese investments based on the number of Japanese joint ventures include automobiles (including motorcycles and automobile-related sectors), financing (leasing and investment banking), and power (IPPs).

Export Processing Zones

The Export Processing Zones Authority (EPZA) was established in 1980 to boost industrialization, augment the country's export base, create job opportunities, bring in new technology and know-how, and attract foreign investment. At present, there are three export processing zones (EPZs),

Table 3.3 FDI Inflows from East and South Asia, $ Mn

Country/Region	2001	2002	2003	2004	2005
Bangladesh	1.7	0.4	(1.5)	(0.3)	3.4
China, People's Rep. of	0.3	3.0	14.3	0.4	1.7
Hong Kong, China	2.8	5.5	6.3	32.4	24.0
Malaysia	0.9	2.3	1.2	22.1	2.9
Singapore	3.9	3.7	5.1	8.0	9.9
India	0.0	0.0	0.1	0.1	0.5
Korea, Rep. of	0.5	0.2	1.0	1.4	1.6
East/South Asia	10.1	16.7	21.3	64.6	59.8

FDI = foreign direct investment, Rep. = Republic, ( ) = negative value, $ Mn = millions of US dollars.

Source: State Bank of Pakistan, annual reports.

Table 3.4 Net Inflow of FDI from East Asia, $ Mn

Year	Hong Kong, China	Japan	Korea	Singapore	PRC	Total	Total FDI	% Share
1990–1995	62.9	164.6	72.2	0	0	299.7	2785.7	10.76
1996–2000	47.4	138.6	30.8	7.1	0.1	224	2451.7	9.14
2000–2006[a]	21.9	37.3	1.4	8.9	16.3	85.8	3020.2	2.84

FDI = foreign direct investment, PRC = People's Republic of China, $ Mn = millions of US dollars, % = percent.

[a] July to April

Source: State Bank of Pakistan, annual reports.

located in Karachi, Sialkot, and Risalpur, the last two having been set up under public–private joint venture arrangements.

The EPZA has contributed significantly to the Government's drive to attract FDIs by offering a package of incentives and facilities. One milestone EPZA achieved was to convert Saindak Project in the mountainous province of Balochistan into an EPZ operated by the Metallurgical Construction Company of the PRC. Saindak EPZ allowed Pakistan's entry into the world market of metal exports. The Saindak gold and copper project started operation in August 2003 and has already produced more than $45 million of exports in the past year. The Saindak project has the capacity to produce around 20,000 tons of blister copper a year and about 5 tons of gold and silver from indigenous ores, generating foreign exchange revenues of over $45 million annually.

The introduction of Textile City projects—which follow the EPZ model—is also a significant breakthrough, with the creation of a joint stock company called Pakistan Textile City. The Government has a 50% share in this venture, which has a starting capital structure of PRs1 billion ($16.8 million). The textile EPZ will compete in international markets in the post-Multi-Fiber Agreement quota environment and focus particularly on dyeing, processing, and finishing. Similarly, there are plans to set up Marble City, under the EPZ model, at Gaddani, Balochistan to harness the tremendous economic potential for marble and granite production in the area.

Investment Policy

Pakistan's investment policy is one of the most liberal in Asia since all economic sectors are open to FDIs, with the exception of four sectors where prior government permission is required: (i) arms and ammunitions, (ii) high explosives, (iii) radioactive substances, and (iv) secure printing for currency and mint. The major components of the country's investment policy are:

- equal treatment to local and foreign investors;
- 100% foreign equity allowed;
- attractive tax and tariff incentive package; only 5% customs duty and 0% sales tax on import of plant, machinery, and equipment (PME); 50% tax relief (initial depreciation allowance, % of PME cost); no customs duty and sales tax on imported raw materials used in producing for exports;
- remittance of royalties, technical and franchise fees, capital, profits, and dividends allowed;
- protection of foreign private investment through Promotion and Protection Act, 1976; the Protection of Economic Reforms Act, 1992; and the Foreign Currency Accounts (Protection) Act, 1976;
- FDI in the service sector is allowed in any activity subject to condition of prior permission or No Objection Certificate (NOC) or license from the concerned agencies and subject to provisions of respective sectoral policies; and
- no work permits are required for foreign workers (technical and/or managerial) and work visas can be easily acquired.

Investment Agreements (Bilateral and Multilateral)

Pakistan has signed bilateral agreements on promotion and protection of investment with 46 countries (Table 3.5). These agreements provide for such items as:

- national treatment, except in the four sectors identified above;
- equal and/or nondiscriminatory treatment in case of compensation for losses owing to war, other armed conflicts, or state of national emergency;
- free transfer of investments, and income, including profits, dividends, interest income, proceeds of sales or liquidation, repayments of loans, salaries, wages and other compensation etc.; and
- dispute settlement mecanisms.

Merchandise Trade Policy

Composition of Exports

Pakistan's export composition has changed during the last 6 years (Table 3.6). Although the share of primary commodities remained more or less the same, the share of semi-manufactured exports has declined from

15% to 10%, at the same time that the share of manufactured goods has increased from 73% to 79%. This implies that Pakistan's reliance on primary commodities and semi-manufactures for foreign exchange earnings is gradually decreasing.

Trade With East Asian and South Asian Countries: Individual and Collective Trends

Trade With East Asia

Pakistan's exports to East Asian countries, as a percentage of total exports, has been steadily declining, with export shares declining from 22.5% in 1990 to 13.6% in 2005 (Table 3.7, Appendix Table A3.1b for details). The greatest declines came from Singapore and Japan whose respective trade shares have fallen by more than 88%. Japan's case is more pronounced as its ranking in the top Asian importing countries decreased from first to sixth during 1990–2005 periods. In contrast, exports to the PRC and Malaysia show an increasing trend, with exports to the PRC increasing by more than 1,000%, making it the country's biggest trading partner within East Asia.

Imports from East Asian countries have fluctuated around 30% of total imports throughout the period 1990–2005 (Table 3.8, Appendix Table A3.1b for details). However, looking at individual countries, some interesting patterns emerge. Again Japan declined from first to second position as Pakistan's biggest source of imports, while the PRC moved from second to first. The percentage of imports from the PRC increased from 4.6% in 1990 to 14.3% in 2005, while during the same period the percentage for Japan declined from 11.9% to 6.3% during the same period.

Trade with South Asia

Pakistan's intraregional trade has been relatively weak with the overall share of exports to South Asian countries hovering around the 3.5% range during 1990–2005 (Tables 3.9 and 3.10, Appendix Table A3.1c for details). Although the shares of imports from South Asia are even smaller, they have somewhat increased from an average of 1.5% in 1990–1995 to 2.4% in the period 2000–2005.

Sectoral Analysis of Exports and Imports

As Table 3.11 suggests, the percentage share of all major export categories (except rice) has slowly fallen over the years. This decline can indicate

Table 3.5 Pakistan's Bilateral Investment Agreements

S.No.	Name of Country	Signing Date	S.No.	Name of Country	Signing Date
1	Germany	25-Nov-1959	24	Tunisia	18-Apr-1996
2	Sweden	12-Mar-1981	25	Syria	25-Apr-1996
3	Kuwait	17-Mar-1983	26	Denmark	18-Jul-1996
4	France	01-Jun-1983	27	Belarus	22-Jan-1997
5	Korea, Republic of	25-May-1988	28	Mauritius	03-Apr-1997
6	Netherlands	04-Oct-1988	29	Italy	19-Jul-1997
7	PRC	12-Feb-1989	30	Oman	09-Nov-1997
8	Uzbekistan	13-Aug-1992	31	Sri Lanka	20-Dec-1997
9	Spain	15-Sep-1994	32	Australia	07-Feb-1998
10	Turkmenistan	26-Oct-1994	33	Japan	10-Mar-1998
11	United Kingdom	30-Nov-1994	34	Belgo-Luxembourg Economic Union	23-Apr-1998
12	Singapore	08-Mar-1995	35	Qatar	06-Apr-1999
13	Turkey	15-Mar-1995	36	Yemen	11-May-1999
14	Portugal	17-Apr-1995	37	Philippines	11-May-1999
15	Malaysia	07-Jul-1995	38	Egypt	16-Apr-2000
16	Romania	10-Jul-1995	39	OPEC Fund	24-Oct-2000
17	Switzerland	11-Jul-1995	40	Lebanon	09-Jan-2001
18	Kyrgyz Republic	23-Aug-1995	41	Morocco	16-Apr-2001
19	Azerbaijan	09-Oct-1995	42	Bosnia and Herzegovina	04-Sep-2001
20	Bangladesh	24-Oct-1995	43	Kazakhstan	08-Dec-2003
21	UAE	05-Nov-1995	44	Lao PDR	23-Apr-2004
22	Iran	08-Nov-1995	45	Cambodia	27-Apr-2004
23	Indonesia	08-Mar-1996	46	Tajikistan	13-May-2004

Lao PDR = Lao People's Democratic Republic, OPEC = Organization of Petroleum Exporting Countries, PRC = People's Republic of China, UAE = United Arab Emirates.

Source: Board of Investment, Government of Pakistan.

more diversification in Pakistan's exports, and a shift away from primary goods and toward finished ones. This is evidenced by a sharp increase in the percentage of other exports and a sizeable growth in exports of petroleum products (90.2%), chemicals (30.5%), and engineering goods (66.9%). However, the decline in exports of synthetic textile is of concern and could indicate faltering competitiveness.

Table 3.12 illustrates how Pakistan's exports to countries in the SAARC remained low during 1990–2005, although it increased slightly from 3.5%

Table 3.6 Economic Classifications of Exports

Year	Primary commodities		Semi-manufactured goods		Manufactured goods		Total value ($)
	Value ($)	% share	Value ($)	% share	Value ($)	% share	
1999/00	53,833	12	68,208	15	321,637	73	443,678
2000/01	67,783	13	81,288	15	389,999	72	539,070
2001/02	60,346	11	80,438	14	420,163	75	560,947
2002/03	71,194	11	71,323	11	509,777	78	652,294
2003/04	70,716	10	83,361	12	554,959	78	709,036
2004/05	92,018	11	86,483	10	675,586	79	854,088

$ = US dollar, % = percent.

Source: Pakistan Economic Survey (2005–06).

Table 3.7 Pakistan's Exports to East Asia, 1990–2005

Countries	1990		1995		2000		2005		% Growth rates (1990–2005)
	%	$ Mn	%	$ Mn	%	$ Mn	%	$ Mn	
Japan	8.18	457	6.78	542	2.64	234	0.92	130	(71.55)
PRC	1.20	67	1.49	119	2.67	237	5.38	757	1029.85
Hong Kong, China	4.98	278	7.53	602	6.01	533	3.78	532	91.37
Indonesia	0.89	50	1.31	105	1.23	109	0.52	73	46
Korea, Rep. of	2.97	166	3.39	271	2.93	260	1.48	208	25.3
Malaysia	0.52	29	0.58	46	0.6	53	0.53	74	155.17
Philippines	0.63	35	0.38	30	0.43	38	0.2	28	(20)
Singapore	2.17	121	1.1	88	0.61	54	0.23	33	(72.73)
Thailand	0.97	54	0.75	60	0.69	61	0.54	76	40.74
Taipei,China	0	0	0	0	0	0	0	0	
Total	22.5	1,257	23.31	1,863	17.8	1,579	13.56	1,911	52.03

PRC = People's Republic of China, Rep. = Republic, $ Mn = millions of US dollars, % = percent, ( ) = negative value.

Source: Computed from the *Direction of Trade Statistics*, International Monetary Fund.

of total exports in 1990/91 to 4.6% in 2004/05. Pakistan's exports to countries in ASEAN, on the other hand, declined to 2.1% in 2004/05 from 5.1% in 1990/91. The low exports to SAARC and ASEAN countries indicate considerable potential for export expansion in these markets. Similarly, Pakistan's imports from SAARC and ASEAN countries are likewise low.

Between 1990 and 2004, there has been an increase in exports of chemicals, food, and live animals to almost all East Asian countries. In the case of the PRC and Indonesia, export of manufactured goods has also gone

Table 3.8 Pakistan's Imports to East Asia, 1990–2005

Countries	1990		1995		2000		2005		% Growth rates (1990–2005)
	%	$ Mn	%	$ Mn	%	$ Mn	%	$ Mn	
Japan	11.88	877	10.72	1,229	5.66	607	6.32	1,662	89.51
PRC	4.58	338	4.41	506	5.02	538	14.32	3,765	1,013.91
Hong Kong, China	0.41	30	0.43	49	0.56	60	0.59	155	416.67
Indonesia	0.64	47	1.02	117	1.57	168	2.44	641	1,263.83
Korea, Rep. of	2.76	204	2.99	343	3.32	356	1.87	491	140.69
Malaysia	3.32	245	8.45	969	4.09	439	2.75	724	195.51
Philippines	0.01	1	0.03	4	0.06	6	0.06	16	1,500.00
Singapore	3.12	230	1.93	221	2.8	300	2.7	711	209.13
Thailand	1.25	92	0.94	108	1.85	198	2.46	648	604.35
Taipei,China	0.05	4	0	0	0	0	0	0	(100)
Total	**28.01**	**2,068**	**30.94**	**3,546**	**24.92**	**2,672**	**33.51**	**8,813**	**326.16**

PRC = People's Republic of China, Rep. = Republic, $ Mn = millions of US dollars, % = percent, ( ) = negative value.

Source: Computed from the *Direction of Trade Statistics*, International Monetary Fund.

Table 3.9 Exports to South Asia, % of total exports and $ Mn

Country	1990		1995		2000		2005		% Growth rates (1990–2005)
	%	$ Mn	%	$ Mn	%	$ Mn	%	$ Mn	
Bangladesh	1.84	103	1.91	153	1.57	139	0.93	131	27.18
India	0.88	49	0.49	39	0.65	58	1.28	180	267.35
Maldives	0.02	1	0.01	1	0.01	1	0.01	2	100.00
Nepal	0.02	1	0.04	3	0.03	3	0.02	3	200.00
Sri Lanka	1.24	69	0.69	55	0.91	81	1.09	153	121.74
Total	**3.99**	**223**	**3.14**	**251**	**3.18**	**282**	**3.34**	**469**	**110.34**

$ Mn = millions of US dollars, % = percent.

Source: Computed from the *Direction of Trade Statistics*, International Monetary Fund.

up, with the increase being pronounced for the PRC. Imports of machinery and transport equipment from most of East Asia have generally increased during the period under analysis. Imports of animal and vegetable oils have sharply increased from Indonesia.

In South Asia, exports of food and live animals to Bangladesh have increased, but exports destined for India and Sri Lanka have decreased. Exports of manufactured goods have gone up for all South Asian countries except India, while exports of crude materials have experienced a marked

Table 3.10 Source of South Asian Imports, % of total imports and $ Mn

Country	1990		1995		2000		2005		% Growth rates (1990–2005)
	%	$ Mn	%	$ Mn	%	$ Mn	%	$ Mn	
Bangladesh	0.51	38	0.31	35	0.34	36	0.22	57	50.00
India	0.62	46	0.71	81	1.66	178	1.98	520	330.43
Maldives	0	0	0	0	0	0	0	0	0
Nepal	0	0	0.01	1	0.03	3	0.02	4	–
Sri Lanka	0.5	37	0.44	50	0.33	35	0.20	53	43.24
Total	1.64	121	1.46	167	2.35	252	2.41	634	423.97

$ Mn = millions of US dollars, – = no data, % = percent.

Source: Computed from the *Direction of Trade Statistics*, International Monetary Fund.

Table 3.11 Commodity Imports from South Asia, % of total imports and $ Mn

Commodities	1990/1991		1998/1999		2004/2005		% Growth rates (1990/1991– 2004/2005)
	%	$ Mn	%	$ Mn	%	$ Mn	
Cotton	61.0	3,739.91	59.1	4,597.39	57.4	8,260.43	120.87
Leather	9.1	557.92	6.9	536.75	5.8	834.68	49.61
Rice	5.6	343.34	6.9	536.75	6.5	935.42	172.45
Synthetic textile	5.7	349.47	5.1	396.73	2.1	302.21	(13.52)
Sports goods	2.2	134.88	3.3	256.71	2.1	302.21	124.06
Others	16.4	1,005.48	18.7	1,454.67	26.1	3,756.05	273.56
Total	100.0	6,131.00	100.0	7,779.00	100.0	14,391.00	134.73

( ) = negative value, $ Mn = millions of US dollars, % = percent.

Source: Pakistan Economic Survey, various issues.

Table 3.12 Exports and Imports from SAARC and ASEAN

Item	1990/1991		1998/1999		2004/2005		% Growth rates (1990/1991– 2004/2005)
	%	$ Mn	%	$ Mn	%	$ Mn	
Destination of Exports							
SAARC	3.5	214.6	5.0	388.9	4.6	662.0	208.5
ASEAN	5.1	312.7	3.2	248.9	2.1	302.2	(3.4)
Origin of Imports							
SAARC	1.5	92.0	2.2	171.1	3.2	460.5	400.8
ASEAN	8.9	545.7	14.1	1,096.8	10.0	1,439.1	163.7

ASEAN = Association of Southeast Asian Nations, SAARC = South Asian Association for Regional Cooperation, ( ) = negative value, $ Mn = millions of US dollars, % = percent.

Source: Pakistan Economic Survey, various issues.

reduction to all of South Asia, with the exception of Nepal. Imports of chemicals have increased for all countries except Nepal, although Nepal has become a more important supplier of food and live animals. Imports of manufactured goods from India and Sri Lanka have increased.

Import Protection

Pakistan's trade policy has been gradually liberalized. Import quotas were removed in 1980 and further restrictions were eliminated during the 1990s. The tariff structure has also been gradually rationalized. During the period 1983–1994, about 724 items were removed from the negative list. Currently the negative list comprises only 62 products, most of them included on religious, environmental, security, or health grounds. During the period 1988–1991, tariffs were reduced on 1,134 items and increased on 462 items. The maximum tariff rate was reduced from 225% to 100%, and reduced again to 65% in 1995. The number of tariff slabs was reduced from 17 to 10 during the same period. At present, the maximum tariff rate is pegged at 25%, except for automobiles and alcoholic beverages, while the number of tariff slabs has been reduced to five.

Tariff rationalization from 1987 to 1998 resulted in a decline in tariff rates on all categories of imports. Tariff rate on final capital goods fell from 19.5% to 8.3%, from 24.6% to 11.1% for final consumer goods, from 20% to 10% for a number of processed goods, and from 10% to 5% for various kinds of raw materials. Moreover, tariff lines have been brought into lower tariff slabs. About 50% of the tariff lines at present are in the 5% or 10% slab, 15% are at the 20% slab, and 36% are at the 25% slab (Table 3.13). Figure 3.2 positions Pakistan's tariffs relative to those of other South Asian countries.

Revenue from Customs Duties

Despite Pakistan's weak tax base, tax revenues did display an increasing trend in the 1990s, rising up from PRs129.64 billion in 1990/91 to PRs805.60 billion in 2005/06. However, the tax revenue collected from international trade, amounting to PRs88.92 billion in 1995/96, fell in the subsequent periods. The share of customs duties in total tax collection, in fact, has continuously declined since 1990/91 because of trade liberalization in the 1990s. For instance, the share of customs duties in total tax collection was around 39% in 1990/91 compared to only 17% in 2005/06. The general insignificance of customs duties relative to total GDP, however, could be largely traced to the prevalent use of concessions, tax incentives, and the highly complicated system that creates considerable space for administrative discretion (World Trade Organization [WTO] 2001).

Table 3.13 Distribution of Tariff Rates 2001 and 2004

Tariff Rate	Percent of Tariff Lines (2001/02)	Percent of Tariff Lines (2004/05)
5%	10.1	24.99
10%	32.2	24.09
20%	17.2	15.12
25%	39.4	35.8

% = percent.

Source: Pakistan Institute of Development Economics, Tariff Rationalization, 2005.

Figure 3.2 Simple Average Applied Tariff Rates in SAARC Countries

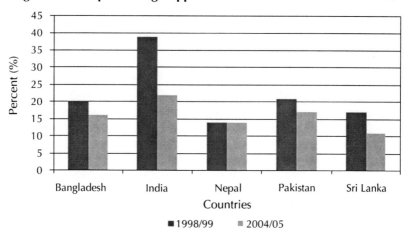

SAARC = South Asian Association for Regional Cooperation, % = percent.

Source: T. Baysan, A. Panagariya, and N. Pigala (2006).

Bilateral and Regional Trade Agreements with East and South Asia

The PRC and Pakistan are on the brink of widening the Silk Road between them by signing an FTA. Pakistan is the only South Asian country to begin talks toward an FTA with the neighboring PRC. An FTA with the PRC could help reduce Pakistan's production costs. Local producers can take advantage of cheaper raw materials and machinery from the PRC, as well as the PRC's booming market for exports given its rapidly growing middle class. Currently, 70% of Pakistani exports to the PRC are cotton yarn and cotton fabric. Other exports include leather products, minerals, and seafood. The PRC's main shipments to Pakistan include machinery equipment, chemicals, electronics, and footwear. The early harvest program under the

Pakistan–PRC FTA is largely geared toward agricultural products, particularly rice, mangoes, potatoes, onions, dates, and apricots.

As a first step toward an FTA, an initial agreement with Malaysia has also been signed to remove tariffs on scores of heavily traded products such as fish, fabric, fruit, and machines. The two countries exchanged a list of 239 products that will fall under the agreement; most of these items will be traded with no tariffs. The duties on others will be reduced to 5%. There is likewise a provision for an early harvest program intended to provide impetus for an early conclusion to bilateral FTA negotiations (Appendix Table A3.3). Pakistan will extend the benefits on 125 Malaysian products, covering 5.49% of imports by value. The items include machinery, mechanical equipment, plastic products, chemical products, rubber, timber products, and live animals. Malaysia, in turn, will waive or reduce duties on 114 Pakistani items, which account for 10.97% of Malaysia's total imports from Pakistan by value. Items covered will include textile clothing, agricultural products, jewelry, and citrus and dried fruit. Malaysia's major exports to Pakistan are palm oil, margarine, and telecommunications equipment. Pakistan's main exports to Malaysia are fresh, chilled, and frozen fish; rice; textile yarn; and fabrics.

To boost the economic and trade relations with the countries of East Asia, Pakistan aims to secure the status of full-dialogue partnership with ASEAN and to conclude bilateral FTAs with its member countries. The status of full dialogue partnership would strengthen Pakistan's overall economic relationship with ASEAN, increase its exports, establish joint ventures, and attract more investment. As shown earlier, trade among ASEAN members has roughly doubled in the last decade.

Three rounds of negotiations have also been held on the Pakistan–Singapore FTA. Progress has been made on the key issues: trade in goods, rules of origin, trade in services, investment, government procurement, customs, and legal issues. Negotiations are also being undertaken with Thailand. The two countries in May 2005 decided to form a joint study group that will start technical talks on the FTA, which will likewise have an early harvest provision. Major Thai export products to Pakistan include chemicals, automobile parts and accessories, plastics, filaments, rubber, electric appliances, iron and steel, glass, and copper. The major imports include cotton, mineral fuel, oil wax, fish, organic chemical, oilseeds, fruits, leather, optical apparatus, and pharmaceutical products. The establishment of the Thai–Pakistan Chamber of Commerce (TPCC) in Bangkok in January 2005 is another milestone in the history of economic relations between the two countries. Investment cooperation between Pakistan and Thailand will focus on potential areas of mutual benefit, such as information technology (IT), telecommunications, construction, automobile parts, food processing, fisheries, agriculture, hotels, and real estate.

Pakistan is in trade talks with Indonesia, with which it already has a comprehensive economic partnership. The two countries signed the Framework Agreement on Comprehensive Economic Partnership (FACEP) in November 2005, with the agreement becoming a fully fledged FTA soon. As a fast-track strategy, a preferential trade agreement (PTA) would be negotiated in the near future by the relevant ministries. There remains considerable untapped potential to diversify trade and further increase investments, taking advantage of existing complementarities.

The total annual trade volume between Pakistan and the Republic of Korea was almost $1 billion in 2005. The Republic of Korea invested more than $21 million in Pakistan's industrial, construction and transport sectors, including joint ventures with Pakistani entrepreneurs. The Government is seeking more investment from the Republic of Korea in infrastructure development, IT, electrical goods, and home appliances.

Pakistan, aside from being a member of the SAFTA, which became effective in January 2006, has also intensified discussions with other trading partners toward bilateral FTAs. An FTA was signed with Sri Lanka in March 2005.

Given that South Asia is one of the least integrated and most highly protected regions of the world, with Pakistan still having considerable tariff peaks, regional and bilateral FTAs carry considerable risks of adverse trade diversion effects. The economic justification for FTAs with too many small countries is also questionable. It is therefore critical that Pakistan continues to reduce its trade barriers through unilateral policy reforms that will reduce the average level and dispersion of import tariffs. The strategy of continuing with unilateral trade liberalization will allow Pakistan to better manage its regional integration objectives by helping to minimize whatever adverse trade diversion effects FTAs might bring.

Like many other FTAs, SAARC also has a provision for a sensitive list, which covers those commodities not subject to tariff reduction measures. This list consists of 1,254 commodities for Bangladesh (24% of the tariff lines offered by Bangladesh); 157 for Bhutan (3% of total tariff lines); 884 for India (16.9% of total tariff lines); 671 for the Maldives (12.8% of total tariff lines); 1,310 for Nepal (25.5% of total tariff lines); 1,183 for Pakistan (22.6% of total tariff lines); and 1,065 for Sri Lanka (20.3% of total tariff lines) (Figure 3.3).

Infrastructure in Pakistan

Infrastructure plays a central role in achieving higher growth rates. There is strong evidence in the literature with reference to the higher returns of

Figure 3.3 Percentage Share of Sensitive List Items in Total Tariff Lines

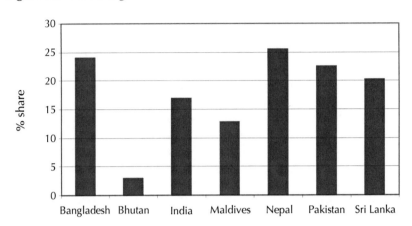

% = percent.

Source: www.saarc-sec.org

infrastructure to investment and therefore growth. Transport and communication, being important elements of infrastructure services, are essential to maintaining higher growth rates and competitiveness. Pakistan's transport and communication sector accounts for about 11% of GDP, 16% of fixed investment, 6% of employment, and about 15% of the Public Sector Development Program.

An Overview of Trade-Related Infrastructure

Road transport is a backbone of Pakistan's transport system, accounting for 90% of national passenger traffic and 96% of freight movement. The 9,518-kilometer (km) national highway and motorway network comprises 37% of the total road network and carries 90% of Pakistan's total traffic. Pakistan, with about 155 million people, has a reasonably developed transport system. However, Pakistan's road density is low when compared with other developed and developing countries (Table 3.14). Pakistan has a road network covering 257,683 km, including 165,762 km high-type roads and 92,578 km low-type roads. The total length of roads, which was 218,345 km in 1995/96, increased to 258,340 km in 2005/06. The total length of high-type roads nationwide increased by 40% since 1995/96.

The *Global Competitiveness Report 2006* ranked Pakistan 67th in terms of infrastructure quality, while Malaysia ranked 19th, Thailand ranked 30th, and Singapore ranked second (Table 3.15).

Pakistan railways, the most effective transport system in the country, plays a vital role in generating development opportunities. During the period 1995–2006, the railways' share of passenger traffic declined from 10.9% to 9.9% and the share of freight traffic declined from 6% to 3.9%.

Karachi Port is the premier port of Pakistan, and it handles more than 65% of the entire trade. It is a deep natural port with an 11-km-long approach channel providing safe navigation to 75,000 dead-weight-ton (DWT) tankers and modern container vessels. The port has 30 dry and 3 liquid product handling berths, including a dedicated container terminal at the east and west wharves. Karachi Port has also handled cargo volume of 28.6 million tons during 2004/05. Port Qasim is the second deep seaport of Pakistan. The private sector has actively been involved in all the economic activities at Port Qasim. Container, commercial, and

Table 3.14 Road Performance of Pakistan

Item	Units	2004
Road Network		
Length of total roads	km	257,683
Motorways	km	367
Highways	km	7,086
Secondary/regional	km	243,847
Road Access		
Access to all season road	% of rural development	76
Total number of vehicles	number	4,787,343
Goods transported annually by road	tons/km-yr	107 Bn
Passenger transported annually by road	passenger/km-yr	108 Bn
Road Finance		
Annual road expenditure	$ Mn	333.55
Annual maintenance expenditure	$ Mn	12.49
Annual road budget	$ Mn	489.80
Affordability		
Average pump price for super gasoline	$/liter	0.72
Average pump price for diesel fuel	$/liter	0.41
Annual license fees	$ per local currency	4.11
Road Safety and Environment		
Annual fatalities in road activities	fatalities per 10,000 vehicles	18.50

Bn = billion, km = kilometer, km-yr = kilometer-year, Mn = million, $ = US dollar, % = percent.

Source: The South Asia Energy and Infrastructure (SASEI) 2005.

Table 3.15 Ranking of Infrastructure Competitiveness, 2005–2006

Country	Overall infrastructure quality	Railway infrastructure development	Port infrastructure quality	Airport infrastructure quality
Pakistan	67	39	52	59
India	59	21	61	46
Sri Lanka	74	61	56	75
PRC	65	33	55	89
Malaysia	19	17	13	16
Thailand	30	40	37	31
Singapore	2	9	1	1

PRC = People's Republic of China.

Source: The *Global Competitiveness Report 2005–06.*

oil terminals are all privately operated. The Gwadar deepwater port is Pakistan's third-most important port, and is located at the corner of the Persian Gulf. A comprehensive master plan for the development of this port is now under way.

A modern terminal complex has been established at Lahore airport. A new Islamabad airport will be established at a total cost of Rs18 billion on 3,200 acres of land, while the new international airport at Gwadar will be constructed at a cost of Rs3650 million. Another international airport is under construction at Sialkot, the hub for the leather and surgical goods industries. As far as port efficiency indicators are concerned, Figure 3.4 shows South Asia to be lagging behind East Asia.

As for intraregional trade, the lack of cross-border transit points in South Asia presents significant trade obstacles. The lack of integrated transport networks in the region raises cargo shipping costs. For example, the per-container cost of imports from East Asia and Pacific countries is $1,037.1 and for South Asian countries $1,494.9 as against only $882.6 for countries in the Organisation for Economic Cooperation and Development (OECD) (Table 3.16). Table 3.17 shows the cost of trade for Pakistan.

Customs and Procedural Issues

It is not only the lack of integrated transport systems, port congestion, and other infrastructural bottlenecks that raise trading costs, but also the complicated customs clearance procedures and other nontransparent administrative procedures. The average time required for customs clear-

Figure 3.4 Port Efficiency Indicators (Maritime and Air)

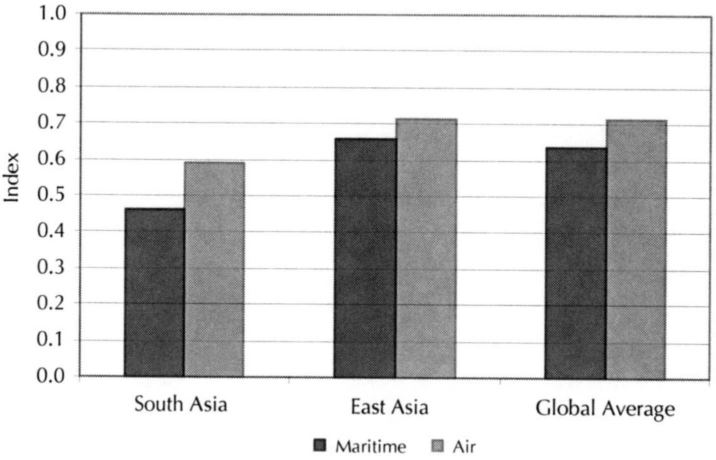

Source: Wilson, Mann, Otsuki (WMO) database 2004.

Table 3.16 Cost of Trade

Region/ Economy	Documents for export (number)	Time for export (days)	Cost to export ($/container)	Documents for import (number)	Time for import (days)	Cost to import ($/container)
East Asia and Pacific	6.9	23.9	884.8	9.3	25.9	1,037.1
South Asia	8.1	34.4	1,236.0	12.5	41.5	1,494.9
Middle East and North Africa	7.1	27.1	923.9	10.3	35.4	1,182.8
OECD	4.8	10.5	811.0	5.9	12.2	882.6

OECD = Organisation for Economic Cooperation and Development, $ = US dollar.

Source: Doing Business Indicators, World Bank.

ance by sea, for instance, is longer in both South Asia and East Asia than the average for developed countries (Figure 3.5). SAARC has approved a Customs Action Plan to collectively address these issues. To begin with, Pakistan has initiated a Customs Valuation Information System (CVIS), through which the importers can access exchange data on their consignments.

Table 3.17 Cost of Trade for Pakistan, 2006

Item	Duration (days)	Cost ($)
Nature of Export Procedures		
Documents preparation	7	42
Inland transportation and handling	12	670
Customs clearance and technical control	2	201
Ports and terminal handling	3	83
Total	**24**	**996**
Nature of Import Procedures		
Documents preparation	11	50
Inland transportation and handling	2	201
Customs clearance and technical control	4	84
Ports and terminal handling	2	670
Total	**19**	**1,005**

$ = US dollar.

Source: Doing Business, World Bank.

Figure 3.5 Average Days Required for Customs Clearance by Sea

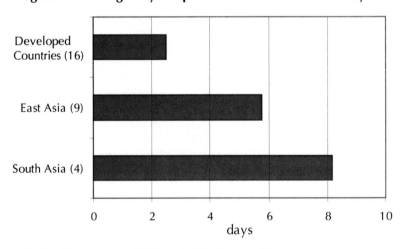

Notes: Calculated from International Exhibition Logistics Associates data.
Developed countries include Australia, Belgium, Denmark, Germany, Finland, France, Great Britain, Italy, Netherlands, Norway, Portugal, Sweden, United States, Canada, and Japan.
East Asia includes People's Republic of China; Hong Kong, China; Indonesia; Malaysia; Philippines; Singapore; Taipei,China; Thailand; and Viet Nam.
South Asia includes Bangladesh, India, Pakistan, and Sri Lanka.

Source: World Bank (2004).

Trade and Foreign Investment in Services

The efficient provision of services is basic to the efficiency of manufacturing, as services account for 10–20% of production costs in addition to trading costs such as communications, transport, trade finance, insurance, and distribution (Hodge and Nordas 1999). International trade in services is estimated to be worth more than $1 trillion a year, accounting for more than 20% of all international trade. For Pakistan's economy, services have played a pivotal role, growing at 8.8% in 2005/06 as compared to 8.0% in 2004/05. This growth is due to considerable development in the finance and insurance sector, better performance in wholesale and retail trade, and fast growth in the transport and communications sector.

Finance and insurance sector growth in the services sector dropped to 23.0% during 2006 as compared to 30% in 2005. The value added in the wholesale and retail trade sector dropped to 10% compared to 11% the previous year. The transport, storage, and communications sector grew by 7% compared to 3.5% in 2004/05.

Trade in services grew worldwide during 2003/04. Table 3.18 shows the relative importance of trade in services in terms of absolute values and of its percentage shares of total GDP for East and South Asia.

Table 3.18 Trade in Services, 2003/04

Country/Region	Services Exports (BOP, $ Mn)		Services Imports (BOP, $ Mn)		Trade in Services (% of GDP)	
	2003	2004	2003	2004	2003	2004
East Asia						
China, People's Republic of	4,673	6,243	5,530	7,213	6	7
Hong Kong, China	4,655	5,516	2,612	314	46	52
Korea, Republic of	3,295	4,142	4,038	5,017	12	13
Singapore	3,457	4,118	3,317	4,069	73	71
Indonesia	529	1,762	1,740	2,850	10	18
Malaysia	1,357	1,676	1,753	1,907	30	30
Philippines	3,299	4,100	5,024	5,383	10	11
Thailand	1,904	2,062	2,307	2,760	24	26
South Asia						
Bangladesh	101	108	171	193	5	5
India	2,339	–	2,570	–	8	–
Pakistan	2,96	274	329	533	8	8
Sri Lanka	141	152	167	190	17	17
World	**189,644**	**225,546**	**183,915**	**220,129**	**10**	**11**

BOP = balance of payments, GDP = gross domestic product, $ Mn = millions of US dollars, – = no data available, % = percent.

Source: World Development Indicators.

In East Asia, Hong Kong, China and Indonesia showed the biggest percentage increases. Singapore's trade in services as compared to GDP declined, while that of the Republic of Korea, Malaysia, and Philippines remained more or less the same. Services exports showed mixed growth. Pakistan's services exports decreased, while Sri Lanka's and Bangladesh's exhibited a slight improvement.

Workers' remittances, the second largest source of foreign exchange inflows after exports, continued to rise. Workers' remittances totaled $4.15 billion during 2004/05 as against $3.82 billion in the previous year, an increase of 8.52%. The US continues to be the single largest source of workers' remittances, accounting for 31.17%, followed by the United Arab Emirates with 17.16% of total remittances for 2004/05 (Table 3.19).

Most of the sectors in services have been fully opened to FDI, with full foreign ownership permitted under Pakistan's 1997 investment policy. There is great potential for growth as a result, especially for mobile telecommunications, which have witnessed strong growth in recent years. The withdrawal of the exclusive rights of the Pakistan Telecommunication Company Limited (PTCL) by the end of 2003 also creates greater market space for private and foreign industry players. Pakistan needs to develop a highly available telecommunications infrastructure. Some 36 digital transit exchanges have been connected through an optical fiber system that

Table 3.19 Remittances, 1999–2005, $ Million

Country	1999/00	2000/01	2001/02	2002/03	2003/04	2004/05
Bahrain	29.36	23.87	39.58	71.46	80.55	91.22
Canada	3.86	4.90	20.52	15.19	22.90	48.49
Germany	10.47	9.20	13.44	26.87	46.52	53.84
Japan	1.58	3.93	5.97	8.14	5.28	6.51
Kuwait	135.25	123.39	89.66	221.23	177.01	214.78
Norway	5.60	5.74	6.55	8.89	10.19	18.30
Qatar	13.29	13.38	31.87	87.68	88.69	86.86
Saudi Arabia	309.85	304.43	376.34	580.76	565.29	627.19
Sultanate of Oman	46.42	38.11	63.18	93.65	105.29	119.28
United Arab Emirates	147.79	190.04	469.49	837.87	597.48	712.61
United Kingdom	73.27	81.39	151.93	273.83	333.94	371.86
United States	79.96	134.81	778.98	1,237.52	1,225.09	1,294.08
Other countries	56.79	88.40	293.28	727.64	567.93	507.27
Total	913.49	1,021.59	2,340.79	4,190.73	3,826.16	4,152.29

$ = US dollar.

Source: State Bank of Pakistan.

links about 2,000 cities. The capacity of these digital transit exchanges has increased from 73,126 to 311,400 ports to handle the additional load.

Despite a liberal overall policy toward FDI, there remain some general limitations applied to market access and national treatment, particularly pertaining to the commercial presence or the presence of natural persons. Moreover, foreign commercial presence in certain sectors (e.g., insurance and banking) is subject to equity limitations and other conditionalities.

For worldwide communications, new category exchanges were installed in Islamabad and Karachi. In 1993, there were only 2,529 international telephone circuits, although that number had risen to 14,500 circuits as of June 2003. Pakistan also linked to Southeast Asia–Middle East–Western Europe 3, a submarine fiber-optic cable that links more than 39 countries from Western Europe to the Far East.

Financial Sector

Before 1990, the government and national institutions dominated Pakistan's financial sector. During the 1990s, the financial sector was liberalized through the sale of more than 50% of the shares in government-owned banks, and through allowing the operation of domestic private banks. The total of private domestic banks operating in the country increased from 10 in 1991 to about 23 at present. Foreign banks were operating in the country before 1990, and now there are about 14 foreign banks in Pakistan.

Exchange and payment reforms were initiated also in 1991 to provide an enabling environment for international trade, foreign exchange mobilization, and foreign investment. The upper limits for remittances for various activities abroad were relaxed, some restrictions were removed, and money changers were allowed to buy and sell foreign currency. Limits on the handling and use of foreign exchange were relaxed for exporters and importers.

In recent years, Pakistan has also witnessed a surge in private capital inflows especially in the form of remittances from abroad. This has resulted in a significant accumulation of reserves. Remittance inflows have now reached close to $4.1 billion. Portfolio investment in Pakistan has likewise been rising. To deepen the capital market, 10-year Pakistan Investment Bonds as the benchmark for corporate bond issues, commercial paper, and debt instruments of different tenures have been made available. An independent securities and exchange commission was incorporated in 1997. To make the financial matters and procedures compatible with international best practices, the State Bank of Pakistan and the Securities and Exchange Commission of Pakistan (SECP) have adequately developed their management structure, technical expertise, technology, and enforcement capacity. New and separate prudential regulations are being introduced with respect to corporations, consumers, and small and medium-sized enterprises (SMEs).

The financial services sector is where most of the liberalization has already taken place. There has been improved international cooperation on agreed standards, including methods of supervision. Nationality-based restrictions on market access have been eliminated, and full national treatment for foreign-based financial service providers have been granted. According to the State Bank of Pakistan, financial assets grew by 70% over the past 5 years and reached PRs5.1 trillion, equivalent to 80% of GDP. The banking sector grew faster than nonbank sectors, currently accounting for 71% of financial industry assets. Market capitalization of the stock exchange has also grown steadily, recently peaking at 44% of GDP relative to 10.3% in June 2000.

Pakistan is focusing on the next phase of financial sector reforms, which would involve (i) further consolidation and restructuring of the banking sector; (ii) strengthening of risk management; and (iii) diversification of the financial sector through further development of the equity and debt markets which, while fairly vibrant, need to play a more significant role in meeting the country's financing requirements.

Regulatory Regime

Various government agencies oversee commercial and financial regulatory regimes, including the SECP, the Central Board of Revenue (CBR), the Board of Investment (BOI), and the State Bank of Pakistan. Equity markets are regulated by the 1969 Securities and Exchange Ordinance and by the 1971 Securities and Exchange Rules. A Takeover Ordinance was recently enacted and 12 takeovers took place under this law during fiscal year (FY) 2004.

Competition law in Pakistan falls under the jurisdiction of the Monopoly Control Authority, an independent regulatory authority that lacks enforcement capacity. The broad-based market liberalizations have reduced market entry barriers, but concentration in numerous industrial sectors remains relatively high. Two private airlines compete with state-owned Pakistan International Airlines (PIA) and the Government permits them to fly choice trunk routes and to undercut PIA on fares. In retail food sales, the Government has used pricing at its several-hundred-unit Utility Stores Corporation chain to influence prices of essential foodstuffs. Market leaders in the cement and sugar industries are alleged to have formed cartels.

The Government has introduced lead-free petrol to control air pollution, and Pakistan is now among the world's largest users of compressed natural gas vehicles. The Securities and Exchange Ordinance regulates the capital markets. Pakistan regulates business activity through laws that cover competition, intellectual property, insurance, banking, financial markets, and investment protection. International investors have expressed concern about the ineffective implementation and enforcement of these laws.

Pakistan and the General Agreement on Trade in Services

Pakistan has been able to ratify several of its commitments under the General Agreement on Trade in Services (GATS), particularly those covered by the extended negotiations on financial and basic telecommunication (Fourth Protocol) services (WTO 2001). It has also approved the Schedule of Specific Commitments in 47 activities within the financial (banking and insurance), business, communications, construction, engineering, health, tourism, and travel services. Pakistan still maintains MFN exemptions under GATS Article II for financial services to respect reciprocity requirements, Islamic financing transactions, and joint ventures among Economic Cooperation Organization (ECO) countries. These exemptions also apply for telecommunications services to preserve preferential treatment for operators in countries that have signed bilateral agreements on accounting rates with the Pakistan Telecommunication Company Limited.

Pakistan has regularly voiced its concerns regarding the lack of significant market-access gains accorded to developing countries and the poor implementation of Article IV of the GATS, which provides for increasing participation of developing countries. Given the comparative advantage of many developing countries such as Pakistan in labor-intensive services, Pakistan saw fit to propose means to further enhance the commitments made on the movement of natural persons (Mode 4).

Conclusions and Policy Implications

Pakistan is increasingly seeking to strengthen its trade and economic relations, particularly with the countries of South and East Asia. It is a signatory to the South Asian Free Trade Area, which came into force in July 2006, and it has also developed a policy to strengthen ties with East Asia as set out in the Strategic Vision East Asia initiative in 2003. Against this backdrop, this study has provided an analysis of Pakistan's trade and investment links with East and South Asian countries. The textiles and clothing sector, for instance, presents considerable opportunities for growth in Pakistan's intraregional trade relations. Textiles and clothing represent a share of about 25% in value added and 38% of the workforce in the manufacturing sector, and constitutes about 70% of total exports. However, the textiles sector in Pakistan economy is largely cotton-based, and with an increasing trend toward synthetic and blended fabrics there is a need to shift current spindle utilization toward synthetic fibers.

The removal of textile and clothing quotas under the Multi-Fiber Agreement since 2005 seems to have benefited Pakistan. Exports of textiles that had increased at a rate of only 1.2% in the first half of 2004/05 registered an 11.4% increase in the second half of the year, a time during which MFA quota restrictions were removed. As a matter of fact during the last 2 months of FY2004/05, exports registered growth above 20%. However, it needs to be noted that some textiles products might have been adversely affected instead. Cotton yarn attracted considerable investments over the last few years but witnessed a decline in the exports. Art silk and synthetic textiles exports also fell because the industry suffered from high duties on inputs. However, with the changes in the duty drawback systems in the 2005/06 budget, it is likely that exports of synthetic textiles will increase.

In Pakistan, the five products having potential for export growth are blue jeans, shrimp, marble tiles, powdered milk, and auto radiators. The first two are major export items, and the last three are new and/or potential exports. As proxies for similar products and activities, the five items cover a spectrum of the key economic activities that offer potential for export diversification and economic growth, including textile and apparel, fisheries, mining, agribusiness, and light engineering.

With a view to promoting foreign investment in the export sector, Pakistan has established EPZs in Karachi and Lahore. These zones offer better infrastructure facilities as well as various other incentives, including tax holidays and unrestricted repatriation of capital and profits.

The investment cooperation between Pakistan and countries of South and East Asia should focus on potential areas of mutual benefit such as IT, telecommunications, construction, automobile parts, food processing, fisheries, agriculture, hotels, and real estate. It must be noted, however, that the cost of doing business is an important determinant of foreign investment. In the case of Pakistan, the cost of doing business is significantly above the Asian and global averages. Pakistan shows a similarly weak standing with respect to the cost of contract enforcement. The World Bank's recently completed Investment Climate Assessment reveals that red tape in general is such a burden on efficiency that Pakistani managers spend 10% of their time dealing with Government regulations—more than twice as much as in Sri Lanka or Turkey. Ranked against 156 other countries in 2004 in the quality of regulation, for instance, Pakistan lost some ground from its 1998 standing. Moreover, corruption is perceived to be on the rise.

The remaining deficiencies in Pakistan's investment environment and the resulting gaps in its international competitiveness cited earlier are also reflected in the international competitiveness rankings reported annually by the World Economic Forum's (WEF) *Global Competitiveness Report*. According to the report, Pakistan's 2005 standing in growth competitiveness (as measured by the quality of the macroeconomic environment, public institutions, and technology) is very low, ranking 83 out of 117 countries, surpassing only Bangladesh and Sri Lanka in South Asia. With respect to business competitiveness (based on the quality of the microeconomic dimensions of the business environment, as well as company operations and strategy), Pakistan ranks 66 out of 116 countries.

Pakistan's export policy plays an important role in determining the pattern of trade. The export policy is focused on encouraging export-led growth through the development of an efficient, competitive, and diversified export sector. To this end, the Government provides a variety of incentives including income and sales tax concessions, exemption from customs duty on imported intermediate inputs and capital goods, and easy access to credit facilities. Exporters are allowed rebates on customs duty, sales tax, and surcharges through the duty drawback facility. The duty drawback rates are standardized as a percentage of the free-on-board value of exports or a specific amount per unit of goods exported. Recently, duty drawback rates of some 300 items have been enhanced. In addition, all direct and indirect exporters are allowed to import inputs through bonded warehousing facilities and other temporary import schemes without payment of customs duty and sales tax, or the withholding of income tax.

The Government has significantly liberalized the trade regime through tariff cuts and rationalization, as well as by removing import quotas, import surcharges, and regulatory duties. State enterprises that used to have control over imports and exports of certain products have mostly been eliminated. The unweighted (i.e., simple) average statutory tariff has fallen from 47.1% in 1997/98 to 14.4% in 2005/06 (World Bank 2006).

Tariff dispersion has increased, rising from about 45% of the simple average tariff in 1997/98 to over 76% following the 2005/06 changes. Despite the recent cuts in tariffs on cars, their duty rates are still two to three times higher than the normal maximum customs duty rate, and the rates on motorbikes are almost four times higher at 90%. Imports of final consumer goods are subject to the normal maximum tariff rate of 25%. Other trade barriers that adversely affect resource allocation include the domestic content requirements in the highly protected automobile industry and the withholding income taxes that are higher when applied on imports than on domestic sales. Finally, with the FY2006 budget, five new tariff slabs have been introduced (3%, 6.5%, 7%, 14%, and 15%), applying mostly to inputs for the textile and apparel sector.

Poor quality, high priced services not only affect the current operations of manufacturers but also discourage future investment by locals and foreigners. This may be one major factor constraining the flow of FDIs to developing countries, despite these countries' supply of cheap labor. The liberalization programs for sectors such as financial services, telecommunications, transport, and professional services would go a long way toward improving the commodity-producing sectors. However, this program must be accompanied by measures to strengthen the domestic services sector. These may include human resource development and technological capacity-building to ensure that professional and quality standards are met. More specifically, the following initiatives may be considered.

- Upgrade of all the telecommunications infrastructure.
- A coherent pro-competitive regulatory framework for goods and services.
- Government support to help service firms, particularly SMEs to improve the quality of the services they provide.
- A presence in major markets.
- The capacity to exploit the opportunities offered by regional markets.

IT-related services such as back-office processing and call centers have opened new vistas where services can be provided at a distance. Obviously, the success of IT exports depends on improvements in communications and transport services.

Improvements in the customs as well as tax and other administrations must complement tariff-reduction policies. This process should be designed and implemented in close consultation with the stakeholders: businesses, farmers, investors, traders, and others.

Trade facilitation involves a wide range of initiatives, such as reforms in the regulation and harmonization of standards, improvements to efficiency in customs, and improvements in regional transport infrastructure. Countries need to adopt a coherent strategy to harmonize their policies, focusing in particular on transport and transit systems and customs procedures. Domestic regulatory procedures and institutional structures based on international best practices can improve transparency and introduce professionalism in border clearance procedures. Streamlining regulations on technical barriers and liberalizing transport and telecommunications regimes can also facilitate trade. Collective action to raise capacity in trade facilitation through upgrading ports and introducing IT for processing trade documents would lower transaction costs and expand trade across the region.

Reducing tariffs alone are not sufficient to promote economic ties with other countries in the region. Improving customs, tax, and other administrations must complement tariff reduction policies. What is needed is a regulatory environment that facilitates trade through reducing the transaction costs associated with the movement of goods and services across borders. There should be a shift from the manual system of operations to a fully automated and information-based system.

The improvement of transport logistics will have an important role in enhancing Pakistan's export competitiveness. Transport logistics need wider roads and safer, less-polluting trucks. Upgrades could take place through reductions in duties on imported trucks and parts. Pakistan's trunk road will also need upgrading by widening the Karachi–Lahore highway, exclusive port-access roads, and truck terminals on the peripheries of major cities. Rail transport, especially for containers moving between Karachi and Lahore, should be encouraged to reduce the burden on highways. Efficient terminal operations should be in place. Excessive overhead costs need to be reduced for movement of containers in bond to inland container depots. There is a need to enhance the efficiency of the port-community information system.

In summary, there is considerable potential to strengthen trade and investment links among South and East Asian countries. Regional trading arrangements among these countries will help individual economies to grow faster through greater international trade, investment, and domestic competition. A regional trade agreement (RTA) may also act as a stepping stone to multilateral trade liberalization by providing an opportunity to experiment with trade liberalization on a limited scale.

While Pakistan's economy has opened, as evidenced by lower average tariff rates, sectors such as engineering goods remain protected by policy. Other sectors such as construction, retail, entertainment, and leisure remain underdeveloped because of policy neglect and regulatory failures. Several sectors in the economy, such as cement, sugar, and flour are not competitive because the incumbents use the regulatory and pricing regimes to their advantage. The major constraint to new investment and trade in Pakistan may therefore be uncompetitive market structures (Haque 2006).

References

Asian Development Bank (ADB). Various issues. *Asian Development Outlook*. Manila: ADB.

Baysan T., A. Panagariya, and N. Pigala. 2006. Preferential Trading in South Asia. *World Bank Policy Research Working Paper* 3813. Washington, DC: World Bank.

Bergman L., C. Doyle, J. Gual, L. Hultkrantz, D. Neven, L. Roller, and L. Waverman. 1998. *Europe's Network Industries: Conflicting Priorities-Telecommunications*. London: Centre for Economic Policy Research (CEPR).

Board of Investment, Government of Pakistan. *Investment Indicators*. Islamabad.

Grossman, G. M., and E. Helpman. 1991. *Innovation and Growth in the World Economy*. Cambridge, MA: MIT Press.

Hertel, T., and W. Martin. 2000. Liberalizing Agriculture and Manufactures in a Millennium Round: Implications for Developing Countries. *The World Economy* 23(4): 455–469.

Haque, N. U. 2006. Beyond Planning and Mercantilism: An Evaluation of Pakistan's Growth Strategy. *The Pakistan Development Review* 45(1): 3-48.

Hodge, J. 2000. Liberalizing Communications Services in South Africa. *Development Southern Africa* 17 (3): 373–87, September.

Hodge, J., and H. Nordas. 1999. *Trade in Services: The Impact on Developing Countries*. Report to Norwegian Foreign Ministry.

Hoekman, B. 2002. The WTO: Functions and Basic Principles. *Development, Trade, and the WTO, A Handbook, Part I-IV*. Washington, DC: World Bank.

International Monetary Fund (IMF). Various issues. *Direction of Trade Statistics*. Washington, DC: IMF.

———. Various issues. *International Financial Statistics*. Washington, DC: IMF.

Krueger, A. O. 1999. *The Developing Countries and the Next Round of Multilateral Trade Negotiations*. Available: www.worldbank.org/wbiep/trade/seattle.html

Krugman, P. 1996. *Rethinking International Trade*. Cambridge, MA: MIT Press.

Pakistan Institute of Development Economics (PIDE). 2005. *Tariff Rationalization*. Islamabad: PIDE.

Pakistan, Government of. 2001–02. *Pakistan Labor Gazette*. Ministry of Labor, Manpower and Overseas Pakistanis.

———. Various issues. *Economic Survey*. Finance Division.

———. 2004–05. *Household Income and Expenditure Survey*.

State Bank of Pakistan. Various issues. *Foreign Assets and Liabilities*. Karachi: State Bank of Pakistan.

———. Various issues. *Annual Report*. Karachi: State Bank of Pakistan.

United Nations Conference on Trade and Development (UNCTAD). 2000. Positive Agenda and Future Trade Negotiations. New York.

Viner, J. 1950. *The Customs Union Issue*. New York: Carnegie Endowment for International Peace.

World Bank. 2004. South Asia Regional Integration. *Trade Facilitation and Regional Integration: Accelerating the Gains to Trade with Capacity Building*. Washington, DC.

———. 2005. *The South Asia Energy and Infrastructure (SASEI)*. Washington, DC.

———. Various issues. *Trade Across the Border*. Washington, DC.

———. Various issues. *World Development Indicators*. Washington, DC.

World Economic Forum. 2005. *Global Competitiveness Report*. Geneva.

Word Trade Organization (WTO). 2001. *Trade Policy Review of Pakistan*. Geneva: WTO.

Yepes, T. 2003. *Expenditure on Infrastructure in East Asia Region, 2006–2010*. ADB-Japan Bank for International Cooperation-World Bank Study. Washington, DC: World Bank.

Appendix Tables

Table A3.1a Pakistan's Trade Data, $ Mn

Item	1990	1995	2000	2007
Exports (World Total)	5,587	7,991	8,870	19,353
Imports (World Total)	7,383	11,461	10,721	39,205

$ Mn = millions of US dollars.

Source: International Monetary Fund. *Direction of Trade Statistics* (December 2008).

Table A3.1b Pakistan's Trade with East Asia

Item	1990	1995	2000	2007
Exports ($ Mn)				
Japan	457	542	234	227
China, People's Republic of	67	119	237	1,005
Hong Kong, China	278	602	533	576
Indonesia	50	105	109	43
Korea, Republic of	166	271	260	446
Malaysia	29	46	53	76
Philippines	35	30	38	39
Singapore	121	88	54	49
Thailand	54	60	61	62
Taipei,China	0	0	0	170
Total	**1,257**	**1,863**	**1,579**	**2,693**
Exports (%)				
Japan	8.18	6.78	2.64	1.2
China, People's Republic of	1.2	1.49	2.67	5.2
Hong Kong, China	4.98	7.53	6.01	3.0
Indonesia	0.89	1.31	1.23	0.2
Korea, Republic of	2.97	3.39	2.93	2.3
Malaysia	0.52	0.58	0.6	0.4
Philippines	0.63	0.38	0.43	0.2
Singapore	2.17	1.1	0.61	0.3
Thailand	0.97	0.75	0.69	0.3
Taipei,China	0	0	0	0.9
Total	**22.5**	**23.31**	**17.8**	**13.9**

continued on next page

Table A3.1b (continued)

Item	1990	1995	2000	2007
Imports ($ Mn)				
Japan	877	1,229	607	1,716
China, People's Republic of	338	506	538	6,363
Hong Kong, China	30	49	60	188
Indonesia	47	117	168	1,029
Korea, Republic of	204	343	356	746
Malaysia	245	969	439	1,383
Philippines	1	4	6	43
Singapore	230	221	300	931
Thailand	92	108	198	728
Taipei,China	4	0	0	411
Total	**2,068**	**3,546**	**2,672**	**13,538**
Imports (%)				
Japan	11.88	10.72	5.66	4.4
China, People's Republic of	4.58	4.41	5.02	16.2
Hong Kong, China	0.41	0.43	0.56	0.5
Indonesia	0.64	1.02	1.57	2.6
Korea, Republic of	2.76	2.99	3.32	1.9
Malaysia	3.32	8.45	4.09	3.5
Philippines	0.01	0.03	0.06	0.1
Singapore	3.12	1.93	2.8	2.4
Thailand	1.25	0.94	1.85	1.9
Taipei,China	0.05	0	0	1.0
Total	**28.01**	**30.94**	**24.92**	**34.5**

$ Mn = millions of US dollars, % = percent.

Source: International Monetary Fund. *Direction of Trade Statistics* (December 2008).

Table A3.1c Pakistan's Trade with South Asia

Item	1990	1995	2000	2007
Exports ($ Mn)				
Bangladesh	103	153	139	179
India	49	39	58	518
Maldives	1	1	1	5
Nepal	1	3	3	3
Sri Lanka	69	55	81	162
Total SAARC	**223**	**251**	**282**	**867**
Exports (%)				
Bangladesh	1.84	1.91	1.57	0.9
India	0.88	0.49	0.65	2.7
Maldives	0.02	0.01	0.01	0.03
Nepal	0.02	0.04	0.03	0.02
Sri Lanka	1.24	0.69	0.91	0.8
Total SAARC	**3.99**	**3.14**	**3.18**	**4.5**
Imports ($ Mn)				
Bangladesh	38	35	36	88
India	46	81	178	886
Maldives	0	0	0	5
Nepal	0	1	3	4
Sri Lanka	37	50	35	61
Total SAARC	**121**	**167**	**252**	**1,044**
Imports (%)				
Bangladesh	0.51	0.31	0.34	0.2
India	0.62	0.71	1.66	2.3
Maldives	0	0	0	0
Nepal	0	0.01	0.03	0.01
Sri Lanka	0.5	0.44	0.33	0.01
Total SAARC	**1.64**	**1.46**	**2.35**	**2.7**

SAARC = South Asian Association for Regional Cooperation, $ Mn = millions of US dollars, % = percent.

Source: International Monetary Fund. *Direction of Trade Statistics* (December 2008).

Table A3.2 Early Harvest Programs of Pakistan and the People's Republic of China (1 January 2006)

			Stage-wise tariff lines		
Pakistan's offer list of zero tariffs	PRC's offer list of zero tariffs	Common list of zero tariffs	Products with MFN rates higher than 15%	Products with MFN rates between 5% and 15%	Products with MFN rates lower than 5%
A total of 386 tariff lines at 8-digit level	A total of 644 tariff lines at 8-digit level	A total of 100 tariff lines at 8-digit level	10% by 1 January 2006, 5% by 1 January 2007, and 0% by 1 January 2008	5% by 1 January 2006, 0% by 1 January 2007	0% by 1 January 2006

MFN = most favored nation, PRC = People's Republic of China, % = percent.

Source:

Table A3.3 Early Harvest Program between Pakistan and Malaysia (1 October 2005)

List of products and tariff preferences granted by Malaysia	List of products and tariff preferences granted by Pakistan	Exemption from customs duty on imports from Malaysia notified by CBR Pakistan
There are 114 tariff lines on the list (which include textiles and clothing, agricultural products, and jewelry.	There are 125 tariff lines in the list (which include machinery, chemical products, mechanical equipment and appliances, plastic products, rubber products, and timber products).	There are a total of 125 products, out of which 49 products are exempted from customs duty and 76 of which face 5% customs duty.

CBR = Central Board of Revenue (Pakistan), FTA = free trade agreement.

Source: Official text of FTA.

Table A3.4 South Asian Free Trade Area (1 January 2006)

Sensitive lists (negative list)	Schedule for tariff reduction	Mechanism for compensation of revenue loss for less-developed countries	Rules of origin	Technical assistance for less-developed member countries
No reduction of tariff on those tariff lines included on the sensitive list. Bangladesh has 1,254 tariff lines (24% of total lines); Bhutan 157 (3%); India 884 (16.9%); Maldives 671 (12.8%); Nepal 1,310 (25.5%); Pakistan 1,183 (22.6%); and Sri Lanka 1,065 (20.3%).	India, Pakistan, and Sri Lanka will bring down their customs tariffs to 20% by 1 January 2008. Less-developed member states (Bangladesh, Bhutan, Maldives, and Nepal) would reduce their customs tariff to 30%.	To be enforced 1 year after implementation of tariff reduction and remain operative for 4 years. Compensation only on revenue loss on import of products where tariff reduction is made by less-developed member countries. The extent of compensation will be as follows: 1st and 2nd year - Not more than 1% of customs duty collected. 3rd year -Not more than 5% of customs duty collected. 4th year -Not more than 3% of customs duty collected.	Rules of origin under the South Asian Free Trade Area (SAFTA) required qualifying products for preferential duty benefits. Criteria are as follows: For developed member countries: 40% value addition plus change in tariff heading at 4 digits. For less-developed member countries: 30% value addition plus change in tariff heading at 4 digits.	Advisory services. Capacity building in metallurgy, standards testing. Training of trade officers. Training in sanitary and phytosanitary measures, technical barriers to trade, and exports of agricultural-based products.

FTA = free trade agreement, % = percent.

Source: Official text of FTA.

Table A3.5 Free Trade Agreement between Pakistan and Sri Lanka (1 June 2005)

Pakistan's offer and reservations				Sri Lanka's offer and reservations		
Negative list	Immediate tariff concession	Tariff-rate quota	Common margin of preference	Negative list	Immediate tariff concession	Tariff-rate quota
540 HS tariff lines at the 6-digit level. Products on the negative list will not enjoy tariff concessions.	206 HS tariff lines at the 6-digit level. Sri Lanka will receive 100% duty-free access for these products in the Pakistan market, effective immediately.	Tariff-rate quotas (TRQ) are specific quantities of products on which the importing country would agree to grant duty-free access or preferential duties, when imported from the other contracting party to the agreement. The products imported in excess of the agreed TRQ will be subject to normal tariffs.	The products listed in Attachment IV are entitled to receive a preferential duty margin of 20% on the applied MFN duty rate with no quantitative restrictions.	697 HS tariff lines at the 6-digit level that will not enjoy any tariff concessions.	Sri Lanka has listed a total of 102 HS tariff lines at the 6-digit level, on which Sri Lanka will receive 100% duty-free access.	Sri Lanka has granted Pakistan tariff-rate quotas on 6,000 tons of basmati rice and 1,000 tons of potatoes per calendar year (January–December) on a duty-free basis. However, import of potatoes is permitted only during Sri Lanka 's off season (two thirds to be imported during June–July and one third during October–November each year).

HS = harmonized code, MFN = most favored nation, % = percent.

Source:

Table A3.6 Trade Facilitation

Measures	Undertaken	Units
Single administrative documents (SAD)	No	Yes or No
Harmonized code (HS)	Yes	Yes or No
EDP systems	ACP	Name of System, e.g., ASYCUDA
Electronic data interchange	20% to 40%	% of ship's inward manifests submitted electronically by shipping line to customs
Direct trader input	20% to 30%	% of import declarations that are inputted by customs agent or consignee directly through designated terminals
Internet input	NA	% of import shipments for which declarations are inputted through internet
Green channel	90%	% of shipments that are cleared with submission of documents but without inspection
Risk management	Yes	% of shipments for which a computer system uses profiling to determine if goods should be inspected
Electronic banking	15%	% of duty and taxes can be paid through electronic transfer from consignee's bank
Electronic signature	Yes	Customs officials can approve declaration using electronic signature rather than physical signature
Private-bonded warehouses	Yes	Import cargo can be moved directly to private warehouses and stored under customs bond for subsequent clearance
Bonded factories	No	Manufacturers (not located in a free trade zone) can receive imported inputs without clearing customs, store them, process them, and export them without paying taxes

ACP = automated clearance procedure, ASYCUDA = Automated System for Customs Data, EDP = electronic data processing, NA = not applicable, % = percent.

Notes:
(i) To complete this, it will be necessary to speak with a customs official familiar with national customs operations or possibly through the association of customs brokers.
(ii) The percentages are estimates (best guess) and at minimum indicate few, some or most.
(iii) The term shipment refers to a consignment of goods for which there is a single declaration, i.e., % of shipments can be stated as % of declarations.

Bangladesh

Mohammed Ali Rashid

Introduction

Bangladesh became an independent nation on 16 December 1971. Since then, the country has made impressive progress in some areas of economic development. Per capita income has more than tripled, human development has experienced remarkable progress, and the incidence of income and/or consumption poverty has nearly halved. But major challenges remain. Per capita income, which stands at $441, is low even by South Asian standards. Poverty is still rather high even though it has been declining. A number of human development indicators are still low even by standards of low-income economies. The development challenges for Bangladesh are quite daunting but by no means insurmountable.

Bangladesh must achieve faster pro-poor economic growth through more trade and investment growth, among other things, to hasten the process of poverty alleviation. While trade and investment flows can be expected to grow under the multilateral framework of the World Trade Organization (WTO), the experiences of many countries and subregions in different parts of the world indicate that significant benefit in this regard can be reaped through regional integration. East Asia and South Asia have been two of the fastest growing subregions in the world in recent times, with annual average growth rates of 6.9% and 5.8%, respectively, over the past decade. While Bangladesh has economic cooperation arrangements with the countries of South Asia, enhancing its economic cooperation with the East Asian countries would greatly benefit the country in terms of increased volumes of trade and foreign investment.

The objective of this study is to analyze existing trade and investment links between Bangladesh and the countries of South Asia and East Asia with the aim of devising policies for further strengthening and expanding these linkages, particularly with East Asian countries in view of their higher stage of development and hence larger potential benefits from economic integration. Of particular importance in this regard is the identification of constraints to greater economic cooperation, policy-induced and otherwise, and ways of overcoming these obstacles. Hence, this paper will examine the policy regimes in Bangladesh pertaining to merchandise trade, services trade, foreign direct investment (FDI), and trade-related infrastructure. Particular attention will be paid to trade facilitation issues and infrastructure since empirical research has shown that these constitute more serious impediments to expansion of trade and investment among countries than do border measures. The paper ends by making some policy recommendations to promote economic cooperation between Bangladesh and the countries of South Asia and East Asia, particularly the latter.

Economic Structure and External Orientation

External Orientation

Bangladesh adopted an export-led growth strategy in the early 1980s and implemented various policy reforms to make its economy more outward oriented. As a result, both exports and imports increased rapidly. Compared with an average annual growth of 8% in export value in the 1980s, export value increased by 11% in the 1990s. On the other hand, average annual growth of import value rose from 3.6% in the 1980s to 11% in the 1990s. As a result, the export-gross domestic product (GDP) ratio increased from 6.4% in 1991/92 to 14.4% in 2004/05. The import/GDP ratio also increased from 11.3% to 21.9% during this period. However, there has been a chronic deficit in the trade balance, although the trade deficit/GDP ratio appears to show a declining trend. The current account deficit has been much smaller than the trade deficit because of a healthy inflow of workers' remittances; in fact, the current account deficit/GDP ratio has improved from -0.4% in 1991/92 to 0.3% in 2003/04.

With regard to recent initiatives taken by Bangladesh to enhance its exports to historically important trading partners, it should be noted that the Government has been making concerted lobbying efforts, in collaboration with the private sector, to gain duty-free access for its exports in the United States (US). Duty-free market access for Bangladesh's exports may be achieved once the bill entitled Tariff Relief Assistance for Developing Economies (TRADE) Act of 2005, which is under consideration in the US Congress, is passed. With regard to enhancing trade with its partners in the South Asian Association for Regional Cooperation (SAARC), the Government of Bangladesh is actively participating in the implementation of the South Asian Free Trade Area (SAFTA) Agreement. The SAFTA Agreement, whose implementation started 1 July 2006, provides that countries not classified as a least developed country (LDC) (i.e., India, Pakistan, and Sri Lanka) will provide market access to exports of LDC member states such as Bangladesh at 0–5% tariff at the end of 3 years of implementation of the Tariff Liberalization Programme (TLP) of the Agreement (i.e., from 1 July 2009). That is, Bangladesh can expect to get duty-free access to India, Pakistan, and Sri Lanka from 1 July 2009, and this should hopefully lead to an expansion of Bangladesh's exports to these countries, if other conditions are propitious.[1] The Government of Bangladesh is aware of the potential of increasing exports to the rapidly growing markets in East and Southeast Asia. However, the Government has adopted no specific policies to achieve this objective aside from joining the Bay of Bengal Initiative for Multi-Sectoral Technical and Economic Cooperation (BIMSTEC), a regional trade agreement (RTA) that includes Thailand.

Economic Structure and GDP Growth Rates

Some macroeconomic indicators of the Bangladesh economy are presented in Appendix Table A4.1. Compared to the 1980s, GDP growth accelerated in the 1990s. Between 1980 and 1985, the GDP growth rate was 3.72% and the growth rate remained unchanged during the second half of the 1980s (Appendix Table A4.2). In contrast to the average growth rate of 3.7% achieved during the decade of the 1980s, the average GDP growth rate increased to 4.8% during the 1990s. The growth rate was 4.4% during the first half of the 1990s, but then it accelerated to 5.2% during the second half of the decade. The average GDP growth rate increased slightly to 5.3% during the period 2000–2005. Because of large increases in production in agriculture, industry, and service sectors, the growth rate increased to 6.3% in 2003/04. However, massive floods caused serious damage to crop production, and despite an increase in output in the industry and service sectors, GDP growth declined to 5.4%. According to the projection of Medium-Term Macroeconomic Framework (MTMF), GDP growth is expected to rise to 6.0% in 2005/06 and to 6.5% in 2006/07.

Per capita GDP grew about 1.6% per annum during the 1980s. The growth rate of per capita GDP rose to 2.4% during the first half of the 1990s, then accelerated to 3.8% during the second half of the decade. Two factors were responsible for this: (i) a slowdown in population growth from about 2.2% during the 1980s to 1.8% during the 1990s, and (ii) a sustained increase in GDP growth. The growth rate of per capita GDP further increased to 3.9% during the period 2000–2005. Per capita GDP increased from $298 in 1991/92 to $441 in 2004/05.

---

[1]   Here reference is being made to nontariff barriers (NTBs), trade facilitation, and increased connectivity. These issues are addressed later in this chapter.

Compared to this, India's average GDP growth rate was nearly 6% during the 1980s and 1990s, and it exceeded 8% during the period 2003–2006; the growth rate of per capita GDP was even faster. Pakistan's GDP growth rate, although lower than that of Bangladesh during the early part of the new century, reached 8.6% by 2005, while per capita income growth was 4.1% in this year. Economic growth in the People's Republic of China (PRC) was phenomenal, with average GDP growth of 9.6% in 1990–2005; as a result, per capita GDP in the PRC rose from $342 to $1,700 during this period. These statistics indicate that Bangladesh is lagging behind significantly in terms of growth not only compared to East Asian countries, such as the PRC, but also behind its South Asian neighbors such as India and Pakistan.

A sustained increase in domestic savings and investment has been responsible for the observed growth in GDP. The gross domestic savings rate has increased from about 14% in 1991/92 to 20% in 2004/05. During this period, the gross national savings rate has increased from about 17% to nearly 26%; a healthy inflow of remittances sent by Bangladeshis working abroad has caused the gross national savings rate to significantly exceed the gross domestic savings rate. Dependence on foreign aid has been reduced significantly as a result of the increase in domestic and national savings; currently, the foreign aid-GDP ratio stands at less than 2%. The investment/GDP ratio has risen from a little over 17% in 1991/92 to 24.5% in 2004/05. The increase in total investment has been mainly driven by an increase in private investment. The private investment-GDP ratio rose from about 10% in 1991/92 to 18.3% in 2004/05. On the other hand, the public investment/GDP ratio declined from 7% to 6.2% during this period.

All three broad economic sectors—agriculture, industry, and services—contributed to the growth acceleration of the 1990s. As Table 4.1 shows, the share of agriculture in GDP has declined from 33% in 1979/80 to about 22% in 2004/05. During this period, the share of industry in GDP increased from about 17% to little over 28%. The share of services has remained more or less unchanged during this time at around 49%.

Appendix Table A4.2 shows that the growth of agricultural GDP accelerated from an average of 2.5% in the 1980s to an average of 3.2% in the 1990s. During this time period, industrial GDP growth increased from 5.8% to 7.0%, and the service sector GDP growth rose from 3.7% to 4.5%. The three sectors, however, performed differently in the first and second halves of the 1990s. Thus, agricultural growth was weak during the first half of the decade but picked up strongly during the second half. On the other hand, industrial sector growth was strong during the first half of the decade but declined during the second half. Services sector growth increased in the second half compared to the first half of the decade. Dur-

Table 4.1 Structural Transformation of Broad Sectoral Shares in GDP, % (constant 1995/96 prices)

Sector	1979/80	1984/85	1989/90	1994/95	1999/00	2004/05	2005/06	2006/07
Agriculture	33.21	31.46	29.52	26.02	25.58	21.91	21.8	21.1
Industry	17.08	18.70	20.78	24.28	25.70	28.44	29.0	29.8
Service	49.72	49.84	49.70	48.70	48.72	49.65	49.2	49.1
Total	100.0	100.0	100.0	100.0	100.0	100.0	100.0	100.0

GDP = gross domestic product, % = percent.

Source: Bangladesh Bureau of Statistics (BBS).

ing the period 2000–2004, agriculture sector growth declined sharply, while the growth of industry and service sectors increased. This clearly shows a lack of complementarities in sectoral growth, a phenomenon that has prevented Bangladesh from achieving higher GDP growth rates.

A disaggregated picture of agriculture and manufacturing growth is presented in Appendix Table A4.3. The crop subsector, accounting for about 70% of agricultural value-added, occupies a central position in Bangladeshi agriculture. Over the years, the growth in crop production was almost entirely due to increased production of food grains. It has been pointed out that there exists unexploited potential for achieving higher agricultural growth through crop diversification (Mahmud et al. 2000). The fishery subsector has recorded remarkable growth of about 8% during the 1990s compared to about 2.5% during the 1980s. It is important to note that apart from garments, frozen shrimp was the only rapidly growing export commodity in the 1990s.

Growth of the manufacturing sector increased in the 1990s, with an average growth rate of 6.9% that was maintained during the period 2001–2005. This growth, however, declined slightly to 6.7% in the period 2000–2004. The growth of large-scale manufacturing has been driven mainly by the ready-made garment (RMG) industry. Excluding the RMG industry, the growth of large- and medium-scale manufacturing industry dropped to 4.3% during the 1990s (Mahmud 2006). Thus, growth in large- and medium-scale manufacturing has been mainly export led. The small-scale manufacturing subsector has also become vibrant since the 1990s, but production of this subsector is mainly for the domestic market.

A large share of GDP originates from the informal sectors outside crop agriculture; these activities comprise small-scale processing and manufacturing, as well as various informal services. According to the Labor Force Survey 1999/2000, these informal activities provide employment to about three quarters of the country's nonagricultural labor force. The growth rates of these informal activities accelerated in the 1990s and contributed substantially to the acceleration of overall GDP growth (Mahmud 2006).

Openness

As a result of the trade policy reforms that Bangladesh has implemented, the economy has become more open than before. The trade-GDP ratio, a commonly used measure of economic openness, rose from 19.9% in 1993/94 to nearly 37% in 2004/05.[2] By contrast, the PRC's trade dependency increased from 35% in 1990 to 65% in 2005. This indicates that Bangladesh's trade policy reforms need to be further speeded up to accelerate the process of export-led growth.

Labor Cost

Bangladesh is pursuing an export-led growth strategy. Thus, external competitiveness is crucial to achieving sustained growth. Since its exports are highly labor intensive, the main determinant of competitiveness is unit labor cost (e.g., the ratio between labor cost per worker to productivity). Table 4.2 compares the wages and productivity of the manufacturing sector in Bangladesh with those of India and Sri Lanka.

It is evident that between the mid-1980s and the late 1990s, the manufacturing labor cost per worker in Bangladesh increased by nearly 21% but the value added per worker declined by 6%. As a result, value added per dollar of labor cost declined, reflecting an increase in unit labor cost. By contrast, value added per dollar of labor cost has increased in India and Sri Lanka, indicating a decline in unit labor cost.

Poverty

Bangladesh has witnessed a modest poverty reduction rate of around 1 percentage point a year since the early 1990s. Two alternative estimates of the poverty headcount ratio show poverty at the national level declining from 58.8% in 1991/92 to 49.8% in 2000, and from 49.7% in 1991/92 to 40.2% in 2000. Consideration of other data sources tends to support the latter estimate. Rural poverty declined from 52.9% to 43.6%, while urban

---

[2]   Two other measures of economic openness are also often employed: (i) export propensity and (ii) import penetration. Export propensity is defined as the ratio of exports of goods and services to gross domestic product (GDP), while import penetration is estimated as the percentage of imports of goods and services to domestic demand plus trade surplus (or deficit). It has been estimated that in Bangladesh the export propensity has increased from 8.3% in 1990 to 17.5% in 2000, while import penetration has risen from 16.7% to 23% during the same period. Also, the degree of international openness, in terms of all three measures, is higher for Bangladesh than for India and Pakistan, although it is lower than for Sri Lanka (see Shahabuddin et al. 2004).

Table 4.2 Wages and Productivity in Manufacturing Sector

Country	Average hours worked per week (1)		Labor cost per worker in manufacturing ($ per year) (2)		Value added per worker in manufacturing ($ per year) (3)		(3) / (2) * 100	
	1980–1984	1995–1999	1980–1984	1995–1999	1980–1984	1995–1999	1980–1984	1995–1999
Bangladesh	–	52	556	671	1,820	1,711	327	255
India	46	–	1,035	1,192	2,108	3,118	204	262
Sri Lanka	50	53	447	604	2,067	3,405	462	564

$ = US dollar, – = no data available.

Source: World Bank (2000)

poverty declined from 33.6% to 26.4% between 1991/92 and 2000.[3] The situation for the poorest improved during this period, although the proportion of the population belonging to this category remained quite high at around 20% in 2000.

While absolute poverty measured by the headcount index has declined over the 1990s, this has been associated with a rise in inequality. Consumption expenditure inequality as measured by the Gini index increased over the 1990s from 30.7% to 36.8% in urban areas, and from 24.3% to 27.1% in rural areas. Overall, the Gini index of inequality at the national level rose from 0.259 to 0.306 during this period.

Thus, Bangladesh has moved from a situation of lower growth with equality in the 1980s to a situation of higher growth with inequality in the 1990s.

Foreign Direct Investment Regime

Since independence, Bangladesh has come a long way in liberalizing its foreign investment regime to attract more FDIs. Policies toward FDIs in Bangladesh are stated in the Industrial Policy, whose major objective is to attract FDIs in both export and domestic market-oriented industries, in order to make up for the deficient domestic investment resources, acquire evolving technology, and gain access to export markets.

The first Industrial Investment Policy of Bangladesh, announced in 1973, was very restrictive, allowing foreigners to take only minority equity

---

[3] The higher estimate of poverty is that of the World Bank (2002a). The lower estimate, which has found wide acceptance, has been made by Sen (1995, 1998).

stakes in public enterprises.[4] The Revised Industrial Investment Policy of 1974 permitted foreign investors to collaborate with both Government and local private entrepreneurs in all industries except some basic industries. Major policy changes were introduced in the Revised Industrial Policy of 1975 whereby foreign investors received equal treatment to local investors. This principle of equal treatment was subsequently included in the Foreign Private Investment (Promotion and Protection) Act 1980, which continues to be the legal framework for foreign investment in Bangladesh. The FDI policy was increasingly liberalized in subsequent industrial policies of the Government.

Foreign Direct Investment Approval Regime and Investment Incentives

Foreign investors do not require any prior Government approval to invest in Bangladesh except that they must register at the Board of Investment (BOI).[5] There is no limit on foreign equity participation, nor is there any limit on repatriation of profit and income. No distinction is made between local and foreign investors in matters of fiscal and other incentives. Export processing zones (EPZs) have been created to attract FDIs by providing ready infrastructure and allowing the import of raw materials on a duty-free basis. FDIs are encouraged in all industrial activities, including service industries, but with the exception of industries included in the list of reserved industries, ready-made garments, banks, insurance companies, and other financial institutions.[6] Pre-registration clearance is required for investment in ready-made garments and the other sectors mentioned.

Foreign investment in Bangladesh is well protected by the Foreign Private Investment (Promotion and Protection) Act of 1980. The Act inter alia ensures the following:

- The Government will accord fair and equitable treatment to foreign private investment which will enjoy full protection and security in Bangladesh.

---

[4] In keeping with the Government development philosophy of having an economy dominated by the public sector, industrial ownership was dominated by the public sector and the private sector was allowed only a minor role.

[5] The discussion on rules and regulations governing foreign private investment in Bangladesh, incentives to foreign investors, etc. has been drawn from the Board of Investment (BOI) (2004).

[6] The industries included on the reserved list are: (i) arms and ammunition and other defense equipment and machinery, (ii) forest plantation and mechanized extraction within the bounds of the Reserved Forest, (iii) production of nuclear energy, and (iv) security printing (currency notes) and minting.

- In the event of losses of foreign investment owing to civil commotion, insurrection, etc., the foreign investor will be indemnified/compensated in the same manner as the local investor.
- Foreign private investment will not be expropriated or nationalized, except for a public purpose against adequate compensation.
- The transfer of capital and the returns from it as well as proceeds from liquidation (in the event of liquidation) are guaranteed.

The protection of foreign private investments is also provided under the bilateral investment treaties signed by Bangladesh with 24 countries.[7] Furthermore, Bangladesh is a signatory to agreements under the Multilateral Investment Guarantee Agency (MIGA), the Overseas Private Investment Corporation (OPIC) of the US, and the International Center for Settlement of Investment Disputes (ICSID). Bangladesh is also a member of the World Intellectual Property Organization's (WIPO) permanent committee on development cooperation related to intellectual property, therefore, it ensures adequate protection for intellectual property rights. The major fiscal and nonfiscal incentives provided to foreign investors in Bangladesh are shown in Table 4.3.

Let us first examine the fiscal incentives. Tax holiday facilities are available in the existing industry for 5 or 7 years, depending on the location of the industrial enterprise. Accelerated depreciation allowance in lieu of a tax holiday is provided only in new industrial undertakings at 100% on the cost of machinery for the first year only. For 100% export-oriented industries, no import duty is charged for capital machinery and parts amounting to a maximum of 10% of the value of such machinery. For other industries, an import duty of 7.5% ad valorem is payable on capital machineries and parts imported for initial installation or Balancing, Modernization and Rehabilitation (BMR) and/or Balancing, Modernization, Rehabilitation, and Expansion (BMRE) of existing industries. Value-added tax (VAT) is not payable for imported capital machinery or parts. Double taxation can be avoided on the basis of bilateral Double Taxation Avoidance Treaties (DTTs). Expatriate employees working in industries specified in the relevant schedule of the Income Tax Ordinance are exempted from payment of income tax for up to 3 years.

Business in Bangladesh may be conducted by companies formed and incorporated locally or by companies incorporated abroad but registered in Bangladesh. Incorporation options for a foreign investor include (i) setting up a 100% foreign-owned company in Bangladesh, (ii) setting up a joint venture with a Bangladeshi company and/or investor, (iii) establishing

---

7   In addition to the United States (US) and member countries in the European Union, most East and Southeast Asian countries have bilateral investment treaties with Bangladesh.

Table 4.3 Major Incentives Provided to Foreign Investors

Fiscal incentives	Nonfiscal incentives
• Tax holiday • Accelerated depreciation allowance instead of tax holiday • Concessionary income tax in lieu of tax holiday and accelerated depreciation allowance • Concessionary duty on imported machinery • Avoidance of double taxation • Remittance of royalty, technical know-how, technical assistance fee	• 100% foreign equity allowed • Unrestricted exit policy • Full repatriation facilities of dividend and capital in the event of exit • Permanent Residence Permit on investing $75,000 and citizenship offer for investing $500,000

$ = US dollar, % = percent.

Source: Board of Investment, Bangladesh (2004).

the company's place of business as Bangladesh, (iv) setting up a branch or a subsidiary of a foreign company in Bangladesh, and (v) setting up a Bangladeshi company or participating in a Bangladeshi company that has already been formed. The incorporation options show that there are no ownership restrictions on foreign investment in Bangladesh.

Export Processing Zones

An EPZ has been defined as a territorial or economic enclave in which goods may be imported and manufactured and reshipped with a reduction in duties and minimal intervention by customs officials. As indicated earlier, the Government of Bangladesh set up EPZs primarily to attract export-oriented FDIs. The Bangladesh Export Processing Zone Authority (BEPZA) is the Government agency responsible for promoting, attracting, and facilitating foreign investment in the EPZs.[8]

At present there are two fully operating EPZs—one in Chittagong and the other near Dhaka—both of which have already attracted a wide range of investors. Another four EPZs have started operation; these are located in (i) Mongla, a southern port city; (ii) Comilla, which lies between Dhaka and Chittagong; (iii) Ishwardi, near the Jamuna Bridge; and (iv) Nilphamari (named Uttara EPZ), near Syedpur airport. Two other EPZs, one at Adamjee near Dhaka and the other at Karnaphuli in Chittagong, are nearing completion.

The primary objective of setting up EPZs is to provide special areas where potential investors may find congenial investment climates free from cum-

---

[8] The discussion on export processing zones (EPZs) is based on Bangladesh Export Processing Zone Authority (BEPZA) (2002) and unpublished documents of BEPZA.

bersome procedures. The following three types of investment can be made in an EPZ: (i) type A, 100% foreign-owned (includes Bangladeshi nationals ordinarily resident abroad); (ii) type B, joint ventures between foreign and Bangladeshi entrepreneurs resident in Bangladesh; and (iii) type C, 100% locally owned. There is no restriction on the extent of foreign ownership. All foreign investment in the EPZs is protected and guaranteed by (i) the 1980 Foreign Private Investment (Promotion and Protection) Act; (ii) the operation of insurance and finance programs under the OPIC of the US; (iii) security and safeguards available under MIGA, of which Bangladesh is a member; and (iv) the availability of arbitration facility of the ICSID.

The incentives provided by the Government of Bangladesh to attract FDIs to EPZs are shown in Table 4.4.

Geographical Focus and Resources of Investment Promotion Agencies

The two specialized government institutions that shoulder the responsibility for promoting foreign private investments are the BOI and the BEPZA.

Table 4.4 Incentives Offered in Export Processing Zones

Fiscal incentives	Nonfiscal incentives
• Tax holiday for 10 years	• 100% foreign ownership permissible
• Duty-free import of construction materials	• Nondiscriminatory treatment of foreign investors
• Duty-free import of machineries, office equipment, spare parts, etc.	• No ceilings on foreign or local investment
• Duty-free import and export of raw materials and finished goods	• Full repatriation of capital and dividends allowed
• Relief from double taxation	• Foreign currency loan from abroad under direct automatic route
• Exemption from dividend tax	• Nonresident Foreign Currency Deposit (NFCD) accounts permitted
• Generalized System of Preference (GSP) facility available	• Operation of Foreign Currency Account by Types B and C investors allowed
• Duty-free import of 2–3 vehicles	• Secured and protected bonded area
• Expatriates exempted from income tax for 3 years	• Offshore banking available
• Accelerated depreciation on machinery or plant allowed	• Freedom from import and export policy restrictions
• Remittance of royalty, technical, and consultancy fees allowed	• Back-to-back letters of credit (L/C)
• Duty- and quota-free access to European Union, Canada, Norway, Australia, etc.	• Import from Domestic Tariff Area (DTA) permitted
	• 10% sale to DTA permissible
	• Customs clearance at factory site
	• Others

% = percent.

Source: Bangladesh Export Processing Zone Authority.

The BOI was established by the Investment Board Act of 1989 to promote and facilitate domestic and foreign investments in the private sector. It is headed by the prime minister and is a part of the Prime Minister's Office. It is therefore a powerful body and does not suffer from a shortage of resources. The general perception is that it is an efficient organization. It does not have any overseas offices at present. However, the BOI plans to establish three overseas offices soon. Outbound missions are sent from time to time to attract foreign investments from major investing countries. It was not immediately clear whether BOI had any dedicated marketing resources at its disposal.

BEPZA was established by the Bangladesh Export Processing Zones Authority Act of 1980. The prime minister is the chairman of BEPZA's board of governors. BEPZA's major objective is to promote investments (local and foreign) in the country. It does not have any overseas offices. Outbound missions are sent from time to time to attract foreign investments in the EPZs.

Merchandise Trade Policy

Trade Performance and Pattern

Trade policy reforms were initiated in Bangladesh in the mid-1980s and the pace of reform accelerated in the 1990s, particularly during the first half of the decade. As a result of import liberalization, imports grew rapidly during the 1990s; at the same time, exports also increased rapidly. The trade balance still continued to be in deficit, although the trade deficit-GDP ratio began to decline because of a faster growth of exports compared to imports (Table 4.5, Appendix Table A4.1 for details).

Bangladesh achieved an impressive double-digit export growth rate of 11% during the 1990s compared to 8% in the 1980s. Export growth declined somewhat in the early part of the new millennium but recovered in 2003/04 (export growth rate of 16%) and 2004/05 (13.8%). This robust growth of exports is primarily attributable to continuing trade liberalization and the Multi-Fiber Agreement (MFA) quota system in operation in garment-importing developed countries, particularly the European Union (EU) and the US.

As in the case of exports, import growth slowed down in the early part of the new millennium, but picked up again in 2002/03 (import growth rate of 15.5%), 2003/04 (18.4%), and 2004/05 (22.1%). Although the trade balance was continuously in deficit because of rapid increasing imports, the current account balance has experienced a small surplus since 2000/01 (except in 2004/05) because of continuing inflows of workers' remittance

Table 4.5 Total Exports and Imports of Bangladesh, $ Mn

Fiscal year	Exports	Imports	Balance of trade
1990/91	1,661	3,470	(1,809)
1991/92	1,904	3,463	(1,559)
1992/93	2,383	4,071	(1,688)
1993/94	2,534	4,191	(1,657)
1994/95	3,473	5,834	(2,361)
1995/96	3,882	6,947	(3,065)
1996/97	4,418	7,162	(2,744)
1997/98	5,161	7,524	(2,363)
1998/99	5,313	8,018	(2,705)
1999/00	5,752	8,403	(2,651)
2000/01	6,467	9,335	(2,868)
2001/02	5,986	8,540	(2,554)
2002/03	6,548	9,658	(3,110)
2003/04	7,603	10,903	(3,300)
2004/05	8,654	11,870	(3,216)
2005/06	10,526	13,301	(2,775)
2006/07	12,178	15,511	(3,333)

$ Mn = millions of US dollars, ( ) = negative value.

Sources: Export Promotion Bureau (EPB) and Bangladesh Bank (BB).

from abroad. During 2000/01, Bangladesh faced a severe balance of payments situation as a result of an increase in the trade deficit and a decline in workers' remittance, largely attributable to a global economic slowdown.

The composition of the export and import baskets reveals several features. In the case of exports, Bangladesh has made some progress in shifting from a resource-based to a process-based export structure; however, the extreme concentration in the exports of ready-made garments remains. In the early 1980s, more than 84% of exports came from industrial supplies (e.g., jute and jute goods, and leather). In the 1990s and thereafter, the concentration has been in consumer goods (mainly ready-made garments), which accounted for 80% of exports in 2000. This shows the extremely narrow base of the country's export sector. In the case of imports, a shift toward the increased share of consumer goods can be observed, from 2.2% of total imports in 1981 to 7.5% in 2000.

Historically, the US and the EU have been the major destinations of Bangladesh's exports. In 2004/05, about 28% of Bangladesh's exports were destined for the US market, about 56% for the EU (having increased from 17.4% in 1981/82 and 39.1% in 1990/91), and 1.4% for Japan. Exports to the SAARC countries, on the other hand, have declined over time, from 8.7% in 1980 to 1.7% in 2003. Several factors may have been responsible for this. Estimates suggest that, with the exception of India and Sri Lanka, the pattern of comparative advantage is quite similar across South Asia. Moreover, both India and Pakistan exhibit an anti-regional bias in their trade structures. Poor connectivity and weak trade facilitation have made matters worse. Bangladesh's exports to East Asian countries have been very small as a percentage of its total exports.

Country-wise, imports of Bangladesh display a pattern quite opposite to that exhibited by exports. The major sources of Bangladesh's imports are East and South Asian countries, with India being the largest source (14.7% of total imports in 2003), the PRC occupying the second position (11%), followed by Singapore (8.4%). The shares of other Asian countries were Japan 5.1%; Hong Kong, China 4.0%; Republic of Korea 3.9%; Taipei,China 3.4%; and Malaysia 2.3%. By contrast, the US' share in Bangladesh's total imports in 2003/04 was only 2.0%.

The commodity composition of Bangladesh's exports has undergone significant change during the 1990s. This is seen from an examination of Table 4.6.

Table 4.6 shows that the share of manufactured goods in total exports increased from 82.2% in 1990/91 to 93.2% in 2006/07, with a corresponding decline in the share of primary commodities. The export growth

Table 4.6 Changing Commodity Composition of Exports, % share of total export

Commodity classification	1990/ 91	1994/ 95	1999/ 2000	2000/ 01	2001/ 02	2002/ 03	2003/ 04	2004/ 05	2005/ 06	2006/ 07
Primary commodities										
Frozen food	10.29	8.81	5.98	5.62	4.61	4.91	5.13	4.86	4.4	4.3
Tea	1.41	0.95	0.31	0.33	0.29	0.24	0.21	0.18	0.1	0.1
Raw jute	6.22	2.27	1.25	1.04	1.02	1.26	1.05	1.11	1.4	1.2
Others	0.50	0.99	0.61	0.50	0.50	0.65	0.89	1.34	1.5	1.4
Total	**18.42**	**13.02**	**8.15**	**7.49**	**6.51**	**7.06**	**7.28**	**7.49**	**7.3**	**6.9**
Industrial goods										
Ready-made garments	45.03	64.27	75.66	75.15	76.57	75.02	74.79	74.16	75.1	75.6
Leather	8.31	5.82	3.39	3.93	3.46	2.92	2.78	2.55	2.4	2.2
Jute goods	17.03	9.18	4.62	3.54	4.04	3.39	3.24	3.55	3.4	2.6
Fertilizer and chemical products	3.56	3.14	2.68	2.30	1.66	1.53	1.60	2.28	2.0	1.8
Others	8.25	4.57	5.50	7.59	7.76	10.08	10.31	9.97	9.8	11.0
Total	**82.18**	**86.98**	**91.85**	**92.51**	**93.49**	**92.94**	**92.72**	**92.51**	**92.7**	**93.2**

% = percent.

Source: Export Promotion Bureau (EPB).

of manufactured goods was remarkable at 13.4% per annum, while the annual growth rate of primary exports was only 4.3%. The growth of manufactured exports was mainly concentrated in ready-made garments, with woven garments accounting for nearly 56% of export growth and knitwear for another 31% (Shahabuddin et al. 2004). As a result of this remarkable growth, the share of garments (woven plus knit) in total exports rose from 45% in 1990/91 to an average of 75% during the period 2000–2005. The growth trend in knitwear is particularly strong because this subsector was coming off a low base. The export share of nontraditional manufactured commodities such as garments has increased at the cost of traditional exports of raw jute, jute goods, and leather. Changes in volume rather than in price primarily explain the growth of exports during the 1990s.

Table 4.7 shows that the major imported commodities are capital machinery, textiles and articles thereof, petroleum products, food grains (rice and wheat), raw cotton and yarn, edible oil, iron and steel, and plastic and rubber. Imports of EPZs are industrial raw materials and intermediate goods and capital machineries. Thus, the bulk of Bangladesh's imports are industrial raw materials, intermediate goods, and capital machinery, all of which are required for maintaining or accelerating industrial growth.

Prior to achieving self-sufficiency in food grain production in the late 1990s, Bangladesh had to import some rice to meet domestic demand. Crude petroleum and petroleum products are also major import items. Imports of raw cotton and yarn have increased rapidly due to increasing demand from the domestic textile industry and the export-oriented knitwear industry. Heavy imports of textiles mainly cater to the needs of the export-oriented woven garments industry.

Table 4.8 shows the changing pattern of imports into Bangladesh. Industrial raw materials, intermediate goods, and capital machinery have comprised the bulk of imports coming into Bangladesh; however, their combined share in total imports has declined from about 64% in both 1990/91 and 1995/96 to about 47% in 2004/05, almost entirely because of a decline in import of capital machineries. In fact, the decline in capital goods imports started in the late 1990s because of a deceleration in industrial growth, and picked up again in 2001/02. It may also be noted that since imports into EPZ consist of capital machineries and industrial raw materials, their share should be added to the figures noted above to get a complete picture of imports of producer goods in Bangladesh. The share of food grain imports has declined with the achievement of self-sufficiency in food grain production at the end of the 1990s; since then, food grains have been imported only when there has been a shortfall in domestic production because of natural calamities such as floods. Imports of consumer goods other than food grains have started to rise in the new millennium, mainly because of the Government's policy of import liberalization.

Table 4.7 Commodity Composition of Imports, $ Mn

Commodities	1990/ 91	1995/ 96	1999/ 2000	2000/ 01	2001/ 02	2002/ 03	2003/ 04	2004/ 05	2005/ 06	2006/ 07
1. Food grains	297	586	381	349	186	409	431	574	418	581
2. Milk and milk products	72	53	60	62	59	61	61	86	–	–
3. Spices	19	23	18	15	13	32	30	42	–	–
4. Oilseeds	16	89	90	64	72	64	73	86	90	106
5. Edible oil	153	179	256	218	251	364	471	440	473	583
6. Sugar	–	6	10	46	23	104	110	220	–	–
7. Cement	75	171	80	–	–	–	–	–	–	–
8. Clinker	–	–	59	106	150	144	139	170	210	240
9. Crude petroleum	144	166	232	273	242	267	252	350	604	524
10. Petroleum products	204	290	406	566	481	620	770	1,252	1,400	1,709
11. Chemical products	125	201	278	339	335	353	406	510	–	–
12. Pharmaceuticals	1	20	27	33	39	44	45	41	–	–
13. Fertilizer	90	97	140	129	107	109	150	332	342	357
14. Dyeing and tanning materials	20	55	71	91	87	86	109	132	–	–
15. Plastic and rubber and articles thereof	–	–	230	261	250	281	367	477	–	–
16. Raw cotton	88	185	277	360	312	393	583	666	742	858
17. Yarn	52	296	300	322	283	270	323	393	501	582
18. Textiles and articles thereof	411	1,086	1,196	1,291	1,063	1,106	1,295	1,571	–	–
19. Staple fiber	12	–	43	39	39	41	57	75	76	97
20. Iron, steel, and other base metal	97	322	393	464	413	455	479	679	–	–
21. Capital machinery	1,231	1,968	314	482	554	548	729	1,115	1,539	1,929
22. Imports of EPZ	–	261	665	685	627	727	887	952	–	–
23. Others	372	888	2,838	3,054	2,866	3,035	3,016	2,825	8,351	9,591
Total imports	**3,470**	**6,947**	**8,374**	**9,335**	**8,540**	**9,658**	**10,903**	**13,147**	**14,746**	**17,157**

– = no data available, EPZ = export processing zone, $ Mn = millions of US dollars.

Source: Bangladesh Bank (BB).

At this point it may be instructive to note Bangladesh's revealed comparative advantage (RCA). Using the Balassa RCA index, the World Bank (2002a) found that Bangladesh enjoys a comparative advantage in about 7.51% of all 4-digit Standard International Trade Classification (SITC) commodities, and in only about 5% commodities did it have a relatively high comparative advantage in 1998. While it does not have any comparative advantage in capital-intensive or high-value products, it is potentially competitive in a large variety of garment products, fish, leather, and jute goods. It also has a comparative advantage in only 15% of commodities under textile yarn and fabric categories at SITC 4-digit levels. The limited

Table 4.8 Changes in Composition of Imports, % of total imports

Broad category of import	1990/91	1995/96	1999/2000	2004/05
1. Food grains	8.6	8.4	4.5	4.4
2. Consumer goods other than food grains[a]	7.1	4.0	4.4	6.3
3. Fuel[b]	10.0	6.6	7.6	12.2
4. Industrial raw materials and intermediate goods (other than EPZs)[c]	28.4	36.0	37.7	38.7
5. Capital machinery (other than EPZs)	35.5	28.3	3.7	8.5
6. Imports into EPZs	–	3.7	7.9	7.2

– = no data available, EPZ = export processing zone, % = percent.

[a] Consumer goods other than food grains includes milk and milk products, spices, edible oil, sugar, and pharmaceuticals.
[b] Fuel includes petroleum and petroleum products.
[c] Industrial raw materials and intermediate goods include oilseeds, cement, clinker, chemical products, fertilizer, dyeing and tanning materials, plastic and rubber and articles thereof, raw cotton, yarn, textile and articles thereof, staple fiber, and iron and steel and other base metal.

Source: Calculated from Table 4.7, Bangladesh Bank (BB).

scope of actual exports, as noted above, seems to be consistent with these findings.

Regarding the geographic distribution of Bangladesh's trade flows, particularly with respect to East and South Asia, a regional distribution of Bangladesh's exports is shown in Tables 4.9 and 4.10. ASEAN+3 consists of the members of the Association of Southeast Asian Nations (ASEAN) plus Japan, PRC, and Republic of Korea. East Asia consists of ASEAN+3 together with Hong Kong, China and Taipei,China. South Asia is taken to consist of Bangladesh, India, Nepal, Pakistan, and Sri Lanka.

Table 4.9 shows some interesting features of Bangladesh's exports to East and South Asia. First, the proportion of total exports of Bangladesh destined for East Asia (4.7% in 2005/06) and South Asia (2.3% in 2005/06) are relatively small. Second, the shares of both these regions have declined between 1993/94 and 2005/06, with the share of ASEAN+3 falling from 5.6% to 3.2%, while the share of East Asia dropped from 8.5% to 4.7%. Estimates of geographic RCA (World Bank 2002a) of Bangladesh exports show that the Balassa RCA for Developing Asia (which includes East Asian countries) has dropped from 1.0999 in 1988 to 0.4261 in 1998. This indicates that Bangladesh's exports are in a disadvantageous position relative to the East Asian countries and this explains the declining share of these countries in Bangladesh's exports, as noted above. Third, the top three

Table 4.9 Bangladesh's Exports to East Asia and South Asia, % of total exports

Region	1993/ 94	1996/ 97	1999/ 2000	2000/ 01	2001/ 02	2002/ 03	2003/ 04	2004/ 05	2005/ 06
ASEAN+3[a]	5.78	4.82	3.36	2.80	2.58	2.72	2.60	2.9	3.2
East Asia[b]	8.48	7.54	4.94	4.71	4.60	4.58	4.20	4.3	4.7
South Asia[c]	2.36	2.72	2.72	1.59	1.36	1.51	1.59	1.9	2.3

ASEAN = Association of Southeast Asian Nations, % = percent.

[a] ASEAN+3 includes the 10 ASEAN members (Brunei Darussalam, Cambodia, Indonesia, Lao People's Democratic Republic, Malaysia, Myanmar, Philippines, Singapore, Thailand, and Viet Nam) plus Japan, the People's Republic of China, and the Republic of Korea.
[b] East Asia is ASEAN+3; Hong Kong, China; and Taipei,China.
[c] South Asia includes the following South Asian Association for Regional Cooperation member countries: India, Nepal, Pakistan, and Sri Lanka.

Source: Bangladesh Bank (BB).

East Asian importing economies for Bangladesh's exports are, in order of descending importance, Hong Kong, China; Japan; and Singapore. Some countries such as the Lao People's Democratic Republic (Lao PDR) and Viet Nam import very little from Bangladesh. Fourth, India is the major importing country in South Asia of Bangladeshi products; imports by Nepal are insignificant. Fifth, the major commodities exported by Bangladesh to the major East Asian importing countries (i.e., Hong Kong, China; Japan; and Singapore) are virtually the same in each case. These are fish and crustaceans, raw hides and skins, and textile and textile articles. These items are also the major exports of Bangladesh to India. Once again, this reflects the rather narrow export base of Bangladesh at present. The export basket must be diversified if Bangladesh is to increase its exports to these two regions.[9]

The geographic concentration of Bangladesh's exports is brought out in sharp relief in Table 4.10. It shows that two regions, the EU and the North American Free Trade Agreement (NAFTA), account for almost 88% of Bangladesh's exports. The reason behind this is the high degree of market concentration of Bangladesh's exports of garments to the EU and the US. The very low shares of exports to countries in ASEAN and the SAARC are particularly of interest for this present study.

The major commodities exported to East and South Asia (as defined in this study) are listed in Table 4.11. This shows that the major exports of Bangladesh to East Asia are primary products such as shrimps, hides, skins, and mineral products. Textile products are virtually the only manu-

---

[9] There are other factors that influence Bangladesh's export to these two regions, particularly South Asia.

Table 4.10 Destination Pattern of Bangladesh's Exports, % of total exports

Bloc/Group/Community	2002/03	2003/04	2004/05	2005/06
European Union (EU)	52.4	58.3	57.2	54.6
North American Free Trade Agreement (NAFTA)	34.2	29.4	30.4	31.9
Organization of Islamic Conference (OIC)	4.5	4.2	4.2	5.5
Other Asian Countries	4.0	3.8	3.7	3.7
Asian Currency Unit Member Countries	2.7	2.6	3.0	3.2
South Asian Association for Regional Cooperation (SAARC)	1.8	1.9	2.3	2.7
Other European Countries	1.9	1.9	1.7	2.0
Organization of Petroleum Exporting Countries (OPEC)	1.9	1.5	1.6	2.0
Association of Southeast Asian Nations (ASEAN)	1.6	1.3	1.5	1.7
Other Countries	0.9	0.8	1.0	0.8

% = percent.

Notes:
(1) The percentage shares add up to more than 100% because of inter-classification of individual country into different bloc/group/community. For example, Indonesia is included in the OIC and also in ASEAN and OPEC; and
(2) Exports of export processing zones are not included.

Source: Bangladesh Bank (BB).

factured goods exported to this subregion in any significant amount. This indicates clearly that Bangladesh must develop new manufactured exports in order to increase its exports to East Asia. A similar picture is observed for exports to South Asia, which are dominated by primary products such as fish and tea. Again, textiles are the only major manufactured export. The other things to note from Table 4.11 are the small percentage shares of the major exports of Bangladesh in total bilateral trade with the respective East or South Asian country (with the exception of Pakistan and Sri Lanka). The reason is that Bangladesh imports much more from each country than it exports. Imports from Pakistan and Sri Lanka are much less, and hence the larger percentage shares of Bangladesh's major export commodities in total bilateral trade with these two countries.

It would be instructive at this stage to look at some more precise measures of geographic concentration of Bangladesh's exports during the 1990s. Estimates of Herfindhal and Finger-kreinin market concentration indices of Bangladesh's exports made by Shahabuddin et al. (2004) show that the former index increased from 0.16171 in 1989/90 to 0.19648 in 1999/2000, while the latter index rose from 0.69561 to 0.70593 during the same period. Calculation of the symmetric Balassa geographic specialization index for Bangladesh by the same authors shows that the index is positive and has increased from 0.25 to 0.57 for bilateral trade with the EU, and from 0.59

Table 4.11 Major Commodities Exported to East Asia and South Asia by Bangladesh in 2004

Country	Major export commodities			
East Asia				
China, People's Republic of	fish & crustaceans value[a] = $1,724 share[b] = 0.15%	plastic & articles thereof value = $2,817 share = 0.24%	raw hides & skins value = $5,329 share = 0.46%	textiles & textile articles value = $11,389 share = 1.00%
Hong Kong, China	fish & crustaceans value[a] = $9,353 share[b] = 1.78%	raw hides & skins value = $76,878 share = 14.63%	textiles & textile articles value = $5,841 share = 1.11%	
Japan	fish & crustaceans value = $18,806 share = 3.57%	raw hides & skins value = $17,703 share = 3.36%	textiles & textile articles value = $14,355 share = 2.72%	footwear value = $5,732 share = 1.09%
Singapore	mineral products value = $19,429 share = 2.08%	textiles & textile articles value = $3,661 share = 0.4%		
South Asia				
India	fish & crustaceans value = $6,311 share = 0.38%	mineral products value = $6,630 share = 0.40%	products of chemical or allied industries value = $1,271 share = 0.08%	plastic & articles thereof value = $1,294 share = 0.08%
	raw hides & skins value = $1,897 share = 0.11%	textiles & textile articles value = $32,312 share = 1.95%		
Pakistan	tea value = $12,756 share = 8.16%	textiles & textile articles value = $27,539 share = 17.62%		
Sri Lanka	textiles & textile articles value = $2,548 share = 13.49%	base metals & articles of base metal value = $4,992 share = 26.42%		

$ = US dollar, % = percent.

[a] value is in thousands of US dollars.
[b] percentage share in total bilateral trade.

Source: Calculated from Bangladesh Bank (BB) data.

to 0.75 for trade with the US over the period 1989/90–1999/2000. Thus, Bangladesh's export trade is geographically specialized in these two regions and specialization has increased over time. However, the index has a negative value for Japan, PRC, Republic of Korea, and India; this indicates that Bangladesh's exports are in a disadvantageous position in these markets. Hence, questions arise as to what extent export promotion efforts have been sufficient with regard to East and Southeast Asia.

Shahabuddin et al. have also estimated a gravity model for Bangladesh's trade flow for the period 1990–1999. Their estimates show that Bangladesh has a significant export bias with its traditional partners the US and the EU. Of the SAARC countries, India, Pakistan, and Sri Lanka have registered positive but small effects. Higher positive effects are observed with Indonesia and Singapore among ASEAN countries. There is also a significant positive effect in the case of Japan and the PRC. Interestingly, the South Asia Preferential Trade Agreement (SAPTA) has a negative coefficient in the fixed effect model, indicating that SAPTA has yet to provide benefits to Bangladesh.

As illustrated in Tables 4.12 and 4.13, in the case of Bangladesh's imports, the picture is quite opposite to that of its exports.

Table 4.12 shows that East Asian countries are the major sources of Bangladesh's imports, although the shares of South Asian countries are likewise significant. The share of ASEAN+3 has increased from 30.4% in 1992/93 to 33.5% in 2005/06; the share of East Asia has increased from 37.7% in 1992/93 to 40.9% in 2005/06. During this period, the share of South Asia in Bangladesh's imports has risen from 10.9% to 15.9%. This is primarily attributable to rising imports from India.

Table 4.14 provides a more detailed picture of Bangladeshi's imports from seven East Asian countries: PRC; Hong Kong, China; Republic of

Table 4.12 Bangladesh's Imports from East Asia and South Asia, % of total imports

Region	1992/ 93	1995/ 96	1999/ 2000	2000/ 01	2001/ 02	2002/ 03	2003/ 04	2004/ 05	2005/ 06
ASEAN+3[a]	30.37	33.44	32.31	34.25	36.27	35.55	35.15	33.1	33.5
East Asia[b]	37.71	42.18	42.36	43.78	45.08	43.44	42.57	40.4	40.9
South Asia[c]	10.91	17.83	11.08	13.85	12.83	14.91	15.86	16.4	13.6

ASEAN = Association of Southeast Asian Nations, % = percent.

[a] ASEAN+3 includes the 10 ASEAN members (Brunei Darussalam, Cambodia, Indonesia, Lao People's Democratic Republic, Malaysia, Myanmar, Philippines, Singapore, Thailand, and Viet Nam) plus Japan, the People's Republic of China, and the Republic of Korea.
[b] East Asia is ASEAN+3; Hong Kong, China; and Taipei,China.
[c] South Asia includes the following South Asian Association for Regional Cooperation member countries: India, Nepal, Pakistan, and Sri Lanka.

Source: Calculated from Bangladesh Bank (BB) data.

Table 4.13 Major Sources of Bangladesh's Imports, % of total imports

Country/Region	1999/ 2000	2000/ 01	2001/ 02	2002/ 03	2003/ 04	2004/ 05	2005/ 06	2006/ 07
China, People's Republic of	6.78	7.59	10.28	9.71	10.99	12.49	14.1	15.0
Hong Kong, China	5.43	5.12	5.16	4.48	3.97	4.3	4.2	4.4
India	9.95	12.38	11.93	14.06	14.69	15.44	9.3	13.2
Japan	8.18	9.06	7.67	6.26	5.06	4.25	4.4	4.0
Korea, Republic of	3.81	4.4	4.05	3.45	3.85	3.24	3.3	3.2
Malaysia	1.29	1.58	1.70	1.75	2.34	2.10	2.3	2.0
Singapore	8.37	8.83	10.2	10.35	8.35	6.75	5.8	6.0
Taipei,China	4.61	4.41	3.65	3.4	3.46	3.34	3.2	2.8
United States	3.88	2.66	3.06	2.31	2.07	2.50	2.3	2.2
Others	47.69	43.65	42.29	44.22	45.21	45.58	47.7	47.3
Total	**100**	**100**	**100**	**100**	**100**	**100**	**100**	**100**

% = percent.

Source: Bangladesh Bank (BB).

Korea; Japan; Malaysia; Singapore; and Taipei,China. The PRC's share has increased sharply while Japan's has declined appreciably. Also, there has occurred a remarkable increase in India's share; Tables 4.12 and 4.13 taken together show clearly that India has almost totally dominated Bangladesh's imports from South Asia.

An analysis of Bangladesh's merchandise trade would remain incomplete without referring to the country's informal border trade with neighboring India. Since the early 1990s, several studies have been undertaken in this area and all of these have come up with estimates of substantial informal trade between the two countries. A very recent study (Bakht and Sen 2002) estimated illegal imports from India in 1997 at $1.08 billion (where official imports in 1999 were $1.02 billion). While illegal imports from India were somewhat higher than legal imports, Bangladesh's exports to India through unofficial channels are estimated to be several times higher than its official exports. The above study estimated unofficial exports from Bangladesh to India to be $250.0 million in 1997 while exports through official channels in 1999 were $50.0 million. The commodity composition of illegal imports from India into Bangladesh changed in the 1990s. The top five informal imports from India in 1993/94 were cattle, cotton saree fabric, sugar, pulses, and fish. In 1997/98, the top five informal imports from India were cattle, wrappers, cotton saree fabric, silk saree fabric, and rice.

The main incentive for informal imports from India lies in border price differentials, which have been declining because of trade liberalization in the two countries but are still high enough to provide incentives for illegal trade. Some factors that have been identified for the persistence of

**Table 4.14 Major Commodities Imported by Bangladesh from East Asia
and South Asia in 2004**

Country	Major export commodities			
East Asia				
China, People's Republic of	vehicles & transport equipment value[a] = $24.63 share[b] = 2.13% Products of chemical or allied industries value[a] = $132.94 share[b] = 11.52%	machinery & mechanical appliances value[a] = $265.55 share[b] = 23.01%	base metals & articles of base metal value[a] = $40.14 share[b] = 3.48%	textiles & textile articles value[a] = $546.69 share[b] = 47.37%
Hong Kong, China	mineral products value[a] = $22.42 share[b] = 4.27%	textiles & textile articles value[a] = $315.63 share[b] = 60%	machinery & mechanical appliances value[a] = $17.71 share[b] = 3.37%	
Japan	products of chemical or allied industries value[a] = $18.90 share[b] = 3.59%	base metals & articles of base metal value[a] = $99.72 share[b] = 18.93%	vehicles & transport equipment value[a] = $210.64 share[b] = 38.27%	
Korea, Republic of	plastics, rubber & articles thereof value[a] = $40.44 share[b] = 9.38% machinery & mechanical appliances value[a] = $65.85 share[b] = 15.28%	paper & paperboard value[a] = $66.16 share[b] = 15.35%	textiles & textile articles value[a] = $130.35 share[b] = 30.24%	base metals & articles of base metal value[a] = $70.98 share[b] = 16.47%
Malaysia	animal or vegetable fats and oils value[a] = $108.15 share[b] = 41.50%	textiles & textile articles value[a] = $33.38 share[b] = 12.81%	plastics, rubber & articles thereof value[a] = $24.37 share[b] = 9.35%	products of chemical or allied industries value[a] = $19.50 share[b] = 7.48%
Singapore	animal or vegetable fats and oils value[a] = $143.45 share[b] = 15.37% vehicles & transport equipment value[a] = $69.15m share[b] = 7.45%	mineral products value[a] = $309.26 share[b] = 33%	products of chemical or allied industries value[a] = $56.45 share[b] = 6.05%	Machinery & mechanical appliances value[a] = $128.81 share[b] = 13.80%

continued on next page

Table 4.14 (continued)

Country	Major export commodities			
Taipei,China	plastics, rubber & articles thereof value[a] = $33.19 share[b] = 8.47%	textiles & textile articles value[a] = $217.05 share[b] = 55.40%	machinery & mechanical appliances value[a] = $72.58 share[b] = 18.53%	
South Asia				
India	vegetable products value[a] = $518.70 share[b] = 31.39%	prepared foodstuff value[a] = $106.43 share[b] = 6.44%	mineral products value[a] = $145.96 share[b] = 8.83%	products of chemical or allied industries value[a] = $132.75 share[b] = 8.03%
	plastics, rubber & articles thereof value[a] = $68.07 share[b] = 4.12% vehicles & transport equipment value[a] = $91.83 share[b] = 5.56%	textiles & textile articles value[a] = $253.75 share[b] = 15.36%	base metals & articles of base metal value[a] = $88.94 share[b] = 5.38%	machinery & mechanical appliances value[a] = $138.37 share[b] = 8.37%

[a] Value is in millions of US dollars.
[b] Percentage share in total bilateral trade.

Source: Calculated from Bangladesh Bank (BB) data.

border price differentials are restrictive trade policy, overvalued exchange rate, demand for mass consumption goods, high transaction cost in official trade, and productivity differences.

Only a limited number of commodities are illegally exported to India from Bangladesh. Of these, gold is the most important item. Other informal exports include video cassette recorders, other electronic items, synthetic yarn, textiles, copper, and brass. All of these are imported at lower rates of duty than India's, then illegally exported to India. Indigenous items in the informal export basket have included fish, cow hides, jute, fabric woven with imported synthetic yarn, and fertilizer. Nontariff barriers (NTBs) in India (such as the high costs of documentation, wide variations in the method of assessment of duties, and other factors) along with factors such as inadequate physical infrastructure at the border checkpoints, lack of transit rights, high landed cost, and lack of financial infrastructure have contributed to poor access to India Bangladeshi exports.

Summing up the discussion in this section, it is observed that exports of Bangladesh to both East Asia and South Asia have declined over time, the decline being larger in the former case. Factors which are likely to have caused a fall in exports to East Asia include (i) a loss of competitive advantage of Bangladesh's exports; (ii) a very narrow range of export items, which prevented the possibility of increasing some exports to compensate for declining demand for other exports; and (iii) the growth of regionalism in East Asia. With regard to Bangladeshi exports to South Asia, it is important to note that India has been the major export market, with exports to other South Asian countries being small (negligible for some, such as Bhutan). Similarities in comparative advantage and weak trade complementarities have constrained the growth of Bangladesh's exports to this region. Bangladesh's exports to South Asia recorded a small increase in the second half of the 1990s after the implementation of SAPTA in 1995, but declined subsequently. The reasons for this decline, as is well documented in the literature on SAPTA, included (i) often meaningless tariff preferences being exchanged on products that had little relevance to actual trade; (ii) stringent rules of origin requirements that were difficult for the least developed country (LDC) members to meet; (iii) relatively long negative lists; (iv) stringent product standards; and (v) most importantly, NTBs. Some of these factors had a constraining effect particularly on Bangladesh's exports to India. Also, the narrow range of Bangladesh's export commodities acted as a serious barrier to the growth of its exports to South Asia.

Imports of Bangladesh have increased from both East and South Asia. An important reason behind this is the import liberalization policy undertaken quite vigorously in Bangladesh during the 1990s, particularly the first half of that decade. Another important factor was the acceleration of industrial growth in Bangladesh during the 1990s, particularly stemming from the garments industry. As Table 4.14 shows clearly, much of the imports were industrial inputs, particularly those required by the expanding export-oriented garment industry, as well as pharmaceuticals, plastics, and metal products.

Import Protection

Considering Bangladesh's trade policy, as indicated earlier, Bangladesh adopted trade policy reform in the mid-1980s with the aim of accelerating exports by reducing the economy's anti-export bias. Reforms consisted of liberalizing and rationalizing the tariff structure, eliminating quantitative restrictions and other nontariff and paratariff barriers to imports, and introducing direct export promotion measures.

The average tariff rate and the number of tariff bands have been reduced over time. There were 18 tariff bands in 1990/91, ranging from 0% to 350%; the number of tariff slabs was brought down to four in 2004/05, ranging from 0% to 25%. To simplify the tariff structure, operative and statutory tariff rates have been equalized since 2001/02. Both the weighted and unweighted tariff rates have been reduced; as Table 4.15 shows, the unweighted average customs duty rate has been brought down from 47.4%

Table 4.15 Average Rate of Customs Duty, %

Fiscal year	Unweighted average	Import-weighted average
1992/93	47.4	23.6
1993/94	36.0	24.1
1994/95	25.9	20.8
1995/96	22.3	17.0
1996/97	21.5	18.0
1997/98	20.7	16.0
1998/99	20.3	14.1
1999/2000	19.5	13.8
2000/01	18.6	15.1
2001/02	17.1	9.7
2002/03	16.5	12.4
2003/04	15.6	11.5
2004/05	13.5	9.6

% = percent.

Note: This data was reported in the Government of Bangladesh's Report by Bangladesh for World Trade Organization's Trade Policy Review of Bangladesh in September 2006.

Source: National Board of Revenue, Ministry of Finance.

in 1992/93 to 13.5% in 2004/05, while the import-weighted average duty rate came down from 23.6% to 9.6% during this time. As shown in Table 4.16, the tariff structure is still cascading in nature, with higher tariffs imposed on final consumer goods and lower tariffs on capital goods, raw materials, and intermediate inputs. The rate of tariff decline has also been fastest for capital goods, which is understandable given Bangladesh's heavy dependence on imported capital goods. Tariffs for consumer goods have been brought down significantly. According to estimates from the WTO, the simple average applied tariff rate declined significantly from 58% in 1992/93 to 22.2% in 1999/2000 (WTO 2000).

Import tariffs by product are shown in Table 4.17. Some important features of Bangladesh's tariff regime may be noted. First, the bound tariff rates have been kept at high levels compared to the applied rates. This gives rise to a fear of backsliding in the ongoing process of tariff liberalization. Ideally, the bound rates should be low and close to the applied tariff rates to demonstrate a country's commitment to tariff reform. Second, industrial tariffs are generally higher than agricultural tariffs, reflecting the Government's intention to protect import-substituting manufacturing industries. For example, rice is grown on 75% of the country's cultivable land but attracts a tariff rate of 5%. The following tariff rates are set: 25% on dairy products, 21% on textiles, 25% on wearing apparel, 81%

Table 4.16 Average Rate of Customs Duty by Type of Commodity, %

Fiscal Year	1999/ 2000		2000/ 01		2001/ 02		2002/ 03		2003/ 04		2004/ 05		2005/ 06		2006/ 07	
Commodity Classification	UW	W	UW	W	UW	W	UW	W	UW	W	UW	W	UW	W	UW	W
Primary goods	15.6	13.6	15.7	14.9	20.1	9.43	20.98	11.92	19.90	11.28	17.61	8.99	17.8	6.9	16.6	4.7
Intermediate goods	17.1	15.1	17.7	15.0	15.6	16.18	14.89	15.86	14.44	15.12	12.46	12.72	12.2	9.3	10.6	8.4
Capital goods	16.1	9.9	11.3	10.4	7.0	3.26	8.03	7.97	7.85	6.42	7.28	5.22	7.5	5.2	6.2	4.3
Final consumer goods	31.0	16.5	29.6	20.3	26.0	13.96	22.94	11.72	21.27	10.68	18.22	15.08	18.1	13.4	17.2	13.0

UW = unweighted average, W = weighted average, % = percent.

Source: National Board of Revenue (NBR), Ministry of Finance.

on petroleum products, and 49% on electronic equipment. This feature of Bangladesh's tariff regime is also observed in Table 4.16. Third, the percentage of bound tariff lines is higher for agricultural products compared to industrial products, reflecting the Government's intention to raise tariffs on certain industrial products in the future, if and when the need arises. It is interesting to note that only 3% of tariff lines are bound for textiles and paper products, and 5% for chemical, rubber, and plastic products even through there are large imports of these products. Perhaps the political influence wielded by owners of these industries contributes to the relatively high tariff rates and the very low proportion of bound tariff rates for these industries.

Tariff reforms reduced nominal protection from 89% in 1990/91 to 17% in 2002/03. However, NTBs and relatively high tariff dispersion have nullified much of the liberalizing effect of tariff reform. In addition to customs duties, other taxes and charges are applied to imports (e.g., supplementary duty, infrastructure development surcharge, VAT, and advanced VAT [AVAT] at the rate of 1.5% since 1 September 2004). When these taxes and charges are imposed on imports in addition to customs duty, the commodity concerned ends up with substantial protection since none of these taxes is applied in a trade-neutral manner.[10]

Effective protection rates (EPRs) for different sectors and products have been calculated by the World Bank (1999), the WTO (2000), and Bangladesh Tariff Commission (BTC) (2001). The overall level of EPR has

[10] Rashid (2005) has shown that in the case of an imported product that is subject to the highest customs duty rate of 25% (typical of many imported consumer goods), the nominal protection rate increases from 25% when customs tariff is the only protective instrument used to 108% when paratariff measures are combined with tariff protection.

163

**Table 4.17 Import Tariffs by Product in Bangladesh, Trade Year 2004;
Tariff Year 2006**

GTAP sector number	GTAP sector description	Bound rate (trade weighted)	MFN rate (trade weighted)	Imports value ($ '000)	Tariff lines	% of tariff lines that are bound
01	PDR - Paddy rice	175.89	5.04	4,977	2	100.00
02	WHT - Wheat	15.00	6.00	249,037	2	100.00
03	GRO - Cereal grains n.e.c.	200.00	0.92	45,030	10	100.00
04	V_F - Vegetables, fruits, nuts	155.08	12.17	232,047	91	91.30
05	OSD - Oil seeds	154.72	0.52	79,714	19	100.00
06	C_B - Sugar cane, sugar beet	0.00	0.00	0	1	100.00
07	PFB - Plant-based fibers	199.96	0.03	566,589	4	57.14
08	OCR - Crops n.e.c.	192.32	20.42	53,263	65	98.39
09	CTL - Bovine cattle, sheep and goats, horses	165.82	5.51	1,380	9	100.00
10	OAP - Animal products n.e.c.	150.76	11.84	6,105	58	94.00
12	WOL - Wool, silkworm cocoons	126.17	3.83	370	7	100.00
13	FRS - Forestry	193.12	6.02	46,736	15	58.33
14	FSH - Fishing	200.00	24.3	592	4	6.82
15	COA - Coal	na	13.00	53,339	0	0.00
16	OIL - Oil	na	6.00	76,071	0	0.00
17	GAS - Gas	na	0.00	0	0	0.00
18	OMN - Minerals n.e.c.	25.00	10.53	58,352	1	1.08
19	CMT - Bovine meat prods	40.96	24.49	945	32	100.00
20	OMT - Meat products n.e.c.	196.95	7.43	1,301	33	67.35
21	VOL - Vegetable oils and fats	199.99	5.60	538,955	57	100.00
22	MIL - Dairy products	113.94	24.97	65,737	20	83.33
23	PCR - Processed rice	200.00	6.00	136,399	2	100.00
24	SGR - Sugar	199.97	25.00	108,719	7	100.00
25	OFD - Food products n.e.c.	199.88	10.85	88,317	217	74.81
26	B_T - Beverages and tobacco products	200.00	25.00	8,138	31	100.00
27	TEX - Textiles	193.35	21.16	1,546,775	20	3.28
28	WAP - Wearing apparel	na	24.83	117,329	0	0.00
29	LEA - Leather products	na	15.50	13,942	0	0.00
30	LUM - Wood products	50.00	22.40	12,182	10	10.31
31	PPP - Paper products, publishing	29.95	16.92	208,539	5	3.27
32	P_C - Petroleum, coal products	na	81.06	538,903	0	0.00
33	CRP - Chemical, rubber, plastic products	64.36	10.70	1,069,392	61	4.95
34	NMM - Mineral products n.e.c.	50.00	337.48	186,636	1	0.61
35	I_S - Ferrous metals	50.00	10.92	306,862	2	0.93
36	NFM - Metals n.e.c.	15.00	10.48	139,690	3	1.62
37	FMP - Metal products	27.47	15.51	56,135	11	4.93
38	MVH - Motor vehicles and parts	na	17.90	182,248	0	0.00
39	OTN - Transport equipment n.e.c.	8.65	794.34	345,784	17	19.05
40	ELE - Electronic equipment	48.67	39.81	263,947	7	5.04
41	OME - Machinery and equipment n.e.c.	30.21	6.20	1,074,283	36	4.06
42	OMF - Manufactures n.e.c.	50.0	16.93	52,203	1	0.56

GTAP = Global Trade Analysis Project, MFN = most favored nation, na = not available, n.e.c. = not elsewhere classified, $ = US dollar, % = percent.

Note: Data is from Trade Analysis and Information System (TRAINS) of the United Nations Conference on Trade and Development (UNCTAD). Specific tariffs have been converted to ad valorem equivalents.

declined from 93% in 1992/93 to 45% in 1995/96. However, EPRs varied widely among sectors, with manufacturing sectors by and large receiving more protection than agricultural products. According to the WTO (2000), the export-oriented textiles and clothing sectors, as well as processed food and tobacco products, are accorded relatively high levels of protection, whereas protection is negligible for chemical fertilizers and pharmaceuticals. BTC (2001) estimates of EPRs for highly export-oriented firms were considerably lower than those for nonexport-oriented firms. Textiles, apparel, and leather processing were found to receive relatively little effective protection.

The coverage of all quantitative restrictions was brought down from 15.6% of four-digit tariff headings in 1991 to 5.1% in 2003. For trade-related quantitative restrictions, the coverage declined from 6.4% of four-digit tariff headings in 1991 to 1.9% in 2003.[11] The Import Policy (2003–06) proposed to slash the number of items covered by quantitative restrictions by almost half but also added many procedural restrictions, thus leaving in place many trade-related quantitative restrictions (World Bank 2004).

There are other NTBs as well. While import licenses are not required for any imports, for instance, prior permission is required for any import in excess of $5,000. Moreover, in addition to the standard letter of credit authorization import procedure, a permit, clearance, or prior permission may be required for a number of imported products. An import permit is required from the Chief Controller of Imports and Exports (CCIE) in certain cases. All importers are required to register with the CCIE (except for enterprises located in EPZs). Some categories of restricted items can be imported only by registered industrial consumers. Many of the clearance requirements for items on the restricted list are, however, based on health and safety grounds. In addition to a letter of credit, a private importer requires six to seven documents such as proof of membership in a trade association.

Exclusive importing rights or state trading constitutes another NTB in some cases. The Trading Corporation of Bangladesh (TCB) has the exclusive right to import salt and exclusive substances (Harmonized System Code [HS] 36.01 to 36.04) for commercial use. The import of salt and sugar is usually banned except in case of shortage. The Bangladesh Sugar and Food Industries Corporation (BSFIC) is the exclusive importer of sugar.

There are also shipping restrictions. All shipments of imported goods are required to use Bangladeshi flag vessels, except shipments of up to 20 tons (t) for an individual, shipments up to 10 t for a group of importers, and for imports by export-oriented industries.

There are 1,612 standards in Bangladesh of which about 8% are compulsory. Testing and certification procedures for compulsory standards,

---

[11] The nontrade-related quantitative restrictions are based on religious, social, environmental, and health grounds.

however, are the same for domestic and imported products. There is no laboratory accreditation scheme in Bangladesh. However, there are some multinational companies operating in Bangladesh whose certificates are accepted in the country. Bangladesh does not as yet participate in any bilateral mutual recognition agreements with its trading partners in the areas of standards, testing, or certification.

There are detailed labeling and packaging requirements that have to be fulfilled by all importers. For example, imports of milk food with fat content and baby food must be packed in tin containers; imported nonfat dried milk must be packaged in bags or tins.

Sanitary certificates and radioactivity test certificates are required for imports of food and edible products. The Bangladesh Atomic Energy Commission conducts radioactivity tests on samples upon arrival of food items and issues clearance certificates for release of the items by the customs authority. Foreign certifications of radioactivity tests are also accepted. All expenses incurred for the tests are borne by the importers.

Export Promotion

Bangladesh uses various measures to promote export growth. These are noted below.

Duty concessions on imported raw materials and intermediate inputs are provided for under different export promotion schemes. Under the Duty Drawback facility, 100% export-oriented firms are entitled to a refund of all duties and taxes paid on imported raw materials according to a flat rate determined by customs (using input-output tables). Under the Special Bonded Warehouse (SBW) scheme, exporting firms are authorized to import and stock under bond duty-free imports. Around 90% of users of the SBW facility are garments exporters and the rest are exporters of leather, toys, and jewelry. Firms operating in the EPZs are entitled to duty-free import of raw materials, capital machinery, and construction materials; they are also permitted to retain foreign exchange earnings.

Various tax concessions are also provided to exporters. Export businesses enjoy rebates of up to 50% on their taxable incomes. Exporters of handicrafts and cottage industry products are exempted from payment of income tax from their export earnings. Rebates on VAT are provided for export-related services such as carriage and freight service and telephone communications. VAT on jute cloth and bags used in packing export goods is refundable.

There are three types of export finance available in Bangladesh. These are (i) pre-shipment financing in local currency by commercial banks, (ii) pre-shipment financing in foreign currency by commercial banks through the Export Development Fund, and (iii) back-to-back letter of credit facilities. There are four export insurance schemes that cover risk domestically and abroad. These are: (i) the Export Credit Guarantees (ECG) Scheme, used at the pre-shipment stage; (ii) ECGs used at the post-shipment stage; (iii) export payment risk policies (comprehensive guarantee); and (iv) whole turnover pre-shipment finance guarantees.

All the export promotion measures are general in nature and have not been explicitly designed to specifically promote trade with East Asian and South Asian countries. However, exporters to these two regions are nevertheless benefiting from the region-neutral export promotion measures.

Government Revenue Role of Tariffs

The Government of Bangladesh relies heavily on import tax for its revenue. Table 4.18 shows that since 2000, half of Government tax revenue has been obtained from taxes at the import level, which in turn is dominated by customs duties (27% share in total tax revenue). It is important to note that the share of income tax has on average been about 18%. The heavy dependence on trade taxes has slowed down the process of tariff liberalization during the second half of the 1990s, and has constrained tariff reform in general. This has also influenced Bangladesh's position in its bilateral and regional trade negotiations. Such a constraint can be relieved only by exploring other revenue sources and increasing other taxes such as the income tax and tax on domestic production and consumption. A determined effort is also needed to reduce inefficiency and corruption of its tax-collecting organ (i.e., the National Board of Revenue).

Tax policy reforms were introduced in the mid-1990s, and these have yielded some fruit in terms of marginal increases in the income tax-total

Table 4.18 Sources of Tax Revenue, % of total revenue

Type of Tax	2002/03	2003/04	2004/05	2005/06	2006/07
Import duty	28.2	27.1	26.4	24.4	23.8
VAT (at import level)	17.4	16.8	17.8	18.3	18.0
Supplementary duty (at import level)	5.4	6.4	6.2	5.1	3.5
Total import tax	51.0	50.3	50.4	47.8	45.3
Excise duty	1.3	0.6	0.5	0.6	0.6
VAT (local)	15.5	16.5	17.0	18.9	20.1
Supplementary duty (local)	13.3	13.5	12.3	14.4	13.0
Income tax	17.9	18.0	18.9	17.4	19.9
Other taxes and duties	1.0	1.1	0.8	0.8	0.9

VAT = value-added tax, % = percent.

Source: National Board of Revenue.

tax revenue ratio; clearly, the reform process has to be implemented much more vigorously so that the problem of massive tax evasion can be quickly overcome. Finally, this would call for addressing problems of a political economic nature that are adversely affecting collection of income tax and other domestic taxes. Thus, in the ultimate analysis, it is a governance challenge.

Regional Trade Agreements

Bangladesh is a member of several RTAs.[12] For each of these agreements, the approach to liberalization of trade in goods, coverage of the agreement, rules of origin (ROO) criteria, and a list of sensitive products are summarized below.

The Asia-Pacific Trade Agreement (APTA) is a preferential trading arrangement that began as the Bangkok Agreement in 1975 and was recently revised and renamed APTA. The member countries are Bangladesh, India, Sri Lanka, PRC, Republic of Korea, and Lao PDR. APTA came into force from 1 July 2006. The objective of the Bangkok Agreement was to promote economic development through trade cooperation among the developing member countries of the United Nations Economic and Social Commission for Asia and the Pacific (UNESCAP) through the adoption of mutually beneficial trade liberalization measures. Concessions are given in a phased manner through negotiations among members and set out in each member country's national list of concessions. LDCs are granted special tariff concessions. The agreement includes some standstill measures that require member states not to introduce or increase the incidence of customs duties and NTBs on products of current or potential export interest to other member states. Furthermore, appropriate measures for cooperation in customs administration and adoption of common tariff nomenclature as well as exchange of trade information are envisaged in the agreement. The agreement also provides for adoption of emergency safeguard measures and consultations in case of "serious injury" to specific sectors of a member state through a surge in imports from other member states. External tariffs with the rest of the world are not coordinated among member states, and there is no provision for investment cooperation. Three rounds of trade negotiations have been concluded, the latest one in 2004. Tariff concessions have been operational from 1 July 2006 under the revised agreement (signed in November 2005).

SAPTA came into existence in April 1993 and became operational in December 1995. The members of SAPTA are Bangladesh, Bhutan, India, Maldives, Nepal, Pakistan, and Sri Lanka. The basic instrument for trade

---

[12] Bangladesh has notified the World Trade Organization about its membership in these regional trade agreements.

liberalization in SAPTA has been the exchange of concessions relating to tariffs, paratariffs, nontariff measures, and direct trade measures. Various approaches to tariff liberalization—such as product-by-product liberalization, across-the-board tariff reductions, sectoral approaches, and direct measures—are allowed under the agreement. LDCs including Bangladesh, Bhutan, Maldives, and Nepal have been accorded special treatment (i.e., deeper concessions) by the non-LDCs (India, Pakistan, and Sri Lanka). The agreement allows for the temporary suspension of concessions in case of "serious difficulties" including balance of payments problems (primarily serious injury caused by import surge from other member countries). There are provisions for dispute settlement and consultations.

SAFTA became operational on 1 July 2006, superseding SAPTA. The long-term objective of SAFTA is to achieve free trade in South Asia by 2016. Across-the-board tariff reduction is to occur in two phases. In the first phase (1 July 2006–1 July 2008), non-LDCs (India, Pakistan, and Sri Lanka) will reduce their maximum tariff rates to 20%. In the second phase (1 July 2008–1 July 2013) they will reduce tariffs to 0–5% (2014 for Sri Lanka). Non-LDC members will reduce tariffs to 0–5% for exports from LDCs within 3 years of the agreement becoming operational. LDC members (Bangladesh, Bhutan, Nepal, and Maldives) will reduce maximum tariffs to 30% in the first phase (1 July 2006–1 July 2008), and to 0–5% in the second phase (1 July 2008 to 1 July 2016). The ROO include (i) a change in tariff heading of the final product at the four-digit and six-digit levels of the HS Code, (ii) minimum domestic value addition of 40% for non-LDC members and 30% for LDC members, and (iii) regional cumulation at specified rates. Separate sensitive lists for non-LDC and LDC members have been given by each member state. The sensitive lists appear to be relatively large. Bangladesh has identified 1,254 items as sensitive, while India has earmarked 763 goods; Pakistan 1,183 goods; Sri Lanka 1,065; Bhutan 157; Maldives 671; and Nepal 1,299. There is a provision for technical assistance and compensation for revenue losses to LDC members.

A framework agreement to form an FTA under BIMSTEC was concluded on 8 February 2004. The members of the BIMSTEC FTA are Bangladesh, Bhutan, India, Nepal, Sri Lanka, and Thailand. Parties to the framework agreement negotiated and concluded three agreements: (i) an Agreement on Trade in Goods, (ii) an Agreement on Trade in Services, and (iii) an Agreement on Investment. There are two tracks for tariff liberalization, fast and normal. For products included under the fast track, developing country members such as India, Sri Lanka, and Thailand will reduce or eliminate their applied most-favored nation (MFN) tariff rates to mutually agreed specified rates[13] between 1 July 2006 and 30 June 2009 for developing

---

[13]   Still under negotiation.

country partners, and between 1 July 2006 and 30 June 2007 for LDC partners (Bangladesh, Bhutan, Myanmar, and Nepal). For products on the normal track, the tariff liberalization time frame for developing country members (LDC members) is 1 July 2007 to 30 June 2012 for developing country members and 1 July 2007 to 30 June 2010 for LDC members mentioned above. Products on the negative list will not be subject to liberalization. It is envisaged that modalities for liberalizing NTBs and detailed procedures for safeguard measures and rules of origin will be established through future negotiations. The agreement also envisages investment cooperation, and trade liberalization in services with substantial sectoral coverage through a positive list approach. Other areas identified for future cooperation include trade facilitation in the areas of customs cooperation, standards and technical regulations, and technical assistance for capacity-building measures in LDC members (Bangladesh, Bhutan, Myanmar, and Nepal).

Bangladesh is also a member of two other RTAs—the D-8 Preferential Trade Agreement (popularly known as D-8) and the Trade Preferential System among the Organization of Islamic Conference (TPS-OIC). The D-8 PTA was established in 1997 by Bangladesh, Egypt, Indonesia, Iran, Malaysia, Nigeria, Pakistan, and Turkey. The group was formed to accelerate economic growth and development among member countries through enhanced cooperation. A framework agreement on trade preferential system among the members was signed in 1997. Negotiations have been completed for signing the PTA. A framework agreement on TPS-OIC was agreed in 1991. Only 23 of the OIC's 57 members signed the agreement. As of January 2004, 14 countries including Bangladesh have signed the framework agreement. Bangladesh signed the agreement in 1997 and ratified it in January 2004. Member countries have decided that tariffs would be reduced to agreed slabs (25%, 15%, and 10%) in four installments by developing country members and six installments by LDC members. Moreover, LDC members would be given 3-year grace period to implement tariff reductions. Table 4.19 summarizes the features of the major regional agreements of which Bangladesh is a member.

As far as the potential benefits of these agreements are concerned, the experience of SAPTA shows that while Bangladesh's imports from the South Asia region have increased, its exports actually declined. Two factors had primarily constrained export expansion from Bangladesh under SAPTA: (i) most of the tariff concessions offered by partner countries had little relevance to the pattern of actual or potential exports, and (ii) the potential trade-creating effect of preferential tariffs was largely negated by erection of various NTBs. The problem was compounded by a very narrow export basket of Bangladesh. The implication is that the extent of benefits derived by Bangladesh from SAFTA will be largely influenced by the

Table 4.19 Summary of Features of Regional Agreements of which Bangladesh is a Member

Name of agreement	Approach to liberalization of trade in goods	Coverage of agreement	Rules of origin (ROO)	Sensitive products
APTA	Providing other members concessions subject to conditions of origin; restrictions on trade reduced in phased manner; partial approach to liberalization; negative list; members whose economies are less developed are granted special concessions; refraining from introducing or increasing customs duties and nontariff import barriers on products of current or potential export interest to other members; scope for review and modification of national list of concessions.	Trade in goods; cooperation in customs administration; exchange of trade information.	Specific ROO requirements have to be fulfilled by a product to be eligible for preferential tariff treatment.	Products included on the negative list are excluded from tariff concessions.
SAFTA	Full, across-the-board tariff liberalization in two phases; negative list approach; less-developed members allowed more time for liberalization.	Trade in goods; provision to consider in the future adoption of trade facilitation and other measures to support and complement SAFTA.	Changes in tariff heading of the final product; minimum domestic value addition of 40% for non-LDC members and 30% for LDC member states; and regional cumulation at specified rates.	Tariff liberalization not applicable to tariff lines included in the sensitive list; separate sensitive lists for non-LDC and LDC member states given by each member state.
BIMSTEC	Progressive elimination of tariffs and nontariff barriers in substantially all trade in goods; fast track and normal track approaches to liberalization; negative list approach.	Trade in goods; trade in services; investment cooperation; and trade facilitation.	Being negotiated.	The number of products on the negative list will be subject to a maximum ceiling to be mutually agreed among member states.

APTA = Asia-Pacific Trade Agreement, BIMSTEC = Bay of Bengal Initiative for Multi-Sectoral Technical and Economic Cooperation, FTA = free trade agreement, LDC = least-developed country, SAFTA = South Asian Free Trade Agreement.

Source: Official texts of FTA.

following factors: (i) elimination of NTBs by partner countries; (ii) intra-regional investment flows that will enhance the export supply capability of Bangladesh; and (iii) improving connectivity in the subregion through developments of trade-related infrastructure and stronger trade facilitation measures.

Bangladesh's experience with the Bangkok Agreement (which later became the APTA) has been less than encouraging. There is data that shows that Bangladesh's exports to the Bangkok Agreement countries have declined over time. Imports have, however, increased from three partner countries: India, Republic of Korea, and PRC. The APTA has been energized with the accession of the PRC. The extent to which Bangladesh can benefit from this will depend mainly on how quickly it can develop new and competitive export items.

Infrastructure and Trade Administration

As conventional trade barriers are lowered, transaction costs related to transport, transit, nontariff measures, and customs procedures assume increasing importance. These transaction costs, which often exceed import tariffs, can be reduced through trade facilitation measures such as modernization of customs procedures and port infrastructure; harmonization of standards, technical regulations and regulatory requirements; simplification of trade-related administrative procedures and documents; and use of modern technology to exchange information efficiently and in a transparent manner.[14]

In the foregoing sections of this chapter, the tariff and NTBs to imports and the availability of trade finance in Bangladesh are discussed. In this section, how the lack of connectivity due to poor transport and infrastructure, problems of transit, and inefficiency of customs have acted as barriers to trade by raising transaction costs are examined.

Overview of Trade-Related Infrastructure

Bangladesh has an extensive transport system comprising 236,728 km of roads; 2,700 km of railways; 6,000 km of waterways; two major seaports (Chittagong and Mongla); three international airports; and nine domestic airports. Despite a high-density road network, poor road conditions and lack of transportation seriously impair economic activity. Poor construction of roads and bridges, lack of maintenance of roads and waterways, and

---

[14] Various studies show the large benefits to be derived from trade facilitation. Thus, a study by UNCTAD finds that a 1% reduction in the cost of maritime and air transport services could increase Asian GDP by $33.3 billion.

lack of integration of different modes of transportation make long-haul transport very difficult.

The road network consists of 3,086 km of national highways; 1,751 km of regional highways; 13,877 km of district roads; 35,582 km of subdistrict roads; 45,055 km of union roads; and 137,377 km of village roads. However, still there is inadequate transport to meet demand. The Government has implemented a strategic transport policy to create a more efficient transport system for passengers and freight over 30 years. The objective is to introduce an integrated multimodal transport system to ease interchange and reduce the transport costs of goods for export.

Chittagong Port is the largest seaport in Bangladesh, handling around 80% of seaborne merchandise imports and 75% of merchandise exports. The port is an integral part of the subregional transport and logistics chain connecting Bangladesh, northeastern India, Bhutan, and Nepal to Europe, North America, and Southeast Asia. The port is plagued with labor problems, poor management, and lack of equipment. The cargo yards are severely congested as containers are filled and emptied in port, and cargo handling equipment is often out of commission for want of spare parts.

Unsatisfactory conditions at Chittagong Port are because of a host of factors. The port's container terminal, for instance, handles only 100–105 lifts per berth a day, well below the United Nations Conference on Trade and Development (UNCTAD) productivity standard of 230 lifts a day. While the port's capacity is to handle 0.2 million 20-foot equivalent units (TEUs) per year, it handled 0.69 million TEUs in 2004. Ship turnaround time is 5–9 days, significantly above the 1-day standard of more efficient ports. Handling charges for a 20-foot container have been estimated at $640 (of which $250 is for unofficial tolls) compared to $220 in Colombo and $360 in Bangkok. Customs procedures at the port require more documents and hence take longer time than at other regional ports. Results of surveys show that Bangladeshi firms reported an average 11.7 days to get their shipment of goods through customs, compared to 3.4 days in Malaysia, 7.5 days in the PRC and India, and 10.2 days in the Philippines.

Presently Bangladesh has prioritized improving the operation and security of Chittagong Port. In 2003, a project was launched to build a new container terminal to increase port capacity. While this project was expected to be completed by 2005, the work has not yet been completed as of this writing.

With adequate infrastructure, the Chittagong Port would be able to handle another 500,000 TEUs. The Chittagong Port Authority states that the container handling capacity of the port is 200,000 TEUs, but current volume exceeds its capacity by three times. With the construction of the new infrastructure, the annual container handling capacity would substantially increase and the cargo handling capacity would quadruple.

The Asian Development Bank (ADB) also sanctioned a loan of $31 million in 2004 to increase the efficiency and security of the Chittagong Port. The objectives of this project are (i) installation of a computer-based system for managing container terminal operations and documents processing, (ii) improvements to internal traffic circulation, (iii) construction of an oil waste management facility, (iv) activation of the Automated System for Customs Data (ASYCUDA)++ management system linked to the Chittagong Port Authority's computer system, (v) installation of container scanners needed to meet new security initiatives, and (v) construction of an access-controlled link from the ADB-funded port access road to the container terminals.

Mongla Port is the second seaport situated in southwestern Bangladesh at the confluence of the River Passur and Mongla, about 131 km upstream from the Bay of Bengal. The port is well protected by the natural mangrove forest of the Sunderbans. Basically, the entire western part of Bangladesh is its hinterland and neighboring countries of Bhutan, Nepal, and border areas of India are also considered Mongla Port's natural hinterlands.

Although Mongla Port has greater capacity to handle larger shipments than does Chittagong Port, the absence of regular dredging has made the channel almost inaccessible for oceangoing vessels. The port, in fact, often remains closed. Anecdotal evidence points to the fact that the port is under the threat of falling idle as fewer and fewer ships berth there.

To ease the movement of import and export items through land ports, the Government of Bangladesh has declared 13 land customs depots along Bangladesh's borders with India, Nepal, and Myanmar as land ports. These are Akhawra, Banglabandha, Benapole, Bhomra, Bibirbazar, Birol, Burimari, Darshana, Haluaghat, Hili, Sonamasjid, Tamabil, and Teknaf. The Government established the Bangladesh Land Port Authority in 2001 to manage cargo handling at land ports.

The Bangladesh Land Port Authority has taken steps to develop five land ports—Banglabandha, Bibirbazar, Birol, Hili, and Sonamasjid—through private operators. Benapole, through which more than 80% of official bilateral trade between Bangladesh and India takes place, is among the better-developed land ports in Bangladesh. It has about 18.2 hectares (ha) of land that house 30 godowns (warehouses) with capacity for 21,500 t of cargo. Its truck terminal can accommodate 1,000 trucks. It may be noted that in the case of Petrapole on the Indian side, there has been little development of infrastructure, resulting in long queues for crossing the border and hampering Bangladesh's exports to India.

The development of the land port at Benapole, however, has not solved all the problems related to trade facilitation. Rather than encouraging the movement of cargo to a location close to the final destination where the customs formalities can be completed, customs reportedly creates delays at the border. Recent studies have shown that at Benapole–Petrapole the cumulative loss of time in (i) loading at the point of origin in India, (ii) transportation, (iii) unloading at Benapole, (iv) parking, (v) customs, (vi) crossing the border, and (vii) reloading, is 99 hours as against the ideal time of 29.6 hours.

Customs Procedures

Since the early 1990s, Bangladesh has taken a number of steps to improve its customs administration and customs clearance procedures. In 1992, under a project funded by the World Bank ASYCUDA was introduced at Dhaka Customs House and partially at Chittagong customs.[15] Further initiatives were taken in 1999 to streamline and automate the customs clearance procedures under the Customs Administration Modernization (CAM) project also funded by the World Bank. ASYCUDA has since been installed at five major customs houses: Dhaka and Chittagong customs houses, the Dhaka inland container depot, Mongla customs house, and Benapole customs house.

Bangladesh introduced the pre-shipment inspection (PSI) system of customs valuation and made it mandatory in February 2001. The designated PSI agent is responsible for certifying the price, quantity, and HS Code designation of an imported product. This has considerably reduced the import clearance time and the harassment faced by importers. With the introduction of the PSI system, physical inspection of consignments has been reduced from 100% in 1999 to around 10% at present. It has also simplified inspection procedures and reduced the average time to clear cargo that has proper documentation from 10 days to 5 days (World Bank 2005).

Import clearance procedures have likewise been simplified by reducing the number of signatures required for clearance of import and export consignments and cutting down the frequency of inspection of the consignments. The number of signatures required for clearing an import shipment has been reduced from 25 to 5 in 2002. Average processing time for clearance of goods has also been reduced to 1–3 days for imports and 3–8 hours for exports; at present, only 10% of import consignments are inspected (World Bank 2005b).

The Customs Act has been amended, and a single administrative document covering export and import has been developed. However, more changes

---

[15] Automated System for Customs Data (ASYCUDA) is a computerized customs management system developed by UNCTAD that covers most foreign trade procedures. The system handles manifests, customs declarations, accounting procedures, and transit and suspense procedures.

are required to make customs procedures more efficient. An electronic monitoring system needs to be developed. Also, for speedy customs clearance of goods, it is essential to shift from the transaction-based process to a process that uses risk management and post-clearance audit.

Cumbersome customs documentation and inspection procedures cause delays in border crossing (Table 4.20). This is a problem not only with Bangladesh but South Asia as a whole. Each country requires different documents such as transit export and import declarations. Exporters must prepare separate documents at each side of the border. Furthermore, the region uses different classification systems for commodities. This leads to a lack of transparency and problems in product classification in trade. There are also other administrative problems that slow down border crossing.

The present status of trade facilitation measures in Bangladesh is shown in Table 4.21.

Table 4.20 Border Documentation in South Asia

Border Point	Documents
India to Bangladesh	For India customs: Customs export declaration, bill of lading, invoices, packing lists, letter of credit For Bangladesh customs: Importer passbook, and for goods destined for export processing zones bonded warehouse license, risk and duty bond
Nepal to India	For Nepal customs: Customs export declaration; duty insurance certificate; invoice; packing list; certificate of origin; certificates of registration (income tax, value-added tax, corporate tax); letter of credit For India customs: customs transit document, duty insurance, invoice, packing list, letter of credit, certificate of origin
Bangladesh to Nepal	For Bangladesh customs: Export registration certificate, invoice, letter of credit, packing list, certificate of origin, truck receipt For Nepal customs: Customs import declaration, invoice, packing list, certificate of origin, import license, letter of credit, health/quarantine certificate, equipment interchange receipt, and duty insurance coverage for containers
Bangladesh ports	Exports: export bill of entry, invoice, packing list, export permit, undertaking by company of export of outpass statement on letterhead, risk bond
India ports	Imports: customs transit declaration, bill of lading, invoice, packing list, certificate of origin, import license, letter of credit, health/quarantine certificate, equipment interchange receipt and duty insurance coverage for containers Exports: customs transit document

Source: U. Subramaniam and J. Arnold (2001).

Table 4.21 Summary of Trade Facilitation Measures in Bangladesh

Area	Status
Single Administrative Document (SAD)	Introduced in 1994 with the introduction of the Automated System for Customs Data (ASYCUDA) Computerized Customs Declaration Processing System.
Harmonized Code	Introduced in 1988. Last updated in 2002. Bangladesh is a signatory to the convention.
Electronic data processing (EDP) systems	Customs declarations and payments are processed under EDP through ASYCUDA, developed by UNCTAD and used in more than 80 countries. Four major customs stations—Chittagong, Dhaka (covering both the Kamalapur inland container depot and the airport), Benapole, and Mongla—operate ASYCUDA live. Other land customs stations operate on a post-entry basis.
	ASYCUDA is being continually upgraded and the last such major upgrade was made in 2002. National Board of Revenue (NBR) is in the process of upgrading it further by migrating from ASYCUDA++ version to ASYCUDA World, which is Windows-based, more user-friendly, and runs on a more secure operating system (Linux).
Electronic data interchange (EDI)	Currently no system of electronic submission of manifest is in place. A project has been undertaken, under an Asian Development Bank loan, to activate the manifest module of ASYCUDA. This will enable shipping agents to submit their manifests electronically. The system is expected to be in place by the end of 2007.
Direct trader input	Introduced in 2002. Currently all declarations relating to exports and all imports of 100%-export–oriented garment factories are processed under direct trader input. Imports of garments factories constitute almost 60% of total import declarations.
	Process is underway to bring the other remaining commercial imports under direct trader input shortly.
Internet input	No provision to submit declarations through the internet. NBR is actively working to launch remote direct trader input to enable consignees to submit declarations through the internet.
Green channel	Provisions are in place but not yet activated. Initially, major export-oriented garment industries were to be given this facility. Accordingly, a list of factories with clean track records was sought from Bangladesh Garments Manufactures and Exporters Association (BGMEA) which is yet to be provided.
	Risk management is being applied as a basis for targeting.

continued on next page

Table 4.21 (continued)

Area	Status
Risk management	Currently, most of the commercial imports are imported under the Pre Shipment Inspection (PSI) regime. Under the current regulations, pre-shipment inspection (PSI) agencies are to certify, through a document called the Clean Report of Findings (CRF), the commercial description, quality, quantity, HS Code designation, and transaction value. Customs authorities carry out the assessment in line with the CRF. Only 10% of the issued CRFs are manually selected for inspection on a random basis.

For consignments not falling under PSI, risk management is applied. Selectivity parameters are determined by a group of senior customs officers and are fed into the computer system. The range of consignments to be selected for inspection varies from 5% to 10%. |
| Electronic banking | Not yet implemented.

A task force, comprising experts from Central Bank, major commercial banks, and NBR, is working on a needs assessment to develop a common platform for connecting banks and customs houses through electronic transactions. |
| Electronic signature | Although the Assessed Bill of Entry (approved declarations) and its corresponding assessment notice (notice showing amount of duties and taxes to be paid) and release order (printed as soon as the payment is made effective) are system-generated, a signature is issued by the concerned clerks in charge of those sections. This is not required by any regulation but is practiced to prevent document forgery. |
| Private-bonded warehouses | NBR has approved a policy for storing imported cargos in private-bonded warehouses instead of at ports. The consignments can directly be removed from the port area's hook point under customs bond to private-bonded warehouses near (20 km maximum) the port. These goods can be subsequently released after customs assessment and payment of duties and taxes. This scheme has yet to be implemented as the necessary infrastructure (ASYCUDA connectivity, security arrangements, handling equipment, etc.) has not been developed.

However, edible oil and petroleum oil are currently enjoying such facilities. Consignments are directly released from the oil tankers through pipelines to private-bonded tankers near the jetty. |
| Bonded factories | All 100%-export–oriented garments and accessories-manufacturing enterprises, irrespective of their locations, enjoy bond facilities. No duties or taxes are applied at any stage of their import, processing, or subsequent export. |

continued on next page

Table 4.21 (continued)

Area	Status
	Selected heavy industries (steel, edible oil, sugar, etc.) and manufacturing products for home consumption are also enjoying the bond facility for its liquidity support. These entities import their raw materials duty-free under home consumption bond facilities while clearing them from the ports. The taxes due are paid when the raw materials are moved from the warehouse to the factory floor. The duties are paid in accordance with the quantity removed from the warehouse.
	All factories must use their raw materials under bond facility within a limited time period. Generally, this time period is 1 year, but this varies depending on the nature of the product in question.

UNCTAD = United Nations Conference on Trade and Development.

Source: National Board of Revenue (NBR).

Trade Transport Corridors of Bangladesh

The two major transport corridors that play important roles in Bangladesh's international trade are the ones that connect Dhaka with the Port of Chittagong and with West Bengal in India. Other corridors are Bangladesh's connections with northeastern India, and with Bhutan and Nepal.[16]

Chittagong–Dhaka Corridor

The Chittagong–Dhaka corridor, Bangladesh's principal transport corridor, provides potential subregional links to northeast India, via the Jamuna Bridge to West Bengal, and to Bhutan and Nepal through India. Because of its strategic location, Bangladesh can play a significant role in the subregional transport system by providing direct and shorter transport links by rail, water, and road. Chittagong Port can be the gateway to promote trade in the region. Development of the inland distribution system by road, rail, and inland water transport will help accelerate export-led growth in Bangladesh and the integration of Bangladesh's economy with those in northeastern South Asia. The upgrade of the Chittagong Port infrastructure is particularly important from the perspective of subregional cooperation of Bangladesh with the states of eastern India.

The primary mode for freight movements on the Chittagong–Dhaka corridor is road transport, which faces major bottlenecks. The road con-

---

[16] The analysis of these is based on Kumar and Mukherjee (2006); in this study, field surveys were conducted in Bangladesh, Nepal, and West Bengal.

necting Dhaka and Chittagong is a combination of two-lane and four-lane segments. At present, medium-sized trucks (7–10 t in payload) operate over two-lane asphalt roads (5.5 meters wide) at relatively low average speeds. The result is relatively low distance coverage—of 200–400 km per day. This causes frequent congestion, with transit times of 6–7 hours, implying an average travel speed of 35–40 km/hr.

Semitrailers are rare on this corridor because of their costs, poor road conditions, congestion, and weight limits on the bridges. Most of the vehicles used for transporting goods are trucks with four and six fixed axles. Despite traffic congestion and other problems, roadways still account for more than 80% of the total cargo moving between Dhaka and Chittagong. The containers that arrive at Chittagong are unpacked and transported in break-bulk in small trucks to Dhaka. The reason for this anomaly is high rail freight charges. It takes almost 8 hours for a container to travel from Chittagong to Dhaka by rail, while roadways transport vehicles travel within 4.5–5 hours.

The cost difference between rail and road for container traffic between Chittagong and Dhaka has to be compared. A shipper who books a container delivery to the Dhaka inland container depot has to pay the shipping line an extra $350 for a 20-foot container or $550 for a 40-foot container for Chittagong–Dhaka movement by rail. Of this, Bangladesh Railway charges only $120–180 for a 20-foot container (depending on the quantity of cargo) and $200 for a 40-foot container. Despite claiming high charges, Bangladesh Railway does not guarantee the safety of goods on this route. Truckers, by contrast, charge $80–100 for an amount of break-bulk cargo equivalent to a 20-foot container load. Since the cost difference is very high, the shippers and exporters prefer to transport goods in break-bulk and unload at Chittagong Port.

The rail line between Dhaka and Chittagong is mainly single meter-gauge track, although the segment between Dhaka and Tongi is dual gauge. In Bangladesh, railways (which are publicly operated) continue to suffer from overstaffing, poor maintenance, and old rolling stock, as well as poor utilization of equipment. There is also a significant problem with track maintenance, especially in areas prone to flooding. Rail traffic has been declining in both relative and absolute terms. Between 1974/75 and 1996/97, there has been a 40% decline in tonnage, and the market share of railways decreased to 7% of total tonnage.

Facilities at Chittagong Port are unsatisfactory, and poor port logistics is one of the major bottlenecks in enhancing Bangladesh's export competitiveness. Because of the relatively small volume of cargo handled and the distance between Chittagong and the major shipping routes, the main mother shipping vessels do not serve Chittagong Port. Goods are carried from the port in feeder vessels to either Singapore or Colombo to load, and then on to their mother vessels. The turnaround time for containers is high, discouraging shipping agents from sending containers to Bangladesh. Sometimes feeder vessels do not reach Chittagong Port directly because of congestion there. Feeder vessels may wait at the outer anchorage for 1–2 days before reaching the port (maximum waiting time is 72 hours). Delays are also caused by poor coordination between feeder and mother vessels. This results in average waiting time of a week in Singapore.

The transshipment of cargo from Chittagong to Singapore or Colombo port adds to the time and cost of trade. The rates and times for shipments to Europe and the US east coast are comparable to those for Viet Nam and the PRC (despite the greater distances) for cargo transshipped at Singapore. For transshipment to East Asia and Pacific countries, Bangladesh would be at a competitive disadvantage relative to the PRC and often to Viet Nam.

The problems of Chittagong Port are exacerbated by (i) labor shortages, (ii) frequent strikes, (iii) lack of requisite container services from the port, (iv) inefficient transportation from the port to other parts of the country because of poor roads, (v) poor railway service, (vi) periodic unavailability of containers, and (vii) lack of proper inland distribution of cargo from the port. There is a one-stop information facility at the port, but it is not sufficient to provide the requisite information to exporters and importers. Moreover, the adoption of manual processes, resulting from lack of computerization and automation in the port, makes the work slow and cumbersome. The port workers take "speed money" of 200–400 takas (Tk) ($3–6) per day. An estimated $30 has to be paid in speed money to various port functionaries to facilitate the process.

Dwelling time is 1 day for exports and 15–16 days for imports. Import clearance takes 4–5 days, while export clearance takes 4–5 hours. In Singapore, a vessel is cleared of goods in 6 hours, while vessel unloading takes about 72 hours in Chittagong because of lack of modern scientific instruments. Even shipments coming from Kolkata to Chittagong come through Singapore, taking about 15 days and costing about $1,800 per container. Using the shortest possible route to import would bring down the cost. This would require the building of proper infrastructure to support trade. The freight charges are also very high (almost 25–30% of the commodity price). A lack of warehouses can cause goods to pile up in the open air, creating numerous problems, particularly during the rainy season. There is congestion in the shipping yard as the number of berths at the port is inadequate.

West Bengal–Dhaka Corridor

The West Bengal–Dhaka corridor includes a route via Petrapole in India and Benapole in Bangladesh, and rail routes via Dorsana, Rohanpur, Benapole, and to a lesser extent Biral. The road infrastructure in this corridor suffers from some major drawbacks. Benapole, which is situated near the border with India (the other side of the border is Petrapole in India), is about 7 hours drive from Dhaka. The road is congested and the river bridges are narrow; as a result, only one vehicle at a time can move in a given direction. Moreover, the road is in bad condition as a result of poor maintenance. Even though there is a railway line from Benapole to Jessore, railway services are almost nonexistent due to lack of investment.

The land port facility at Benapole is operated by the Government. Although there are government warehouse facilities at the port, they are insufficient in number to meet demand. As a result, Indian trucks coming to Bangladesh to release goods get stranded in sheds and yards.

The total storing capacity of the Benapole land port is 31,650 t while about 6,000–7,000 t of goods are handled daily through the port. About 75% of the export and import handling work is carried out manually and only 25% is done with equipment. There is only one exit and entry route for the warehouse, which often results in congestion during the peak hours. The warehouses are small, so that it becomes difficult for other trucks to pass when one truck is being unloaded. It takes on an average 2 days to unload from an Indian truck and reload in a Bangladeshi truck in the warehouse. All these factors cause considerable delays.

To make Benapole port more functional, four more warehouses with 1,200 t of capacity are going to be built. Carriage and freight agents say that proper infrastructure at the port is lacking. The port lacks space and equipment for unloading and reloading, including warehouse facilities and separate terminals for loading and unloading trucks in warehouses. As a result, trucks are stranded in queues. Forklifts and other equipment are old, and most are out of order. Carriage and freight agents say it still requires 20–25 signatures for an import shipment and 7–8 for an export shipment. If pre-shipment inspection is done, then the consignments get customs clearance the next day, but for other consignments it takes 3–4 days to complete customs procedures. According to carriage and freight agents, an average of 200–300 trucks are processed for import and 100–150 trucks for export each day.

Bangladesh–Northeastern India Corridor

It is generally believed that because of geographical proximity, strategic position, close cultural and historical bond, and above all economic complementarities, there is huge potential for promoting trade and investment between Bangladesh and seven northeastern states of India. The seven state capitals are 1,080–1,680 km from the nearest Indian port city of Kolkata. These cities are much closer to Dhaka and Chittagong than they are to Kolkata. Also, this region is characterized by poor infrastructure and transport; consequently, transportation cost of goods to and from this region to rest of India and within the region is prohibitively higher than that of any strategic part of Bangladesh. The potential for beneficial trade and investment relations between Bangladesh and northeast India is undeniable.

However, the physical infrastructure necessary for facilitating trade between northeast India and Bangladesh (as well as Nepal and Bhutan) is largely absent. Indeed, it has been argued that the links are weaker today than they were at the time of partition of British India in 1947. The Stilwell Road is now a mere muddy track and the rail links with Bangladesh are severed. As a result, the transport cost of export and import between Bangladesh and India is much higher than in any other part of the world. A large part of trade, therefore, takes place through informal channels. One of the essential requirements to promote trade, investment, and tourism between the two countries is to develop an effective transport network to facilitate the smooth movement of goods and people.

Bangladesh–Nepal Corridor Through the Phulbari–Banglabandha Transit Route

The transit facility for Nepal and Bangladesh through India is very poor. There is a 45-km stretch of pothole-ridden road through India connecting the Nepal border with Bangladesh. But there are inadequate customs facilities and testing laboratories in this region. The transit facility is virtually non-existent. The transit agreement is signed by India with Nepal only, and not with Bangladesh. Bangladesh has no input regarding the transit facility.[17]

There is a procedural problem on this transit route as no foreign vehicles are allowed on Bangladeshi roads. Nepalese trucks come to the Bangladesh border, release their goods, and return empty. Moreover, Nepalese trucks are allowed access only on certain dedicated routes within India and only at fixed hours of the day.

There is also no banking facility near Kakarvita and entrepreneurs have to go to Siliguri for banking activities. Samples are sent to Kolkata for testing, which takes about a week, and this causes further delay in the process. Port infrastructure is very bad and customs facilities are inadequate.

For exporting or importing through Bangladesh, the cargos have to cross two borders: (i) the Indian border near Kakarvita, and (ii) the Phulbari and Banglabandha border near Bangladesh. Undergoing customs and other export or import procedures delays the consignments. Reportedly, there are problems with the documentation process in Bangladesh.

---

[17] India's indifference toward facilitating Bangladesh–Nepal trade transit is probably attributable to the fact that it wants transit route through Bangladesh to its northeastern states. In addition, India also wants to utilize the transit route to gain entry into countries such as Myanmar and the PRC.

The access road from the inland container depot in Dhaka to Chittagong Port is in bad condition. The documents required in India and Bangladesh also vary widely, and this creates hassles for exporters and importers.

The Phulbari–Banglabandha transit route is not properly operational as the 45-km road that passes through India does not have adequate infrastructure for easy movement of cargo. Although the Government of Bangladesh has already set up immigration office at Banglabandha, India is yet to do the same. Indian border security personnel only opens the borders for 2 hours a day. The Government of India has not developed the 2-km-long mud road between Nepal and the Indian border, making the maneuvering of vehicles slow and difficult.

Trade Finance

There are three types of export finance available in Bangladesh: (i) pre-shipment financing in local currency by commercial banks, (ii) pre-shipment financing in foreign currency by commercial banks through the export development fund, and (iii) back-to-back letter of credit facilities. There are four export insurance schemes that cover risk domestically and abroad: (i) an export credit guarantee (ECG) scheme at the pre-shipment stage, (ii) the ECG scheme at the post-shipment stage, (iii) the export payment risk policy (comprehensive guarantee), and (iv) the whole turnover pre-shipment finance guarantee.

Cost to Trade of Infrastructure Deficiencies

The World Bank (2005b) has documented some of the costs associated with deficiencies in infrastructure that seriously affect firms in Bangladesh. In fact, Bangladesh fares worse than its neighboring countries on general measures of infrastructure, according to this study. In a ranking of Malaysia, Thailand, Indonesia, PRC, Sri Lanka, India, Philippines, Viet Nam, and Bangladesh by overall quality of infrastructure, Bangladesh ranks last.

Electricity is the biggest concern. With generating capacity comes short of needs, supply is notoriously unreliable and power outages common. Access to reliable power is a prime concern for most manufacturing firms. Firms reported losing more than 3% of production on average as a result of problems with the electricity grid. This is because firms are forced to rely heavily on generators, which cost at least $20,000. While firms reported paying about Tk4 per kilowatt-hour (kWh) from the electricity grid, they pay more than Tk6 per kWh to use their own generators.

According to results of firm-level surveys, transport is a bigger problem in Bangladesh than in some comparator countries such as the PRC and Pakistan. According to the *Global Competitiveness Report 2001/02* (World

Economic Forum 2002), Bangladesh ranked 70th of 75 countries for roads and 72nd for ports. Although Bangladesh outperformed Sri Lanka, India, and Philippines in the rankings for roads, it ranked lower than any of the comparator countries for ports. India ranked 57th on ports and the PRC 51st. Chittagong port is considered one of the most inefficient and costly ports in Asia.

Results of surveys also show that the average time required for imports to clear ports and customs in Bangladesh is 12 days; exports take 9 days. Regression analysis suggests that import delays are correlated with lower profits, while customs delays for exports are associated with slower growth in sales and employment and lower investment. While imports are typically delayed longer than exports, firms tend to be hurt more by export delays. Each day that exports are delayed in customs is associated with a 0.3-percentage-point reduction in investment and a 0.2-percentage-point reduction in sales and employment growth. These figures suggest that the average wait of 9 days for exports reduced sales and employment growth by nearly 2 percentage points and investment by 2.7 percentage points. Given the average growth rate among the surveyed firms of sales (11%), employment (9%), and investment (9%), delays for exports reduced the sales and employment growth rates and the investment rate by nearly a quarter.

Service Sector Trade and Foreign Direct Investment Policies

As is well known, FDI inflows act as a catalyst in the development process, mainly through (i) supplementing domestic resources to augment investment, (ii) acting as a vehicle for technology transfer, and (iii) helping to increase exports. With this in mind, the Government of Bangladesh has designed a liberal and attractive FDI policy, which has been examined above. In this section, the magnitude and patterns of FDI inflow in Bangladesh are analyzed, as well as the magnitude and patterns of services trade. Services trade throughout the world, particularly in developed countries, has been growing faster than trade in goods in recent times. It is therefore important to examine whether this has been happening in Bangladesh. For both FDI and service trade, the major focus in examining Bangladesh is on East Asia and South Asia, in keeping with the objective of this study.

Foreign Direct Investment Performance

The inflow of FDI to Bangladesh has been low even by South Asian standards. FDI inflows into Bangladesh have on average been lower than in India, Pakistan, or Sri Lanka. This is shown in Table 4.22.

Table 4.22 FDI Inflows into Bangladesh: A Comparative Picture, $ Mn

Country	1993	1994	1995	1996	1997	1998	1999	2000	2001	2002	2003
East Asia											
China, People's Republic of	27,515	33,787	35,849	40,180	44,237	43,751	38,753	38,399	44,241	49,308	53,505
Hong Kong, China	–	–	–	–	–	2,220	5,208	2,572	12,432	(7,781)	8,133
Indonesia	2,004	2,109	4,346.0	6,194	4,677	(356)	(2,745)	(4,550)	(3,278)	(1,513)	(597)
Korea, Republic of	(752)	(1,652)	(1,776.2)	(2,345)	(1,605)	673	5,136	4,284	1,108	(224)	100
Malaysia	5,006	4,342	4,178.2	5,078	5,136	2,163	3,895	3,788	554	3,203	2,473
Philippines	1,238	1,591	1,478.0	1,517	1,222	2,287	1,725	1,345	989	1,792	319
Singapore	2,534	3,973	7,123.7	1,616	1,158	5,150	8,846	11,400	(8,590)	1,727	5,626
Thailand	1,804	1,366	2,068.0	2,336	3,895	7,315	6,103	3,366	3,892	953	1,949
South Asia											
Bangladesh	14	11	1.9	14	139	190	180	280	78	52	102
India	550	973.3	2,143.6	2,426	3,577	2,635	2,169	2,496	3,768	3,700	4,269
Nepal	–	–	–	19	23	12	–	–	–	(1)	15
Pakistan	349	421.0	722.6	922	716	506	532	308	383	823	534
Sri Lanka	194	166.4	56.0	120	430	193	176	173	172	196	229

FDI = foreign direct investment, – = no data available, ( ) = negative value, $ Mn = millions of US dollars.

Source: World Bank, Global Development Finance 2005 Website.

Table 4.22 shows that FDI inflows into South Asia have been much less than to East Asia, with the exception of India. Within South Asia, Bangladesh has received the lowest amount of FDIs aside from Nepal. FDIs in Bangladesh started from very low levels in the early 1990s, then recorded some increase in the later half of the decade when they reached $0.28 billion,[18] before falling again to $0.05 billion in 2002 (then recovering slightly to $0.1 billion in 2003). Compared to this, FDI inflows into India, for example, have increased gradually to reach $4.27 billion in 2003. Even in politically disturbed Sri Lanka, FDIs have been larger than in Bangladesh and continues to grow.

The major reason for this underperformance is probably the high cost of doing business in Bangladesh. A comparative picture in this regard is presented in Table 4.23.

On average, seven procedures taking a combined 30 days are involved in starting a business in Bangladesh. However, the cost of even these relatively few procedures is extremely high in Bangladesh, and in fact higher than in PRC, India, Sri Lanka, or Thailand. The same cost, expressed as a share of per capita gross national product (GNP), is higher in Bangladesh than in any other country (except Niger in the comparator group, which is not shown in Table 4.23). A complementary measure based on surveys of executives corroborates that starting a business is more onerous in Bangladesh than in any comparator country in Asia. The average cost of enforcing a contract in Bangladesh is almost three times its per capita GNP, the highest such ratio among the comparator group.

Table 4.23 Cost of Doing Business: Bangladesh vis-à-vis Comparator Countries

Country	Starting a business				Enforcing contracts			
	No. of procedures	Duration (days)	Cost ($)	Cost (% GNI per capita)	No. of procedures	Duration (days)	Cost ($)	Cost (% GNI per capita)
Bangladesh	7	30	272	75.5	15	270	973	270.3
India	10	88	239	49.8	11	365	456	95.0
Sri Lanka	8	58	154	18.3	17	440	64	7.6
PRC	11	46	134	14.3	20	180	301	32.0
Malaysia	8	31	959	27.1	22	270	687	19.4
Thailand	9	42	144	7.3	19	210	586	29.6

PRC = People's Republic of China, GNI = gross national income, $ = US dollar, % = percent.

Source: World Bank. 2005. *Bangladesh Growth and Export Competitiveness Report 2005.*

[18] This was when substantial amounts of foreign direct investment (FDI) from the US and the United Kingdom began to enter the gas and power sectors in Bangladesh.

Persistent corruption is probably another major factor deterring FDI in Bangladesh. According to the US Department of Commerce report, business people consider Bangladesh Customs to be a thoroughly corrupt organization in which officials routinely exert their power to influence the tariff value of imports and to expedite or delay import and export processing at the ports. Unhelpful treatment of business people by some government officials, coupled with the adverse investment climate, high start-up and operational costs, all tend to counteract the Government's numerous investment incentives. In addition to the above, poor infrastructure, backward and costly port facilities, unsatisfactory energy supply, and political instability resulting in labor unrest have also discouraged foreign investments in Bangladesh.[19]

It would be interesting to investigate the relationship between trade and investment inflows in Bangladesh. When FDIs move into a host economy with the motive of market access (horizontal FDI), these are generally involved in import-substituting activities and therefore act as a substitute to trade.[20] When the objective of FDI is cost reduction and access to natural resources, it occurs as a part of a production networking scheme where the production process is fragmented to take advantage of low cost and productivity differentials (vertical FDIs). In such cases, FDIs are generally involved in export industries. This link between FDIs and trade can be investigated by examining the sectoral distribution of FDIs in Bangladesh. Since most of the export-oriented industries are located in EPZs, data on FDIs in the EPZs as recorded by BEPZA can be used as a close proxy for export-oriented or vertical FDIs. On the other hand, FDIs coming into import-substituting industries and service industries are registered with the BOI, and hence can be treated as vertical FDIs.

Table 4.24 shows that the manufacturing sector received 73.4% of registered FDIs during the period 1991–1995, while the service sector absorbed 26.6%. However, this process was reversed in the second half of the 1990s when the share of manufacturing in FDI inflows declined to 25% while the share of the services sector rose to about 75%. This pattern has been maintained subsequently; in 2005, the share in FDIs of the manufacturing sector was 26%, and of the service sector 74%. Proposed FDIs in the manufacturing and services sectors have mostly been in import-substituting industries such as cement, textiles, chemicals and agro-based manufactures, and services such as power and gas, telecommunications, and container terminals.

---

19 This information was gathered through interviews with foreign investors and from findings of a survey of local and foreign investors carried out by the Bangladesh Enterprise Institute (BEI) and CUTS. See CUTS (2003).

20 One important reason for such FDI would be high trade costs or barriers to trade, and hence this is often called tariff jumping FDI.

Table 4.24 Sectoral Distribution of FDI Approval in Bangladesh, $ Mn

Sectors	1991–1995[a]	1996–2001[b]	2005[c]
Manufacturing	2,378.497	2,488.402	221.7
Agro-based	156.489	277.612	63.5
Food and allied	22.445	18.295	–
Textile and apparel	675.546	373.782	96.5
Leather and leather products	46.601	34.929	0.7
Chemicals	1,224.820	1,564.848	3.9
Engineering	230.046	154.091	1.7
Glass and ceramics	10.826	35.302	–
Printing and packaging	8.755	6.740	–
Miscellaneous	2.969	22.804	55.4
Services	862.262	7,330.602	623.7
Telecommunications	221.225	1,613.717	278.8
Container terminals	33.435	324.127	–
Industrial parks	484.374	0.000	–
Leasing firms	1.453	182.392	–
Hotels and motels (5-star)	0.300	561.972	–
Aircraft cargo services	0.000	202.914	–
Airport terminals	0.000	1,333.084	–
Oil and gas	0.000	859.732	181.1
Power generation	0.000	1,115.279	27.2
Water treatment plants	0.000	369.687	–
Others	–	–	136.6
Total	**3,240.759**	**9,819.004**	**845.4**

FDI = foreign direct investment, – = no data available, $ Mn = millions of US dollars.

Sources: [a] Unpublished data of the Board of Investment (BOI); [b] BOI Survey; [c] Bangladesh Bank Enterprise Survey, 2006.

Foreign Presence in the Services Sector

Foreign investment is present in Bangladesh's services sector. Natural gas is an important resource for the economic development of Bangladesh. It helps to supply about 70% of primary commercial energy and 45% of final commercial energy demand. With declining foreign aid in the 1990s, the Government liberalized the gas sector, leading to increasing FDI inflows since 1996/97. The reason why Bangladesh's gas sector is particularly attractive for FDIs is that the ratio of exploration to discovery is 2.8:1 in Bangladesh, while it is much higher (14:1) in neighboring West Bengal in India. The official estimate of gas reserves in Bangladesh is

13.79 trillion cubic feet (TCF), of which a little less than 4 TCF has already been consumed. Since the sector was opened up to private investment, it has attracted more than $400 million in exploration and development.

The power sector was also opened up for local and foreign private investments in the late 1990s and since then has attracted considerable foreign investment. The Power Development Board's Power System Master Plan envisages raising power generation capacity from the present level of 2,900 megawatts (MW) to 10,000 MW by 2015, relying primarily on FDIs.

Bangladesh has one of the lowest telephone penetration rates in the world. The Government deregulated the telecommunication sector in 1991 to attract private operators to run the mobile cellular phone system, operate rural telephone exchanges, provide paying and trunking facilities, and become Internet service providers. This attracted foreign telephone companies such as Norway's Telenor and Malaysia's Telekom Malaysia International.

Foreign Direct Investment in Export Processing Zones

About 80% of total investments in EPZs are foreign in origin. Data on distribution of investment, employment, and exports originating in the EPZs is presented in Table 4.25.

The table shows that cumulative FDIs in the EPZs up to June 2006 have been about $780 million, directed mostly toward textiles and textile-related industries. The share of EPZs in total export earnings has increased from 0.02% in 1983/84 to 15.49% in 1999/2000, and to 18% in 2001/02. EPZs employ about 150,000 workers, most of them in ready-made garments (woven and knit) and textiles.

Foreign Direct Investment by Source

Finally, the sources of inbound FDI to Bangladesh are considered. Table 4.26 shows that ASEAN+3 and East Asia were dominant sources of FDIs coming into Bangladesh during the period 1991–1995; Malaysia and Japan were the major investing countries. During this time, the EU had a share of about 12% while South Asia's share was only 6.7% (India having a share of 4%). The picture changed sharply during 1996–2001 when the UK's share rose to 12.4% and that of the US rose to 19%, while the shares of East Asia 1 declined sharply to 16.5%, and East Asia 2 also declined sharply to 24.2%. There were particularly rapid reductions in FDIs from both Malaysia and Japan. South Asia's share fell further to 3.1%. The picture has remained more or less unchanged in 2005. The main reason behind this change in pattern has been large US and UK investments in the gas sector since the second half of the 1990s.

Table 4.25 Investment, Employment, and Exports from EPZs, cumulative up to June 2006

Industry	No. of Units	Investment		Employment		Export (2001/02)	
		Industry Total ($ Mn)	EPZ (% of total)	Industry Total (Nos.)	% of EPZ Total	Total Industry Export ($ Mn)	% of Total Export from EPZs
Garments	49	252.317	25.75	95,345	53.62	501.778	46.59
Textile	26	240.369	24.53	20,322	11.43	177.086	16.44
Terry towel	16	34.459	3.52	4,422	2.49	22.989	2.14
Knits and other textiles	21	87.450	8.92	19,187	10.79	115.779	10.75
Garment accessories	31	77.926	7.95	5,950	3.35	14.933	1.39
Caps	7	42.800	4.37	12,391	6.97	–	7.50
Tents	4	22.627	2.31	5,049	2.84	–	4.76
Electric and electronics	15	51.333	5.24	2,899	1.63	23.419	80.832
Leather and footwear	12	51.275	5.23	5,185	2.92	33.225	51.294
Metal products	11	20.238	2.06	805	0.45	8.287	0.77
Plastic foods	13	20.815	2.12	1,013	0.57	13.011	1.21
Paper products	2	0.831	0.08	109	0.06	1.064	0.10
Fishing reels and golf clubs	1	31.238	3.19	566	0.32	15.018	1.39
Rope	2	6.105	0.62	408	0.23	2.847	0.26
Agricultural products	10	2.786	0.28	293	0.16	–	–
Service-oriented industries	3	4.917	0.50	452	0.25	–	–
Miscellaneous	19	32.416	3.31	3,413	1.92	15.486	1.44
Total	**242**	**979.893**	**100.00**	**177,809**	**100.00**	**1,077.05**	**100.00**

EPZ = export processing zone, – = no data available, $ Mn = millions of US dollars, % = percent.

Note: Total investment by Bangladeshi enterprises is $199.4 million, total number of local enterprises is 56, and employment generated by them is 33,365.

Source: Unpublished data from Bangladesh Export Processing Zone Authority.

Insofar as FDIs in the EPZs are concerned, a slightly different picture is observed (Table 4.27). FDIs from East Asia have dominated throughout the 1990s and thereafter. The share of East Asian countries in total FDIs in the EPZs up to June 2006 has been nearly 83%, with the Republic of Korea being the dominant investor with a share of nearly 36%, followed by Japan (16%) and the PRC (15.6%). These countries have invested in Bangladesh's EPZs to take advantage of low wages. The share of South Asian countries

Table 4.26 Distribution of FDI by Source Country, $ Mn

Country/Region	1991–1995		1996–2001		2005		2006	
	Value ($ Mn)	% of Total	Value ($ Mn)	% of Total	Value ($ Mn)	% of Total	Value ($ Mn)	% of Total
South Asia	216.346	6.68	308.863	3.14	32.4	3.83	–	–
India	135.906	4.19	244.802	2.49	2.7	0.32	–	–
ASEAN	1,206.263	37.22	888.039	9.04	132.1	15.63	141.9	17.9
ASEAN+3	2,112.14	65.17	1,620.71	16.51	210.0	24.84	218.6	27.6
Singapore	232.930	7.19	476.543	4.85	97.5	11.53	97.5	12.3
Malaysia	945.787	29.18	391.770	3.99	33.1	3.91	44.5	5.6
Japan	763.936	23.57	320.217	3.26	46.5	5.50	22.8	2.9
China, People's Republic of	42.990	1.33	64.920	0.66	1.6	0.19	–	–
Korea, Republic of	98.952	3.05	347.539	3.54	29.8	3.52	53.9	6.8
East Asia	2,145.986	66.22	2,378.213	24.22	274.5	32.47	266.0	33.6
Hong Kong, China	23.727	7.32	718.762	7.33	53.1	6.28	47.4	6.0
Taipei,China	10.119	0.31	38.741	0.39	11.4	1.35	–	–
European Union	402.880	12.43	1,576.007	16.05	190.1	22.49	–	–
United Kingdom	233.206	7.20	1,218.784	12.41	152.8	18.08	70.5	8.9
United States	89.058	2.75	1,877.409	19.12	141.8	16.77	175.7	22.2
Total	3,240.759	100.00	9,819.004	100.00	845.3	100.00	792.4	100.00

– = no data available, ASEAN = Association of Southeast Asian Nations, ASEAN+3 = ASEAN plus Japan, People's Republic of China (PRC), and Republic of Korea, FDI = foreign direct investment, $ Mn = millions of US dollars, % = percent.

Notes: Total FDI inflow in 2006 includes FDIs of $17.9 million from "other countries."

Source: Board of Investment, Bangladesh.

**Table 4.27 FDI Inflows into EPZs Classified by Source Country,
cumulative to June 2006**

Country/Region	Unit (Nos.)	Value ($ Mn)	% of Total
South Asia	18	8.369	1.07
India	13	4.493	0.58
ASEAN	9	78.636	10.07
East Asia	117	644.630	82.59
Singapore	2	6.332	0.81
Malaysia	6	71.791	9.20
Japan	24	127.353	16.32
China, People's Republic of[a]	25	122.089	15.64
Korea, Republic of	59	278.302	35.66
Taipei,China	10	38.250	4.90
European Union	23	68.946	8.83
United Kingdom	10	26.768	3.43
United States	12	46.864	6.00
Total	**186**	**780.475**	**100.00**

ASEAN = Association of Southeast Asian Nations, FDI = foreign direct investment, $ Mn = millions of US dollars, % = percent.

[a] People's Republic of China includes Hong Kong, China.

Source: Unpublished data from Bangladesh Export Processing Zone Authority.

has been very low at 1%; this is probably because of the fact that in these countries wage costs are similar to those in Bangladesh.

Service Sector Trade

Services trade in Bangladesh as recorded in the balance of payments is shown in Table 4.28.

Being an LDC, it is not surprising that the volume of trade in services has been very small compared to merchandise trade (Table 4.28). Nonetheless, the volume of services trade has increased alongside the growth of the economy. Export of services has increased from a very low level of $3.4 million in 1990/91 to $165.5 million in 2004/05. However, imports during the same period grew much faster, from $185.3 million to $242.7 million, resulting to a chronic deficit in the balance of services trade.

The major item of service export of Bangladesh is government services. This refers to service expenditure by foreign diplomatic missions and international organizations in Bangladesh. There are no other notable service exports from Bangladesh. There are four major service imports in Bangladesh: shipment of freight, travel or tourism, insurance services,

Table 4.28 Service Sector Trade in Bangladesh, $ Million

Service Items	1990/91		1997/98		2000/01		2002/03		2004/05	
	Export	Import	Export	Import	Export	Import	Export	Import	Export	Import
Shipment of freight and other transportation services	1.01	142.12	0.75	143.81	0.50	161.91	0.38	183.30	0.33	181.20
Travel	0.14	0.78	0.41	3.38	0.25	10.82	0.16	15.83	0.30	21.49
Communication services	0.00	0.00	0.00	0.04	0.02	0.10	0.00	0.02	0.00	0.02
Construction services	0.00	0.00	0.07	0.00	0.00	0.00	1.61	0.00	0.80	0.00
Insurance services	0.00	0.00	0.00	15.95	0.00	18.09	0.00	20.36	0.02	20.18
Financial services	0.00	0.00	0.14	0.18	0.12	0.15	0.04	0.05	0.13	0.03
Computer and information services	0.00	0.00	0.00	0.02	0.00	0.04	0.02	0.00	0.07	0.00
Royalties and license fees	0.00	0.00	0.00	0.36	0.00	0.04	0.00	0.05	0.00	0.00
Other business services	0.00	0.00	0.70	0.45	1.74	1.40	2.60	0.85	2.24	1.13
Entertainment, cultural, and recreational services	0.00	0.00	0.00	0.00	0.00	0.00	3.61	0.12	0.00	0.00
Government services (not included elsewhere)	2.27	42.43	101.66	10.16	155.69	12.31	65.85	24.51	161.62	18.63
Total	3.42	185.34	103.65	174.43	158.32	204.85	74.26	245.09	165.51	242.69

Source: Bangladesh Bank, balance of payments statistics.

and government services (expenditures of Bangladesh diplomatic personnel, diplomatic and trade missions, and military expenditures abroad). Between 1990/91 and 2004/05, imports of transportation services (mainly freight transportation) increased from $142.1 million to $181.2 million, tourism services increased from $0.8 million to $21.5 million, and insurance services increased from nil to $20.2 million, and government services increased from $185.3 million to $242.7 million.

Remittances

Although services exports, as recorded in the balance of payments, have been very small in Bangladesh, exports of labor ("temporary movement of natural persons," according to the terminology in the General Agreement on Trade in Services [EGATS]) has been substantial and has earned Bangladesh a considerable amount of foreign exchange in the form of remittances. In fact, remittance earnings have been the second source of foreign exchange earnings for Bangladesh after merchandise exports. The amount and pattern of remittance earnings are reported in Table 4.29.

Table 4.29 shows that inflow of remittances into Bangladesh has increased at a very rapid rate, rising from $1.2 billion in 1994/95 to $3.8 billion in 2004/05. In fact, in 2004/05 remittances constituted 45% of total merchandise exports. Overseas Bangladeshi workers to the Middle East are mainly unskilled. In recent years, Saudi Arabia, United Arab Emirates, Kuwait, US, and UK have been the major importers of labor from Bangladesh. Also, the export of labor to South and East Asian countries has been comparatively small; as Table 4.29 shows, only Malaysia and Singapore import some labor from Bangladesh.

Employment of Bangladeshis in East Asia (Malaysia, Republic of Korea, and Singapore) gradually increased from about 2% of total overseas employment of Bangladeshis in 1990 to about 35% in 1996, but then the proportion of Bangladeshis working in East Asia began to decline, reaching 5% in 2005. The decline began with the East Asian financial crisis, but employment of Bangladeshis remained low despite the economic recovery experienced in East Asia. During the first half of the 1990s, the bulk of Bangladeshis working in East Asian countries were employed in Malaysia. The pattern changed from the second half of the decade when the majority of Bangladeshis were employed in Singapore.

Regulatory Regime in Service Sectors

The priority service sectors in Bangladesh are power and energy, telecommunications, and banking. The salient features of the regulatory regime in these sectors are presented below.

Prior to the Government's Fifth Five-Year Plan (1997–2002), private investment was not allowed in the energy sector. However, from the Fifth Plan onwards, the government monopoly in the gas sector ended and private investment, both local and foreign, has been encouraged to meet the gas shortages. The primary requirement is that foreign private investors enter into a production-sharing contract with the Government. Also, foreign private investors are not allowed to export gas. Similarly, the power sector was opened to private investment from the late 1990s and there has been considerable foreign investment in this sector since then. The electricity tariff, however, is solely determined by the Government. The major objectives of regulation in the energy sector are to ensure a competitive environment, protect consumer interests, curb abuse of monopolies, and ensure environmental protection.

The telecommunications sector has been open to private investment since 1991. As a result, there has been substantial foreign investment in this sector as well. While services such as mobile cellular phones, paging

Table 4.29 Remittances to Bangladesh, by Country ($ Mn)

Year	Saudi Arabia	UAE	Qatar	Oman	Bahrain	Kuwait	US	UK	Malaysia	Singapore	Others	Total
1994/95	477	81	72	81	34	175	102	47	50	3	75	1,198
1995/96	498	84	53	82	30	174	115	41	74	4	61	1,217
1996/97	587	90	53	94	32	211	157	56	95	7	93	1,475
1997/98	589	107	58	88	32	213	203	66	78	8	84	1,525
1998/99	685	125	64	92	39	230	239	54	68	13	96	1,706
1999/2000	916	130	64	93	42	245	241	72	54	12	81	1,949
2000/01	920	144	63	84	44	247	226	56	31	8	60	1,882
2001/02	1,148	233	91	103	54	286	356	103	47	14	65	2,501
2002/03	1,245	327	114	114	64	339	458	220	41	31	100	3,062
2003/04	1,386	373	114	119	61	361	468	298	37	32	123	3,372
2004/05	1,510	442	136	131	67	407	557	376	26	48	148	3,848
2005/06	1,697	561	176	165	67	494	761	556	21	65	239	4,802
2006/07	1,735	805	233	197	80	681	930	887	12	80	339	5,979

UAE = United Arab Emirates, UK = United Kingdom, US = United States, $ Mn = millions of US dollars.

Source: Bangladesh Bank.

and trunking facilities, and internet services were opened up for private investment, until very recently the state-run Bangladesh Telephone and Telegraph Board (BTTB) had a monopoly on residential land-line services. Regulations are meant to ensure that the network facilities of government operator are not bypassed, and that certain services are reserved for exclusive supply by the government operator.

The Government closely monitors the banking sector. The major aim of regulation (for example, maintaining capital adequacy ratios) is to bring dynamism in the sector and to provide more security to depositors. Although there are several foreign banks operating in Bangladesh, the Government has not opened up the financial sector for foreign participation in its Schedule of Specific Commitments under the GATS.

The General Agreement on Trade in Services and Bangladesh

Finally, restrictions imposed on the import of services are considered. In its Schedule of Specific Commitments under the WTO's GATS, Bangladesh has opened up two service sectors for foreign participation: (i) five-star hotels and lodging services; and (ii) telecommunications.[21] In the case of five-star hotels and lodging services, there are two limitations to market access: (i) foreign equity of up to 100% is allowed, but commercial presence requires that foreign service providers incorporate or establish the business locally in accordance with the relevant provisions of Bangladesh laws, rules, and regulations; and (ii) employment of foreign natural persons for the implementation of the foreign investment will be agreed upon by the contracting parties and approved by the Government and such personnel will be employed in upper management and specialized jobs only.

With regard to telecommunication services, the only limitation on market access is that foreign natural persons should be employed in upper management and specialized jobs only. The limitation on national treatment is that certain subsidies and tax benefits may only be extended to national operators. Furthermore, Bangladesh submitted two Article II (MFN) exemptions for telecommunication services.

Policy Implications

The analysis presented in the foregoing sections has several policy implications for promoting economic integration between Bangladesh and the other South Asian economies as well as the economies of ASEAN+3 and East Asia (includes ASEAN+3; Hong Kong, China; and Taipei,China). Some

---

[21] For details, see Rashid (2006).

broad policy recommendations to accelerate this process of economic integration are presented in this section.

Despite being a member of SAFTA, Bangladesh's exports to South Asian countries are very small in proportion to its total exports, although it is the single most important importing country in SAFTA. This is because of the rather narrow export base of Bangladesh and the lack of trade complementarities in the South Asia region. The problem has been compounded by poor trade-related infrastructure and transport, cumbersome customs procedures, and the existence of NTBs.

The problem created by weak trade complementarily can be at least partly overcome through more intraindustry trade. The potential for intraindustry trade exists. As shown by Vona and Abd-EL indices of the extent of intraindustry trade over the period 1989–1998, intraindustry trade has increased in Bangladesh during the period 1989–1998 at both the 6-digit and 4-digit product levels, although most of them have a small share (less than 3%) of total trade. For this potential to be realized, investment flows across the region have to be facilitated together with the creation of a conducive policy environment for interindustry trade. However, little emphasis has been placed on investment cooperation in SAFTA, and this needs to be changed in order to promote increased trade flows in the South Asia region.

Bangladesh already has significant trade links with East Asia. But, as noted earlier, while East Asian countries are a major source of imports to Bangladesh, the latter's exports to the former are small. Bangladesh has economic cooperation schemes with some of the major East Asian countries (namely under APTA and now BIMSTEC). Apparently, participation in such schemes has not helped Bangladesh to increase its exports to East Asia. Once again, this could be primarily attributable to Bangladesh's limited export capacity.

Therefore, Bangladesh urgently needs to diversify its export basket to increase its exports to South and East Asia. To achieve this, Bangladesh must not only accelerate industrial growth in particular, but also diversify its industrial production base. To facilitate export of agricultural-based products, the growth and diversity of the agricultural sector need to be enhanced. It is generally recognized that Bangladesh has the potential to increase exports of agricultural-based products (e.g., fruit and vegetables, and canned fruit juice). Appropriate policies must be designed to reach this potential.

FDIs can play a crucial role in export expansion of Bangladesh. There already exists substantial FDIs from East Asian countries in export-oriented industries located in the export processing zones of Bangladesh. Although Bangladesh's FDI policy regime is undoubtedly attractive and liberal, the country has not been enough to attract FDIs. What is equally important to attract FDIs is that other complementary factors—such as good roads, port facilities, reliable power supply, cooperating bureaucracy, good law and order, and a corruption-free administrative system—are present as well. It is the responsibility of the Government to ensure that a conducive environment for FDIs is created through the adoption of appropriate policies. At the same time, it is equally important that investment cooperation be strengthened among South Asian countries, and, to the extent possible, between the regions of South Asia and East Asia, particularly under the aegis of SAFTA, BIMSTEC, and APTA.

The pace of liberalization of Bangladesh's merchandise trade regime has been satisfactory by any standards, particularly during the first half of the 1990s. The speed of liberalization has, however, faltered since the late 1990s, particularly in terms of reducing paratariff barriers. This needs to be rectified immediately, although Bangladesh's dependence on trade taxes may make the task difficult in the short run.

While Bangladesh should take immediate steps to further liberalize its merchandise trade regime, by the same token, the other countries of South Asia must follow suit. In particular, countries such as India still have in place many NTBs that Bangladeshi exporters say are restricting their market access in India. Such NTBs should immediately be eliminated, either unilaterally or under the framework of SAFTA. At the same time, the size of the sensitive lists of member states of SAFTA must be reduced as quickly as possible. Furthermore, the present ROO criteria under SAFTA appear to be restrictive and should be liberalized. All these steps would contribute significantly toward promoting intraregional trade in South Asia.

Bangladesh has followed a rather restrictive policy with regard to the import of services. However, it should be noted that Bangladesh, as an LDC member of the WTO, is allowed to open only a few service sectors. Even though many service sectors have not been included in the country's Schedule of Specific Commitments, some of these sectors (e.g., financial services) are more or less open for foreign participation. In any case, Bangladesh should selectively open up more service sectors in its own interest.

Customs procedures have been reformed in Bangladesh and show a marked improvement from 10 years ago. Having said this, it should be said that there is still scope for further simplification and improvement. The Government must take appropriate steps in this regard to further facilitate trade, particularly the modernization of the Chittagong Port. Some investment has already been made in this area with assistance from ADB, although more is required. Also, administrative reforms in the port have to be implemented urgently.

The poor condition of roads, railways, and inland water transport in Bangladesh has also hindered trade. These have to be improved as quickly as possible, especially the Dhaka–Chittagong corridor and the other corridors used for trade purposes. This would call for heavy investment, and donor agencies such as the World Bank and ADB should come forward to help Bangladesh. Problems with transit between Bangladesh and India need to be quickly solved.

Finally, other South Asian governments, especially India, must reciprocate government initiatives with regard to trade facilitation. Bangladeshi exporters complain that factors including cumbersome customs procedures, stringent and improperly administered product standards, and poor road conditions at the border land ports like Petrapole have hindered market access for Bangladesh's exports. It is urgent that these impediments to trade be removed.

In the light of the above discussion, the following specific policy recommendations are made to strengthen economic cooperation between Bangladesh and the countries of South Asia and East Asia:

Strategic Regional Orientation

East Asia has been growing rapidly for more than two decades, and Bangladesh must make strong efforts to benefit from this. Bangladesh should therefore make concerted attempts to forge bilateral FTAs with the dynamic economies of East Asia (such as the PRC and Japan). The PRC has already formed bilateral FTAs with India and Pakistan. Bangladesh should also strive to form bilateral FTAs with India, Pakistan, and Sri Lanka. According to newspaper reports, India is keen to form a bilateral FTA with Bangladesh. Bangladesh should also try to maximize its benefits from SAFTA, BIMSTEC, and APTA.

Foreign Direct Investment Regime and Policy

The Government of Bangladesh must take immediate steps to reduce the cost of doing business in the country to attract more FDIs from East and South Asia, and also from other countries. This would require policies such as those to eliminate government corruption, improving Chittagong Port facilities, improve power supply, ensure good law and order situation, and ensure political stability. While the FDI regime and policy is attractive, unless the above improvements are made, FDIs will continue to avoid Bangladesh.

The Government may consider providing special incentives to foreign investors from East Asia and South Asia. This could be done easily once bilateral FTAs are formed.

Merchandise Trade Regime and Policy

The process of trade liberalization should be accelerated. This will not only help to expand and diversify exports, it will also help to attract more export-oriented FDIs. Tariffs should be further reduced and rationalized, and non-tariff and paratariff barriers should be eliminated as quickly as possible.

Services Regime and Policy

Bangladesh should selectively open up more service sectors for foreign participation under the GATS for its own interest. In turn, this would attract more FDIs from East and South Asia in the services sectors of Bangladesh.

Customs Procedures and Trade Facilitation

Customs procedures should be further simplified and improved. This would entail, among other things, (i) installation of an electronic monitoring system, and (ii) shifting from the transaction-based process of customs clearance to the risk-management and post-clearance audit processes.

Transport Initiatives

The poor condition of roads, railways, and inland water transport in Bangladesh has hindered trade. These need to be improved as quickly as possible, particularly the Dhaka–Chittagong corridor. Chittagong Port facilities need urgent improvements.

Other Policy Issues

There should be faithful implementation by non-LDC members of SAFTA to reduce tariffs to 0–5% for exports of LDC members by 1 July 2009.

SAFTA member states must remove nontariff and paratariff barriers to intraregional trade.

The ROO criteria under SAFTA should be relaxed to enable less-developed member states to gain greater benefits from tariff liberalization.

The size of the sensitive lists under SAFTA should be reduced to maximize the benefits of tariff liberalization.

Greater emphasis must be placed on investment cooperation under the SAFTA.

Appendix Tables

Table A4.1 Macroeconomic Indicators

Indicator	1991/92	1994/95	1998/99	1999/2000	2000/01	2001/02	2002/03	2003/04	2004/05	2005/06	2006/07
GDP growth (%)	5.0	4.9	4.9	5.9	5.3	4.4	5.3	6.3	5.4	6.6	6.4
GDP growth per capita (%)	3.0	3.1	3.6	4.9	3.7	2.9	4.0	4.3	4.1	4.3	4.5
Per capita GDP ($)	298.0	313.0	354.0	357.0	371.0	372.0	389.0	418.0	441.0	447.0	482.0
Gross domestic saving (% of GDP)	14.1	12.7	17.7	17.9	18.0	18.2	18.2	19.5	20.0	20.3	20.5
Gross national saving (% of GDP)	16.9	16.3	22.3	23.1	22.4	23.4	23.7	25.4	25.8	27.6	29.1
Total investment (% of GDP)	17.3	19.1	22.2	23.0	23.1	23.2	23.2	24.0	24.5	24.7	24.3
Private investment (% of GDP)	10.3	12.4	15.5	15.6	15.8	16.8	16.5	17.8	18.3	18.7	18.7
Public investment (% of GDP)	7.0	6.7	6.7	7.4	7.3	6.4	6.7	6.2	6.2	6.0	5.6
Total government revenue (% of GDP)	8.3	9.3	9.0	8.5	9.0	10.2	10.3	10.2	10.4	10.8	10.6
Total government expenditure (% of GDP)	12.7	14.6	13.8	14.7	14.1	14.8	13.8	13.4	13.9	14.7	14.3
Overall budget balance (% of GDP)	(4.5)	(5.2)	(4.8)	(6.2)	(5.1)	(4.7)	(3.5)	(3.2)	(3.5)	3.9	3.7
Exports (% of GDP)	6.4	9.2	11.6	12.2	13.6	12.5	12.5	13.5	14.4	16.8	17.8
Imports (% of GDP)	11.3	15.4	17.5	17.8	19.9	18.0	18.6	19.3	21.9	21.5	22.9
Trade balance (% of GDP)	(4.9)	(6.2)	(5.9)	(5.6)	(6.1)	(5.4)	(4.3)	(4.1)	(7.5)	(6.8)	(4.8)
Current account balance (% of GDP)	(0.4)	(1.8)	(0.9)	0.0	(2.2)	0.5	0.6	0.3	(0.9)	(1.3)	(1.4)
Real effective ER (1990=100)	95.4	90.9	104.4	102.6	101.2	101.5	97.0	93.4	90.3	86.9	89.0
Rate of inflation (%, year on year)	4.6	8.8	8.9	3.9	1.6	2.8	4.4	5.8	6.5	7.2	7.2

ER = exchange rate, GDP = gross domestic product, $ = US dollar, % = percent, ( ) = negative value.

Sources: Bangladesh Bank, Bangladesh Bureau of Statistics, and Ministry of Finance.

Table A4.2 Sectoral GDP and Per Capita GDP Growth Rates, annual average at constant 1995/96 prices (%)

Sector	1980/81–1984/85	1985/86–1989/90	1990/91–1994/95	1995/96–1999/00	2000/01–2004/05	1980/81–2003/04
Agriculture	2.68	2.40	1.55	4.88	2.13	2.77
Industry	5.70	5.86	7.47	6.44	7.48	6.51
Service	3.83	3.58	4.15	4.81	5.73	4.33
Total GDP	3.72	3.74	4.39	5.21	5.32	4.41
Per capita GDP	1.54	1.58	2.36	3.83	3.91	2.54

GDP = gross domestic product, % = percent.

Source: Bangladesh Bureau of Statistics (BBS).

Table A4.3 Disaggregated Growth of Agriculture and Industry Sectors, annual average at constant 1995/96 prices (%)

Sector	1980/81–1984/85	1985/86–1989/90	1990/91–1994/95	1995/96–1999/00	2000/01–2004/05	1980/81–1999/00	1990/81–1999/00
Agriculture	2.68	2.40	1.55	4.88	2.13	2.54	3.22
Crops and vegetables	2.69	2.69	0.43	3.86	1.53	2.69	1.72
Fishery	3.06	1.64	7.86	8.56	1.43	2.35	8.21
Others	2.40	2.21	2.53	3.30	–	2.31	2.92
Industry	5.70	5.86	7.47	6.44	7.48	5.75	6.96
Manufacturing	4.69	5.27	8.20	5.59	6.89	4.98	6.90
Large and medium scale	4.44	5.43	8.41	5.49	6.66	4.94	6.95
Small scale	5.41	4.89	7.69	5.87	7.46	5.15	6.78
Construction	6.44	5.59	6.27	8.80	8.46	6.02	7.54
Others	11.50	10.68	6.43	4.90	–	11.09	5.67

– = no data available, % = percent.

Source: Bangladesh Bureau of Statistics (BBS).

References

Bakht, Z., and B. Sen. 2002. Border Trade of Bangladesh. Mimeo, Manila: Asian Development Bank (ADB).

Bangladesh Bank. Various years. *Annual Report.* Available: www.bangladeshbank.org/

Bangladesh Economic Processing Zone Authority (BEPZA). 2002. *Information for Investors.* Dhaka: BEPZA.

Bangladesh Tariff Commission. 2001. *Review of Relative Protection.* Dhaka: Government of Bangladesh.

Bhattacharya, D., and S. Hossain. 2006. An Evaluation of the Need and Cost of Selected Trade Facilitation Measures in Bangladesh: Implications for the WTO Negotiations on Trade Facilitation. *Asia-Pacific Research and Training Network on Trade (ARTNet) Working Paper Series* No. 9, April.

Board of Investment (BOI). 2004. *Bangladesh Investment Handbook.* Dhaka: BOI.

CUTS. 2003. Investment Policy in Bangladesh–Performance and Perceptions. Discussion Paper. Jaipur.

Kumar, P., and C. Mukherjee. 2006. Trade Facilitation Needs Assessment in *South Asia: A Case Study of Eastern Sub-Region.* CUTS Centre for International Trade, Economics & Environment (CUTS-CITEE).

Mahmud, W. 2006. Employment, Incomes and Poverty: Prospects of Pro-Poor Growth in Bangladesh. In *Growth and Poverty: The Development Experience of Bangladesh,* edited by S. Ahmed and W. Mahmud. Dhaka: The University Press Limited.

Mahmud, W., et al. 2000. Agricultural Diversification: A Strategic Factor for Growth. In *Out of the Shadow of Famine: Evolving Food Markets and Food Policy in Bangladesh,* edited by R. Ahmed. Baltimore: Johns Hopkins University Press.

Rashid, M. A. 2005. Bangladesh. In *South Asian Free Trade Area: Opportunities and Challenges.* New York: United States Agency for International Development (USAID) and Nathan Associates Inc.

––––––. 2006. SAFTA: Trade Liberalization Program (Tariff Measures): Some Issues. Paper presented at the Final Meeting on Regional Economic Cooperation in South Asia. Kathmandu, 14–16 August 2006; organized by CUTS-CITEE in association with Friedrich Ebert Stiftung (FES).

Sen, B. 1995. Recent Trends in Poverty and its Dynamics. In *Experiences with Economic Reform: A Review of Bangladesh's Development 1995.* Dhaka: Centre for Policy Dialogue and The University Press Limited.

––––––. 1998. Politics of Poverty Alleviation. In *Crisis in Governance: A Review of Bangladesh's Development 1997.* Dhaka: Centre for Policy Dialogue and The University Press Limited.

Shahabuddin, Q., et al. 2004. Trade and Foreign Direct Investment Performance During Policy Reform in Bangladesh. In *Economic Reform and Trade Performance in South Asia*, edited by O.H. Chowdhury and W. Geest. Dhaka: The University Press Limited.

Subramaniam, U., and J. Arnold. 2001. *Forging Subregional Links in Transportation and Logistics in South Asia*. Washington, DC: World Bank.

World Bank. 1999. *Bangladesh Trade Liberalization: Its Pace and Impacts*. Dhaka: World Bank.

_____. 2000a. *Foreign Direct Investment in Bangladesh: Issues of Long-Run Sustainability*.

_____. 2000b. *World Development Indicators 2000*. Washington, DC: World Bank.

_____. 2002a. *Poverty in Bangladesh: Building on Progress*. Washington, DC: World Bank (South Asia Region). Report No. 24299-BD.

_____. 2002b. Trade Can CD-ROM.

_____. 2004. *Bangladesh Development Forum Economic Update*. Report No. 29118-BD. Washington, DC.

_____. 2005a. *Global Development Finance 2005*.

_____. 2005b. *Bangladesh Growth and Export Competitiveness Report*.

World Bank and Bangladesh Enterprise Institute. 2003. *Improving the Investment Climate in Bangladesh*. Washington, DC.

World Trade Organization (WTO). 2000. *Trade Policy Review: Bangladesh*. Geneva: WTO.

Nepal

Binod Karmacharya and Nephil Maskay

Introduction

Nepal is a landlocked country of 23 million people with an area of 147,181 square kilometers (km). The country lies on the southern slopes of the Himalayas, bordering only two countries: the Tibet Autonomous Region of the People's Republic of China (PRC) to the north and India to the east, south, and west. The geographical situation facing Nepal presents a formidable challenge to domestic economic growth and development. Nepal has an open border with India, but for access to the world economy, the nearest seaport is that of Kolkata in India and is more than 900 km away from the country's border. Most of Nepal's terrain is mountainous or hilly, and only 20% of the total land area is arable. These factors contribute to country's high transport costs, hindering market development and creating a near-complete dependence on India for trading routes. The open border with India and the high cost of access to the markets of the rest of the world have been decisive factors in putting Nepal in this situation of de facto integration with India.

Figure 5.1 Map of Nepal

Source: http://ncthakur.itgo.com/map.htm

Nepal and the PRC have remained close friends and neighbors, with diplomatic relations being established in 1955. An agreement was signed between the two countries in 1961 to construct a 120-km highway linking Kathmandu to the border of the PRC's Tibet Autonomous Region and on to Lhasa. It was a remarkable achievement during the Cold War and amidst an atmosphere of unease and tensions in the region. This highway is the most important road link between the two countries. Through this route, trade volume between the two countries has expanded rapidly. Imports of manufactured products from the PRC have increased significantly and the land route to the PRC via the Tibet Autonomous Region is emerging as an important outlet for regional trade. It could not be used as a trade route between India and the PRC in the past due to the Cold War, although Nepal has been the traditional corridor for trade between them. However, with the advent of new era of economic dynamism in Asia, Nepal has enormous potential to be a transit country for trans-Himalayan trade between the PRC and India.

Prior to the mid-1980's Nepal had adopted a closed protectionist regime. This led to substantial state control in country's economic activities and the growth of public enterprises. The country changed from a closed protectionist regime in the mid-1980s to a liberal, open economy. The move for greater integration with the global economy can be most saliently seen in the country becoming the 147th member of the World Trade Organization (WTO) in April 2004.

Nepal has also made conscious efforts to foster deeper economic integration with its historical trade partner India and with other regional partners in South and East Asia. Nepal is a party to a number of bilateral and regional preferential trading agreements (PTAs), the most important of these being a Nepal–India PTA, the South Asian Free Trade Area (SAFTA), and the Bay of Bengal Initiative for Multi-Sectoral Technical and Economic Cooperation (BIMSTEC). Nepal also has limited preferential trade agreements with Pakistan and the Tibet Autonomous Region.

These reforms have contributed to the transformation of Nepal's agriculture-based economy, with the trade–gross domestic product (GDP) ratio increasing from close to zero to nearly 60% by the end of the 1990s. However, this figure fell markedly after 2001 because of a global economic slowdown and escalating domestic political instability. Nepal needs to attain long-lasting peace, to resolve its political stalemate, and to press ahead with effective reform plans and policies in order to improve its external aspirations and achieve economic growth.

Against this background, the purpose of this study aims to (i) analyze Nepal's present status of economic cooperation with South and East Asian countries, (ii) identify Nepal's potential to enhance such cooperation, (iii) highlight constraints to exploit such identified potentials, and (iv) recommend the policy measures to address such constraints but which are largely dependent on the decade-long political instability which prevails in the country.

The study has been structured into six sections in order to fulfill the above-mentioned purpose of the study. This section provides general introduction to the study. In section 5.2, Nepal's economic structure and external orientation is discussed. Section 5.3 overviews Nepal's FDI regime, with emphasis on East and South Asia; section 5.4 examines Nepal's merchandise trade policy with South and East Asia; section 5.5 deals with trade infrastructure and administration issues with East and South Asia; and section 5.6 analyzes Nepal's service-sector trade with emphasis on East Asia and FDI policies with emphasis on South Asia. Section 5.7 concludes with proper policy recommendations.

Economic Structure and External Orientation

External Orientation

Nepal has undergone three distinct phases in the evolution of its trade policy regime during the post-war period, moving from a free-trade regime (1923–1956) to a closed protectionist regime (1956–1986), and then back toward an open liberal regime (1986 onwards). Nepal had a policy of virtually free trade prior to the mid-1950s. Nepal has embarked on periodic development planning exercises since 1956. In the next three decades until 1985, Nepal followed restrictive trade policies while maintaining relatively open trade relations with India. To attain its economic development goals, Nepal followed interventionist, protectionist, state-led policies, which resulted in a large public sector, the dominance of state corporations, and a relatively closed economy.

In response to a balance of payments and fiscal crisis in the mid-1980s, Nepal started implementing economic policy reforms. These reforms progressed in four different phases in next two decades with the Government having opened the economy to trade in goods and services, technology, and investment. In the first phase (1985/86), expenditure and tax policies were improved and the currency devalued. Likewise, structural reforms, aided by an International Monetary Fund (IMF) program, included attempts to liberalize the import regime, the introduction of duty drawback and bonded warehouse schemes, and relaxation of industrial licensing. In the second phase, which took place from the early 1990s,[1] the tax base was

---

[1]   Nepal's ability to integrate with the global economy itself is influenced by India's integration with the latter. Accordingly, Nepal's dramatic policy reforms in the early 1990s became possible when India opened itself further to the global economy (Karmacharya 2003).

broadened, revenue administration improved, and trade and industrial policies were further liberalized. There was a steady reduction in tariffs, with quantitative restrictions virtually dismantled. In addition, Interest rates were also liberalized and banking-sector entry facilitated. Likewise, the foreign exchange system was unified and the current account liberalized.[2] Privatization was introduced, with entry being liberalized by the new investment act. After stalling in the middle 1990s, the third reform phase around 1997 liberalized the agricultural sector, introduced a neutral value-added tax (VAT), and strengthened local governments. In the most recent reform phase since 2000, the Government has improved tax policy and administration, introduced a medium-term expenditure framework, and commenced the process of financial sector reform (this includes restructuring the management of Nepal's two main commercial banks, both of which are troubled; strengthening financial sector regulations; and combating corruption).

Recent Initiatives with Historical and Regional Trading Partners

During the last two decades, Nepal also made conscious efforts to foster deeper economic integration with its historical trade partner India, regional partners, and with the global economy. The trade and transit treaties agreed with India in mid-1990s have provided Nepal with access to the vast Indian market and to the Kolkata port. Likewise, Nepal had completed its accession to the WTO in April 2004. Being the first least-developed country to join the WTO through the regular accession process, Nepal faces considerable opportunities as well as challenges in enhancing its capacity and competitiveness. Nepal had also participated in the South Asian Free Trade Area (SAFTA) and is a signatory to other important regional cooperation initiatives such as the Bay of Bengal Initiative for Multi-Sectoral Technical and Economic Cooperation (BIMSTEC).

In recent years, efforts have been made to improve transport links to the PRC in order to provide transit route for India–PRC trade, which is beneficial to both countries.

GDP Per Capita and GDP Growth Rate

Nepal's problem—with difficult initial conditions in terms of its geography, a feudal history, and a late start in development in 1960s—was

---

[2]   This was also reflected in the country having accepted the 8th Article of the IMF's Articles of Association.

compounded by the policies that it followed in the two decades to 1985. Between 1965 and 1985, per capita income growth was stagnant at around 0.6% (Table 5.1) but with the additional burden of Nepal's rising population and without the benefits of the Green Revolution taking place in the countries of the South. Policy reforms starting in the mid-1980s significantly improved the economy. First, per-capita income growth accelerated markedly after reforms were launched in the mid-1980s (Table 5.1) and the economy diversified (Table 5.2). Second, the share of agriculture fell from 64% of the economy in the mid-1970s to less than 40% at the beginning of the 21st century; in the same period the share of industry increased from 12% to 21%. Third, this diversification led to significantly lower volatility in incomes. As the sources of growth moved away from agriculture toward industrial and services sectors (finance and construction) and irrigation expanded, the dependence of the economy on rainfall declined. The standard deviation of per capita GDP fell from nearly 4 in the period of 1965–1985 to around 1.5 in the second period. It is evident that achieving successful stabilization and better fiscal, financial and external sector policies helped to improve economic performance. Nevertheless, a considerable reform agenda remains pending. This progress faces serious threats from an extended period of political instability and domestic conflict[3] since the mid-1990s, and a more competitive environment abroad. As a result, growth has faltered in the last 4 years in comparison to countries in both South Asia and ASEAN (Table 5.1). If past gains are to be sustained, Nepal needs to achieve long-lasting peace, resolve the political stalemate, and press ahead with its reform agenda.

---

[3] The country witnessed three general elections and 15 changes in government over the period 1990–2005, each averaging only about 11 months in duration. The disenchantment with democracy as it was practiced since 1990 and exclusion of certain regions and ethnic groups and castes from benefits of growth and human development fueled a Maoist insurgency, which started in 1996 and has escalated since 2001. The dismissal of the coalition government by King Gyanendra on 1 February 2005 polarized the political scene and united the political parties and the Maoists. A mass uprising throughout the country, led by a seven-party alliance and backed by the Communist Party of Nepal-Maoist (CPN-M) compelled King Gyanendra's government to resign and reinstate the dissolved House of Representatives on 24 April 2006. In the wake of these historic political changes, the CPN-M declared a unilateral ceasefire for 3 months effective 26 April 2006, which was quickly reciprocated by the new government, paving the way for peace talks. Recent developments hold promise for restoring lasting peace and stability in Nepal. The transition to lasting peace and democracy will, however, be very challenging and carries significant risks. At the local level, in several instances CPN-M is maneuvering for control of the political and development space. The political process ahead—particularly agreeing on a process and modality for constituent assembly elections and disarmament, demobilization, and reintegration of the insurgent forces to ensure free and fair elections—will be very challenging.

Table 5.1 Economic Performance Indicators Throughout the Reform Process

Year	Growth (%)			External sector (% of GDP)		
	Real GDP Per Capita Income	Real GDP	Population	Merchandise Export to GDP	Merchandise Import to GDP	Total trade of Goods and NFS to GDP
1990–1997	2.1	5.1	2.3	8.3	25.9	50.1
1998–2005	1.1	3.4	2.34	12.9	28.9	53.8
Pre–reform						
1965–1985	0.6	2.6	2.1			
Reform						
1985–2001	2.5	4.8	2.4			
2002	-2.5	-0.3	2.24	14.3	27.4	50.5
2003	0.9	3.1	2.24	11.6	27.7	49.8
2004	1.3	3.5	2.23	11.6	28	52.1
2005	0.2	2.4	2.26	11.8	28.7	51.1

GDP = gross domestic product, NFS = nonfactor services.

Source: Economic Survey, Ministry of Finance (2005).

Table 5.2 GDP Composition, % GDP, Period Average

Sectors	1975–1977	1999–2001
Agriculture, fisheries, and forestry	64.2	39
Industry	10.6	20.4
Manufacturing	4.8	9
Electricity, gas, water	0.3	0.8
Construction	5.4	10.1
Services	25.2	40.7
Trade, restaurants, hotels	4.1	11.2
Transport, communication, storage	5.4	8.5
Financial and real estate	8.5	10.1
Community and social services	7.2	10.9

Source: Estimated from Central Bureau of Statistics (CBS).

Measure of Openness

Nepal's reforms of the early 1990s increased its economic integration with the world economy. These reforms have contributed to a rise in Nepal's trade-GDP ratio, which was close to 60% by the end of 1990s. However, this fell markedly after 2001 because of the global economic slowdown and the escalating violence of the Maoist insurgency (Table 5.1). Nepal is among South Asia's most open and trade-dependent economies. Also, the trade-GDP ratio in similarly sized economies is about 80%, indicating further potential for trade growth. Nepal's proximity to large economies such as the PRC and India also offers opportunity for trade. Moreover, Nepal's export share in the world market, including products where Nepal has a comparative advantage, is still less than 0.2%, suggesting significant potential for growth.

Unit Labor Cost

Despite economic policy reforms, the competitiveness of Nepal's economy is low as measured by firm-level surveys in manufacturing, and aggregate productivity estimates. While Nepal clearly has an advantage in terms of low wages, this is more than offset by low labor productivity (Table 5.3).

Table 5.3 Index of Unit Labor Cost of Nine Asian Countries, 1999

Country	Labor cost per worker[a]	Value added per worker[b]	Unit labor cost (ULC)[c]	Annual % change in ULC (1990–1999)
Nepal	100	100	100	-3.7
India	130	205	81	-2.3
PRC	180	271	72	-1.1
Bangladesh	110	130	90	
Indonesia	120	276	87	-0.1
Thailand	480	390	94	-2.3
Sri Lanka	160	195	105	4.5
Malaysia	960	909	93	-0.1
Philippines	600	742	93	-2.7

ULC = unit labor cost.

[a] average labor cost per worker manufacturing
[b] value added per unit of labor
[c] labor cost per unit of output manufacturing, according to the internationality accepted definition of the US Department of Commerce.

Source: Nepal Trade Competitiveness Study (2004)

As a result, Nepal's unit labor costs (ULC) are among the highest in the region, even though Nepal has comparative advantage in a range of agricultural and manufacturing products. While ULCs declined in 1990s, this could not be sustained, partly because of the appreciation in the real effective exchange rate (by about 14%) at the end of the 1990s. Key factors contributing to low competitiveness and productivity in Nepal's economy are (i) labor market rigidities, (ii) the limited technology transfer mechanisms such as firm training and FDI, (iii) high infrastructure and transactions costs, (iv) a poor business climate, and (v) insufficient human capital.[4]

Poverty Headcount Ratios

Poverty is deep and pervasive in Nepal, with wide disparity across regions. However, the incidence of poverty declined dramatically, falling from 42% in 1995/96 to 31% in 2003/04 (Table 5.4). Both measures of poverty—the headcount rate and the poverty gap—improved. Thus, the incidence of poverty in Nepal declined by about 11 percentage points (or 26%) over the course of 8 years, a decline of 3.7% per year. Progress occurred in both rural and urban areas, although it was much greater in urban areas. The incidence of poverty in urban areas declined from 22% to 10%, a change of 9.7% per year. While poverty in rural areas also declined appreciably— from 43% to 35%, at 1 percentage point per year—its incidence remains higher than in urban areas.

Table 5.4 Poverty in Nepal, 1995/96 and 2003/04, %

Item	Head-count rate (%)			Poverty gap (x100)		
	1995/96	2003/04	% Change	1995/96	2003/04	% Change
Nepal	41.8	30.9	-26	11.8	7.5	-36
Urban	21.6	9.6	-56	6.6	2.2	-67
Rural	43.3	34.6	-20	12.1	8.5	-30

Source: Central Bureau of Statistics (various years)

The decline in poverty was driven by growth in per capita consumption expenditure and income which, in turn, was driven by increase in remit-

---

4 Estimates of total factor productivity based on firm-level data shows that average levels of productivity in Nepal are lower than in other least-developing countries. The average level of firm productivity (using a total factor productivity index) in Nepal's manufacturing sector was estimated at 53% (measured against the most efficient benchmark) compared with a mean level of productivity in other least developing countries ranging from 60% to 70%.

tances, higher agricultural wages, increased connectivity, urbanization, and a decline in the dependency ratio (World Bank, 2005). Household survey data show that real per capita expenditure increased in real terms by 42% between 1995/96 and 2003/04. Per capita income increased by 41% in real terms and the structure of income changed substantially with income from remittances, nonagricultural entrepreneurial activities, and wage and property income rising. Remittances increased dramatically to $794 million in 2003/04, up from $203 million in 1995/96, to an equivalent of 12% of Nepal's GDP. Agricultural wages rose 25%, nonagricultural unskilled wages rose 20%, and skilled wages more than doubled. Nepal's road network increased 6.7% between 1995/96 and 2003/04. Urbanization moved workers from low-productivity jobs in rural areas to higher-productivity activities in urban areas. The dependency ratio declined; the number of nonworking people per working adult fell between 1995/96 and 2003/04 as a result of the decline in fertility that began in the 1980s. In urban areas, the number of working males per household increased the most.

Foreign Direct Investment Regime: Brief Overall With an Emphasis on East and South Asia

Foreign Direct Investment Performance and Potential New Sectors

FDI performance in Nepal is limited to inbound flows because Nepal has a very strict policy regarding investments by Nepalese in foreign countries. Under the present system, until and unless someone gets permission from the Government and that permission is published in a gazette, nobody can make a foreign investment abroad. A major issue presently under discussion and debate is regarding the relaxation of the above-mentioned restriction, which is based on legal provisions made almost five decades ago. Taking into consideration the present situation, the present analysis is limited to inbound FDI.

There have been FDI inflows into Nepal for many years. However, a significant increase has been noted only from the early 1990s with liberalization of the domestic economy. During this period, private sector participation and FDI were institutionalized withthe enactment of the Foreign Investment and Technology Transfer Act (FITTA) of 1992 and the Industrial Enterprise Act (IEA) of 1992,[5] the two main acts governing FDI

---

[5] IEA and the FITTA were amended in 1996 and 1997, respectively.

into Nepal. There was also liberalization of the exchange rate regime in which the currency was made partially convertible in the current account in March 1992 and subsequently made fully convertible in February 1993. The overall trade reform program during that time was complemented by the amendment of a bilateral trade treaty with India in 1996 that allowed India to import goods manufactured in Nepal (except those on the negative list) free of import duty with no quantitative restrictions. This encouraged Indian investment in Nepal (Rana and Pradhan 2003). These measures created a conducive investment environment and had led to an upward trend of FDI approval until 2000–01.

After 2000/01 however, FDI approval began to decline, the period 1990–2001 saw annual FDI approvals worth $27.7 million, while the period 2002–2005 saw $24.73 million in FDI approvals. The reversal in FDI approval is attributed to deterioration in the investment climate due to growing political instability, which badly affected the economic and commercial activity (Acharya, 2005). The effect on the domestic economy was magnified with the revision of the Nepal–India Trade Treaty in 2002, which withdrew the highly favorable provisions of the earlier treaty in 1996, and led to a substantial drop volume of exports, resulting in the closure of many industries targeting the Indian market.[6]

The trend of aggregate FDI and its three major components—agriculture, manufacturing, and services—during 1990–2005 is presented in Table 5.5.

Regional Foreign Direct Investment Commitments

FDI commitments can also be viewed in terms of FDI originating from SAARC and countries in ASEAN+3. SAARC provided 41.17% of FDI while ASEAN+3 provided 21.43% of total FDI. Regarding the sectoral shares, FDI in agriculture is highest from the ASEAN+3 region and FDI in manufacturing is highest from SAARC. It is worth noting that India, the country with the largest FDI commitments of 39.76%, had more FDI commitment than the whole of ASEAN+3. The percentage share of FDI up to 2005 is presented in Table 5.6.

FDI to Nepal is less than its neighboring countries and regions. Nepal's FDI-GDP ratio stands at 2.1% in 2004, which is far below neighboring countries India (5.9%) and the PRC (15%) (UNCTAD, 2005).[7] Nepal has the lowest FDI-GDP ratio in SAARC. This suggests that there is scope for increasing FDI flows into the country.

---

[6]   Rana et al. 2005.
[7]   UNCTAD. 2005. *World Investment Report*. New York.

Table 5.5 FDI in Nepal, 1990–2005

Year	Agriculture			Total Manufacturing			Total Service			Total FDI		
	No. of Est	FDI	Emp	No. of Est	FDI	Emp	No. of Est	FDI	Emp	No. of Est	FDI	Emp
1990	0	0.00	0	17	3.86	7,526	13	9.79	1,989	30	13.65	9,515
1991	0	0.00	0	18	9.32	2,679	5	0.17	295	23	9.49	2,974
1992	2	0.12	35	23	8.30	4,485	13	5.26	1,095	38	13.68	5,615
1993	0	0.00	0	38	15.85	8,182	26	46.82	5,691	64	62.68	13,873
1994	5	0.57	368	20	19.86	3,033	13	7.48	1,333	38	27.91	4,734
1995	1	0.25	65	14	8.12	1,774	4	1.04	547	19	9.42	2,386
1996	1	0.48	270	24	12.36	3,102	22	26.46	4,660	47	39.29	8,032
1997	1	0.02	73	29	13.58	5,757	47	28.43	3,517	77	42.03	9,347
1998	0	0.00	0	25	5.81	1,855	52	23.65	2,481	77	29.46	4,336
1999	1	0.07	0	19	10.72	1,291	30	13.54	855	50	24.33	2,146
2000	0	0.00	0	31	6.92	3,567	40	13.07	1,136	71	19.99	4,703
2001	1	0.13	31	54	24.21	5,234	41	17.02	1,615	96	41.37	6,880
2002	2	0.06	144	37	11.41	2,285	38	3.97	1,302	77	15.45	3,731
2003	0	0.00	0	27	4.31	1,279	47	18.74	2,293	74	23.06	3,572
2004	0	0.00	0	22	12.50	276	56	24.86	1,868	78	37.36	2,144
2005	1	0.10	37	25	16.62	2,072	38	6.33	3,467	64	23.06	5,576
Average 1990–1998	1	0.16	90	23	10.78	4266	22	16.57	2401	46	27.51	6757
Average 1999–2005	1	0.05	30	31	12.39	2286	41	13.93	1791	73	26.37	4107
Average 1990–2005	1	0.11	64	26	11.49	3400	30	15.42	2134	58	27.04	5598

Emp = employment generated, FDI = foreign direct investment, no. of est = number of establishments.

Note: Classification based on Government GDP standards. FDI is in $ million; Number of Establishment and Employment are in number.

Source: Department of Industries (2006).

Box 5.1: FDI Statistics in Nepal

The Department of Investment under the Ministry of Industry is the sole agency responsible for administration and implementation of inbound FDI. When bringing in FDI, the government reporting system simply requires data on the amount of FDI approved with details such as the country of origin, the amount of FDI, and employment potential. However, this data does not provide an accurate account on the actual FDI flows and on whether the FDI enterprises are in operation. This implies that there may not be a correspondence between reported and actual FDI flows.

Table 5.6 Share of ASEAN and SAARC Countries in Total FDI, 2005

Country/ Region	Agriculture	Manufacturing	Service	Total FDI
ASEAN+3[a]	50.98	17.60	24.17	21.43
	7.25	10.14	10.92	10.57
Hong Kong, China	0.00	1.33	2.42	1.94
Japan	43.73	0.46	5.62	3.54
Korea	0.00	4.28	2.92	3.50
Malaysia	0.00	0.02	0.12	0.07
Philippines	0.00	0.43	0.00	0.19
Singapore	0.00	0.16	2.15	1.28
Thailand	0.00	0.78	0.01	0.34
South Asia	15.76	50.55	34.18	41.17
Bangladesh	0.00	1.69	0.10	0.78
India	15.76	47.85	33.74	39.76
Pakistan	0.00	1.01	0.09	0.49
Sri Lanka	0.00	0.00	0.25	0.14
Rest of the world	33.25	31.85	41.65	37.39
Total	100.00	100.00	100.00	100.00

[a] Brunei; Cambodia; Indonesia; the Lao People's Democratic Republic; Myanmar; Taipei, China; and Viet Nam in ASEAN+3 have made no investments and are therefore excluded from the table.

Source: Department of Industries (2006).

Potential New Sectors for Foreign Direct Investment in Nepal

The United Nations Convention on Trade and Development's (UNCTAD) Investment Policy Review of Nepal of 2003[8] identified the following sectors of potential FDI flow for the coming 20 years, breaking them down into the short, medium, and long term.

- In the short term, the potential sectors are tourism, some manufacturing industries, and herbal products. It has been emphasized that FDI inflows are subject to the Government of Nepal coming out with appropriate investment promotion packages for these sectors. Measures should focus on infrastructure development for tourism, establishment of special economic zones, involvement of the private sector in the development of industrial estates, ceilings on individual land ownership (to help cultivate plant species for commercial scale), reasonable plant royalties, and reductions to import duties on capital equipment.
- In medium term, the potential sectors are hydropower and agriculture. The study emphasizes that improvements to the investment framework in these sectors are necessary. For instance, efforts should be made toward making the Nepal Electricity Authority[9] more efficient and creditworthy, as well as ensuring that air links for domestic agricultural industries are economical.
- In the long term, more FDI is expected in industries such as IT-based services, business and financial-based services, and manufacturing. In due course, the study suggests that the Government should gradually privatize public enterprises in order to create an investment-friendly environment.

Foreign Direct Investment Approval Regime

Acquiring FDI approval in Nepal is lengthy and complex. For example, foreign investors are required to undertake such measures as (i) incorporating at the Company Registrar's Office; (ii) registering the industry at the Department of Investment; (iii) registering at Inland Revenue Office to obtain a Permanent Account Number; and (iv) obtaining permission for trademarks, patents, and designs if necessary.

---

[8] UNCTAD. 2003. *Investment Policy Review* UNCTAD/ITE/IPC/MISC/2003/1, United Nations, New York

[9] The Nepal Electric Authority is the sole state-owned institution authorized to distribute electricity in the country.

To facilitate the above-mentioned procedures, the One Window Committee (OWC) was constituted at the Ministry of Industry, Commerce and Industry. The purpose of the OWC is to make available the facilities and concessions to be enjoyed by any industry under this Act. For the OWC, the Department of Investment acts as a secretariat that has also published a manual on foreign investment procedures. However, the OWC has problems. Its administrative stature is not high enough, so its decisions are not considered final.

Currently there is no board of investment, but there is an Investment Promotion Board (IPB). The board consists of members from related line ministries and the private sector, and the governor of the Nepal Rastra Bank; the director-general of the Department of Industries (DOI) acts as the member secretary. The board is tasked to (i) render necessary cooperation in formulating and implementing the country's industrial law, policies, and regulations; (ii) maintain coordination between the policy level and the implementation level; (iii) take necessary action against the complaints from the OWC; (iv) control environmental and health problems that may arise from industries; and (v) make necessary recommendations to the Government.[10] The major problems that foreign investors face are delays in decision making, mainly attributed to difficulty in regularly convening the IPB, which is composed of high-ranking government officials.

These problems have made FDI approval in Nepal a demanding process. It is thus essential to develop a truly one-window system that would have the mandate to harmonize requirements for documents such as licenses, income tax, customs, and company registration.

Investment Incentives and Tax Concessions

To attract FDI, Nepal has made a number of investment incentives and tax concessions (Maskay et al. 2005). These incentives (Box 5.2) are broadly targeted (not focused by region or by country).

There are additional incentives to attract FDI. For example, the Government has committed to arrange the necessary infrastructure (e.g., roads, warehouses, electricity, water, sanitation, and telecommunications) required to establish industries as well as to provide government land or industrial districts for their establishment. Likewise, the Industrial Enterprises Act has made the provision for recruiting required man-

---

[10]   In addition to the One Window Committee and the Investment Promotion Board, the country also had a Board of Investment (BOI). However, the existence of these two separate bodies (IPB and BOI) with similar functions made the FDI approval regime confusing and problematic (Pant and Sigdel, 2004). Because of this, the government recently dissolved the BOI.

Box 5.2: Incentives and Tax Concessions

Income Tax Exemption. Corporate tax will not exceed 20% of profits with a maximum of 5% income tax imposed on dividends earned out of investment in any industry. Export earnings are taxed at 40% of the income tax imposed on other industries, with the tax amount not exceeding 0.5% of the total export amount.

Income Tax Deductions. Income tax rebates to industries other than tobacco and beverages established and operating in remote and undeveloped regions; provision of depreciation on the fixed assets; industries other tobacco and beverages utilizing 80% or more local raw materials and employing all Nepalese citizens are granted a rebate of 10% on income tax; deduction for capital expenditure or expanding its installed capacity by 25% or more; additional income tax rebate of 10% for that year if a single industry provides direct employment to 600 or more Nepalese citizens through the year; and reduction from the taxable income for the investment on pollution control process and equipments. There is also a provision to capitalize the pre-operation cost incurred by the industry for skill development and training; 10% of the gross profit may be deducted against taxable income on account of technology and efficiency improvement; 5% of gross income to be deducted against taxable income on account of spent on advertising.

Concessional Customs Duties. Provision of 5% duty rate and 50% rebate on customs duties with full exemption from sales tax for manufacturing industries importing plant, machinery, and equipment required for direct production processes falling under chapter 84 of the harmonized customs (HS) classification; bonded warehouse facilities to export-oriented industries. Provision of entry into the pass book without paying any customs duty.

Excise Duty Rebate and Refund. A rebate of 35% on excise duty for 10 years from the date of operation for industries established and operating in remote areas, 25% in undeveloped areas, and 15% in under-developed areas, and special tax concessions for industries utilizing locally available raw materials, chemicals, and packing materials.

Duty Drawbacks. Provision of refund on duty and taxes levied on raw materials, auxiliary raw materials etc. used in producing goods for export.

Source: Industrial Enterprise Act (1992) and Budget Speech (2006-07).

power either from among Nepalese citizens. If those industries cannot be operated with Nepalese citizens, expatriates or foreign nationals can be appointed with prior approval from the Department of Labor. Expatriates or foreign nationals can be employed for a maximum period of 5 years, with a provision for an additional 5 years. Likewise, as per commitments under Nepal's accession to the WTO, the total number of foreign nationals working in an organization should not exceed 15% of local employment. This commitment is expected to liberalize further after 5 years in the WTO.

Despite these commitments, there are a number of issues regarding government policy. First is the confusion regarding tax concessions; the Income Tax Act of 2002 has removed tax concessions for industry mandated under the Industrial Enterprise and Foreign Investment Acts. Second are the bureaucratic rules and processes, which force foreign investors to face unnecessary complications and long waiting periods for receiving duty drawbacks on re-exported goods. Third, there is the need to examine whether foreign investors can undertake external commercial borrowing and in what modality; this will make investments more competitive. Fourth, domestic labor laws are not investment-friendly. Fifth, the Government of Nepal has not made substantial progress in reforms to the legal framework governing foreign investment or labor. Such reforms could attract FDI and harmonize the legal process as per commitments under the WTO. Sixth, the Government imposes export tax that hampers the competitiveness of local industries.

Investor Protection and Ownership Restrictions

There are certain provisions that ensure investor protection and stabilize expectations.

- Investor protection is guaranteed by the Industrial Enterprise Act, which has stated that there will be no nationalization of privately owned industries.
- Foreign investors can own up to 100% equity in private firms and are entitled to repatriate the investment amount and other earnings. Further, to facilitate business transactions, foreign exchange restrictions have been relaxed. Foreigners and companies are allowed to open and operate foreign exchange accounts in any of the domestic commercial banks.
- Likewise, there is the provision for business visas for foreign investors for up to 5 years. Provisions also exist for providing nontourist visas to carry out studies for investment along with residential visas for foreign investors.

However, there have been difficulties with implementing these provisions. For example, there is no smooth transfer of foreign capital. Likewise, the Foreign Investor Visa Card is not being honored in letter and spirit; foreign investors are treated unequally and placed in the same category as tourists. Also, no clear policy governs competition or consumer rights.

Ownership Restrictions

There are certain ownership restrictions imposed on FDI under the 1992 Foreign Investment Act; that is, FDI is permitted in all industries except in statutory state monopolies and those reserved exclusively for national investors. Specifically, ownership is restricted in cottage industries, services (such as beauty parlor, hair cutting, tailoring, and driver training), real estate, film (in the national language and other recognized languages of the nation), retail business, some tourist businesses (nonstar-rated hotels, travel agencies, trekking agencies, and white-water rafting), pony trekking, horseback riding, internal courier services, agriculture-based enterprises (poultry, fish, and beekeeping), explosive gunpowder, and consultancy services (such as management, accounting, engineering, and legal services).

Procedures for Settlement of Investor–State Disputes in Nepal

Procedures for the settlement of disputes between foreign and national investors are provided in the Foreign Investment Act and the 2005 Procedural Manual for Foreign Investment in Nepal. In the case of industries with up to NRs500 million in fixed assets, the DOI will settle the dispute amicably by mutual consultation with the disputing parties and give decision. If any party is dissatisfied with the decision, the dispute will be settled by arbitration in accordance with Nepal Arbitration Law, which follows the rule of United Nations Commission on International Trade Law (UNCITL). The complainant in such a case has to appeal to the Appellate Court for nomination of an arbitrator who will review the DOI decision. The Foreign Investment Act stipulates that such arbitration will be held in Kathmandu. However, for industries with fixed asset investment above $7.7 million, disputes may be settled according to the Foreign Investment Agreement document signed by all concerned parties of the agreement. Settlement of disputes regarding intellectual property, industrial designs, patents, or trademarks is covered by the Patent, Design and Trade Mark Act 1965 (with amendment of 2005 ordinance). According to this Act, the DOI is authorized to settle the dispute and, if necessary, impose fines.

Settlement of investor–state disputes is facilitated by the fact that Nepal is a signatory to the Convention on the Settlement of Investment Disputes between States and Nations and Other States and a member of the International Centre for the Settlement of Investment Disputes, the World Intellectual Property Right Organization (WIPRO), and the Multi-lateral Investment Guarantee Agency (MIGA). Nepal has also entered into bilateral investment treaties with France, Germany, the United Kingdom, and Mauritius. Nepal has also entered into double taxation trade treaties with nine countries: India, the PRC, Pakistan, Sri Lanka, Thailand, Norway, Mauritius, Austria, and the Republic of Korea.

Nevertheless, the major issue is that the present mechanism for settling disputes over FDI is ineffective and costly (Rana and Pradhan 2005).

Export Processing Zones and Special Economic Zones

There is presently no EPZ or special economic zone operating in Nepal. However, the importance of EPZs has been acknowledged by the Government, which has approved the construction of one in Bhairhawa (in western Nepal at an India border checkpoint). This is targeted to be operational in the near future. Similarly, a law related to EPZs is in the process of enactment. This law will fully exempt industries established in EPZs from paying income tax for the first 5 years, with a 50% exemption in the years thereafter.

Investment Agency Geographical Focus and Resources

At present, Nepal does not have a policy providing for an external investment agency. A first step in this direction was taken when the country took a more active economic diplomacy stance. In this regard, an Economic Diplomacy Coordination Committee was formed under the chairmanship of the prime minister, and an Economic Diplomacy Standing Committee was formed under the chairmanship of the foreign minister. In addition, a Multilateral Economic Affairs Division was established at the Ministry of Foreign Affairs. This division has been given more responsibility in terms of foreign trade, FDI, tourism, foreign employment, and investment programs related to nonresident Nepalese. Despite these activities, there is serious lack of focus in economic diplomacy policymaking as evidenced by weak coordination between Nepal and SAARC, ASEAN+3, BIMSTEC, and other nations in the subregion.

Other Issues Raised by Firms

Along with the above-mentioned issues, other concerns have also been raised: (i) discrimination by government officials between foreign and national investors, (ii) the need to allow outbound FDI in other countries by developing necessary laws and regulations, (iii) and the need to tap nonresident Nepalese for FDI.

Merchandise Trade Policy with Emphasis on East and South Asia

Trade Performance and Patterns

Exports

Exports have grown at an average rate of 11.8% per annum during the last 15 years, with an annual growth at 13% during the period 1990–1997 and 11% during the period 1998–2005 (Table 5.7). The country's improved business environment during the first period due to the economic reforms contributed to better export growth. The deteriorating export performance during the second period could be attributed to the softening of world demand; policy changes in importing countries; faltering competitiveness; rising transport costs; and the Maoist insurgency, which seems to have deepened the effects of external shocks. Weak demand seems to have affected Nepal's exports to third countries, particularly those destined toward the US and Germany.

Nepal, like other South Asian countries, still depends on a few exports and a few markets. In the past decade, Nepal has become even more dependent on the same few markets with 90% of its exports going to India, Germany, and the US (Table 5.7). While the shares of Nepal's exports to Germany and the US have declined from 56% in 1990 to 18% in 2005, it increased threefold to India during this period. Thus, India is Nepal's largest export market, accounting for two thirds of Nepal's total exports in 2005. This rise is due to (i) the long porous border between the two countries, (ii) the free movement of people and capital, (iii) a preferential trade agreement between two countries, and (iv) the pegging of the Nepalese rupee to the Indian rupee. Over the past decade, integration with India has increased as the Indian economy has expanded and Nepal's exports to third-country markets have stalled. There is limited success in penetrating other regional markets, despite membership in the SAFTA (Karmacharya, 2005b). In the last 15 years, Nepal's exports to other South Asian countries accounted for only 1% of its exports. The share of Nepal's exports to East Asian countries increased from 3.4% in 1990 to about 4.7% in 2005. Nepal's major export partner in East Asia is the PRC (through the Tibet Autonomous Region), accounting for 3.1% of its total exports in 2005.

Manufacturing now dominates Nepal's exports, though exports of agricultural products have increased in recent years (Table 5.8). Data for the years 1990, 1997, and 2005 indicate that manufacturing goods account for about 80% of Nepal's exports while primary goods cover the remaining 20%. Nepal's exports until recently were concentrated in three items:

Table 5.7 Direction of Nepal's Export Trade, 1991–2005

Country/Region	$ '000			Share (%)			Growth Rate (%)		
	1991	1998	2005	1991	1998	2005	1991–1998	1998–2005	1991–2005
East Asia	5860.33	12824.87	38512.8	3.4	3.17	4.66	11.84	17.01	14.39
ASEAN	817.71	530.63	2100.44	0.47	0.13	0.25	-5.99	21.72	6.97
Brunei	5.23	12.49	8.62	0	0	0	13.23	-5.16	3.63
Cambodia	0	0	1.5	0	0	0	N/A	N/A	N/A
Indonesia	26.14	2.09	14.12	0.02	0	0	-30.29	31.37	-4.3
Lao PDR	0	0	0	0	0	0	N/A	N/A	N/A
Malaysia	2.83	80.54	175.46	0	0.02	0.02	61.37	11.76	34.29
Myanmar	0	0.68	0.15	0	0	0	N/A	-19.02	N/A
Philippines	0.4	5.18	63.67	0	0	0.01	44.34	43.09	43.71
Singapore	743.01	423.09	626.08	0.43	0.1	0.08	-7.73	5.76	-1.22
Thailand	40.09	6.52	1101.95	0.02	0	0.13	-22.85	108.1	26.7
Viet Nam	0	0.03	108.87	0	0	0.01	N/A	223.4	N/A
Japan	679.04	2629.32	7524.57	0.39	0.65	0.91	21.34	16.21	18.74
PRC	2820.96	9147.56	26561.5	1.63	2.26	3.22	18.3	16.45	17.37
Tibet	2820.96	9140.32	25809.23	1.63	2.26	3.13	18.29	15.99	17.13
Korea	1349.84	254.59	506.62	0.78	0.06	0.06	-21.2	10.33	-6.76
Hong Kong	192.78	262.77	1819.66	0.11	0.06	0.22	4.52	31.84	17.39
Taipei,China	0	0	0	0	0	0	N/A	N/A	N/A
South Asia	42365.14	146679.12	562225.85	24.54	36.2	68.09	19.41	21.16	20.28
Bangladesh	48.25	8762.61	4091.1	0.03	2.16	0.5	110.25	-10.31	37.32
India	39747.66	132730.49	554829.82	23.03	32.76	67.2	18.8	22.67	20.72
Sri Lanka	2368.48	4427.48	78.93	1.37	1.09	0.01	9.35	-43.75	-21.6

continued on next page

Table 5.7 (continued)

Country/Region	$ '000			Share (%)			Growth Rate (%)		
	1991	1998	2005	1991	1998	2005	1991–1998	1998–2005	1991–2005
Germany	63757.13	100345.32	43906.51	36.94	24.76	5.32	6.69	-11.14	-2.63
United Kingdom	3948.46	4685.73	14768.07	2.29	1.16	1.79	2.48	17.82	9.88
France	1379.98	7166.51	8689.17	0.8	1.77	1.05	26.53	2.79	14.05
Saudi Arabia	0.28	0.37	68.66	0	0	0.01	3.97	111.1	48.13
Rest of World	22572.1	28844.85	51026.65	13.08	7.12	6.18	3.57	8.49	6
Total	172605.14	405206.19	825677.92	100	100	100	12.97	10.7	11.83

ASEAN = Association of Southeast Asian Nations.

Source: Trade Promotion Center (2005)

Table 5.8 Nepal's Structure of Merchandise Exports, 1991–2005

Product	Value ($ Mn)				Share (%)				Growth (%)			
	1991	1998	2005		1991	1998	2005		1991–1998	1998–2005	1991–2005	
Exports	172.61	405.21	825.68		100	100	100		12.97	10.7	11.83	
Food and live animals	23.05	46	98.36		13.35	11.35	11.91		10.37	11.47	10.92	
Tobacco and beverages	0.26	0.34	0.44		0.15	0.08	0.05		3.63	4.09	3.86	
Crude materials and inedible	7.29	7.17	12.4		4.22	1.77	1.5		-0.23	8.13	3.86	
Crude material and lubricants	0	0.31	0.06		0	0.08	0.01		N/A	-21.01	N/A	
Animal and vegetable oil and fats	4.72	31.46	71.31		2.73	7.76	8.64		31.14	12.4	21.41	
Vegetable ghee	0	23.27	65.2		0	5.74	7.9		N/A	15.86	N/A	
Chemicals and drugs	0.41	28.99	51.72		0.24	7.15	6.26		83.52	8.62	41.19	
Manufactured goods, classified	100.75	171.39	402.12		58.37	42.3	48.7		7.88	12.96	10.39	
Hides and skins	4.92	6.15	7.91		2.85	1.52	0.96		3.23	3.68	3.45	
Woolen carpets	87.22	124.97	83.84		50.53	30.84	10.15		5.27	-5.54	-0.28	
Machinery and transport equipment	0	0.85	2.92		0	0.21	0.35		132.35	19.19	66.42	
Miscellaneous manufactured articles	36.11	118.7	186.21		20.92	29.29	22.55		18.53	6.64	12.43	
Readymade garments	31.55	103.31	93.85		18.28	25.5	11.37		18.47	-1.36	8.1	
Woolen and pashmina goods	0	0	25.34		0	0	3.07		N/A	N/A	N/A	
Not classified	0	0	0.13		0	0	0.02		N/A	N/A	N/A	

N/A = not applicable.

Source: Economic Survey, Ministry of Finance.

garments, carpets, and pashmina, which together accounted for more than 70% of Nepal's exports in the early 1990s. However, the share of these three products declined to about 25% in 2005. Vegetable ghee, chemicals, and drugs are now some new major exports, accounting for about 15% of Nepal's exports in 2005.

Garments are exported almost exclusively to the US, although they are being increasingly traded to India. Carpets are primarily destined for Germany and vegetable ghee to India. Table 5.9 shows that some top four major exports to East Asian countries in 2005 include raw hides and skins (largest to the PRC, followed by Thailand and Malaysia), garments (Japan followed by Hong Kong, China; the Republic of Korea; Singapore; and Malaysia), works of art and antiques (Japan followed by Hong Kong, China; Singapore; and Thailand), and carpets (Japan; the Republic of Korea; Hong Kong, China; and Singapore).

Nepal's dependence on a limited number of exports and markets has made it vulnerable to external shocks arising from shifting external demand and policy. The end of the Agreement on Textiles and Clothing has been a significant shock for Nepal. The phasing out of the quota-based trade in textiles from the beginning of 2005 has adversely affected garment exports. Similarly, the carpet industry has lost its large market in recent years due to declining demand, price controls, long order cycles, and greater competition. Nepal's growing dependence on India as a destination for its exports is also risky. Its renewed trade treaty with India is more restrictive than its 1996 predecessor. The renewed treaty imposes more stringent rules of origin and tariff-rate quotas, requires clearly specified safeguard clauses, and requires that Nepal submit information about the basis for its calculating rules of origin to the Government of India annually. This change in policy from free to restricted trade has had an immediate negative effect on Nepal's export performance.

Imports

Imports have grown at an average rate of 10% per year during the last 15 years, with an average annual growth of 13.4% during the period 1990–1997 and about 7% during the period 1998–2005. Nepal's import sources are slightly more diversified than its export markets. More than 10 countries supply 90% of Nepal's imports. Despite a concerted effort in the 1970s to diversify its foreign trade partners, Nepal still turned to India for more about 60% of its imports in 2005 compared to about 33% in 1990 (Table 5.10). This increase came from the corresponding decline in Nepal's share of imports to East Asian countries. For example, Nepal's share of imports from East Asian countries has declined from 41% in 1990 to about 26% in 2005. The substantial decline in import share is largely due to the drop of

Table 5.9 Nepal's Major Exports to East and South Asia, 2004/05

Country	Vegetable ghee	Readymade garments	Carpets	Groats and meal	Homeo-pathic medicine	Raw hides and skins	Spike-nard oil	Works of art and antiques	Cardamom	Spectacle lenses	Machinery and parts
East Asia	0	1,522,041	899,722	386,290	3,457	1,886,596	7,701	967,886	184,964	124,335	295,983
ASEAN	0	82,628	34,419	386,290	230	364,401	7,701	220,027	184,964	116,715	3,704
Brunei	0	0	2,352	0	0	0	0	0	0	0	0
Cambodia	0	0	0	0	0	0	0	0	0	0	1,498
Indonesia	0	2,556	0	0	0	0	7,701	0	0	0	0
Lao PDR	0	0	0	0	0	0	0	0	0	0	0
Malaysia	0	32,974	3,992	0	42	24,110	0	48,565	0	0	0
Myanmar	0	0	0	0	159	0	0	0	0	0	0
Philippines	0	0	0	0	0	0	0	9,281	0	0	0
Singapore	0	31,018	21,041	0	0	0	0	92,036	184,964	2,981	2,206
Thailand	0	9,935	7,034	386,290	14	340,292	0	69,625	0	65,005	0
Viet Nam	0	6,145	0	0	14	0	0	520	0	48,729	0
Japan	0	1,287,798	361,094	0	1,404	0	0	603,125	0	0	0
PRC	0	3,367	56,391	0	0	525,765	0	34,340	0	7,556	86,314
Korea	0	68,238	359,495	0	1,823	0	0	1438	0	64	0
Hong Kong, China	0	80,010	88,323	0	0	996,429	0	108,956	0	0	205,965
Taipei,China	0	0	0	0	0	0	0	0	0	0	0
South Asia	65,202,532	5,151,507	24,290	1,941,924	147,098	4,800,464	0	1,420,978	10,816,782	29851	6,859
Bangladesh	0	0	0	1,941,924	0	0	0	318	0	11,363	0
India	65,202,532	5,143,460	0	0	98,453	4,744,023	0	1,419,128	8448,664	0	0
Pakistan	0	61	24,290	0	48,646	0	0	1,448	2,368,118	18,487	0
Sri Lanka	0	7,986	0	0	0	56,441	0	84	333,169	0	6,859
Rest of the world	0	87,178,927	82,917,282	0	18,331	1,227,429	8,494	56,451,87	333,169	11,443	1,518,164
Total	65,202,532	93,852,475	83,841,294	2,328,214	168,886	7,914,489	16,195	8,034,051	11,334,915	165,629	18,21,007

Source: Trade Promotion Centre

Table 5.10 Direction of Nepal's Import Trade, 1991–2005

Country	$'000			Share in total imports (%)			Growth rate (%)		
	1991	1998	2005	1991	1998	2005	1991–1998	1998–2005	1991–2005
East Asia	222739.63	538616.29	542844.71	41.05	41.09	25.82	13.44	0.1	6.57
ASEAN	91765	256352.49	268646.54	16.91	19.56	12.78	15.81	0.7	7.97
Brunei	4.35	6392.25	386.64	0	0.49	0.02	183.5	-33	37.79
Cambodia	0	45.1	0.82	0	0	0	N/A	-43.6	N/A
Indonesia	2133.11	19903.3	73456.22	0.39	1.52	3.49	37.58	20.5	28.76
Lao PDR	2.97	0	0.08	0	0	0	-100	N/A	-22.45
Malaysia	5337.29	17131.86	39674.77	0.98	1.31	1.89	18.13	12.75	15.41
Myanmar	0.28	385.85	87.23	0	0.03	0	180.8	-19.14	50.68
Philippines	22.06	696.08	504.98	0	0.05	0.02	63.74	-4.48	25.06
Singapore	78903.2	186162.05	108956.68	14.54	14.2	5.18	13.05	-7.37	2.33
Thailand	4834.58	25564.08	43847.64	0.89	1.95	2.09	26.86	8.01	17.06
Viet Nam	527.17	71.93	1731.49	0.1	0.01	0.08	-24.76	57.53	8.87
Japan	73094.98	40524.08	36079.2	13.47	3.09	1.72	-8.08	-1.65	-4.92
PRC	37883.86	77590.96	180860.51	6.98	5.92	8.6	10.78	12.85	11.81
TAR	12127.1	16227.13	64767.92	2.23	1.24	3.08	4.25	21.86	12.71
Korea	12105.47	27422.96	39165.26	2.23	2.09	1.86	12.39	5.22	8.75
Hong Kong, China	7890.33	136725.8	18093.21	1.45	10.43	0.86	50.3	-25.09	6.11
Taipei,China	0	0	0	0	0	0	N/A	N/A	N/A
South Asia	182263.97	414169.56	1212976.3	33.59	31.6	57.7	12.44	16.59	14.5

continued on next page

Table 5.10 (continued)

Country	$ '000			Share in total imports (%)			Growth rate (%)		
	1991	1998	2005	1991	1998	2005	1991–1998	1998–2005	1991–2005
Bangladesh	62.9	5384.48	2893.21	0.01	0.41	0.14	88.83	-8.49	31.45
India	181598.13	401135.49	1207260.2	33.46	30.6	57.43	11.99	17.05	14.49
Pakistan	302.64	5621.87	2346.65	0.06	0.43	0.11	51.8	-11.73	15.75
Sri Lanka	300.3	2027.72	476.22	0.06	0.15	0.02	31.37	-18.7	3.35
Other Major Trading Partner	36325.26	96228.14	120870.21	6.69	7.34	5.75	14.93	3.31	8.97
US	3801.99	19995.02	24807.9	0.7	1.53	1.18	26.76	3.13	14.34
Germany	11582.17	22070.84	22094.47	2.13	1.68	1.05	9.65	0.02	4.72
United Kingdom	3575.51	19332.02	20424.3	0.66	1.47	0.97	27.26	0.79	13.26
France	16953.88	6824.86	9401.59	3.12	0.52	0.45	-12.19	4.68	-4.12
Saudi Arabia	411.71	28005.41	44141.94	0.08	2.14	2.1	82.73	6.72	39.64
Rest of world	101341.71	261766.57	225609.79	18.67	19.97	10.73	14.52	-2.1	5.88
Total	**542670.6**	**1310781**	**2102301**	**100**	**100**	**100**	**13.43**	**6.98**	**10.16**

TAR = Tibet Autonomous Region

Source: Trade Promotion Centre

imports from Japan from about 14% of total imports in 1990 to about 2% in 2005, followed by Singapore with a decline in import share from 15% in 1990 to 5% in 2005. However, Nepal's share of imports from the PRC increased during this period from about 7% in 1990 to about 9% in 2005. Among Nepal's top six East Asian import trading partners in 2005 are the PRC, followed by Singapore, Indonesia, Thailand, the Republic of Korea, and Japan. Imports from other countries in the SAARC make up about 1% of Nepal's imports.

Significant changes have occurred in Nepal's import structure (Table 5.11). Manufacturing has become the most important sector since the last decade although its share in total imports declined from 37% in 1997 to 25% in 2005. Fuels have the second largest share of imports at 20% in 2005. Machinery and transport equipment, which accounted for the largest import share at 26% in 1990, have dropped to third position at 18% in 2005. Table 5.12 shows that Nepal's top four import items from East and South Asia are machinery and parts (the largest importer being India followed by the PRC; Singapore; Japan; the Republic of Korea; Thailand; Hong Kong, China; Malaysia; and Indonesia), vehicles and spare parts (the largest importer being India, followed by Japan and the Republic of Korea), palm oil (the largest importer being Indonesia, followed by Singapore and Malaysia), and textiles (the largest importer being India followed by the PRC and Thailand).

Import protection

Average Import Tariff

Historically, Nepal's trade regime has been shaped by its long and open border with India. Its close links with India and dependence on India for transit routes have resulted in a special economic relationship. While providing opportunities for increased exports and agricultural and industrial growth that remain to be fully exploited, these links have constrained policy choices in Nepal. Nepal has been subjected to adverse spillover effects of India's inward-looking, inefficient industrial system. The disparities in the prevailing economic policies of both India and Nepal, India's relatively high tariff structure, the porous borders between the two countries, and Nepal's wish to keep a lower tariff structure all serve as incentives to smuggle third-country goods from Nepal to India. To mitigate this smuggling, Nepal developed an elaborate structure of quantitative restrictions, import licenses, and other administrative controls that govern private and foreign transactions. Following the adoption of liberalization measures in India during early 1990s, the constraints on policy choices have lessened.

Table 5.11 Nepal's Structure of Merchandise Imports, 1991–2005

Product	Value ($ Mn)			Share (%)			Growth (%)		
	1991	1998	2005	1991	1998	2005	1991–1998	1998–2005	1991–2005
Imports	**542.67**	**1310.78**	**2102.30**	**100.00**	**100.00**	**100.00**	**13.43**	**6.98**	**10.16**
Food and live animals	42.54	72.59	138.13	7.84	5.54	6.57	7.94	9.63	8.78
Tobacco and beverages	6.00	11.77	14.28	1.11	0.90	0.68	10.10	2.80	6.39
Crude materials and inedible	47.04	102.74	157.62	8.67	7.84	7.50	11.81	6.30	9.02
Crude material and lubricants	53.23	140.46	420.92	9.81	10.72	20.02	14.87	16.97	15.92
Animal and vegetable oil and fats	17.33	29.84	84.62	3.19	2.28	4.02	8.07	16.06	11.99
Chemicals and drugs	71.29	163.14	269.76	13.14	12.45	12.83	12.55	7.45	9.97
Manufactured goods, classified	139.04	480.14	521.06	25.62	36.63	24.79	19.37	1.18	9.90
Machinery and transport equipment	139.97	246.46	369.37	25.79	18.80	17.57	8.42	5.95	7.18
Miscellaneous manufactured articles	26.18	58.53	106.21	4.83	4.47	5.05	12.18	8.89	10.52
Not classified	0.05	5.10	20.33	0.01	0.39	0.97	95.52	21.83	54.34

Source: Economic Surveys, Ministry of Finance (various issues).

Table 5.12 Nepal's Major Imports from East and South Asia in 2005 (Selecting Top from Individual Country)

Country/Region	Value of Products ($)									
	Petroleum products	Machinery and parts	Palm oil	Textiles	Jute and related fibers	Parts of airplanes and helicopters	Sugar	Perfume and cosmetics	Edible vegetables and roots	Vehicles and spare parts
East Asia	0	114388873	87497131	41166723	194	5923135	2909140	2864814	783944	22984811
ASEAN	0	35046354	87497131	23028685	0	5230848	1103110	2027541	654727	1322639
Brunei	0	20554	0	0	0	327169	0	0	0	0
Cambodia	0	811	0	0	0	0	0	0	0	0
Indonesia	0	3118029	52513879	1527710	0	0	0	394510	0	0
Lao PDR	0	0	0	0	0	0	0	0	0	0
Malaysia	0	4289606	11918314	486006	0	54336	0	178992	0	282560
Myanmar	0	0	0	0	0	0	0	0	87225	0
Philippines	0	41069	0	0	0	44798	192336	11745	0	0
Singapore	0	20084896	23064938	2542591	0	4777324	910107	324484	554653	729826
Thailand	0	6808917	0	18466442	0	27220	666	1117810	12849	310253
Viet Nam	0	682472	0	5936	0	0	0	0	0	0
Japan	0	15001624	0	1041291	0	10757	0	31715	0	9751409
PRC	0	48498401	0	14343903	194	0	1407316	56415	128629	4884293
Korea	0	11367180	0	1010659	0	0	0	3798	0	6904207
Hong Kong, China	0	4475314	0	1742185	0	681530	398714	745344	588	122264
Taipei;China	0	0	0	0	0	0	0	0	0	0

continued on next page

Table 5.12 *(continued)*

Country/Region	Petroleum products	Machinery and parts	Palm oil	Textiles	Jute and related fibers	Parts of airplanes and helicopters	Sugar	Perfume and cosmetics	Edible vegetables and roots	Vehicles and spare parts
South Asia	374855134	59284622	0	30704558	1404087	0	793249	5499914	11786080	71991007
Bangladesh	0	602381		49883	1404087	0	0	5445	0	0
India	374855134	58562588	0	29713080	0	0	793249	5399437	11738397	71990155
Pakistan	0	29115	0	941595	0	0	0	7147	47684	853
Sri Lanka	0	90539	0	0	0	0	0	87884	0	0
Rest of world	0	43426290	0	6656663	0	10431206	6383375	1395485	2774642	4656739
Total	**374855134**	**217099785**	**87497131**	**78527944**	**1404281**	**16354342**	**10085764**	**9760213**	**15344666**	**99632557**

Value of Products ($)

Source: Trade Promotion Centre

236

Box 5.3: Informal Trade

Unrecorded or informal trade is an important aspect of Nepal's trade with India. It operates both through and outside legal channels. Informal trade through legal channels is carried out through false invoicing, which partially evades export and import tariffs, domestic taxes, and nontariff barriers. Informal trade through unofficial channels totally evades tariffs, taxes, and nontariff barriers. Such trade takes place along Nepal's border with India. The following discussion concerns only the border crossings of goods between Nepal and India and is based on estimates from Indian and Nepalese territories (Taneja, Sarvananthan, Karmacharya, and Pohit 2004).

Estimates of India-Nepal Informal Trade: Contrary to the belief that informal trade between India and Nepal takes place largely from Nepal to India, recent studies show that informal trade takes place in both directions (Table 5.13). In fact, data suggest that informal exports from India to Nepal in 2000/01 averaged $180 million, while those from Nepal to India averaged $157 million. This data implies that Nepal has a slight deficit in informal trade. Estimates of total two-way informal trade range between $368 million (Nepalese estimates) and $408 million (Indian estimates).

Table 5.13 Summary Estimates of Formal and Informal Trade Balance, 2000-2001 ($ Mn)

Item	Export (X)	Imports (M)	X+M	X-M
Indian Territory				
Formal	141	255	396	-114
Informal	180	228	408	-48
Share of informal trade to formal trade (%)	128	89	103	54
Nepalese Territory				
Formal	359	614	973	-255
Informal	157	211	368	-54
Share of informal trade to formal trade (%)	44	34	38	21

Notes: The reference period for India (formal and informal) is April 2000–March 2001; for Nepal, June/July 2000–May/June 2001 (formal), and April/May 2000–March/April 2001 (informal).

Sources: Karmacharya, B. K. 2002a; Taneja, N., M. Sarvananthan, B.K. Karmacharya, and S. Pohit. 2004.

The conventional position is that informal trade is a response to trade and domestic policy distortions. This holds true for goods exported from Nepal to

India that originated in third countries. The difference in tariffs prevailing between Nepal and India in these goods vis-à-vis rest of the world is wide-ranging (5–30%). Furthermore, Nepal's trade regime has few nontariff barriers. Tariffs differences might not be such a strong influence on informal imports from India, which consist mostly of rice and other unprocessed food products that face no tariff or nontariff barriers in Nepal. Factors other than policy-related distortions are apparently more important in influencing informal trade. A survey by Taneja and Pohit (2000) showed that trade policy barriers such as tariffs and quantitative restrictions between Nepal and India were less significant than institutional factors—quick realization of payments, no paperwork, no procedural delays, and lower transport costs—in driving traders to informal channels. Taneja and Pohit (2000) also showed that informal traders bear relatively low transaction costs in comparison to formal traders. Most informal traders bear transaction costs of less than 10% of turnover, few bear costs of more than 20%, and none bear costs of more than 30%. Formal traders may bear total transaction costs of more than 30% of their turnover.

The reforms of the early 1990s appear to have simplified the tariff structure and substantially reduced tariff levels and variation. The unweighted average customs duty in 2005 was 14%, with most items falling within the range of 10–20% (Table 5.14. The prevailing applied tariff rates ranged from 5% to 80% (with intermediate tariffs at 5%, 10%, 15%, 25%, and 40%). The high tariff rate of 80% on vehicles is largely for revenue-raising purposes. The Government has imposed an excise tax on vehicle imports since 2000. Since no vehicles are manufactured or assembled in Nepal, the tariff and excise rates are equivalent.

In addition, Nepal also imposes other duties and charges on imports, ranging from 2.5% to 11.5% on industrial goods and from 2.5% to 14.5% on agricultural products. This has resulted to a cascading tariff rate structure.

Nontariff Barriers

Nontariff barriers are imposed on a few sensitive and banned items. These include narcotics such as opium and morphine, liquor of more than 60% alcohol content, beef and beef products, and other items related to defense and communication. Nepal does not have any import quota restrictions.

As part of its accession to the WTO, Nepal has made extensive commitments to liberalize trade. In return for the rights associated with WTO membership, Nepal agreed to ensure that all its trade-related laws conform with WTO obligations. Nontariff barriers and other duties and charges are to be eliminated and there would be full implementation of the Agreement on Customs Valuation, the Agreement on Technical Barriers to Trade, the Agreement on Sanitary and Phytosanitary Measures, the Agreement on Trade Related Aspects of Intellectual Property Rights (TRIPS), and the Agreement on Rules of Origin. Nepal has bound almost all its tariff rates, with most bindings at or above current applied rates. Nepal accepted an average tariff binding of 42% in agricultural products and around 24% in industrial goods

Table 5.14 Nepal Average Customs Duty by Main Categories of Goods, %

Chapter numbers	Main category of goods	2001/02	2002/03	2005/06
1–10	Live animals	10.5	10.5	10.8
11–20	Grains, vegetable extracts, sugars	16.7	16.7	16.8
21–30	Beverages, tobacco, mineral fuels, pharmaceuticals	13.6	11	11.6
31–40	Fertilizers, cosmetics, soaps, chemicals, plastics	20.6	16.5	16.4
41–50	Rawhides, skins, wood, paper, silk	11.7	12.2	13.4
51–60	Wool, cotton, manmade fibers, carpets	11.2	11.6	11.8
61–70	Clothing, footwear, ceramics, glassware, stoneware	20.1	21.3	22.2
71–80	Iron, steel, copper, nickel, aluminum, lead, zinc, tin	12.9	13	12.9
81–90	Tools, machinery, vehicles, aircrafts	11.9	11.8	11.5
91–91	Clocks, musical instruments, arms, furniture, art	21.1	21.6	21.5
	Total number of items	5321	5346	5367
	Average customs duty	14.4	13.7	14

Source: Customs Tariff Schedules, Ministry of Finance (various issues).

Main Instruments for Export Promotion

Nepal provides duty drawback and bonded warehouse schemes for its exporters. The bonded warehouse facilities were initially limited to garment producers exporting to third countries (i.e., non-India markets) and only for fabrics, not accessories. The facility is presently extended to (i) producers exporting garments to India and third countries, (ii) producers exporting nongarment products to third countries, and (iii) other producers exporting a minimum of 80% of their nongarment production to India.

All exports are subject to an export service fee of 0.5% of the free-on-board value to cover the costs of services provided by customs and other trade facilitation agencies. As such, it should not be a major disincentive to exporters. Raw hides and unprocessed wool are also subject to some export restrictions to encourage domestic value addition. Sugar exports are restricted, except to the EU. Although the export valuation system has been abolished, the Government still fixes the reference price in case of carpets exports for the purpose of customs valuation. For carpets of up to 80 knots, the reference price is fixed at $32; carpets beyond 80 knots face a reference price at $75. Sales tax was replaced by single rated value added tax in the year 1997 for both domestically produced and imported goods. The value added tax has been increased from 10% to 13%. Export earnings are subjected to income tax. The Government has proposed to establish export-processing zones, which are an important component in the Government's export promotion strategy. Feasibility studies are currently being conducted for proposed sites at Bhairawa, Nuwakot, Paachkhal, and Birgunj.

Regional Agreements

Nepal is party to various bilateral and regional preferential trading agreements (PTA). Most important of these include a Nepal–India PTA, SAFTA, and BIMSTEC.

Nepal–India Preferential Trade Agreement

This treaty was signed in 1996 and was renewed in 2002. It allows for (i) exemption of primary products from import duties and quantitative restrictions on a reciprocal basis; (ii) duty-free access for Nepalese manufactures to India, largely without quantitative restrictions, except for sensitive items; and (ii) preferential access for Indian manufactured exports without quantitative restrictions. The renewed treaty of March 2002 introduced more stringent rules of origin, tariff-rate quotas, and safeguard clauses. New provisions for rules of origin cover value-added requirements of 30% of ex-factory prices (from March 2003) and changes in tariff heading (CTH) at the four-digit level of the Harmonized System code. For Nepalese manufactured exports that do not meet the CTH criteria, the new provision requires products to have undergone a "sufficient manufacturing process within Nepal," which is determined case by case, in order to qualify for preferential access. Under the amended clause of the renewed treaty, India imposes the following fixed annual tariff-rate quotas on Nepal's exports: 100,000 tons (t) for vegetable ghee, 10,000 t for acrylic yarn, 10,000 t for copper, and 2,500 t for zinc oxide. If exports exceed the quotas, which are lower than recent export levels, they are subject to most favored nation (MFN) treatment. In addition, exporters of vegetable ghee must channel their products through India's state trading company and pay a service charge. The new treaty also provides safeguards against damages to domestic producers due to an export surge. Nepal's exports to India are subject to a countervailing duty that makes the prices of these exports comparable to those of Indian counterparts. Trade transactions are in local currencies. Nepal, however, permits imports of few intermediate inputs or machinery for local industry from India against payment in a convertible currency.

South Asian Free Trade Area (SAFTA)

The SAFTA members are Bangladesh, Bhutan, India, the Maldives, Nepal, Pakistan, and Sri Lanka. Members are committed to removing tariffs over 10 years beginning in 2006, with least-developed countries (LDCs) such as Nepal (along with Bangladesh, Bhutan, and the Maldives) having a delayed reduction schedule (Table 5.15). In the first phase of SAFTA implementation, Nepal will face maximum tariffs of 20% in India, Pakistan, and Sri Lanka and 30% in LDCs by 2009. In the second phase of implementation, Nepal will face maximum tariffs of 5% in India and Pakistan by 2013, Sri Lanka by 2014, and LDCs by 2016.

Certain products are excluded from tariff liberalization under SAFTA. These are the sensitive products kept on the negative lists (Table 5.16) Nepal and other countries (Bangladesh and India) have kept separate negative lists

Table 5.15 Phase Out of Tariff Liberalization Program under SAFTA

Phase	Countries	Existing Tariff Rates	Tariff rates proposed under SAFTA	Year to be completed
First Phase	India, Pakistan and Sri Lanka	20% & above	20% (Max)	2008
		Below 20%	Annual reduction of 10%	2008
	Bangladesh, Bhutan, Maldives and Nepal	30% & above	30% (Max)	2008
		Below 30%	Annual reduction of 5%	2008
Second Phase	India and Pakistan	20% or below	0–5%	2013
	Sri Lanka	20% or below	0–5%	2014
	Bangladesh, Bhutan, Maldives and Nepal	30% or below	0–5%	2016

SAFTA = South Asia Free Trade Agreement.

Source: Derived from Annex of the Agreement available at http://www.saarc-sec.org/main.php

for LDCs and non-LDCs. Nepal's sensitive list is guided mainly to minimize the revenue loss from tariff liberalization. India's sensitive lists include mainly goods from agriculture, textiles, chemicals, leathers, and small-scale industry.

SAFTA's Rules of origin are based on a change of tariff classification at the heading level Harmonized System (HS 4-digit), and allows for regional

Table 5.16 Sensitive (Negative) List of items (under HS 6-digit) by countries under SAFTA

Country	Sensitive list for		Total
	LDCs	Non-LDCs	
Bhutan		157	157
Bangladesh	1,249	1,254	2,503
India	7,63	884	1,647
Maldives	671		671
Nepal	1,300	1,350	2,650
Pakistan		1,183	1,183
Sri Lanka		1,065	1,065

HS = Harmonized System of Commodity Trade Classification of 1996, LDC = Least Developed Countries,

SAFTA = South Asia Free Trade Agreement.

Source: Derived from Annex of the Agreement available at http://www.saarc-sec.org/main.php

cumulation. Moreover, import content of the products will be not more than a specified percentage (Table 5.17). As the LDCs members, import content of the exportable products originating from Nepal should not exceed 70% of its free-on-board value thus implying a minimum 30% of domestic value added (DVA). There are some product specific rules that stipulate the need for both change in tariff classification (HS 4-digit) or subheading (HS 6-digit) and value-added content of 25%, 30%, 40%, and 60% depending upon the product. SAFTA has also established a mechanism for compensation of revenue loss, where non-LDCs members are expected to provide compensation to the LDCs for loss of customs revenue due to its tariff concessions.

Bay of Bengal Initiative for Multi-Sectoral Technical and Economic Cooperation (BIMSTEC)

Nepal is also a signatory to the BIMSTEC FTA, formed in 1997 and consisting of Bangladesh, India, Myanmar, Sri Lanka, and Thailand. Nepal and

Table 5.17 Rules of Origin (import content/value-added) under SAFTA

Item	Rules of origin	Cumulative rules of origin
Products exported from India & Pakistan	Value of imported material does not exceed 60% free-on-board value of exported products, implying minimum 40% value-added in exporting country	
Products exported from Sri Lanka	Value of imported material does not exceed 65% free-on-board value of exported products, implying minimum 35% value-added in exporting country	Minimum 20% value-added in exporting country provided total regional value addition is not less than 50%
Products exported from least-developed countries (Bangladesh, Bhutan, the Maldives, and Nepal)	Value of imported material does not exceed 70% free-on-board value of exported products, implying minimum 30% value-added in exporting country	

SAFTA = South Asia Free Trade Agreement.

Source: Derived from Annex of the Agreement available at http://www.saarc-sec.org/main.php

Bhutan were admitted in February 2004. The agreement aims for broad economic integration in goods, services, and investment. The accord on trade in goods was to be launched in July 2006, but was put on hold because of many unresolved issues. Agreements on trade in services and investment promotion were agreed to be launched in the future. Complete elimination of tariffs is undertaken via fast or normal tracks. Least-developed countries will have more time to eliminate some tariffs.[11] (Table 5.18). Unlike the SAFTA, the BIMSTEC-FTA has no provision for the compensation of losses due to tariff reductions or eliminations.

Other Agreements

Under a limited preferential trade agreement with Pakistan, Nepalese tea has duty-free access to Pakistan. Under a preferential trade agreement with the Tibet Autonomous Region in the PRC, imports from the PRC that enter Nepal through the region enjoy a 10% rebate on customs duty. This

---

[11] NLDM includes India, Sri Lanka, and Thailand.

does not include goods for which specific duties apply. The South Asian Growth Quadrangle—Bangladesh, Bhutan, India, and Nepal—was formed in 1996 under the charter of the SAARC to accelerate economic development among the four countries.

Table 5.18 BIMSTEC FTA Tariff Reduction Schedules

More Developed Member Countries		Least-Developed Member Countries	
2006–09 Fast Track	Tariffs on products from least developing and non-least developing countries reduced to zero.	2006–07 Fast Track	Tariffs on products from least developing countries reduced to zero.
2007–10 Normal Track	Tariffs on products from non-least developing countries reduced to zero at equal annual rate.	2006–11 Fast Track	Tariffs on products from non-least developing countries reduced to zero.
2007–12 Normal Track	Tariffs on products from least developing countries reduced to zero at equal annual rate.	2007–15 Normal Track	Tariffs on products from least developing countries reduced to zero at equal annual rate.
		2007–17 Normal Track	Tariffs on products from non-least developing countries reduced to zero at equal annual rate.

Nepal's bilateral agreement with India is more attractive than the SAFTA or the BIMSTEC. The main attraction is nonreciprocal, zero-tariff access to India's markets for Nepal's manufacturing products. Nepal thus prefers to continue trading with India under the bilateral agreement. This is especially true because SAFTA's sunset clause phases out compensation for revenue loss, while BIMSTSEC-FTA has no provision at all for compensating revenue loss. The bilateral FTA also remain more attractive as the nature and the extent of its safeguard measures in terms of rules or origin and sensitive lists are more liberal than those under SAFTA. The bilateral FTA is also believed to allow Nepalese exporters to be the first movers into the Indian market. At present, Nepal's access to India's markets for its manufacturing products is the least restricted of anywhere in the world.

Government Revenue Role of Tariffs

Share of Tariffs and Other Trade Taxes in Government Revenue

Trade taxes—import tariffs, export taxes, Indian excise refunds, and other duties and charges—are some of the major sources of Government revenue in Nepal. Import tariffs account for the largest share in the total of the components of Government trade taxes. However, their share in the total Government revenue has declined over the last 15 years. For example, the share of import tariffs in total Government revenue declined from about 23% during the period 1990–1997 to about 19% during the period 1998–2005 (Table 5.19).

Table 5.19 Share of Customs Tariffs and Other Trade Taxes in Total Government Revenue 1990–2005

Year	Percentage of Total Government Revenue			
	Import-Related Tax	Export-Related Tax	Indian Excise Refund	Other Customs Income
1998	21.31	0.66	3.35	0.5
1999	20.67	1.01	3.24	0.63
2000	20.89	1.01	3.1	0.21
2001	21.25	1.01	2.98	0.43
2002	19.19	1.82	3.37	0.72
2003	18.79	1.52	4.22	0.79
2004	17.11	0.85	6.23	0.77
2005	17.54	1.00	3.12	0.74
1990–1997[a]	23.1	0.96	2.97	0.07
1998–2005	19.27	1.13	3.8	0.62
1990–2005	20.32	1.08	3.57	0.47

[a] Average of the period

Source: Economic Review, Ministry of Finance (various issues).

The share of other trade taxes in total government revenue has slightly increased during this period. For example, the share of export taxes in total government revenue has increased from 0.96% during the period 1990–1997 to 1.13% during the period 1998–2005. Likewise, the share of other duties and charges in total government increased from 0.07% during the period 1990–1997 to 0.62% during the period 1998–2005.

Implications for Approach to Trade Agreement

The potential impact of Nepal's market access commitments under accession to the WTO are estimated to bring about a revenue loss of about $55 million due to the continued implementation of applied rates (before WTO accession) and elimination of other duties and charges, particularly on imports of rice and tariffs on motor vehicles (Sauve, 2005). This accounts for about one quarter of Nepal's total customs revenue in 2004. The sectoral incidence of tariff cuts and foregone revenues show that the biggest losses would result from the elimination of other duties and charges on imports of rice (a revenue fall of $5.5 million) and from the lowering of tariffs on motor vehicles from the applied tariff of 130% to the bound tariff rate of 40% (a decrease of about $15 million). Estimates of overall trade creation would be equivalent to $89 million in the same sectors where customs revenue would be the highest.

Nepal's revenue losses from joining SAFTA or the BIMSTEC FTA are likely to be small for two main reasons. Firstly, both SAFTA and BIMSTEC FTA have allowed negative lists to limit the adverse effect on revenue from tariff reductions. Secondly, Nepal is unlikely to integrate its bilateral agreement with India into SAFTA and BIMSTEC FTA for the reasons discussed above. Since India is Nepal's single largest importer, it accounted for 62% of Nepal's total tariff revenue in 2004 (Karmacharya, 2005a). Other SAFTA and BIMSTEC countries have negligible shares in Nepal's tariff revenues.

Trade Infrastructure and Administration Issues with Emphasis on East Asia and South Asia

Overview of Trade-Related Infrastructure

Nepal, along with Bhutan, is one of the least-developed landlocked countries in South Asia. It is bounded by India in the east, west, and south and by the PRC to the north. Due to Nepal's geographical location and traditional ties with India, its overseas trade commonly passes through India's land and seaports. Mountainous terrain on the Nepal–PRC border has curtailed trade with the Tibet Autonomous Region. The dependence of Nepal on India in terms of trade is substantially greater than that associated with other landlocked countries (MOICS 2004),[12] although under the WTO agreement, Nepal is assured to have freedom of transit facilities. Due to this geographical reality, Nepal's overseas trade infrastructure and administration have mainly focused on improving custom procedures, as well as infrastructure and trade transit with India. Transit between the two countries is governed by the Nepal–India Transit Treaty. Because of deepen-

---

[12]   MOICS. 2004. *Nepal Trade and Competitiveness Study*. Kathmandu.

ing political and economic ties between India and the PRC, Nepal has now been recognized as a potential transit route to be developed between India and the PRC.

Road and Rail

Road transport is the main means of travel between India and Nepal. Presently Nepal has nearly 18,000 km road, of which nearly 28% are paved. Of these, there are 15 highways totaling 3,027 km and 51 feeder roads totaling 1,832 km,[13] forming the Strategic Road Network (SRN). The SRN connects the major towns, administrative centers, and border gateways of the country. The construction of roads in Nepal has increased substantially. Between 1993 and 1998, in particular, Nepal's road network experienced one of the highest growth rates in the region, expanding an average annual 4.6% (UNESCAP, 2003).

However, many communities in Nepal are still not linked to the SRN; giving them they have limited access to regional and national markets. Fifteen of the country's 75 districts do not have roadway facilities; these districts are mainly in the mountainous western regions of the country. The conditions of the roads are an important concern for the speedy flow of goods in trade. In 2004, approximately 23% of roads in the SRN were in poor condition. Likewise, many studies have emphasized the need to upgrade and reconstruct the roads in Nepal (Nepal 2006 and ESCAP 2003). The Nepal Road Board (NRB), an autonomous body consisting of representatives from relevant government institutions and the private sector, has been formed to collect taxes and fees from road users on all highways and to maintain roads. However, the effective interinstitutional relationship between Ministry of Finance and the NRB has to be established. While the Ministry of Finance collects transport levies, fees, and other road taxes which provide the NRB with funds for roads expenditures, the ministry incurs delays in the collection of taxes and fees, thus delaying the flow of funds and adversely affecting the NRB's activities. Likewise, transit via India faces constraints from poor road conditions, specifically those leading to the Indian state of Bihar.

Nepal's terrain has not made it feasible to operate an extensive rail network. A 51-km narrow-gauge railway from Jaynagar to Jaleshwore exists, but it is not equipped to handle large quantities of cargo. A 5.4-km broad-gauge railway track connecting Raxual with the Birgunj inland clearance depot was completed in March 2001, made possible through financial assistance from India.

---

[13] Four of the national highways and five of the feeder roads are partially completed.

Air Transport

Nepal has limited access to overseas destinations by air. Nepal has 50 domestic airports (only nine with paved runways) and one international airport: Tribhuvan International Airport (TIA), 5.56 km east of Kathmandu. The average number of takeoffs and landings per day at TIA for 2006 has been recorded at 280. There are currently 13 international and 16 domestic airlines operating out of TIA.

In order to facilitate cargo movement, the Civil Aviation Authority of Nepal has built up an air cargo complex for trade traffic. This terminal is 10,200 square meters in size, and has a capacity of 24,000 t for exports and 12,000 t for imports. However, being in the first phase of construction, the airport can currently only handle 16,000 t of exports and 10,000 t of imports. Nonetheless, the capacity of phase 1 is anticipated to be sufficient to meet the domestic demand for the coming decade.

Ports

The dominant port for entry of Nepal's cargo is Kolkata in India. It is the nearest port from the Nepalese border, some 618 km away. Nepal is also using the Chittagong and Khulna-Chalna ports in Bangladesh for overseas trade since 1976. However, the use of these ports is limited as they are farther than Kolkata. Moreover, these ports have poor infrastructure, congested facilities, and long transit procedures.

Nepal has three inland clearance depots (ICDs); one each at the Birgunj, Biratnagar, and Bairahawa border points. These depots are expected to reduce transport costs, thus boosting competitiveness, and promote competitive transport service. The ICDs of Biratnagar and Bairahawa have been in use since July 2000. However, Birgunj ICD started only in July 2004, 2 years after its completion, due to the lack of agreement with the Indian railway authorities on transit facilities. The Government has contracted the management of these depots to a private entity, the Inter State Multi Model Transport Ltd. Another depot is also under construction at the eastern border point Kakervita, a transit route to Bangladesh, under financial assistance from ADB.

There are various infrastructural impediments for enhancing cross-border trade. Clearly, the poor road conditions between Nepal and India increase the cost of trade. The international airport is also characterized by congestion, long delays, and irregular maintenance of infrastructure. Conditions at Kolkata Port are likewise less than ideal, given the absence of a testing laboratory (the nearest is 1,000 km away), post office, and other required infrastructure. Shipping agents in Nepal are concentrated in Kathmandu, leading to information delays between the depots and the shipping agents. Lastly, there is a need for roads to and from the depot in Birgunj (alongside rail-based depots) to ease the congestion of cargo.

Customs and Procedural Issues That May be Open to Trade Facilitation

Customs procedures are a main component of trade facilitation. In Nepal, customs procedures are governed by the Customs Act 1962, the last amendment of which took place in 1997. The customs procedures of this Act have not yet been simplified and harmonized as outlined by the Kyoto Convention and as required by the WTO.[14] To facilitate customs collections and strengthen the institutional capacity for speedier clearance, effective revenue collection and consistency with international standards, the Government, with technical assistance from Asian Development Bank (ADB), introduced the Automated System for Customs Data (ASYCUDA) software in 1996 (Box 5.4). Despite these efforts, customs offices are still plagued by poor performance, weak administration, and clearance delays.

Box 5.4: Automated System for Customs Data (ASYCUDA) in Nepal

Currently, ASYCUDA is used in 10 customs offices in Nepal: Kakerbhita, Biratnagar, Birgunj, Birgunj, Gaur, Bairahawa, Krishnanagar, Nepalgunj, Tatopani, and the Tribhuvan International Airport. Only a limited set of modules (i.e., goods declaration, processing, and accounting of payment) are being used. Other modules (i.e., selectivity, cargo information, broker declaration, transit, and direct trade input) have not yet been activated. This is partly due to the difficulty of data exchange between customs offices at different locations. Consequently, ASYCUDA has only marginally improved the custom clearance time. Moreover, the implementation of this software has also been problematic since it was designed as a computerization exercise rather than a customs reform program.

This motivated customs reform, through the 3-year Customs Modernization Plan, which tried to balance customs control with trade facilitation (Rajkarnikar et al. 2006). The plan has identified seven reform areas: valuation, customs simplification, the harmonization of customs process, the

---

[14] Trader needs to submit 15 types of documents for export and 11 types of documents for import. Likewise, five officials are needed for custom clearance.

development of physical facilities, risk management, customs integrity, and reforms to the passenger clearance process and personnel training.[15] Some progress has been achieved, such as (i) the development in September 2003 of the working procedures for customs clearance; (ii) the development of a number of manuals for customs valuation and post-clearance audit;[16] (iii) the undertaking of 130 post-clearance audits in 2006, with selected modules being tested in some custom offices; and (iv) the utilization of the Harmonized Commodities Code for commodities classification and tariff calculation. However, amendments to the Customs Act have remained in draft form for the last 2 years in the absence of parliamentary approval.

The installation of the ASYCUDA system in the Dhangadi Customs Office is currently in progress. Furthermore, a program to use electronic data interchange (EDI) to exchange data between custom offices at different locations is under negotiation with ADB. The installation of EDI will facilitate electronic submission of declaration, computerized processing of custom documents, and computerized risk management, linking of the cargo status report between various agencies. None of these measures is currently available.

There are also various issues that hamper key trade facilitation measures. One is poor customs infrastructure, which is partly due to the irregular maintenance of its machinery. There have also been continued delays in the release of cargo due to time-consuming valuation, tariff classification, and checking of goods. Corruption is also rampant and the opening hours quite rigid: customs offices close at 5 pm, and cargo arriving thereafter has to wait until the next day.

Trade Finance

In Nepal, commercial banks are the only financial intermediates participating in trade finance. Trade in goods is generally financed through letters of credit or cash against documents. Banks generally provide pre-shipment and post-shipment loan to trader in three forms: export finance, cash against documents, and discounting of letters of credit. Export credit is mostly in the form of trade loans, which are provided for 90 days to traders against security of stock or valuable assets. The commission rate on letters of credit is around 0.25% and banks demand 5% cash margins as security. Likewise, traders must first obtain a Business Credibility Requirement License from the DOI to open a letter of credit

---

[15] DOC. 2001. *Three Years Customs Reform and Modernization Action Plan* (2003–2006). Kathmandu: MOF/GON (then HMG)

[16] DOC 2006. Preparation of Valuation and PCA Manuals in *Nepalese Custom News Bulletin*. Kathmandu.

at a commercial bank. This license lists the items that the traders are legally permitted to import and export, and which banks are allowed to provide them with trade financing. Traders are also required to provide various documents to the Central Bank of Nepal, so that they may monitor foreign exchange transactions. More details on trade financing are provided in Table 5.20.

Table 5.20 Trade Financing

Item	Interest Rate (%)	Period	Form of Security
Per trade			
Export finance	12	90 days	Stock or assets in kind
Export guarantees	NRs5,000	6 months	5% cash margin
Export credit insurance	NA	NA	NA
Letter of credit	0.25	1 years	5% cash margin
Post shipment			
Discounting letter of credit	LIBOR	1 years	Stock or assets in kind

LIBOR = London inter-bank offered rate. NA = not applicable.

Source: Bank official

Currently, there are 18 commercial banks in Nepal with a total of 381 branch offices. Rastriya Banijya Bank is the only state-owned commercial bank, while the Government owns a minority stake in the Nepal Bank Limited, Nepal's first commercial bank. Privately owned commercial banks are fully computerized and have electronic data transfer, making them quicker in providing services than Nepal Bank or Rastriya Banijya Bank.

Some of the major problems surrounding trade financing are the foreign exchange restrictions imposed by the central bank and the lack of an export credit insurance geared toward minimizing the risks involved in trade credit.

Key Transport Corridors Relevant To East and South Asia Trade

There are nine border crossing points with the PRC and 22 with India, with 15 authorized land routes for passage of goods via Kolkata. Tatopani is the only border crossing that allows trade with the PRC, while Birgunj (main port), Biratnagar, Bhairahawa, Kakarbhitta, and Nepalgunj are the trading points with India. At Kolkata Port, exports are loaded onto feeder vessels, which are then transported to Singapore and in some cases to Colombo, for transshipment to destinations in Europe, the Middle East, East Asia, and the Americas. Likewise as mentioned earlier, Nepal has been recognized as a potential transit route to be developed between India and the PRC due to growing political and economic ties between these countries.

Kathmandu–Birgunj (Nepal)–Raxaul (India)–Kolkata/Haldia

This is the main road corridor for Nepal, accounting for almost 70% of its total trade (Nepal 2006). The only rail-based inland clearance depot was developed in 2004 at Birgunj. It is currently available for cargo movement.

Box 5.5: Nepal North-South Transit Corridor Between the PRC and India

There have been significant recent developments in political and economic relations between India and the PRC. India-PRC trade is expected to increase from $13 billion annually at present to over $30 billion by 2010. India has requested Nepal to provide transit traffic freedom rights for trade with the PRC. Nepal has also initiated exercises to tap its ideal geographical location to develop serve as a transit route between these two countries.

A study committee on trade transit came up with eight possible transit routes, and identified six other routes for future development. Subsequently, there have also been many studies commissioned to assess the prospective transit routes between the PRC and India. For example, an ADB study estimated that 10% trade between the PRC and India will be diverted from sea to land through Nepal in the initial phase. The study also finds that the cost per ton is 40% higher by land, but takes half the time it would by sea. However, as the PRC railway starts operating trains to Lhasa, transport costs will drop, in turn reducing the cost differentials between transit and sea routes. Transit routes would become more attractive given the much shorter travel time. The ADB study recommended a new feasibility study to further develop one more corridor (the fast track) for speedy traffic between Kathmandu to Birgunj as the present corridor between those locations is inadequate over the long term.

Biratnagar, opposite Jogbani in India, is Nepal's closest border point to the Kalkota seaport. This route is 618 km long. Biratnagar is connected to Kathmandu and connected by a 548-km road; the length of the Kathmandu–Biratnagar (Nepal)–Jogbani (India)–Kolkata/Haldia corridor is 1,166 km. The corridor is Nepal's second-most-used trade route. Bhairahawa, opposite Sunauli in India, is the major route for passengers travelling by road. This point is mostly used for bilateral trade with India. Biratnagar accounts for 16%, and Bhairahawa accounts for 10% of total trade. Kakarbhitta, opposite Panitanki (Silguri) in India, is an important gateway not only to India but to Bangladesh and Bhutan. The Bangladesh corridor goes through the Phulbari–Banglabandh corridor. The Kakarbhitta border point is also a potential transit point to Bhutan via Jaigaon and Pheuntsholing.

There are a number of physical barriers to the Kathmandu–Birgunj (Nepal)–Raxaul (India)–Kolkata/Haldia Corridor: (i) the long distance from Kathmandu to Birgunj (276 km), in addition to a number of single-lane bridges from Hetauda to Pathalaiya that threaten to become bottlenecks as traffic increases; (ii) congestion at the Birgunj border point as the customs yard for road-based cargo is inadequate; (iii) bad road conditions, particularly in India's Bihar state, reduce truck speeds to 20 km/hr over an approximately 180-km section, adding a day to total travel time.

There is also a number of nonphysical barriers to the Kathmandu–Birgunj (Nepal)–Raxaul (India)–Kolkata/Haldia Corridor. There is the absence of bills-of-lading provided by the shipping lines.[17] Customs are also inflexible regarding the timing of arrival of goods for example, if cargo arrives after 3 pm; it is not processed on the same day because the Customs Office closes at 5 pm. Nepalese manufactured goods have free access to the Indian market, but foodstuffs are required to pass through Indian quarantine. This leads to delays at the borders, sometimes as long as 10–12 days, as samples are sent to Kolkata for testing. The Indian Standards Institute does not readily accept standards set by its counterpart, the Nepali Standards Bureau, and this causes problems. There are also very high insurance and bond prices are charged by Indian Customs when associated with sensitive cargo, even though these do not reflect the losses sustained. Abandoned Nepali cargo cannot easily be disposed of at Kolkata or Haldia ports. There is lack of security in some of the remoter areas along the corridor, preventing trucks from traveling at night. Finally, there is no computerization at the borders and documents are processed manually.

There are no nonphysical barriers to passenger movement between India and Nepal. However, more formal arrangements in the form of a comprehensive motor vehicle agreement governing movement of personal and commercial passenger vehicles would be required in order provide a predictable and easily understood system of fees, information on the number of days to be allowed in other country's territory, and the number and frequency of bus services between designated points.

---

[17] This means that the importer has to separately arrange for land transportation, increasing the overall door-to-door costs. The reasons for the lack of through-bills are the lack of a suitable legal framework, traffic imbalances, reliability of transport services, and the availability of container transport resources. In essence, the present conditions favor unstuffing containers in Kolkata/Haldia rather than carrying them through to Nepal.

Air Corridors

Currently, four countries in SAARC (India, Bhutan, Pakistan, and Bhutan) and five of the countries in ASEAN+3 grouping (the PRC, Japan, Thailand, Singapore, and Malaysia) are connected directly with Nepal by air. Nepalese and Sri Lankan authorities have agreed to establish direct flight links, but details on which cities will be connected and the flight schedules in question have not been settled. The Kathmandu-Delhi air route is Nepal's main air route. The direct air corridors with SAARC and ASEAN+3 countries are listed in Table 5.21.

Table 5.21 Direct Air Corridors from Nepal to SAARC and ASEAN+3 Countries

Country	Air corridor	Flight schedule
SAARC Country		
India	Kathmandu–Delhi	Daily
India	Kathmandu–Kolkata	4 days a week
India	Kathmandu–Mumbai	2 days a week
India	Kathmandu–Varanasi	3 days per week
Bangladesh	Kathmandu–Dhaka	4 days a week
Pakistan	Kathmandu–Karachi	2 days a week
ASEAN+3		
Thailand	Kathmandu–Bangkok	Daily
Singapore	Kathmandu–Singapore	4 days a week
Malaysia	Kathmandu–Kuala Lumpur	4 days a week
PRC	Kathmandu–Lhasa	3 days a week
Japan	Kathmandu–Osaka	4 days a week

SAARC = South Asian Association for Regional Cooperation, ASEAN = Association of Southeast Asian Nations.

Source: Nepal Tourism Board

Traders in Nepal also use the air-to-sea shipment method. Cargo is generally transported to Singapore by air, then transhipped to its final destination.

Other Issues Linked to Transport Costs

The cost–time analysis of trade transit measures the effectiveness of activities for trade facilitation. The time required during transit and cost incurred will be measured to calculate the flow of goods and the financial impact due to delays in trade. For this purpose, the key corridor of overseas trade (Kathmandu–Birgunj/Raxual (India)–Kolkata/Haldia) has been chosen. The breakdown of time and cost of trade transit in this corridor is presented in Table 5.22. The analysis estimates that the average transit cost to transport cargo from Kathmandu to Kolkata port is $4.55 per hour. Delay in transport transit due to customs clearance and poor road conditions add extra trade costs.

Table 5.22 Breakdown of Time and Cost for Exporting Containerized Cargo Using the KTM–Birgunj–Kolkata Road Corridor (Per 20-Foot Equivalent Unit Container)

Item	Distance (km)	Cumulative distance (km)	Average transit time (hours)	Cumulative transit time (hours)	Average cost ($)	Cumulative cost ($)
Kathmandu–Birgunj	298	298	18	18	250	250
Birgunj–Raxaul (border)	6	304	27	45	124	374
Raxaul–Kolkata Port Trust	960	1264	120	165	525	899
Kolkata port clearance[a]			60	225	125	1024
Total	1264		225		1024	

[a] Time at Kolkata Port refers to clearance time for export cargo; cost refers the cost other than port duty.

Source: Economic and Social Commission for Asia and the Pacific of United Nations (ESCAP), (2003).

Box 5.6: India-Nepal Trade Meeting

At the 2006 Nepal-India trade meeting, Nepal raised the impact of the increase in tariffs levied on Nepalese goods by India. The Government has also proposed for Indian assistance on the development of India-trade transit, railway networks, and other economic infrastructure in southern Nepal. The India-Nepal transit treaty was renewed on March 2007 for a period of 5 years.

Other issues are (i) uncertainty among traders due to delays in amendments to the Nepal–India Transit Treaty, (ii) significant documentation requirements for transit transport (i.e., the Nepal–India treaty requires 15 for import procedures and 22 documents for export procedures), and (iii) time-consuming verification of vessel content. As an example to illustrate (iii), the import general manifest is submitted generally after the arrival of the shipping vessel, and there is considerable time lost in locating the imported cargo consistent with the bill of lading or delivery order. The Government should also initiate a feasibility study on the use of the Chennai Port or Nawa Sewa Port as alternatives to Singapore in order to reduce transport time.

Service Sector Trade and Foreign Direct Investment Policies With Emphasis on East and South Asia

Foreign Direct Investment Performance (Inbound and Outbound) and Potential Sectors

As mentioned earlier, our focus here is on inbound FDI since outbound flows are presently restricted. The discussion elaborates on the earlier presentation regarding FDI into Nepal, with focus on the services sector.

FDI for 1990–2005 is provided in Table 5.23. FDI commitments in eservices have two distinct trends: the period up to 2001, when the average commitment reached $16.06 million; and after 2001, when commitments declined to $13.84 million. FDI commitments into Nepal can be separated into three components: energy, tourism (other than restricted tourism sector in FITTA 1992),[18] and other services. Unsurprisingly, the tourism sector was the major contributor and accounted for an average share of 42% of total service FDI during the period 1990–2005.

FDI commitments in services can also be viewed in terms of FDI originating from countries in the SAARC and ASEAN+3; SAARC captured of FDI 34.92% and ASEAN+3 24.26%. As for shares in individual sectors, FDI in other services is highest in SAARC and FDI in tourism is highest in ASEAN+3.

Service Trade Flow by Sector and Partner as Far as Possible

When examining Nepal's external services trade flows, it is worth keeping in mind that services trade is captured in the current account. This discussion has to be balanced with data realities. First, Nepal only began compiling its balance of payments (BOP) data in the International Monetary Fund (IMF Version 5) from 2000. While earlier data is available, it does not fully capture services-related flows. Second, services trade flows are disaggregated only into the broad headings of transportation, travel, government

---

[18]   FDI in tourism is mainly concentrated in star-rated hotels, restaurants, and bars.

Table 5.23 FDI Flows into the Services Sector (1990–2005)

Year	Energy			Tourism			Other services			Total services		
	No of Est	FDI	Emp	No of Est	FDI	Emp	No of Est	FDI	Emp	No of Est	FDI	Emp
1990	0	0.00	0	7	9.32	753	6	0.47	1,236	13	9.79	1,989
1991	1	0.01	8	3	0.15	258	1	0.02	29	5	0.17	295
1992	0	0.00	0	9	4.52	967	4	0.73	128	13	5.26	1,095
1993	2	14.97	2,664	15	8.47	2,015	9	23.39	1,012	26	46.82	5,691
1994	0	0.00	0	7	6.01	752	6	1.47	581	13	7.48	1,333
1995	0	0.00	0	3	0.42	516	1	0.62	31	4	1.04	547
1996	1	18.96	1,240	13	6.54	1,730	8	0.96	1,690	22	26.46	4,660
1997	0	0.00	0	18	8.22	1,515	29	20.21	2,002	47	28.43	3,517
1998	0	0.00	0	28	17.29	1,883	24	6.36	598	52	23.65	2,481
1999	2	7.67	108	13	2.92	560	15	2.95	187	30	13.54	855
2000	1	0.31	27	17	2.37	611	22	10.39	498	40	13.07	1,136
2001	3	5.27	352	19	7.17	684	19	4.57	579	41	17.02	1,615
2002	1	0.06	16	13	1.18	317	24	2.73	969	38	3.97	1,302
2003	3	5.77	344	24	1.26	541	20	11.71	1,408	47	18.74	2,293
2004	1	0.56	4	23	1.65	261	32	22.65	1,603	56	24.86	1,868
2005	0	0.00	0	12	0.52	254	26	5.81	3,213	38	6.33	3,467
Average 1990–98	1	3.77	435	11	6.77	1,154	10	6.02	812	22	16.57	2,401
Average 1999–2005	2	2.81	122	17	2.44	461	23	8.69	1,208	41	13.93	1,791
Average 1990–2005	1	3.35	298	14	4.88	851	15	7.19	985	30	15.41	2,134

No of Est = number of establishments, FDI = Foreign Direct Investment, Emp = employment generated.

Note: FDI is in $ million; number of establishments and jobs created are in number.

Source: Department of Industries (2006).

services, and other services (e.g., insurance). Third, remittance flows are captured only in the income subaccount of the current account because Nepal has not yet begun capturing short-term remittance information.[19]

---

[19] The BOP classifies these receipts into two categories: (i) persons outside the country for less than 12 months are recorded under the current account's income subaccount as compensation to employees; and (ii) persons outside for more that 12 months are recorded under the current account's current transfers subaccount as workers' remittances. The study uses remittances to capture the total flow because of data limitations.

Finally, Nepal does not provide BOP data broken down by partner. Nepalese BOP statistics for the period 2001–2006 are provided in Table 5.25.

Table 5.24 Percentage Share of ASEAN and SAARC countries in Service Sector FDI on the Basis of FDI up to 2005

Country/Region	Energy-based services	Tourism	Other services	Total services
A. ASEAN +3				
PRC	27.64	3.90	7.94	10.74
Hong Kong, China	0.00	4.97	1.92	2.51
Japan	0.65	14.92	2.10	5.47
Malaysia	0.00	0.16	0.14	0.11
Philippines	0.00	0.00	0.00	0.00
Korea	0.00	4.11	3.47	3.54
Singapore	0.00	6.59	0.37	2.07
Thailand	0.00	0.00	0.01	0.01
Total A	**28.28**	**34.65**	**15.96**	**24.46**
B. South Asia				
Bangladesh	0.00	0.00	0.20	0.16
India	0.00	18.98	57.47	34.44
Pakistan	0.00	0.03	0.17	0.09
Sri Lanka	0.00	0.00	0.50	0.24
Total B	**0.00**	**19.01**	**58.35**	**34.92**
C. Rest of World	**71.72**	**46.33**	**25.70**	**40.62**
Total (A+B+C)	**100.00**	**100.00**	**100.00**	**100.00**

ASEAN = Association of Southeast Asian Nations.

Note: Brunei; Cambodia; Indonesia; the Lao People's Democratic Republic; Myanmar; Taipei,China; and Viet Nam have no FDI commitments and are therefore excluded from table.

Source: Department of Industries (2005).

Current account trends for the period 2001–2006 show some structural changes. Remittance flows, generating 33% of current account income in the last 6 years, have helped sustain the economy in the face of political instability. In spite of a difficult environment, the tourism sector has been able to retain its significant role in services export and accounted for an average of 7% of current account income during the same period. The main services import is transport, accounting for an average of 6% of total current account expenditure. The variation in net services is seen during the period 2001–2006 and could be traced to fluctuations in services credit (largely in the tourism business) during the period 2001–2006 (tables 5.26 and 5.27) (Khanal and Kanel, 2005).

Table 5.25 Services Trade Flow ($ Mn) 2001–2006

Item	2001	2002	2003	2004	2005	2006
Current account	272.90	236.23	149.31	197.83	160.21	191.86
Current account credit	2331.14	2028.43	2050.80	2473.88	2706.35	3227.07
Current account debit	-2058.24	-1792.21	-1901.49	-2276.05	-2546.14	-3035.21
Balance on goods	-764.59	-694.05	-903.62	-1052.74	-1190.15	-1545.12
Goods: exports f.o.b.	945.26	754.21	652.54	748.45	832.03	876.32
Goods: imports f.o.b.	-1709.85	-1448.26	-1556.15	-1801.19	-2022.18	-2421.44
Services: net	126.00	51.23	90.62	122.98	-28.23	-86.78
Services: credit	403.92	305.78	340.90	465.05	360.84	370.19
Travel	158.70	112.57	151.02	245.93	145.21	133.46
Government, n.i.e.	103.13	115.69	85.15	96.81	94.43	104.14
Other	142.09	77.52	104.73	122.30	121.19	132.59
Services: debit	-277.93	-254.55	-250.28	-342.07	-389.07	-456.97
Transportation	-126.08	-115.17	-110.79	-127.15	-147.13	-177.18
Travel	-74.77	-74.55	-79.34	-135.81	-134.50	-166.95
Other	-77.07	-64.83	-60.15	-79.11	-107.44	-112.84
Income: net	23.04	-7.87	-8.69	-22.82	22.71	68.96
Income: credit	74.10	55.89	57.68	52.06	107.57	159.71
Income: debit	-51.06	-63.76	-66.37	-74.88	-84.86	-90.75
Transfers: net	888.46	886.92	970.99	1150.41	1355.88	1754.80
Current transfers: credit	907.87	912.56	999.68	1208.32	1405.91	1820.84
Grants	163.16	164.55	177.94	265.05	292.42	263.94
Workers' remittances	639.52	618.32	696.79	793.98	909.54	1365.98
Pensions	85.45	107.57	94.19	107.14	173.50	168.17
Other (Indian Excise Refund)	19.72	22.12	30.75	42.15	30.46	22.75
Current transfers: debit	-19.41	-25.64	-28.69	-57.91	-50.04	-66.04

f.o.b. = Free on Board, n.i.e. = National Income and Expenditure.

Note: Grant and Indian Excise Refund are not service export

Source: Nepal Rastra Bank

Table 5.26 Tourism Flows 1991–2005, number

Country/Region	1991–1998a	1999	2000	2001	2002	2003	2004	2005
A. Major ASEAN+3								
PRCb	-	5,638	7,139	8,738	8,715	7,562	13,326	21,170
Indonesia	337	538	979	532	514	824	668	687
Japan	25,186	38,893	41,070	28,830	23,223	27,412	24,231	18,460
Malaysia	1,863	2,953	3,486	3,787	2,777	8,197	7,266	5,269
Philippines	417	609	685	411	388	468	342	264
Korea	3,239	5,370	8,880	11,568	8,798	13,200	10,827	10,300
Singapore	2,975	5,140	5,743	2,933	1,818	3,165	3,164	3,075
Thailand	2,738	4,872	8,709	5,312	4,694	11,129	14,648	13,508
Total A	**36,755**	**64,013**	**76,691**	**62,111**	**50,927**	**71,957**	**74,472**	**72,733**
B. SAARC								
Bangladesh	4,016	9,262	8,731	7,742	5,507	5,031	14,607	20,201
India	112,678	140,661	95,915	64,320	66,777	86,363	90,326	96,434
Pakistan	2,782	3,534	2,620	2,319	1,241	761	2,020	1,753
Sri Lanka	3,235	12,432	16,649	9,844	9,805	13,930	16,124	18,770
Total B	**122,710**	**165,889**	**123,915**	**84,225**	**83,330**	**106,085**	**123,077**	**137,158**
C. Other Asian	**18,738**	**19,891**	**23,926**	**18,653**	**14,413**	**22,003**	**20,838**	**20,391**
D. Other than Asian	**183,046**	**241,711**	**239,114**	**196,248**	**126,798**	**138,087**	**166,910**	**145,116**
Total	**361,249**	**491,504**	**463,646**	**361,237**	**275,468**	**338,132**	**385,297**	**375,398**

ASEAN = Association of Southeast Asian Nations, SAARC = South Asian Association of Regional Cooperation.

a - Average of 1991 to 1998
b - A separate record for PRC tourists started only in 1999, before that the arrivals recorded as Other Asian category.

Source: Ministry of Tourism

Table 5.27 Average Duration of Stay of Foreign Tourist (in days)

Item	1991–1998a	1999	2000	2001	2002	2003	2004	2005
Duration of stay	10.93	12.80	11.88	11.93	7.92	9.60	13.51	9.10

a Average of 1991–1998

Source: Ministry of Tourism

Assessment of Future Potential

There are two important studies on service-sector trade flows in Nepal. The first, the Nepal Trade Competitiveness Study, has identified the potential for services in terms of trade flows and FDI. Likewise, a 2003 study from the United Nations Convention on Trade and Development (UNCTAD) has also identified the potential of certain services exports in Nepal: tourism, hydropower, and labor.

Tourism. Studies have identified the tourism sector as the most competitive service sector in Nepal. Comparative advantages include the country's landscape, and its religious and cultural attractions. This can be reflected in Table 5.26, which shows tourism flows, and Table 5.27, which details the duration of stays. Although wide fluctuations have been seen in terms of tourist flows and duration of stays due to decade long political instability, the sector has contributed 11% of the country's foreign exchange earnings over the last 10 years.

Examination of Table 5.26 suggests that tourists from India constitute the largest share of visitors, with an average of 27% of total tourist arrivals in 1990–2005. Japan is next, with an average share of 7% in the period 1990–2005; tourists from ASEAN+3 account for an average share of 13% and from SAARC 32%. The share of ASEAN+3 and SAARC gradually rose in the same period as compared to other Asian and non-Asian tourists. Tourist flows from various regions over time are presented in Figure 5.2.

Figure 5.2 Regional Tourist Flows 1990, 1998, and 2005

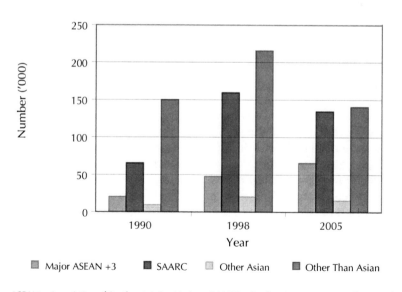

ASEAN = Association of Southeast Asian Nations, SAARC = South Asian Association of Regional Cooperation

261

The Government has acknowledged the increasing tourist flows and made an effort to promote this sector through a Tourism Master Plan. The priority is to remove the ban on ownership for overseas tour operators and travel agencies, and to establish tourism development zones (GON Economic Survey, 2006).

For tourism to play a leading role, there are some areas which necessitate more attention, namely: (i) the facilitation of the entry of tourists; (ii) the initiation of a dynamic and effective marketing campaign to reverse the negative image of decade-long political instability; (iii) the development of eco-toursim , and religion-based tourism to attract tourists particularly from India, Sri Lanka, Thailand, Japan, the Republic of Korea, and Myanmar.

Hydropower. Studies have also pointed to the hydropower as a potential export earner. This is because Nepal is the second richest country in term of hydropower with an approximate 83,000 megawatts (MW) of potential hydropower, of which 44,000 MW having been identified as economically viable. However, the country has only marginally exploited this resource: the total hydropower generated at the end of 2005 is only 0.67% of total capacity and 1.27% of economically viable capacity. At the end of 2005, there were only 15 FDI establishments in hydropower which sell electricity to Nepal Electricity Authority (NEA).

In order to improve hydropower production and attract FDI and private-sector participation, the Government has issued a Hydro Power Development Policy in 2001 and amended the 1992 Electricity Act. However, success in terms of attracting FDI and hydroelectric power production is marginal. The underexploitation of hydropower resources is primarily responsible for the high cost of development, which the Government can not afford to shoulder without private and foreign donor participation.[20] Private participation is hampered because of limited incentive-enhancing policy measures, limited transmission links with India, the NEA's poor payment administration to private electricity providers, and longstanding political instability.

Recently the Nepalese and Indian private sector have taken the initiative to organize the Hydro Power Expo in Kathmandu. In the course of this expo, Nepal was able to negotiate with India the establishment of transmission lines between the two countries. However, local investors doubt whether the substantial flow of needed FDI could be realized without government policy action geared at creating an investor-friendly environment.

Other pending issues are the need to (i) establish transmission links with the Indian grid given the fact that India will be the largest energy consumer, (ii) to develop transregional energy infrastructure and the resolution of water-sharing issues, (iii) review the Hydro Power Development

---

[20]   Most government-owned hydropower stations were established through soft loans from international donor agencies.

Policy 2001, and (iv) undertake administrative reforms in Nepal Electronic Authority.

Remittances. Remittances of overseas workers are important sources of export earnings. In 2004 it had accounted for 7.15% of total GDP, and presently this contribution has increased. The growing importance of remittances is shown in Table 5.28.

Table 5.28 Flow of Remittances to Nepal, 1990–2004

Year	Remittances ($)	% change in remittance	Remittances as % of GDP
1990–1998 (average)	40.87	8.60	1.05
1999	85.04	46.42	1.71
2000	101.29	19.11	1.98
2001	207.95	105.30	3.87
2002	267.58	28.67	4.96
2003	344.43	28.72	5.58
2004	476.89	38.46	7.15

Source: Ministry of Labor and Transportation

As earlier mentioned, labor from Nepal is traditionally exported to India. However, since 1990, there has been a significant diversification of Nepalese labor flows away from India, particularly since 1998. In that year, for instance, some 7,745 workers went to countries other than India; this had increased by 300% the following year and continued to rise. Table 5.29 shows the total labor supply flow to countries other than India in 2005 was 138,838, but official records show that there were 591,400 persons working abroad based on permits granted by the Government. The data on overseas Nepalese workers is probably grossly underestimated, since the 1950 bilateral trade treaty eliminated restrictions for employment in India. Anecdotal evidence suggests that this figure could be adjusted upwards by a magnitude of five or more. Looking at official records, almost half of these recorded workers are working in Malaysia.

Despite the importance of labor exports, there have not been any systematic efforts to promote labor skills given that Nepalese labor exports are for relatively low-skilled jobs. It is only recently that the Government has started some technical and vocational training focused on foreign employment. The informal channel of labor supply is mushrooming in Nepal and labor exploitation is much more rampant in informal sectors. Problems include (i) an inadequate legal framework to punish illegal recruiters, (ii) a dearth of bilateral agreements with labor-importing countries, and (iii) the absence of institutions geared to promote more bona fide recruitment channels.

Other Potential Sectors. In the long run, Nepal was also identified as an offshore services center, especially to serve India. These services could include offshore financial services for Indian residents, and the provision of professional and back-office facilities. Nepal's core attributes are a temperate climate, low wage costs, a smaller and more accessible bureaucracy, and an attractive expatriate lifestyle. Likewise, a central bank study in 2005 identified communications, education, and health services as other long-term sectors with potential.

Table 5.29 Labor Flows to Major Countries Other than India, 2003–05

Country/Region	2003		2004		2005	
	No. of Labor Supply	% Share	No. of Labor Supply	% Share	No. of Labor Supply	% Share
A. Major ASEAN +3						
Malaysia	43,812	41.70	45,760	42.90	66,290	47.75
Korea	712	0.68	1,324	1.24	325	0.23
Hong Kong, China	564	0.54	672	0.63	178	0.13
Total A	**45,088**	**42.92**	**47,756**	**44.77**	**66,793**	**48.11**
B. Other major countries						
Saudi Arabia	17,990	17.12	16,875	15.82	13,359	9.62
Qatar	26,850	25.56	24,128	22.62	41,952	30.22
UAE	12,650	12.04	12,760	11.96	12,503	9.01
Bahrain	818	0.78	606	0.57	258	0.19
Kuwait	907	0.86	3,194	2.99	1,686	1.21
Total B	**59,215**	**56.36**	**57,563**	**53.97**	**69,758**	**50.24**
C. Others	754	0.72	1,341	1.26	2,287	1.65
Total (A+B+C)	**105,057**	**100.00**	**106,660**	**100.00**	**138,838**	**100.00**

ASEAN = Association of Southeast Asian Nations.

Source: Ministry of Labor and Transport

Export of Services

There is an increasing role of services in the Nepalese economy as reflected in its increasing share in total GDP from 35% in 1991 to 39% in 2005. Prior to economic liberalization, very few services were traded. At present, services trade contributes 43% to overall trade income and 17% share of total GDP. Furthermore, it employs about 7.5% of the total labor force.

A direct impact of services export is poverty alleviation. Remittance inflows have increased the income of receiving households from 23% to 32% and contributed to reducing poverty from 42% in 1996 to 31% in 2004.

Box 5.7: Nepal as an Offshore Financial Center

A study by Collins and Associates has highlighted the potential for Nepal to become an offshore financial center because of its ideal time zone and geographical location. The International Financial Transactions Act was enacted in 1998 but is presently not functional. The Government needs to identify and publish a date in the Nepal Gazette from which the Act will take effect.

Collins & Associates initiated the concept of an International Financial Services Center in Nepal in the mid-1990's which was again recently reinitiated.

Regulatory Regime for the Service Sector (Focus on Priority Sectors)

Nepal's legislation generally complies with the provisions of articles II and XVII of the General Agreement on Trade in Services (GATS) concerning MFN and national treatment. However, exceptions exist with regard to the number of activities, as described on the services sectoral classification list. For example, employment in any industry, including all services, must give priority to Nepalese nationals, although foreigners are permitted to work in Nepal on technical areas, particularly with regards to the transfer of technology. Furthermore, foreign professionals working in Nepal are required to join the relevant Nepalese professional associations.[21]

During Nepal's accession to the WTO, some laws, regulations, and administrative decisions were not found in conformity with those of the WTO. In this regard, Nepal has submitted its legislation action plan to WTO and is presently revising 26 laws, 6 regulations, and 10 administrative decisions. Among them, the 2002 Income Tax Act, the Foreign Exchange (Regulation) Act, the Copyright Act, and the Nepal Chartered Accountant Act have all been approved by parliament and are now in force.

---

[21] Accordingly, architects and all types of engineers must be registered with the Nepal Engineering Council; accountants are required to be registered with Nepal Chartered Accountants Institute. Lawyers who appear before courts in Nepal are required to be registered with Nepal Bar Council. Practitioners of third country and international law who do not appear before courts in Nepal are not required to join the Bar Council.

It is important to note that the procedures for settling disputes between foreign and national investors, or other concerned local industries, are outlined in the Foreign Investment Act and the 2005 Procedural Manual for Foreign Investment.

A major issue facing Nepal is significant legal reforms have been stalled since 2002, in large part due to political instability. During the above-mentioned period, the amended acts have been enforced only as ordinances that may last 6 months. This has brought uncertainty regarding the status of those laws.

GATS and Regional Commitments – Sensitivities in Services Trade Negotiations Between East and South Asia

The country has made a number of multilateral commitments under GATS. These mainly deal with FDI flows. As the country negotiates for greater liberalization with WTO member countries, it is essential that the country take stock of its future commitments in regard to regional commitments. In SAARC, Nepal has made the most liberal commitments in services, while in the case of SAFTA and BIMSTEC, no firm commitments have yet been made.

With regard to sector-specific negotiations, it is important for Nepal to have an assessment of its strengths. There are three important sectors highlighted: tourism, hydropower, and labor. For tourism, appropriate facilities need to be created in order to foster regional tourism. The second round of BIMSTEC tourism minister's roundtable, for instance, emphasized the need to develop the regional tourism among its member countries. Agreement was further reached on the development of the BIMSTEC Tourism Information Centre, BIMSTEC Tourism Fund, Buddhist circuit tour package and ecotourism. For hydropower, the main customer will be India so it is essential to develop a consensus on both a national and regional strategy. For labor export, Malaysia is presently the most important destination, thus it is important to ensure facilitation channels.

Policy Implications for Trade Cooperation with East and South Asia

Strategic Regional Orientation (Focus on East Asia and South Asia)

As a landlocked country situated between two of the largest and most rapidly growing economies in the world—the PRC and India—Nepal has much to gain from accelerated economic integration. Given the greater importance of the Indian economy to Nepal, a key question is what appropriate policies

Nepal can adopt in order to benefit from its proximity to these large, fast-growing economies. First, Nepal needs to broaden its agreement with India to attract Indian investment. The aim should be to facilitate the infusion of Indian capital and technology in a way that will enhance Nepal's own indigenous capital, labor, and resources. To this end, Nepal could pursue the proposed Bilateral Investment Promotion and Protection Agreement to provide further assurances on investment and trade rights to foreign investors. Efforts to forge a formal agreement should be further complemented by advertising efforts to attract Indian investments. Nepal, for instance, should make a special effort to underscore its preferential access to Europe through the everything-but-arms (EBA) initiative. Second, economic diplomacy with the central Indian government needs to be extended to the neighboring Indian states to ensure market access and transit rights. This is important as the Indian state governments wield discretionary powers that can often disrupt trade. Third, Nepal needs to harmonize border procedures, documentation, special economic zones (SEZ) rules, product standards, and customs software with India, in order to facilitate exports even to East Asian countries. Fourth, Nepal could facilitate Indian interests in Nepal by proceeding to build the Tibet–India transit routes, and in return Nepal can request more transit routes and shipping facilities at a variety of Indian ports.

Nepal should also make optimum use of the opportunities arising from rapid economic transformation taking place in the PRC's Tibet Autonomous Region. The Tibet Autonomous Region is increasingly integrated with more prosperous and developed provinces in the PRC, and improved rail and road networks link Lhasa with the major cities in the PRC. The development of international transit routes through Nepal, connecting India and the PRC, would also have major implications for transport development in Nepal as well as possibly significant implications for economic and social development.

Nepal's access to the large markets in India and the PRC may be strategically used to attract FDI from other South and East Asian countries.

Current Comparative and Competitive Advantage, and Likely Future Trends

Nepal has several assets that would make it potentially more competitive. These include (i) a comparative advantage in producing a number of agriculture and manufacturing products (garments, carpets, pashmina, food products such as vegetables, spices and herbs, tea, and honey); (ii) proximity to the large and fast-growing economies of India and the PRC; (iii) the availability of preferential access to Europe and India; (iv) hydroelectric resources that could be exported to energy-constrained India and Bangladesh; (v) its natural beauty, climate, and important religious and cultural sites that draw tourists; and (vi) its growing pool of educated labor. In particular, duty-free entry to Europe under the EBA initiative and preferential access to India combine with lower wages and a better investment climate than some neighboring Indian states to potentially attract foreign and Indian investments.

As for opportunities offered by tourism, South Asia Subregional Economic Cooperation (SASEC) and BIMSTEC, which have set out several action plans based on ecotourism and Buddhism-related tours, could promote Nepal's tourism with East and South Asian countries. However, to exploit this potential, there is a need for better security conditions. Recent initiatives toward the removal of travel agencies and trekking from the FDI negative list are particularly encouraging. Moreover, the limited capacity and poor financial condition of the state-owned Nepal Airlines has to be addressed.

Nepal has enormous potential in hydropower that could be harnessed to meet domestic and regional energy demand. Although its estimated generation potential is 44,000 MW, Nepal currently generates only around 1% of this and trades negligible amounts. The challenge is to develop new capacity to meet growing domestic and export demand, including through foreign investment. On the supply side, transmission links with the Indian and subregional grids could be established. There is also a need to lower the costs of power by reducing system losses (24%), and by encouraging greater private sector participation in power generation and distribution. On the demand side, South Asia—India in particular—has large energy deficiencies. The establishment of the Power Trading Corporation in India is an encouraging development. The promotion of more commercial and private-led power exchanges, the ratification of the Power Trade Agreement, and the reactivation of the Power Exchange Committee between India and Nepal would be helpful.

Higher incomes in East Asia and India and rising education levels in Nepal have increased demand for Nepalese workers abroad. A formal memorandum of understanding has been signed with Malaysia and ratified by Nepal. Similar talks are under way with Hong Kong, China and with the Republic of Korea. Nepal needs to extend employment-seeking talks to countries such as Japan, where the aging of its population will require it to import more foreign labor in the future. Efforts could be made to reduce transaction costs for migrants through more effective regulation of manpower agencies and through the improvement of access to finance from the formal financial system.

Foreign Direct Investment Regime and Policy

Nepal's location between two heavily populated countries with fast-growing economies, its topography, abundant biodiversity, and rich culture and heritage suggest that there is scope for attracting FDI. Unfortunately, Nepal does not have a concrete FDI promotion strategy. The first step in the development of such strategy is the streamlining of the approval regime by strengthening the Investment Promotion Board and the One Window Committee, keeping open the possibility of moving toward the formation of a Board of Investment. The amendment of the Industrial Enterprise Act and the Foreign Investment Act is also needed in order to remove inconsistencies. An important goal is to make investment incentives competitive with those in other comparable countries. Finally, investor confidence should be built up through further strengthening and institutionalization of the current FDI dispute settlement mechanism (for instance, through the establishment of an investment dispute tribunal).

Other policy reforms could be beneficial. First, Nepal needs a stronger bureaucracy in general and a tax administration in particular, since their inefficient performance nullifies many incentives for FDI. Second, the foreign exchange regime could be enhanced by abolishing exchange controls and allowing access to long-term financing. Third, Nepal requires rules governing export processing zones that will harmonize the regulatory regime with those in major trading partners such as India and the PRC. Fourth, market-driven labor reforms are needed, under which wages and benefits are more consensual and flexible with safeguards appropriate for all parties concerned. Fifth, the necessary roads, communication, and energy infrastructure are needed to facilitate FDI. Sixth, economic diplomacy could enhance FDI cooperation among countries in the SAARC, ASEAN+3, and BIMSTEC. Seventh, laws could be enacted to facilitate investments from nonresident Nepalese. Eighth, FDI outflows could be explored as well, and the corresponding rules, regulations, and safeguards implemented.

Merchandise Trade Regime and Policy

External sector adjustments are needed to exploit the existing opportunities and restore the growth of exports. Nepal has to undertake significant trade policy and behind-the-border reforms to improve the business climate.

First, the remaining anti-export bias has to be corrected by reducing the cascading nature of the current tariff structure. Second, improvements in duty drawback are needed, since the current system, implemented through the passbook scheme, is not working well. In fact, some exporters do not even claim duty drawback on their imported inputs because of the high transaction costs involved in claiming duty privileges. Third, addressing trade and exchange rate issues has become important since the gains of the 1990s are now eroding. In the more competitive environment, Nepal's exchange rate, pegged to the Indian rupee, will require continuous review. Fourth, improvements in customs, trade facilitation, standards and quality, infrastructure and transport, and business support will be crucial. Fifth, regulatory reforms in labor markets, specifically in garments, carpets, and agriculture, have made in order to remove price and other entry restrictions. Sixth, emergency actions need to be taken to minimize the adverse effects of on garment exports of the end of the Multi-Fiber Agreement. These would include lowering transport costs sharply by activating a container-train service running through Birgunj, providing EPZ facilities sooner at border points such as Birgunj, facilitating the relocation of industries there, cutting down port handling time in Kolkata, and speeding up customs transactions. These measures are needed to make Nepal more competitive both within and outside the region.

Services Regime and Policy

Services trade is an important engine for facilitating economic growth and development. To foster services trade in Nepal, it is essential that commensurate policy and regulatory regime changes be made. For tourism, the Government should (i) expedite the development of the Tourism Master Plan to include new strategies (e.g., more diversified and region-specific tourism products, including the religious tourism plan mentioned above) not limited to adventure tourism; (ii) facilitate the flow of tourists by eliminating visa requirements and reducing charges (abolishing visa requirements among SAARC and eventually ASEAN+3); (iii) create adequate transit and airline links (e.g., make airfares more economical by reassessing navigation and ground handling charges, and addressing the limited capacity and poor financial condition of the state-owned Nepal Airlines); and (iv) develop a focused, innovative, and effective marketing strategy (priority should be given to improve the Nepal Tourism Board's marketing activities and the funding for promotion, and improving the service standards and codes of practice under the Ministry of Tourism as the industry regulator). Tourists from ASEAN+3 and SAARC largely focus on religious sites such as Lumbini, the birthplace of Buddha. Unfortunately, these sites are underdeveloped as tourist destinations.[22]

For hydropower the Government should (i) review the 2001 Hydro Power Development Policy and the 1992 Electricity Act, as they are not able to improve hydropower production, attract private sector or foreign participation, and promote electricity export; (ii) make the Nepal Electricity Authority, the sole owner of transmission lines, efficient in dealing with power purchase agreements, whose absence prohibits the initiation of hydropower projects; (iii) enhance the energy network with neighboring countries, especially India; and (iv) initiate mechanisms to finance large energy projects.

---

[22] Lumbini is the destination of many tourists from the PRC, Japan, Myanmar, Thailand, and Sri Lanka. Many Hindus from India also visit religious sites in Nepal.

Despite the importance of labor exports, there have not been any systematic efforts to strengthen this sector. Toward this end, there is a need to (i) amend the 1985 Foreign Employment Act and the 1999 Foreign Employment regulation;[23] (ii) formulate agreements with countries pertaining to employment of Nepalese workers; (iii) establish an institution to facilitate the development of regular and legal recruitment channels; (iv) educate the workers on their rights and privileges to limit exploitation; (v) enhance economic diplomacy and ensure that the diplomatic mission of Nepal assist workers in settling their problems overseas; (vi) facilitate the remittance of funds by reducing administrative requirements and cost; (vii) enhance the monitoring and supervision of labor flows; and (viii) provide the necessary training for foreign employment.

A critical impediment of services trade is related to payments, which face foreign exchange restrictions. It is essential that regulations be put in place to ensure that payments (also those transacted electronically) occur in a way that creates certainty to service providers. This may entail some liberalization of the capital account.

Customs Procedures and Trade Facilitation

Customs procedures are the main components of trade facilitation. The present customs procedures in Nepal are time consuming. Custom legislations and procedures should be reviewed in a way that would make them more consistent with the requirements of the Kyoto Convention and the WTO.

Other recommendations are to (i) strengthen customs infrastructure and human resources; (ii) develop uniform and simplified customs procedures; (iii) reform the incentive structure of custom officials to reduce corruption; (iv) reconceptualize the implementation of ASYCUDA as a reform-facilitating measure rather than solely as a computerization exercise; (v) establish electronic data interchange between relevant institutions; (vi) establish a road-based inland clearance depot in Birgunj; (vii) reorganize the institutional structure to enhance private sector participation in customs reform; (viii) improve the operating time of the major customs offices, and (ix) develop a grading system to evaluate the facilitation provided by custom officers.

Transport Initiative

Nepal commonly uses India's roads and sea ports for trade because of its geographical location and traditional links with India. These transit routes are governed by the transit treaty between India and Nepal. Amendments to

---

[23] This law allows Nepali nationals aged 18 or above to work abroad with permission from the Government of Nepal.

the treaty are necessary. Current issues are (i) the improvement of current transit procedures by using combined bills of landing for easy port clearance; (ii) bilateral discussion of common transit-related problems such as poor road infrastructure in various Indian states; and (iii) the need for Government to (a) make gradual improvements in road-planning capacity, with the clear assignment of responsibilities from central to local levels in order to bring all communities into the Strategic Road Network; (b) foster effective inter-institutional relationships, especially between the Ministry of Finance and the Road Board; (c) improve the international passenger terminal, in terms of maintenance work and the work schedule at peak times; (d) improve the institutional requirements in various shipping ports, for instance, by setting up government representative offices at the inland clearance depots; and (e) to expedite the assessment of transit corridors and transit procedures between the PRC and India, which will enhance the integration of those two countries and consequently between the SAARC and ASEAN+3.

Other Policy Issues

The dynamic structure of Nepal's economic relations also requires a flexible policy perspective. In this regard, other policy issues include the need to (i) emphasize economic diplomacy to enhance Nepal's effective coopera-tion with East and South Asia; (ii) reform national institutions, such as the Ministry of Industry, Commerce and Supply, enabling the establishment of a public–private consultation system; and (iii) initiate fuller foreign exchange convertibility to facilitate both inbound and outbound flows of FDI.

References

Acharya, K. P. 2005. *An Assessment of Economic Cost of the Ongoing Armed Conflict in Nepal: An Empirical Examination of the Period 1990–2005.* Presented at the NEFAS/FES Seminar in Kathmandu, Nepal on Cost of Armed Conflict in Nepal. 29–30 September 2005.

Department of Customs. 2001. *Three Years Customs Reform and Moderniza-tion Action Plan (2003–2006).* Kathmandu: Government of Nepal.

_____. Various Issues. *Nepalese Custom News Bulletin.* Ministry of Finance. Kathmandu: Government of Nepal.

Department of Industries. 1992. *Foreign Investment and Technology Transfer Act 1992 and Industrial Enterprises Act 1992.* Kathmandu: Government of Nepal.

_____. 2005. *Procedural Manual for Foreign Investment in Nepal.* Kathmandu: Government of Nepal.

_____. 2006. *Industrial Statistics.* Kathmandu: Government of Nepal.

Federation of Nepalese Chambers of Commerce and Industry and World Bank. 2000. The Business Environment and Manufacturing Performance in Nepal. Washington D.C.: World Bank.

Karmacharya, B. K. 2003. Trade Policy Regime, Growth and Poverty: The Nepalese Experience. In *Trade Policy, Growth and Poverty in Asian Developing Countries*, edited by K. Sharma. London: Routledge Publications.

_____. 2005a. Performance of Nepal's Foreign Trade. In *Readings in Nepalese Economy*, edited by M. Dahal. Kathmandu: Hira Publications.

_____. 2005b. South Asian Free Trade Area: Country Paper on Nepal. In *South Asian Free Trade Area: Opportunities and Challenges.* Washington D.C.: United States Agency for International Development.

Khanal, D. R. and N. R. Kanel. 2005. *Macroeconomic Policies, Shocks and Poverty Reduction in Nepal.* Kathmandu: Institute for Policy Research and Development.

Maskay, N. M., R. K. Panta, and B. P. Sharma. 2005. Foreign Investment Liberalization and Incentives in Selected Asia-Pacific Developing Countries: Implications for the Health Service Sector in Nepal. Report Submitted to Asia Pacific Research and Training Network on Trade (ARTNeT) Secretariat.

Ministry of Finance. Various Issues. *Economic Survey.* Kathmandu: Government of Nepal.

_____. Various Issues. *Budget Speech.* Kathmandu: Government of Nepal.

Ministry of Industry, Commerce and Supplies. 2004. *Nepal Trade and Competitiveness Study.* Kathmandu: Government of Nepal

Nepal Rastra Bank. 2005. *Nepal's WTO Service Sector Commitments and Its Impact on the Balance of Payments Situation.* Available: http://www.nrb.org.np

_____. Various Issues. 2002. *Quarterly Economic Bulletin.* Kathmandu: National Planning Commission. 2002. *The Tenth Plan.* Government of Nepal.

Nepal, V. N. 2006. *Policy Reorientation Study on Transit Trade of Nepal.* Kathmandu: Economic Policy Network. Ministry of Finance and Asian Development Bank. Nepal Resident Mission.

Onta, I. R. 2005. *Strategic Approach to North-South Connectivity.* Kathmandu: Economic Policy Network, Ministry of Nepal and Asian Development Bank: Nepal Resident Mission.

Pant, B. and B. D. Sigdel. 2004. *Attracting Foreign Direct Investment: Experiences and Challenges.* NRB Working Paper, NRB/wp/1. 26 April 2004: Kathmandu: Nepal Rastra Bank.

Pohit, S. and N. Taneja. 2002. India's Informal Trade with Bangladesh and Nepal: A Qualitative Assessment. Working Paper No. 58. New Delhi: Indian Council for Research on International Economic Relations.

Rahmatullah, M. 2006. Nepal North-South Transit Corridor Study. Report submitted to Asian Development Bank.

Rajkarnikar, P. R., N. M. Maskay and S. R. Adhikari. 2005. The Need for and Cost of Selected Trade Facilitation Measures Relevant to the WTO Trade Facilitation Negotiation: A Case Study of Nepal. Report Submitted to Asia Pacific Research and Training Network on Trade Secretariat.

Rana, Madhukar S. J. B. and Stalin Pradhan. 2005. *Implementation Evaluation of Foreign Direct Investment Policy in Nepal.* Kathmandu: Economic Policy Network, Ministry of Finance and Asian Development Bank. Nepal Resident Mission.

Sauvé, P. 2005. Economic Impact and Social Adjustment Cost of accession to the WTO: Cambodia and Nepal. *Asia-Pacific Trade and Investment Review.* 1(1): 27–49.

Taneja, N., M. Sarvananthan, B. K. Karmacharya, and S. Pohit. 2004. India's Informal Trade with Sri Lanka and Nepal: An Estimation. *South Asia Economic Journal* 5(1): 27–54.

United Nations Conference on Trade and Development. 2003. *Investment Policy Review* UNCTAD/ITE/IPC/MISC/2003/1. New York: United Nations.

_____. 2003. *Report of the Working Party on the Accession of the Kingdom of Nepal* to the WTO WT/ACC/NPL/16. New York: United Nations.

_____. 2005. World Investment Report. New York: United Nations.

United Nations Economic and Social Commission for Asia and the Pacific. 2003. *Transit Transport Issues in Landlocked and Transit Developing Countries.* New York: United Nations.

World Bank. 2005. *Nepal Development Policy Review.* Sector Report No 29382. Washington D.C.: World Bank.

_____. 2004. Making Services Work for the Poor. In *World Development Report.* Washington D.C.: World Bank.

Online Resources

Asian Highway available at: http://www.unescap.org/ttdw/index.asp?MenuName=AsianHighway

Bay of Bengal Initiative for Multi-Sectoral Technical and Economic Cooperation. Available at: http://www.bimstec.org

Nepal Rastra Bank. Available at: http://www.nrb.org.np

South Asian Association for Regional Cooperation Secretariat Available at: http://www.saarc-sec.org/main.php

Trade Promotion Centre of Nepal. Available at: http://www.tpcnepal.org.np

World Trade Organization. Available at: http://www.wto.org

Appendix Table

Table A5.1 Synopsis of Customs Facilitation in Nepal, 2006

Item	Response
Single administrative document	Yes
Harmonized Code (HS)	Yes
EDP system	ASYCUDA
EDI (% of ship's inward manifests submitted electronically by shipping line to customs)	No
Direct trader input (% of import declarations that are input by customs agent or consignee directly through designated terminals)	No
Internet input (% of import shipments for which declarations are input through internet)	No
Green channel (% of shipments that are cleared with submission of documents but without inspection)	Less than 1%a
Risk management (% of shipments for which a computer system uses profiling to determine if goods should be inspected)	Less than 1%a
Electronic banking (% of duty and taxes can paid through electronic transfer from consignee's bank)	No
Electronic signature (customs officials can approve declaration using electronic signature rather than physical signature: Yes or No)	No
Private bonded warehouses (import cargo can be moved directly to private warehouse and stored under customs bond for subsequent clearance: Yes or No)	Yes
Bonded factory manufacturers (not located in free trade zones) (can receive imported inputs without clearing customs, store them, process them, and export them the product without paying taxes: Yes or No)	Yes

EDP = Electronic Data Processing, EDI = Electronic Data Interchange , ASYCUDA = Automated System for Customs Data.

[a] Green channels and risk management have been conducted in few customs offices on a test basis but are not used for day-to-day work.

Source: Interview with custom official.

Sri Lanka

Dushni Weerakoon[24]

Introduction

As in many other contemporary developing countries, Sri Lanka's economic policy regime in the 1960s and 1970s saw a gradual shift toward inward-looking dirigiste policies, prompted by deteriorating international terms of trade for its primary export commodities (tea, rubber, and coconuts). However, the country witnessed a marked shift in economic policy thinking from the late 1970s, when it adopted an outward-oriented liberal market economic policy regime, becoming the first country in South Asia region to do so. The policy program included many of the standards reforms of a structural adjustment program, including liberalization of trade and payments, rationalization of public expenditure, dismantling of controls on prices and interest rates, promotion of private sector development, promotion of foreign investment, and financial sector reforms.[25]

The structural transformation of the Sri Lankan economy following the reforms—moving it away from a predominantly agricultural economy to one driven by industrial and services sector growth—set the pattern for its trade and investment links with the rest of the world. The emergence of an export-oriented garment industry strengthened Sri Lanka's trade and investment links with East Asia—as a major source of imports and foreign direct investment (FDI)—while its export interests were primarily focused on the developed countries in Europe and North America. Apart from the early emergence of the garments industry, industrial transformation has remained limited in the two decades of reform because Sri Lanka's investment climate has been hurt by unfavorable political and policy developments. The most dynamic sector of economic activity has been services, encouraged particularly since the early 1990s by the trend toward privatization of public utilities and other state-owned economic enterprises. As a

---

[24] The author wishes to thank Suwendrani Jayaratne, Project Intern, Institute of Policy Studies of Sri Lanka, for her excellent research assistance.
[25] These policy reforms have been well documented. See Lal and Rajapatirana (1989), Cuthbertson and Athukorala (1991), Athukorala and Jayasuriya (1994).

result, the composition of FDI into Sri Lanka has also changed over time, with the majority of foreign investment seeking opportunities in service-related activities.

Although Sri Lanka's trade and investment links with South and East Asia are still rather limited, they indicate both the potential and the manner in which future developments will occur in a rapidly integrating Asian trade and investment environment. East Asia is a significant source of FDI to Sri Lanka, both in the early stages of concentration in the garments industry, and later diversifying into service-related activities such as telecommunications. More recently, Sri Lanka's economic relations with India have been transformed on the back of improved bilateral political relations between the two countries. Supporting such developments, Sri Lanka has already entered into several bilateral and regional trade agreements across South Asia whilst being a party to ongoing negotiations on agreements that include countries in East Asia.

The most significant change in Sri Lanka's trade and investment relations recently has been the emergence of India as a major trade and investment partner. The expansion of the Indian economy can be viewed as a potential link to strengthen Sri Lanka's trade and investment relations with the rest of Asia. India, with its Look East Policy, is already well on the way to cementing stronger engagement with the economies of East Asia, particularly the People's Republic of China (PRC). In view of such developments, this paper reports on an initial exploration of these and related issues, documenting the nature of Sri Lanka's trade and investment relations with East and South Asia, and emerging trade and investment links within regional groupings with particular attention to India–Sri Lanka links.

Economic Structure and External Orientation

Sri Lanka began its post-independence economic development with expectations of being a star performer in Asia. It had relatively high per capita gross domestic product (GDP) and, significantly, had human development indicators well above countries with a similar per capita GDP. Its failure to keep up with the fast-growing East Asian economies has been variously attributed to its decision to increasingly close its economy to international trade and investment from the 1960s. Economic policy inconsistencies brought on by frequent changes of government have also been blamed for the country's poor economic performance until the emergence of an open economic policy regime in the 1980s (Kelegama, 1998).

The outward reorientation in trade and investment policy in the late 1970s saw a marked change in the country's external position. Export performance improved dramatically—albeit from a relatively low base—to increase from an average of 15% of GDP prior to liberalization to an average of 30% of GDP in the 1990s. Given the relatively limited resource base of the economy, import growth continued to outstrip export growth, leading to sustained deficits on the trade balance. Overall, the economy remains fairly open as indicated by the export-import GDP ratio of over 70%. This is relatively high compared to South Asia but much lower in respect of most East Asian economies.

Much of the early focus to improve the country's outward orientation relied on unilateral tariff reforms. Sri Lanka was slow to pursue preferential trade initiatives. An early opportunity to emulate the successes of East Asian economies and strengthen its economic links with the region was lost when Sri Lanka declined to join the Association of Southeast Asian Nations (ASEAN) at its inception in 1967. Sri Lanka in the 1960s had achieved levels of economic development on par with—or in instances well above— many contemporary developing countries. Sri Lanka's decision to opt out of ASEAN appears to have been based primarily on ASEAN's military and defense implications (Kodikara, 1982).

Following the implementation of economic reforms in the late 1970s, Sri Lanka made a formal application for membership in ASEAN in May 1981. However, Sri Lanka's economic development by the late 1970s lagged well behind East Asia, and its application was declined on the basis that the grouping's membership was primarily a geographical one (Kodikara 1982). Following the establishment of a sectoral dialogue partnership with India in 1993, Sri Lanka reapplied for the membership as a full dialogue partner. Sri Lanka was said to be politically acceptable, but the application was turned down on the grounds that the country would not be able to satisfy the general criteria or conform to ASEAN guidelines. From an economic point of view, Sri Lanka's trade with ASEAN as a whole or its individual members was not considered substantial enough. Further, Sri Lanka's domestic market was also considered small, unlike, for example, India's. India was considered to be economically beneficial to ASEAN because of its large domestic market, external trade, investment, and the potential for expanding economic cooperation.

Another key preferential trade policy initiative pursued by Sri Lanka in the early 1990s was to strengthen bilateral trade and investment linkages with India. Sri Lanka proposed the establishment of a preferential trade agreement, but India did not receive it with much enthusiasm at the time (Jayawardena et al. 1993). The subsequent decision taken in 1993 to accelerate trade cooperation through a wider regional framework under the South Asian Association for Regional Cooperation (SAARC) served to push the bilateral agenda more or less to the background until the late 1990s. Thus, from the mid-1990s, Sri Lanka's external trade policy orientation was confined to forging closer links with the South Asian region. Sri Lanka became a party to the South Asian Preferential Trade Agreement (SAPTA), which was initiated in December 1995. This was, however, a limited agreement with minimal liberalization on a preferential basis.

Table 6.1 Economic Performance, %

Annual average growth rate	1990–1997	1998–2005
Per capita GDP growth	4.0	3.0
GDP growth	5.3	4.4
Agriculture	1.4	1.3
Industry	7.1	4.5
Services	5.8	5.5
Exports	11.8	4.6
Imports	10.5	6.8

Source: Central Bank of Sri Lanka, Annual Report (various issues).

The slow progress of the SAPTA initiative led to a discussion within the SAARC of accelerating liberalization among countries willing to do so. However, deteriorating bilateral relations between India and Pakistan from mid-1998 prompted by nuclear tests by both countries halted SAARC official contact until January 2002. In the interim, Sri Lanka signed a bilateral FTA with India and began negotiations on a similar agreement with Pakistan. With the resumption of the SAARC Heads of State Summit in 2002, the much-awaited South Asia Free Trade Agreement (SAFTA) was finalized in 2004.

Sri Lanka's external trade relations with East Asia have moved at a much slower pace. While it was a party to the Bangkok Agreement since its inception in 1975, the Bangkok Agreement had little effect in terms of the coverage or depth of preferential tariff reductions and as a tool of strengthening trade links with East Asia was largely ignored. While the accession of the PRC in 2001—and subsequent renaming of the Bangkok Agreement to the Asia-Pacific Trade Agreement (APTA) in 2005—was expected to give a boost to the pact, its scope still remains very limited. Of more immediate interest is likely to be the reactivation of the Bay of Bengal Initiative for Multi-Sectoral Technical and Economic Cooperation (BIMSTEC), which was set up in 1997.[26] The framework agreement signed in February 2004

---

[26] Originally termed Bangladesh-India-Myanmar-Sri Lanka-Thailand Economic Cooperation.

infused some dynamism to the notion of building a bridge between South Asia and East Asia through a regional pact. The BIMSTEC FTA was scheduled to begin implementation in 2006/07.

Despite opening up the economy to trade and investment, Sri Lanka has been less than successful in reaping the full benefits primarily due to adverse developments on the political front. Since the mid-1980s, Sri Lanka has been engaged in a costly separatist civil conflict that has drained long-term investor confidence in the economy (Arunatilake et al 2001). While GDP growth has averaged around 5% per annum in the last two decades, it is well short of the country's potential (Table 6.1). High defense expenditures (averaging 5–6% of GDP) have been a costly burden on scarce resources, contributing to a fiscal deficit averaging around 9% per annum over the last decade that has undermined confidence in the macroeconomic environment.

The most dynamic sector has been services, which has come to account for nearly 56% of GDP and 44.8% of total employment (Table 6.2). The services sector has been driven by growth in banking, telecommunications, and retail trade. Industry has come to account for 27% of GDP and 24.5% of total employment. Much of Sri Lanka's industrial sector activities are concentrated in the textile and garments sector, which alone accounts for nearly 40% of industrial output albeit with a gradual decline from over 45% in 1998. Agricultural share in GDP has declined progressively to around 17% by 2005, accounting for 30.7% of total employment.

Table 6.2 Structure of the Sri Lankan Economy

Item	1990	1998	2005
Composition of GDP (%)			
Agriculture	26.3	21.1	17.2
Industry	26.0	27.5	27.0
Services	47.7	51.4	55.8
Exports ($ mn.)	1984	4798	6347
Imports ($ mn.)	2686	5890	8863
Exports/GDP (%)	24.8	31.9	27.4
Imports/GDP (%)	33.6	39.2	38.3

Source: Central Bank of Sri Lanka, Annual Report (various issues).

While Sri Lanka has made measured progress in raising per capita income growth to over 3% per annum on average over recent decades, there has been limited headway in poverty reduction. The national poverty headcount[27] at 22.7%—relatively high for a country with a per capita income of over \$1,000—has shown only a modest decline from 26.1% in 1990/91 (Table 6.3). In more recent years, there is also increasing evidence to suggest that income inequality in the country has also been on the increase, with significant inequities in poverty reduction across sectors and provinces of the country. During the decade 1990/91–2002, the poverty gap between the urban sector and the rest of the country widened, while there was also a significant increase in poverty in the estate sector (primarily the tea for export).

Table 6.3 Poverty Headcounts for Sri Lanka

| | 1990/91 | 1995/96 | 2002 | Gini coefficient of per capita expenditure | |
				1990/91	2002
National	26.1	28.8	22.7	0.34	0.42
Urban	16.3	14.0	7.9	0.37	0.44
Rural	29.4	30.9	24.7	0.30	0.39
Estate	20.5	38.4*	30.0	0.24	0.33

Note: Comparability for estate headcount for 1995/96 with that for other years may be affected by the fact that the 1995/96 survey was sampled differently for the estate sector.

Source: World Bank (2004).

Sri Lanka needs to raise its long-term growth rate to 7–8% if inroads are to be made in alleviating poverty. This would require that the current rate of investment of around 25% of GDP rise to 30–35%. With a national savings rate of around 23%—assisted by worker remittances—Sri Lanka will have to depend on raising more FDI from the current inflow averaging around 1% of GDP per annum. While the economy has seen a progressive recovery more recently—to record a GDP growth rate of 6% in 2005 and an expected growth rate close to 7% in 2006—Sri Lanka's economy is increasingly hamstrung by supply-side rigidities, particularly in key areas of infrastructure. While the orientation of economic policy has remained unchallenged and incremental reforms have taken place, the progress has not been entirely free of policy reversals and setbacks. Political developments[28]—particularly the rise of coalition politics—have hampered Sri Lanka from substantive reforms to address the remaining supply-side rigidities.

---

[27] Based on official poverty lines.
[28] The country has experienced five elections in the period 1999—2005.

Foreign Direct Investment Regime

Inflows of FDI to Sri Lanka have averaged only around 1% of GDP per annum, although there was an increase in the early part of the 1990s with the implementation of a privatization program. Given the advantages of a skilled labor force and relatively low levels of red tape, its poor performance in matching levels of FDI coming into the neighboring countries in East Asia has been attributed primarily to political instability. A prolonged civil conflict from the early 1980s has continued to undermine long-term investor confidence. A second phase of trade and investment liberalization in the early 1990s saw a strong positive response in FDI inflows. However, it tapered off with the subsequent escalation of political instability, lending credence to the argument that political instability has been the primary reason for modest levels of inbound FDI (Athukorala and Rajapatirana, 2000).

Table 6.4 Realized Foreign Investment (Cumulative as at end 2005)

Categories	No. of Enterprises	Foreign Investment	
		($ mn)	As % of total BOI investment in category
Food, beverages, and tobacco	147	164.2	61.9
Textiles, wearing apparel, and leather	483	296.5	66.0
Wood and wood products	28	55.0	95.6
Paper and paper products	28	7.7	44.5
Chemical, petroleum, rubber, and plastic products	143	186.5	66.8
Nonmetallic mineral products	62	94.2	53.6
Basic metal products	-	-	-
Fabricated metal products, machinery and transport equip.	92	96.2	79.4
Manufactured products (n.e.s.)	167	82.3	72.8
Services	721	1,304.2	58.1
Total	**1871**	**2,286.7**	**61.4**

BOI = Board of Investment, Mn. = million, n.e.s. = not elsewhere specified

Source: Central Bank of Sri Lanka, Annual Report (2005).

Competing demands for scarce resources have meant that over time, public investment spending has suffered, leading to significant bottlenecks in infrastructure development. Such behind the border constraints to FDI include poor infrastructure. For example, poor infrastructure in electricity and transport sectors has been cited as the top constraint to doing business in Sri Lanka (World Bank, 2005).

As of the end of 2005, cumulative realized FDI according to Board of Investment (BOI)[29] data stood at around $2.3 billion spread across a total of 1,871 enterprises (Table 6.4). The initial spurt of FDI came primarily into the manufacturing sector with the take-off of garments exports. Initially, more than one half of manufacturing FDI was concentrated in textile- and garment-related sectors. Service-related FDI overtook manufacturing from the end of the 1990s with increased opportunities in such sectors as telecommunications and property development. Privatization has been an important channel of FDI into Sri Lanka from the early 1990s, particularly with regard to FDI inflows in to services.

The overwhelming dominance of textile and clothing in FDI inflows into manufacturing has been changing—albeit slowly—over the years. FDI in the sector has dropped to about 30% of total manufacturing FDI in recent years (Table 6.5). There has been a notable increase of FDI in other labor-intensive activities such as footwear, travel goods, plastic products, gems and jewelry, rubber-based products, and ceramics. The data is not adequate to determine accurately the degree to which noninfrastructure-related investments outside the textile and garments sectors are export- or home-market oriented, but there are indications that significant amounts of FDI have come in to set up export platforms that exploit the relatively low labor cost advantages of Sri Lanka with its generally high levels of literacy and investments in human capital.

FDI in Sri Lanka is dominated by a handful of countries. The East Asian region has been an important source of FDI for Sri Lanka. Much of the initial inflow of FDI came into the garments industry as East Asian countries began to take advantage of quota opportunities afforded to Sri Lanka by the US and the European Union (EU). The East Asian region accounted for over two thirds of total FDI, with the Republic of Korea; Hong Kong, China; Japan; and Singapore being the key sources. While garments-related manufacturing FDI has slowed more recently, other East Asian economies such as Malaysia have emerged as significant investors, particularly in the services sector. Malaysia, for example, was the single largest source of FDI in 2005/06 bringing about $100 million into the telecommunications sector (accounting for 90% of total Malaysian FDI). Another key development has been the emergence of India as a significant source of investment. At times, tense political relations with India have discouraged more active

---

[29] Formerly the Greater Colombo Economic Commission (GCEC) set up in 1978 and reconstituted as the Board of Investment in 1992.

Indian involvement in the economy. However, with a marked improvement in bilateral relations since the late 1990s, Indian investment has picked up sharply. The principle sectors for Indian investment have been steel, cement, rubber products, tourism, and information technology (IT). While outbound FDI from Sri Lanka is fairly limited, it has also been concentrated primarily in India.[30]

Table 6.5 Foreign Direct Investment in Manufacturing, 1995–2004

Item	Cumulative 1995–1999		Cumulative 2000–2004	
	No of Projects	Foreign Investment ($ mn)	No. of Projects	Foreign Investment ($ mn)
Food, beverages, and tobacco	71	18.2	32	24.3
Textile, wearing apparel, and leather products	147	69.2	180	105.6
Wood and wood products	10	4.3	8	16.9
Paper, paper products, printing, and publishing	13	2.1	9	1.5
Chemicals, petroleum, coal, rubber, and plastic	62	19.8	57	34.2
Nonmetallic mineral products	35	20.0	27	17.4
Fabricated metal, machinery, and transport equipment	18	18.5	55	73.1
Other manufactured products, n.e.s.	97	31.0	54	43.1
Total manufacturing	**453**	**183.1**	**422**	**316.0**

Source: Sri Lanka's BOI.

The BOI is responsible for the approval and facilitation of foreign investment throughout the country, other than for investments made by purchasing shares in the Colombo Stock Exchange, or for investments in a number of activities which are regulated by other statutory agencies. A key objective in setting up the BOI was to offer superior regulatory, tax, and administrative treatment to eligible—usually large—investors. All other investors are subject to the general regime and to administration by the line ministries agencies, the outcome of which has been the creation of a

---

[30] Ceylon Biscuits Ltd (confectionary), KIK (electric panel builders), Bodyline Private Ltd. (apparel), and Damro Exports Ltd. (prefabricated furniture) are among the successful Sri Lankan investors in India.

dual regime. FDI approval is in general handled by the BOI and is, with some exceptions, automatic.

Table 6.6 Share of Asian FDI in Sri Lanka, % share in total FDI

Country/Region	Cumulative 1978–1995	2005
ASEAN+3	54.1	48.8
Korea	32.7	1.7
Japan	11.7	1.4
Singapore	6.4	10.7
Malaysia	0.2	34.7
PRC	0.5	0.3
East Asia[a]	66.7	55.1
Hong Kong, China	11.9	5.4
Taipei,China	0.6	0.7
South Asia	2.1	6.6
India	1.2	6.2

[a] Refers to ASEAN+3 plus Hong Kong, China and Taipei,China; SAARC excludes Afghanistan, Bhutan, and the Maldives.

Sources: Sri Lanka BOI.

The BOI was created with wide powers to grant tax relief and administrative discretion for larger or priority investors. The BOI offers an array of incentives to both local and foreign investors. Minimum investment amounts, export requirements, and employment levels are qualifying conditions that may be applied. Fiscal incentives are available to approved investors. While incentives are liable to change over time, typically they have taken the form of (i) an initial tax holiday, often for 5 years, followed by a short period of a concessional income tax rate (e.g., 10% for 2 years) and a long-term concessional rate of 15–20% depending on the industry; (ii) zero dividend tax and dividend withholding tax (DWT) during the tax holiday and for 1 year thereafter; and (iii) import duty exemptions on capital equipment in some industries and zero duties on raw materials in export manufacturing. No country is given special treatment.

The fiscal-incentive-based system of attracting FDI has drawn its share of criticism. It discriminates against small and medium-sized enterprises (SMEs) that may not be able to meet the minimum investment required to qualify for such incentives. The most vocal criticism, however, has been that such incentives discriminate against investors who are ineligible for such concessions and thus face a far higher tax burden. It has been estimated that the tax burden could be as high as 50–100% (UNCTAD, 2004). In addition, Sri Lanka's deteriorating revenue generation has been partly ascribed to the provision of generous tax breaks without instituting compensatory revenue measures.

Box 6.1: FDI Approval Regime

Foreign investors are not permitted to invest in the following activities: (i) money lending, (ii) pawnbroking, (iii) retail trade with capital of less than $1 million, (iv) personal services other than for the export or tourism sectors, (v) coastal fishing, (vi) education of students who are citizens of Sri Lanka and below 14 years of age, and (vii) award of local educational degrees.

Foreign investment of only up to 40% of equity in a company is permitted in the following areas: (i) production of goods where Sri Lanka's exports are subject to internationally determined quota restrictions; (ii) growing and primary processing of tea, rubber, coconut, cocoa, rice, sugar, and spices; (iii) mining and primary processing of nonrenewable national resources; (iv) timber-based industries using local timber; (v) deep-sea fishing; (vi) mass communications; (vii) education; (viii) freight forwarding; (ix) travel agencies; and (x) shipping agencies. If foreign ownership exceeds 40%, the BOI grants approval on a case-by-case basis.

The percentage share of foreign investment is subject to approval of the relevant regulatory authority in the following business activities: (i) air transport, (ii) coastal shipping, (iii) industrial undertakings in the Second Schedule of the Industrial Promotion Act No. 46 of 1990,[8] (iv) large-scale mechanized mining of gems, and (v) lotteries.

Sri Lanka maintains a relatively liberal FDI regime. It has been estimated that nearly 60% of FDI by value and 45% by the number of projects has been undertaken by wholly foreign-owned enterprises (UNCTAD, 2004). Nevertheless, certain limitations, conditions, and qualifications pertain specifically to some forms of commercial presence by foreign investors through the imposition of a negative list (Box 6.1).

---

[31] Namely, any industry manufacturing arms, ammunitions, explosives, military vehicles, equipment, aircraft, or other military hardware; any industry manufacturing poisons, narcotics, alcohol, dangerous drugs and toxic, hazardous or carcinogenic materials; any industry producing currency, coins, or security documents.

While the overall regime is fairly liberal, there is room in rationalizing the scope of FDI entry. Restrictions on the entry of education establishments, and air transportation appear to be somewhat arbitrary while there is too much discretionary power in granting approval on a case-by-case basis.

Foreign investment in Sri Lanka is guaranteed by Article 157 of the Constitution, which ensures the commitments of bilateral investment protection agreements (BPIAs).[32] Sri Lanka is currently a signatory to approximately 25 BPIAs, covering essentially the principle home country investors in Sri Lanka. The BPIAs typically include national treatment, most favored nation (MFN) treatment, arbitration, and guarantees against nationalization or expropriation. Sri Lanka is a party to the Convention on the Settlement of Investment Disputes (ICSID) and the UN Commission on International Trade Law (UNCITRAL). While Sri Lanka is not a party to the UN Convention on the Recognition and Enforcement of Foreign Arbitral Awards (New York Convention), it was referred to in the Greater Colombo Economic Commission (GCEC) Law and has been enshrined in the Arbitration Act. Foreign arbitral awards are enforced in Sri Lanka.

Export processing zones (EPZs) were set up with the intention of providing a more conducive environment for FDI through better infrastructure and less red tape. The establishment of EPZs, eight of which are spread across the country,[33] is particularly encouraged through the provision of infrastructure and security. However, under current government policies, foreign investors are allowed to establish factories in almost any part of the country and still receive tax incentives. About 80% of BOI firms, in fact, are estimated to operate outside EPZs (World Bank, 2004). The share of EPZs in total export earnings has risen from 8.7% in 1980 to over 30% by 2000 (UNCTAD, 2004). Foreign investment accounts for approximately 60% of total investment in the EPZs.

While the BOI has likely helped to facilitate the entry and operations of new large investors, it has not been quite as successful in promoting and attracting new FDI. Sri Lanka's annual inflows of FDI have stagnated near 1% of GDP over the last two decades. While it is difficult to assess the extent of the BOI's role in this underperformance, the organization has come under some criticism. The BOI is considered to be heavily overstaffed and too centralized in carrying out its functions. On the other hand, the nature of the fiscal incentives offered to BOI companies has necessitated a large bureaucracy to approve and monitor size-based incentives.

---

[32] Sri Lanka is also a founder member of the Multilateral Investment Guarantee Agency (MIGA) of the World Bank which provides guarantees against noncommercial risks, such as those arising out of political changes or political instability.

[33] With the exception of two zones, all are within 65 kilometers (km) of Colombo.

There does not appear to be a specific strategy to attract investment by region or by sector. The policy goal seems to be that of targeting countries and regions that have conceded preferential market access to Sri Lanka (i.e., to support export growth into specific markets by attracting FDI from those regions). Thus, the focus at present is to attract FDI mainly from the US, the EU, and India. While the common reason cited is the size of these markets, concessions offered to Sri Lanka under the EU's General System of Preferences (GSP) plus scheme or the India–Sri Lanka FTA, for example, appear to play a significant role. For example, the BOI is of the view that some of the areas for future Indian investments could include IT and business process outsourcing, tourism, textiles and accessories, automotive parts and components, rubber, medical products and pharmaceuticals, and education.

While the BOI also claims to be looking strategically at countries like Malaysia, it seems more to be following the market than leading the investment drive. While the BOI has no country offices or other persons working in foreign countries to promote investment, it is said to have desk officers assigned to particular countries from which they have responsibility for promoting inward investment. It appears that a more strategic approach is needed to tap into emerging markets in East Asia.

Merchandise Trade Policy

Trade Performance and Patterns

Sri Lanka's export earnings, which recorded a healthy growth in excess of 10% per annum, slowed considerably during the period 1998–2005. This is largely due to external factors such as the downside effects of the East Asian financial crisis and a global economic slowdown, and also the adverse impacts of domestic policy challenges during the period 2000–2002 (Table 6.1). Export earnings have recovered to an average of around 9–10% during the period 2003–2006. Garments have been the mainstay of export earnings since the mid-1980s, accounting for half of total export earnings. The continued overdependence on garments is a key weakness of the manufacturing sector. It has been widely argued that the lack of a suitable industrial strategy—in the belief that price incentives generated from trade policies would be sufficient—has been a major contributory factor for the limited diversification of manufactured exports (Athukorala and Rajapatirana, 2000). Political instability has also meant that Sri Lanka has been more successful in attracting more "footloose" FDI into sectors such as garments rather than long-term investment in high-value-added manufactures.

Reflecting the overt concentration of exports, there has been little change in the composition of Sri Lanka's exports over the period under review (Table 6.7). Articles of apparel and clothing accessories (knitted as well as not knitted) plus coffee, tea, mate, and spices have been the major categories of exports from 1998 to 2005. During the period 1998–2005, both knitted and non-knitted articles of apparel alone (HS chapters 61 and 62) accounted for more than 40% of total exports. However, by 2005 there has been a slight decrease in the export share of knitted and not-knitted

Table 6.7 Top 10 Exports in Selected Years

HS Codes	Description	Value of exports ($ Mn)			Share of total exports (%)		
		2005	1998	1990	2005	1998	1990
62	Non knitted articles of apparel, etc.	1,600	1,450	443	26.4	32.4	23.5
61	Knitted articles of apparel, etc.	1,103	649	175	18.2	14.5	9.3
09	Coffee, tea, mate, and spices	887	816	531	14.6	18.3	28.2
40	Rubber and articles thereof	435	211	106	7.2	4.7	5.7
71	Pearls, precious stones, etc.	320	118	172	5.3	2.7	9.2
74	Copper and articles thereof	155			2.6		
15	Animal or vegetable fats	142			2.4		
99	Manufactures, n.e.s	117			1.9		
85	Electrical machinery, etc.	104			1.7		
03	Fish, crustaceans, etc.	102	98	22	1.7	2.2	1.2
42	Leather articles, etc.		141			3.2	
63	Other made up textile articles		97			2.2	
84	Machinery and mechanical appliances		93			2.1	
64	Headgear and parts thereof		62			1.4	
08	Edible fruits, nuts, etc.			48			2.6
27	Mineral fuels, oils, etc.			28			1.5
53	Other vegetable textile fibers, etc.			18			1.0
69	Ceramic products			15			0.8
	Total	6,066	4,472	1,885			

HS = Harmonized System of commodity trade classification of 1996, Mn = million, n.e.s. = not elsewhere specified.

Source: Compiled from Department of Customs, External Trade Statistics (various years).

articles of apparel taken together. In the same period, Sri Lanka has seen new sectors of exports emerging in the top 10 items. Copper, animal or vegetable fats and oils, and electrical machinery are some export items that were not among the major 10 export items in 1990 and 1998 that appeared in the top 10 in 2005.

Table 6.8 Top 10 Imports in Selected Years

HS	Description	Value of Imports ($ Mn)			Share of Total Imports (%)		
		2005	1998	1990	2005	1998	1990
27	Mineral fuels, oils, etc.	1,098	335	331	13.4	6.2	12.1
84	Machinery and mechanical appliances	598	506	177	7.3	9.3	6.5
87	Vehicles other than railways, etc.	574	371	170	7.0	6.8	6.2
52	Cotton	515	395	122	6.3	7.3	4.5
85	Electrical machinery	507	402	135	6.2	7.4	4.9
60	Knitted or crocheted fabrics	382	250		4.7	4.6	
39	Plastics and articles thereof	318	172		3.9	3.2	
71	Natural or cultured pearls, stones, etc.	306	168	93	3.7	3.1	3.4
55	Manmade staple fibers	288	320	128	3.5	5.9	4.7
72	Iron and steel	249			3.1		
10	Cereals		168	127		3.1	4.6
17	Sugar and sugar confectionery			131			4.8
48	Pulp			77			2.8
	Total	**8,182**	**5,444**	**2,749**			

HS = Harmonized System of commodity trade classification of 1996, mn = million.

Source: Compiled from Department of Customs, External Trade Statistics (various years).

The major import items have changed little during the period 1990–2005; changes in import composition are perhaps even smaller than those in exports (Table 6.8). Imports have been concentrated in serving the export-oriented garment industry. Raw materials for the garments sector such as cotton, manmade staple fibers, and knitted or crocheted fabric have together accounted for a significant share of total imports. Collectively, the share increased from just over 9% in 1990 to nearly 18% in 1998 before declining more recently to around 15%. The heavy import dependence of the garment industry highlights the need to invest in the development of local input suppliers. The other major import items are machinery and mechanical appliances and vehicles. Iron and steel are also emerging as major import items.

Sri Lanka's exports are mainly destined for the US and the EU (Table 6.9). In contrast, the share of East Asia in total exports is minimal and has actually declined progressively over time. This is primarily due to reduced shares of exports going to Japan and the Republic of Korea while new export markets have failed to emerge in the region. By contrast, the export share to countries in the SAARC has increased significantly between 1998 and 2005 solely as a result of a sharp expansion in exports to India, which is largely due to the implementation of the India–Sri Lanka FTA from 2000.

Table 6.9 Direction of Export Trade

Regions/Countries	Value of Exports ($ mn)			Share of Total Exports (%)		
	2005	1998	1990	2005	1998	1990
US	1,953	1,780	488	32.2	40.2	25.9
EU	1,875	1,252	505	30.9	28.0	26.8
ASEAN+3	549	529	186	9.1	11.8	9.9
East Asia	620	588	210	10.2	13.2	11.2
Japan	140	185	101	2.3	4.1	5.4
Korea	225	228	5	3.7	5.1	0.3
Singapore	702	382	44	1.2	0.9	2.4
PRC	279	86	3	0.5	0.2	0.2
SAARC	608	69	62	10.0	1.6	3.3
India	550	33	20	9.1	0.8	1.1
Pakistan	42	26	32	0.7	0.6	1.7
Total	**6,066**	**4,472**	**1,885**			

EU = European Union, Mn = million PRC = People's Republic of China, SAARC = South Asian Association for Regional Cooperation.

Source: Compiled from Department of Customs, External Trade Statistics (various years).

The composition of Sri Lanka's exports to Asia has undergone some changes over the years. In the early 1990s exports were still dominated by the traditional products such as tea and cultured pearls (Table 6.10). There was a marked shift in this composition by 2005, with exports of copper and animal and vegetable oils dominating the export basket. This is largely a reflection of the growing importance of India as a dominant export market. Other sectors that have opened up include aluminum product exports, machinery and mechanical appliances, and organic chemicals.

Table 6.10 Top 10 Exports to Asia

HS	Description	Value of exports ($ mn)			Share of total exports to Asia (%)		
		2005	1998	1990	2005	1998	1990
74	Copper and articles	153			12.5		
15	Animal or vegetable fats	142		6.6	11.6		2.4
09	Coffee, tea, mate, and spices	87	61	48.6	7.1	9.2	17.8
71	Natural and cultured pearls	55	38	71.0	4.5	5.8	26.0
40	Rubber and articles	49	22	14.7	4.0	3.4	5.4
85	Electrical machinery	49	26		4.0	4.0	
76	Aluminum and articles	44			3.6		
03	Fish and crustaceans	41	72	15.6	3.4	10.9	5.7
84	Machinery and mechanical appliances	38	83	6.8	3.1	12.6	2.5
29	Organic chemicals	24			2.0		
27	Mineral fuels and oils		11.2	24.0		1.7	8.8
55	Man made staple fibers		11.1			1.7	
53	Other vegetable textile fabrics		9.9			1.5	
61	Knitted articles of apparel		9.8			1.5	
72	Iron and steel			10.1			3.7
12	Oilseeds			7.6			2.8
62	Articles of apparel			6.8			2.5
	Total	**1,228**	**658**	**273**			

HS = Harmonized System of commodity trade classification of 1996.

Source: Compiled from Department of Customs, External Trade Statistics (various years).

Despite the existence of an Export Development Board (EDB), Sri Lanka lacks a targeted export promotion strategy. For the most part, the strategy appears to be to look to expand market opportunities where Sri Lanka has entered into preferential trade agreements. While this may make sense in terms of key agreements such as the India–Sri Lanka FTA, it makes less sense when applied to other agreements such as the FTA with Pakistan or the SAFTA, where market access opportunities are recognized to be fairly limited.

In terms of East Asian economies, the EDB cites the PRC, Japan, the Republic of Korea, and Singapore as countries that hold potential market access opportunities. However, there appears to be a lack of strategic planning in terms of identifying products with export potential and devising means of accessing markets for those products. There seems to be an overreliance on trade agreements as a means of breaking into East Asian markets. For example, the perception remains that it would be difficult for a country like Sri Lanka to break into a regional bloc market such as ASEAN unless some form of a preferential trade initiative is negotiated.

In some sectors, production links have been established through inflows in FDI. The case of investments in the rubber sector is of particular interest since Sri Lanka, being a net exporter of natural rubber, had been seeking greater access to the protected but growing Indian market, with little success. On the other hand, the increased penetration of the transport equipment market by India has led to a large influx of Indian-made vehicles, creating opportunities for firms to supply rubber products, such as tires, for these vehicles. To the extent that further liberalization or preferential measures may ease Sri Lanka's access to Indian rubber and rubber goods markets, there is clearly an opportunity developing for export-oriented investments in Sri Lanka that can target the Indian market. The following case study of a tire manufacturing joint venture with an Indian firm is interesting in this light (Box 6.2).

The initial trade liberalization in Sri Lanka permitted India's early penetration (especially by its tire manufacturers) into the vehicle market. The privatization program in Sri Lanka also provided investment opportunities to capitalize on cheap Sri Lankan natural rubber.

In terms of imports into Sri Lanka, the experience in relation to trade with Asia is somewhat different to that of exports. East Asia has long been an important source of imports to Sri Lanka (Table 6.11). For example, Japan was the single most important source of imports until India overtook Japan in the mid-1990s. ASEAN and other East Asian economies such as Hong Kong, China have also played a key role as a source of imports for Sri Lanka's garments industry, which is heavily dependent on imported fabrics originating from the East Asian region. The PRC more recently increased its share of imports into Sri Lanka. The most significant change to import trade in more recent years, however, has been India's enormous gains in the Sri Lankan market, where it accounts for more than 20% of total imports. Thus, the overall trend is that Sri Lanka is becoming more dependent for its imports on South Asia and East Asia while lessening its dependence on the rest of the world.

Box 6.2: Joint Venture in Tire Manufacturing

Ceat Pvt Ltd. is the flagship company of one India's largest companies: RPG enterprises, which has two joint-venture operations in Sri Lanka. The first was with Associated Motorways Pvt Ltd. (AMW) in 1993 creating Associate Ceat (Pvt) Ltd. ACPL), while the second occurred in 1999, between ACPL and Kelani Tyres Pvt Ltd. (Kelani Tyre).

In 1993 Ceat and AMW of Sri Lanka entered into a joint venture operation to produce. The ACPL produced tires for local and export markets, and was successful in capturing the market segments in ties for light trucks and three-wheeled vehicles within a short time. In also started making truck tires within 24 months of operation under the brand name of Ceat. Ceat's well-developed distribution channels provided an added advantage for AMW in this venture. The reasons cited for Ceat to invest in Sri Lanka were (i) the strategic location of Sri Lanka in accessing global markets; (ii) an abundant natural rubber supplies; and (iii) the privatization of a number of state-owned firms, including the Tyre Corporation in 1990, offered opportunities to obtain local assets with well established brand-name recognition.

In expanding its future operations, ACPL entered into a second joint venture operation with Kelani Tyres in January 1999. At present the joint venture company is exporting tires to South America, Pakistan, Bangladesh, Mauritius, and Nepal. Many of the reasons for this second joint venture (Kelani-Ceat) were seen as being mutually beneficial to both parties, including: (i) to avoid competition between the two main players in the market for local tires, ACPL and Kelani Tyres; (ii) to improve viability after the Government of Sri Lanka reduced the import duty on imported tires, making locally produced tires less competitive and encouraging horizontal integration; (iii) to obtain economies of scale; (iv) to capitalize on the high demand for pneumatic tires; (v) to obtain Kelani's established brand in the domestic market, while capitalizing on Ceat's brand prominence internationally. Therefore, the joint venture could increase positive gains through expansion into the domestic and export markets.

Table 6.11 Direction of Import Trade

Regions/Countries	Value of Imports ($ Mn)			Share of Total Imports(%)		
	2005	1998	1990	2005	1998	1990
US	200	218	242	2.4	4.0	8.8
EU	1.267	969	449	15.5	17.8	16.3
ASEAN+3	2.658	1.990	947	32.5	36.6	34.5
East Asia	3.571	2.743	1.223	43.6	50.4	44.5
Singapore	726	296	104	8.9	5.4	3.8
Hong Kong, China	637	391	121	7.8	7.2	4.4
PRC	620	215	120	7.6	4.0	4.4
Japan	373	529	332	4.6	9.7	12.1
Malaysia	327	183	113	4.0	3.4	4.1
Taipei,China	274	360	155	3.4	6.6	5.6
Indonesia	215	173	39	2.6	3.2	1.4
Korea	207	433	127	2.5	8.0	4.6
Thailand	165	139	86	2.0	2.6	3.1
SAARC	1.540	617	181	18.8	11.3	6.6
India	1.417	528	119	17.3	9.7	4.3
Pakistan	113	86	53	1.4	1.6	1.9
Total	**8.182**	**5,444**	**2,749**			

Mn = million, EU = European Union, PRC = People's Republic of China, SAARC = South Asian Association for Regional Cooperation.

Source: Compiled from Department of Customs, External Trade Statistics (various years).

Despite the increase in share of imports from the Asian region as a whole, the composition of imports to Sri Lanka from the region has not changed significantly over time (Table 6.12). East Asia and India have been important sources of vehicles, cotton and other textile fabric, and machinery imports. More recently, imports of plastics, iron and steel, and animal and vegetable fats and oils have gained ground.

Import Protection

Sri Lanka has progressively rationalized and liberalized its import regime. The reforms saw the removal of export and import controls and export duties, a gradual reduction of tariffs, the elimination of licensing requirements for agricultural imports, and the binding of agricultural tariffs, and

Table 6.12 Top 10 Imports from Asia

HS	Description	Value of Imports ($ mn)			Share of Total Imports to Asia (%)		
		2005	1998	1990	2005	1998	1990
87	Vehicles other than railway	552	346	158	10.8	10.3	11.3
27	Mineral fuels, oils	475	120	78	9.3	3.6	5.6
52	Cotton	470	352	118	9.2	10.5	8.4
84	Machinery and mechanical appliances	408	322	99	8.0	9.6	7.1
60	Knitted or crocheted fabric	316	218	70	6.2	6.5	5.0
85	Electrical machinery	265	184	67	5.2	5.5	4.8
55	Manmade staple fibers	235	289	119	4.6	8.6	8.5
39	Plastics and articles	230	124		4.5	3.7	
72	Iron and steel	194			3.8		
15	Animal or vegetable fats and oils	148			2.9		
59	Coated textile fabrics		94			2.8	
54	Manmade filaments		84	53		2.5	3.8
17	Sugar and sugar confectionery			77			5.5
31	Fertilizers			42			3.0
	Total	**5,111**	**3,361**	**1,405**			

HS = Harmonized System of commodity trade classification of 1996, mn = million.

Source: Compiled from Department of Customs, External Trade Statistics (various years).

textile and apparel tariffs at modest rates. The tariff structure was rationalized progressively up to 2000 but there was some interruption to this policy direction with the reintroduction of multiple bands in the following years due primarily to revenue pressures. Further moves to rationalize the tariff system have since seen the reintroduction of a five-band tariff structure of 0%, 2.5%, 6%, 15%, and 28% in 2005. Duty on basic raw materials is kept at the lowest tariff level while finished products are placed at the highest tariff level. Agriculture is also afforded tariff protection under the highest bands. The average applied tariff rate is estimated to be 6.4% (agriculture average applied tariff of 63.7% and industry average applied tariff of 6.0%).[34] Applied tariff rates in agriculture remain fairly high due to the application

---

[34]   Source: http://www.macmap.org

of specific duties on key commodities. Nevertheless, the average tariff on imports in 2005 was estimated at 4.3%. Available official estimates of the effective rate of protection (ERP) for import-competing manufacturing is estimated to have declined from 70% in 1991 to 56% in 2002 (World Bank, 2004). Although there are no official estimates of ERP for export-oriented production, some estimates suggest a rise from 30% in 1991 to 37% in 2003 (World Bank, 2004). These trends point to a reduction in the incentive bias against exports during this period.

Despite efforts to rationalize the tariff structure, revenue consider-ations led to the introduction of various other duties, such as surcharges, specific duties, duty waivers, and exemptions. An import surcharge of 10% and a paratariff in the form of a Ports and Airports Development Levy (PAL) of 3% of cost, insurance, and freight. value of imports are in place. In addition, a total of around 370 items at the six-digit level of the HS Code remain under import control for reasons of health, national security, and environment protection, among others. However, such para-tariffs and nontariff barriers (NTBs) are applied across the board and do not discriminate against particular trading partners either in South Asia or East Asia.

Export Promotion

While export duties have been phased out in all sectors, traditional exports such as tea, coconuts, and coconut products are subject to export taxes which are supposed to be earmarked to finance specific activities (e.g., research and development, export promotion, and to support small-scale land holders). In addition, about 30 categories of exports continue to remain under license with the objective of environmental protection and preservation of antiques.

Sri Lanka offers several incentive programs (e.g., duty exemptions, drawbacks, fiscal incentives administered through EPZs) to promote exports. Some of the incentives are contingent on export performance. At present there are three main incentive schemes in operation: a drawback scheme,[35] a temporary importation for export processing (TIEP) scheme [36] and the manufacture-in-bond scheme.[37] These schemes include bonded warehouse facilities for imported capital and intermediate goods, and the

---

[35] Duties paid on imported materials used to manufacture or process goods in Sri Lanka may be partially or fully rebated or refunded once the final good is exported.

[36] The TIEP scheme allows indirect and direct exporters to import inputs without payment of fiscal levies.

[37] Manufacturers who establish a manufacturing-in-bond warehouse can avoid paying duties and taxes at the time of importation.

refund of duties and other fiscal levies on imported inputs used in the manufacture of exports.

There is no state agency or bank that provides loans or equity finance to exporters. The Sri Lanka Export Credit Insurance Corporation (SLECIC) offers post-shipment financing at market interest rates to small exporters who are unable to obtain bank loans. The SLECIC also acts as the Government's export credit insurer. The main agency for export promotion and development of exports in the country is the Sri Lanka Export Development Board (EDB). Its role is to assist producers and exporters of goods and services (including professional services) to identify and penetrate new markets, as well as to develop goods and services that will meet market demands. Although the EDB did have trade offices in countries such as the Netherlands, the Maldives, and Japan, they have since been closed down since the Government thought it unnecessary to have such offices given the presence of commercial attaches at embassies and the high cost involved in maintaining overseas offices.

The EDB is financed primarily through public funds and roughly two thirds of the funds allocated to the EDB is estimated to be spent on administrative costs. While the remaining one third of funds is spent on providing assistance to exporters, no information is available on the effectiveness of EDB promotional and developmental activities. The high cost of administration alone has cast doubt on the cost effectiveness of the EDB in delivering such assistance (WTO 2004). Nevertheless, there appears to be a lack of specific targets—by product, country, or region—to focus on developing export opportunities for the country in the medium and long terms.

Regional Agreements

Sri Lanka began to participate proactively in regional and bilateral trade initiatives from the mid-1990s (Table 6.13). In 1995, it became a member of the South Asian Preferential Trade Agreement (SAPTA), which was superseded by the South Asia Free Trade Agreement (SAFTA) in 2006. It is also a signatory to the Bangkok Agreement and BIMSTEC. With the entry of the PRC and the Republic of Korea to the Bangkok Agreement, Sri Lanka is expected to move toward an FTA under the Asia–Pacific Trade Agreement (APTA). BIMSTEC has already concluded a framework agreement to establish an FTA, expected to be implemented 2007. Bilateral FTAs to which Sri Lanka is a signatory include the India–Sri Lanka FTA and the Pakistan–Sri Lanka FTA.

A third round of tariff liberalization under the Bangkok Agreement produced a consolidated list of concessions that covers 4,857 tariff lines, including special concessions (587 tariff lines) offered to least-developed countries (LDCs) (Table 6.14). Sri Lanka has offered preferential treatment

Table 6.13 Summary of Regional Trade Agreements

Agreement	Scope	Coverage	Approach
BA	Preferential	Partial	Positive list
SAPTA	Preferential	Partial	Positive list
ISFTA	FTA	Partial	Negative list
PSFTA	FTA	Partial	Negative list
SAFTA	FTA	Partial	Negative list
BIMSTEC	FTA	Partial	Negative list

BA = Bangkok Agreement, SAPTA = South Asian Preferential Trade Agreement, ISFTA = India–Sri Lanka Free Trade Agreement, PSFTA = Pakistan–Sri Lanka Free Trade Agreement, SAFTA = South Asia Free Trade Agreement, BIMSTEC = Bay of Bengal Initiative for Multi-Sectoral Technical and Economic Cooperation.

on 427 tariff lines (and an additional 72 for LDCs). The Bangkok Agreement by and large has been dormant since its inception and has had very limited impact, if any at all. Negotiations toward the SAPTA too have been limited both the depth and scope of tariff cuts offered. In fact, it has been estimated that on average only 8.4% of tariff lines in the case of imports from non-LDCs (and 6.2% in the case of imports from the LDCs are covered by the tariff concessions in the three rounds concluded by 1998 (World Bank, 2004). In reality, products imported under SAPTA concessions translated to only 15% of total imports between member countries in the SAARC.

The defining bilateral FTA to emerge in the region was the India–Sri Lanka FTA (ISFTA) concluded in December 1998. Under the ISFTA, India agreed to remove tariffs on 1,351 products.[38] It also submitted a negative list of 429 items and agreed to phase out the tariffs on the remaining items over a span of 3 years; a 50% reduction in Indian customs duties in the first year; a 75% reduction in the second year; and a 100% reduction in the third year. Sri Lanka would, therefore, have duty-free access to the Indian market (excluding those items coming under the negative list) three years after the FTA becomes operative.

In return, Sri Lanka submitted a negative list consisting of 1,180 items and granting immediate duty-free access to India on 319 items. A 50% margin of preference was offered on an additional 889 items, with the preferential reduction raised to 70%, 90% and 100% over a 3-year period. The duty on the remaining items (excluding those that do not fall within

---

[38]   The products were to be named within 60 days of the signing of the agreement. However, the exchange of lists was delayed until March 2000 due to various reasons, including some opposition by both Indian and Sri Lankan interest groups.

Table 6.14 Coverage Offered by Sri Lanka under Trade Initiatives, No. of Tariff Lines at HS 6-Digit

Agreement	Preference	Negative list	Immediate zero duty	Residual list
BA	427 (additional 72 for LDCs)			
SAPTA	155 (additional 44 for LDCs)			
ISFTA		1,180	319	50% margin of preference on 889 items. Preferential reduction rose to 100% over 3 years. Duty on balance items phased out over 8 years.
PSFTA		697	102	Duty on balance items phased out over 5 years.
SAFTA		1,065		Reduce tariffs on balance items to 20% within 2 years; reduced further to 0–5% over next 5 years.

BA = Bangkok Agreement, SAPTA = South Asian Preferential Trade Agreement, ISFTA = India–Sri Lanka Free Trade Agreement, PSFTA = Pakistan–Sri Lanka Free Trade Agreement, SAFTA = South Asia Free Trade

Source: Respective Agreements

Sri Lanka's negative list) are expected to be phased out over an 8-year period: 35% of the existing duty level by the end of the first three of the 8 years; 70% of the existing duty level by the end of the 6th year; and 100% removal of duties by the end of the 8th year. Thus, India will have duty-free access to the Sri Lankan market (excluding those items on the negative list) after 8 years of implementation of the FTA.

Pakistan reacted with a proposal of an FTA with Sri Lanka, the framework agreement of which was signed in July 2002. The Pakistan–Sri Lanka FTA came into operation in June 2005. Pakistan maintaining a negative list of 540 items while granting immediate duty-free entry on 206 products and agreeing to eliminate duties on other products over a 3-year period. In return, Sri Lanka was permitted to maintain a negative list of 697 items while granting immediate duty-free entry on 102 products and agreeing to phase out tariffs on a further 4,527 items over 5 years.

After much delay, the framework agreement on the SAFTA was finalized in 2004 and negotiations were completed for the treaty in July 2006. The approach adopted in SAFTA is a commitment toward a top-down reduction of tariffs where member states that are not LDCs are required to reduce exiting tariffs to 20% in 2 years of implementation of the agreement, and thereafter to further reduce tariffs to a range of 0–5% in the next 5 years.[39] LDC member countries are required to reduce existing tariffs to 30% in 3 years and further ensure a reduction to a range of 0–5% in the next 8 years. One of the key constraining factors of the SAFTA negotiations is the allowable size of the negative list. The final decision was to retain a sensitive list of 20% of tariff lines for non-LDC member states and a close approximation of that for the LDC member countries. Negative lists have ranged from 157 tariff lines in the case of Nepal to 1,249 tariff lines in the case of Bangladesh.[40]

Table 6.15 Comparative Rules of Origin

Item	SAFTA	ISFTA	PSFTA
Single Country ROO			
DVA (% of FOB)			
India and Pakistan	40%	35%	35%
Sri Lanka	35%	35%	35%
LDCs	30%		
CTH	4-digit	4-digit	6-digit
Cumulative ROO			
Minimum Aggregate Content	50%	35%	35%
Input from Exporting Country	20%	25%	25%
Derogation from General Rule	DVA: 25%, 30%, 40%, or 60% CTH: at 4- or 6-digit level Process: PSR	Being negotiated under CEPA	Not applicable

SAFTA = South Asian Preferential Trade Agreement, ISFTA = India–Sri Lanka Free Trade Agreement, PSFTA = Pakistan–Sri Lanka Free Trade Agreement, ROO = Rules of Origin, DVA = Domestic Value Addition, FOB = Free on Board, LDCs = Least-developed countries, CTH = Change of Tariff Headings, PSR = Product Specific Rules, CEPA = Comprehensive Economic Partnership Agreement.

Source: Respective agreements.

Another important provision of trade agreements is the rules of origin (ROO). Under the South Asian Preferential Trade Agreement (SAPTA),

---

[39] Sri Lanka is given an additional year in recognition of its status as a small, vulnerable economy.

[40] Bhutan has submitted a negative list of 157 tariff lines, the Maldives has submitted 671, Pakistan 1,183, and Sri Lanka 1,065 tariff lines. Bangladesh submitted a negative list of 1,254 and 1,249 tariff lines for members that are non-LDCs and those that are LDCs, respectively. India submitted a negative list of 884 and 763 tariff lines, and Nepal a negative list of 1,310 and 1,301 tariff lines for non-LDCs and LDCs, respectively.

preferences will be granted for products meeting the domestic value addition (DVA) criteria requiring 50% DVA from the member countries of the SAARC that are non-LDCs and 40% for the LDC member countries (Table 6.15). Due to concerns that the DVA criteria were too stringent, these were relaxed in 1998 to 40% for non-LDC members and 30% for LDC members.

The India–Sri Lanka Free Trade Agreement (ISFTA) saw a departure from using DVA as the sole criteria and introduced a change of tariff heading (CTH) at the HS 4-digit level to be applied in tandem. However, the DVA percentage under the ISFTA was more liberal at 35% as against the 40% applied under the SAPTA. Nevertheless, the ROO criteria under ISFTA encountered some problems as there were specific products that were not able to meet a DVA and CTH simultaneously. For example, a product such as tea was able to meet the DVA of 35% with some processing but could not meet CTH at the 4-digit level (CTH only took place at the 6-digit level).[41] In recognition of such problems applicable to specific products, the joint consultative mechanism under the ISFTA has further allowed certain products to be eligible under more relaxed set of ROOs.

With this experience in mind, Sri Lanka negotiated DVA of 35% and CTH at the 6-digit level under the PSFTA. However, this was not to be the case under SAFTA negotiations. Given that DVA was the sole criteria used in the SAPTA, the LDC members were largely in favor of similar ROO being carried over. However, on the basis that SAPTA and SAFTA are essentially different in concept—the former being a preferential agreement while the latter having broader implications in terms of moving toward zero-duty rates—an argument was put forward for a more comprehensive ROO criteria. As such, DVA of 40% is required of the non-LDC member countries of India and Pakistan, 35% is required of Sri Lanka (as a small economy), and 30% is required of LDCs, in combination with a CTH at the 4-digit level. However, derogation from the General Rule has been permitted under the SAFTA agreement as there are some products that may undergo substantial transformation and allow the DVA criteria to be met without CTH at 4-digit level and vice versa. There is also provision for cumulation of regional value-added with a minimum aggregate content of 50% with the proviso that the minimum input from the exporting country should be 20%.

There have been many instances where ROO have been flouted in the implementation of such agreements, particularly with respect to the ISFTA. The main problem area has been in the exports of two key products: a derivative of palm oil (*vanasthpathi*) and copper wire from Sri Lanka to India under preferential tariff treatment. In fact, these two items accounted

---

[41]   To overcome this shortcoming, derogation from the General Rule is being negotiated under the CEPA.

for the bulk of increased trade between India and Sri Lanka following the signing of the ISFTA. Most of the firms that set up ventures under the BOI to export vanaspahi and copper wire to India were Indian-owned companies that imported raw material from countries such as Malaysia and re-exported to India without meeting the ROO criteria. At the behest of India, concessions offered under the BOI to several such companies were withdrawn, and the monitoring of ROO was made more stringent.

The treatment of sensitive lists under the FTAs has been quite constraining (Table 6.16). Sri Lanka has placed all its agricultural products on the sensitive lists of its agreements, despite the fact that the bulk of imports from South Asia are in the mineral products sector. While agricultural products account for only 18.5% of total imports from the rest of South Asia into Sri Lanka, nearly 500 agricultural tariff lines (i.e., nearly 50% of all tariff lines on the sensitive list) are on Sri Lanka's negative list under SAFTA. Most of the agricultural and food items exported from India have considerable potential for rapid market penetration in Sri Lanka, but are currently under high specific import duties and have been excluded from concession lists of all FTAs, which Sri Lanka is negotiating.

Clothing and textiles constitute the majority of tariff lines on the negative lists of India, Pakistan, Bangladesh, and Nepal, be it under their bilateral FTAs or SAFTA. Given that this is one area where South Asia has some complementarities—with both Pakistan and India having substantial bases for fabric manufacturing, and garments exporters such as Bangladesh and Sri Lanka lack such access—the decision by most countries to protect their textile and clothing sector through sensitive lists appears somewhat short-sighted. India and Pakistan have also attempted to safeguard their respective machinery and mechanical goods sectors through the application of the sensitive-list provisions.

Moreover, the treatment of sensitive lists also seems to be somewhat ad hoc. The application of sensitive list to actual trade that is taking place suggests that many tariff lines have been placed on the sensitive list without due care. For example, in placing all agricultural items on Sri Lanka's sensitive list, tariff lines covering such items as purebred breeding horses have been placed in Sri Lanka's negative list without much rationale. At the time of implementation of the ISFTA, for example, it was found that of Sri Lanka's total tariff lines of 1,180, only 623 products were actually being imported from India. Similarly, of the 419 tariff lines imposed by India, imports from Sri Lanka accounted for only 50 tariff lines (Weerakoon and Wijayasiri, 2001). Based on bilateral trade data at the beginning of implementation of ISFTA in 2000, more than 44% of Indian exports to Sri Lanka fell within Sri Lanka's sensitive list. Conversely, only 13% of Sri Lankan exports to India fell within the Indian negative list (Table 6.17).

Table 6.16 Sector Coverage of FTA Sensitive Lists

Sector	ISFTA		PSFTA		SAFTA					
	India	Sri Lanka	Pakistan	Sri Lanka	Bangladesh	India	Maldives	Pakistan	Nepal	Sri Lanka
01–05 Live animals, animal products	0	156	6	51	25	27	58	21	83	90
06–14 Vegetable products	3	232	6	68	44	179	56	51	145	204
15 Animal or vegetable fats and oils	1	40	22	6	6	32	4	29	17	37
16–24 Prepared foodstuffs	17	168	34	94	74	67	53	36	105	165
25–27 Mineral products	0	19	0	7	17	8	8	7	21	22
28–38 Chemical products	0	23	35	20	62	34	24	77	57	22
39–40 Plastics and rubber	97	73	86	60	67	95	126	119	77	84
41–43 Leather products	0	14	0	3	13	0	0	1	13	25
44–46 Wood products	6	6	2	5	7	0	10	20	0	2
47–49 Paper products	12	55	11	40	57	13	16	49	60	49
50–63 Textile articles	293	22	191	16	391	302	20	293	494	20
64–67 Footwear	0	32	11	29	13	17	0	16	26	30
68–70 Stone, plaster, cement	0	42	9	38	26	9	10	29	45	36
71 Pearls	0	3	3	3	1	0	14	0	0	3
72–83 Base metal	0	114	42	102	114	60	190	134	66	114
84–85 Machinery and mechanical goods	0	81	48	58	160	27	33	210	82	69
86–89 Transport equipment	0	42	27	40	57	4	40	73	39	37
90–92 Optical, photographic equipment	0	8	2	7	36	2	3	7	0	7
93 Arms and ammunition	0	0	0	0	0	0	0	0	0	0
94–96 Misc. manufactured articles	0	50	5	50	84	3	6	11	2	49
97–99 Works of art	0	0	0	0	0	0	0	0	3	0
Total	429	1180	540	697	1254	885	671	1183	1335	1065

ISFTA = India–Sri Lanka Free Trade Agreement, PSFTA = Pakistan–Sri Lanka Free Trade Agreement, SAFTA = South Asia Free Trade Agreement.

Source: Respective agreements.

Table 6.17 Partner Country Sensitive Lists under ISFTA and PSFTA

Sector		ISFTA		PSFTA	
		% of Indian Exports Subject to Sri Lankan SL	% of Sri Lankan Exports Subject to Indian SL	% of Pakistan Exports Subject to Sri Lankan SL	% of Sri Lankan Exports Subject to Pakistan SL
01–05	Live animals, animal products	17.5		98.9	
06–14	Vegetable products	99.2		72.5	23.6
15	Animal or vegetable fats and oils	84.9		2.3	100.0
16–24	Prepared foodstuffs	35.4		81.6	
25–27	Mineral products	74.4		14.1	
28–38	Chemical products	5.9		2.0	
39–40	Plastics and rubber	52.6	91.4	43.5	
41–43	Leather products	61.5		25.4	
44–46	Wood products	35.3			
47–49	Paper products	74.3	9.3	60.0	
50–63	Textile articles	1.9	21.5	...	
64–67	Footwear	93.5		18.8	
68–70	Stone, plaster, cement	75.0		19.4	
71	Pearls				
72–83	Base metal	25.4		0.7	
84–85	Machinery and mechanical goods	18.0		10.7	
86–89	Transport equipment	76.8		9.0	
90–92	Optical and photographic equipment	4.8			
93	Arms and ammunition				
94–96	Misc. manufactured articles	56.0		12.6	
97–99	Works of art				
	Total	**44.1**	**13.6**	**15.4**	**24.5**

ISFTA = India–Sri Lanka Free Trade Agreement, PSFTA = Pakistan–Sri Lanka Free Trade Agreement, SL = Sensitive List.

Note: Sri Lanka has maintained a much smaller sensitive list under the PSFTA given that Pakistan is not a major source of imports. Only around 15% of current imports from Pakistan fall within Sri Lanka's sensitive list. By contrast, around 25% of Sri Lanka's exports to Pakistan are restricted under the PSFTA's sensitive list.

Source: Estimated using data from Department of Customs, External Trade Statistics, Sri Lanka; Weerakoon and Wijayasiri (2001) for ISFTA estimates.

A similar assessment of the impact of the sensitive lists under SAFTA shows that nearly 53% of total imports from the region in 2004 are excluded from tariff liberalization (Table 6.18). While it is very much a static estimate, it nevertheless highlights the very limited nature of negotiations to open up the region to free trade. The restrictiveness with which the sensitive lists have been applied becomes abundantly clear by looking at a country-by-country breakdown of import trade by countries in the SAARC. Paradoxically, Pakistan which has maintained the largest number of tariff lines on its sensitive list amongst the member countries which are non least-developing countries—a total of 1,183 tariff lines as against a list of 884 by India and 1,065 by Sri Lanka—has the lowest application of goods on its sensitive list by value of imports from the rest of the region. Just over 17% of Pakistan's total imports from SAFTA member countries are excluded from the tariff liberalization process. By contrast, India and Sri Lanka have restricted up to 38% and 52%, respectively, of their total imports from SAARC under the sensitive list category. The LDC member countries by and large have protected up to 65%–75% of their imports from South Asia, from the SAFTA tariff liberalization process. It becomes quite apparent that SAFTA has begun with an even more limited approach to liberalizing trade in the region than anticipated.

The degree of restrictiveness of the sensitive lists looked at from an export perspective confirms the nature of imbalances. Although Pakistan has restricted only 17% of total imports from SAARC under its sensitive list, more than 34% of Pakistan's exports to the member countries of SAFTA fall within the respective sensitive lists of its trading partners (Table 6.18). While India has excluded 38% of its imports from SAARC countries, a slightly higher proportion of total Indian exports of around 57% are excluded under the sensitive lists of its trading partners in SAFTA. Sri Lanka, on the other hand, has restricted around 52% of imports from SAARC countries and in turn, a comparable 47% of its exports to the rest of the region are subject to the sensitive lists of member countries.

In the absence of a meaningful opening up of trade in a regional context, bilateral agreements will continue to provide more favorable market access to Sri Lanka. Under SAFTA, for instance, Sri Lanka faces an Indian sensitive list that is almost twice that of what has been offered under the bilateral deal. Compounding the problem is that the bilateral FTAs are scheduled to be fully implemented well ahead of the timeframe set out under the SAFTA treaty.

The emergence of BIMSTEC (inclusive of five of the seven member countries of SAFTA) will also pose its own challenges to the SAARC. In 2007, BIMSTEC is scheduled to launch the implementation of an FTA, which is generally expected to move much faster than SAFTA. The framework agreement includes provision for fast-track liberalization as well as for the inclusion of services and investment negotiations from 2007. Five of the SAFTA members are represented in BIMSTEC, and some of those members also have separate bilateral FTAs with their largest regional trading partner within those groups, i.e., India. The net result of these alternative bilateral agreements and BIMSTEC may eventually be something that will approximate free trade within the region except for Pakistan.

Table 6.18 Trade Restriction under SAFTA

Country	Value of Imports from SAARC Subject to Negative List (%)	Value of Exports to SAARC Subject to Negative List (%)
Bangladesh	65.0	22.0
India	38.4	56.5
Maldives	74.5	57.6
Nepal	64.0	46.4
Pakistan	17.2	34.0
Sri Lanka	51.7	47.0
Total	**52.9**	

SAARC = South Asian Association for Regional Cooperation, SAFTA=South Asia Free Trade Agreement

Source: Weerakoon and Thennakoon (2006).

Following the implementation of the ISFTA, additional areas of cooperation under a CEPA are being envisaged. The facilitation of trade in services and investment and the pruning of the sensitive lists are among the extensions being considered. Progress has been slow, however, due to the overall implementation problems under the ISFTA.

Sri Lanka's exports to India have seen a significant increase since the implementation of the FTA with India. In absolute terms, export earnings increased from $55 million in 2000 to $560 million by 2005. In fact, growth in export earnings to India has far outstripped total export earnings for the country since 2001 (Table 6.19). Much of the increase is observed for products whose tariffs have reached zero by 2003 (Table 6.19). As a proportion of total trade, the share of Sri Lankan exports to India receiving such preferential treatment had risen to nearly 96% by 2005.

However, a breakdown of the composition of trade receiving zero duty preference suggests that the increase of exports has been concentrated in a handful of export items (Table 6.20). The most significant expansion has come in the sector of base metals where predominantly Indian investors established manufacturing bases in Sri Lanka to export copper and exploit the preferential tariff treatment afforded under the ISFTA. Copper and copper articles had jumped from a share of just 3.5% of Sri Lanka's total exports to India in 2001 to nearly half of all exports by 2003.

Table 6.19 Sri Lankan Exports to India under ISFTA Categories

	Average 1999–2000	2001	2002	2003	2004	2005
Negative list	10.5	6.9	3.6	2.7	5.8	2.4
No. of items	37	34	51	53	69	69
Zero duty	77.6	86.0	94.0	94.3	92.0	95.7
No. of items	300	383	469	560	664	723
Residual list[a]	11.8	7.1	2.4	2.9	2.2	1.8
No. of items	63	73	100	99	154	162
Growth in exports (%)						
India	15.7	25.7	144.2	45.1	54.7	47.2
Total exports	19.8	-12.8	-2.4	9.2	12.2	10.2

No. = number

Note: [a] - Includes tariff rate quotas on textiles and tea.

Source: Estimated using data from Department of Customs, External Trade Statistics, Sri Lanka.

The other item of significant export expansion has been vegetable oil, which increased its share of exports to India from 1% in 2002 to more than a quarter of total exports by 2005. Again, the main export item of interest is vanaspati (a hydrogenated vegetable oil similar to ghee), where Indian investors established processing plants in Sri Lanka to make use of the preferential tariff treatment to export to India.

Sri Lanka's shipments of vanaspati under the FTA with India have been a cause of contention in bilateral trade relations. Similar problems have emerged in the case of copper, pepper, and bakery shortening. It has been argued that exports of vanaspati from Sri Lanka is flooding the Indian market and destabilizing the domestic Indian industry. During trade negotiations in 2003, both countries had agreed to cap vanaspati shipments from Sri Lanka to 250,000 tons (t), but subsequently India has demanded that such imports should be capped at 100,000 t, a demand Sri Lanka was reluctant to meet. Consequently, India unilaterally decided to restrict imports of vanaspati oil from Sri Lanka, appointing the National Agricultural Cooperative Marketing Federation of India Ltd. (NAFED) the sole agency for such imports. While the issue is still under negotiation, such a policy is likely to adversely affect local vanaspati factories and could even lead some to close down. Other forms of obstacles such as the prevalence of state sales taxes, customs delays, and quality checks (sometimes requesting additional quality requirements that do not exist in the agreement) faced by Sri Lanka exporters to India have been cited as examples of obstacles to the free flow of goods, even under the FTA.

Table 6.20 Composition of Exports Receiving Zero Duty Treatment Under ISFTA, %

Sector		Average 1999–2000	2001	2002	2003	2004	2005
01–05	Live animals, animal products	1.7	0.5	0.1	0.3	0.2	0.2
06–14	Vegetable products	40.5	28.1	26.3	9.0	7.3	6.2
15	Animal or vegetable fats and oils	5.0	1.9	1.0	2.4	4.5	25.6
16–24	Prepared foodstuffs	1.0	1.2	0.4	0.8	0.9	0.6
25–27	Mineral products	5.0	24.4	5.2	0.5	0.3	0.5
28–38	Chemical products	0.7	1.2	1.1	2.7	5.3	6.3
39–40	Plastics and rubber	0.9	0.7	0.9	1.6	1.7	1.1
41–43	Leather products	0.0	0.1	0.7	0.6	0.7	0.4
44–46	Wood products	0.1	0.0	0.7	1.7	2.3	2.0
47–49	Paper products	7.6	8.4	3.8	3.8	3.3	2.7
50–63	Textile articles	0.0	0.0	0.0	0.0	0.0	0.0
64–67	Footwear	0.2	0.1	0.0	0.0	0.1	0.0
68–70	Stone, plaster, cement	0.7	2.4	0.8	2.3	3.6	1.7
71	Pearls	0.2	0.1	0.1	0.3	0.4	0.5
72–83	Base metal	11.6	11.2	47.6	55.1	43.8	39.9
	Copper and articles thereof	(1.5)	(3.5)	(42.3)	(49.2)	(32.1)	(27.7)
84–85	Machinery and mechanical goods	2.0	4.0	3.4	12.2	15.5	6.8
86–89	Transport equipment	0.1	0.4	0.3	0.1	0.8	0.1
90–92	Optical, photographic equipment	0.1	0.1	0.4	0.1	0.1	0.1
93	Arms and ammunition	0.0	0.0	0.0	0.0	0.0	0.0
94–96	Misc. manufactured articles	0.3	1.4	1.1	0.9	1.1	1.2
97–99	Works of art	0.0	0.0	0.0	0.0	0.0	0.0
	Total residual list	**77.6**	**86.0**	**94.0**	**94.3**	**92.0**	**95.7**

Source: Estimated using data from Department of Customs, External Trade Statistics, Sri Lanka

Overall, the impact of Sri Lanka's preferential agreements on strengthening trade flows has been fairly minimal. To a large extent, this reflects the very narrow scope of liberalization adopted under most agreements as a result of the long sensitive lists of items excluded from preferential tariff treatment. Additionally, Sri Lanka has concentrated its preferential negotiations on countries in South Asia that hold limited potential for creating significant trade complementarities, perhaps with the exception of India.

Government Revenue Role of Tariffs

Sri Lanka has witnessed a persistent decline in total government revenue since the mid-1990s. A sharp contraction of the economy in 1996 initiated the decline, but it continued with the transition to a goods and services tax (GST) in 1998, replacing the existing business turnover tax. The GST, however, was introduced at a non-revenue-neutral rate of 12.5% as against the required revenue-neutral rate of 16%. In 2002, the GST was replaced by a new value added tax (VAT), compounding the necessary administrative adjustments. The downward trend in the tax-GDP ratio was reversed only in 2005, albeit marginally. Sri Lanka has also witnessed a shrinking of the contribution made by import duties to total revenue, declining from 5.2% of GDP in 1990 to less than 2% by 2005 (Table 6.21).

Table 6.21 Government Revenue

Item	1990	1998	2005
Tax revenue	19.0	14.5	14.2
Income taxes	2.3	2.0	2.2
General sales & turnover tax	6.3		
Turnover tax		1.6	
GST		2.3	
VAT			5.9
Excise tax	2.5	3.0	3.3
Import duties	5.2	2.8	1.9
Export duties	0.8	0.0	0.0
Other taxes	1.9	2.9	1.0
Non tax revenue	2.1	2.7	1.8
Total revenue	**21.1**	**17.2**	**16.1**

GST = Goods and Services Tax, VAT = Value Added Tax.

Source: Central Bank of Sri Lanka, Annual Report (various issues).

Revenue considerations are likely to have an impact on the approach to bilateral and regional trade initiatives. Already, there is increasing evidence that the implementation of the ISFTA and its revenue implications are causing some concern to the finance authorities. In April 2006, Sri Lanka was due to offer tariff concessions of up to 70% on the reserve list of items, but this was pushed back to September 2006 due to procedural delays. This led to discussions on how to best tackle the revenue effects of the ISFTA on Sri Lanka, given the fact that India accounts for over 17% of the country's total imports. One policy being considered is the imposition of an additional tax applicable on imports from all countries in order to compensate for the lost revenue. Whilst in the strictest terms, such a move will not be a contravention of the obligations of Sri Lanka under the ISFTA, it will nevertheless offer domestic competitors some additional protection from Indian imports.

Additional revenue measures such as the extension of excise duties to consumer durables have also been implemented to boost revenue while the Government is also continuing to impose an import surcharge. Such measures, however, can prove damaging in the long term. Tariff measures imposed on an ad hoc basis—and with limited regard for the overall structure and incentive implications of the tariff system—can prove counterproductive if they undermine the predictability and consistency of the policy regime. Many temporary taxes, such as the imposition of excise duties on select luxury goods, tend to become entrenched in the system over time. For instance, a temporary import surcharge introduced in 2001 for duration of 6 months has continued into 2005, albeit with a reduction in the surcharge progressively from 40% at the time of implementation to 10% at present. The current policy regime in Sri Lanka does suggest that revenue considerations will play a critical role in moderating the pace of negotiations of future FTAs.

Infrastructure and Trade Administration

Overview of Trade-Related Infrastructure

The fiscal constraints under which the Sri Lankan economy has been functioning have left limited resources for needed public investment in economic infrastructure. Public investment in transport and communication, for example, was at 1.3% of GDP in 1990 and remained at that level in 2005. While the Government is promoting private investment in infrastructure—largely on a build-own-operate or build-own-transfer basis—the lack of suitable pricing policies has often deterred private-sector entry.

The road network is the backbone of Sri Lanka's transport sector. The country has a fairly dense road network of 1.5 km per square km of land area. However, only 10% of the paved road network is estimated to be in good condition because of poor maintenance (World Bank, 2004). Recurrent public spending on transport and communications, which stood at 0.8% of GDP in 1990, had declined to 0.5% of GDP in 2005, indicative of the limited resources diverted to maintenance. In addition, despite substantial expansion of traffic demand, the country has seen little investment in improving road trunks, upgrading of roads, and construction of new national highways (World Bank, 2004). According to the World Bank Investment Climate Survey, road quality was considered the biggest problem by 36% of respondents, with 33% citing access to roads as the next problem (World Bank, 2005).

According to estimates, about $870 million will be required during the period 2004–2008 for the rehabilitation and maintenance of Sri Lanka's road network and a further $665 million for new planned expressways (World Bank, 2004). Work has commenced on two expressways, one linking Colombo with the airport and the other with the Southern Province, but this will not be completed until at least 2008. Rehabilitation of the A9 highway to the Northern Province commenced in 2002, but has been put on hold temporarily following the escalation of violence in 2006. Other road projects in the pipeline include the Colombo–Kandy expressway and an outer-circle highway in Colombo, but funding for these has yet to be finalized.

While Sri Lanka Railways (SLR) used to play a dominant role in the country's transport sector, the importance of rail transport has declined progressively in recent decades. The rail system's shares in passenger and freight transportation are presently estimated to be only about 8% and 5% respectively. The railways continue to face serious competition from road transportation, and have been adversely affected by the country's two-decade-long civil war. Since 1989, security threats have led to the suspension of services on the only two profitable lines: the Northern Line beyond Vavunia and the Talaimannar Line.

While Sri Lanka has several large ports (such as Galle, Trincomalee, and Kankasanthurai) and harbors, the country's premier commercial port is Colombo. It has three container terminals: the state-owned Jaye Container Terminal and the Unity Container Terminal, both operated by SLPA; and the South Asia Gateway Terminal, which is operated by P&O Ports of Dubai. Structural reforms within the SLPA (including the trimming of its workforce) have improved productivity, while aggressive marketing has resulted in a sharp increase in its market share. In 2005, container traffic rose to 2.5 million 20-foot equivalent units (TEUs), which is close to its capacity limits. The construction of a new south harbor (scheduled to be completed in 2009) to serve very large ships will significantly increase the capacity of the Colombo port. There are plans for a total of four new container terminals to be built by 2020, which could further boost capacity to

12 million TEUs. In addition, funding has been secured from the PRC for the construction of a new port in Hambantota in the south of the country.

Figure 6.1 Quality of Ports

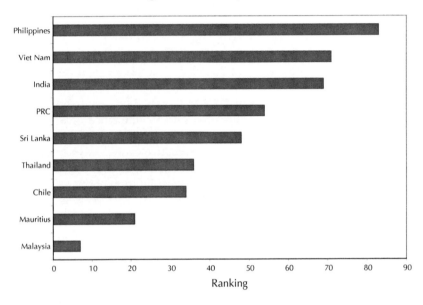

Source: World Bank (2005).

Sri Lanka's ports are considered to be relatively efficient due in large part to reforms that introduced competition in the main Colombo port in the mid-1990s, and allowed the private sector to build and operate a new terminal. In a survey of port quality, Sri Lanka's ports outperformed those of the PRC, India, and the Philippines, although they ranked below those of Malaysia and Thailand. These rankings have been supported by the findings of Investment Climate Surveys carried out by the World Bank (2005) which shows that clearing imports through ports and customs takes less time in Sri Lanka (4 days on average) than in the PRC (7), India (10), and the Philippines (10), although more time than in Malaysia (3). However, the surveys also find that it takes more time to clear exports through ports and customs in Sri Lanka than in the PRC, India, and the Philippines.[42]

---

[42] Delays in the food and beverages sector are largely to account for the relatively poor performance. When this sector is excluded, the average time to clear exports falls to around 2 days, close to that of Malaysia (World Bank, 2005).

At present, the SLPA uses electronic data systems to some extent in order to avoid port congestion and to reduce paper work. The vessel turn-over time has improved significantly, and Colombo has become one of the best ports in the region in terms of transshipment rates. The SLPA personnel interviewed suggests that they expect to increase the number of containers discharged per day to 65 from the current level of 35 and improve their service to compete with other ports in the region.

Customs Issues

Despite reforms in the 1990s and improvements in customs operations, customs procedural issues still remain an area for urgent reform. The three main policy reforms undertaken include: (i) adoption of the Sri Lanka Automated Cargo Clearance Systems (SLACCS); (ii) implementation of the WTO/GATT Valuation Agreement; and (iii) simplification and harmonization of customs procedures.

An electronic data interchange (EDI) system was established in Sri Lanka in 2004 under a project named Sri Lanka Automated Cargo Clearance System (SLACCS). EDI facilities for electronic submissions of import documents have been available to entities registered under the BOI since 2004, while export submissions commenced in May 2005. For non-BOI entities, submissions through EDI have started on an experimental basis only.

Those who have so far availed themselves of EDI facilities were large-scale traders. The approved partner of EDI in Sri Lanka is E-services Lanka Ltd., which provides a secure e-commerce gateway for electronic submission of Customs Declarations and allied documentation. At present 400 clients are using the system, including 60 large-scale clients. Nearly 5,000 import-related transactions are carried out through E-services Lanka, but the service has been recently enhanced to handle export entries as well.

According to the Department of Customs, only 40 companies use EDI through customs for their transactions at present. The lack of awareness among traders of the benefits of the system and the high cost of electronic data communication prevailing in Sri Lanka are some of the barriers to improving EDI facilities. The new system has not been well accepted by the intermediary participants such as clearing agents, because of the losses they expect to incur from further improvements. Lack of coordination between different government agencies and widespread bureaucratic problems were also identified as a key barrier in setting up a fully implemented and interlinked EDI system.

The Automated System for Customs Data (ASYCUDA) system for lodging entries with customs and assessing them has been in operation since 1994 while ASYCUDA++ has been in use since 1998. Since then, automation of bonded warehouse stock control has been established. At present, a valuation database is being set up as a tool for risk management for front-line officers.

Customs clearance in Sri Lanka consists of three channels. The green channel operates for low-risk declarations, and goods are released without calling for documents or cargo examination. In the yellow channel, medium-risk consignments are cleared upon examining the required documents without cargo examination. High-risk declarations are cleared in the red channel, with examination of both documents and cargo. Additionally, as an incentive for good compliance, so-called gold-card holders are provided with fast-track clearance. With regard to green and yellow consignments, it is expected that customs clearance will be given prior to the arrival of the vessel, provided that reporting of the manifest by the shipping agent is ensured at least 2 days prior to the arrival of the vessel. This type of customs clearance is expected to result in zero time clearance as far as the customs clearance procedure is concerned.[43]

In general, cargo is cleared within a maximum period of 3–4 days. Nevertheless, interviews suggest that the average time required for clearance through customs is even higher due to factors including congestion at the port, non-availability of customs officials for inspection, operation hours of customs and ports, and poor port handling facility. The respondents indicated that many of the government offices were closed at night and on Sundays, further reducing the effective operating hours.

In terms of customs documentation, Sri Lanka has committed to introduce international standards. However, stakeholders are of the view that import-export processes still require a considerable amount of documentation at the customs and ports, although most large-scale industries appear to feel less burdened than do smaller players.

The administrative procedures are also found to be complex, and the collection of trade-related information is considered time consuming and costly. The perception was that the laws and administrative rulings were not easily accessible. In addition, both stakeholders and officials were of the view that sudden changes in rules, regulations, and policies were not promptly communicated to the affected parties.[44] There is also no single-window policy where transactions that involve several government agencies may be handled in one location.

According to stakeholders, the most time-consuming links in the chain of trade procedures are the acquisition of various refunds such as duty drawbacks, obtaining different licenses and export/import codes, clearance

---

[43]   With the support of the US, the SLPA is going to introduce a "mega port concept" for security processing which might add to delays. Under this new concept, exports to US are subjected to additional inspection procedures, which consist of a new technological mechanism for screening containers.

[44]   However, Sri Lanka Customs was found to publish new amendments to laws without delays but it was noted that government procedure takes time in publishing information through gazette notifications.

through customs, getting remittances through banks, and the final dispatch of export consignments (in order of the time taken for the process).

Service Sector Trade and Foreign Direct Investment Policies

Services account for more than 55% of Sri Lanka's GDP, employing nearly 45% of the labor force. The key area of service sector activity is in retail trade, although its contribution in overall services has been declining over time (Table 6.22). Transport and communication services constitute the second largest sector, although the most dynamic has been the growth of financial and business services, which have increased their share in total services from 9.5% in 1990 to nearly 18% by 2005.

Table 6.22 Sectoral Distribution of Services

Item	1990	1998	2005
Wholesale and retail trade, hotels and restaurants	44.6	41.9	36.3
Import trade	15.9	17.4	16.7
Export trade	3.5	4.7	3.9
Domestic trade	25.2	19.8	15.0
Transport, storage, and communication	20.7	21.7	26.4
Transport			14.3
Cargo handling			1.9
Post and telecommunications			10.3
Financial services, real estate, and business services	14.7	18.5	21.8
Financial services	9.5	14.8	17.9
Real estate	5.2	3.7	3.9
Public administration	11.4	10.2	15.5
Other services, n.e.s.	8.6	7.7	0.0
Total	**100.0**	**100.0**	**100.0**

n.e.s. = not elsewhere specified.

Source: Central Bank of Sri Lanka, Annual Report (various issues).

Foreign Direct Investment Performance

About 60% of total FDI is accounted for by FDI in services, spread largely in construction, energy, telecommunications, and port services. In turn, cumulative foreign investment in energy and telecommunications together make up more than 60% of FDI in the services sector in the period 2000–2004 (Table 6.23). The predominance of services-related FDI is evident from the fact that of the 20 largest foreign investors in the country, most are in the services sector (Table 6.24). Of these large investors, there is a FDI significant presence in services-related activities from both the East and South Asian region. Japanese investments, for instance, are to be found in sectors such as telecommunications, energy, port services, and construction.

There is likewise significant Indian FDI in services to be found in the leisure, health, IT training, and other professional services sectors. The BOI is targeting this Indian FDI, especially in IT and business process outsourcing (BPO), tourism, and education. A proposed four-hectare offshore shopping complex and an airport-related BPO zone in Sri Lanka are viewed as representing investment opportunities for Indian entrepreneurs.

Table 6.23 Foreign Direct Investment in Services, 1995–2004

	Cumulative 1995–1999		Cumulative 2000–2004	
	No. of Projects	Foreign Investment ($ Mn)	No. of Projects	Foreign Investment ($ Mn)
Housing property development	36	107.0	23	32.9
Container service warehousing and freight forwarding	18	6.5	15	50.1
Computer software development and data entry operations	24	5.8	53	15.5
Hotels, restaurant services and entertainment complex	42	10.8	28	13.3
Hospital services and medical centers	3	0.3	6	8.1
Educational training institutions	19	1.8	38	1.8
Management consultancy firms	2	0.0	1	0.0
Trading and buying houses	11	2.0	17	4.2
Telecommunication, TV and radio communication network	14	164.3	11	103.9
Garment washing, screen printing	20	2.7	21	5.0
Power	8	31.5	22	168.6
Ports	0	0.0	0	0.0
Others	21	113.6	37	83.3
Total services	**218**	**446.2**	**272**	**441.8**

Mn = million, No. = number.

Source: BOI, Sri Lanka.

Table 6.24 Top 20 Foreign Investments

Enterprise	Product	Country	Investment ($ Mn)
Sri Lanka Telecom (1997)	Fixed-line telecom	Japan	236
Lanka Bell (1997)	Wireless telecom network	Singapore and United Kingdom	148
Colombo Power (2000)	Barge-mounted power plant	Japan	141
Lanka Cellular (1993)	Cellular phone service	Singapore	141
South Asia Gateway Terminals (1999)	Port services	Australia and United Kingdom	131
JAIC Lanka (1997)	Apartments	Japan	127
Overseas Realty (1996)	Property development	Hong Kong, China; and Singapore	119
Kabool Lanka (1990)	Yarn	Korea	118
MTN Networks (1995)	Cellular phone network	British Virgin Islands and Finland	117
AES Kelanitissa (1999)	Power generation	US	107
Shell (1995)	Gas	Netherlands	103
Ansell Lanka (1990)	Surgical gloves	Australia	96
Air Lanka (1998)	Airline	United Arab Emirates	77
Prima Ceylon Ltd (2001)	Food processing	Singapore	70
Asia Power (1998)	Power generation	United Kingdom	64
Suntel (1996)	Wireless telecom network	Sweden	50
Colombo Dockyard	Port services	Japan	43
Ace Power Generation (1999)	Utility	Finland and United Kingdom	33
Orient Lanka (1996)	Trading	United Kingdom	31
North Pole Lanka (1992)	PVC manufacture	Korea	27

Mn = million, PVC = polyvinyl chloride.

Source: UNCTAD (2004).

As far as outbound FDI from Sri Lanka in services is concerned, it appears that the attention of the domestic business community has been limited very much to the immediate South Asian region, particularly India and Maldives for tourism and India and Bangladesh for banking. Sri Lanka's hotel and leisure sector has already expanded in to the Maldives beginning in 1993. More recently, pioneering efforts are underway to enter the Indian hotel industry, as well.[45] One of Sri Lanka's premier domestic private banks expanded its operations to Bangladesh in 2004, while another is at present looking at entering the Indian market.

Services Trade Flows by Sector

Sri Lanka's tourism industry has been one of the most adversely affected by the civil disturbances since the early 1980s. A steady recovery with the implementation of a ceasefire agreement in 2002, which saw tourist arrivals peak in 2004, suffered a setback with the December 2004 tsunami and escalation of violence from 2005 (Table 6.25). Earnings from travel, which have been irregular through the years, increased to $513 million in 2004 (or 35% of total services income).

Sri Lanka has long been catering to lower-end of package tours, primarily attracting tourists from Europe to the country's beach resorts. Regional tourism is dominated by a handful of countries. Although Hong Kong, China figured as an important source of tourists in 1990, many of those tourists were likely to be in the country for business reasons, also given that the expansion of the local garments industry has had significant links with Hong Kong, China.

While tourist arrivals from Japan have been declining, those from India have been surging. Increased trade relations between the two countries, enhanced air links, and a decision by Sri Lanka to extend visas on arrival to Indian nationals in 2003 (extended to all countries in SAARC in 2004) were key factors. Air travel has been greatly facilitated with the liberalization of air travel between the two countries after the adoption of an open skies policy in 2003. By 2005, the largest number of tourist arrivals has been recorded from India, accounting for 21% of total tourist arrivals and 51% of total tourist arrivals from Asia. A survey carried out by the Sri Lanka Tourist Board of departing Indian tourists found that the majority (65%) came for vacation purposes with the vast majority (85%) being single-destination travelers visiting only Sri Lanka.[46] Sri Lanka also receives a fair amount of tourists regionally from the Maldives.

The Sri Lanka Tourist Board (SLTB) has said that the it is focusing on are the PRC; Hong Kong, China; Japan; Malaysia; Thailand; Singapore; and the Philippines. As far as India is concerned, lifestyle and shopping

---

[45] For example, Aitken Spence Hotel Management of Sri Lanka has signed agreements with India's Anant Raj Industries Ltd. to manage a hotel in New Delhi. In addition, it has entered into a joint venture with Floatels India Ltd. to build a resort in Kerala.

[46] Sri Lanka Tourist Board. 2004. A Survey of Departing Indian Tourists. The survey included 1,000 interviews (see www.sltbstatistics.org).

are the main areas being promoted. Religious tourism is also being targeted.

Table 6.25 Tourist Arrivals, % of total arrivals

	1990	1998	2004	2005
Europe	59.4	64.6	52.8	43.1
UK	7.3	17.4	18.8	16.9
Germany	19.9	19.4	10.3	8.4
Asia	33.6	26.2	35.0	40.7
India	4.4	9.8	18.6	20.6
Maldives	2.5	1.9	2.7	4.5
Japan	7.5	3.6	3.5	3.1
Malaysia	0.9	1.1	1.8	2.1
Singapore	1.8	1.5	1.5	2.0
Pakistan	2.6	2.8	1.7	2.0
PRC	0.3	0.4	1.6	1.8
Korea	0.8	0.5	0.8	1.1
Taipei,China	n.a.	0.9	0.3	0.5
Bangladesh	0.3	0.4	0.3	0.4
Indonesia	0.4	0.7	0.3	0.3
Hong Kong, China	9.4	1.0	0.3	0.2
Nepal	0.1	0.2	0.2	0.2
Total arrivals	**297,888**	**381,063**	**566,202**	**549,308**

n.a. = not applicable.

Note: Tourist arrivals figures in 2005 were affected by the December 2004 tsunami. Aid workers have also tended to be categorized as tourists.

Source: Ceylon Tourist Board, Annual Statistical Report (various issues).

Export Role of Services

As in the case of many developing countries, Sri Lanka suffers from a dearth of statistics on services trade. However, available data suggests that the transportation and travel sectors have been the key sectors of export service income for the country (Table 6.26). Together, the two sectors have accounted for over 70% of service income in recent times. In 2005, earnings from services exports accounted for 20% of total export earnings from goods and services.

Telecommunication services, insurance and other business services, construction services, and computer and information services have recently emerged as important income earners in the service sector. Information gathered from IT companies operating in the export sector suggests that many are targeting the US and the United Kingdom.

Table 6.26 Service Trade Flows, $ Mn

Sector	1994		1998		2005	
	Credit	Debit	Credit	Debit	Credit	Debit
Transportation	293	155	402	263	673	470
Travel	231	169	230	202	429	314
Telecommunication	n.a.	n.a.	n.a.	n.a.	44	19
Insurance	21	13	34	18	73	34
Other business	176	197	224	253	188	322
Government expenditure, n.i.e.	25	19	25	34	21	37
Computer and information	n.a.	n.a.	n.a.	n.a.	82	-
Construction	n.a.	n.a.	n.a.	n.a.	29	6
Other services	n.a.	n.a.	n.a.	n.a.		
Total	**745**	**566**	**914**	**770**	**1540**	**1202**

n.a. = not available, n.i.e. = national income and expenditure.

Source: Central Bank of Sri Lanka, Annual Report (various issues).

Export destinations are also sector-specific. Companies engaged in developing software for airlines, for example, export their services to the Middle East (e.g., Dubai and Oman), Denmark, Japan, and Pakistan. While Sri Lanka does not appear to be exporting currently to East Asia, many companies have expressed intentions to do so in the future.

Firms engaged in direct software exports consider that Sri Lanka's IT exports will emerge as a major services export earner for the following reasons: (i) availability of knowledge and skills in the sector; (ii) a high literacy rate; and (iii) availability of English language skills. Further, other resources related to the IT sector that could be exploited include the fact that, apart from the United Kingdom, Sri Lanka has the highest number of Chartered Institute of Management Accountants (CIMA) qualified people. IT companies can use these individuals when expanding or starting finance-related IT services. The Government is therefore called on to assist the industry further developing infrastructure, increasing the number of IT graduates, and providing fiscal incentives for those setting up operations in Sri Lanka.

The computer and IT sector has emerged rapidly in recent years and has strong potential for future expansion. Since 1995, 50 software development companies have begun operations in Sri Lanka. There is a significant Indian presence in the IT sector in Sri Lanka. Tata Infotech and ApTech India, for example, have entered into a technical partnership to provide IT training in Sri Lanka. A Sri Lankan company (JKH) and an Indian business process outsourcing (BPO) firm (Raman Roy Associates) have recently announced plans to establish a joint BPO investment in India, the first of its kind.

Private worker remittances have proved to be an important source of foreign exchange earnings for Sri Lanka. Remittances became the second largest source of export earnings from the early 1990s (after gross earnings from garments), overtaking tea as a key source of export earnings for Sri Lanka. There has been a steady increase in the number of persons leaving the country for foreign employment in the period 1990–2005. Accordingly, total private and/or worker remittances have increased steadily to an average of around 6–7% of GDP (Table 6.27). The higher remittances inflow in 2005 was an exception related to inbound money transfers following the December 2004 tsunami.[47]

Table 6.27 Private Remittances, % share

Region	1990	1998	2005
Middle East	54.3	61.2	56.8
North America	19.7	7.6	6.5
EU	11.4	13.5	18.5
South Asia	0.8	0.8	1.0
Southeast Asia	5.6	1.9	2.0
Far East Asia	4.9	6.2	4.5
Other	3.3	8.8	10.7
Total	100.0	100.0	100.0
Remittances as % of GDP	5.0	6.3	8.3

EU = European Union, GDP = Gross Domestic Product.

Source: Central Bank of Sri Lanka, Annual Report (various issues).

The largest share of earnings inflow is from the Middle East, which employs mostly unskilled female labor. However, since the late 1990s, there has been an increase in the share of remittances originating from Europe,

---

[47] The distribution of remittance inflows shows no variation, however.

as more skilled and professional workers find their way to these countries. By contrast, it is also notable that the share of private remittances from North America has been decreasing over the period.[48]

The share of remittances originating from the Asian region has declined progressively from 11.3% in 1990 to 7.5% by 2005. The sharpest decline has come from Southeast Asia, where Sri Lanka had a mix of skilled professional and unskilled domestic workers. The low levels of remittances from South Asia may be attributed to the abundance of relatively cheap labor in those countries, although there has been a sharp increase in Sri Lanka workers taking up managerial positions in Bangladesh's garment industry.

Trade and Foreign Direct Investment Restriction in Services

In Sri Lanka, the preferred mode of service liberalization has tended to be a liberal FDI regime permitting the commercial presence of service providers.[49] As such, Sri Lanka has removed most limits on foreign capital ratios, except for a few specified sectors under the Exchange Control Act, and has instituted liberal foreign remittance regulations. Nevertheless, existing regulations applicable to areas such as residence requirements and domestic procurement may inhibit the commercial presence of service suppliers across most sectors.

In the case of residence requirements, the Department of Immigration and Emigration (DIE) issues 1-year renewable residence visas (which include authorization to work) on the recommendation of the relevant line ministry or the BOI. Approval is subject to certain sector-specific commitments such as a minimum volume of investment. Additionally, under the Resident Guest Scheme, a self-employed investor who invests $200,000, or a foreign professional with exceptional skills needed in Sri Lanka, is granted a 5-year resident visa. However, neither the DIE nor the sponsoring agencies appear to have guidelines or categorized occupations and professions for which foreign hire will be sponsored on a routine basis.

Sri Lanka also retains certain sector-specific restrictions applicable to trade in services. While Sri Lanka does not maintain restrictions regarding the establishment of foreign financial service providers, approval, reg-

---

[48]   Canada took in the second-largest contingent of refugees from Sri Lanka (after India) following the escalation of violence from the mid-1980s. Ties to Sri Lanka, and thus the need for financial resources, are likely to have weakened over time.

[49]   In April 2002, for example, Sri Lanka announced new sectors open to foreign investors (even up to 100% of equity capital). These included sectors such as construction of residential buildings and roads, supply of water, mass transportation, production and distribution of energy and power, professional services, and permitting branch or liaison offices of companies incorporated outside Sri Lanka.

istration, and licensing related to banks and other financial institutions are subject to an economic needs test. Moreover, some restrictions on the supply of financial services exist in accordance with provisions governing the Exchange Control Law. Individual foreign investors, for instance, are excluded from participating in the domestic debt market. Sri Lankan nationals are also not permitted to buy insurance from companies that are not registered in Sri Lanka under the provisions of the Insurance Act of 2000, unless explicit permission is obtained from the Insurance Board of Sri Lanka (IBSL). This measure has been relaxed with respect to travel and health insurance, where insurance can be taken from an insurer licensed or registered overseas irrespective of whether it is registered with the IBSL. In addition, Sri Lankan investors are not permitted to borrow freely from abroad and are subject to the Exchange Control Act. Exceptions are granted by the BOI. Under prudential requirements, commercial banks are permitted to borrow abroad up to 15% of capital and reserves.

In the tourism sector, although the establishment of tourism related facilities is allowed, there is a 40% limit in foreign investment in travel-related services. In transport, Sri Lanka maintains entry restrictions on FDI in freight forwarding and shipping agencies. Under BOI regulations, automatic approval for foreign investment in these areas is permitted only up to 40% of equity. Foreign ownership in excess of 40% has to be approved on a case-by-case basis.

GATS and Regional Commitments

Sri Lanka has made a series of commitments on several sectors of services under the WTO General Agreement on Trade in Services (GATS) (tourism- and travel-related services, financial services such as banking and insurance, and telecommunications). In the Uruguay Round, Sri Lanka made specific commitments regarding tourism only. Subsequently, it participated in the extended negotiations on basic telecommunications and financial services and accepted the GATS Fourth Protocol (basic telecommunications) in 1997 and Fifth Protocol (financial services) and 1999.[50] As far as ongoing negotiations are concerned, Sri Lanka has submitted its request list to 18 countries mainly in professional, computer-related, health-related, social, transport, and transport auxiliary services although it has not made any new offers.

Sri Lanka is gradually incorporating trade in services in the ongoing negotiations for the Comprehensive Economic Partnership Agreement

---

[50] Sri Lanka adopted the Reference Paper on Regulatory Principles as an additional commitment to the GATS.

(CEPA) with India. The negotiations in the services sector are progressing in line with the GATS framework and its positive-list approach.[51] Services under negotiation for initial discussions include information and communication technology, tourism and leisure, construction and engineering, health, transport and logistics services. Liberalization of financial services is likely to be carried out in relation to Mode 3, with deeper concessions granted through national treatment. Any measure under Mode 1 is expected to pose significant difficulties given implications on capital account liberalization (CBSL, 2005).

Sri Lanka's initial requests to India were relatively limited, focusing primarily in tourism and travel, retailing, IT, audiovisual, maritime transport, and other business services. By contrast, India's initial requests are more extensive, covering a wide range of professional services (health, accounting, architecture, IT, construction, and engineering). Discussions with industry professional bodies in Sri Lanka have suggested little enthusiasm for opening up such service sectors to India.

Policy Implications for Promoting Cooperation with East Asia and South Asia

Sri Lanka's evolving patterns of trade and investment with South and East Asia reflect the interaction of fundamental economic forces driving global trade and investment. Though the extent of these trade-investment links between Sri Lanka and East Asia are still rather limited, they indicate both the potential and the manner in which future developments will occur in a more liberal trading and investment environment in the Asian region. Sri Lanka's exports of merchandise goods to East Asia have remained limited over time with the overt concentration of the country's export basket in garments, and which are heavily dependent on the US and EU markets. However, with the anticipated global post-Multi-Fiber Agreement (MFA) restructuring of the garments industry, the outlook for maintaining Sri Lanka's market share remains uncertain. Sri Lanka needs to diversify its industrial export base, although some evidence of this already occurring with the limited decline in the share of garments exports. Preferential trade initiatives have proven useful to some extent in this exercise, with the bilateral FTA between India and Sri Lanka encouraging some amount of joint-venture activities. Nevertheless, in order for such links to be further developed and expanded regionally, the domestic policy environment is quite critical. At present,

---

[51]   Air services are excluded from the scope of the GATS. However, India and Sri Lanka have already liberalized air services through a bilateral open skies policy and prefer to bring air services under the CEPA, as India and Singapore did in their 2005 CECA.

Sri Lanka's trade and investment policy framework appears not to focus on any regional strategy, preferring instead to rely on preferential agreements to foster closer economic links. Needless to say, some preferential trade initiatives are perhaps undertaken more for political rather than economic reasons, as shown by the limited scope for preferential liberalization in the FTAs currently negotiated or are in the process of being negotiated.

Strategic Regional Orientation

Sri Lanka lost an early opportunity to strengthen its economic integration with East Asia when the country decided not to enter ASEAN at its inception. With the liberalization of the Sri Lankan economy in the late 1970s, East Asia has, nevertheless, emerged as an important source of FDI and imports to Sri Lanka. Regional agreements such as the proposed FTAs within the BIMSTEC and APTA frameworks hold opportunities in the future for accessing East Asian markets in both goods and services. Nevertheless, domestic institutional arrangements in Sri Lanka—providing both export and investment support—appear at present not to have a clear intent to target the East Asian region, apart from negotiating market access through preferential trade initiatives. While such agreements do have some scope for facilitating linkages and market access, Sri Lanka's policy on preferential liberalization has been to adopt a cautious approach that is likely to limit any meaningful expansion in trade and investment opportunities with the rest of East Asia.

However, Sri Lanka is increasingly building a strategic economic relationship with India. Stronger political relations between the two countries from the end of the 1990s has been cemented by the implementation of a bilateral agreement on free trade in goods, with negotiations under way to deepen and expand the agreement to include trade in services and investment. India has emerged as a major source of FDI and a significant trading partner for Sri Lanka. With the anticipated expansion of the Indian economy, Sri Lanka is looking to attract more Indian FDI by way of joint ventures in both goods and services. Already such enterprises exist in the production of rubber tires to service the rapidly expanding automobile sector in India. As India further orients itself toward East Asia through its Look East Policy, Sri Lanka can use emerging production networks with India to expand market integration with the East Asian region as well.

Current Comparative and Competitive Advantage, and Likely Future Trends

Sri Lanka has an important export-based clothing industry that has grown not only because of the country's natural comparative advantage but equally because of guaranteed quotas for its exports in the US and the EU. The lifting at the beginning of 2005 of textile and garment import quotas in the US and EU has brought both an opportunity—to exceed quota levels—and a risk of market-share loss to new competitors. Sri Lanka is fast losing its comparative advantage in low-cost labor in the garments industry and was cited by US manufacturers as a likely victim of the garment boom in the PRC (USITC, 2004). Two years into the new trading regime, the impact has been less dramatic than originally expected, but the long-term consequences remain uncertain (Kelegama, 2005).

While export diversification has been limited, there has nevertheless been some expansion of exports in rubber-based products, ceramics, and electrical machinery, and new sectors of export activities have emerged in connection with bilateral FTAs. Export diversification is likely to be tied in closely to progress in raising the current modest volume of inbound FDI. Political stability will be determinant. However, several behind-the-border constraints to attracting more FDI—including poor infrastructure and investor-unfriendly regulations such as those governing labor market participation in particular—have also been identified as requiring urgent policy attention.

Foreign Direct Investment Regime and Policy

Political instability and the implied policy instability have inhibited the inflow of FDI to a significant degree in Sri Lanka. Further, poorly developed infrastructure facilities put Sri Lanka at a disadvantage relative to the East Asian countries that had already embarked on extensive expansion and modernization of their infrastructure facilities. Nevertheless, in some sectors there have been some important investments.

The outward orientation of trade policies and liberal investment policies combined to generate incentives for export-oriented investors to locate in Sri Lanka. Foreign investments have also been attracted by the privatization of state-owned economic enterprises, particularly public utilities currently enjoying significant monopoly power in domestic markets.

The East Asian region has historically been an important source of inbound FDI to service Sri Lanka's export-oriented garment industry. More recently, some East Asian economies such as Malaysia have emerged as key investors in services related sectors such as telecommunications. In addition, India has become an important investor over time in both merchandise and services sectors, with a significant increase in services-related investment from the 1990s. While Sri Lanka's FDI regime remains fairly liberal, there does not appear to be a concerted effort to promote more strategic FDI partnerships. The BOI appears to be concentrating more on the US and the EU (as well as India) as key potential sources. However, there is less emphasis on East Asia, which could be detrimental to Sri Lanka's interests in the longer term. Countries such as the PRC and Malaysia hold significant potential as sources of FDI that could strengthen a trade-investment nexus, allowing Sri Lanka to benefit more from the anticipated growth expansion of the East Asian region.

Merchandise Trade Regime and Policy

While Sri Lanka has undertaken significant liberalization of its trade regime, the tariff structure remains littered with import surcharges, specific duties for agricultural products, ad hoc duty exemptions, and the introduction of preferential tariffs under various FTAs. Since 2001, the number of tariff bands has expanded with adjustments being made primarily on revenue considerations. Engagement in preferential trade agreements has been, and will continue to be, the preferred option to obtain market access. Sri Lanka's focus to gain preferential market access through regional and bilateral deals is presently aimed at South and East Asia. In fact, there appears to be an almost singular focus on gaining market access through FTAs that might be to the detriment of efforts being paid to unilateral reforms to further rationalize the prevailing tariff regime in the country.

Despite the emphasis on negotiating FTAs, the overall picture is one that shows quite limited tariff liberalization through bilateral and/or regional trade initiatives. While the limitations of the regional liberalization process in particular have been overcome to some extent through bilateral FTAs, the latter also suffer from extensive coverage of sensitive lists. Nevertheless, some improvements in bilateral trade between India and Sri Lanka have been witnessed following the signing of an FTA that holds some promise for regional initiatives such as the proposed FTA under BIMSTEC and APTA. Such agreements—if meaningfully liberalized—can be used to forge trade links between South and East Asian countries in the future.

However, domestic export supply constraints also have to be addressed for Sri Lanka to fully benefit from enhanced market access opportunities provided by regional agreements. This includes the provision of a predictable and consistent domestic tariff policy regime, a stable macroeconomic environment, and improved infrastructure facilities. Within such a framework, trade policy and promotion should also be geared to identifying potential market opportunities and products to cater to emerging markets. In this context, a more strategic positioning of Sri Lanka's trade interests in East Asia is desired if the country is to benefit from the expected economic expansion of the Asian region—led by the PRC and India—in the coming years. At present, the institutional arrangements do not appear to be providing such a region-focused approach.

Services Regime and Policy

The services sector has been the most dynamic sector of activity in the Sri Lankan economy. Services-related activities received a boost with the implementation of privatization measures in utilities such as telecommunications that saw larger amounts of services-related FDI. Asian countries such as Malaysia and India have emerged as major investors in services-related activities, including telecommunications, health, IT-related training, and tourism. While FDI policies with regard to the services sectors have seen substantial liberalization—as in financial services, for instance—other sectors such as education continue to be constrained by limitations on foreign participation. India, for example, has expressed interest in establishing educational institutes in Sri Lanka, but such efforts require domestic deregulation measures to be implemented.

Some export sectors such as IT related business process outsourcing have in recent years emerged as areas of export earnings where collaborative efforts in IT-related training have been established between Sri Lankan and Indian companies. But moves to encourage services related market integration with East Asia and South Asia will require some liberalization and deregulation of services in the domestic economy. Gradual liberalization in the services sector is envisaged under the preferential trade agreements currently under negotiation between India and Sri Lanka and proposed to be included in the SAFTA and the BIMSTEC. However, from Sri Lanka's perspective, the market openings being considered are fairly limited. For instance, there appears to be considerable domestic opposition to opening up professional services under Mode 4 even under regional deals.

Customs Procedures, Trade Facilitation, and Transport Initiatives

Sri Lanka has initiated reforms in customs procedures and trade facilitation measures such as the introduction of ASYCUDA, and EDI facilities. While there have been many reforms to improve the efficiency of customs clearance, customs operations still remain a fairly time consuming operation for businesses. The usage of EDI facilities remains very limited given the lack of awareness of traders regarding benefits of the system and the high cost of electronic data communication prevailing in Sri Lanka.

As indicated by the 2005 World Bank Investment Climate Survey, transport problems have been identified as a major bottleneck for both urban (20% of respondents) and rural (46%) businesses. It has long been recognized that expanding access to roads and improving their quality would have immense benefits on all sectors, including tourism, agribusiness, and industrial exports. The lack of funding to undertake the development of major highways—and delays in implementing infrastructure projects where concessional funding has been available—has been a hallmark of poor infrastructure spending in Sri Lanka. Nevertheless, fresh initiatives, such as the Southern Highway, have been taken in order to improve road access in the coming years.

Sri Lanka's Colombo port is a key link in the international sea routes to the rest of Asia. While the port of Colombo is considered to be more efficient than those of some of its competitors in the Asian region, there is scope for improving efficiency. There are an estimated 25 moves per hour at the Colombo port, compared to 100 per hour in Singapore. Nonetheless, the relatively high efficiency of Sri Lanka's ports has been attributed in part to the reforms that introduced competition in the mid-1990s by allowing private-sector participation in the operation of terminals. Restructuring of the Sri Lanka Ports Authority to unbundle the management of ports and the operation of terminals is considered one means by which efficiency of port operations can be improved.

References

Arunatilake, N., S. Jayasuriya and S. Kelegama. 2001. The Economic Cost of the War in Sri Lanka. *World Development*, 29(9):1483–1500.

Athukorala, P., and S. Jayasuriya. 1994. *Macroeconomic Policies, Crises, and Growth in Sri Lanka, 1969–90*. World Bank: Washington DC.

Athukorala, P. and S. Rajapatirana. 2000. *Liberalization and Industrial Transformation: Sri Lanka in International Perspective*. New Delhi: Oxford University Press.

Central Bank of Sri Lanka. Various years. *Annual Report*. Colombo: Central Bank of Sri Lanka.

Cuthbertson, A. G. and P. Athukorala. 1991. Sri Lanka. In *Liberalising Foreign Trade: The Experience of Indonesia, Pakistan and Sri Lanka*, edited by D. Papageorgiou, M. Michaely, and A. M. Choksi. Cambridge: Basil Blackwell.

Cuthbertson, S. 2003. *Tariff and Trade Policy Framework for Sri Lanka*. Colombo: Tariff Advisory Council.

Jayasuriya, S. and D. Weerakoon. 2001. FDI and Economic Integration in the SAARC Region. In *Trade, Finance and Investment in South Asia*, edited by T. N. Srinivasan. New Delhi: Social Sciences Press.

Jayawardena, L., L. Ali, and L. Hulugalle. 1993. Indo-Sri Lanka Economic Cooperation: Facilitating Trade Expansion through a Reciprocal Preference Scheme. Study Group Series No. 9, World Institute for Development Economics Research of the United Nations University, Helsinki, Finland.

Kelegama, S. 1998. Economic Development in Sri Lanka during the 50

Years of Independence: What Went Wrong? Occasional Paper No. 53, Research and Information System for the Non-Aligned and Other Developing Countries, New Delhi, India.

_____. 2005. Ready Made Garment Industry in Sri Lanka: Facing the Global Challenge. *Asia-Pacific Trade and Investment Review* 1(1):51–67.

Kodikara, S. U. 1982. *Foreign Policy of Sri Lanka: A Third World Perspective.* New Delhi: Chanakya Publications.

Lal, D. and S. Rajapatirana. 1989. *Impediments to Trade Liberalisation in Sri Lanka.* London: Trade Policy Research Center.

United Nations Conference on Trade and Development. 2004. *Investment Policy Review Sri Lanka.* New York and Geneva: United Nations.

United States International Trade Commission. 2004. *Textile and Apparel Assessment of the Competitiveness of Certain Foreign Suppliers to the US Market.* Washington DC: USITC.

Weerakoon, D. and J. Thennakoon. 2006. SAFTA: Myth of Free Trade. *Economic and Political Weekly* 41(37):3920–3923.

Weerakoon, D. and J. Wijayasiri. 2001. Regional Economic Cooperation in South Asia: A Sri Lankan Perspective. *International Economic Series* 6. Colombo: Institute of Policy Studies.

World Bank. 2004. *Sri Lanka: Development Policy Review.* Washington DC: World Bank.

_____. 2005. *Sri Lanka: Improving the Rural and Urban Investment Climate.* Washington, DC: World Bank.

World Trade Organization. 2004. *Trade Policy Review of Sri Lanka: Report by the Secretariat.* Geneva: WTO.

People's Republic of China

Zhang Yunling[52]

Introduction

The People's Republic of China (PRC) has achieved great success in developing its economy since it conducted economy-wide reforms and opened itself to the outside world. In less than three decades, the PRC has become a leading world economy, the second largest in terms of foreign direct investment (FDI) inflows, the third largest in foreign trade, the fourth largest in gross domestic product (GDP), and an important engine for global economic growth. One of the key factors for the PRC's success has been its integration into the world economic system, enabling it to use global market resources (markets, capital, and technology). Accession to the World Trade Organization (WTO) has made the PRC economy more open, transparent, and integrated into the world economic system. The PRC's new regional strategy, that is forming free trade agreements (FTAs), as well as its foreign investment strategy, have deepened, and the PRC will continue to intensify its economic integration and cooperation with its partners.

The Asia and Pacific region is the source of most of the PRC's FDI inflows, as well as the principal destination of its exports, with the United States (US) and Japan the two largest markets. East Asia accounts for half of the PRC's foreign trade and more than 70% of FDI inflows. The PRC's trade with South Asia is still small in volume, but it is growing quickly. With the emergence of the Indian economy, trade and services between the PRC and India have increased very rapidly in recent years.

Economic relations between East and South Asia used to be very weak. This now seems to be changing with Indian economic dynamism and the country's active Look East policy. Considering its geographical location and its economic expansion, the PRC can play an important and special role in

---

[52] This paper is based on research conducted jointly by Dr. Zhao Jianglin, Dr. Li Shujuan, Dr. Li Wei, Dr. Lu Bo, and Dr. Liu Xiaoxue.

bridging East and South Asian regions through trade, investment, services, technology, and broad economic cooperation.

The PRC's External Economic Relations

Economic Progress

The PRC has achieved great success since economic reform and opening to the world began in 1978. The PRC's average GDP growth was 9.7% during the period 1979–2007 (Figure 7.1). With its economy already robust and still growing, the PRC has one of the fastest GDP growth rates in the world and became the fourth largest economy in 2007. In the next decade, GDP growth may flag slightly but the economy is still expected to maintain its dynamism.

Figure 7.1 People's Republic of China GDP Growth 1990–2007, %

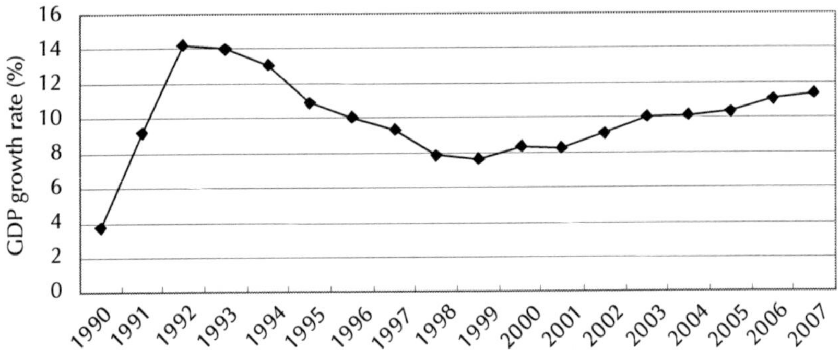

GDP = gross domestic product, % = percent.

Sources: *China Statistical Yearbook* (1991–2007 versions) and www.stats.gov.cn

The rise in the PRC's GDP per capita has been equally rapid. In 1990, the PRC's GDP per capita was only $342 based on market exchange rate weights. This doubled to a little more than $700 in 1997, and had more than three times again by 2007, when per capita GDP reached $2,482 (Figure 7.2).

As a consequence, the PRC has made strides in poverty reduction as well. The number of people living below the poverty line in rural areas fell from 250 million in 1978 to less than 100 million in 1990, dropping again to 26.1 million by 2004. At the same time, the headcount ratio, which is the number of poor people as a proportion of the total rural population, also dropped from 30.7% in 1978 to 10.0% in 1990 and 2.8% in 2004 (Figure 7.3). As a result, the PRC met the United Nations' Millennium Development Goal on poverty in advance.[53]

Figure 7.2 People's Republic of China GDP Per Capita at Current Market Prices 1990–2007, $

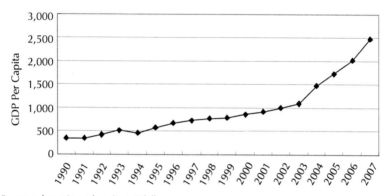

GDP = gross domestic product, $ = US dollar.

Sources: China Statistical Yearbook (1991–2007 versions) and www.stats.gov.cn/

External Economic Relations

Economic Openness

The PRC's trade dependency ratio increased from 35.0% in 1990 to 66.3% in 2007, and the ratio of exports and imports to total GDP also rose from less than 20.0% in 1990 to more than 37.1% and 29.2% respectively in 2007. This shows the economy's growing dependency on the external market, as well as its increasing integration into the world market (Figure 7.4).

The size of FDI inflows to the PRC has grown significantly, with the share of FDI stock in GDP as high as 23.4% in 2007. But the share of FDI inflows into the PRC as a percentage of gross fixed capital formation (GFCF) is decreasing, to 4.1% in 2007 from a peak in 1994. This implies FDIs are becoming less important than domestic investments in terms of overall investments.

---

[53]   The United Nations' (UN) Millennium Development Goals adopted in 2000 required that the poverty level be reduced by half by 2015.

Figure 7.3 Aggregate Poverty Headcount and Poverty Headcount Ratio (or Incidence of Poverty) in Rural People's Republic of China (1978–2007)

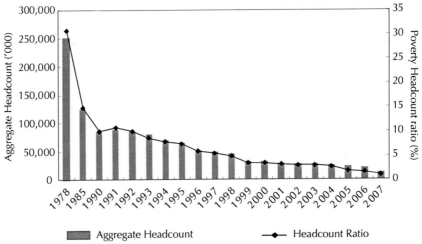

Source: National Bureau of Statistics of the People's Republic of China, Statistical Bulletin on Poverty Monitoring in the PRC's Rural Areas. Available: www.stats.gov.cn

Figure 7.4 People's Republic of China Economic Openness in Terms of Trade (%)

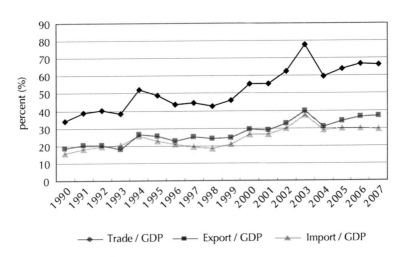

GDP = gross domestic product, % = percent.

Sources: China Statistical Yearbook (1991–2007 versions) and www.stats.gov.cn/

However, FDIs remain critical in supporting economic growth in the PRC. With economic progress, FDIs may even induce structural adjustments, such as the shift from labor-intensive to capital- and technology-intensive sectors. Although the PRC Government will remain open toward FDIs, it will be introducing selection criteria to manage the impact of FDIs on the rest of the economy.

Figure 7.5 People's Republic of China Economic Openness in Terms of FDIs (%)

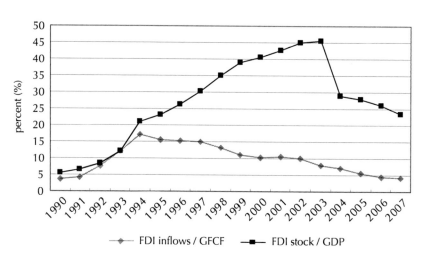

FDI = foreign direct investment, GDP = gross domestic product, GFCF = gross fixed capital formation, % = percent.

Sources: China Statistical Yearbook (1991–2007 versions) and www.stats.gov.cn/

External Economic Cooperation

The PRC has actively pursued a number of FTAs with its trading partners (Table 7.1). The China–ASEAN (Association of Southeast Asian Nations) FTA was the PRC's first FTA initiative after joining the WTO in 2000, introducing the concept of an early harvest program that liberalized trade on 600 farm products. An agreement with ASEAN on trade in goods was signed in 2005, on service in 2007, while the provisions covering investment are still under negotiation. A new progress was made in April 2007 following the signing of the PRC–New Zealand FTA which is the first FTA for the PRC with a developed economy. Subsequently, more FTAs with countries in East Asia, and the Asia and Pacific region were initiated. The PRC has also actively participated in some regional cooperation institutions, such as the Asia–Pacific Economic Cooperation (APEC) forum; 10+3 (ASEAN plus PRC, Japan, and Republic of Korea); the Shanghai Cooperation Organization (SCO); and the Asia–Pacific Trade Agreement (formerly known as the Bangkok Agreement). More recently, the PRC has made new efforts to improve economic relations with South Asia. An FTA signed with Pakistan in 2005, for instance, also included an early harvest program. A feasibility study toward a PRC–India FTA is now underway. The PRC became an observer of the South Asian Association for Regional Cooperation (SAARC)

Table 7.1 FTA Initiatives with Regional Partners

Initiative	Signing Time	Partners	Trade weight (%) 2005
CEPA	2003, Signed in 2005	Hong Kong, China	9.60
CEPA	2004, Signed in 2005	Macao, China	0.10
China–ASEAN FTA	Framework agreement, 2002; Early harvest program, 2005; Trade in goods, 2005; trade in service, 2007	ASEAN (10 members)	9.20
Early Harvest Program for the Free Trade	Signed in 2005	Pakistan	0.30
PRC–Pakistan FTA	Signed in 2006	Pakistan	0.30
PRC Chile–FTA	Signed in 2005	Chile	0.50
PRC–GCC	Framework agreement in 2004, under negotiation	Gulf Cooperation Council (5 members)	2.40
PRC–New Zealand FTA	Negotiation from 2004	New Zealand	0.20
PRC–Australia FTA	Negotiation from 2005	Australia	1.90
PRC–Iceland FTA	Negotiation from 2006	Iceland	0.01
PRC–Norway FTA	Negotiation from 2006	Norway	0.17
PRC–SACU FTA	Study from 2005	South African Customs Union (5)	0.50
PRC–Korea FTA	Study from 2006	Republic of Korea	7.90
PRC–Indian FTA	Agreed study from 2005	India	1.30
PRC–Singapore FTA	Agreed study from 2006	Singapore	2.30

ASEAN = Association of Southeast Asian Nations, CEPA = Closer Economic Partnership Arrangement, FTA = free trade agreement, GCC = Gulf Corporation Council, PRC = People's Republic of China, SACU = South African Customs Union, % = percent.

Sources: Ministry of Commerce of the People's Republic of China (www.mofcom.gov.cn) and Ministry of Foreign Affairs of the People's Republic of China (www.fmprc.gov.cn).

Table 7.2 Other Regional Economic Arrangements

Initiatives	Date of assignment	Partners	Trade weight (%) 2005
Asia–Pacific Trade Agreement (Bangkok Agreement)	2005	Bangladesh, India, Republic of Korea, Lao People's Democratic Republic (Lao PDR)	9.4
East Asia FTA	2005, in research (jointly)	ASEAN, Japan, Republic of Korea (12 members)	30.0
SCO FTA	Proposed in 2005	Shanghai Cooperation Organization members (5 members)	2.7
Free Trade Area of the Asia–Pacific	Initiated by the US in 2006	APEC members (20)	67.6
Greater Mekong Subregion, Strategic Framework of Facilitation on Trade and Investment	2005	Cambodia, Lao PDR, Myanmar, Thailand, and Viet Nam	2.2
Joint Declaration on the Promotion of Tripartite Cooperation	2003	Japan and Republic of Korea	20.8
ACD (Asia Cooperation Dialogue)	2002	21 members	32.8

APEC = Asia–Pacific Economic Cooperation, ASEAN = Association of Southeast Asian Nations, FTA = free trade agreement, SCO = Shanghai Cooperation Organization, % = percent.

Sources: Ministry of Commerce of the People's Republic of China (www.mofcom.gov.cn) and Ministry of Foreign Affairs of the People's Republic of China (www.fmprc.gov.cn).

in 2006, which opens a new avenue for broadening economic ties with the rest of South Asia.

Strengthening economic relationships with trading partners is one of the PRC's major regional strategies. Experience shows these agreements appear to have facilitated trade and opened up new markets. The "noodle bowl effect"—caused by the different and overlapping rules of origins (ROOs)—is, however, a cause for concern. These ROOs may instead create some new barriers to trade. FTAs also provide venues that help improve relations with its regional partners in general. For example, the China–ASEAN FTA has had a clearly positive impact on political ties between the PRC and ASEAN countries.

Foreign Direct Investment Inflows and the PRC's FDI Management

Foreign Direct Investment Inflow to the PRC

The PRC has adopted FDI-friendly policy since opening its economy to the outside world starting in the late 1970s. However, despite various measures to attract FDIs in the early period of 1979–1983, FDI inflows in the PRC were modest, totaling a few hundred million dollars annually and mainly directed toward four special economic zones (SEZs). Starting from the early 1990s, however, the PRC has attracted substantial amounts of FDIs, with inflows amounting to $4.4 billion in 1991, $11 billion in 1992, and $28 billion in 1993. Consequently, the PRC became the largest FDI recipient among all developing countries and the world's second largest FDI recipient after the US. This trend of rapid growth continued in the following years. The PRC's annual FDI inflows increased to $45 billion in 1998 and to $74.8 billion in 2007.

**Figure 7.6 FDI Inflows in the People's Republic of China
(1979–2007)**

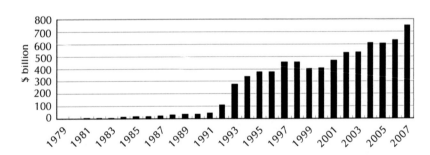

FDI = foreign direct investment, $ = US dollars.

Source: Foreign Investment Department of the Ministry of Commerce of the People's Republic of China.

By 2007, total accumulated FDIs in the PRC had reached $759.8 billion. As shown in Figure 7.7, from 1997 to 2006, Hong Kong, China; Taipei,China; and Macao, China were the major investors, accounting for 42% of the total accumulated FDI inflows, followed by Japan (8.6%), ASEAN (6.4%), and Republic of Korea (6.2%). Although FDIs from East Asia have declined in recent years, the region remains the leading foreign investor in the PRC. FDI inflows from the US (7.8% of total FDI) and the European Union (EU) (8.6%) are also sizable. The combined share of the rest of the world is only 20.5%.

By the end of 2006, the Asia 10 economies (Hong Kong, China; Macao, China; and Taipei,China; Indonesia; Japan; Republic of Korea; Malaysia; Philippines; Singapore; and Thailand) shared 63.2% of the PRC's total accumulated FDIs ($321.3 billion).

Table 7.3 People's Republic of China FDI Inflows by Sector 2005 ($ Mn)

Sector	Projects	Contractual	Utilized
Primary industry	1,310.0	4,853.6	1,072.3
Manufacturing	28,928.0	127,357.3	42,452.9
Service Sector	13,763.0	56,853.6	16,799.5
Total	**44,001.0**	**189,064.5**	**60,324.7**

FDI = foreign direct investment, $ Mn = millions of US dollars.

Source: Ministry of Commerce of the People's Republic of China.

Figure 7.7 FDI Sources to the People's Republic of China

Realized FDI stock by Source Areas in the PRC, 1997–2006

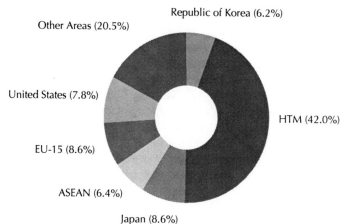

ASEAN = Association of Southeast Asian Nations; EU = European Union; FDI = foreign direct investment; HTM = Hong Kong, China; Taipei,China; and Macao, China; % = percent

Source: Calculated from the reports issued by the China National State Statistical Bureau, 1997–2007.

FDIs from South Asia to the PRC are still small, although the growth rate is considerable. From 1990 to 1997, the annual growth rate of the PRC's FDI inflows was 171.1%, while the annual growth rate of FDI inflows from South Asia was 557.1% and from East Asia[54] 166.8% (Tables 7.4 and 7.5).

The unprecedented growth of FDIs has been accompanied by the PRC's outstanding progress in foreign trade and economic development. In general, FDIs have (i) brought in capital, technology, and management know-how; (ii) stimulated reforms to state-owned enterprises; (iii) upgraded workforce skills; (iv) generated employment; (v) increased tax revenue; and (vi) ultimately contributed to the growth of output and incomes (Table 7.5). In addition to its important role in the PRC's economic growth, FDIs have also helped accelerate the PRC economy's transition to a market system and integration with the world economy.

The PRC's Foreign Direct Investment Management

Many laws and regulations have been promulgated since the late 1970s when the PRC opened its economy to the outside world. Examples include the Sino-Foreign Equity Joint Venture Law of PRC (1979), Sino-Foreign Cooperative Joint Venture Law (1986), and the Wholly Foreign Owned Enterprise Law (1988). Together with their implementing rules, and several revisions thereafter, these are the main rules and principles governing FDIs in the PRC. The Catalogue for the Guidance of Foreign Investment Industries is another important regulation acting as the framework from which the state approves FDI projects and grants concessions. Foreign commercial enterprises must conduct their investments according to this catalogue, which classifies various business sectors into four categories: encouraged, permitted, restricted, and prohibited.

The PRC regulates FDI at different levels, with the State Council being the highest governing body agency. The National Development and Reform Commission (NDRC) and its local counterparts are in charge of approving FDI projects. According to Interim Foreign Investment Project Ratification Administrative Procedures promulgated by NDRC in 2004, projects with a total investment of $100 million or more in the encouraged or permitted categories, or $50 million or more in the restricted category, must be reported to NDRC for ratification; applications for projects in the encouraged or permitted categories, where the total investment amount is $500 million or above, or in the restricted category where the total invest-

---

[54] South Asia includes Bangladesh, India, Nepal, Pakistan, and Sri Lanka. East Asia includes the Association of Southeast Asian Nations (ASEAN) 10, Japan, Republic of Korea, as well as Hong Kong, China; Macao, China; and Taipei,China.

Table 7.4 People's Republic of China FDI Inflows from East Asia and South Asia 1990–2006, ($ Mn)

Country (area)	1990	1992	1997	2000	2001	2002	2003	2004	2005	2006
South Asia	0	12	12	123	182	520	235	376	385	672
ASEAN 10	605	2,759	34,280	28,446	29,840	32,397	29,254	30,405	31,054	33511
Korea, Republic of		1,195	21,424	14,896	21,518	27,207	44,885	62,479	51,683	38949
Japan	5,034	7,098	43,265	29,159	43,484	41,901	50,542	54,516	65,298	45981
ASEAN+3	5,638	11,052	98,969	72,500	94,842	101,505	124,682	147,400	148,035	118441
Hong Kong, China	18,800	75,071	206,320	155,000	167,173	178,609	177,001	189,983	179,488	202329
Macao, China	334	2,020	3,946	3,473	3,211	4,684	4,166	5,464	6,005	6029
Taipei,China	2,224	10,505	32,894	22,963	29,799	39,706	33,772	31,175	21,517	21358
East Asia	26,997	98,648	342,128	253,936	295,025	324,504	339,621	374,021	355,045	348157
Total	34,871	110,075	452,570	407,148	468,776	527,429	535,047	606,300	603,246	630,205

ASEAN = Association of Southeast Asian Nations, FDI = foreign direct investment, $ = US dollars.

Notes: South Asia includes Bangladesh, India, Nepal, Pakistan, and Sri Lanka. ASEAN+3 includes ASEAN 10, Japan, and Republic of Korea. East Asia includes ASEAN+3, and Hong Kong, China; Macao, China; Taipei,China; and People's Republic of China.

Source: *People's Republic of China. Customs Statistics Yearbook, 1990–2007.*

ment is $100 million or above, will be submitted to the State Council for final verification (after the NDRC has examined and verified the application). For encouraged or permitted category projects, where the total investment is below $100 million and restricted category projects, where the total investment is below $50 million, investments must be ratified by the local NDRC; of these, restricted category projects must be ratified by a provincial-level NDRC, and this ratification right cannot be delegated to lower-level bodies.

Table 7.5 Contribution of People's Republic of China FDI Inflows to Economic Growth, 1993–2006

Year	Realized FDI ($ Mn)	Shares of FDI in fixed assets investments (%)	Contribution of FDI to industrial output value (%)	Share of FDI in exports (%)	Contribution of FDI to tax (%)
1993	27,520	12.1	9.2	27.5	5.7
1994	33,780	17.1	11.3	28.7	8.5
1995	35,720	15.7	14.3	31.5	11.0
1996	41,730	15.1	15.1	40.1	11.9
1997	45,260	14.8	18.6	41.0	13.2
1998	45,460	13.2	24.0	41.1	14.4
1999	40,320	11.2	27.8	45.5	16.0
2000	40,720	10.5	22.5	47.9	17.5
2001	46,880	10.5	28.1	50.1	19.0
2002	52,740	10.1	33.4	52.2	20.5
2003	53,500	8.0	40.8	55.5	20.9
2004	60,600	7.2	27.8	57.4	20.8
2005	60,300	5.6	22.2	58.3	–
2006	63,000	4.6	15.9	58.2	–

FDI = foreign direct investment, $ Mn = millions of US dollars, – = no data, % = percent.

Sources: www.fdi.gov.cn; www.mofcom.gov.cn

However, it is the Ministry of Commerce (MOFCOM) of the People's Republic of China and its local counterparts that are the main regulatory bodies in charge of examining and approving FDIs. The scope of MOFCOM's responsibilities mainly cover the formulation of corresponding laws and regulations, examination and approval of the establishment of capital increases over the $100 million benchmark for foreign-invested enterprises within the encouraged and permitted categories, as well as the capital increase over $50 million for the enterprises within the restricted category. As for projects within the encouraged and permitted categories where capital increase does not exceed $100 million, and firms in restricted categories where the capital increase does not exceed $50 million, approvals can be handled by the local units of MOFCOM. To attract more FDIs, the PRC provides many kinds of incentives, such as access to information and technology assistance, facilitation of financing, tax incentives, an investment guarantee program, and establishment of export processing zones (EPZs). Among them, tax incentives are the primary measures, which are dispensed with in a complex system involving national and local levels. Moreover, exemptions, reductions, and refunds are granted depending on the business type, sector, and location of the investment.

This complexity arises from the manner in which these incentives are intended to serve regional economic development and industrial development goals. Tax incentives, for instance, are used to channel FDIs toward targeted regions. The income tax on foreign-invested enterprises (FIEs) located in SEZs, state new- and high-tech industrial zones, or economic and technological development zones face 15% tax. Those located in coastal economic open zones, SEZs, or in the old urban districts of cities where economic and technological development zones are located pay 24%. Those engaged in projects such as energy, communications, ports, and dock are also taxed at 15%. Income taxes can be still reduced by 15% after a 3-year period, provided they are listed in the state-encouraged projects and located in the central and western regions of the country. Moreover, FIEs engaged in manufacturing production and/or software development, with a production timeframe of more than 10 years, may avail themselves of a 2-year income tax exemption and a further 3-year 50% reduction on the income tax payable from the first profit-making year.

Tax concessions are also provided to promote exports. In addition to the 2-year tax exemption and 3-year tax reduction treatment, FIEs producing for export will be allowed a reduced income tax rate of 50% as long as their annual exports account for 70% or more of their total sales volume. Technology-intensive FIEs are also encouraged. For certified technologically advanced enterprises belonging to state-encouraged production projects, a 50% tax reduction is available for a further 3 years after the above-mentioned 5-year tax holiday expires.

To encourage the reinvestment of profits, a 40% tax refund on taxes paid on the reinvested amount is provided for enterprises in operation for a period of no less than 5 years. Once again, taxes can still be further reduced by 15% after a 3-year period, provided they are listed as being among the state-promoted projects and located in the central and western regions.

Other FDI incentives are given by way of exemptions from value-added tax, to those considered as having transferred advanced technology. Equipment imported for foreign- or domestic-invested projects that are encouraged and supported by the state shall enjoy tariff and import-stage value-added tax exemption. FIEs and research centers will be exempt from paying tariffs on imported equipment, technology, and replacement parts.

The PRC's open-door policy toward FDIs is illustrated by the market-access commitments it has entered into in both industrial and services sectors, allowing full foreign ownership of individual enterprises in a range of sectors. There are, however, ownership restrictions on 31 strategic sectors identified as restricted in the Catalogue for the Guidance of Foreign Investment Industries. In 32 sectors, some foreign participation is allowed, but PRC partners must be the controlling shareholders.

Special Economic Zones

There are five SEZs in the PRC: Shenzhen, Zhuhai, Shantou, Xiamen, and Hainan Province. The SEZs represented a major initial attempt to attract foreign capital, advanced technology, and managerial expertise, and to develop export-oriented industries. These SEZs are characterized by a minimum of bureaucracy; good infrastructure; generous tax holidays for manufacturing units; and unlimited duty free imports of raw, intermediate, final, and capital goods.

SEZs have experienced four development phases: the start-up stage (1980–1985), when the necessary infrastructure was laid out; the stage during which export-oriented processing industries were developed (1986–1995); and the upgrading stage, when the shift of industrial structures were encouraged, from labor-intensive industries to technology-intensive and high value-added industries (1995 and beyond).

As more and more cities and regions in the PRC are opened to outside world, the preferential policies exclusive to SEZs were extended (for example, coastal open cities and high-tech and industrial development zones). In particular, the PRC's entry into the WTO in 2001 required that these SEZs develop themselves not on the basis of the application of preferential policies.

The PRC's five SEZs proved to be very successful in attracting FDIs and boosting exports. A significant part of FDIs to the PRC is concentrated there, and the zones have contributed the lion's share of the PRC's total foreign trade. The value of foreign trade through Shenzhen SEZ, for example, reached more than $710 billion during the period 1999–2005, 13.3% of the PRC's total foreign trade in the same period. During the period 1999–2004, the Shenzhen SEZ attracted over $18 billion in FDIs, 5.0% of the PRC's total inbound FDIs.[55]

Outbound Foreign Direct Investment

The PRC has increasingly invested overseas as well. While the PRC's FDI outflows are still very small relative to global flows, the rate of growth is

---

[55] Sources: www.sztj.com/pub/sztjpublic/tjgb/; www.stats.gov.cn/; Ministry of Commerce of the People's Republic of China (PRC).

high, with the amount of investments rising from $0.3 billion in 1991 to $18.7 billion in 2007. By the end of 2007, the cumulative stock of the PRC's FDIs exceeded $93.7 billion. It is predicted that during the 11th Five-Year Plan (2006–2010), total outbound FDIs will reach a total of $83.8 billion, averaging $16.8 billion per year.

The PRC's outbound FDIs are widely distributed among 163 countries/ regions. The 2005 Statistical Bulletin of China's Outward Foreign Direct Investment (Non-Finance Part), released by the Ministry of Commerce and the National Bureau of Statistics, shows the PRC's FDI outflows to South Asia and East Asia during 2003–2005 and is listed in Table 7.6.

To implement the Government's strategy to invest abroad, a series of policies has been introduced in six areas: (i) creation of incentives; (ii) streamlining administrative procedures, including greater transparency of rules and decentralization of authority to local levels of government; (iii) easing of capital controls; (iv) relaxing foreign exchange controls; (v) providing information and guidance on investment opportunities; and (vi) giving credit support to key overseas investment projects encouraged by the Government. These policies are outlined in a series documents, such as the Provisions on Approval Matters Relating to Investment and Establishment of Enterprises Abroad issued by MOFCOM on 1 October 2004 (similar rules for Hong Kong, China and Macao, China issued in August 2004); Interim Administrative Provisions on Approval of Offshore Investment Projects, issued by NDRC on 9 October 2004; Circulars on Foreign Exchange Issues Relating to Foreign-Funded Mergers and Acquisitions and Offshore Investment by Individuals issued by State Administration of Foreign Exchange in January 2005 (No. 11) and April 2005 (No. 29), repealed and replaced by Circular No. 75 (effective 1 November 2005); Catalogue of Countries and Industries for the Direction of Investments Abroad (I), issued by MOFCOM and Ministry of Foreign Affairs on 8 July 2004; and the Circular on Credit Support Policy to Key Offshore Investment Projects Encouraged by the State, issued by NDRC and China Import and Export Bank on 27 October 2004.

The PRC's Merchandise Trade and Policy

The PRC's Foreign Trade

Foreign trade has grown rapidly since 1990; total trade increased from $115.4 billion in 1990 to $2.2 trillion in 2007, growing an average annual 18.9%. Exports increased from $62.06 billion to $1,218 billion, also growing an average annual 19.1%; imports increased from $53.4 billion to $955.8 billion or up 18.5% average annual (see Table 7.7 and Figure 7.8).

Table 7.6 People's Republic of China Outbound FDIs 2003–2005, $ Mn

Economy/Area	2003	2004	2005
SAARC	**11.42**	**4.46**	**17.06**
Brunei Darussalam	–	–	1.50
Cambodia	21.95	29.52	5.15
Indonesia	26.80	61.96	11.84
Lao PDR	0.80	3.56	20.58
Malaysia	1.97	8.12	56.72
Myanmar	–	4.09	11.54
Philippines	0.95	0.05	4.51
Singapore	–	47.98	20.33
Thailand	57.31	23.43	4.77
Viet Nam	12.75	16.85	20.77
ASEAN-10	**122.53**	**195.56**	**157.71**
Korea, Republic of	8.92	40.23	588.82
Japan	7.37	15.30	17.17
Subtotal	**16.29**	**55.53**	**605.99**
Hong Kong, China	1,148.98	2,628.39	3.419.70
Macao, China	31.71	26.58	8.34
Bangladesh	1.41	0.76	0.18
India	0.15	0.35	11.16
Nepal	–	1.68	1.35
Pakistan	9.63	1.42	4.34
Sri Lanka	0.23	0.25	0.03
Subtotal	**1,180.69**	**2,654.97**	**3,428.04**
Total of the above	**1,330.93**	**2,910.52**	**4,208.80**
Total outflow	**2,854.65**	**5,497.99**	**12,261.17**

ASEAN = Association of Southeast Asian Nations, FDI = foreign direct investment, Lao PDR = Lao People's Democratic Republic, SAARC = South Asian Association for Regional Cooperation, – = no data, $ Mn = millions of US dollars.

Sources: *2005 Statistical Bulletin* of the People's Republic of China's Outward Foreign Direct Investment (Non-finance Part), released by the Ministry of Commerce and the National Bureau of Statistics.

Trade with East Asia has grown faster than the PRC's overall trade, rising from $67.14 billion in 1990 to $923.12 billion in 2007. Imports have increased from $27.19 billion to $460.20 billion in 2007, while exports increased from $62.06 billion to $ 1,218 billion during the same period.[56]

Table 7.7 Growth of the People's Republic of China Foreign Trade

Year	Export ($ Bn)	Growth (%)	Import ($ Bn)	Growth (%)	Export + Import ($ Bn)	Growth (%)
1990	62.06	18.1	53.35	(9.8)	115.41	3.4
1991	71.91	15.8	63.79	19.5	135.7	17.6
1992	85.0	18.3	80.61	26.3	165.61	22.0
1993	91.76	8.0	103.95	28.9	195.71	18.2
1994	121.04	31.9	115.69	11.2	236.73	20.9
1995	148.77	22.9	132.08	14.2	280.85	18.6
1996	151.07	1.5	138.84	5.1	289.9	3.2
1997	182.7	20.9	142.36	2.5	325.06	12.1
1998	183.76	0.5	140.17	(1.5)	323.92	(0.4)
1999	194.93	6.1	165.72	18.2	360.65	11.3
2000	249.21	27.8	225.1	35.8	474.31	31.5
2001	266.15	6.8	243.61	8.2	509.77	7.5
2002	325.57	22.3	295.2	21.2	620.77	21.8
2003	438.37	34.6	412.84	39.9	851.21	37.1
2004	593.37	35.4	561.42	36	1,154.79	35.7
2005	762.0	28.4	660.12	17.6	1,422.12	23.2
2006	968.9	27.2	791.4	19.9	1,760.4	23.8
2007	1,218.0	25.7	955.8	20.8	2,173.8	23.5

$ Bn = billions of US dollars, % = percent, () = negative value.

Source: People's Republic of China Customs Statistics Yearbook, 1990–2007.

With an average annual growth rate of 23.6% for exports and 28.9% in imports, the PRC's trade is increasingly oriented toward South Asia (Bangladesh, India, Nepal, Pakistan, and Sri Lanka) as well. Trade jumped from $1.17 billion to $50.8 billion from 1990 to 2007, with exports rising from $0.96 billion to $34.9 billion, and imports from $0.21 billion to $15.9 billion (see Table 7.9).

---

[56] If East Asia includes Hong Kong, China and Taipei,China, the PRC's total trade with the region grew from $67.14 billion to $654.69 billion (with an annual average growth rate of 16.4%); exports from $39.95 billion to $315.5 billion (14.8%); and imports from $27.19 billion to $339.18 billion (18.3%).

Figure 7.8 Growth of the People's Republic of China Foreign Trade

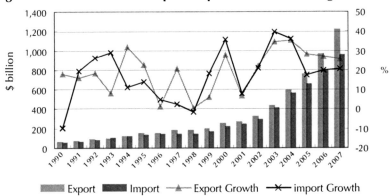

$ = US dollar, % = percent.

Source: People's Republic of China *Customs Statistics Yearbook*, 1990–2007.

Table 7.8 People's Republic of China Trade with East Asia, $ Bn and %

Year	Export ($ Bn)	Import ($ Bn)	Total Trade ($ Bn)	Share of total export (%)	Share of total inport (%)	Share of total trade (%)
1990	39.95	27.19	67.14	64.36	50.97	58.17
1991	49.62	36.14	85.76	69.0	56.66	63.2
1992	57.02	47.14	104.15	67.08	58.47	62.89
1993	47.51	58.31	105.81	51.77	56.09	54.07
1994	67.74	64.35	132.09	55.97	55.62	55.8
1995	84.71	72.57	157.28	56.94	54.94	56.0
1996	84.4	76.52	160.93	55.87	55.12	55.51
1997	100.81	79.81	180.62	55.18	56.06	55.57
1998	89.62	79.1	168.72	48.77	56.43	52.09
1999	93.32	92.34	185.67	47.87	55.72	51.48
2000	119.85	121.82	241.67	48.09	54.12	50.95
2001	127.41	126.18	253.59	47.87	51.79	49.75
2002	152.55	162.04	314.6	46.86	54.89	50.68
2003	195.74	225.09	420.83	44.65	54.52	49.44
2004	258.66	296.18	554.84	43.59	52.75	48.05
2005	315.5	339.18	654.69	41.4	51.38	46.04
2006	385.68	393.06	778.74	39.80	49.66	44.24
2007	462.92	460.20	923.12	38.01	48.15	42.47

$ Bn = billions of US dollars, % = percent.

Note: ASEAN+3 includes the 10 Association of Southeast Asian Nations (ASEAN) countries—Brunei Darussalam, Cambodia, Indonesia, Lao People's Democratic Republic, Malaysia, Myanmar, Philippines, Singapore, Thailand, Viet Nam—and Japan and Republic of Korea; East Asia includes ASEAN; Japan; Republic of Korea; Hong Kong, China; and Taipei,China.

Sources: People's Republic of China *Customs Statistics Yearbook*, 1990–2007 and Ministry of Commerce.

Table 7.9 People's Republic of China Trade with South Asia

Year	Export ($ Mn)	Import ($ Mn)	Total Trade ($ Mn)	Balance ($ Mn)	Share of Total Export (%)	Share of Total Import (%)	Share of Total Trade (%)
1990	957.24	212.3	1,169.54	744.94	1.54	0.4	1.01
1991	1,096.75	225.09	1,321.84	871.66	1.53	0.35	0.97
1992	1,066.73	284.49	1,351.22	782.24	1.26	0.35	0.82
1993	1,384.74	529.91	1,914.65	854.83	1.51	0.51	0.98
1994	1,735.19	508.53	2,243.72	1,226.66	1.43	0.44	0.95
1995	2,479.45	667.66	3,147.11	1,811.79	1.67	0.51	1.12
1996	2,193.46	1,102.17	3,295.63	1,091.29	1.45	0.79	1.14
1997	2,621.28	1,349.79	3,971.07	1,271.49	1.43	0.95	1.22
1998	2,560.71	1,332.18	3,892.89	1,228.53	1.39	0.95	1.20
1999	2,909.28	1,047.76	3,957.04	1,861.52	1.49	0.63	1.10
2000	3,773.27	1,884.50	5,657.77	1,888.77	1.51	0.84	1.19
2001	4,201.71	2,313.31	6,515.02	1,888.40	1.58	0.95	1.28
2002	5,422.62	2,883.66	8,306.28	2,538.96	1.67	0.98	1.34
2003	7,159.64	4,885.01	12,044.65	2,274.63	1.63	1.18	1.42
2004	11,157.45	8,360.09	19,517.54	2,797.36	1.88	1.49	1.69
2005	15,893.16	10,725.21	26,618.37	5,167.95	2.09	1.62	1.87
2006	23,277.3	11,426.6	34,703.9	11,850.7	2.40	1.44	1.97
2007	34,911.11	15,913.21	50,824.33	18,997.90	2.87	1.66	2.34

$ Mn = millions of US dollars, % = percent.

Note: South Asia includes Bangladesh, India, Nepal, Pakistan, and Sri Lanka.

Sources: People's Republic of China *Customs Statistics Yearbook, 1990–2007* and Ministry of Commerce.

Trade Direction

Although the PRC's exports are predominantly destined for Asian markets, exports to North America have grown the fastest, increasing their share from 9% of total exports in 1990 to 20.7% in 2007. Exports to Asia fell correspondingly, from as high as 71.77% to 46.63% during the same period (Table 7.10). However, this change is largely due to goods being exported directly from the mainland; previously, a large share of exports was coursed through the ports of Hong Kong, China.

Table 7.10 Share of the People's Republic of China Exports by Region, %

Year	Asia	Africa	Europe	Latin America	North America	Oceania
1990	71.77	2.09	14.98	1.26	9.04	0.86
1991	74.14	1.39	13.07	1.11	9.39	0.9
1992	71.91	1.53	13.37	1.27	10.88	0.94
1993	57.36	1.66	17.9	1.94	19.79	1.34
1994	60.68	1.45	15.54	2.03	18.89	1.42
1995	61.84	1.68	15.45	2.12	17.64	1.28
1996	60.4	1.7	15.8	2.07	18.73	1.3
1997	59.62	1.76	15.85	2.52	18.94	1.31
1998	53.43	2.21	18.19	2.9	21.82	1.45
1999	52.62	2.11	18.2	2.7	22.77	1.6
2000	53.09	2.02	18.25	2.88	22.18	1.57
2001	52.96	2.26	18.5	3.09	21.66	1.53
2002	52.31	2.14	18.19	2.91	22.81	1.62
2003	50.78	2.32	20.14	2.71	22.39	1.66
2004	49.8	2.33	20.63	3.07	22.45	1.71
2005	48.09	2.45	21.74	3.11	22.92	1.69
2006	47.03	2.75	22.23	3.72	22.61	1.65
2007	46.63	3.06	23.64	4.23	20.70	1.73

% = percent.

Source: People's Republic of China *Customs Statistics Yearbook*, 1990–2007.

Imports from Asia have accounted for more than half of the PRC's total imports since the 1990s. The import share from Asia has increased from 54.37% in 1990 to 64.86% in 2007 (see Table 7.11). In 2007, the East Asian share of the PRC's total trade was 42.47%; of exports, 38.0%; and of imports, 48.2% (see Table 7.8). In contrast, trade with South Asia did not experience obvious growth, with shares of total trade at 2.34%; of exports, 2.87%; and of imports, 1.66% in 2007 (see Table 7.9).

Table 7.11 Share of the People's Republic of China Imports by Region, %

Year	Asia	Africa	Europe	Latin America	North America	Oceania
1990	54.37	0.69	24.07	2.83	15.12	2.78
1991	58.93	0.67	19.91	2.45	15.13	2.73
1992	60.83	0.63	19.97	2.36	13.43	2.55
1993	60.2	0.97	23.07	1.86	11.61	2.27
1994	59.44	0.77	21.64	1.94	13.66	2.52
1995	59.09	1.08	21.05	2.25	14.23	2.29
1996	60.1	1.05	19.92	2.6	13.49	2.84
1997	62.09	1.73	18.09	2.65	12.86	2.58
1998	62.11	1.05	18.77	2.13	13.7	2.24
1999	61.36	1.43	19.7	1.81	13.16	2.53
2000	62.79	2.47	18.12	2.4	11.6	2.61
2001	60.42	1.97	19.87	2.75	12.41	2.58
2002	64.47	1.84	18.1	2.82	10.46	2.31
2003	66.11	2.03	16.89	3.62	9.27	2.08
2004	65.82	2.79	15.86	3.88	9.27	2.37
2005	66.89	3.19	14.61	4.06	8.52	2.73
2006	66.38	3.64	14.51	4.32	8.46	2.69
2007	64.86	3.80	14.61	5.34	8.41	2.97

% = percent.

Source: People's Republic of China *Customs Statistics Yearbook*, 1990–2007.

Trade Protection

The PRC's average applied most-favored nation (MFN) tariff level was 9.8% in 2007, with the average MFN tariff rates for agricultural products set at 15.2% and nonagricultural products set at 8.95%. In accordance with the Information Technology Agreement (ITA), tariffs for all ITA products have been eliminated since January 2005, as well as nontariff measures such as import quotas, import licenses, and import tendering. The administration of the tariff rate quota system has been further improved and the amount of quotas gradually fell in line with the commitments made. Quotas for vegetable oils, for instance, were abolished on 1 January 2006, as committed. In line with the Foreign Trade Law as amended in April 2004, the Government of the People's Republic of China liberalized the state trading rights in July 2004, six months ahead of schedule, and on 1 January 2005, state trading for silk was abolished. Designated trading was also eliminated on schedule.

Some concerns from the PRC's trading partners remain, however. The insufficient correspondence between PRC and international standards, for instance, leads to higher compliance costs for foreign companies operating in the PRC market. Entry for foreign small and medium-sized enterprises (SMEs)

Table 7.12 People's Republic of China Tariff Levels

GTAP sector number	GTAP sector description	Bound rate (trade weighted), %	MFN rate (trade weighted), %	Imports value ($ '000)	Tariff lines	% of tariff lines that are bound
1	PDR – Paddy rice	65.00	33.00	113	3	100
2	WHT – Wheat	65.00	33.00	762,135	3	100
3	GRO – Cereal grains n.e.c.	3.11	1.56	435,566	15	100
4	V F – Vegetables, fruits, nuts	12.12	12.11	1,125,849	147	100
5	OSD – Oil seeds	2.52	2.47	7,999,611	32	100
6	C B – Sugar cane, sugar beet	10.00	20.00	382	2	100
7	PFB – Plant-based fibers	39.47	26.67	3,240,170	7	100
8	OCR – Crops n.e.c.	7.77	7.94	609,877	166	100
9	CTL – Bovine cattle, sheep and goats, horses	0.2	0.19	78,379	13	100
10	OAP – Animal products n.e.c.	8.29	8.19	1,746,949	189	100
12	WOL – Wool, silk-worm cocoons	37.09	19.17	1,152,845	15	100
13	FRS – Forestry	1.18	0.21	3,308,296	43	100
14	FSH – Fishing	10.72	11.60	181,278	75	100
15	COA – Coal	4.00	3.99	1,385,368	7	100
16	OIL – Oil	0.00	0.00	47,722,873	2	100
17	GAS – Gas	5.75	0.00	190	2	100
18	OMN – Minerals n.e.c.	0.4	0.38	29,435,841	113	100
19	CMT –Bovine meat prods	10.6	10.60	350,025	31	100
20	OMT – Meat Products n.e.c.	10.15	2.10	402,910	73	100
21	VOL – Vegetable oils and fats	8.86	13.19	3,241,240	54	100
22	MIL – Dairy products	9.03	9.03	494,302	24	100
23	PCR – Processed rice	62.73	33.00	195,966	2	100

continued on next page

Table 7.12 (continued)

GTAP sector number	GTAP sector description	Bound rate (trade weighted), %	MFN rate (trade weighted), %	Imports value ($ '000)	Tariff lines	% of tariff lines that are bound
24	SGR – Sugar	49.7	32.32	386,057	9	100
25	OFD – Food products n.e.c.	9.94	9.88	5,225,242	379	100
26	B T – Beverages and tobacco products	14.19	14.11	473,240	34	100
27	TEX – Textiles	8.75	8.55	17,979,650	816	100
28	WAP – Wearing apparel	15.41	15.27	1,257,007	294	100
29	LEA – Leather products	8.2	8.13	4,278,022	101	100
30	LUM – Wood products	2.67	2.46	3,092,660	166	100
31	PPP – Paper products, publishing	2.81	2.48	11,028,193	381	100
32	P C – Petroleum, coal products	6.64	6.53	14,018,668	78	100
33	CRP – Chemical, rubber, plastic products	7.05	7.51	89,441,971	1626	100
34	NMM – Mineral products n.e.c.	11.22	11.02	3,730,665	200	100
35	I S – Ferrous metals	4.66	4.65	29,043,889	232	100
36	NFM – Metals n.e.c.	3.8	3.79	25,046,014	230	100
37	FMP – Metal products	9.01	9.01	6,923,700	276	100
38	MVH – Motor vehicles and parts	14.81	17.75	14,524,342	169	100
39	OTN – Transport equipment n.e.c.	3.19	3.6	8,520,968	134	100
40	ELE – Electronic equipment	1.23	1.56	172,463,862	274	100
41	OME – Machinery and equipment n.e.c.	6.94	6.67	143,701,867	1426	100
42	OMF – Manufacturers n.e.c.	13.65	12.66	2,710,957	231	100

GTAP = Global Trade Analysis Project, MFN = most-favored nation, n.e.c. = not elsewhere classified, $ = US dollar, % = percent.

Notes: Data are from United Nations Conference on Trade and Development Trade Analysis and Information System and specific tariffs have been converted to ad valorem equivalents.

is hindered by the costly process of applying for China Compulsory Certification (CCC) mark exemptions, as they are required to submit their applications to the Beijing offices of Certification and Accreditation Administration of China (CNCA) in person. In addition, some laboratories responsible for testing imported products are affiliated with domestic competitors; this not only increases the risk of industrial espionage, but could also lead to even higher compliance costs due to more stringent sanitary and phytosanitary measures.

Export Promotion

Trade promotion has been an important policy in the PRC's economic development strategy. The main measures are (i) export credits and export credit insurance; (ii) assistance for exporters to explore international markets; (iii) setting up institutions to promote trade by developing foreign trade relations, sponsoring exhibitions, and providing information and advisory services; and (iv) facilitating exports of SMEs.

The most direct and effective measure in the PRC's export promotion is the 1985 export value-added tax (VAT) refund system, which partially or completely refunds the levied domestic taxes to export-oriented enterprises.

Table 7.13 Summary of the People's Republic of China VAT Refund Policy

Phases	Period	Average refund rate (%)
1	January 1985–December 1993	11.20
2	January 1994–June 1995	16.63
3	July 1995–December 1995	12.90
4	1997	8.29
5	1998	9.24
6	January 1999–June 1999	11.80
7	July 1999–December 2003	15.00
8	January 2004–Present	12.00

VAT = value-added tax, % = percent.

During the latest VAT refund policy readjustment, some changes were made. Sectors in agricultural products, ships, automobiles and key parts, medical appliances, and some mechanical and electronics products will continue to enjoy their full refund rate of 17%. These sectors are either high-tech intensive and high value-added products encouraged by the Government for the structural adjustment of exports, or as a means to protect strategic sectors that may still lack international competitiveness, such as agricultural products and automobiles. Some sectors that previously enjoyed the full refund rate—such as clothing, textiles, desktop computers and peripherals, home electrical appliances, some electrical parts and articles, and apparatus and instruments—experienced a reduction in their refund rates. The Government has also abolished the refund for some resources products in order to discourage the exports of these products.

Two major institutions deliver export finance, insurance, and guarantees. The Export-Import Bank of China (China Eximbank) is a state policy bank whose mandate is to provide financial support to promote the exports of goods such as mechanical and electronic products and high-tech and new-tech products. The China Export & Credit Insurance Corporation (SINOSURE) is the only policy-oriented PRC insurance company specializing in export credit insurance. SINOSURE provides export credit insurance, export financing facilitation, information, and receivables management services as ways of promoting PRC exports, especially those in high-tech or high value-added capital goods. SINOSURE also offers coverage against political and various commercial risks.

MOFCOM publishes information online to help export enterprises, especially SMEs. A list of key export brands is made, including products in the mechanical and electrical industry, textiles, light industry, arts and crafts, food and food processing, metals, minerals, and chemicals and pharmaceuticals aiming at enhancing the competitiveness of PRC enterprises in the international market. Exporters on the list will enjoy various types of assistance such as export credit insurance through SINOSURE. Some special funds are also provided especially to promote the exports of SMEs, such as the International Market Exploration Fund for SMEs, established in 2000.

The PRC has also used its tax system to encourage foreign investment. Foreign firms enjoy lower tax rates (15% and 24%) than domestic companies (33%) and also have access to tax holidays if they invest in targeted sectors or regions in the past. Considering that exports by FDI enterprises account for over half of the PRC's total export, such tax and preferential policies play an important role in export expansion. However, from 2007, the dual tax treatments have been unified into one system for local and foreign companies.

The PRC Free Trade Agreement Strategy

Since joining the WTO, the PRC has been active in negotiating a number of FTAs that go well beyond tariff liberalization. These FTAs are often comprehensive in nature, with institutional harmonization and broader economic cooperation (such as investment cooperation, training, research and development, and education).

As a developing country, the PRC has adopted a gradual liberalization approach in concluding FTAs, beginning with less sensitive products in an early harvest program. Tables 7.14 to 7.16 summarize the nature, scope, and the rules of origin of the PRC's FTAs.

Table 7.14 Summary of Approaches to Free Trade Agreements (FTAs)

Agreement	Approach
China–ASEAN FTA	The Association of Southeast Asian Nations (ASEAN) and the People's Republic of China (PRC) implemented the Early Harvest Program from 1 January 2004, and the tariff rates of these products had already been reduced to zero by 1 January 2006.
	In November 2004, the PRC and ASEAN concluded PRC–ASEAN Framework Agreement on Comprehensive Economic Cooperation – Agreement on Trade in Goods. In line with the agreement, the PRC and ASEAN started full tariff reduction as from July 2005.
	Negotiations on trade in goods within China–ASEAN FTA are in the form of negative list, meaning products not listed in the sensitive list are regarded as normal products.
	Products within the FTA can be simplified into two categories: tariff lines in the normal track, whose ultimate tariff rate will be reduced to zero; and tariff lines in sensitive track, whose ultimate tariff rate will not be reduced to zero.
	ASEAN 6 (Brunei Darussalam, Indonesia, Malaysia, Philippines, Singapore, and Thailand) and the PRC shall each reduce their tariff rates to 0–5% not later than 1 July 2005 at least for 40% and not later than 1 January 2007 at least for 60% of their tariff lines in the normal track. They shall eliminate all their tariffs for tariff lines in the normal track not later than 1 January 2010, with flexibility to tariffs on same tariff lines, not exceeding 150 tariff lines, but eliminating them not later than 1 January 2012.
	Cambodia, Lao People's Democratic Republic, Myanmar, and Viet Nam shall each eliminate all their tariffs for tariff lines placed in the normal track not later than 1 January 2015, with flexibility to tariffs on some tariff lines, not exceeding 250 tariff lines, eliminating them not later than 1 January 2018.
Closer Economic Partnership Arrangements (CEPAs) with Hong Kong, China and Macao, China	The PRC signed CEPAs with Hong Kong, China and Macao, China special administrative regions on 29 June 2003 and 17 October 2003, respectively. Under both agreements, from 1 January 2004, the PRC began to implement a staged elimination of tariffs on imports originating in Hong Kong, China and Macao, China, and will fully eliminate tariffs on imports originating in Hong Kong, China and Macao, China not later than 1 January 2006.
	Respective Supplementary Agreements to the two CEPAs were signed in 2004 and 2005, expanding the coverage of CEPAs. The PRC agreed to eliminate tariffs on additional products imported from Hong Kong, China and Macao, China from 1 January 2005, and market access requirements for Hong Kong, China service suppliers would be further relaxed. The implementation of CEPAs and their supplements spurred the liberalization of trade in goods and services and the facilitation of trade and investment between the mainland PRC and Hong Kong, China and Macao, China.
PRC–Chile FTA	The PRC and Chile signed the PRC–Chile Free Trade Agreement on 18 November 2005. The two countries began tariff reduction process for trade in goods in the later half of 2006. 74% of Chile's tariff

continued on next page

Table 7.14 (continued)

Table 7.14 Summary of Approaches to Free Trade Agreements (FTAs)

Agreement	Approach
	lines will be immediately reduced to zero tariff rate on the date the Agreement enters into force, and 63% of the PRC's tariff lines will be reduced to zero by 1 January 2007. There are also two other categories of products which are applicable for tariff reduction for Chile and the PRC: Year 5 category, meaning import customs duties shall be removed in five equal annual stages and shall be duty-free by 1 January 2010; and Year 10 category, meaning import customs duties shall be removed in ten equal annual stages and duty-free by 1 January 2015. Ninety-seven percent of tariff lines will be reduced to zero tariff rate by 2015, but the two countries each maintain below 3% of tariff lines as exclusion products, which are not subject to tariff elimination. In addition, on the request of either party, the two countries shall consult to consider accelerating the elimination of import customs duties set out in their Schedule.
PRC–Pakistan FTA	In April 2005, the PRC and Pakistan launched FTA negotiations and signed the Agreement on the Early Harvest Program (EHP) for the Free Trade Agreement, which entered into force on 1 January 2006. While negotiations of the PRC–Pakistan FTA are still in process, the EHP shall be implemented from 1 January 2006. Products in the EHP will be reduced to zero not later than 1 January 2008.
PRC-New Zealand FTA	The decision to begin negotiations on a bilateral FTA came in November 2004 following a joint feasibility study which determined that there would be demonstrable benefit to both countries in entering an FTA. Fifteen rounds of negotiation were then held between late 2004 and late 2007. The FTA was signed on 7 April 2008 in Beijing.

Source: Official texts of FTAs.

Table 7.15 Summary of Coverage of Free Trade Agreements (FTAs)

Agreement	Coverage
China–ASEAN	The agreement is comprehensive, including not only trade in goods, but also trade in services and investment. The priority cooperation is in five fields, including agriculture, mutual investment, information and communication, Mekong Valley development, and human resources development. Currently, the negotiations on trade in services and investment are still going on.
PRC–Chile	The agreement mainly covers trade in goods and cooperation. Cooperation includes economic cooperation; small and medium-sized enterprises; cultural cooperation; education; research, science and technology; labor, social security, and environmental cooperation; intellectual property rights (IPR); investment promotion; and mining and industrial cooperation.
CEPAs with Hong Kong, China and Macao, China, China	The agreement is comprehensive, including liberalization of trade in goods and services and the facilitation of trade and investment between the mainland and Hong Kong, China and Macao, China.

continued on next page

Table 7.15 (continued)
Table 7.15 Summary of Coverage of Free Trade Agreements (FTAs)

Agreement	Coverage
PRC–Pakistan	Currently, the negotiation has not been finished, and only liberalization of trade in goods in the form of Early Harvest Program is launched.
PRC–New Zealand	The agreement is comprehensive, including liberalization of trade in goods and services and the facilitation of trade and investment, also including IPR, standards, and trade disputes.

ASEAN = Association of Southeast Asian Nations, CEPA = Comprehensive Economic Partnership Arrangements, PRC = People's Republic of China.

Source: Official texts of FTAs.

Table 7.16 Summary of Rules of Origin (ROO)

Agreement	Approach
China–ASEAN	Products must be wholly produced or obtained in Association of Southeast Asian Nations (ASEAN) countries, or the content of products originating in any one of the ASEAN countries should be no less than 40% of total content, or the value of the non-originating parts or components used in the manufacture of the products must be no more than 60% of the free-on-board value of the product. The country of origin is defined as the country where the last manufacturing operation takes place. In addition, goods must enter the People's Republic of China (PRC) directly.
CEPAs with Hong Kong, China	Products must be wholly produced in Hong Kong, China or have Hong Kong, China content of at least 30% of value added; in addition, the final stage of processing must be carried out in Hong Kong, China.
CEPAs with Macao, China	Products must be wholly produced in Macao, China or have Macao, China content of at least 30% of value added or have resulted in a change in the HS 4-digit tariff heading, in addition, the final stage of processing must be carried out in Macao, China.
PRC–Chile FTA	Products must be wholly obtained or produced in Chile; or produced in Chile using non-originating materials that conform to a regional value content not less than 40%, except for the goods listed in the Annex 3 of the Agreement.
PRC–Pakistan FTA	Products must be wholly produced or obtained in Pakistan or the value of the non-originating parts or components used in the manufacture of the products must be no more than 60% of the free-on-board value of the product.
PRC–New Zealand FTA	In general a product can qualify as 'originating' under the PRC–NZ FTA if: it is wholly obtained or wholly produced in either PRC or New Zealand, or it is produced entirely in either or both PRC and New Zealand, from materials that conform to the provisions of the ROO Chapter, or the good is manufactured in either or both PRC and New Zealand using inputs from other countries, and meets the product-specific ROO, and the other requirements specified in the ROO Chapter.

FTA = foreign trade agreement, HS = Harmonized System of commodity trade classification of 1996.

Source: Official texts of FTAs.

Except for the agreements with the territories of Hong Kong, China and Macao, China, all concluded FTAs carry a sensitive-product clause.[57] The PRC–ASEAN FTA, for instance, allows for a maximum ceiling of 400 tariff lines at the Harmonized System of commodity trade classification (HS) 6-digit level and 10% of the total import value (based on 2001 trade statistics) for the ASEAN 6 (Brunei Darussalam, Indonesia, Malaysia, Philippines, Singapore, and Thailand) and the PRC; and 500 tariff lines at the HS 6-digit level for ASEAN's newer members (Cambodia, Lao People's Democratic Republic [Lao PDR], Myanmar, and Viet Nam), with no import value ceiling requirements. Tariff lines on the sensitive track are further broken down into sensitive and highly sensitive lists.[58]

The PRC and ASEAN started the early harvest program in January 2004 and tariff reductions from 20 July 2005. This seems to have led to benefits reflected by the growth in trade. PRC–ASEAN trade grew by 35% in 2004 ($105.88 billion in value), and 23.1% in 2005 ($130.37 billion). Products covered by the early harvest program grew even faster from 2003/04, with exports increasing by 31.2% and imports by 46.6%.

The PRC has begun negotiations or carried out FTA feasibility studies with developed countries such as Australia, New Zealand, and Iceland.[59] Australia, for instance, is more interested in the single package approach on agriculture, manufacture, investment, trade in services, government procurement, and intellectual property rights. The protection of intellectual property rights is a particular concern among the PRC's trade partners. From the PRC's side, energy cooperation is one of its key priorities.

Services Trade and Policy

Services Trade
The share of services in the PRC's total trade is still very low, accounting for about 10.3% of total trade in 2007, and with a value $250.9 billion, it

---

[57] Agreements with the PRC territories of Hong Kong, China and Macao, China differ from those with ASEAN. First, Hong Kong, China and Macao, China have few original products, and their gains are mainly in the concessions in trade in services provided by the PRC. Such gains are not directly reflected in the trade account, however. Secondly, these two partners are the PRC's Special Administrative Regions, and as such have been granted special preferences.

[58] For sensitive products, tariff rates will be reduced to 20% by January 2012, and subsequently to 0–5% by January 2018 (liberalization for Cambodia, Lao People's Democratic Republic [Lao PDR], Myanmar, and Viet Nam is delayed to 2015 and 2020). For highly sensitive products, tariff rates must not be more than 50% by January 2015 for the ASEAN 6 (Brunei Darussalam, Indonesia, Malaysia, Philippines, Singapore, and Thailand) and the PRC, and January 2018 for Cambodia, Lao PDR, Myanmar, and Viet Nam.

[59] The PRC demands market economy status recognition from its free trade partners. In some cases, this has become a precondition to launching negotiations toward free trade agreements.

represents about 7.7% of the PRC's GDP. Services imports outpaced that of exports, resulting in a deficit of $5.6 billion in 2000 and $7.6 billion in 2007. (see Tables 7.17 and 7.18).

Table 7.17 People's Republic of China Trade in Services and Goods, 1998–2007

Year	Total Trade ($ Bn)	Change (%)	Trade in Services ($ Bn)	Change (%)	Trade in Goods ($ Bn)	Change (%)
1998	377.0	(0.8)	53.1	(3.3)	323.9	(0.4)
1999	415.8	10.3	55.1	3.8	360.7	11.3
2000	539.8	29.8	66.5	20.7	474.3	31.5
2001	582.4	7.9	72.6	22.7	509.8	7.5
2002	646.8	11.1	86.6	19.3	560.2	9.9
2003	953.2	47.4	102.0	17.8	851.2	5.2
2004	1,283.4	34.6	128.6	26.1	1,154.8	35.7
2005	1,580.3	23.1	158.2	23.0	1,422.1	23.2
2006	1,952.2	23.5	191.8	22.1	1,760.4	23.8
2007	2,424.7	24.2	250.9	30.9	2,173.8	23.5

$ Bn = billions of US dollars, % = percent, () = negative value.
Sources: Ministry of Commerce of the People's Republic of China and State Administration of Foreign Exchange.

Table 7.18 Balance of Service Trade 1998–2007, $ Bn

Year	Service Trade		
	Export	Import	Balance
1998	24.1	29.0	(4.9)
1999	23.8	31.3	(7.5)
2000	30.4	36.0	(5.6)
2001	33.3	39.3	(6.0)
2002	39.7	46.8	(7.1)
2003	46.7	55.3	(8.6)
2004	58.9	69.7	(10.8)
2005	74.4	83.8	(9.4)
2006	91.4	100.3	(8.9)
2007	121.7	129.3	(7.6)

$ Bn = billions of US dollars, () = negative value/trade deficit.

Source: State Administration of Foreign Exchange.

The strength of the PRC's service sector is mainly in traditional services and low value-added projects. For example, exports of transport and tourism services accounted for over half of the PRC's services exports in the past decade. Banking, insurance, consulting, information, advertising, and technology- and knowledge-intensive high value-added services are still in their primary stages of development.

The tourism sector earned a significant surplus, while the transport sector—the second biggest service export sector—had a sizeable deficit. The deficit in transport services widened from $7.9 billion in 2002 to $13 billion in 2005. In 2005, transport, tourism, and other commercial services accounted for nearly 80% of the total receipts and payments of services.

Table 7.19 shows the service trade value and changes in 2005 by sectors. In 2005, services exports totaled $74.4 billion while imports reached $83.8 billion, implying an increase of 19% and 16% respectively during the 2004/05 period. Tourism is the major source of the PRC's service trade surplus. Tourism income was $29.3 billion, with a year-on-year increase of 14%, accounting for 39% of total services income. Tourism outlays totaled $21.8 billion, $7.5 billion less than tourism income. Transport earned $15.4 billion in 2005 (up by 28% from 2004), accounting for 21% of total services income.

Table 7.19 People's Republic of China Services Trade 2005

Item	Imports & Exports		Exports		Imports		Balance
	Value ($ 100 Mn)	Change (%)	Value ($ 100 Mn)	Change (%)	Value ($ 100 Mn)	Change (%)	Value ($ 100 Mn)
1. Transport	438.7	20	154.3	28	284.5	16	(130.2)
2. Tourism	510.6	14	293.0	14	217.6	14	75.4
3. Communication	10.9	19	4.9	10	6.0	28	(1.2)
4. Construction	42.1	50	25.9	77	16.2	21	9.7
5. Insurance	77.5	19	5.5	44	72.0	18	(66.5)
6. Financial services	3.0	31	1.5	55	1.6	15	(0.1)
7. Computer and information	34.6	20	18.4	12	16.2	30	2.2
8. Royalties and license fees	54.8	16	1.6	(33)	53.2	18	(51.6)
9. Consulting	115.1	46	53.2	69	61.8	31	(8.6)
10. Advertising	17.9	16	10.8	27	7.2	2	3.6
11. Film/AV	2.9	33	1.3	227	1.5	(12)	(0.2)
12. Other commercial services	262.7	8	168.8	6	93.9	11	75.0
13. Government services	11.2	23	4.9	31	6.2	17	(1.3)
Total	1,582.0	18	744.0	19	838.0	16	(93.9)

AV = audio and video, Mn = million, $ = US dollar, () = negative value.

Source: State Administration of Foreign Exchange.

The income from film, audio, and video grew the fastest in 2005 with a rate of 227%. Next came construction, growing by 77%, and consulting, which grew by 69%. In 2005, income from sales of broadcasting rights for the 2008 Olympic Games, and for exports of films and other audio and video, totaled $130 million, an increase of 227% from 2004.

Table 7.20 People's Republic of China Trade in Construction, Labor, and Design

Year	Total value $ Mn	Value					
		Contractual Construction		Labor service		Designing	
		$ Mn	% of total	$ Mn	% of total	$ Mn	% of total
1976–88	6,090	4,970	81.6	1,120	18.4	–	–
1679–2005	172,810	135,810	78.6	35,600	20.6	1,400	0.8
1989	1,690	1,480	88.0	200	12.0	–	–
1990	1,870	1,640	88.1	220	11.9	–	–
1991	2,360	1,970	83.4	390	16.6	–	–
1992	3,050	2,400	78.8	650	21.2	–	–
1993	4,540	3,670	80.8	870	19.2	–	–
1994	5,980	4,880	81.7	1,100	18.3	–	–
1995	6,590	5,110	77.5	1,350	20.4	130	2.0
1996	7,700	5,820	75.6	1,710	22.2	160	2.1
1997	8,380	6,040	72.0	2,170	25.8	180	2.2
1998	10,130	7,770	76.7	2,280	22.5	90	0.9
1999	11,240	8,520	75.9	2,620	23.3	90	0.8
2000	11,330	8,380	74.0	2,810	24.8	130	1.2
2001	12,140	8,900	73.3	3,180	26.2	60	0.5
2002	14,350	11,190	78.0	3,070	21.4	90	0.6
2003	17,230	13,840	80.3	3,310	19.2	90	0.5
2004	21,370	17,470	81.7	3,750	17.6	150	0.7
2005	26,790	21,760	81.2	4,800	17.9	230	0.8
2006	35,700	30,000	37.9	5,370	12.3	330	45.4
2007	47,860	40,600	35.3	6,770	26.0	490	48.5

– = no data, $ Mn = millions of US dollars, % = percent.

Sources: National Bureau of Statistics and the Ministry of Commerce of the People's Republic of China.

The PRC's service trade partners are mainly Hong Kong, China and the United States (US), contractual construction and labor services being the principal sectors. Since 1995, designing services export plays important role in the PRC's service exports as well.

Table 7.21 People's Republic of China Contractual Construction in East Asia 1998–2006

Country	1998		1999		2000		2001		2002		2003		2004		2006	
	Value	%	Value	%	Value	%	Value	%	Value	%	Value	%	Value	%	Value	%
Japan	–	–	–	–	20	0.2	20	0.2	50	0.4	30	0.2	50	0.3	136.7	0.5
Korea, Rep. of	–	–	–	–	–	–	10	0.1	10	0.1	90	0.7	100	0.6	321.5	1.1
Hong Kong, China	1,830	19.8	1,970	23.1	2,030	24.2	1,700	19.1	2,140	19.1	2,640	19.1	2,430	14.6	1,754.9	5.9
Macao, China	130	1.4	120	1.4	100	1.2	60	0.7	80	0.7	170	1.2	200	1.2	792.3	2.6
Taipei,China	–	–	–	–	–	–	–	–	20	0.2	50	0.4	30	0.1	181.9	0.6
ASEAN	1,840	19.9	1,180	13.8	1,250	14.9	1,270	14.3	1,640	14.6	1,760	12.7	2,230	12.8	3,875.3	12.9
Singapore	590	6.4	530	6.2	650	7.8	510	5.7	540	4.8	500	3.6	630	3.8	832.5	2.8
Malaysia	160	1.8	90	1.0	90	1.1	70	0.8	130	1.1	230	1.7	200	1.2	430.1	1.4
Thailand	270	2.9	110	1.3	90	1.0	110	1.3	180	1.6	110	0.8	170	0.9	625.2	2.1
Philippines	50	0.6	60	0.7	40	0.5	70	0.8	70	0.6	100	0.7	130	0.7	189.0	0.6
Indonesia	20	0.2	20	0.3	10	0.1	30	0.3	80	0.7	140	1.0	260	1.5	709.3	2.4
Brunei Darussalam	40	0.4	20	0.2	10	0.1	–	–	–	–	–	–	–	–	9.1	0.0
Viet Nam	60	0.7	70	0.8	70	0.8	90	1.1	150	1.3	160	1.2	280	1.6	552.0	1.8
Lao PDR	150	1.6	80	1.0	90	1.1	100	1.1	140	1.2	100	0.7	130	0.8	151.9	0.5
Cambodia	10	0.1	20	0.2	20	0.2	40	0.4	60	0.5	40	0.3	60	0.4	98.3	0.3
Myanmar	490	5.3	190	2.3	180	2.1	250	2.8	290	2.6	370	2.7	330	1.9	277.9	0.9

ASEAN = Association of Southeast Asian Nations, Lao PDR = Lao People's Democratic Republic, – = no data.

Note: Value is in millions of US dollars ($ Mn) and % is the percentage share of total.

Sources: National Bureau of Statistics and the Ministry of Commerce of the People's Republic of China.

Table 7.22 People's Republic of China Labor Service Exports to East Asia, 1998–2006

Country	1998 Value ($ Mn)	1998 Share of Total (%)	2000 Value ($ Mn)	2000 Share of Total (%)	2002 Value ($ Mn)	2002 Share of Total (%)	2004 Value ($ Mn)	2004 Share of Total (%)	2006 Value ($ Mn)	2006 Share of Total (%)
Japan	330	13.7	380	13.6	540	17.7	800	21.4	1,088.9	25.9
Korea, Republic of	100	4.3	220	7.7	200	6.6	280	7.3	313.8	6.1
Hong Kong, China	190	7.9	220	7.9	170	5.6	220	5.9	237.1	4.0
Macao, China	130	5.6	120	4.4	110	3.6	130	3.5	137.7	4.8
Taipei,China	110	4.5	120	4.2	90	3.1	70	2.0	73.4	1.3
ASEAN	470	19.7	670	23.7	660	21.4	540	14.3	470.2	9.2
Singapore	340	14.0	550	19.7	550	17.8	430	11.4	398.3	7.8
Malaysia	20	0.7	20	0.6	20	0.8	10	0.3	26.2	0.2
Thailand	10	0.3	10	0.3	10	0.4	40	1.0	7.8	0.1
Philippines	10	0.4	–	0.1	–	0.1	–	0.0	1.0	0.0
Indonesia	30	1.1	30	1.0	20	0.5	20	0.6	8.0	0.3
Brunei Darussalam	–	0.0	–	0.0	–	0.0	–	0.0	0.5	0.0
Viet Nam	10	0.5	20	0.7	20	0.8	20	0.5	15.8	0.6
Lao PDR	–	0.1	–	0.1	–	0.0	–	0.1	0.3	0.0
Cambodia	30	1.4	30	1.1	20	0.7	10	0.4	10.8	0.3
Myanmar	30	1.2	10	0.3	10	0.3	–	0.1	1.7	0.0

ASEAN = Association of Southeast Asian Nations, Lao PDR = Lao People's Democratic Republic, $ Mn = millions of US dollars, % = percent, – = no data.

Sources: National Bureau of Statistics and the Ministry of Commerce of the People's Republic of China.

In South Asia, Pakistan is one of the most important markets for the PRC's contractual construction service exports. Up to the end of 2004, PRC companies contracted 383 projects of construction, and exported machinery services. Total contractual value from 1992 to 2004 was more than $6.8 billion, in which construction contributed a total of $730 million. The PRC's exports of construction and labor to Sri Lanka totaled $610 million and the contractual value was $880 million as of 2003. The PRC also exported construction and labor to Bangladesh since the 1980s, and in 2006, contractual value of construction exported to Bangladesh was $485 million. New construction contracts in 2004 amounted to $2.19 billion, a 90% increase from the previous year. New contracts between the PRC and India in 2004 reached $0.51 billion; contracts between the PRC and Pakistan totaled $1.3 billion, representing an increase of 217% from the previous year.

Table 7.23 People's Republic of China Contractual Construction and Labor Services to South Asia 2002–2006, $ Mn

Country	2002	2003	2004	2005	2006
India	597.9	315.5	504.7	412.9	1,133.6
Pakistan	546.8	408.1	1,303.1	751.42	987.97
Bangladesh	181.3	363.7	193.8	613.97	496.04
Sri Lanka	47.9	52.0	152.7	90.3	131.32
Nepal	20.6	7.3	27.2	14.45	51.92
Maldives	0.03	–	9.7	7.94	1.86

$ Mn = millions of US dollars, – = no data.

Sources: National Bureau of Statistics and Ministry of Commerce of the People's Republic of China.

Foreign Direct Investment in the PRC's Service Sectors

The PRC's FDI inflows are mainly concentrated in manufacturing sectors, which account for about 70% of total FDI inflows. FDI inflows in services rose from $12 billion in 2001 to $19.9 billion in 2006. In the financial services sector, 14 new foreign banks invested in the PRC with total assets reaching $49.6 billion, from the period of the PRC's accession to the WTO in 2001 until the end of 2003.

During the period 1994–2005, the total assets of foreign banks increased from $11.8 billion to $87.7 billion, representing a more than sevenfold increase. In 2005, FDI inflows in banking, insurance, and securities totaled $11.8 billion. The number of foreign-invested insurance companies

Table 7.24 FDI Inflows to the People's Republic of China Manufacturing and Service Sectors, 2001–2006

	2001		2002		2003	
	Value ($ Mn)	Share (%)	Value ($ Mn)	Share (%)	Value ($ Mn)	Share (%)
Manufacturing	30,907	65.9	36,800	69.8	36,936	69.7
Service[a]	11,988	25.6	14,011	26.6	13,136	24.6

	2004		2005		2006	
	Value ($ Mn)	Share (%)	Value ($ Mn)	Share (%)	Value ($ Mn)	Share (%)
Manufacturing	43,017	71.0	42,453	70.4	40,077	63.6
Service[a]	12,228	20.2	11,679	19.4	19,915	31.6

[a] excluding finance service.

Source: Ministry of Commerce.

Table 7.25 Foreign Financial Institutions in the People's Republic of China, 1990–2003

Year	Foreign banks	Branches of foreign banks	Other financial institutions	Investing banks	Foreign insurance companies
1990	–	4	2	–	–
1991	–	13	–	–	2
1992	2	14	1	–	2
1993	4	26	–	–	–
1994	1	16	1	–	2
1995	1	16	–	1	–
1996	1	15	1	–	2
1997	1	13	1	–	1
1998	1	10	–	–	–
1999	–	9	–	–	–
2000	–	4–2[a]	–	–	8
2001	–	7	–	–	3
2002	1[a]	19[a]	1[a]	–	5
2003	–	10	3[a]	–	9
Total	**12**	**156**	**4**	**1**	**36**

[a] Closed institutions, – = none.

Source: Ministry of Commerce.

increased from 14 in 2000 to 40 in 2005, which accounts for 7% of the PRC's total market share. Up to end of 2005, 72 foreign banks from 21 countries and regions have established 254 affiliates in the PRC, and 177 foreign banks from 40 countries and regions have established 240 representative offices. There were 40 foreign insurance companies investing by the end of 2005, representing half of the total 82 insurance companies in the PRC. Their revenues have rapidly expanded; 29 times faster relative to their domestic counterparts.

During the period 1992–2005, 1,341 foreign-owned distribution enterprises had been registered in the PRC, with foreign-owned retail shops numbering 5,657. In 2005, the market share of foreign-owned supermarket chains accounted for over a quarter of the total retail market in the PRC. During 1997–2003, there were 2,243 foreign-operated construction enterprises, with a contractual FDI value of $11.4 billion ($7.5 billion of which is used).

FDIs in services are mainly concentrated in real estate ($6 billion in 2004, accounting for 48.7% of the total utilized FDIs in services), computer service, construction, retail, hotel and catering, warehousing, and water transport.

Foreign Direct Investment Policy in Service Sectors

Consistent with the PRC's commitments to the WTO, more than 60% of services have been opened up to foreign investors. The degree of openness in developed countries generally comes to 80%, whereas in developing and transitional economies the figure averages 20–40%. In the case of the PRC, the level of market access for foreign services suppliers has been significantly increased. By the end of 2005, 62% of the PRC's service sector had opened to the outside world, with the liberalization in telecommunications, accounting, and education services offering the most market access opportunities.

Since the PRC's accession to the WTO, more than 40 laws and regulations have been enacted in the field of banking, insurance, law services, security, retail, transport, tourism, and education. The Foreign Trade Law, which came into force in July 2004, allowed foreign-invested enterprises to have full trading rights. The PRC's Catalogue for the Guidance of Foreign Investment was revised in 2004, containing the redefinition of the restricted and prohibited foreign investment sectors. On 16 April 2004, the PRC promulgated the Measures for the Administration of Foreign Investment in the Commercial Sector, simplified the procedures for approving FDI. In 2005, the PRC further revised its laws and regulations governing leasing and market concessions for finished oil, franchising, auction, auto brand sales, and forwarders for civil aviation and international freight.

Restrictions on ownership and location in finance, insurance, and security services have been eliminated. However, foreign financial institutions that wish to establish subsidiaries in the PRC should have total assets of more than $10 billion at the end of the year prior to filing the application. A branch of a foreign bank, on the other hand, needs to have total assets of

Table 7.26 People's Republic of China FDI Inflows to Service Sector 2005, $ Mn

Sectors	Projects	Contractual value	Utilized FDIs
Power, gas, and water production and supply	390	3,502.2	1,394.4
Construction	457	2,566.8	490.2
Transport, warehousing, post, and telecommunications	734	5,224.0	1,812.3
Information, computer service, and software industry	1,493	4,512.1	1,014.5
Wholesale, retailing	2,602	4,344.0	1,038.5
Hotel and catering	1,207	2,736.7	560.2
Financing	40	551.4	219.7
Real estate	2,120	19,400.3	5,418.1
Leasing and commercial services	2,981	8,580.1	3,745.1
Scientific research, technical services, and geological survey	926	1,755.0	340.4
Water, environment, and public utility management	139	921.3	139.1
Resident service and other services	329	1,366.2	260.0
Education	51	159.7	17.8
Health, social security, and social welfare	22	164.6	39.3
Cultural, sports, and entertainment	272	1,069.3	305.4
Public management and social organization	–	–	3.7
Total (all sectors)	**13,763.0**	**56,853.7**	**16,798.7**

FDI = foreign direct investment, $ Mn = millions of US dollars, – = not applicable.

Source: Ministry of Commerce of the People's Republic of China.

more than $20 billion at the end of the year prior to filing the application. A PRC–foreign joint-venture finance company or bank must meet a lower minimum of $10 billion at the end of the year prior to filing the application. Foreign financial institutions wishing to engage in local currency trading are required to have operated in the country for 3 years, and profitably for 2 consecutive years prior to the application.

Foreign companies are allowed to provide health, group, and pension and annuities insurance to foreigners and PRC nationals without quantitative or locational restrictions. Foreign nonlife insurers are allowed to have a wholly-owned subsidiary, but cannot engage in statutory insurance business. The investors should be a foreign insurance company that has been established for at least 30 years, that has a representative office in the PRC for 2 consecutive years, and that possesses total assets of more than $5 billion at the end of the year prior to application. Insurance brokers should have total assets of more than $200 million.

Foreign securities institutions may engage directly (without intermediaries who are PRC nationals) in B-share business (stock open to foreign currency business only). Representative offices of foreign securities institutions may become Special Members of all PRC stock exchanges. Joint ventures, with foreign minority ownership not exceeding one third, are allowed to engage in underwriting yuan-denominated A shares, and in underwriting and trading of hard-currency B and H shares, as well as government and corporate debt instruments.

Wholly foreign-owned enterprises are allowed to undertake construction projects financed by (i) foreign investments and/or grants, (ii) loans of international financial institutions, or (iii) international tendering according to the terms of loans. The same is true for Sino–foreign joint construction projects, as long as the foreign share is at least 50% of total venture. There are also projects where foreign expertise would be needed, or projects that would be difficult to implement by enterprises from the PRC that are operating alone. In utilities networks (gas, heat, water supply, and water drainage) the PRC partner must be the majority shareholder.

Wholly foreign-owned subsidiaries can freely establish in the service sectors of packaging, maintenance and repair of office machinery and equipment, rental and leasing, taxation, architecture, advertisement, management consultation, and luxury hotels (real estate). Foreign courier services can set up wholly foreign-owned subsidiaries, except for those currently reserved for the PRC's postal agencies.

Foreign majority ownership and/or joint ventures are permitted in services related to event organization, photography, translation and interpretation, high-standard real estate projects (that is, apartments and office buildings), and medical treatment.

International law firms are also allowed to provide legal services as long as they are conducted via their representative offices.[60] For basic telecommunication services, joint ventures are allowed, but the foreign stake may not exceed 49%. In the construction and operation of cinemas, production of broadcasting and TV programs, publishing, and filmmaking, a partner from the PRC must again hold the majority of shares. For

---

[60] All representatives shall be resident in the PRC no less than 6 months each year. The representative office shall not employ PRC-registered lawyers outside of the PRC.

offshore oilfield services, foreign firms must enter into partnerships with their PRC counterparts; for instance, onshore oil field services have to be undertaken in cooperation with the China National Petroleum Corporation (CNPC).

In recent years, the PRC has stepped up its efforts in services trade legislation to offer more opportunities to foreign investors. For example, administration of the PRC's foreign trade in services involves various government departments that could play positive roles in promoting development of services trade, but there are difficulties in coordination. A complete legislation system in service sectors has not been set up; in general, the PRC's trade in services is characterized by imperfect laws and regulations.

In the WTO negotiations on trade in services, the PRC was mainly asked to (i) reduce the minimum asset limit for banks, insurance companies, and telecommunication companies; (ii) simplify the approval procedure; and (iii) open the sectors of legal and postal services.

The PRC has submitted more than 30 proposals and position papers in the WTO negotiations, which had played a positive and constructive role in advancing the negotiations, bridging understanding among WTO members, and narrowing differences. In February 2006, the PRC joined three requests on water transport, movement of natural persons, and eliminating the MFN exceptions initiated by other WTO members. In the negotiations in March and May of 2006, the PRC initiated bilateral requests from 29 WTO members including the Brazil, Canada, the EU, India, Japan, and US on more than 10 sectors including construction, water transport, health, education, and tourism.

Infrastructure and East–South Asia Link

PRC Infrastructure Improvement

In the 1990s, the burgeoning international trade aggravated the long-standing shortage of transport capacity in the PRC. This prompted the Government to launch the PRC's largest ever investment package for infrastructure construction in the late1990s. During the 9th Five-Year Plan period (1995–2000), the total investment in transport infrastructure construction reached 1.0 trillion yuan (CNY), of which CNY885.8 billion is for highways, CNY42.1 billion for coastal ports, and CNY23.1 for inland water.[61] It turned

---

[61] Ministry of Communications of the People's Republic of China. The Current Status of China's Transport and Its Development Objectives During the 10th Five-Year Plan, 29 March 2001.

out to be the program with the best record in scale, speed, and quality of the construction. Since then, there has been a great leap forward in supply of transport services in the PRC.

Road

The PRC's highway infrastructure has grown very quickly. The increase in mileage is enormous, with the total mileage of highway reaching 1.94 million kilometers (km) by the end of 2005, while the total mileage of expressway open to traffic has surpassed 41,000 km.

The improvement of highways, combined with the increase of carrying capacity of vehicles and the upgrading of technology have greatly improved the capacity and service quality of transportation. In 2005, the gross volume of passenger transport was 16.97 billion persons and the turnover reached 929.2 billion persons per km, and the gross volume for cargo transport was 13.4 billion t with turnover of 869.3 billion t-km. The average cargo transport distance has risen to 64.79 km. The rapid rise of highway express transport significantly improved the efficiency of transport services, and strengthened the fundamental position of highway transport in the integrated transport system.[62]

Rail

Rail is one of the dominant freight transportation modes in the PRC. Importantly, the PRC's energy supply is heavily dependent on railways. For example, 40% of the freight tonnage moved by rail is coal, and about 70% of the PRC's coal moves by rail. With the high increase in energy demand, pressure has been put on the rail infrastructure to move high-quality coal through longer distances out of the northern PRC to southern manufacturing areas. The Government therefore reached the decision to speed up the construction of railways in the late 1990s. By 2005, the total operating railway mileage in the PRC had reached 75,437 km, and is now ranked as the longest among the Asian countries. A railway transportation network has been constructed as well as modernized. The mileage of double-tracking railways is 25,566 km, with the rate of double-tracking reaching 33.9%. With the Qinghai–Tibet Railway running into operation in 2006, railway services are available in all the provinces, autonomous regions, and municipalities.

The coast of the PRC is more than 18,000 km long, and its rivers total 220,000 km. This provides the ideal conditions for developing inland river

---

[62] All the statistics came from 2005 Road and Waterway Transportation Statistics Report by the Ministry of Communications of the People's Republic of China.

transport and ocean shipping. In the 1990s, the construction of ports was a key focus for infrastructure development, and was in fact, supported by a series of Government priority policies. For instance, the PRC allows foreign companies to build and operate berths in the form of joint ventures and engage in (i) loading and unloading business, (ii) cargo storage, (iii) disassembling and packaging services, and (iv) related passenger and cargo transport services by land and water. Foreign companies are also allowed to enter into partnership with their PRC counterparts to engage in loading and unloading business by leasing, or to build special harbors and waterways for cargo owners with exclusive foreign funds. These measures have promoted port construction, so that by the end of 2004, the total number of ports in the PRC reached 1,430, with annual cargo capacity of 4.17 billion t.

Table 7.27 Berths and Turnover of Top 10 Foreign Trade Seaports, 2004/05

Ports	Number of Berths (with handling capacity over 10,000 tons)	Total Foreign Trade Volume ('000 tons)	Imports ('000 tons)	Exports ('000 tons)
Shanghai	74	158,360	90,910	67,450
Qingdao	37	121,280	88,000	33,290
Tianjin	52	107,920	51,820	56,100
Ningbo	26	102,330	83,810	18,510
Shenzhen	47	88,650	38,210	50,440
Guangzhou	37	59,040	40,640	18,390
Qinhuangdao	33	53,610	9,540	44,070
Dalian	57	49,210	30,560	18,650
Rizhao	19	33,660	18,850	14,810
Xiamen	23	28,480	12,970	15,510

Source: People's Republic of China Statistical Yearbook 2005.

Ocean shipping in the PRC is divided into two major navigation zones: the northern zone and the southern zone. The northern one has Shanghai and Dalian as centers, and the southern one has Guangzhou and Shenzhen as centers. There are 11 major coastal harbors in the PRC, with an annual cargo capacity of over 100 million t. Shanghai Harbor ranks the first among the trade harbors in the world (with an annual cargo capacity of 400 million t). The other three main harbors are Ningbo (269 million t), Guangzhou (250 million t), and Tianjin (241 million t). With regard to cargo and container handling capacity, the PRC has retained the first place in the world in the past 3 years. By the end of 2005, the cargo turnover for imports and exports amounted to 1.37 billion t, and the container turnover in more than 20 seaports reached 70 million t.

Air

Airports play an increasing role in connecting the PRC with the outside world. In 2004, there were 133 airports operating scheduled flights, 39 of them with an annual passenger volume of over 1 million and cargo turnover of over 10,000 t. The PRC also has 244 international air routes connecting 38 countries and 80 foreign cities. In 2005, the total volume of passenger traffic reached 284.35 million, and cargo turnover by air reached 6.33 million t. Its capacity in handling passenger and goods ranks the third place in the world.

In the next 5 years, the Government will continue to invest large amounts into building transport infrastructure.

The PRC and South Asia Transport Cooperation

Transport between the PRC and South Asia is busier and more convenient than ever. In contrast with the past, when there were no air links between

Table 7.28 Passenger and Cargo Transport of Top 10 Airports in the People's Republic of China, 2005

Airport	Passenger transport	Rank	Cargo transport (tons)	Rank
Beijing	41,004,008	1	782,066.0	2
Shanghai / PuDong	23,664,967	2	1,857,119.8	1
Guangzhou	23,558,274	3	600,603.9	3
Shanghai / Hong qiao	177,797,365	4	359,594.5	5
Shenzhen	16,283,071	5	466,476.4	4
Chengdu	13,899,929	6	251,017.9	6
Kunming	11,818,682	7	196,530.2	7
Hangzhou	8,092,641	8	165,917.9	8
Xian	7,942,034	9	83,256.1	15
Haikou	7,027,397	10	60,590.3	19

Source: www.caac.gov.cn

Table 7.29 People's Republic of China Transportation Development

Transport Type	Length of transport routes	Transport Equipment Units	Government investment plans (11th Five-Year Plan, 2006–2010)
Rail	74,408 km (track in operations)	528,000 rail containers	• Annual investment will be about $8 billion by 2010.
Road	1.87 million km (highways)	8.93 million vehicles (average capacity is about 2 tons)	• Half of the rail investment is planned for western PRC projects, including the world's highest railway that will link Qinghai and the Tibet Autonomous Region.
Sea	34,000 (shipping berths)	1,500 vessels (capacity of 37 million DWT)	• Annual investment will be about $80 billion by 2010.· • Plan to double the number of deepwater berths.· • Specific deepwater port projects include Shanghai, Dalian, Qingdao, Tianjin, and Shenzhen.
Inland water	123,300 km	210,000 vessels	• Annual investment will be about $1.1 billion by 2010.
Air	2.05 million km (civil aviation routes)	890 airplanes	• Construction or renovation of about 35 airports.

DWT = dead weight ton, km = kilometer, PRC = People's Republic of China, $ = US dollar

the PRC and India, there are now nine scheduled flights between India and the PRC every week. Some air and road links connect the PRC with Bangladesh, Nepal, Pakistan, and Sri Lanka.

The PRC has taken new initiatives to improve its transport corridors with South Asia. The PRC and India, for instance, agreed to jointly work toward enhancing direct air and shipping links, tourism, and people-to-people contacts. A memorandum of understanding was also signed that will pave the way for a major liberalization of civil aviation links between the PRC and India. The PRC and Pakistan agreed to initiate the renovation project of the Karakoram Highway, the only overland connection between the two countries. The 809-km highway, whose location is 600 to 4,700 meters (m) above sea level, was built in 1978 for special geopolitical reasons but was not adequately maintained. Since 2005, a plan was designed to widen the highway from 10 m to 30 m, tripling its capacity. The PRC and Bangladesh agreed to open a direct air link between Beijing and Dhaka via Kunming. Both sides were also committed to complete the final phase of the Kunming–Chittagong road link.

During the 11th Five-Year Plan period (2006–2010), the PRC plans to extend the Qinghai–Tibet Railway from Lhasa to Shigatse, and then through Shigatse to Yadong, a small border town near India. A railway through Shigatse to Nilamu, a land port of entry to Nepal, is also under consideration. A railway from Dali to Ruili, a border town near Myanmar, is still being studied.[63]

Facilitation Measures

In recent years, the PRC's General Administration of Customs (GAC), together with other concerned ministries, has focused in establishing a modern customs system. The chief priority of the reforms is clearance handling.

The project is divided into the following two phases.

Phase 1 (1998–2002). The PRC made great strides in improving its customs clearance. Progress was achieved in various areas such as screening, supervision of administration authorities, standardization of goods, transportation enterprises management, and modernization of physical facility in some key ports customs. Progress was also made in establishing fast customs clearance procedures in ports and accelerating the movement of goods. Strides were also made toward nationwide use of fast customs-transfer operation and incorporation of the one-stop, single-window approach to customs-transfer between inland and ports or between different customs. The PRC piloted a paperless customs clearance project, implemented the E-customs Project network connecting national customs, increased customs administration effectiveness via the E-ports Project of data exchange, and networked joint inspection between different government departments and different regions. All of these measures enhanced overall performance in ports administration and the efficiency of import and export procedures.

Phase 2 (2004–2010). The PRC has planned to establish a "smart" customs service based on best practices. The service aims to be professionally managed, highly efficient, and resistant to corruption. To achieve these targets, the PRC has made great efforts in the following aspects: (i) adopting

---

[63] The Stilwell Road (or the Ledo Road) was built by the US during World War II and named after British commander General Joseph Warren Stilwell, Chief of Staff of the Allied Forces. This 60-year-old road, now in disrepair, connects Ledo in Assam to Kunming in the PRC via Myanmar. At present, most of the trade between Yunnan Province and India is shipped by sea, traveling more than 6,000 kilometers (km). The road would trim the distance from Yunnan to India to 1,220 km. The PRC actively supports reviving this road link and has begun to upgrade the part of the road in its territory. Reviving the entire length of the Stillwell Road will require strong political will and confidence building among India, Myanmar, and the PRC to ensure effective cooperation in rebuilding the road.

the WTO valuation agreement principles,[64] and (ii) promoting automation and information technology in customs clearance via developing E-customs, E-Ports. Paperless clearance procedures have been expanded in most customs districts, speeding up the procedures for customs clearance. At the same time, a nationwide integrated quarantine and inspection operation management system named CIQ 2000 has been set up. The system computerized fees, quarantine, inspection, certification of customs clearance, and compilation of customs statistics. It also provides electronic declaration, bill transfer, and customs clearance services.

Policy Recommendations

Because of its geographical location, large market, and high economic growth, the PRC can play an important role in strengthening economic relations between East and South Asia.

This study shows that the PRC has achieved great progress in both its economic development and external relations. In the past two decades, as an emerging giant economy, the PRC has been in a key position to develop East Asian production and service networks through trade and FDI. The PRC economy is expected to maintain its dynamism and become even more integrated with other parts of the world.

The PRC and South Asia have rapidly developed their trade and investment relations in the past decade. By 2005, the PRC became the third largest export market and the first largest import market for India. The PRC has also become an important destination for Indian FDIs, especially in software. As for the rest of South Asia, the PRC and Pakistan have initiated talks toward a FTA, starting with an early harvest program. The PRC became an observer of the SAARC in 2005, while a liberalization package has also been introduced in the Asia–Pacific Trade Agreement (formerly known as the Bangkok Agreement).

Trade and investment between the PRC and South Asia is rapidly growing, although the absolute size of this exchange is still rather limited because of a proliferation of tariff and non-tariff barriers.

The following are the policy recommendations to emerge from this study:

---

[64] On 23 November 2003, the State Council issued the Import and Export Duty Statute for the purpose of readjusting and improving the customs valuation system. In addition, a series of capacity-building measures was also undertaken, including translation and publishing of the Customs Valuation Agreement and other important documents in Chinese, as well as research and introduction of the best international customs management practices.

Bilateral Relations

* The PRC and India are two of the largest developing countries with fast economic growth in the world. However, trade disputes have emerged and threatened to become serious because of trade imbalances and an increasing number of antidumping cases initiated by the Government of India against PRC exports. To promote trade, it is highly necessary for the two countries to reduce tariff and non-tariff barriers and improve overall governance. The two countries have agreed to study the possibility of a possible FTA to cover a comprehensive package of economic cooperation measures. This agreement could be opened to other South Asian countries as well.

* The PRC and Pakistan are traditional trade partners and signed an FTA in 2006. Their relations continue to develop although at a slightly more modest rate than the PRC's relations with other South Asian countries. Pakistan's trade deficit is also worsening because of its limited export capacity to the PRC. To improve the trade and investment environment between the PRC and Pakistan, it is important to help to enhance the capacity of Pakistan companies exporting to the PRC. An FTA between the two countries is a good step in this direction. The PRC should offer more help to Pakistan especially in the field of and do more in capacity building for the country. The two sides should further expand their economic cooperation in the areas of energy and manufacturing through more FDIs from the PRC. The Government of Pakistan proposed to be an energy corridor and the PRC has shown strong interest in supporting and cooperating in this field. PRC companies can expand in the special industrial zone that the two governments agreed to initiate in Pakistan. Pakistan should significantly improve its trade and investment environment, especially through improving security.

* Trade relations between the PRC, Bangladesh, and Sri Lanka have developed quickly in recent years. But Bangladesh and Sri Lanka are running widening trade deficits with the PRC, mainly because of their similar export structures and their enterprises' low export capacity. PRC firms still complain that the tariff levels in those two countries are still high, and there also many non-tariff taxes and fees. The financial systems of Bangladesh and Sri Lanka need to be improved as well. In recent years, many PRC firms have invested in Bangladesh and Sri Lanka, either through FDIs or project contracts. However, the size of these investments is still limited. The three countries should strengthen their cooperation in improving the business environment and initiate

feasibility studies toward FTAs. The PRC should provide assistance to those two countries for enhancing their export capacity and economic development.

Regional Cooperation

The PRC and South Asia have developed their economic relations under a regional framework. For instance, the PRC became an observer of the SAARC, which provides a venue to discuss trade and investment facilitation programs, among other issues. However, political inertia could slow down the SAARC free-trade process. Thus, the PRC should explore other avenues to enhance its integration with the region.

The Bangkok Agreement initiated by the United Nations Economic and Social Commission for Asia and the Pacific (UNESCAP) in 1975 with six members (Bangladesh, PRC, India, Republic of Korea, Lao PDR, and Sri Lanka) from East and South Asia is one of the major arrangements that brings the PRC together with other East and Southeast Asian countries. The Bangkok Agreement was renamed the Asia–Pacific Trade Agreement in 2005 and has since lowered tariffs on about 4,000 items by about 30%.

The PRC should continue to promote greater subregional cooperation with Bangladesh, India, and Myanmar, which could be helpful for policy dialogue, improvement of infrastructure, and development cooperation.

Infrastructure

The land connection between the PRC and South Asia is in the PRC's southern and southwestern provinces, especially Yunnan and Sichuan. The current infrastructure is underdeveloped and unable to support the increasing exchanges between the PRC and South Asia. Effort should be made to improve infrastructure in the following three areas:

- The PRC and Pakistan agreed to improve the Karakoram Highway, the only road link between the two countries. The PRC and India may consider rehabilitating the Stilwell Road, which was built during World War II, to link the PRC with Myanmar and India. The roads connect Yunnan–Myanmar–Bangladesh (reach to Chittagong port, the second largest city of Bangladesh) could also be considered.
- Sea links are potentially more important than roads. The PRC and South Asian countries should develop modern port networks.[65]

---

[65] It would be feasible to connect the PRC with ports in Southeast and South Asia through improved road–port links.

- The PRC and South Asian countries have increased their air links, but current air capacity is far from sufficient. More passenger jet and cargo lines should be developed quickly.

References

Asia–Pacific Economic Cooperation (APEC) Business Advisory Council, Finance Working Group. 2004. *Proposal to support Financial Services Liberalization: Supporting the WTO Negotiations on Financial Services.* Available: www.abaconline.org/v4/download.php?ContentID=2164

China National State Statistical Bureau. 2005. *China's Yearbook of Statistics* (1997–2005 versions). People's Republic of China.

Chen, W., and W. Li. 2005. An Evaluation of the Need and Cost of Selected Trade Facilitation Measures in China—Implications for the WTO Negotiations on Trade Facilitation. Asia–Pacific Research and Training Network on Trade (*ARTNeT*) *Working Paper.*

Drewry Shipping Consultants Limited. 2003. *China's Transport Infrastructure and Logistics.*

Frost, S. 2004. Chinese Outward Direct Investment in Southeast Asia: How Much and What Are the Regional Implications? *City University of Hong Kong Working Paper* 67. Available: www.cityu.edu.hk/searc/WP67_04_Frost.pdf

Ho, O.C. 2004. Determinants of Foreign Direct Investment in China: A Sectoral Analysis. Paper submitted for the 16th Annual Conference of the Association for Chinese Economics Studies, Australia (ACESA), Brisbane, QLD, 19–20 July.

Huang, Z. 2002. Working Together to Open up a New Prospect for China–ASEAN Cooperation on Transport. Speech delivered at the First China–ASEAN Transport Ministers' Meeting, People's Republic of China, 20 September.

Ministry of Commerce. 2000. *China's WTO Commitments in Services Sector.* People's Republic of China.

_____. 2004. *Measures for the Administration on Foreign Investment in Commercial Sector.* People's Republic of China.

_____, Department of Foreign Capital Utilization. 2005. *China's Foreign Investment Report 2005.* People's Republic of China.

_____, Department of WTO Affairs. 2006. *The New Round of WTO Negotiations on Trade in Services.* June. People's Republic of China.

_____, State Development and Reform Commission. 2004. *Catalogue for the Guidance of Foreign Investment Industries.* People's Republic of China.

Ministry of Commerce and China National State Statistical Bureau. 2006. *Statistical Bullet of China's Outward Foreign Direct Investment.* Available:

http://aaa.ccpit.org/Category7/mAttachment/2006/Dec/19/asset
000070002035118file1.pdf

Ministry of Communications. 2001. *The Current Status of China's Transport and Its Development Objectives During the 10th Five-Year Plan*. 19 March. People's Republic of China.

_____. 2005. *Road and Waterway Transportation Statistics Report*. People's Republic of China.

Spear, A., C. Nailer, and S. He. 2006. China Infrastructure: Sectoral Plans, Reforms and Financing. *Department of Foreign Affairs and Trade, Australia, Briefing Paper Series* 6.

World Trade Organization (WTO). 2005. *World Trade Developments in 2005*. Available: www.wto.org/english/res_e/statis_e/its2006_e/its06_general_overview_e.pdf

Zhang, J. 2005. Targeted Foreign Direct Investment Promotion Strategy—Attracting The Right FDI for Development. Paper submitted for the First Annual Conference on Development and Change held in Neernrana, India, 2–4 December.

Zhang, K. H. 2001. What Attract Foreign Multinational Corporations to China? *Contemporary Economic Policy* 19(3): pp. 336–346 (July).

_____. 2002. Why Does China Receive So Much Foreign Direct Investment? *China & World Economy* 3: pp. 49–58.

Thailand

Suthiphand Chirathivat and Chayodom Sabhasri

Introduction

Policies of economic growth led by exports and foreign direct investment (FDI) have been the main driving forces behind Thailand's economic progress. Trade and FDI performance has increased considerably since the second half of the 1980s, even accounting for the sluggish period around the 1997/98 financial crisis. While economic ties with the Association of Southeast Asian Nations (ASEAN); the People's Republic of China (PRC); Hong Kong, China; Japan; the Republic of Korea; and Taipei,China have considerably strengthened, links with South Asia remain weak. There is much room for improvement, therefore, especially given Thailand's geographical position and potential to serve as a bridge between East and South Asia. Increasing FDIs from both the PRC and India could likewise be first steps toward deepening economic relationships between the two Asian subregions.

Thailand is actively taking part in a number of regional trade agreements, at both the multilateral and bilateral levels. In addition to the ASEAN Free Trade Area, Thailand has bilateral free trade agreements (FTAs) with Australia, India, and New Zealand, as well as a regional trading agreement under the China–ASEAN FTA. Thailand has also been unilaterally reducing its tariff barriers, as evidenced by a fall in average applied tariff rates. The Government also implements trade and investment promotion programs that include (i) the provision of financial facilities and bilateral financial arrangements; (ii) the establishment of overseas export promotion offices; and (iii) the launching of investment privileges such as export processing zones (EPZs), special economic zones (SEZs), and industrial estates. As a result, Thailand has considerable potential to be a hub for regional production networks for industries such as automobiles, chemical products, and electrical and electronic products. These production networks could deepen the economic relationships among Thailand, ASEAN, PRC, India, and Japan.

Thailand has liberalized most of its service sector as the Government realizes the heavy dependence of the country on developing services support for various manufacturing sectors. Trade travel and transportation services, for instance, are rapidly increasing in importance, especially between East and South Asia. FDIs in oil exploration and real estate have also been increasing, particularly from Japan and Singapore.

This paper illustrates how Thailand can serve as a corridor linking its Asian neighbors. Proposals such as liberalizing trade and investment, raising the logistics system to international standards, and improving trade-related infrastructure, are particularly urgent.

The chapter has the following sections: (i) an overview of the Thai economy, with an emphasis on its external orientation; (ii) an analysis of FDI performance and policies, and potential sectors for FDI growth; (iii) an investigation of the merchandise policy, and the features of Thailand's regional trade agreements; (iv) a discussion on infrastructure and trade administration issues related to East and South Asia; (v) an analysis of trade and FDI policies; (vi) policy implications for promotion of East and South Asia from Thailand's perspectives; and (vii) a conclusion.

Regional Economic Integration and Trade Negotiation Strategies

Thailand has increasingly been focused on the formation of regional trade arrangements, also as a means of efficiently restructuring its economy to cope with globalization. It is clear that trade liberalization is increasingly being pursued through FTAs. The policy objectives seemed to be particularly geared toward keeping Thailand's standing in its key markets (the United States [US] and Japan), strengthening trade ties with the emerging markets such as the PRC and India, and gaining entrance to new markets such as Australia, Bahrain, New Zealand, and Peru.

Trade negotiations are also guided by sectoral strategies. In agriculture, the focus is on processed food and fast-growing agricultural products. These products are typically placed on sensitive product lists to allow for a longer period of adjustment. In the manufacturing sector, items with high potential for export include automobiles and parts, electronics, electrical appliances, fashion items, and furniture. These items are receiving significant policy attention. The positive-list approach, on the other hand, is applied to the service sector. Thailand considers itself internationally competitive in only a few service industries, such as tourism and health care. Information and communications technology, logistics, entertainment, and repair services will receive more attention in the future, while banking, insurance, communication, and transportation are less competitive and are seen to be requiring special treatment.

The historical trading partners of Thailand are ASEAN, European Union (EU), Japan, and US. However, with changes in the global division of labor, the PRC has become very important as well. With the China–ASEAN FTA, trade and investment relationships within the region are expected to intensify. Nevertheless, Japan will remain a key FDI and trading partner given its solid foothold in Thailand since the 1980s.

Economic Structure

The Thai economy could be considered as having recovered from the 1997/98 financial crisis by 2000, having done so through a variety of policy measures such as Government spending cuts, higher value-added tax, higher interest rates, and more stable exchange rates. New investment promotion policies were launched and more aggressive trade policies have been implemented to increase export earnings.

Figure 8.1 Trade Balance, $ Billion

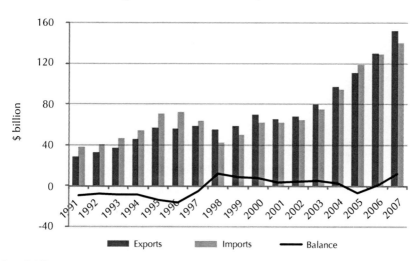

$ = US dollar.

Source: Thai Customs Department.

As shown in Figure 8.1, Thailand experienced trade deficits for several years up to 1998. When the Thai baht was devalued at the end of the 1980s, Thailand received a large amount of FDIs, especially from Japan. These FDI inflows resulted in higher export growth, but because of the low local content of these exports, the trade deficit persisted as imports of raw materials and capital goods continued to rise. The trade deficit rose further between 1995 and 1997 because of the high imports of consumption and luxury goods, the devaluation of renminbi in the PRC, and a weak Japanese economy.

The import structure has changed since 1998, with the import share of fuel and lubricated oil continuously increasing, except when the oil price hiked in 2007. The recent oil price hike and the dependency on imported materials and capital goods resulted to a deteriorating trade balance (Figure 8.2).

Figure 8.2 Structure of Imports, %

% = percent.

Source: Thai Customs Department.

Figure 8.3 GDP Growth, %

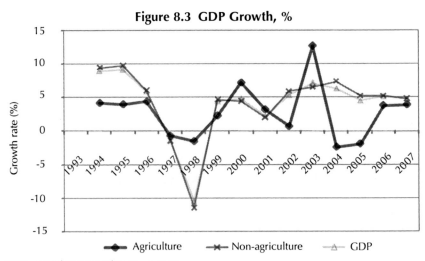

GDP = gross domestic product, % = percent.

Sources: National Economic and Social Development Board and Bank of Thailand.

Global economic improvement since 2002 led to the recovery of the Thai economy since 2002. Manufacturing exports have become the main driving force in the economy, that sector accounting for approximately 90% of gross domestic product (GDP). Figure 8.3 shows the almost perfect correlation between overall economic growth and manufacturing performance.

During the period 1997–2000, GDP per capita was constant, but as a sign of full economic recovery, it rebounded by 99.5% in US dollar terms from 2001 to 2007 (Figure 8.4). The key engine for growth was export performance.

Figure 8.4 GDP Per Capita, $

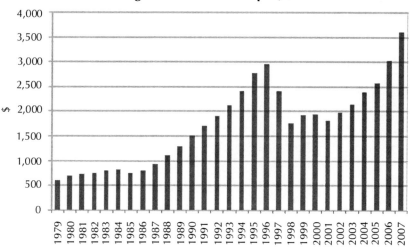

GDP = gross domestic product, $ = US dollar.

Sources: National Economic and Social Development Board and Bank of Thailand.

The growing importance of international trade in the Thai economy is reflected by the increasing amount of trade in proportion to total GDP. This measure of the degree of openness rose from 80% to 149% during the period 1993–2005 (Figure 8.5).

In the past, one of the key advantages of Thai industry was its relatively low labor costs, especially for skilled workers. The unit labor cost (national standard minimum wage rate) shown in Figure 8.6 was very low in 1990 and the wage rate was slightly below $3 per day. However, the wage rate has continuously increased since then. Between 1990 and 1996 unit labor cost increased by 73.7%, and by 37.6% during the period 1997–2007. Nonetheless, the unit labor cost moved in narrow range of $3.5 to $4.8 between 1998 and 2007 due to almost constant nominal wages and a stable exchange rate. From the beginning of 2006, the baht has been strengthening against the US dollar, leading to higher unit costs in US dollar terms.

Figure 8.5 Degree of Openness, % of Trade to GDP

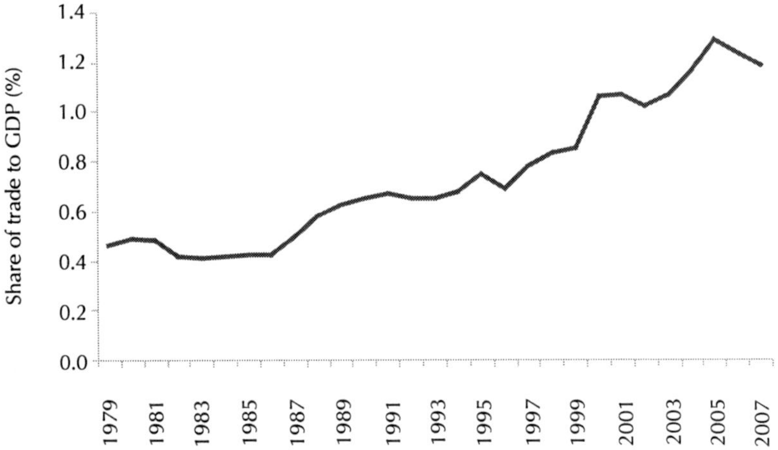

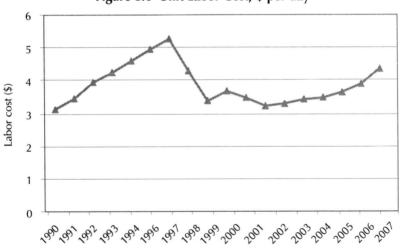

GDP = gross domestic product, % = percent.

Source: Thai Customs Department.

Figure 8.6 Unit Labor Cost, $ per day

$ = US dollar.

Source: Ministry of Labor.

As the economy grew, the poverty headcount ratio dropped between 1990 and 1996 (Figure 8.7). During the Asian financial crisis of 1997/98, poverty incidence slightly increased, only to fall below its lowest level since 1990.

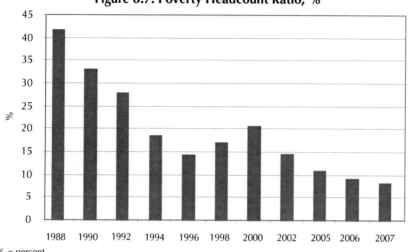

Figure 8.7: Poverty Headcount Ratio, %

% = percent.

Source: National Economic and Social Development Board.

Foreign Direct Investment Regime

Foreign Direct Investment Performance and Potential New Sectors

Data shows that inbound FDI stock[1] has accumulated in the past 15 years, except during the 1997/98 financial crisis. Outward flows are rather minimal. Total FDIs rose considerably during the period 1997–1999, reaching $50 billion in 2004, and with inflows increasing particularly in industries such as machinery and transportation equipment, electrical appliances, trade, and services. Investments in real estate, however, have substantially slowed down. Because the local firms were short of capital, and the baht was rather weak, the inflows of FDI were rather substantial. The capital outflows are insignificant as compared to the capital inflows. The only years with larger outflows were 1994 and 1996, when Thailand liberalized its financial sector.

Before 1990, Japan was the major source of net FDIs. The US managed to match Japan's contributions in 1996 (Figure 8.10) although its net FDIs (and that of the EU) dropped sharply, turning into net outflows between

---

[1] The following analysis is based on the United Nations Conference on Trade and Development definition of foreign direct investment (FDI) stock. It is defined as the value of the share of their capital and reserves (including retained profits) attributable to the parent enterprise, plus the net indebtedness of affiliates to the parent enterprises.

2002 and 2004. After the 1997/98 Asian financial crisis, ASEAN—especially Singapore—became almost as important an investment partner as Japan. FDIs from the PRC are rather limited, while those from Hong Kong, China are substantial but fluctuating (Figure 8.10).

Figure 8.8 FDI Inward Stock, $ Million

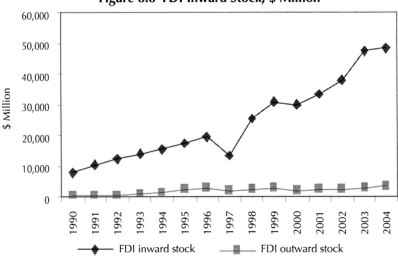

FDI = foreign direct investment, $ = US dollar.

Source: Bank of Thailand.

Figure 8.9 Inflows and Outflows of FDIs, $ Million

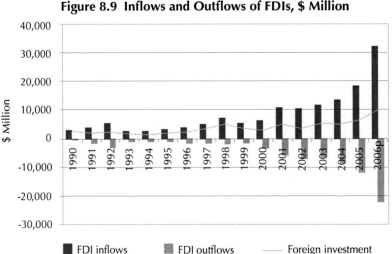

FDI = foreign direct investment, p = provisional, $ = US dollar.

Source: Bank of Thailand.

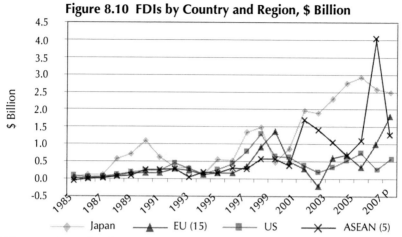

Figure 8.10 FDIs by Country and Region, $ Billion

ASEAN = Association of Southeast Asian Nations, EU = European Union, FDI = foreign direct investment, p = provisional, US = United States, $ = US dollar.

Note: 1) Prior to May 2004, EU comprises 15 countries: Austria, Belgium, Denmark, Finland, France, Germany, Greece, Ireland, Italy, Luxembourg, Netherlands, Portugal, Spain, Sweden, and United Kingdom. 2) Prior to 1999, ASEAN comprises 5 countries: Brunei Darussalam, Indonesia, Malaysia, Philippines, and Singapore.

Source: Bank of Thailand.

As shown in Figures 8.11 and 8.12, FDIs are concentrated in real estate, trade, machinery and transport equipment, electrical appliances, and chemicals.

Figure 8.11 Net FDI Flows by Sector, $ Million

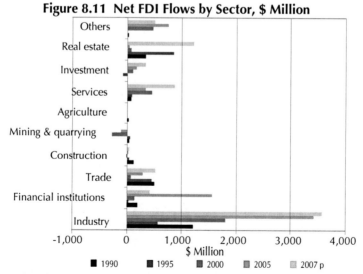

FDI = foreign direct investment, p = provisional, $ = US dollar.

Source: Bank of Thailand.

Figure 8.12 FDIs by Industrial Sector, $ Million

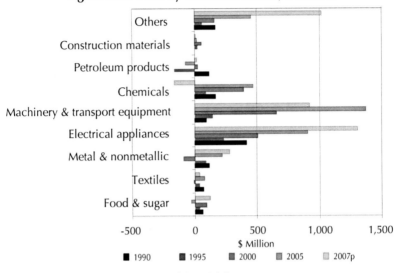

FDI = foreign direct investment, p = provisional, $ = US dollar.

Source: Bank of Thailand.

FDI inflows substantially increased from $29.3 billion to $80.2 billion from the pre-crisis (1990–1997) to post-crisis (1998–2005) period. The pattern of FDI inflows changed its structure post-crisis, with less in financial institutions, construction, and real estate and more in machinery and transport equipment, and services. After the crisis, FDI outflows increased from $11.6 billion to $42.6 billion, particularly concentrated on electrical appliances.

Looking at FDI inflows from East Asia, most come from Singapore; Japan; and Hong Kong, China. The post-crisis FDI inflows from Singapore increased by three times and from Japan doubled, while FDIs from the Philippines, Malaysia, Republic of Korea, and PRC also increased, although the total was insignificant. Most of the FDIs from South Asia originated from India and Pakistan, while Thai investments went only to India. Thai FDI outflows mainly went to Singapore; Japan; and Hong Kong, China.

Asian FDIs to Thailand shows different patterns; Japanese FDIs are concentrated in electrical appliances, and machinery and transport equipment; Republic of Korea invests primarily in electrical appliances and services; Hong Kong, China in services and real estate; Taipei,China in textiles and electrical appliances; PRC in the upstream textiles; Malaysia and Singapore in electrical appliances (pre-crisis) and transport and travel (post-crisis); India in financial institutions and services; Pakistan in trading; and Nepal and Bangladesh in housing and real estate.

As for FDI outflows to Asian countries, Thailand has to date largely invested in trade and electrical appliances in Singapore, in electrical appliances and machinery and transport equipment in Japan, and in the food sector in India. The pattern of Thai investment in Asia is largely Japanese in origin.

Foreign Direct Investment Approval Regime

The Board of Investment (BOI) is Thailand's main architect of the investment promotion policy (Box 8.1). Investment promotion policies are geared toward (i) enhancing the efficiency and effectiveness of tax privileges; (ii) providing small and medium-sized industries with various privileges; and (iii) giving high priority to investments in agriculture, projects related to technological and human resources development, public utilities and infrastructure, and environmental protection.

The BOI also pays special attention to low-income regions and areas with inadequate investment facilities. Privileges are dispensed according to the following criteria:

- The value added should not be less than 20% of sales revenue, except for projects in electronic products and parts and processed agricultural products.
- The ratio of liabilities to registered capital should not exceed 3:1 for a newly established project.
- Modern production processes and new machinery should be used, and in cases where old machinery is used its efficiency must first be certified by designated institutions.
- Adequate environmental protection systems should be installed.

The BOI offers tax and nontax incentives for promoted projects. Tax-based incentives include corporate income tax exemptions or reduction of import duties on machinery and raw materials, while nontax incentives include permission to bring in foreign workers, own land, and take or remit foreign currency abroad.

Export Processing Zones and Special Economic Zones

There are two categories of industrial estates (for further details see www. ieat.go.th): the (i) general industrial zones, and (ii) EPZs. The Industrial Estate Authority of Thailand offers privileges for industrial operators in EPZs. Incentives include exemption from the payment of (i) surcharge, import duty, value-added tax (VAT), and excise tax on imported machinery, components, and material imported for factory construction; (ii) surcharge

Box 8.1 Board of Investment Privileges by Investment Promotion Zone

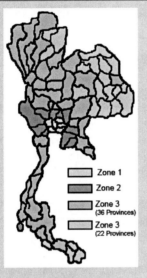

Zone 1
Zone 2
Zone 3
(36 Provinces)
Zone 3
(22 Provinces)

Zone 1: includes Bangkok, Samut Prakan, Samut Sakhon, Nakhon Pathom, Nonthaburi, and Pathum Thani (Bangkok and 5 provinces)

Zone 2: includes Ang Thong, Ayutthaya, Chachoengsao, Chon Buri, Kanchanaburi, Nakhon Nayok, Phuket, Ratchaburi, Rayong, Samut Songkhram, Saraburi, and Suphanburi (12 provinces)

Zone 3: encompasses the remaining 58 provinces

1. Project in Zone 1
- 50% reduction of import duty on machinery that is subject to import duty of not less than 10%.
- Corporate income tax exemption for 3 years for projects located within industrial estates or promoted industrial zones, provided that such a project with capital investment of 10 million baht (B) or more (excluding cost of land and working capital) obtains ISO 9000 or similar international standard certification within 2 years from its start-up date, otherwise the corporate income tax exemption will be reduced by 1 year.

2. Project in Zone 2
- 50% reduction of import duty on machinery that is subject to import duty of not less than 10%.
- Corporate income tax exemption for 3 years for projects located within industrial estates or promoted industrial zones, provided that such a project with capital investment of B10 million or more (excluding cost of land and working capital) obtains ISO 9000 or similar international standard certification within 2 years from its start-up date, otherwise the corporate income tax exemption will be reduced by 1 year.
- Exemption of import duty on raw or essential materials used in the manufacturing of export products for 1 year.

3. Project in Zone 3
- Exemption of import duty on machinery.

continued on next page

Box 8.1 (continued)

Box 8.1 Board of Investment Privileges by Investment Promotion Zone

- Corporate income tax exemption for 8 years provided that a project with capital investment of B10 million or more (excluding cost of land and working capital) obtains ISO 9000 or similar international standard certification within 2 years from its startup date, otherwise the corporate income tax exemption will be reduced by 1 year.
- Exemption of import duty on raw or essential materials used in the manufacturing of export products for 5 years.

Table 8.1 Foreign Direct Investments from South Asia; ASEAN+3; Hong Kong, China; and Taipei,China ($ Mn)

Item	Year	Inflows	Outflows	New Flows
South Asia	1990–1997	–	–	–
	1998–2005	37	14	23
	2006	–	–	–
	2007	–	–	–
ASEAN	1990–1997	6,507	4,649	1,857
	1998–2005	20,681	14,934	5,748
	2006	–	–	4,071
	2007	–	–	1,245
PRC + Japan + Republic of Korea	1990–1997	6,181	1,130	5,051
	1998–2005	12,699	5,445	7,254
	2006	–	–	2,678
	2007	–	–	2,536
Hong Kong, China + Taipei,China	1990–1997	5,865	2,123	3,743
	1998–2005	3,930	1,288	2,642
	2006	–	–	(53)
	2007	–	–	534
World Total	1990–1997	29,295	11,610	17,684
	1998–2005p	80,149	42,640	37,509
	2006	–	–	10,031
	2007	–	–	7,451

ASEAN+3 = Association of Southeast Asian Nations plus People's Republic of China (PRC), Japan, and Republic of Korea; p = provisional; $ Mn = millions of US dollars; – = data not available; ( ) = negative value.

Source: Bank of Thailand.

Table 8.2 Foreign Direct Investments from ASEAN Member Countries, $ Mn

Item	Year	Inflows	Outflows	New Flows
Indonesia	1990–1997	57.9	0.9	57.0
	1998–2005	22.1	2.9	19.2
	2006	–	–	(5.3)
	2007	–	–	6.7
Malaysia	1990–1997	82.4	20.4	62.0
	1998–2005	276.4	99.1	177.3
	2006	–	–	326.7
	2007	–	–	245.8
Philippines	1990–1997	–	–	17.3
	1998–2005	232.8	17.7	215.1
	2006	–	–	0.8
	2007	–	–	6.6
Singapore	1990–1997	6,346.2	4,626.1	1,720.1
	1998–2005	20,109.6	14,807.9	5,301.7
	2006	–	–	3,722.1
	2007	–	–	978.4
ASEAN	1990–1997	6,506.6	4,649.4	1,857.2
	1998–2005	20,681.4	14,933.8	5,747.6
	2006	–	–	4,071.1
	2007	–	–	1,244.5

ASEAN = Association of Southeast Asian Nations, $ Mn = millions of US dollars; – = data not available,
( ) = negative value.

Source: Bank of Thailand.

Table 8.3 Foreign Direct Investments from ASEAN+3; Hong Kong, China; and Taipei,China ($ Mn)

Item	Year	Inflows	Outflows	New Flows
PRC	1990–1997	36.9	32.2	4.7
	1998–2005	81.9	23.6	58.2
	2006	–	–	43.9
	2007	–	–	8.5
Japan	1990–1997	5,999.2	1,089.0	4910.2
	1998–2005	12,344.1	5,390.1	6,954.1
	2006	–	–	2,583.6
	2007	–	–	2,492.2

continued on next page

Table 8.3 (continued)

Item	Year	Inflows	Outflows	New Flows
Korea, Republic of	1990–1997	144.7	9.0	135.6
	1998–2005	273.0	31.3	241.6
	2006	–	–	50.8
	2007	–	–	35.6
Hong Kong, China	1990–1997	4,604.0	1,837.8	2,766.2
	1998–2005	2,815.6	1,020.4	1,795.2
	2006	–	–	(16.5)
	2007	–	–	439.9
Taipei,China	1990–1997	1,261.4	284.9	976.6
	1998–2005	1,114.5	267.7	846.9
	2006	–	–	(80.1)
	2007	–	–	85.2

ASEAN+3 = Association of Southeast Asian Nations plus People's Republic of China (PRC), Japan, and Republic of Korea; $ Mn = millions of US dollars; – = data not available; ( ) = negative value.

Source: Bank of Thailand.

Table 8.4 Foreign Direct Investments from South Asia, $ Million

Item	Bangladesh	India	Nepal	Pakistan	Sri Lanka	South Asia
	1998–2005	1998–2005	1998–2005	1998–2005	1998–2005	1998–2005
Inflows	1.0	20.1	0.6	12.5	3.1	37.1
Outflows	–	13.7	–	0.3	0.2	14.2
Net	1.0	6.4	0.6	12.2	2.8	23.0

– = data not available, $ = of US dollars.

Source: Bank of Thailand.

under the law on promotion of investment import duty, VAT, and excise tax on raw materials; (iii) export duty, VAT, and excise tax for exported goods; and (iv) taxes and duties for local goods utilized for production.[2]

The EPZs are highly concentrated in central and eastern provinces, while there are only a few places in the north and south. No EPZs are located in the northeast.[3]

---

[2] See: www.ieat.go.th/menu02/2.1.30.5.0.0.0.0.0.0_en.php3

[3] Central Region Industrial Estates at Baan Wa High-Tech (Ayudthaya Province); Bangpa-In (Ayudthaya Province); Bangpoo (Samut Prakarn Province); and Lat Krabang (Bangkok). Eastern Region Industrial Estates at Laem Chabang (Chonburi Province); Hemaraj (Chonburi Province); and Gate-Way City (Chachoengsao Province). Northern Region Industrial Estates at Phichit (Phichit Province); and Northern Region Industrial Estate (Lam Phun Province). Southern Region Industrial Estate at Southern Export Processing Zone (EPZ) (Song Khla Province).

Table 8.5 Investment Promotion Certificates Issued, 2003–2007

Economy	2003		2004		2005		2006		2007	
	Number of Projects	Value ($ Bn)	Number of Projects	Value ($ Bn)	Number of Projects	Value ($ Bn)	Number of Projects	Value ($ Bn)	Number of Projects	Value ($ Bn)
Total FDI (Foreign no less than 10%)	484	4.01	654	6.50	718	9.41	719	9.02	781	10.27
100% foreign	231	1.73	324	2.74	349	2.49	364	2.42	405	4.33
Japan	236	2.02	334	2.68	348	4.06	317	2.37	332	3.75
Taipei,China	43	0.33	53	0.24	44	0.14	60	0.49	53	0.26
Hong Kong, China	10	0.06	25	0.17	14	0.24	22	0.10	19	0.13
Korea, Republic of	36	0.05	46	0.19	27	0.04	25	0.09	40	0.15
China, People's Republic of	5	0.01	11	0.09	11	0.03	12	0.04	16	0.07
India	10	0.04	7	0.01	12	0.01	13	0.01	13	0.10
ASEAN-4	66	0.34	93	0.73	120	0.61	80	0.92	109	1.24
Singapore	41	0.23	60	0.52	81	0.43	57	0.45	75	0.76
Malaysia	25	0.10	27	0.19	35	0.16	23	0.46	29	0.36
Indonesia	–	0.00	2	0.01	2	0.01	3	0.01	4	0.12
Philippines	–	0.00	4	0.02	2	0.00	1	0.02	1	0.00

ASEAN = Association of Southeast Asian Nations, FDI = foreign direct investment, – = data not available, $ Bn = billions of US dollars, % = percent.

Source: Thailand's Board of Investment.

The Board of Investment and Its Performance

According to the promoted projects by the BOI during the period 2003–2005, the total value of FDI projects where foreign shares were no less than 10% increased more than twofold. FDI projects that were wholly foreign increased from 68.7 billion baht (B) to B102 billion. Although the US and the EU have invested a significant amount of capital, the net flows of FDI from these two regions are not as stable as Japan. More than half of the total FDIs still come from Japan. Meanwhile Singapore is the major FDI source from ASEAN as it accounts for nearly 80% of total FDIs from the ASEAN-4.

Japanese investment projects approved by BOI are found in metal products and machinery, electric and electronic products, chemicals, and paper. The Japanese investments have mostly located in Zone 2 since 2000, while the locations were quite equally distributed before then. Production of one third of the 300-plus Japanese firms is geared toward exports.

Although total FDIs from the PRC are rather small compared to Japan, it is expected that FDIs from the PRC will increase under the China–ASEAN FTA. FDIs from the PRC are scattered among several industries; for instance, metal products and machinery saw PRC investments of $37 million in 2000, while the textile industry saw investments of $116 million in 2001. Total FDIs from the PRC was $59 million in 2000 and $198 million in 2001. In 2003, FDIs were largely directed toward agriculture, with investments reaching $19 million out of the total PRC FDIs of $35 million. In 2004, FDIs in chemicals and paper industries shared nearly 50% of total PRC FDIs to Thailand.

Merchandise Trade Policy with Emphasis on East and South Asia

Direction and Composition of Trade

After the financial crisis of 1997/98, the structure of trading partners changed considerably.

Japan; US; Singapore; Taipei,China; Malaysia; Germany; PRC; Republic of Korea; and Oman were the top import sources of Thailand in 1998. In 2005, the United Arab Emirates, Saudi Arabia, and Australia are ranked among the top countries, replacing Taipei,China; Germany; and Oman. More importantly, European countries such as Germany, France, and United Kingdom (UK) have been losing shares. The share of the US dropped by almost half. The PRC's share has risen more than twofold since the crisis and imports from ASEAN countries, except for Singapore, have increased as well.

Although the US remains the most important market for the Thai exports, its share substantially declined from 22.3% in 1998 to 12.6%

in 2007. The European market—especially Netherlands, UK, Germany, France, Belgium, and Italy—also became less important. Markets in ASEAN have continuously grown well, except for Singapore. While Japan remains the major export destination for Thai products, the PRC and Hong Kong, China are becoming increasingly important as well. For instance, Thailand's exports to the PRC have risen almost threefold since 1997.

Regarding the trade between Thailand and South Asia, Thailand has a persistent and increasing trade surplus with Bangladesh, Pakistan, and Sri Lanka throughout the years. The major exports to Bangladesh consist of (i) manmade fibers, cotton and yarn, and manmade filaments and fabric; (ii) plastic, iron, and steel products; (iii) salt and sugar; and (iv) machinery and electrical machinery. The sole import from Bangladesh is fertilizer. Fish, seafood, and vegetable textile fibers were significant imports in the past, but their values have since dropped. To Pakistan, Thailand's main exports are vehicles, organic chemicals, machinery, plastics, and manmade fibers, while the imports are cotton and yarn fibers, fish and seafood, and organic chemicals. Thai exports with strong potential include machinery, synthetic fibers, and vehicles which nearly doubled in 2005. In the past, Thailand imported some machinery from Sri Lanka, but precious stones are now the only important Sri Lankan import to Thailand. Thai exports to Sri Lanka that have a strong potential for future growth are synthetic fibers, plastics, and salt.

The high export growth of (i) machinery and electrical machinery; (ii) plastic, iron, and steel; and (iii) mineral fuel and oil, gave Thailand a trade surplus with India in 2005. Imports from India consist of precious stones, iron and steel products, copper, organic chemicals, and machinery. The precious stones, mostly from Mumbai and Jaipur, are used as raw materials in Thai gems and jewelry, which are among the top Thai exports. Copper, machinery, automobiles and parts, and certain types of iron and steel products also have high export potential to Thailand. Iron and steel products are likely to receive more attention because of the sizable investments made by India's Tata Steel in recent years.

Thai imports from Nepal are minimal and mostly consist of hides and skins. Thailand exports several items to Nepal, including manmade fibers, knitted apparel, electrical and other machinery, and plastics. Perfume and cosmetic items are exports with strong potential.

Import Protection

Average Tariff Rates. The tariff rates in Thailand are reported under the 7-digit Harmonized System (HS) in four different ways: (i) as specifically announced by the Custom Acts; (ii) at the applied rate; (iii) at World Trade Organization (WTO) bound rates; and (iv) at concession rates under the

Table 8.6 Export Share by Economy (Unit), %

	Country	1998	1999	2000	2001	2002	2003	2004	2005	2006	2007
1	Japan	13.71	14.13	14.70	15.26	14.60	14.19	13.98	13.60	12.63	11.82
2	China, People's Republic of	3.24	3.18	4.07	4.41	5.22	7.11	7.37	8.26	9.04	9.75
3	United States	22.33	21.64	21.36	20.25	19.82	16.99	16.06	15.32	14.99	12.62
4	Malaysia	3.27	3.63	4.07	4.19	4.16	4.84	5.50	5.25	5.10	5.12
5	Singapore	8.62	8.68	8.71	8.07	8.15	7.31	7.28	6.93	6.44	6.27
6	Hong Kong, China	5.11	5.10	5.05	5.07	5.41	5.39	5.12	5.56	5.52	5.64
7	Australia	1.80	2.25	2.35	2.09	2.41	2.70	2.56	2.86	3.35	3.76
8	Taipei;China	3.20	3.50	3.49	2.95	2.89	3.23	2.70	2.45	2.59	2.18
9	United Arab Emirates	1.01	0.97	0.85	0.98	1.05	0.94	1.00	1.06	1.14	1.45
10	Indonesia	1.81	1.66	1.95	2.10	2.47	2.83	3.33	3.59	2.55	3.12
11	Korea, Republic of	1.15	1.56	1.83	1.89	2.05	1.98	1.93	2.04	2.06	1.95
12	Germany	2.86	2.50	2.38	2.42	2.25	2.24	1.87	1.81	1.79	1.89
13	Saudi Arabia	0.65	0.57	0.43	0.54	0.58	0.54	0.64	0.91	0.96	0.90
14	United Kingdom	3.89	3.57	3.43	3.58	3.51	3.22	3.14	2.53	2.62	2.33
15	Philippines	1.41	1.59	1.57	1.78	1.87	2.02	1.90	1.85	1.98	1.91
16	Viet Nam	1.09	0.98	1.22	1.23	1.39	1.58	1.94	2.13	2.37	2.50
17	India	0.52	0.60	0.72	0.74	0.61	0.80	0.95	1.38	1.40	1.75
18	Netherlands	4.00	3.76	3.26	3.13	2.78	2.95	2.69	2.50	2.50	2.50
19	Myanmar	0.64	0.68	0.73	0.55	0.48	0.55	0.63	0.64	0.58	0.63
20	Italy	1.29	1.22	1.22	1.04	1.03	1.19	1.39	1.13	1.15	1.21

% = percent.

Source: Ministry of Commerce Thailand.

Table 8.7 Import Share by Region, %

Region	1998	1999	2000	2001	2002	2003	2004	2005	2006	2007
ASEAN	**15.08**	**15.84**	**16.64**	**16.24**	**16.84**	**16.64**	**16.84**	**18.30**	**18.33**	**17.91**
Brunei Darussalam	0.05	0.29	0.79	0.61	0.70	0.43	0.41	0.17	0.10	0.08
Cambodia	0.06	0.03	0.01	0.02	0.02	0.02	0.03	0.03	0.03	0.03
Indonesia	2.09	2.20	2.08	2.20	2.41	2.34	2.46	2.65	2.67	2.85
Lao PDR	0.07	0.11	0.12	0.14	0.14	0.14	0.12	0.19	0.40	0.34
Malaysia	5.12	4.99	5.40	5.00	5.63	5.99	5.88	6.85	6.58	6.16
Myanmar	0.15	0.22	0.41	1.30	1.40	1.20	1.43	1.51	1.80	1.64
Philippines	1.46	1.62	1.77	1.82	1.67	1.78	1.64	1.59	1.64	1.53
Singapore	5.55	5.92	5.51	4.61	4.49	4.31	4.40	4.55	4.41	4.49
VietNam	0.55	0.46	0.53	0.53	0.37	0.44	0.46	0.75	0.70	0.79
Plus 3	**31.39**	**32.80**	**33.68**	**31.75**	**34.58**	**35.94**	**36.17**	**34.76**	**34.48**	**35.65**
China, People's Republic of	4.25	4.95	5.45	5.99	7.62	8.00	8.66	9.44	10.56	11.59
Hong Kong, China	1.78	1.40	1.43	1.33	1.41	1.42	1.41	1.27	1.20	1.03
Japan	23.66	24.33	24.73	22.33	23.04	24.09	23.71	22.03	19.93	20.28
Korea, Republic of	3.49	3.52	3.50	3.43	3.91	3.85	3.80	3.29	3.98	3.78
SAARC	**1.27**	**1.19**	**1.28**	**1.29**	**1.38**	**1.34**	**1.30**	**1.19**	**1.38**	**1.56**
Bangladesh	0.07	0.08	0.07	0.05	0.04	0.04	0.01	0.02	0.03	0.01
India	1.00	0.90	1.00	1.09	1.20	1.16	1.21	1.08	1.26	1.48
Nepal	0.00	0.00	0.00	0.00	0.00	0.00	0.00	0.00	0.00	0.00
Pakistan	0.11	0.09	0.09	0.09	0.13	0.12	0.06	0.07	0.08	0.05
Sri Lanka	0.09	0.11	0.12	0.06	0.01	0.01	0.01	0.01	0.02	0.03
Taipei,China	**5.21**	**4.69**	**4.68**	**4.20**	**4.49**	**4.26**	**4.22**	**3.81**	**3.96**	**4.10**

ASEAN = Association of Southeast Asian Nations, Lao PDR = Lao People's Democratic Republic, SAARC = South Asian Association for Regional Cooperation, % = percent.

Source: Ministry of Commerce Thailand.

Table 8.8 Export Share by Region, %

Region	1998	1999	2000	2001	2002	2003	2004	2005	2006	2007
ASEAN	**18.16**	**18.60**	**19.36**	**19.33**	**19.91**	**20.60**	**22.01**	**21.99**	**20.83**	**21.36**
Brunei Darussalam	0.09	0.07	0.06	0.06	0.06	0.05	0.06	0.06	0.06	0.06
Cambodia	0.55	0.61	0.50	0.72	0.76	0.86	0.75	0.83	0.95	0.89
Indonesia	1.81	1.66	1.95	2.10	2.47	2.83	3.33	3.59	2.55	3.12
Lao PDR	0.69	0.70	0.55	0.63	0.58	0.57	0.60	0.70	0.78	0.86
Malaysia	3.27	3.63	4.07	4.19	4.16	4.84	5.50	5.25	5.10	5.12
Myanmar	0.64	0.68	0.73	0.55	0.48	0.55	0.63	0.64	0.58	0.63
Philippines	1.41	1.59	1.57	1.78	1.87	2.02	1.90	1.85	1.98	1.91
Singapore	8.62	8.68	8.71	8.07	8.15	7.31	7.28	6.93	6.44	6.27
Viet Nam	1.09	0.98	1.22	1.23	1.39	1.58	1.94	2.13	2.37	2.50
Plus 3	**18.10**	**18.87**	**20.61**	**21.56**	**21.87**	**23.27**	**23.28**	**23.90**	**23.73**	**23.51**
China, People's Republic of	3.24	3.18	4.07	4.41	5.22	7.11	7.37	8.26	9.04	9.75
Hong Kong, China	5.11	5.10	5.05	5.07	5.41	5.39	5.12	5.56	5.52	5.64
Japan	13.71	14.13	14.70	15.26	14.60	14.19	13.98	13.60	12.63	11.82
Korea, Republic of	1.15	1.56	1.83	1.89	2.05	1.98	1.93	2.04	2.06	1.95
SAARC	**1.32**	**1.43**	**1.62**	**1.64**	**1.53**	**1.79**	**2.01**	**2.47**	**2.50**	**2.72**
Bangladesh	0.25	0.28	0.32	0.36	0.34	0.34	0.39	0.36	0.36	0.34
India	0.52	0.60	0.72	0.74	0.61	0.80	0.95	1.38	1.40	1.75
Nepal	0.04	0.03	0.04	0.05	0.03	0.03	0.04	0.02	0.02	0.03
Pakistan	0.28	0.29	0.29	0.27	0.34	0.42	0.45	0.53	0.50	0.43
Sri Lanka	0.24	0.23	0.25	0.22	0.22	0.20	0.19	0.18	0.23	0.18
Taipei,China	**3.20**	**3.50**	**3.49**	**2.95**	**2.89**	**3.23**	**2.70**	**2.45**	**2.59**	**2.18**

ASEAN = Association of Southeast Asian Nations, Lao PDR = Lao People's Democratic Republic, SAARC = South Asian Association for Regional Cooperation, % = percent.

Source: Ministry of Commerce Thailand.

Common Effective Preferential Tariff (CEPT) scheme, the ASEAN Integrated System of Preference (AISP), the Global System of Trade Preference (GSTP), and the Customs Tariff Decree B.E. 2530 (1987). The Minister of Finance can modify the tariff rate with cabinet approval. Moreover, the Minister of Finance can impose an import surcharge of no more than 50% of the tariff rate.

The tariff rates have been reduced four times since 1999, with the bound tariff lines being 72% of all tariff lines in 2003 and the average applied tariff rate, being set at 14.7% (Figure 8.13). While agricultural products (HS 01–24) have the simple average applied rate of 25.4%, the average applied tariff rate for industrial products (HS 25–97) is 12.9%. Tariffs on all agricultural products are bound, except for salt, fuel, fertilizer, transport equipment, rubber products, and iron and steel products. Higher tariff rates are applied to certain products such as tobacco, vegetables, processed foods, transport equipment, shoes, hats, and weapons. The tariff escalation also results in higher costs of imported intermediate and final goods. Tariff escalation can be observed in products such as processed foods, leather products, wood products, paper and pulp, petroleum and coal products,

Figure 8.13 Simple Average Applied MFN Tariff Rates, by HS Section, 2003 and 2006

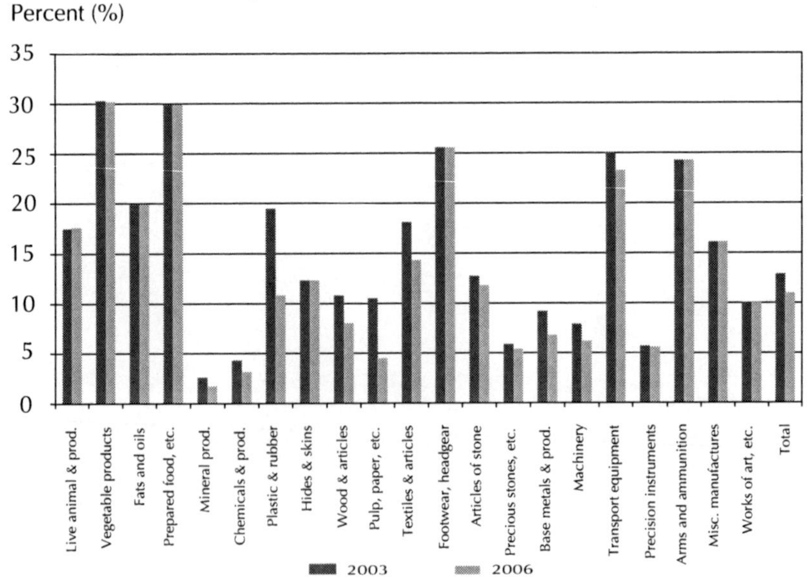

Percent (%)

AVE = ad valorem equivalent, HS = Harmonized System of commodity trade classification, MFN = most favored nation, Misc. = miscellaneous, prod. = products, % = percent.

Note: Including AVEs for *non-ad valorem* rate, as available. Where AVEs are not available, the *ad valorem* part of alternate rates is used. Excluding in-quota rates.

Source: World Trade Organization Secretariat calculations, based on data provided by the Thai authorities.

nonferrous metals, and iron and steel. The WTO expressed concerns about the unbound tariff rates being about 25% of all tariff lines.

Domestic Nontariff Barriers, Especially Affecting East and South Asia Trade. As reported in the WTO's Trade Policy Review of Thailand, import licensing measures and import quotas are still applied on a number of products. The licenses are used for national security, health, and environmental reasons. Non-automatic licensing is applied on 23 items such as agricultural items (under the tariff quota), and processed goods including fish meal, raw silk and silk yarn, jute and kenaf, gunny bags woven of jute or kenaf, used diesel engines, certain buses, chainsaws, used cars and tractors, used motorcycles, marble, plastic waste, building stones, coins in size and weight similar to official coins, and certain antiques or objects of art. For certain garments, intaglio printing machines, and color photocopying machines, automatic licensing applies.

Thailand's Anti-Dumping and Countervailing Act, which provides the legal basis for antidumping and countervailing measures, is implemented by the Department of Foreign Trade. It is tasked to conduct the investigations and make preliminary determinations, including calculations of duty rates. Provisional measures will be imposed with the affirmative determination of dumping and injury to domestic producers.

As of 2003, Thailand imposed countervailing duties on six products from WTO members (Indonesia; Japan; Republic of Korea; and Taipei,China) and three cases of the imported products from non-WTO members. Countervailing duties were also imposed for steel products (particularly from India) in 2003.

Table 8.9 Antidumping Measures, 31 December 2006

Product	Country/customs territory	Date of imposition	Definitive duty in force (c.i.f.), %
H-section	PRC	10 Oct 2002	27.81
Glass block	Indonesia	05 Aug 2005	14.27–50.59
Cold-rolled carbon steel, sheet and strip in coils and cut to length	Kazakhstan	25 Jan 2003	26.36
	Russian Federation	25 Jan 2003	35.80–64.70
Flat-rolled products of stainless steel	Taipei,China	13 Mar 2003	0.00–33.99
	European Community	13 Mar 2003	10.02–25.57
	Japan	13 Mar 2003	0.00–50.92
	Republic of Korea	13 Mar 2003	50.99
Flat hot-rolled steel in coils and not in coils	Algeria	27 May 03	33.26
	Argentina	27 May 03	37.94–53.09

continued on next page

Table 8.9 (continued)

Product	Country/customs territory	Date of imposition	Definitive duty in force (c.i.f.), %
	Taipei,China	27 May 03	3.45–25.15
	India	27 May 03	26.81–31.92
	Indonesia	27 May 03	24.48
	Japan	27 May 03	3.22–36.25
	Kazakhstan	27 May 03	109.25
	Republic of Korea	27 May 03	13.96
	Romania	27 May 03	27.95
	Russian Federation	27 May 03	24.20–35.17
	Slovak Republic	27 May 03	51.95
	South Africa	27 May 03	128.11
	Ukraine	27 May 03	30.45–67.69
	Venezuela	27 May 03	78.44
Citric acid	PRC	09 Jan 2004	28.70–38.10
Cathode ray tubes	Malaysia	22 Oct 2005	7.00

CIF = cost, insurance and freight; PRC = People's Republic of China; % = percent.

Source: Trade Policy Reviews, World Trade Organization.

Table 8.10 Structure of MFN Tariffs in Thailand, %

		2003	2006	Final bound[a]
1	Bound tariff lines (% of all tariff lines)	73.7	73.7	73.7
2	Simple average applied rate	13.0	11.0	27.0
	Agricultural products (HS 01–24)	25.3	24.2	32.3
	Industrial products (HS 25–97)	11.0	8.7	26.3
	WTO agricultural products	25.0	25.0	34.9
	WTO non-agricultural products	11.2	8.8	25.8
	Textiles and clothing	18.6	14.7	28.9
3	Tariff quotas (% of all tariff lines)	1.0	1.0	1.0
4	Domestic tariff "peaks" (% of all tariff lines)[b]	3.9	3.9	0.5
5	International tariff "peaks" (% of all tariff lines)[c]	30.3	25.2	65.4
6	Overall standard deviation of tariff rates	14.3	14.0	14.1
7	Coefficient of variation of tariff rates	1.1	1.3	0.5

continued on next page

Table 8.10 (continued)

		2003	2006	Final bound[a]
8	Duty free tariff lines (% of all tariff lines)	4.1	18.5	2.2
9	Non-*ad valorem* tariffs (% of all tariff lines)	23.1	22.5	18.9
10	Non-*ad valorem* tariffs with no AVEs (% of all tariff lines)	20.3	19.9	18.8
11	Nuisance applied rates (% of all tariff lines)[d]	21.4	12.1	0.1

AVE = ad valorem equivalent, HS = Harmonized System of commodity trade classification, MFN = most favored nation, WTO = World Trade Organization, % = percent.

[a] Implementation of the Uruguay Round was achieved in 2005. Calculations on bound average are based on 4,059 bound tariff lines (representing 73.7% of total lines).
[b] Domestic tariff "peaks" are defined as those exceeding three times the overall simple average applied rate.
[c] International tariff "peaks" are defined as those exceeding 15%.
[d] Nuisance rates are those greater than zero, but less than or equal to 2%.

Note: Calculations include AVEs for non-*ad valorem* rates provided by the authorities to the WTO, as available . In case of non-availability, the *ad valorem* part of alternate rates is taken into account. Calculations do not include in-quota rates.

Source: WTO calculations, based on data provided by the authorities of Thailand.

Export Promotion

Main Instruments for Export Promotion, Geographical Focus, and Resources. There are several government organizations that play a role in export promotion; EXIM Bank is one among them. Its facilities consist of long-term credit for export of capital goods, financial facilities for overseas construction contracts, export credit insurance, and pre-shipment financing for SMEs. Some of these financial facilities are not available at commercial banks, while others are provided as supplements to services at commercial banks. EXIM Bank also provides services that facilitate imports or investment in order to enhance Thailand's export capabilities and promote overseas investment that will help build Thailand's commercial base.

To promote international trade, international trade payment facilitation schemes such as bilateral payment arrangements (BPAs) have been introduced to reduce the reliance on the use of hard currencies in international trade settlements. EXIM Bank will be responsible for the international account settlements with other member countries by netting the Thai importers' bill with exporter's account receivables. Currently, Malaysia, Myanmar, Bangladesh, and Iran are the members of BPAs, while agreements with Cambodia, Indonesia, Lao People's Democratic Republic (Lao PDR), Pakistan, and Philippines are under negotiation. Other services of the bank include confirmation of letters of credit and a revolving trade finance facility.

EXIM Bank also provides export credit insurance to protect exporters from the risks of nonpayment by buyers. Importantly, the bank also promotes Thai investment overseas by giving high priority to Thai firms that are set to benefit from the trade liberalization due to various economic cooperation initiatives such as ASEAN Free Trade Agreement (AFTA), Bay of Bengal Initiative for Multi-Sectoral Technical and Economic Cooperation (BIMSTEC), and the Ayeyawady–Chao Phraya–Mekong Economic Cooperation Strategy (ACMECS).

For medium- and long-term export insurance facilities (against nonpayment from Bangladesh and Qatar), EXIM Bank approved medium-term insurance worth B1,583 million ($38.6 million) in 2005, compared to B135 million ($3.4 million) in 2004, and long-tem insurance worth B1,448 million ($35.3 million) in 2005.

Table 8.11 Business Volume of Facilities for Exporters and Export-Related Business in 2004 and 2005

Item	Working capital loan			Term loan for business expansion			Merchant marine financing		
	2005 ($ Mn)	2004 ($ Mn)	Change (%)	2005 ($ Mn)	2004 ($ Mn)	Change (%)	2005 ($ Mn)	2004 ($ Mn)	Change (%)
New approvals during the year	306.4	315.8	(3.0)	112.4	111.3	1.0	55.4	53.3	3.9
• Credit	287.5	297.2	(3.3)	112.4	111.3	1.0	55.4	53.3	3.9
• Guarantee	18.9	18.6	1.4						
Approvals as of year-end	1,607.6	1,506.0	6.7	312.9	266.2	17.5	145.0	111.2	30.5
• Credit	1,534.6	1,446.2	6.1	312.9	266.2	17.5	145.0	111.2	30.5
• Guarantee	73.0	59.8	22.1						
Outstanding credit facilities as of year-end	725.9	627.6	15.7	231.2	196.1	17.9	146.6	107.5	36.4
Guarantee obligations as of year-end	41.9	66.2	(36.7)						
Business turnover during the year	2,936.2	2,798.0	4.9						

$ Mn = millions of US dollars, % = percent, ( ) = negative value.

Source: EXIM Bank of Thailand.

Figure 8.14 Value of Exports under Medium- and Long-Term Export Insurance by Country, %

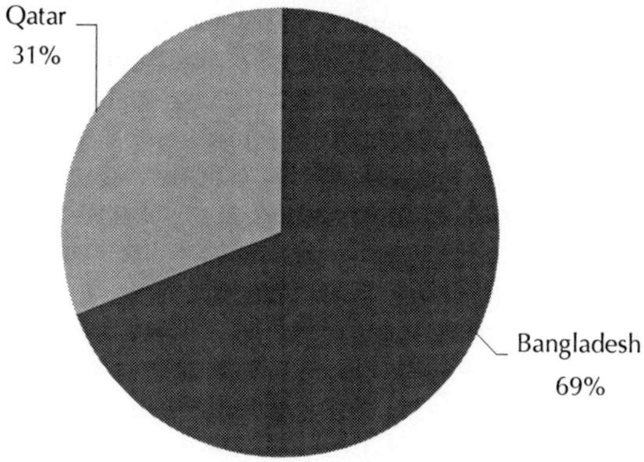

Qatar 31%

Bangladesh 69%

% = percent.

Source: EXIM Bank of Thailand.

Efficiency of Export Promotion with Emphasis on East and South Asia Trade

The Department of Export Promotion (DEP) under the Ministry of Commerce is responsible for promoting the export of both Thai goods and services and expanding Thailand's market share abroad. DEP is also responsible for supporting the distribution network at the international level, hosting exhibitions domestically and abroad, arranging training programs for exporters, developing new products, and serving as a one-stop service for export information and documentation.

Thailand and Regional Trade Agreements

Thailand is currently involved in negotiations toward several bilateral trade agreements. An agreement for closer economic relations with Australia was initiated in May 2002, and was later changed to the Thailand–Australia Free Trade Agreement (TAFTA). The agreement covers goods, services, and investment. Following the completion of TAFTA, an agreement was also concluded with New Zealand in May 2004 and the agreement was concluded in November 2004. The Thailand–New Zealand Closer Economic Partnership Agreement has been implemented since July 2005 and includes liberalization in goods, services, investment, and trade facilitation measures such as e-commerce, intellectual property rights, government procurement, and competitive policy. There is also joint cooperation on sanitary and phytosanitary measures.

A framework agreement was also signed with India in October 2003, which provides for the elimination of tariffs by 2010, and a Closer Economic Partnership Agreement (JTEP) with Japan in December of the same year. The Thailand–India agreement contains an early harvest program that consists of 82 items subject to tariff elimination in September 2006. Tariffs on products classified as normal will be eliminated in 2010. Services and investment issues, as well as information and communications technology, tourism, healthcare, banking, and construction are still under negotiation. The coverage of JTEP includes trade liberalization in goods, services, and investment. The agreement is expected to reduce and/or eliminate tariffs on more than 90% of tradable items, while allowing Thai investors to set up service businesses in Japan. The agreement also provides for technical cooperation in processed foods, iron and steel, textiles, and automobiles.

In December 2002, Thailand signed an FTA with Bahrain, and a Closer Economic Partnership Agreement in Peru. Negotiations for a Trade and Investment Framework Agreement between the US and Thailand started in 2004. The agreement is comprehensive as it covers the liberalization in goods, services, and investment, and negotiations on sanitary and phytosanitary measures, technical barriers to trade, rules of origin, financial services, telecommunications, government procurement, competitive policy, intellectual property rights, e-commerce, and trade facilitation. The last round of negotiations took place in January 2006 and further negotiations are being scheduled.

Thailand is also a member of AFTA, where tariffs will be eliminated in 2010.[4] ASEAN, as a regional grouping, has entered into several regional arrangements, such as framework agreements toward FTAs with the PRC in 2002 and the Republic of Korea in 2005. In the China–ASEAN FTA, an early harvest program has been implemented since January 2004 for products in HS Chapters 1–8. However, Thailand and the PRC reached a bilateral agreement to further accelerate the tariff reduction for products under the HS chapters 7 and 8 in October 2003. Sensitive products, however, will see tariffs eliminated over a longer period. Additionally, new ASEAN members receive special and differential treatment, and are thus given an extended transition period for tariff elimination.

In the case of the Korea–ASEAN FTA, Thailand has raised some objections regarding the exclusion of rice in the list of products to be subjected to regional liberalization. Thailand's request for some compensation due to this exclusion has not received a positive response from the Republic of Korea.

---

[4] Cambodia, Lao People's Democratic Republic (Lao PDR), Myanmar, and Viet Nam will eliminate their tariffs by 2015.

Thailand has also requested the inclusion of some agricultural products and processed foods in return for opening its markets for automobiles and parts, iron sheets, and televisions, and limiting the sensitive list to 10% of its total import value from the Republic of Korea.

For BIMSTEC, liberalization also follows normal and fast tracks. The fast track will include 10% of all 6-digit HS products, while the normal track will have tariff reductions on the zero-tariff and 5%-tariff categories. A negative list is applied to no more than 20% of each country's items, and the list will be used for further negotiations on tariff reductions. The first round of negotiations with the European Free Trade Area (EFTA) began in October 2005 and the comprehensive agreement was proposed with flexibility provisions. Thailand proposed setting up a contact point to prevent problems with sanitary and phytosanitary measures and technical barriers to trade, as well as to create technical cooperation that will allow Thai producers to comply with EFTA's high standards.

Tables 8.12 to 8.15 summarize the provisions of the FTAs that Thailand has implemented with Australia, New Zealand, India, ASEAN plus the PRC, and BIMSTEC. BIMSTEC provisions are still under negotiation.

Recent Free Trade Agreements and Trends in Trade and Investment.
FTAs are a growing trend in Asia. Thailand has completed negotiations and implemented the FTA tariff reductions with East Asian countries and India. Additionally, Thailand has also negotiated with BIMSTEC members for deeper integration and has taken part in ASEAN's agreements with India, Japan, and Republic of Korea.

The ASEAN FTA with the PRC was implemented in October 2003 (the early harvest program) and deepened in June 2005 (normal-track tariff reductions). However, concerns about the nontariff measures remain, in particular sanitary and phytosanitary measures governing the trade in agricultural products. Direct investment flows between the PRC and Thailand are in their nascent stages. FDIs from the PRC are scattered in several industries such as chemical and paper, metal products, and the upstream of textiles industry while FDIs from Thailand to the PRC are in areas such as sugar, processed foods, retailing, and wholesale outlets.

A Thailand–India Free Trade Area agreement is under negotiation but the early harvest program, with a total of 82 items, has been in place since September 2004. The export from Thailand of the program's 82 items increased sharply in 2005 (see Table 8.16)

In November 2007, Japan and Thailand Economic Partnership Agreement was implemented with the tariff reduction of more than 90% of traded items. Moreover, Thai entrepreneurs are now able to set up service business in Japan. Those services includes spa, restaurant, elderly care, and automobile repair shops.

Table 8.12 Summary of Thailand's Free Trade Agreements with Australia

Country and coverage	Negotiation approach	Trade in goods	Services and investment	Rules of origin	Cooperation
Australia 1 January 2005 Comprehensive agreement in trade in goods, services, and investment as well as sectoral cooperation	Reciprocal basis in compliance with WTO. Consider the differences in economic development resulting in special and differential treatment. Requests and offers approach for negation in goods and services.	Australia: 0% tariff for 83% of tariff lines as of January 2005 and 0% for the rest in 2010 and 2015. Thailand: 0% tariff for 49% of tariff lines and 0% for the rest in 2015. Sensitive items for Thailand are beef, pork, milk, butter, tea, and coffee; and for Australia are textiles and garments. Tariff elimination will be within 10, 15, and 20 years with safeguard measure to some items.	Australia allows for 100% investment in all business except newspaper, broadcast, air transportation, and airports. If the capital investment is over $10 million, permission is needed. Thailand allows Australia to be the major shareholder (up to 60%) for specific business such as exhibition center and mining.	Wholly obtained, substantial transformation, and regional value content (40–45%) are applied.	Set up the sanitary and phytosanitary committee; other cooperation includes custom procedure, e-commerce, intellectual property rights, and competition policy.

WTO = World Trade Organization, % = percent.

Source: Official texts of FTAs.

Table 8.13 Summary of the FTA Cases Implemented by Thailand with New Zealand and India

Country and coverage	Negotiation approach	Trade in goods	Services and investment	Rules of origin	Cooperation
New Zealand 1 July 2005 Comprehensive agreement in trade in goods, services, and investment as well as sectoral cooperation	Following the Thailand–Australia Free Trade Agreement (FTA)	New Zealand: 0% of 79% of tariff lines as of July 2005 (pick-up truck, canned tuna, plastic resin, processed grain, gems and jewelry, frozen shrimp, electrical appliance, and glass) and 0% for the rest in 2010 except textiles and garments and shoes in 2015. Thailand: 0% of 54% of tariff lines as of July 2005 (baby foods, woods and wood products, wool, plastic, paper, machinery, sugar, vitamin, animal feeds, vegetable and fruits) and 0% for the rest in 2010. Sensitive items are milk, beef, pork, onion, and seeds.	The negotiation will begin after 3 years of comprehensive economic partnership.	Wholly obtained, substantial transformation, and regional value content (40–45%) are applied.	Set up the sanitary and photosanitary committee; other cooperation includes custom procedure, e-commerce, intellectual property rights, and competition policy.

continued on next page

Table 8.13 (continued)

Country and coverage	Negotiation approach	Trade in goods	Services and investment	Rules of origin	Cooperation
India EHP: 1 Sep 2004 Early harvest program for goods implemented as of September 2004 while the normal track will take more time. Service and investment as well as economic cooperation will be included later.	Completion of the trade in goods while negotiation for services, investment, and economic cooperation shall be completed later.	Two parts of trade in goods: (i) EHP with 82 items (fruits, canned seafood, gems, machinery parts, and some electrical appliances) with the margin of preference 50%, 75%, and 100% starting from March 2004 to September 2006; and (ii) normal track as well as sensitive track (agriculture, textiles, and automobiles and parts) are under negotiation but the tariff elimination will be within 2010.	Have to wait untill the trade in goods is settled.	EHP: (i) Wholly obtained; (ii) combination of substantial transformation and local value–added content such as change at 4-digit HS level (change to subheading from any other headings), provided that there is a local value–added content not less than 40%; and (iii) local value–added content not less than 20–40% depending on the products. Product specific rule is under negotiation.	Joint cooperation in designing the safeguard measure. Priority consultation for the antidumping measure. Dispute settlement process.

EHP = early harvest program, HS = Harmonized System of commodity trade classification, % = percent.

Source: Official texts of FTAs.

Table 8.14 Summary of the FTA Cases Implemented by Thailand with ASEAN and the PRC

Country and coverage	Negotiation approach	Trade in goods	Services and investment	Rules of origin	Cooperation
ASEAN and PRC FTAs January 2004 for Early Harvest Program (EHP) and July 2005 for Normal Track. The coverage of EHP is HS 01–08 products. However, Thailand and the PRC agreed upon the accelerated tariff elimination program and eliminated tariff for the HS 07 and 08 products in October 2003. Trade in services and investments are under negotiation.	Comprehensive for trade in goods, and services and investment	EHP: Thailand and the PRC to eliminate tariff for HS 07 and 08 in October 2003. EHP: ASEAN and the PRC to eliminate tariff for HS 01–08 by January 2006. Two tracks are applied for the tariff elimination: (i) normal track for 6,000 items with tariff elimination within 2010; and (ii) sensitive track for 400 items with 0–5% tariff rate within 2018 and highly sensitive track with 100 items with no more than 50% tariff rate within 2015.	Still under negotiation.	Wholly obtained for agricultural products and 40% ASEAN and PRC content. Product specific rule is applied.	Agriculture, information and communication technology, human resources, Greater Mekong Subregion, investment, product standard, and intellectual property rights.

ASEAN = Association of Southeast Asian Nations, FTA = free trade agreement, HS = Harmonized System of commodity trade classification, PRC = People's Republic of China.

Note that Thai sensitive list consists of agricultural products like milk, potato, garlic, onion, tea, coffee, silk, marble, and automobiles and parts; while the PRC sensitive list consists of corn, rice, vegetable oil, sugar, natural rubber, wood products, paper and pulp, and automobiles and parts.

Source: Official texts of FTAs.

Table 8.15 Summary of the FTA Cases Implemented by Thailand with BIMSTEC

Country and coverage	Negotiation approach	Trade in goods	Services and investment	Rules of origin	Cooperation
BIMSTEC Negotiation for trade in goods was completed in 2004 while trade in services and investment are under negotiation.	Positive list approach is used for trade in services and investment and the special and differential treatment is also applied for less developed countries.	There are two groups of countries: (G1) Thailand, India, and Sri Lanka for one group; and (G2) Bangladesh, Nepal, Bhutan, and Myanmar for another group. Fast track will cover 10% of the HS 6-digit items. Negative list for the normal track is under negotiation.	Under negotiation	Under negotiation	Economic cooperation covers many aspects such as custom procedure, standard and testing, and business travelers.

BIMSTEC = Bay of Bengal Initiative for Multi-Sectoral Technical and Economic Cooperation, FTA = free trade agreement, HS = Harmonized System of commodity trade classification, % = percent.

Source: BIMSTEC.

Table 8.16 Trade in G2 Early Harvest Program Products

	Value ($ Mn)					Growth (%)			
	2003	2004	2005	2006	2007	2004	2005	2006	2007
Thailand–India									
Total	1,508.5	2,049.2	2,805.6	3428	4,730.5	35.8	36.9	21.4	38.0
Exports	638.6	913.6	1,529.7	1,810.1	2,664.4	43.1	67.4	18.3	47.2
Imports	869.9	1,135.6	1,275.9	1,617.9	2,066.1	30.5	12.4	26.8	27.7
Balance	(231.3)	(222.0)	253.8	192.2	598.3	(4.0)	214.3	(21.1)	211.3
Thailand–India FTA									
Total	137.8	217.2	429.8	465.4	451.9	57.6	97.9	8.3	(2.9)
Exports	65.0	147.4	340.7	364.3	373.7	126.8	131.1	6.9	2.6
Imports	72.8	69.8	89.1	101.1	78.2	(4.1)	27.7	13.5	(22.6)
Balance	(7.8)	77.6	251.6	263.2	295.5	1,094.9	224.2	4.6	12.3

FTA = free trade agreement, $ Mn = millions of US dollars, % = percent, ( ) = negative value.

Source: Thailand Customs Department.

In the area of information technology (IT), Infosys Technologies Ltd. of India, EXIM Bank of Thailand, and Yip In Tsoi & Co. Ltd. of Thailand agreed to form a partnership to develop EXIM Bank's core IT platform using a universal banking solution from Infosys. EXIM Bank will deploy the program across its retail and corporate banking, trade finance, and treasury operations. Infosys sees this agreement as an important milestone for India's IT industry in the ASEAN market and the agreement marks the beginning of a highly competitive Thai IT market.[5]

As far as FDI is concerned, Indian multinational corporation (MNC) Aditya Birla Group has invested in Thailand for more than 35 years in several industries, its products selling not only in Thailand but all over the world. The group's investments are in manufacturing rayon (half of production is exported worldwide), synthetics (yarn and yarn spinning, 70% of output directed for exports), textiles (weaving and dyeing), acrylic fiber plants (ranking among the top three global producers), carbon black (the world's largest plant at a single location), chemicals, and hydrogen peroxide (Aditya Birla Group 2006).

Another major investor in Thailand is India's Tata Group. In June 2005, Tata Motors of India, the world's fifth-largest medium and heavy truck manufacturer and the second-largest heavy bus manufacturer, entered a joint venture with Thonburi Automotive Assembly Plant to produce a niche

---

[5] Available at www.infosys.com

pick-up truck for the Thai market. Thailand is the second largest pick-up truck producer in the world after the US and has many truck manufacturers. The venture aims to export pick-up trucks not only to ASEAN but also to the PRC, using the tariff reductions under the China–ASEAN FTA.

Tata Motors' plan was not new to Thailand. Japanese automakers such as Honda, Nissan, and Toyota relocated assembly to Thailand many years ago and also enjoy privileges provided by the BOI. Additionally, Ford, Honda, and Toyota have established research and development centers in Thailand to solidify their investments. Japanese automobile parts are produced in several locations in ASEAN, including Indonesia, Malaysia, and Philippines. Cost and technological advantages are the key factors in determining the location of investment. Assembly of a certain car model will take place in one country but other models will be assembled elsewhere. Under the AFTA and the ASEAN Industrial Cooperation (AICO) scheme, the parts and the assembled automobiles will eventually be traded across borders with no or lower tariffs. Such investment decisions are meant not only to enhance competitiveness through cost efficiency but also to launch the right products in the right markets.

The latest FDI from India was in 2006 when Tata Steel took over Millennium Steel Pcl. Ltd., a Thailand-based steelmaker. Millennium's main products included deformed bars, round bars, angle channels, low-carbon wire rods, high-carbon wire rods, small sections, special bars, and rolled steel. The company changed its name to Tata Steel Thailand Pcl. Tata Steel will also invest more than $130 million in the Thai subsidiary on improvements including a blast furnace.

Gems and jewelry are an area where Thailand and India could strengthen their investment relationship, given that Thailand is already known for producing gems set in both silver and gold and plans to be a trading center for colored stones, while India is rich in rough precious stones and polished small diamonds. Precious stones are already the major (and growing) import to Thailand from India. In 2007, the Indian International Jewelry Show in Mumbai hosted for the first time a Thai pavilion. The Bangkok Gems Fair regularly plays host to more than 500 traders from India.

Despite strong potential for a Thailand–India FTA, there is still much to be done in informing traders and investors regarding local regulations. In India, for instance, regulations can differ by state.

BIMSTEC covers trade and investment in goods and services, and is scheduled to be fully implemented by 2012. Negotiations have been slightly delayed, however. Meetings in 2006 were to consider a proposed accord on free trade in goods within BIMSTEC, but the trade negotiation committee has not been able to set a date to review progress. The rules of origin and a negative list of goods has not been settled either. Trade among members has also not significantly improved, given the similarity of members' production structures and exports (that is, textiles and garments). Whatever increase in trade is because of India's economic expansion and natural gas exports from Myanmar.

There are lessons from the joint investment between ASEAN and Japan that can be applied to strengthen the regional economic relationship with South Asia. The participation of major MNCs is key. Toyota, for instance, has expanded its manufacturing and marketing capacity in Thailand with the investment of $4.1 billion in 2005. Honda also invested $140 million to establish a third two-wheeled-vehicle plant in Indonesia and 4 billion yen (¥) to expand manufacturing capacity at its Thai engine plants from 150,000 to 300,000 engines annually. Nissan also invested ¥50 billion to renew its Thai production facilities and build a new production line for pick-up truck gearboxes.

Importance of Tariffs in Government Revenue

Taxes on income and profits constitute the bulk of government revenues. As expected, the overall tax revenues fell during the economic crisis. Data shows that tariff income is very sensitive to prevailing economic conditions as import tariff revenues decreased from $5 billion in 1996 to $1.76 billion in 1999, the year with the lowest tariff earnings. In 2007, tariff revenues increased to $2.6 billion, but overall the share of tariffs in total government revenues has been decreasing. In 1992, the share was 19% and the share decreased to 9.5% in 1998 and to 6% in 2007. Import tariffs will no longer be an important source of government income in the near future with the implementation of commitments under various FTAs.

Figure 8.15 Structure of Government Revenue, $ Million

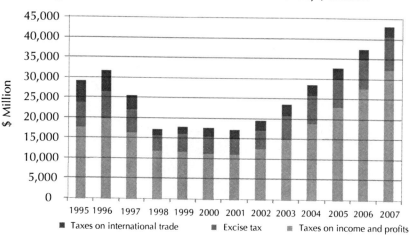

$ = US dollar.

Source: Thai Customs Department.

Figure 8.16 International Tax Structure, $ Million

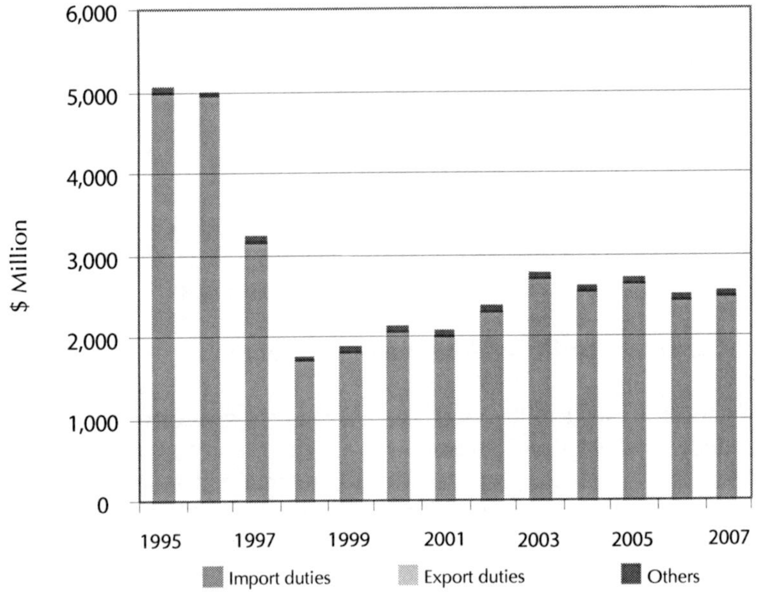

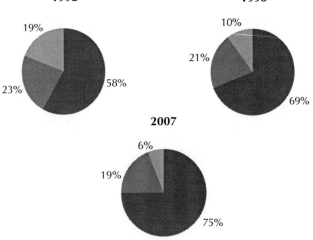

$ = US dollar.

Source: Thai Customs Department.

Figure 8.17 Tax Structure in 1992, 1998, and 2007

1992

19%

23%

58%

1998

10%

21%

69%

2007

6%

19%

75%

■ Taxes on income and profits   ■ Excise tax   ■ Taxes on international trade

% = percent.

Source: Thai Customs Department.

Infrastructure and Trade Administration Issues with Emphasis on East and South Asia

Overview of Trade-Related Infrastructure

The development of Thailand's trade and distribution systems over the years seems to be unmatched by the development of its trade-related infrastructure. Thailand's transport and logistics costs are high relative to trade value. This is because of inadequate transport infrastructure, and slow and costly bureaucratic customs procedures. Moreover, the road and rail systems have not kept pace with overall economic growth. The rail system is often overlooked by Thai policy makers, and has a total track length of only 4,180 kilometers (km). Road transport facilities are often concentrated in major cities like the Bangkok Greater Metropolitan area, which accounts for more than 50% of GDP, and in Nakorn Rachasima, Chiang Mai. This imbalance in land transport development, together with an energy cost and transport bottlenecks such as traffic jams in Greater Bangkok, all explain the high costs in land transport.

Private land transport firms are highly developed, however, and provide all kinds of services using a highly efficient distribution system. The recent Government policy to build up a solid logistics and transport network within the Greater Mekong Subregion (GMS) and BIMSTEC region relies on the private sector to play an increasing role in developing land transport infrastructure.

As for maritime transport and its ports, the main seaport is located at Laem Chabang (and, to a certain extent, Map Taput and the old Klong Toey). Port infrastructure quality is now on a par with neighbors such as Hong Kong, China; Malaysia; and Singapore. Thailand has a strong locational advantage vis-à-vis international sea lanes and shipping routes.

Inland maritime transport provides only a limited support to Thailand's transport needs. The Chao Praya River, the main artery for river transport, has not been fully developed for commercial transport. Thailand is under pressure to develop a transport route along the Mekong River, which connects it with neighboring countries such as the PRC. It is only recently that Thailand has started to develop its transport strategy in connection with GMS members and BIMSTEC, giving impetus to Laemg Chabang as a gateway to all these neighboring regions.

Thailand's main airports (Bangkok, Chiang Mai, Had Yai, Phuket, and Samui) have been adequately developed over the years to respond to the growing needs of the economy. The recent move from the old Don Muang International Airport in Bangkok to the new Suvarnabhumi Airport adds a new dimension to Thailand's air transport history. The 92-year-old airport, which was closed on 28 September 2006, handled around 39 million passengers in 2005—almost 10 million beyond its designated capacity. The new Suvarnabhumi Airport can accommodate 45 million passengers, but that figure could be reached quickly, so the Government plans to build more terminals, especially for budget airlines.[6] As for air cargo transport, total inbound, outbound, and transiting tradable goods have all continued to increase.

Customs Procedures and Issues Open to Facilitation

Thailand has recognized the importance of trade facilitation to support the country's overall trade strategy. An effective trade facilitation system could help the delivery of products overseas, both for manufacturing and processing. Thailand's recent customs reforms (Table 8.17) contain the following features:

- The adoption of a single administrative document and harmonized commodities code since January 2002 (however, customs officials seem to be unsure about the declaration form which is in conformity with the United Nations Key Layout).
- The implementation of electronic data interchange (EDI) since 2000 among shipping lines, freight forwarders, and large shippers, providing a way to electronically settle tariff calculations and payments.
- Familiarity with the use of green channels for clearance of documents (customs officials are not yet acquainted with the use of the Automated System for Customs Data [ASYCUDA]).
- Clearance of inbound re-export cargo with duty drawback, ability to clear goods behind the border at the inland customs (for example, dry port at Lad Krabang), and payment of duties and various customs taxes electronically.

The 1-day clearance project starting in 2004 is also an important element of the customs reform. The objective of the 1-day clearance service is to accelerate the clearance of inbound and outbound cargos so that traders can move their cargos within 24 hours. The customs check for outbound cargo is still around 2 days, while inbound cargo may take 2–4 days. In addition, a single-window e-logistics has been developed to eliminate inefficiencies in administering cross-border transactions and maximize

---

6   According to the Airports Council International, the number of travelers passing through Bangkok was 38.9 million in 2005. It rose to 31.46 million from January to September 2006, a 10.76% increase from the same period in 2005, making Bangkok a rival for Hong Kong, China and Singapore in the world rankings for the busiest airport.

Table 8.17 Status of Customs Reform (Based on Interview)

Customs Reform	Status	Units
Single Administrative Document (SAD)	Yes	Yes or No
Harmonized Code (HS)	Yes	Yes or No
Electronic data processing systems	No	Name of system, e.g., Automated System for Customs Data (ASYCUDA)
Electronic data interchange	70%	% of ship's inward manifests submitted electronically by shipping line to customs
Direct trader input	60%	% of import declarations that are input by customs agent or consignee directly through designated terminals
Internet input	40%	% of import shipments for which declarations are input through internet
Green channel	40%	% of shipments that are cleared with submission of documents but without inspection
Risk management	70%	% of shipments for which a computer system that uses profiling to determine if goods should be inspected: Yes or No
Electronic banking	60%	% of duty and taxes can paid through electronic transfer from consignee's bank
Electronic signature	Yes	Customs officials can approve declaration using electronic signature rather than physical signature: Yes or No
Private bonded warehouses	Yes	Import cargo can be moved directly to private warehouse and stored under customs bond for subsequent clearance: Yes or No
Bonded factories	No	Manufacturers (not located in a free-trade zone) can receive imported inputs without clearing customs, store them, process them, and export the product without paying taxes: Yes or No

% = percent.

Source: The Customs Department.

the value of information and communications technology (ICT) in fulfilling all import, export, and transit-related regulatory and transportation requirements. There is also a reform project called one-stop export service center created in June 2002 within the Export Promotion Department to expedite the process of granting export certificates. The center aims to shorten the application process by 1 week, granting approval to food exports for 1–3 days.

Other new initiatives to facilitate customs clearance are as follows:

- The provision of appeal procedures and due process concerning valuation discrepancies between customs officers and concerned importers (appeals can be made within specified time limits).
- The development of risk management programs to increase the efficiency of post-clearance audit.
- The facilitation of business partnerships such as gold card privileges that provide qualified importers and exporters privileges like exemptions from inspection and duty drawback approval.
- The initiation of the Joint Customs Consultation to provide a venue to discuss and exchange information regarding problems and difficulties faced in the process of fulfilling various customs formalities.

More recently, Thailand has also become active in developing single-stop customs inspections at border crossings with GMS neighbors. The country has also considered a study to develop such a scheme within the BIMSTEC framework. For the moment, there is no national trade facilitation body, although the formation of National Institutional Arrangements for Trade Facilitation is being considered.

Trade Finance

Thailand's foreign exchange regime is generally liberal. However, there are minimum procedures required for accessing foreign exchange for imports and for reporting foreign exchange earnings from exports. The transactions are supported by banks and specialized financial institutions, and a full range of trade financing schemes is available.

With regard to the procedures for arranging foreign exchange, when a shipment arrives in or leaves Thailand, importers and exporters are required to file a goods declaration with supporting documents to customs for cargo clearance. To facilitate the flows and movement of legitimate cargo, the Customs Department provides two clearance systems: manual and electronic. For manual cargo clearance, shipments are inspected on a random basis as specified by the Customs Department. The electronic system, however, requires that cargo under profile be examined as deemed appropriate, regardless of the random rate specified by the Customs Department for the manual system. With exports, if the declaration is properly completed, the Customs Department will assign a declaration number to the exporters who then proceed to warehouses for cargo inspection and release.

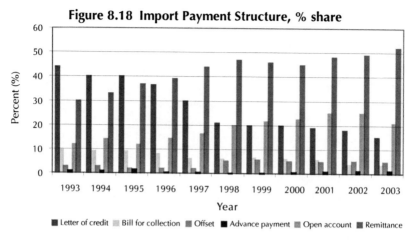

Figure 8.18 Import Payment Structure, % share

% = percent.

Source : Bank of Thailand.

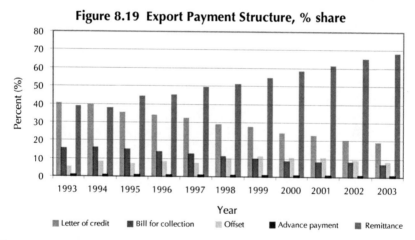

Figure 8.19 Export Payment Structure, % share

% = percent.

Source: Bank of Thailand.

The payment structure for exports and imports has changed over the years. Before the Asian financial crisis of 1997/98, 35–40% of import payments were made through letters of credit (see Figure 8.18). After the crisis, the share of payments undertaken through letters of credit dropped to 15–25%. Payment transfers have increased to 45–55% of total imports. Also for exports, a decrease in the use of letters of credit has been observed, and payment transfers represent 55–70% of total export payments since the crisis.

Table 8.18 Trade Finance Facilities for Thai Exporters

Types of trade finance	Interest rate	Period	Form of Security
1. Pre trade			
1.1 Export Finance			
• Packing credit	According to value and CRR	<180 days	
• Packing credit plus	According to value and CRR		
• Pre-shipment financing (baht, US dollar, and yen)	According to value and CRR	120 days	
• Export supplier's finance	Prime Rate: 0.5% per year	120 days	
• Express export credit	According to value and CRR	90 days	
• Financing facilities for re-export	According to value and CRR		
• Term loan for business expansion	According to value and CRR	5–7 years	
• Long-term credit for export of capital goods	According to value and CRR	<7 years	• Pre-delivery period: 70% of actual amount of loss being costs and expenses incurred in the production • Post-delivery period: 90% of actual amount of loss being the invoiced value of the delivered goods/service
• Merchant marine financing	According to value and CRR	<7 years	
• Trade fair financing	According to value and CRR	1–2 years	
1.2 Export guarantees			
• Buyer/bank risk assessment service	According to value and CRR	90 days	
• Small export bill insurance	According to value and CRR	90 days	• Commercial risk: 70% of actual amount of loss
• Medium- and long-term export insurance	According to value and CRR	180 days	• Political risk: 90% of actual amount of loss

continued on next page

Table 8.18 (continued)

Types of trade finance	Interest rate	Period	Form of Security
1.3 Export credit insurance • Export credit insurance letter of credit policy	According to value and CRR	90 days	• Commercial risk: 85% of actual amount of loss • Political risk: 90% of actual amount of loss
• Export credit insurance policy for D/P, D/A, and O/A	According to value and CRR	<180 days	• Commercial risk: 85% of actual amount of loss • Political risk : 90% of actual amount of loss
1.4 Letter of credit • Export bills under letters of credit	According to value and CRR	-	• Letter of credit sight 7 days
• Letter of credit	According to value and CRR	90 days	
2. Post Shipment • Export Bills under letter of credit	• No guaranteed approval: Prime rate • With guaranteed approval: prime rate minus 0.5%	-	• Noninterest-rate letter of credit sight 7 days
• Export Bills for Collection	• Prime rate	<180 days	• Noninterest-rate D/P 7 days

CRR = Credit Risk Rating, D/A = Documents Against Acceptance, D/P = Documents Against Payment, O/A = Open Account, % = percent.

Sources: Siam Commercial Bank and EXIM Bank of Thailand.

Thai exporters are generally endowed with trade finance facilities such as packing credit facilities for short and longer term (Table 8.18), export guarantees, export credit insurance, and letters of credit. Post-shipment facilities consist of both export bills under letters of credit and export bills for collection.

Key Transport Corridors

Thailand has tabled and implemented various proposals to develop key transport corridors in the region:

- The Asian Highway Network Agreement and the Trans-Asian Railway with the support of the United Nations Economic and Social Commission for Asia and the Pacific. Thailand signed the agreement in April 2004.

- The ASEAN highway initiated in 1997 with the actual ASEAN Transport Action Plan, 2005–2010.
- Greater Mekong Subregion cooperation with three main economic corridors (North–South, East–West, and Southern) as initiated by the Asian Development Bank (ADB).
- Cross-border and sea transport linkage to support trade with neighbors in groups such as ACMECS, BIMSTEC, and Indonesia–Malaysia–Thailand Growth Triangle (IMT-GT).

These new initiatives have substantially transformed regional and domestic transport systems. In the light of Thailand's links to South Asia, the Government has also encouraged the development of new trade lanes via the Andaman Sea using integrated multimodal transport. Within the BIMSTEC priority projects, a feasibility study on enhancing the cooperation on developing short sea shipping between Thailand and India is under way, as is a study on major surface routes and border crossings. This is apart from Thailand–South Asia air travel, which is growing quickly.[7] The total number of flights between Thailand and India now stands at 144 per week.[8]

There are various areas of economic integration that BIMSTEC can address,[9] particularly in the area of infrastructural development. As part of the National Economic and Social Development Plan (2006–2010), it is hoped that the BIMSTEC cooperation framework and development will be part of Thailand's ambition to establish itself as a world-class logistics, trade, and investment center. Indeed, Thailand's logistics development strategy emphasizes such areas as improving and optimizing logistic networks, internationalizing logistics services, enhancing trade facilitation, developing providers of logistics services, and providing personnel training.

The lack of progress in implementing all these plans is still a major concern. The socioeconomic links and environmental impact of transport also need to be addressed. Success in the transport sector still depends on a clean legal framework, a transparent pricing and taxation policy, and a risk sharing and management strategy, all of which would need a closer public–private partnership. Initial public investment is often seen as essential to attract private sector funds to infrastructure development.

---

[7] Thai Airways International actually covers eight destinations in India (Delhi, Kolkata, Chennai, Bangalore, Mumbai, Varanasi, Gaya, Hyderabad), three in Pakistan (Karachi, Islamabad, Lahore), two in Bangladesh (Dhaka, Chittagong), one in Nepal (Kathmandu), and one in Sri Lanka (Colombo).

[8] The expansion will help to achieve the target set by the Thai and Indian governments to have 10,000 airline seats available each week between the two countries within the next 3 years. *Bangkok Post*, 10 January 2007.

[9] For example, sustainable development, poverty reduction, income distribution, productivity improvement, technology transfer, and capacity building.

Table 8.19 Breakdown of Domestic Times and Costs for Large- and Small-Scale Shipments (Days, Baht/FEU)

Activity	Units	Bangkok–Laem Chabang
Outbound		
Loading	Time	1–2 hours
	Cost	B2,400
Transport	Time	4 hours
	Cost	B5,000
Port	Time	Ask carriers
	Cost	B3,900
Customs	Time	2 days
	Cost	B2,700
Inbound		
Port	Time	Ask carriers
	Cost	B800
Customs	Time	2–4 days
	Cost	B3,000
Transport	Time	4 hours
	Cost	B5,000
Unloading	Time	1–2 hours
	Cost	B2,400
Distance	km	200 km

B = baht, FEU = 40-foot equivalent unit, km = kilometer.

Source: Interviews with trucking companies.

To illustrate the recent trends of transport development, the study will concentrate more on domestic transport issues but will keep an eye of underlining the potential for regional development.

Ocean transport is key to Thailand's transport system. Table 8.3 reports a survey that covers the large and small shipments of import/export containers (in 40-foot equivalent units). For exports, ocean freight rates for container for exports to Singapore are cheaper for large shipments than for small shipments. Thai exports usually have to use Singapore as a transshipment port to re-export to the final port destinations. For imports, the features are similar, except for imports from Nhawa Sheva (India) to Port Kelang (Malaysia). Both Thai exports to and imports from Los Angeles/ Long Beach in the US are direct so ocean freight rates for containers are also set for this direct route (Tables 8.20 and 8.21 also show the estimates

Table 8.20 Ocean Freight Rate including THC for Container, $/FEU

Exports from Laem Chabang to						
Item	Rotterdam	Jebel Ali	Singapore	Nhava Sheva	Shanghai	Los Angeles/ Long Beach
Current price	2,000	1,500	400	1,600	800	3,550
Small shipment price	2,300	1,600	450	1,700	850	3,950
Large shipment price	1,800	1,400	380	1,500	700	3,200
Transit time (days)	26	18	3	13	15	18
Transshipment port	Singapore	Singapore	Direct	Singapore	Singapore	Direct
Imports to Laem Chabang from						
	Rotterdam	Jebel Ali	Singapore	Nhava Sheva	Shanghai	Los Angeles/ Long Beach
Current price	150	150	100	400	400	400
Small shipment price	250	200	120	450	1,000	600
Large shipment price	100	100	70	350	900	300
Transit time (days)	19	19	3	13	9	20
Transshipment port	Singapore	Singapore	Direct	Port Kelang	Singapore	Direct

FEU = 40-foot equivalent units, THC = truck haulage cost, $ = US dollars.

Source: Interviews with freight forwarders.

of ocean freight rates for containers). Several considerations are made to reach these estimates: distance to final destination, port stay cost, usual or unusual routes, weight of goods transported, volume transported, types of goods transported, and seasonal demand and supply for shipments.

The estimates for airfreight rates are shown in Table 8.22. It is quoted in US dollars and baht per kilogram for airport-to-airport movements. There are slight discounts for general bulk shipments as compared to normal shipments. These estimates could also vary depending on types, weight, and volumes of goods. For this study, these estimates are collected from major airlines, which offer interesting airfreight rates.

Table 8.21 Estimates of Ocean Freight Rate for Container

	Additional Surcharge for Full Container Load	
Abbreviation	Definition	Unit
SEA	Sea freight	US dollar
BAF	Bunker Adjustment Factor	US dollar
CSF	Carrier Security Fee	US dollar
THO	Terminal Handling Origin	(local currency)
THD	Terminal Handling Destination	(local currency)
B/L	Bill of Lading fee	(local currency)
D/O	Delivery Order fee	(local currency)
CAF	Currency Adjustment Factor	in % of sea freight
YAS	Yen Appreciation Surcharge	Yen
WRS	War Risk Surcharge	US dollar
	Additional Surcharge for Less than Container Load	
Maybe same as above, depending on the company		
CFS	Container Freight Station	(charge per cubic meter)
Discount	Discount usually considered from the number of containers per year	
Volume customer	Customers with cargo moving all over the world and have volume committed with carrier as per container shipper per year	
Large lots	Customers with large number of containers moving once at a time (such as 20–30 containers). Shipment cargo can be waste or non-value cargo such as waste paper, waste plastic, scrap metal, etc.	

% = percent.

Source: Interview with freight forwarders.

Table 8.22 Airfreight Rates for Normal and General Bulk Shipments, per kg

From Bangkok To	Normal rate (per kg up to 45 kg)		General bulk rate			
			(>45 kg)		(>100 kg)	
	$	Baht	$	Baht	$	Baht
New York	2.96	111	2.89	108	2.70	101
Rotterdam	2.54	95	2.49	93	2.49	93
Dubai	1.82	68	1.66	62	1.63	61
Singapore	0.45	17	0.45	17	0.23	16
Mumbai	0.99	37	0.99	37	0.94	35
Beijing	1.47	55	1.18	44	1.09	41
Los Angeles	6.15	230	3.24	121	3.10	116

B = baht, kg = kilogram, $ = US dollar.
Note: Exchange rate of B37.380 = $1 as of 4 September 2006.

Source: Interview with air cargo agents.

As for land transport costs collected from trucking companies, truck haulage rates are shown in Table 8.23 for domestic shipments and for shipments to and from land border crossings. In Thailand, popular modes for truck haulage are loaded 10- and 18-wheel trucks. The operator cost involves mainly unit-related activities and product-sustaining activities.

For border transport, the analysis applies to the usual border transport at the Nongkhai–Vientiane border crossing linking Thailand and the Lao PDR (Table 8.24). With the First International Mekong Bridge and land transport agreement between the two countries, border transport is handled on location. The Thai–Myanmar border transport has similar features.

Table 8.23 One-Way Truck Haulage Rates, Baht

Rate for Distance	50 km		500 km	
	Charges/Ton	Charges/full truck	Charges/ton	Charges/full truck
For a loaded 6-wheel truck	n.a.	n.a.	n.a.	n.a.
For a loaded 10-wheel (10-ton) truck	100	10,000	1,000	10,000
For a loaded 18-wheel (28-ton) truck	71.43	2,000	714.29	20,000

km = kilometer, n.a. = not available.

Source: Interviews with trucking companies.

Table 8.24 Border Transport at Nongkhai–Vientiane

Item	Cost (Baht)			Time		
	Minimum	Typical	Maximum	Minimum	Typical	Maximum
Inbound (wood products, mineral and forestry products)						
Cargo clearance	Thai–Lao PDR land transport agreement (1999)			Thai–Lao PDR land transport agreement (1999)		
Cargo handling	Free pass			Free pass		
Outbound (consumer goods, capital goods, and raw materials)						
Cargo clearance	Thai–Lao PDR land transport agreement (1999)			Thai–Lao PDR land transport agreement (1999)		
Cargo handling	B800	B900	B1,000	1 hour per trip	1.5 hours per trip	2 hours per trip

B = baht, Lao PDR = Lao People's Republic.

Source: Interviews with cargo companies.

Service Sector Trade and Foreign Direct Investment Policies with Emphasis on East and South Asia

Service Trade Flows by Sector and Partner

Services are the largest sector of the Thai economy and their contribution to GDP is important in supporting manufacturing growth, output, and employment (Figures 8.20 and 8.21). Given the openness of its economy, Thailand's trade in services also ranks high in the world. Thailand has maintained a share of around 1% in service exports and imports. Thailand also ranks high among East and South Asia in terms of planned investments in infrastructure services. Since the Asian financial crisis of 1997/98, the country has not been investing much in public infrastructure. Transport and energy rank among the highest priority sectors, followed by telecommunications, water, and sanitation.

Thailand's international trade in services has also grown since 2003. In general, service receipts have surpassed the payments over the years, with a surplus of around $5 billion per year. Thus, the service account has continuously helped to lessen the overall current account deficit. In general, travel, transport, and other services represent the bulk of services receipts as compared to the same share of service payments. It is also noticeable that royalties and license fees have become an important part of service payments, especially since 2002.

Figure 8.20 Thailand's Services Trade, 1993–2007

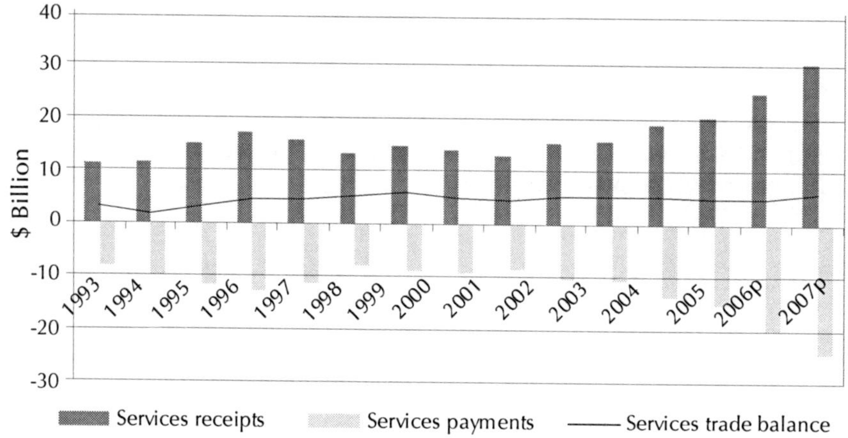

p = provisional, $ = US dollar.

Source: Bank of Thailand.

433

Figure 8.21 Thailand's Income Receipts and Payments, 1993–2007

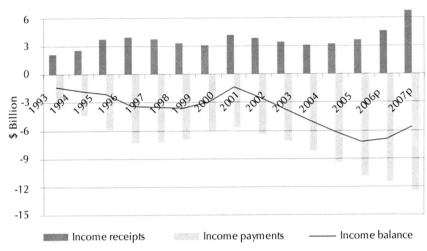

p = provisional, $ = US dollar.

Source: Bank of Thailand.

Thailand's trade in services with East and South Asia has also expanded rapidly in recent years, both in the sides of receipts and payments. Thailand's travel and transport markets have been doing well in the region. Even India has become a source of services receipts for Thailand. However, Thailand incurred a deficit especially for investment income and other services.

Figure 8.22 illustrates the growth of travel and transportation services in South Asia. Arrivals of South Asian tourists in Thailand grew from 224,305 in 2000 to 666,774 in 2007, an increase of 197%. India is the principal tourist market in South Asia, taking a share of almost 76% of the total arrivals from the subregion in 2007. As for Thai tourists in South Asia, Figure 8.24 shows that there is a doubling of flows from 25,512 persons in 2000 to 76,992 persons in 2007.[10]

---

[10] It will take a long period to redress this imbalance. South Asian countries fail to attract more tourists because of poor tourism infrastructure, pricing, and sanitary conditions relative to East Asia.

Figure 8.22 International Tourist Arrivals by Region Residence, 2000 and 2007

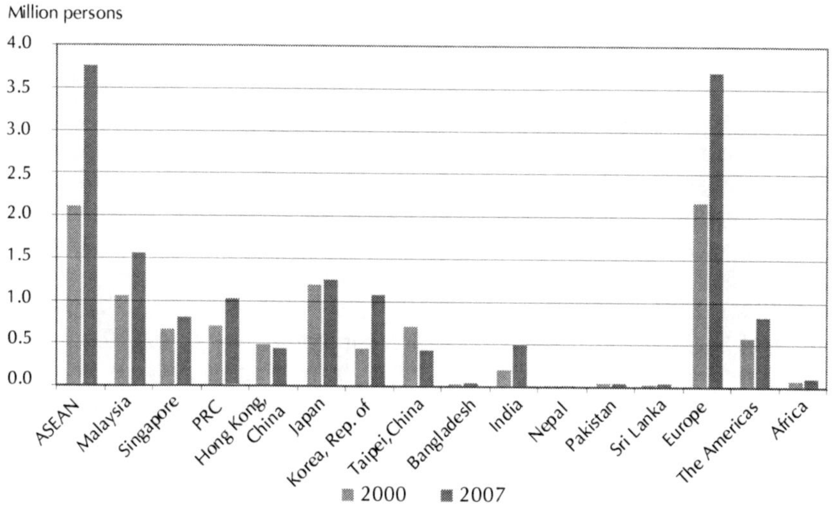

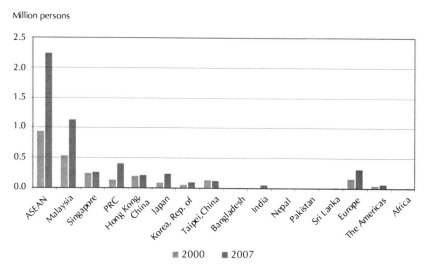

ASEAN = Association of Southeast Asian Nations, PRC = People's Republic of China, Rep. = Republic.

Source: Immigration Bureau, Police Department.

Figure 8.23 Outgoing Thai Nationals by Region of Destination, 2000 and 2007

ASEAN = Association of Southeast Asian Nations, PRC = People's Republic of China, Rep. = Republic.

Source: Immigration Bureau, Police Department.

Service Sector Foreign Direct Investment Performance

The importance of service sector FDIs to economic development is well known. The overall pattern and significance of service sector FDIs, in particular, in East and South Asia is being examined. Analysis is carried out distinguishing between the pre- and post-1997/98 financial crisis periods.

The net providers of FDIs in Thailand for both periods were Hong Kong, China; Japan; Republic of Korea; Singapore; and Taipei,China, with Japan and Singapore being net providers of FDIs since the beginning of 1990. Interestingly, the countries of East and South Asia combined contribute around half of Thailand's FDI net inflows of $15.6 billion between 1998 and 2005, with the PRC, Japan, and Republic of Korea taking a combined share of 23.2%; ASEAN accounting for a combined 18.4%; and Hong Kong, China and Taipei,China a combined 8%. In particular, Singapore played a significant role in service sector FDI projects such as those in trade, oil exploration, other services, and real estate. South Asia's share of FDIs accounted for 0.1%, or around $23 million, during the period 1998–2005.

In terms of subsector net flows of FDIs, countries in the region seem to favor services in trade (86.0% of the total), including transportation, travel, and other services (56.6% of the total); and mining and quarrying, especially oil exploration.

For Northeast Asia, Japan's share is more substantial than PRC's; Hong Kong, China's; Republic of Korea's, or Taipei,China's. The Republic of Korea and Taipei,China started to invest more after the Asian financial crisis in other ASEAN countries such as Indonesia, Philippines, and Viet Nam. For South Asian countries, there seems to be little interest in services investment as their net flows of FDIs reached only $23 million for the period 1998–2005.

Export Role of Services

Looking into the export role of services, the receipts of the tourism industry, totaling $10 billion per year since 2004, represent around half of Thailand's services receipts. Transportation has also benefited from the travel sector as passengers' service receipts also contribute to overall services income. Thailand has also benefited from inward remittances amounting to more than $1 billion per year since 1998.

Thailand has continued to promote exports in these areas where it has a strong comparative advantage. Prospects are also promising as several factors are responsible for the increasing amount of international activity in Thailand's service sector. The overall growth of the national economy, its regional integration with other East and South Asian countries, and technological developments are among the several important factors contributing to this change.

The role of trade in services is also related to various economic activities within and outside Thailand, with the degree of foreign participation varying from one subsector to another. Since the crisis of 1997/98, some subsectors such as banking, wholesaling, and retail have been unilaterally liberalized. Some important sectors such as transportation, telecommunications, construction, and financial services have also considerably expanded because of ever-increasing foreign involvement.

Regulatory Regime and Restrictions

Thailand's services are governed by a regulatory regime that for the most part acts to impede international competition in the sector. However, the 1997/98 crisis did exert some pressure toward liberalization in areas such as banking, retail, wholesaling, and telecommunications.

The Ministry of Commerce has long been in the forefront of managing the regulatory regime for services. Since the financial crisis, some important laws and regulations have been introduced, the most important one being the 1999 Alien Business Act B.E. 2542. This Act replaced an old law designed and enforced during a previous military regime. It lists the business activities in which Thais are to be protected from direct foreign competition. It also separates business activities into three categories: (i) businesses where foreign operators are banned, such as publishing, TV and radio broadcasting, and land transportation; (ii) businesses where permission must be sought because of their potential adverse impact on national security, culture, and tradition; and (iii) businesses in which Thais are deemed not ready to face direct foreign competition. The current list includes important services such as accounting, legal services, architectural services, engineering, construction, agencies, auctioning, commodities trading, retailing (with a value of less than B100 million), advertising, and hotel and tour guides.

For businesses in the third category, the law restricts foreign operators, for instance, by setting limits on their shareholdings. The Ministry of Commerce is entitled to revise the lists every year in response to the changing business environment. For instance, the arrival of foreign retail companies has shown that the minimum investment requirement is too low to adequately protect local retailers from competition.

The Competition Law introduced in 1999 covers services, although its interpretation is still subject to debate and further implementation.

Restrictions to services are by nature nontariff barriers. In the Thai case, they vary greatly from one subsector to another. Some subsectors, like banking, telecommunications, transportation, and professional services, have special rules and regulations governing trade and investment in services. There are also barriers that limit the right to establish foreign affiliates and also other barriers that limit the domestic provision of any type of foreign services.[11]

The General Agreement on Trade in Services and Regional Commitments

Since the beginning of 1995, Thailand has been committed to liberalize 10 out of 12 service sectors as listed in the General Agreement on Trade in Services (GATS) classification system. The 10 sectors, covering more than 100 subsectors, are: (i) business services; (ii) communication services; (iii) construction and related engineering services; (iv) distribution services; (v) environmental services; (vi) financial services; (vii) education services; (viii) tourism and travel-related services; (ix) recreation, culture, and sports; and (x) transport services. With regard to financial services, Thailand's commitments started in March 1999, while the liberalization of basic communications started in 2006.

It should be noted that Thailand's commitments for the above-mentioned 10 sectors do not exceed stipulations in Thai law concerning foreign participation. In other words, these commitments merely mirror the domestic status quo. Foreign operators are permitted provided that foreign equity does not exceed 49% of registered capital. In addition, the number of foreign shareholders must be less than half of the total number of shareholders of the company concerned.

At the regional level, the ASEAN Framework Agreement on Services (AFAS) was initiated right after the Uruguay Round conclusion in December 1995. AFAS adopts the structure and approach of GATS-plus commitments, and must offer new sectors and subsectors not covered under GATS. Negotiations in services trade are being conducted through the Coordinating Committee on Services (CCS). The CCS, established in 1996, listed seven priority sectors after three rounds of negotiations in services:[12] (i) air transport, (ii) business services, (iii) construction, (iv) financial services, (v) maritime services, (vi) telecommunications, and (vii) tourism.

Liberalization under AFAS is undertaken according to a so-called modified common subsector approach, wherein a particular subsector is identified as a common subsector if three or more members are able to make commitments under GATS or AFAS. As in goods trade liberalization, the minus-x approach is applied to AFAS. Under such a formula, two or more members may conduct negotiations and agree to liberalize trade in services

---

[11] Such as local content requirements, licensing exchange restrictions, and limitations on sales.

[12] Round I from 1996 to 1998, round II from 1999 to 2001, and round III from 2002 to 2004.

for specific sectors or subsectors while other members may join whenever they are ready. During the ASEAN Summit in November 2001, leaders mandated the start of negotiations on mutual recognition arrangements (MRAs) to facilitate the flow of professional services under AFAS. The CCS agreed to adopt a sectoral approach to developing MRAs for professional services, and is working with respective professional bodies in member countries. MRAs for professional services could be based on an ASEAN minus-x approach and start with MRAs for architects and engineers.

Future liberalization under AFAS will now take place under the process set by the ASEAN Economic Community (AEC), which aims for the free flow of goods and services by 2020. To achieve this, a high-level task force is to make recommendations on:

- targets and schedules of services liberalization for each sector;
- acceleration of services liberalization in specific sectors through the application of the ASEAN minus-x formula; and
- completion of MRAs for qualifications needed in major professional services by 2008.

For the other regional arrangements made with countries, such as Australia, the PRC, India, New Zealand, and the US, negotiations on services are conducted using a positive-list approach, resulting in limited progress.

Policy Implications for Promoting Cooperation with East and South Asia

Current Comparative and Competitive Advantage and Likely Future Trends

Thailand is well endowed with natural resources and high-quality physical infrastructure. However, the supply of skilled workers is limited and the communication networks are costly. Manufacturing consists mostly of labor-intensive products with rather low value added. Most Thai firms compete by cutting costs rather than improving the production quality and creating product differentiation. They also invest minimally in research and development. FDI is then one of the key drivers of the whole economy and helps to raise the level of competition by enhancing competitiveness. There are some niche industries that are considered highly competitive: the automobile industry, which relies heavily on FDI from Japan and the Republic of Korea; the processed foods industry, which has large numbers of Thai-owned and Japanese MNCs; the fashion industry, which mainly focuses on textiles and garments; gems and jewelry; and tourism.

As far as Thai MNCs are concerned, only a few can invest overseas, and most of them are in the food industry. The best-known Thai MNCs are Charoen Pokphand, which produces chicken; and Mitra Phon, which produces sugar. An exception to the trend of excellence in food production is the MNC Saha Union, which invests in power plants. Most Thai MNCs' investments overseas have taken place in the PRC. MNCs in Thailand's automotive industry are largely from Japan or the Republic of Korea, and local firms are mostly involved in producing auto parts. Overall, Thai MNCs are not large enough to invest significantly in East or South Asia.

However, Thailand's industrial infrastructure makes the country a potential production hub that links East and South Asia, particularly for the automotive industry. As discussed earlier, Indian firm Tata Motors has invested in Thailand to produce small trucks, which will be exported to the rest of ASEAN and the PRC, taking advantage of the preferential schemes afforded by AFTA and the China–ASEAN FTA.

Foreign Direct Investment Regime and Policy

Thailand relies heavily on FDI inflows to drive its economy. The BOI provides incentives such as tax and tariff exemptions. Thailand's geographical location and sound relationships with its trading partners have ensured that FDIs from East and South East remain constant. The PRC recently became active in relocating some of its industries to Thailand to take advantage of the abundance of natural resources and raw materials.

The future role of BOI is to focus on priority sectors, such as those 11 sectors stated in the AEC declaration, and to encourage foreign investors from outside ASEAN to fill in the gaps in the production value chain. This will benefit not only Thailand but also the whole region. BOI regional offices should also provide guidance and information on domestic regulations and measures. FDIs coming from the PRC and India could replicate the initial investment inflows from Japan and the Republic of Korea and may eventually generate new production networks in ASEAN. On the other hand, information on investing in India and the PRC must be supplied to Thai investors. Additionally, Thailand and India should build stronger joint investments in industries such as foods.

The success of FDI policy depends on (i) enhancing Thailand's geographical advantages by lowering the costs of logistics, (ii) improving the industrial infrastructure and human capital, (iii) liberalizing trade and investment regulations, (iv) eliminating nontariff barriers to trade, and (v) allowing the movement of skilled and professional workers.

Merchandise Trade Regime and Policy

Although tariff barriers are significantly removed, nontariff barriers—such as those implied in various sanitary and phytosanitary measures, food safety and quarantine requirements, safety measures and minimum standards requirements—remain in several countries. Another important issue is inconsistent rules of origin (ROO) for FTAs. The AFTA uses the 40% value-added and now contains product-specific rules as well, while the Korea–ASEAN agreement has product-specific rules. The ROOs for the Japan–ASEAN agreement depend on bilateral negotiations between member countries and Japan, and is expected to be a complicated process. India–ASEAN applies 35% value-added plus change in tariff heading. Differences in the ROOs will certainly be an obstacle. In addition, hub countries such as Thailand which have multi-commitments in several FTAs will be particularly hampered in fully have exploiting the advantages of free regional trade.

Clearly, the success of the merchandise trade policy depends heavily on completing and implementing Thailand's FTAs. Several problems such as nontariff measures and the ROOs need to be resolved. Nevertheless, cooperation at the WTO level must progress parallel to regional initiatives to create tighter links between East and South Asia.

Trade in Services

Thailand's trade in services continues to expand with East and South Asia, although the country is far more connected to the former than it is to the latter. However, major changes in the last few years have taken place, with an increase of Thailand's services trade with India in terms of tourist arrivals. Japan continues to play a significant role in net flows of service sector FDI, but Japanese investment has been more concentrated in the manufacturing sector. Singapore has emerged as service sector investor, especially in oil exploration and real estate. East Asia contributes around half of Thailand's FDI net flows. South Asia's share in service sector FDIs for the moment is negligible, but could emerge in the ICT industry, for example.

Thailand has continued to promote the export role of services sectors where the country has strong comparative advantage. Travel or tourism is still doing well with East Asia and even more so with South Asia (especially India). Transportation has also benefited as more travel operations have helped Bangkok to become a regional aviation hub. Since the Asian financial crisis, sectors such as construction, financial services, retail and wholesaling, telecommunications, and transportation have also expanded.

As for the service regulatory regime and restrictions, the Ministry of Commerce has enacted an important and critical law—the Foreign Business Act B.E. 2542—which was set to be amended in 2007.[13] There has also been a Competition Law in place since 1999, but its interpretation is still subject to debate and further improvement. In sum, nontariff measures create restrictions on services, with such measures varying greatly from one subsector to another. Thai policy makers apply a gradual approach to services liberalization and follow much of the country's existing multilateral, regional, and bilateral commitments.

Transport Initiatives

Thailand's roads are generally in good condition. The Asian Highway has been completed, connecting Thailand to neighboring Cambodia, Lao PDR, Malaysia, and Myanmar. For maritime transport, most containerized cargo is transshipped via Singapore, partly because of the draft limitations that exist at Bangkok port. However, Laem Chabang port has begun to receive direct calls in major East–West trade. As for air transport, the new Suvarnabhumi airport replaced the old Don Muang airport, raising capacity to 45 million passengers per year. Thailand has also other major international airports including Chiang Mai, Chiang Rai, Hat Yai, and Phuket.[14]

New transport initiatives are under negotiation. At the national level, improvements were being sought to overall logistic management, an effort to reduce transaction costs and help Thailand turn into a major transport hub. However, most of these recent new initiatives at the national level are pending and being reconsidered under the new government.

Regional initiatives to which Thailand had committed have mostly been pursued. The most important projects include the Asian Highway initiative, signed in April 2004; the ASEAN Highway action plan, for implementation during the period 2005–2010; cooperation among members of the GMS toward establishing various transport corridors; and cross-border transport initiatives carried out under the aegis of organizations such as ACMECS, BIMSTEC, and IMT-GT. Cross-border transport projects such as those involving ACMECs, BIMSTEC, and IMT-GT will remain important for Thailand's transport development.

---

[13] This Foreign Business Act includes a list of business activities in which Thais are protected from direct competition with foreigners.

[14] Railways play a layer role in freight transport with a share of only 2.1% against total freight. Two international routes to Malaysia experience heavy congestion between Laem Chabang and Lat Krabang Inland Container Depot.

Customs Procedures and Trade Facilitation

Thailand's most recent customs reforms include (i) implementation of a single administrative document and a harmonized commodities code, (ii) electronic data interchange (EDI) implementation, (iii) green channels for clearance against documents, and (iv) electronic duty payments. There are also interesting new initiatives, such as 1-day clearance and single window e-logistics, that have helped fulfill import and export transit-related regulations and transport-related requirements.

In general, Thailand's customs control has become more professional and business-friendly. It has business partnerships such as gold card privileges for importers and exporters, as well as joint customs consultations. For land transport control, single-stop customs inspections at border crossings with GMS neighbors are being seriously considered; such privileges could extend to Thailand's partners in the BIMSTEC in the future. In terms of increased transparency, Thailand's customs laws are much improved and are now consistent with the WTO Customs Valuation Agreement.

Trade Finance

Thailand's foreign exchange regime is generally open. However, minimum procedures are required for arranging foreign exchange. Transactions are supported by banks and specialized financial institutions. In general, both domestic and international institutions have a full range of trade finance. Financial procedures are required when a shipment arrives in or leaves Thailand.

The structure of trade finance payment has shifted over the years from letters of credit to payment transfer. There are also various packaging credit facilities for exporters.

Conclusion

Thailand has increased its outward economic orientation over the years. The country has seen the rapid expansion of trade and FDI since the latter part of the 1980s, indicating the increasing importance of international trade and investment in its economy. The result was higher growth, interrupted to some extent during the financial crisis of 1997/98, giving evidence to the dynamic effects of outward-oriented policies on the domestic economy. Trade partners in more developed countries, such as Japan, the EU, and the US, still play important roles in Thailand's trade profile. However, economies such as Republic of Korea; Taipei,China; ASEAN countries such as Singapore and Malaysia; and, more recently, the PRC and India, have come to play crucial roles in further developing trade and production link.

Merchandise trade is quite substantial, totaling over $100 billion since 2005. Apart from ASEAN, the PRC combined with Hong Kong, China in 2005 surpassed Japan as Thailand's main export destination, although Japan is still Thailand's most important source of imports. Thailand's export share to South Asia almost doubled between 1998 and 2005. Thailand's increasing regional integration with Asia suggests a rise of intra-industry trade, especially in the automotive, electrical, and electronic goods sectors.

Trade policy has also been streamlined to cope with the changing trends in Thailand's regional position. The tariff system has been restructured, and average applied tariff rates have been reduced several times since 1999, encouraging more industrial adjustment and greater competitiveness. However, Thailand has recently begun to use nontariff measures and countervailing duties on certain products from East and South Asia. Overall, trade liberalization is in tandem with the multilateral framework of the WTO.

There is also a greater emphasis on regionalism and bilateralism in Thailand's trade policy. Apart from the AFTA, Thailand has made progress with countries such as Australia, the PRC, India, and New Zealand. Negotiations are ongoing toward FTAs with Bahrain, Japan, Peru, US, and BIMSTEC countries. A recent change in the Thai government might delay implementation of some FTAs. Overall, however, the last Government of Thailand (2001–2006) seems to have paid more attention to FTA development as part of Thailand's trade liberalization and as a vehicle for developing the country as a strategic investment location.

With regard to FDIs, total inward stocks reached $50 billion in 2004. The financial crisis of 1997/98 encouraged mergers and acquisitions never seen before in industries such as automobiles, electrical and electronic appliances, finance, retail trade, and other service sectors. Local firms were short of capital, so investment inflows were substantial. Capital outflows generally were insignificant except for a few years before and after the financial crisis. Otherwise, Thailand expects FDI inflows to correspond with the rise of global and regional production networks. Thai overseas investments are mainly concentrated in East Asia.

The US and the EU have invested a significant amount of capital in Thailand. However, the net flows from these two regions are not as stable as those from Japan. In a sense, Japanese FDIs are more committed to Thailand, especially in the manufacturing sector as more than half of Thailand's total FDIs still come from Japan. Singapore, on the other hand, is the major investor from ASEAN, with its share of nearly 80% of the total FDIs from ASEAN. Unlike Japan and Singapore, emerging countries like the PRC and India have also become major investors in recent years. For the PRC in particular, Thailand could help it meet its needs for raw materials and intermediate products. India's Look East policy has helped Indian firms to gain greater benefits from Thailand's regional location advantages and attractive investment environment.

The Government of Thailand is committed to improving the overall investment environment. The main investment promotion agency is the BOI with its tax privileges granted to investors, in addition to other promotional incentives. There are investment incentives linked to production in EPZs, SEZs, and industrial estates. Thailand has sought to promote investments in industries such as agribusiness, automobiles, electronics, fashion, food manufacturing, tourism, and restaurants.

Also, Thailand is gradually implementing services liberalization in most sectors. At present, its trade in services has a 1% share of world trade in services. It has grown substantially, amassing a surplus of around $5 billion per year. Travel, transport, and other services represent the bulk of service receipts. Thailand's trade in services with East and South Asia has expanded quickly, particularly for travel and transportation. East Asian tourists constitute the bulk of Thailand's travel receipts. India has also been catching up quickly to become a major source of tourist arrivals in Thailand, accounting for more than 300,000 visitors in 2005.

As for the service sector FDIs, net flows stem from sectors such as transportation, travel, and other services, as well as mining and quarrying (especially oil exploration). Japan and Singapore have been the most important service providers since the 1990s. Singapore has emerged as an important source of FDIs since the crisis, and it has played a significant role in service-sector areas such as trade, oil exploration, other services, and real estate.

One of the most important laws related to investment is the Foreign Business Act B.E. 2542. There is also the Competition Law, which has been in effect since 1999, but its interpretation is still subject to debate and improvement. As for Thailand's commitments to the GATS, 10 sectors were committed as stipulated by domestic law. Future liberalization under the ASEAN Framework Agreement on Services (AFAS) will take place under the ASEAN Economic Community (AEC). Other regional and bilateral initiatives are limited at present.

The development of key transport corridors connecting Thailand to East and South Asia has become increasingly important. Various proposals are being tabled and implemented. In fact, transport logistics is essential for Thailand's development. With the PRC and India continuing their rapid economic development, the demand for raw materials and intermediate products will further expand. Thailand thus needs to act quickly and reduce its logistic costs to meet these regional needs. Thailand aims to have a world-class logistics system and serve as a major transport hub in Southeast Asia. For these reasons, Thailand needs to improve overall trade-related infrastructure, including customs reform. The aim is to focus on improving the overall competitiveness of various industries that will further link Thailand with East and South Asia.

References

Chirathivat, S. 1995. External Economic Influences, Regional Cooperation and the Role of Thailand as an NIC. In *Thailand's Industrialization and its Consequences*, edited by M. Krongkaew. New York: St. Martin's Press.

———. 2006. ASEAN–China FTA: Background, Implications and Future Development. *Journal of Asian Economics* 13: 98–114.

Chirathivat, S., and S. Mallikamas. 2004. Thailand's FTA Strategy: Current Development and Future Challenges. *ASEAN Economic Bulletin* 21: 37–53.

Chulalongkorn Economics Research Center, Faculty of Economics, Chulalongkorn University. 2004. Thailand and Australia Free Trade Area. Final report prepared for the Ministry of Commerce.

———. 2004. Nontariff Measures as Proactive Import Policy. Final report prepared for Ministry of Commerce.

———. 2005. Strategic Management for Thai Import Policy. Final report prepared for Ministry of Commerce.

———. 2005. The Analysis of ASEAN and China FTA under the Comprehensive Agreement. Final report prepared for Ministry of Commerce.

Chulalongkorn University. 2002. China Accession to WTO and ASEAN–China Free Trade Area: Enhancing Thailand's Competitiveness. Final Report Prepared for Ministry of Commerce, (in Thai).

Chulalongkorn University, Faculty of Economics. 2005a. A Study to Prepare Thailand's Readiness on the Impact of FTA with China. Final report prepared for the Fiscal Policy Institute, Ministry of Finance.

———. 2005b. A Study to Prepare Thailand's Readiness on the Impact of FTA with India. Final report prepared for the Fiscal Policy Institute, Ministry of Finance.

Fukasaku, K., M. Kawai, M. G. Plummer, and A. Trzeciak-Duval. 2005. *Policy Coherence Toward East Asia Development Challenges for OECD Countries*. Organisation for Economic Co-operation and Development (OECD) Publishing.

Swee-Hock, S., S. Lijun, and C. Kin Wah. 2005. *ASEAN–China Relations Realities and Prospects*. Institute of Southeast Asian Studies.

Online Resources

Aditya Birla website. www.adityabirla.com
www.bilaterals.org/article.php3?id_article=6159
Board of Investment website. www.boi.go.th
EXIM Bank of Thailand website. www.exim.go.th
Industrial Estates Authority of Thailand. www.ieat.go.th/menu02/2.1.30
    .5.0.0.0.0.0.0_en.php3
Infosys website. www.infosys.com

Appendix Tables

Table A8.1 Inflows of Foreign Direct Investment from South Asia; ASEAN+3; Hong Kong, China; and Taipei,China (%)

Item	South Asia		ASEAN		PRC + Japan + Korea, Republic of		Hong Kong, China + Taipei,China		Total	
	1990–1997	1998–2005	1990–1997	1998–2005	1990–1997	1998–2005	1990–1997	1998–2005	1990–1997	1998–2005
1. Financial Institutions	n.a.	5.6	49.7	1.2	2.4	1.0	27.0	6.4	18.05	6.01
2. Trade	n.a.	18.6	12.7	55.9	16.1	13.5	25.2	23.2	18.27	25.66
3. Construction	n.a.	0.1	1.7	0.1	7.7	2.1	10.6	2.6	5.44	0.88
4. Mining and quarrying	n.a.	0.0	0.3	10.9	0.2	0.5	0.2	0.1	2.06	5.03
4.1 Oil exploration	n.a.	0.0	0.1	10.8	0.2	0.3	0.0	0.0	n.a.	n.a.
4.2 Others	n.a.	0.0	0.1	0.1	0.0	0.2	0.1	0.1	n.a.	n.a.
5. Agriculture	n.a.	0.3	0.1	0.0	1.0	0.0	0.3	0.7	0.40	0.09
6. Industry	n.a.	4.1	22.9	18.7	61.9	73.9	23.7	27.5	34.68	41.04
6.1 Food	n.a.	0.3	1.3	1.7	3.2	0.9	2.0	1.7	2.30	1.95
6.2 Textiles	n.a.	1.4	0.6	0.3	2.6	1.1	2.5	3.8	1.57	0.89
6.3 Metal based and nonmetallic	n.a.	0.0	1.6	0.9	7.6	9.9	2.2	2.3	3.24	4.34
6.4 Electrical appliances	n.a.	0.0	10.5	6.5	24.6	24.1	5.9	7.9	11.03	11.50
6.5 Machinery and transport equipment	n.a.	0.0	3.5	2.3	10.0	25.6	1.7	1.2	4.10	10.34
6.6 Chemicals	n.a.	0.1	1.9	0.6	6.6	5.0	3.1	1.8	4.77	4.37

continued on next page

Table A8.1 (continued)

Item	South Asia		ASEAN		PRC + Japan + Korea, Republic of		Hong Kong, China + Taipei,China		Total	
	1990–1997	1998–2005	1990–1997	1998–2005	1990–1997	1998–2005	1990–1997	1998–2005	1990–1997	1998–2005
6.7 Petroleum products	n.a.	0.0	0.2	3.5	1.5	0.2	0.3	0.0	2.49	2.68
6.8 Construction materials	n.a.	0.0	0.1	0.1	0.1	0.2	0.6	0.2	0.26	0.34
6.9 Other industry	n.a.	2.3	3.1	2.9	5.9	6.9	5.3	8.6	4.92	4.63
7. Services	n.a.	18.0	3.5	5.9	3.6	3.3	3.1	8.8	3.79	5.81
7.1 Transportation and travel	n.a.	0.1	0.7	1.1	2.2	0.7	1.0	2.3	n.a.	n.a.
7.2 Other services	n.a.	17.8	2.8	4.8	1.4	2.6	2.1	6.4	n.a.	n.a.
8. Investment	n.a.	0.0	5.3	2.7	0.7	0.9	1.8	10.6	1.99	4.06
9. Real estate	n.a.	6.1	3.1	1.5	5.8	0.6	7.1	8.4	14.43	2.78
9.1 Housing and real estate	n.a.	5.7	2.2	0.8	4.1	0.6	6.2	7.1	n.a.	n.a.
9.2 Hotels and restaurant	n.a.	0.4	0.9	0.6	1.6	0.1	0.9	1.3	n.a.	n.a.
9.3 Other real estate	n.a.	0.0	0.0	0.1	0.0	0.0	0.0	0.1	n.a.	n.a.
10. Others	n.a.	47.3	1.0	3.1	0.5	4.1	1.2	11.8	0.88	8.64
Total Percentage (%)	n.a.	100.0	100.0	100.0	100.0	100.0	100.0	100.0	100.0	100.0
Total Value ($ Million)	n.a.	37.1	6,506.6	20,681.4	6,180.8	12,698.9	5,865.4	3,930.1	29,294.6	80,149.2

ASEAN+3 = Association of Southeast Asian Nations plus People's Republic of China (PRC), Japan, and Republic of Korea; n.a. = not available; $ = US dollars; % = percent.

Source: Bank of Thailand.

Table A8.2 Outflows of Foreign Direct Investment to South Asia; ASEAN+3; Hong Kong, China; and Taipei,China (%)

Item	South Asia		ASEAN		PRC + Japan + Korea, Republic of		Hong Kong, China + Taipei,China		Total	
	1990–1997	1998–2005	1990–1997	1998–2005	1990–1997	1998–2005	1990–1997	1998–2005	1990–1997	1998–2005
1. Financial Institutions	n.a.	0.0	62.8	1.9	4.5	0.6	55.5	7.1	36.78	6.69
2. Trade	n.a.	0.6	11.9	64.4	9.0	13.2	22.6	29.4	14.41	35.94
3. Construction	n.a.	0.0	1.5	0.5	3.9	2.4	1.5	0.7	2.30	1.16
4. Mining and quarrying	n.a.	0.0	0.0	9.2	0.5	3.1	0.5	0.1	0.69	8.24
4.1 Oil exploration	n.a.	0.0	0.0	9.2	0.5	3.1	0.3	0.1	n.a.	n.a.
4.2 Others	n.a.	0.0	0.0	0.0	0.0	0.0	0.2	0.0	n.a.	n.a.
5. Agriculture	n.a.	0.0	0.0	0.0	3.6	0.2	0.2	0.2	0.44	0.08
6. Industry	n.a.	92.7	13.0	17.5	53.4	71.5	14.1	29.8	30.78	29.29
6.1 Food	n.a.	85.4	0.5	0.4	2.7	0.9	0.9	1.0	0.92	1.25
6.2 Textiles	n.a.	0.1	0.5	0.1	5.3	1.0	1.9	3.3	1.15	0.55
6.3 Metal based and nonmetallic	n.a.	0.0	0.3	1.1	3.8	8.0	0.4	4.1	1.02	3.14
6.4 Electrical appliances	n.a.	0.0	7.1	8.5	16.1	35.7	4.1	10.3	8.16	11.36
6.5 Machinery and transport equipment	n.a.	0.0	2.3	1.6	4.6	17.0	2.5	0.9	2.12	4.47
6.6 Chemicals	n.a.	0.8	1.2	0.5	5.6	4.5	1.7	2.0	2.90	2.87

continued on next page

Table A8.2 (continued)

Item	South Asia		ASEAN		PRC + Japan + Korea, Republic of		Hong Kong, China + Taipei,China		Total	
	1990–1997	1998–2005	1990–1997	1998–2005	1990–1997	1998–2005	1990–1997	1998–2005	1990–1997	1998–2005
6.7 Petroleum products	n.a.	0.0	0.0	4.0	10.6	1.2	0.8	2.7	9.25	2.78
6.8 Construction materials	n.a.	0.0	0.2	0.0	0.0	0.0	0.0	0.9	0.24	0.18
6.9 Other industry	n.a.	6.5	0.9	1.4	4.6	3.2	1.7	4.7	5.02	2.69
7. Services	n.a.	0.0	2.6	3.2	2.0	1.7	1.3	8.1	2.59	3.98
7.1 Transportation and travel	n.a.	0.0	0.1	0.1	0.8	0.2	0.1	3.0	n.a.	n.a.
7.2 Other services	n.a.	0.0	2.5	3.1	1.1	1.4	1.1	5.0	n.a.	n.a.
8. Investment	n.a.	0.0	7.5	2.4	0.5	5.6	0.9	14.3	4.47	6.09
9. Real estate	n.a.	4.8	0.6	0.4	22.1	0.9	2.3	8.6	4.15	2.32
9.1 Housing and real estate	n.a.	4.8	0.4	0.1	13.5	0.9	2.1	7.1	n.a.	n.a.
9.2 Hotels and restaurants	n.a.	0.0	0.2	0.3	8.6	0.0	0.1	1.5	n.a.	n.a.
9.3 Other real estate	n.a.	0.0	0.0	0.0	0.0	0.0	0.1	0.0	n.a.	n.a.
10. Others	n.a.	2.0	0.1	0.3	0.6	0.8	1.2	1.8	3.39	6.22
Total Percentage (%)	n.a.	100.0	100.0	100.0	100.0	100.0	100.0	100.0	100.0	100.0
Total Value ($ Million)	n.a.	14.2	4,649.4	14,933.8	1,130.2	5,445.0	2,122.6	1,288.1	11,610.4	42,640.0

ASEAN+3 = Association of Southeast Asian Nations plus People's Republic of China (PRC), Japan, and Republic of Korea; n.a. = not available; $ = US dollars; % = percent.

Source: Bank of Thailand.

Table A8.3 Net Flows of Foreign Direct Investment from South Asia; ASEAN+3; Hong Kong, China; and Taipei,China (%)

Item	South Asia 1990–1997	South Asia 1998–2005	ASEAN 1990–1997	ASEAN 1998–2005	PRC + Japan + Korea, Republic of 1990–1997	PRC + Japan + Korea, Republic of 1998–2005	Hong Kong, China + Taipei,China 1990–1997	Hong Kong, China + Taipei,China 1998–2005	Total 1990–1997	Total 1998–2005
1. Financial Institutions	n.a.	9.0	33.1	4.5	2.0	1.4	10.9	6.0	5.76	5.23
2. Trade	n.a.	29.7	16.6	28.7	17.7	13.8	26.6	20.1	20.81	13.98
3. Construction	n.a.	0.2	3.2	(1.0)	8.6	1.8	15.7	3.6	7.51	0.57
4. Mining and quarrying	n.a.	0.0	0.9	15.3	0.2	(1.5)	0.0	0.2	2.96	1.38
4.1 Oil exploration	n.a.	0.0	0.4	15.1	0.2	(1.8)	(0.1)	0.0	n.a.	n.a.
4.2 Others	n.a.	0.0	0.4	0.2	0.0	0.3	0.1	0.2	n.a.	n.a.
5. Agriculture	n.a.	0.5	0.2	0.0	0.4	(0.1)	0.4	0.9	0.38	0.10
6. Industry	n.a.	(50.6)	36.9	21.8	63.8	75.7	29.1	26.4	37.24	54.41
6.1 Food	n.a.	(52.2)	3.8	5.3	3.3	0.9	2.6	2.1	3.21	2.74
6.2 Textiles	n.a.	2.2	0.5	0.5	2.0	1.1	2.9	4.0	1.84	1.28
6.3 Metal based and nonmetallic	n.a.	0.0	4.8	0.3	8.4	11.4	3.2	1.4	4.69	5.71
6.4 Electrical appliances	n.a.	0.0	12.1	1.3	26.5	15.4	6.9	6.8	12.92	11.67
6.5 Machinery and transport equipment	n.a.	0.0	5.3	4.5	11.2	32.1	1.3	1.4	5.39	17.00
6.6 Chemicals	n.a.	(0.4)	3.0	0.8	6.8	5.3	3.8	1.7	6.00	6.07

continued on next page

Table A8.3 (continued)

Item	South Asia		ASEAN		PRC + Japan + Korea, Republic of		Hong Kong, China + Taipei,China		Total	
	1990–1997	1998–2005	1990–1997	1998–2005	1990–1997	1998–2005	1990–1997	1998–2005	1990–1997	1998–2005
6.7 Petroleum products	n.a.	0.0	1.4	2.3	(0.6)	(0.5)	0.0	(1.3)	(1.96)	2.58
6.8 Construction materials	n.a.	0.0	(0.1)	0.1	0.1	0.4	1.0	(0.1)	0.28	0.52
6.9 Other industry	n.a.	(0.2)	6.2	6.5	6.2	9.7	7.4	10.5	4.86	6.84
7. Services	n.a.	29.0	5.5	12.9	4.0	4.5	4.2	9.1	4.58	7.89
7.1 Transportation and travel	n.a.	0.2	2.5	3.1	2.5	1.0	1.5	2.0	n.a.	n.a.
7.2 Other services	n.a.	28.8	3.0	9.8	1.5	3.5	2.6	7.1	n.a.	n.a.
8. Investment	n.a.	0.0	(0.1)	3.0	0.7	(2.6)	2.3	8.8	0.36	1.74
9. Real estate	n.a.	6.9	2.6	4.4	2.1	0.5	9.7	8.3	21.17	3.29
9.1 Housing and real estate	n.a.	6.2	(0.5)	2.6	2.0	0.4	8.5	7.0	n.a.	n.a.
9.2 Hotels and restaurants	n.a.	0.6	3.8	1.5	0.1	0.1	1.3	1.2	n.a.	n.a.
9.3 Other real estate	n.a.	0.0	(0.8)	0.3	0.0	0.0	(0.1)	0.1	n.a.	n.a.
10. Others	n.a.	75.2	1.2	10.6	0.5	6.5	1.1	16.7	(0.77)	11.40
Total Percentage (%)	n.a.	100.0	100.0	100.0	100.0	100.0	100.0	100.0	100.0	100.0
Total Value ($ Million)	n.a.	23.0	1,857.2	5,747.6	5,050.6	7,253.9	3,742.8	2,642.1	17,684.2	37,509.2

ASEAN+3 = Association of Southeast Asian Nations plus People's Republic of China (PRC), Japan, and Republic of Korea; n.a. = not available; $ = US dollars; ( ) = negative value; % = percent.

Source: Bank of Thailand.

Table A8.4 Inflows of Foreign Direct Investment from ASEAN, %

Item	Indonesia 1990–1997	Indonesia 1998–2005	Malaysia 1990–1997	Malaysia 1998–2005	Philippines 1990–1997	Philippines 1998–2005	Singapore 1990–1997	Singapore 1998–2005	ASEAN 1990–1997	ASEAN 1998–2005	Grand Total 1990–1997	Grand Total 1998–2005
1. Financial Institutions	0.0	0.6	0.0	6.0	0.0	2.1	50.9	1.1	49.7	1.2	18.05	6.01
2. Trade	45.3	31.1	28.5	13.2	32.1	1.8	12.1	57.1	12.7	55.9	18.27	25.66
3. Construction	0.0	2.5	8.6	0.1	16.2	0.6	1.6	0.1	1.7	0.1	5.44	0.88
4. Mining and quarrying	5.2	9.6	0.3	1.1	0.0	0.0	0.2	11.2	0.3	10.9	2.06	5.03
4.1 Oil exploration	1.1	0.0	0.1	1.1	0.0	0.0	0.1	11.1	0.1	10.8	n.a.	n.a.
4.2 Others	4.1	9.6	0.2	0.0	0.0	0.0	0.1	0.1	0.1	0.1	n.a.	n.a.
5. Agriculture	0.0	1.8	0.1	0.0	0.0	0.0	0.1	0.0	0.1	0.0	0.40	0.09
6. Industry	39.1	18.7	38.2	19.3	18.3	84.9	22.6	17.9	22.9	18.7	34.68	41.04
6.1 Food	5.7	2.4	1.7	0.6	1.8	82.2	1.3	0.8	1.3	1.7	2.30	1.95
6.2 Textiles	8.0	4.5	1.5	0.0	0.0	0.0	0.5	0.3	0.6	0.3	1.57	0.89
6.3 Metal based and nonmetallic	3.1	0.0	1.0	2.0	0.0	0.0	1.6	0.9	1.6	0.9	3.24	4.34
6.4 Electrical appliances	0.0	0.0	19.0	6.6	1.9	0.1	10.5	6.6	10.5	6.5	11.03	11.50
6.5 Machinery and transport equipment	0.1	0.4	0.5	2.4	0.0	0.3	3.6	2.3	3.5	2.3	4.10	10.34
6.6 Chemicals	0.4	10.4	5.1	0.8	0.0	0.1	1.9	0.6	1.9	0.6	4.77	4.37

continued on next page

Table A8.4 (continued)

Item	Indonesia 1990–1997	Indonesia 1998–2005	Malaysia 1990–1997	Malaysia 1998–2005	Philippines 1990–1997	Philippines 1998–2005	Singapore 1990–1997	Singapore 1998–2005	ASEAN 1990–1997	ASEAN 1998–2005	Grand Total 1990–1997	Grand Total 1998–2005
6.7 Petroleum products	0.0	0.0	0.0	0.0	0.0	0.0	0.2	3.6	0.2	3.5	2.49	2.68
6.8 Construction materials	0.0	0.0	0.0	2.6	0.0	0.0	0.1	0.0	0.1	0.1	0.26	0.34
6.9 Other industry	21.7	1.0	9.4	4.2	14.6	2.2	2.8	2.9	3.1	2.9	4.92	4.63
7. Services	2.0	10.2	2.6	26.9	31.4	5.2	3.4	5.7	3.5	5.9	3.79	5.81
7.1 Transportation and travel	0.0	7.9	0.1	18.8	0.0	0.1	0.7	0.9	0.7	1.1	n.a.	n.a.
7.2 Other services	2.0	2.2	2.5	8.1	31.4	5.1	2.7	4.8	2.8	4.8	n.a.	n.a.
8. Investment	0.6	0.5	0.5	2.1	0.0	1.9	5.4	2.7	5.3	2.7	1.99	4.06
9. Real estate	4.4	6.9	18.7	4.4	0.0	0.6	2.9	1.5	3.1	1.5	14.43	2.78
9.1 Housing and real estate	1.3	6.9	11.0	3.5	0.0	0.6	2.1	0.8	2.2	0.8	n.a.	n.a.
9.2 Hotels and restaurants	3.0	0.0	7.7	0.9	0.0	0.0	0.8	0.6	0.9	0.6	n.a.	n.a.
9.3 Other real estate	0.0	0.0	0.0	0.0	0.0	0.0	0.0	0.1	0.0	0.1	n.a.	n.a.
10. Others	3.6	18.2	2.5	26.7	0.7	2.9	0.9	2.7	1.0	3.1	0.88	8.64
Total Percentage (%)	100.0	100.0	100.0	100.0	100.0	100.0	100.0	100.0	100.0	100.0	100.0	100.0
Total Value ($ Million)	57.9	22.1	82.4	276.4	18.5	232.8	6,346.2	20,109.6	6,506.6	20,681.4	29,294.6	80,149.2

ASEAN = Association of Southeast Asian Nations, n.a. = not available, $ = US dollars, % = percent.

Source: Bank of Thailand.

Table A8.5 Outflows of Foreign Direct Investment to ASEAN, %

Item	Indonesia 1990–1997	Indonesia 1998–2005	Malaysia 1990–1997	Malaysia 1998–2005	Philippines 1990–1997	Philippines 1998–2005	Singapore 1990–1997	Singapore 1998–2005	ASEAN 1990–1997	ASEAN 1998–2005	Grand Total 1990–1997	Grand Total 1998–2005
1. Financial institutions	0.0	0.0	0.1	1.0	52.7	0.0	63.1	1.9	62.8	1.9	36.78	6.69
2. Trade	97.4	22.1	36.7	24.2	17.8	0.1	11.8	64.8	11.9	64.4	14.41	35.94
3. Construction	0.0	0.0	6.1	0.2	0.0	0.7	1.5	0.5	1.5	0.5	2.30	1.16
4. Mining and quarrying	1.8	0.0	5.7	7.0	0.0	0.0	0.0	9.2	0.0	9.2	0.69	8.24
4.1 Oil exploration	0.0	0.0	0.0	7.0	0.0	0.0	0.0	9.2	0.0	9.2	n.a.	n.a.
4.2 Others	1.8	0.0	5.7	0.0	0.0	0.0	0.0	0.0	0.0	0.0	n.a.	n.a.
5. Agriculture	0.0	0.0	0.2	0.0	0.0	0.0	0.0	0.0	0.0	0.0	0.44	0.08
6. Industry	0.0	62.6	45.1	59.9	20.9	95.1	12.9	17.1	13.0	17.5	30.78	29.29
6.1 Food	0.0	2.0	0.4	0.0	0.0	86.8	0.5	0.3	0.5	0.4	0.92	1.25
6.2 Textiles	0.0	42.0	0.0	0.0	0.0	0.0	0.5	0.1	0.5	0.1	1.15	0.55
6.3 Metal based and nonmetallic	0.0	0.0	0.0	0.0	0.0	0.0	0.3	1.1	0.3	1.1	1.02	3.14
6.4 Electrical appliances	0.0	0.0	34.9	57.2	0.0	8.2	7.0	8.2	7.1	8.5	8.16	11.36
6.5 Machinery and transport equipment	0.0	0.0	0.0	0.0	0.0	0.0	2.3	1.6	2.3	1.6	2.12	4.47
6.6 Chemicals	0.0	18.7	9.6	2.2	0.0	0.0	1.2	0.4	1.2	0.5	2.90	2.87

continued on next page

Table A8.5 continued

Item	Indonesia 1990–1997	1998–2005	Malaysia 1990–1997	1998–2005	Philippines 1990–1997	1998–2005	Singapore 1990–1997	1998–2005	ASEAN 1990–1997	1998–2005	Grand Total 1990–1997	1998–2005
6.7 Petroleum products	0.0	0.0	0.0	0.0	0.0	0.0	0.0	4.0	0.0	4.0	9.25	2.78
6.8 Construction materials	0.0	0.0	0.0	0.0	0.0	0.0	0.2	0.0	0.2	0.0	0.24	0.18
6.9 Other industry	0.0	0.0	0.2	0.5	20.9	0.1	0.9	1.4	0.9	1.4	5.02	2.69
7. Services	0.0	14.8	4.7	1.9	0.0	2.9	2.6	3.2	2.6	3.2	2.59	3.98
7.1 Transportation and travel	0.0	0.0	0.0	0.0	0.0	0.0	0.1	0.1	0.1	0.1	n.a.	n.a.
7.2 Other services	0.0	14.8	4.7	1.9	0.0	2.9	2.5	3.1	2.5	3.1	n.a.	n.a.
8. Investment	0.0	0.0	0.0	0.8	0.0	0.0	7.6	2.5	7.5	2.4	4.47	6.09
9. Real estate	0.0	0.0	0.0	2.5	0.0	0.7	0.6	0.4	0.6	0.4	4.15	2.32
9.1 Housing and real estate	0.0	0.0	0.0	0.2	0.0	0.3	0.4	0.1	0.4	0.1	n.a.	n.a.
9.2 Hotels and restaurants	0.0	0.0	0.0	2.3	0.0	0.3	0.2	0.3	0.2	0.3	n.a.	n.a.
9.3 Other real estate	0.0	0.0	0.0	0.0	0.0	0.0	0.0	0.0	0.0	0.0	n.a.	n.a.
10. Others	0.9	0.4	1.5	2.6	8.7	0.5	0.1	0.3	0.1	0.3	3.39	6.22
Total Percentage (%)	100.0	100.0	100.0	100.0	100.0	100.0	100.0	100.0	100.0	100.0	100.0	100.0
Total Value ($ Million)	0.9	2.9	20.4	99.1	1.2	17.7	4,626.1	14,807.9	4,649.4	14,933.8	11,610.4	42,640.0

ASEAN = Association of Southeast Asian Nations, n.a. = not available, $ = US dollars, % = percent.

Source: Bank of Thailand.

457

Table A8.6 Net Flows of Foreign Direct Investment from ASEAN, %

Item	Indonesia		Malaysia		Philippines		Singapore		ASEAN		Grand Total	
	1990–1997	1998–2005	1990–1997	1998–2005	1990–1997	1998–2005	1990–1997	1998–2005	1990–1997	1998–2005	1990–1997	1998–2005
1. Financial institutions	0.0	0.7	0.0	8.8	(3.8)	2.3	35.8	4.4	33.1	4.5	5.76	5.23
2. Trade	44.4	32.5	25.7	7.1	33.1	1.9	15.2	30.4	16.6	28.7	20.81	13.98
3. Construction	0.0	2.8	9.5	0.1	17.3	0.6	3.0	(1.1)	3.2	(1.0)	7.51	0.57
4. Mining and quarrying	5.2	11.0	(1.5)	(2.1)	0.0	0.0	0.8	16.6	0.9	15.3	2.96	1.38
4.1 Oil exploration	1.1	0.0	0.1	(2.1)	0.0	0.0	0.4	16.4	0.4	15.1	n.a.	n.a.
4.2 Others	4.1	11.0	(1.6)	0.0	0.0	0.0	0.4	0.2	0.4	0.2	n.a.	n.a.
5. Agriculture	0.0	2.0	0.1	0.0	0.0	0.0	0.2	0.0	0.2	0.0	0.38	0.10
6. Industry	39.7	12.2	35.9	(3.5)	18.1	84.1	37.0	20.3	36.9	21.8	37.24	54.41
6.1 Food	5.8	2.4	2.1	1.0	1.9	81.8	3.8	2.4	3.8	5.3	3.21	2.74
6.2 Textiles	8.1	(1.1)	1.9	0.0	0.0	0.0	0.2	0.6	0.5	0.5	1.84	1.28
6.3 Metal based and nonmetallic	3.1	0.0	1.4	3.0	0.0	0.0	5.1	0.3	4.8	0.3	4.69	5.71
6.4 Electrical appliances	0.0	0.0	13.7	(21.7)	2.1	(0.6)	12.6	2.1	12.1	1.3	12.92	11.67
6.5 Machinery and transport equipment	0.1	0.5	0.7	3.8	0.0	0.3	5.7	4.7	5.3	4.5	5.39	17.00
6.6 Chemicals	0.4	9.2	3.7	0.1	0.0	0.1	3.0	0.9	3.0	0.8	6.00	6.07

continued on next page

Table A8.6 (continued)

Item	Indonesia 1990–1997	Indonesia 1998–2005	Malaysia 1990–1997	Malaysia 1998–2005	Philippines 1990–1997	Philippines 1998–2005	Singapore 1990–1997	Singapore 1998–2005	ASEAN 1990–1997	ASEAN 1998–2005	Grand Total 1990–1997	Grand Total 1998–2005
6.7 Petroleum products	0.0	0.0	0.0	0.0	0.0	0.0	1.5	2.5	1.4	2.3	(1.96)	2.58
6.8 Construction materials	0.0	0.0	0.0	4.0	0.0	0.0	(0.2)	0.0	(0.1)	0.1	0.28	0.52
6.9 Other industry	22.1	1.2	12.4	6.4	14.1	2.4	5.4	6.8	6.2	6.5	4.86	6.84
7. Services	2.0	9.5	1.9	40.9	33.6	5.4	5.4	12.4	5.5	12.9	4.58	7.89
7.1 Transportation and travel	0.0	9.1	0.1	29.3	0.0	0.1	2.6	2.3	2.5	3.1	n.a.	n.a.
7.2 Other services	2.0	0.4	1.8	11.6	33.6	5.2	2.8	10.0	3.0	9.8	n.a.	n.a.
8. Investment	0.6	0.5	0.7	2.9	0.0	2.1	(0.2)	3.0	(0.1)	3.0	0.36	1.74
9. Real estate	4.5	7.9	24.9	5.5	0.0	0.6	1.7	4.4	2.6	4.4	21.17	3.29
9.1 Housing and real estate	1.4	7.9	14.6	5.4	0.0	0.6	(1.1)	2.6	(0.5)	2.6	n.a.	n.a.
9.2 Hotels and restaurants	3.1	0.0	10.3	0.2	0.0	0.0	3.6	1.6	3.8	1.5	n.a.	n.a.
9.3 Other real estate	0.0	0.0	0.0	0.0	0.0	0.0	(0.8)	0.3	(0.8)	0.3	n.a.	n.a.
10. Others	3.6	20.8	2.8	40.3	0.1	3.1	1.0	9.7	1.2	10.6	(0.77)	11.40
Total Percentage (%)	100.0	100.0	100.0	100.0	100.0	100.0	100.0	100.0	100.0	100.0	100.0	100.0
Total Value ($ Million)	57.0	19.2	62.0	177.3	17.3	215.1	1,720.1	5,301.7	1,857.2	5,747.6	17,684.3	37,509.2

ASEAN = Association of Southeast Asian Nations, n.a. = not available, $ = US dollars, ( ) = negative value, % = percent.

Source: Bank of Thailand.

459

Table A8.7 Inflows of Foreign Direct Investment from East Asia; Hong Kong, China; and Taipei,China (%)

Item	China, People's Republic of 1990–1997	China, People's Republic of 1998–2005	Japan 1990–1997	Japan 1998–2005	Korea, Republic of 1990–1997	Korea, Republic of 1998–2005	Hong Kong, China 1990–1997	Hong Kong, China 1998–2005	Taipei,China 1990–1997	Taipei,China 1998–2005	Grand Total 1990–1997	Grand Total 1998–2005
1. Financial institutions	6.8	0.0	2.5	1.1	0.6	0.0	34.3	8.7	0.4	0.4	18.05	6.01
2. Trade	44.3	14.9	15.9	13.5	18.4	14.8	21.7	23.5	37.8	22.3	18.27	25.66
3. Construction	12.4	5.1	7.4	1.9	18.9	10.0	12.5	2.2	3.4	3.5	5.44	0.88
4. Mining and quarrying	0.3	0.0	0.2	0.5	0.1	0.0	0.2	0.2	0.1	0.0	2.06	5.03
4.1 Oil exploration	0.0	0.0	0.2	0.3	0.1	0.0	0.0	0.0	0.1	0.0	n.a.	n.a.
4.2 Others	0.3	0.0	0.0	0.2	0.1	0.0	0.2	0.2	0.0	0.0	n.a.	n.a.
5. Agriculture	1.3	0.0	1.0	0.0	0.0	0.0	0.0	0.9	1.3	0.0	0.40	0.09
6. Industry	27.4	52.6	62.2	74.8	56.4	43.0	17.1	18.7	47.6	50.0	34.68	41.04
6.1 Food	3.4	2.7	3.2	0.9	0.3	0.2	0.8	1.2	6.4	3.1	2.30	1.95
6.2 Textiles	1.6	26.0	2.7	0.9	0.3	0.0	1.2	1.5	7.1	9.6	1.57	0.89
6.3 Metal based and nonmetallic	2.8	0.1	7.6	10.1	6.7	4.0	1.1	1.5	6.1	4.3	3.24	4.34
6.4 Electrical appliances	0.0	4.3	24.9	24.2	16.1	25.6	4.4	7.0	11.4	10.3	11.03	11.50
6.5 Machinery and transport equipment	0.4	2.4	10.3	26.3	0.0	1.5	2.0	1.0	0.6	1.7	4.10	10.34
6.6 Chemicals	0.0	5.2	6.7	4.9	2.7	5.9	2.5	0.9	5.3	3.9	4.77	4.37

continued on next page

Table A8.7 (continued)

Item	China, People's Republic of		Japan		Korea, Republic of		Hong Kong, China		Taipei,China		Grand Total	
	1990–1997	1998–2005	1990–1997	1998–2005	1990–1997	1998–2005	1990–1997	1998–2005	1990–1997	1998–2005	1990–1997	1998–2005
6.7 Petroleum products	0.0	0.0	1.5	0.2	0.0	0.0	0.4	0.0	0.0	0.0	2.49	2.68
6.8 Construction materials	0.0	0.3	0.1	0.2	0.0	0.0	0.6	0.2	0.7	0.4	0.26	0.34
6.9 Other industry	19.1	11.6	5.2	6.9	30.2	5.8	4.0	5.4	10.1	16.6	4.92	4.63
7. Services	4.6	1.7	3.6	2.9	4.2	20.3	3.4	10.8	2.0	3.8	3.79	5.81
7.1 Transportation and travel	0.4	0.0	2.2	0.6	2.4	4.1	1.2	2.5	0.4	2.1	n.a.	n.a.
7.2 Other services	4.2	1.7	1.4	2.3	1.8	16.2	2.2	8.3	1.6	1.7	n.a.	n.a.
8. Investment	0.9	0.2	0.7	0.9	0.0	0.1	1.9	14.2	1.5	1.5	1.99	4.06
9. Real estate	0.8	3.8	6.0	0.6	0.5	3.4	7.9	10.4	4.1	3.3	14.43	2.78
9.1 Housing and real estate	0.8	3.8	4.3	0.5	0.5	1.8	6.8	9.0	3.8	2.2	n.a.	n.a.
9.2 Hotels and restaurants	0.0	0.1	1.7	0.0	0.0	1.6	1.0	1.3	0.3	1.1	n.a.	n.a.
9.3 Other real estate	0.0	0.0	0.0	0.0	0.0	0.0	0.0	0.1	0.0	0.0	n.a.	n.a.
10. Others	1.3	21.7	0.5	3.8	1.0	8.5	1.0	10.4	1.7	15.3	0.88	8.64
Total Percentage (%)	100.0	100.0	100.0	100.0	100.0	100.0	100.0	100.0	100.0	100.0	100.0	100.0
Total Value ($ Million)	36.9	81.9	5,999.2	12,344.1	144.7	273.0	4,604.0	2,815.6	1,261.4	1,114.5	29,294.6	80,149.2

East Asia = includes People's Republic of China, Japan, and Republic of Korea; n.a. = not available; $ = US dollars; % = percent.

Source: Bank of Thailand.

Table A8.8 Outflows of Foreign Direct Investment to East Asia; Hong Kong, China; and Taipei,China (%)

Item	China, People's Republic of		Japan		Korea, Republic of		Hong Kong, China		Taipei,China		Grand Total	
	1990–1997	1998–2005	1990–1997	1998–2005	1990–1997	1998–2005	1990–1997	1998–2005	1990–1997	1998–2005	1990–1997	1998–2005
1. Financial institutions	3.2	0.0	4.5	0.6	0.5	0.2	64.0	8.4	0.6	2.3	36.78	6.69
2. Trade	49.5	6.0	7.7	13.2	20.5	17.3	19.5	33.1	42.7	15.4	14.41	35.94
3. Construction	13.5	12.4	3.6	2.3	6.0	12.8	1.3	0.7	2.7	0.5	2.30	1.16
4. Mining and quarrying	0.0	1.0	0.5	3.2	0.5	0.0	0.5	0.1	0.7	0.0	0.69	8.24
4.1 Oil exploration	0.0	0.2	0.5	3.2	0.0	0.0	0.3	0.1	0.1	0.0	n.a.	n.a.
4.2 Others	0.0	0.8	0.0	0.0	0.5	0.0	0.1	0.0	0.5	0.0	n.a.	n.a.
5. Agriculture	0.0	0.0	3.7	0.2	0.0	0.0	0.1	0.3	0.3	0.0	0.44	0.08
6. Industry	27.7	74.2	54.0	71.6	70.2	62.3	9.5	21.1	43.9	63.2	30.78	29.29
6.1 Food	0.0	2.8	2.8	0.9	0.0	0.3	1.0	0.5	0.8	3.0	0.92	1.25
6.2 Textiles	0.3	8.5	5.5	1.0	0.0	0.0	1.0	1.5	7.6	10.1	1.15	0.55
6.3 Metal based and nonmetallic	0.0	0.0	3.9	8.0	0.0	9.8	0.3	2.7	1.2	9.5	1.02	3.14
6.4 Electrical appliances	20.0	31.4	15.7	35.6	51.2	39.6	1.5	4.7	21.2	31.6	8.16	11.36
6.5 Machinery and transport equipment	0.0	9.7	4.7	17.2	3.5	0.3	2.8	1.0	0.6	0.2	2.12	4.47
6.6 Chemicals	0.0	21.8	5.7	4.4	9.0	0.0	1.1	0.9	5.2	6.1	2.90	2.87

continued on next page

Table A8.8 continued)

Item	China, People's Republic of 1990–1997	China, People's Republic of 1998–2005	Japan 1990–1997	Japan 1998–2005	Korea, Republic of 1990–1997	Korea, Republic of 1998–2005	Hong Kong, China 1990–1997	Hong Kong, China 1998–2005	Taipei,China 1990–1997	Taipei,China 1998–2005	Grand Total 1990–1997	Grand Total 1998–2005
6.7 Petroleum products	0.0	0.0	11.0	1.2	0.0	0.0	0.9	3.5	0.0	0.0	9.25	2.78
6.8 Construction materials	0.0	0.0	0.0	0.0	0.0	0.0	0.0	1.1	0.0	0.0	0.24	0.18
6.9 Other industry	7.4	0.0	4.5	3.2	6.5	12.3	0.9	5.2	7.2	2.8	5.02	2.69
7. Services	1.9	1.2	2.0	1.7	0.8	4.5	1.4	8.2	0.4	7.6	2.59	3.98
7.1 Transportation and travel	0.1	0.0	0.8	0.2	0.0	1.1	0.1	2.4	0.0	5.4	n.a.	n.a.
7.2 Other services	1.8	1.2	1.1	1.4	0.8	3.4	1.3	5.8	0.3	2.2	n.a.	n.a.
8. Investment	0.4	0.0	0.5	5.6	0.8	0.0	1.1	17.9	0.1	0.6	4.47	6.09
9. Real estate	1.2	0.6	22.9	0.9	0.0	0.0	2.0	10.1	4.4	3.0	4.15	2.32
9.1 Housing and real estate	1.2	0.6	14.0	0.9	0.0	0.0	1.8	8.2	4.3	2.8	n.a.	n.a.
9.2 Hotels and restaurants	0.0	0.0	8.9	0.0	0.0	0.0	0.1	1.9	0.0	0.2	n.a.	n.a.
9.3 Other real estate	0.0	0.0	0.0	0.0	0.0	0.0	0.2	0.0	0.1	0.0	n.a.	n.a.
10. Others	2.6	4.6	0.6	0.8	0.7	2.8	0.7	0.3	4.2	7.5	3.39	6.22
Total Percentage (%)	**100.0**	**100.0**	**100.0**	**100.0**	**100.0**	**100.0**	**100.0**	**100.0**	**100.0**	**100.0**	**100.0**	**100.0**
Total Value ($ Million)	**32.2**	**23.6**	**1,089.0**	**5,390.1**	**9.0**	**31.3**	**1,837.8**	**1,020.4**	**284.9**	**267.7**	**11,610.4**	**42,640.0**

East Asia = includes People's Republic of China, Japan, and Republic of Korea; n.a. = not available; $ = US dollars; % = percent.

Source: Bank of Thailand.

Table A8.9 Net Flows of Foreign Direct Investment from East Asia; Hong Kong, China; and Taipei,China (%)

Item	China, People's Republic of 1990–1997	China, People's Republic of 1998–2005	Japan 1990–1997	Japan 1998–2005	Korea, Republic of 1990–1997	Korea, Republic of 1998–2005	Hong Kong, China 1990–1997	Hong Kong, China 1998–2005	Taipei,China 1990–1997	Taipei,China 1998–2005	Grand Total 1990–1997	Grand Total 1998–2005
1. Financial institutions	31.7	0.0	2.0	1.4	0.6	0.0	14.6	8.9	0.4	(0.2)	5.76	5.23
2. Trade	9.0	18.5	17.7	13.7	18.2	14.4	23.1	18.1	36.4	24.5	20.81	13.98
3. Construction	4.5	2.1	8.3	1.6	19.7	9.6	20.0	3.1	3.6	4.5	7.51	0.57
4. Mining and quarrying	2.1	(0.4)	0.2	(1.6)	0.1	0.0	0.0	0.2	(0.1)	0.0	2.96	1.38
4.1 Oil exploration	0.0	(0.1)	0.2	(1.9)	0.1	0.0	(0.2)	0.0	0.1	0.0	n.a.	n.a.
4.2 Others	2.1	(0.3)	0.0	0.3	0.0	0.0	0.2	0.3	(0.2)	0.0	n.a.	n.a.
5. Agriculture	9.9	0.0	0.4	(0.1)	0.0	0.0	(0.1)	1.3	1.6	0.0	0.38	0.10
6. Industry	25.3	43.8	64.0	77.2	55.5	40.5	22.1	17.3	48.7	45.8	37.24	54.41
6.1 Food	26.7	2.7	3.3	0.9	0.4	0.2	0.7	1.6	8.0	3.2	3.21	2.74
6.2 Textiles	10.9	33.1	2.0	0.9	0.4	0.0	1.4	1.5	6.9	9.5	1.84	1.28
6.3 Metal based and nonmetallic	21.7	0.1	8.4	11.7	7.2	3.2	1.6	0.8	7.5	2.6	4.69	5.71
6.4 Electrical appliances	(136.0)	(6.7)	27.0	15.3	13.7	23.8	6.3	8.3	8.5	3.5	12.92	11.67
6.5 Machinery and transport equipment	3.2	(0.6)	11.5	33.4	(0.2)	1.6	1.5	1.0	0.6	2.2	5.39	17.00
6.6 Chemicals	0.0	(1.5)	6.9	5.3	2.3	6.7	3.3	1.0	5.3	3.2	6.00	6.07

continued on next page

Table A8.9 (continued)

Item	China, People's Republic of 1990–1997	China, People's Republic of 1998–2005	Japan 1990–1997	Japan 1998–2005	Korea, Republic of 1990–1997	Korea, Republic of 1998–2005	Hong Kong, China 1990–1997	Hong Kong, China 1998–2005	Taipei,China 1990–1997	Taipei,China 1998–2005	Grand Total 1990–1997	Grand Total 1998–2005
6.7 Petroleum products	0.0	0.0	(0.6)	(0.5)	0.0	0.0	0.1	(2.0)	0.0	0.0	(1.96)	2.58
6.8 Construction materials	0.0	0.4	0.1	0.4	0.0	0.1	1.0	(0.4)	0.9	0.6	0.28	0.52
6.9 Other industry	98.8	16.3	5.4	9.8	31.7	5.0	6.1	5.5	11.0	21.0	4.86	6.84
7. Services	23.4	2.0	4.0	3.9	4.4	22.4	4.8	12.3	2.4	2.5	4.58	7.89
7.1 Transportation and travel	2.9	0.0	2.5	0.9	2.6	4.5	1.9	2.5	0.5	1.0	n.a.	n.a.
7.2 Other services	20.5	2.0	1.5	3.0	1.8	17.9	2.9	9.7	1.9	1.6	n.a.	n.a.
8. Investment	4.0	0.3	0.7	(2.7)	(0.1)	0.1	2.4	12.1	2.0	1.8	0.36	1.74
9. Real estate	(2.0)	5.1	2.2	0.3	0.5	3.8	11.8	10.6	4.0	3.4	21.17	3.29
9.1 Housing and real estate	(2.0)	5.1	2.1	0.3	0.5	2.1	10.2	9.4	3.7	2.0	n.a.	n.a.
9.2 Hotels and restaurants	0.0	0.1	0.1	0.0	0.0	1.8	1.7	1.0	0.4	1.4	n.a.	n.a.
9.3 Other real estate	0.0	0.0	0.0	0.0	0.0	0.0	(0.1)	0.1	0.0	0.0	n.a.	n.a.
10. Others	(7.9)	28.7	0.5	6.2	1.0	9.2	1.2	16.2	0.9	17.7	(0.77)	11.40
Total Percentage (%)	100.0	100.0	100.0	100.0	100.0	100.0	100.0	100.0	100.0	100.0	100.0	100.0
Total Value ($ Million)	4.7	58.2	4,910.2	6,954.1	135.6	241.6	2,766.2	1,795.2	976.6	846.9	17,684.3	37,509.2

East Asia = includes People's Republic of China, Japan, and Republic of Korea; n.a. = not available; $ = US dollars; ( ) = negative value; % = percent.

Source: Bank of Thailand.

Table A8.10 Inflows of Foreign Direct Investment from South Asia, %

Item	Bangladesh 1998–2005	India 1998–2005	Nepal 1998–2005	Pakistan 1998–2005	Sri Lanka 1998–2005	South Asia 1998–2005	Grand Total 1990–1997	Grand Total 1998–2005
1. Financial institutions	0.0	10.3	0.0	0.0	0.0	5.6	18.05	6.01
2. Trade	0.0	8.7	0.0	40.9	2.4	18.6	18.27	25.66
3. Construction	0.0	0.2	0.0	0.0	0.0	0.1	5.44	0.88
4. Mining and quarrying	0.0	0.0	0.0	0.0	0.0	0.0	2.06	5.03
4.1 Oil exploration	0.0	0.0	0.0	0.0	0.0	0.0	n.a.	n.a.
4.2 Others	0.0	0.0	0.0	0.0	0.0	0.0	n.a.	n.a.
5. Agriculture	0.0	0.0	0.0	1.0	0.0	0.3	0.40	0.09
6. Industry	0.0	2.9	0.0	2.2	21.2	4.1	34.68	41.04
6.1 Food	0.0	0.5	0.0	0.0	0.0	0.3	2.30	1.95
6.2 Textiles	0.0	1.2	0.0	2.2	0.0	1.4	1.57	0.89
6.3 Metal based and nonmetallic	0.0	0.0	0.0	0.0	0.0	0.0	3.24	4.34
6.4 Electrical appliances	0.0	0.0	0.0	0.0	0.0	0.0	11.03	11.50
6.5 Machinery and transport equipment	0.0	0.0	0.0	0.0	0.0	0.0	4.10	10.34
6.6 Chemicals	0.0	0.1	0.0	0.0	0.0	0.1	4.77	4.37
6.7 Petroleum products	0.0	0.0	0.0	0.0	0.0	0.0	2.49	2.68
6.8 Construction materials	0.0	0.0	0.0	0.0	0.0	0.0	0.26	0.34

continued on next page

Table A8.10 (continued)

Item	Bangladesh 1998–2005	India 1998–2005	Nepal 1998–2005	Pakistan 1998–2005	Sri Lanka 1998–2005	South Asia 1998–2005	Grand Total 1990–1997	Grand Total 1998–2005
6.9 Other industry	0.0	1.1	0.0	0.0	21.2	2.3	4.92	4.63
7. Services	0.0	33.3	0.0	0.0	0.0	18.0	3.79	5.81
7.1 Transportation and travel	0.0	0.2	0.0	0.0	0.0	0.1	n.a.	n.a.
7.2 Other services	0.0	33.0	0.0	0.0	0.0	17.8	n.a.	n.a.
8. Investment	0.0	0.0	0.0	0.0	0.0	0.0	1.99	4.06
9. Real estate	55.3	6.3	17.4	2.7	0.1	6.1	14.43	2.78
9.1 Housing and real estate	46.1	6.1	17.4	2.7	0.1	5.7	n.a.	n.a.
9.2 Hotels and restaurants	9.2	0.2	0.0	0.0	0.0	0.4	n.a.	n.a.
9.3 Other real estate	0.0	0.0	0.0	0.0	0.0	0.0	n.a.	n.a.
10. Others	44.7	38.2	82.6	53.3	76.3	47.3	0.88	8.64
Total Percentage (%)	100.0	100.0	100.0	100.0	100.0	100.0	100.0	100.0
Total Value ($ Million)	1.0	20.1	0.6	12.5	3.1	37.1	29,294.6	80,149.2

n.a. = not available, $ = US dollars, % = percent.

Source: Bank of Thailand.

Table A8.11 Outflows of Foreign Direct Investment to South Asia, %

Item	Bangladesh 1998–2005	India 1998–2005	Nepal 1998–2005	Pakistan 1998–2005	Sri Lanka 1998–2005	South Asia 1998–2005	Grand Total 1990–1997	Grand Total 1998–2005
1. Financial institutions	0.0	0.0	0.0	0.0	0.0	0.0	36.78	6.69
2. Trade	0.0	0.6	0.0	0.0	0.0	0.6	14.41	35.94
3. Construction	0.0	0.0	0.0	0.0	0.0	0.0	2.30	1.16
4. Mining and quarrying	0.0	0.0	0.0	0.0	0.0	0.0	0.69	8.24
4.1 Oil exploration	0.0	0.0	0.0	0.0	0.0	0.0	n.a.	n.a.
4.2 Others	0.0	0.0	0.0	0.0	0.0	0.0	n.a.	n.a.
5. Agriculture	0.0	0.0	0.0	0.0	0.0	0.0	0.44	0.08
6. Industry	0.0	96.0	0.0	0.0	0.0	92.7	30.78	29.29
6.1 Food	0.0	88.4	0.0	0.0	0.0	85.4	0.92	1.25
6.2 Textiles	0.0	0.1	0.0	0.0	0.0	0.1	1.15	0.55
6.3 Metal based and nonmetallic	0.0	0.0	0.0	0.0	0.0	0.0	1.02	3.14
6.4 Electrical appliances	0.0	0.0	0.0	0.0	0.0	0.0	8.16	11.36
6.5 Machinery and transport equipment	0.0	0.0	0.0	0.0	0.0	0.0	2.12	4.47
6.6 Chemicals	0.0	0.8	0.0	0.0	0.0	0.8	2.90	2.87
6.7 Petroleum products	0.0	0.0	0.0	0.0	0.0	0.0	9.25	2.78
6.8 Construction materials	0.0	0.0	0.0	0.0	0.0	0.0	0.24	0.18

continued on next page

Table A8.11 (continued)

Item	Bangladesh 1998–2005	India 1998–2005	Nepal 1998–2005	Pakistan 1998–2005	Sri Lanka 1998–2005	South Asia 1998–2005	Grand Total 1990–1997	Grand Total 1998–2005
6.9 Other industry	0.0	6.7	0.0	0.0	0.0	6.5	5.02	2.69
7. Services	0.0	0.0	0.0	0.0	0.0	0.0	2.59	3.98
7.1 Transportation and travel	0.0	0.0	0.0	0.0	0.0	0.0	n.a.	n.a.
7.2 Other services	0.0	0.0	0.0	0.0	0.0	0.0	n.a.	n.a.
8. Investment	0.0	0.0	0.0	0.0	0.0	0.0	4.47	6.09
9. Real estate	0.0	3.2	0.0	0.0	100.0	4.8	4.15	2.32
9.1 Housing and real estate	0.0	3.2	0.0	0.0	100.0	4.8	n.a.	n.a.
9.2 Hotels and restaurants	0.0	0.0	0.0	0.0	0.0	0.0	n.a.	n.a.
9.3 Other real estate	0.0	0.0	0.0	0.0	0.0	0.0	n.a.	n.a.
10. Others	0.0	0.2	0.0	100.0	0.0	2.0	3.39	6.22
Total Percentage (%)	100.0	100.0	100.0	100.0	100.0	100.0	100.0	100.0
Total Value ($ Million)	0.0	13.7	0.0	0.3	0.2	14.2	11,610.4	42,640.0

n.a. = not available, $ = US dollars,   % = percent.

Source: Bank of Thailand.

469

Table A8.12 Net Flows of Foreign Direct Investment from South Asia, %

Item	Bangladesh 1998–2005	India 1998–2005	Nepal 1998–2005	Pakistan 1998–2005	Sri Lanka 1998–2005	South Asia 1998–2005	Grand Total 1990–1997	Grand Total 1998–2005
1. Financial institutions	0.0	32.5	0.0	0.0	0.0	9.0	5.76	5.23
2. Trade	0.0	26.0	0.0	41.7	2.6	29.7	20.81	13.98
3. Construction	0.0	0.8	0.0	0.0	0.0	0.2	7.51	0.57
4. Mining and quarrying	0.0	0.0	0.0	0.0	0.0	0.0	2.96	1.38
4.1 Oil exploration	0.0	0.0	0.0	0.0	0.0	0.0	n.a.	n.a.
4.2 Others	0.0	0.0	0.0	0.0	0.0	0.0	n.a.	n.a.
5. Agriculture	0.0	0.0	0.0	1.0	0.0	0.5	0.38	0.10
6. Industry	0.0	(196.6)	0.0	2.3	22.9	(50.6)	37.24	54.41
6.1 Food	0.0	(188.0)	0.0	0.0	0.0	(52.2)	3.21	2.74
6.2 Textiles	0.0	3.7	0.0	2.3	0.0	2.2	1.84	1.28
6.3 Metal based and non-metallic	0.0	0.0	0.0	0.0	0.0	0.0	4.69	5.71
6.4 Electrical appliances	0.0	0.0	0.0	0.0	0.0	0.0	12.92	11.67
6.5 Machinery and transport equipment	0.0	0.0	0.0	0.0	0.0	0.0	5.39	17.00
6.6 Chemicals	0.0	(1.3)	0.0	0.0	0.0	(0.4)	6.00	6.07
6.7 Petroleum products	0.0	0.0	0.0	0.0	0.0	0.0	(1.96)	2.58
6.8 Construction materials	0.0	0.0	0.0	0.0	0.0	0.0	0.28	0.52

continued on next page

Table A8.12 (continued)

Item	Bangladesh 1998–2005	India 1998–2005	Nepal 1998–2005	Pakistan 1998–2005	Sri Lanka 1998–2005	South Asia 1998–2005	Grand Total 1990–1997	Grand Total 1998–2005
6.9 Other industry	0.0	(11.0)	0.0	0.0	22.9	(0.2)	4.86	6.84
7. Services	0.0	104.6	0.0	0.0	0.0	29.0	4.58	7.89
7.1 Transportation and travel	0.0	0.8	0.0	0.0	0.0	0.2	n.a.	n.a.
7.2 Other services	0.0	103.8	0.0	0.0	0.0	28.8	n.a.	n.a.
8. Investment	0.0	0.0	0.0	0.0	0.0	0.0	0.36	1.74
9. Real estate	55.3	13.0	17.4	2.7	(8.1)	6.9	21.17	3.29
9.1 Housing and real estate	46.1	12.2	17.4	2.7	(8.1)	6.2	n.a.	n.a.
9.2 Hotels and restaurants	9.2	0.8	0.0	0.0	0.0	0.6	n.a.	n.a.
9.3 Other real estate	0.0	0.0	0.0	0.0	0.0	0.0	n.a.	n.a.
10. Others	44.7	119.7	82.6	52.3	82.6	75.2	(0.77)	11.40
Total Percentage (%)	100.0	100.0	100.0	100.0	100.0	100.0	100.0	100.0
Total Value ($ Million)	1.0	6.4	0.6	12.2	2.8	23.0	17,684.3	37,509.2

n.a. = not available, $ = US dollars, ( ) = negative value, % = percent.

Source: Bank of Thailand.

Table A8.13 Thailand's Services Trade, 1997–2007 ($ Million)

Item	1997	1998	1999	2000	2001	2002	2003	2004	2005	2006p	2007p
Services	**4,494**	**5,235**	**5,814**	**4,650**	**4,475**	**5,007**	**5,062**	**5,294**	**4,794**	**4,664**	**5,921**
Services receipts	15,779	13,214	14,653	13,869	13,024	15,391	15,801	19,050	20,165	24,834	30,362
(1) Transportation	2,413	2,674	3,015	3,244	3,059	3,264	3,505	4,349	4,626	5,379	6,369
1.1 Freight	626	469	512	605	610	678	805	1,092	1,200	1,383	1,603
1.2 Passenger	1,394	2,082	2,387	2,447	2,306	2,491	2,601	3,010	2,527	3,223	3,956
1.3 Others	393	123	116	192	143	95	99	247	900	773	810
(2) Travel	7,677	6,202	7,040	7,489	7,077	7,902	7,855	10,057	9,576	13,401	16,669
(3) Government service, n.i.e.	145	81	94	83	92	87	104	108	152	186	233
(4) Other services	5,544	4,257	4,504	3,053	2,796	4,138	4,337	4,536	5,810	5,867	7,092
4.1 Communication services	187	160	144	132	109	134	149	202	258	244	232
4.2 Construction services	34	95	236	230	295	263	188	235	255	336	519
4.3 Royalties and license fees	39	8	21	9	9	8	7	15	17	46	54
4.4 Insurance services [a]	67	51	59	81	87	106	134	138	279	253	312
4.5 Others	5,217	3,943	4,044	2,601	2,296	3,627	3,859	3,946	5,001	4,988	5,974
Services payments	(11,285)	(7,979)	(8,839)	(9,219)	(8,549)	(10,384)	(10,739)	(13,756)	(15,371)	(20,170)	(24,441)
(1) Transportation	(1,426)	(955)	(1,028)	(1,141)	(1,376)	(1,419)	(1,792)	(2,441)	(3,965)	(4,763)	(5,602)
1.1 Freight	(877)	(509)	(469)	(478)	(698)	(506)	(806)	(1,146)	(1,860)	(1,881)	(2,199)
1.2 Passenger	(340)	(288)	(398)	(446)	(412)	(583)	(618)	(824)	(1,117)	(1,577)	(1,745)
1.3 Others	(209)	(158)	(161)	(217)	(266)	(330)	(368)	(471)	(989)	(1,306)	(1,659)
(2) Travel	(3,425)	(1,970)	(2,476)	(2,775)	(2,923)	(3,303)	(2,921)	(4,516)	(3,803)	(4,599)	(5,144)
(3) Government service, n.i.e.	(214)	(126)	(118)	(131)	(135)	(148)	(171)	(168)	(146)	(175)	(252)
(4) Other services	(6,220)	(4,928)	(5,217)	(5,172)	(4,115)	(5,514)	(5,855)	(6,631)	(7,456)	(10,633)	(13,442)
4.1 Communication services	(101)	(55)	(29)	(39)	(146)	(84)	(179)	(143)	(214)	(159)	(169)

continued on next page

Table A8.13 (continued)

Item	1997	1998	1999	2000	2001	2002	2003	2004	2005	2006p	2007p
4.2 Construction services	(207)	(124)	(83)	(105)	(111)	(69)	(152)	(229)	(314)	(581)	(642)
4.3 Royalties and license fees	(634)	(518)	(584)	(709)	(822)	(1,071)	(1,269)	(1,584)	(1,676)	(2,047)	(2,289)
4.4 Insurance services ^{a}	(229)	(188)	(182)	(177)	(198)	(328)	(382)	(356)	(478)	(484)	(504)
4.5 Others ^{b}	(5,049)	(4,043)	(4,339)	(4,142)	(2,838)	(3,962)	(3,873)	(4,319)	(4,774)	(7,362)	(9,839)
Income	**(3,455)**	**(3,594)**	**(2,973)**	**(1,373)**	**(2,454)**	**(3,664)**	**(4,978)**	**(6,121)**	**(7,186)**	**(6,853)**	**(5,667)**
Income receipts	3,749	3,333	3,096	4,234	3,919	3,419	3,152	3,247	3,640	4,661	6,772
(1) Compensation of employees	1,665	1,425	1,463	1,696	1,253	1,380	1,608	1,623	1,187	1,333	1,635
(2) Investment income	2,084	1,908	1,633	2,538	2,666	2,039	1,544	1,624	2,453	3,327	5,137
Of which: Reinvested earnings ^{c}	0	0	0	0	84	65	135	125	249	163	163
Income payments ^{d}	(7,204)	(6,927)	(6,069)	(5,607)	(6,373)	(7,083)	(8,130)	(9,368)	(10,825)	(11,514)	(12,439)
(1) Income on equity	(1,628)	(1,436)	(1,545)	(1,516)	(3,004)	(4,692)	(6,260)	(7,676)	(9,306)	(9,461)	(10,541)
Of which: Reinvested earnings ^{c}	0	0	0	0	(1,175)	(2,388)	(3,316)	(4,223)	(4,501)	(4,165)	(4,165)
(2) Income on debt	(5,576)	(5,491)	(4,524)	(4,091)	(3,369)	(2,391)	(1,870)	(1,692)	(1,519)	(2,053)	(1,898)
Inward remittances ^{e}	**1,207**	**1,198**	**1,182**	**1,440**	**1,004**	**1,153**	**1,256**	**1,517**	**1,184**	**1,423**	**1,628**

n.i.e. = not included elsewhere, p = provisional, ( ) = negative value, $ = US dollars.
^{a} Including insurance on goods. ^{b} Including compensation of employees. ^{c} Reinvested earnings have been recorded as part of direct investment in financial account, and its contra entry recorded as "investment income" in current account. The series have been revised back to 2001. ^{d} Investment income only. ^{e} Since 1 April 2004, Bank of Thailand has changed the data submission method from foreign transactions report to electronic data set.

Source: Bank of Thailand.

Table A8.14 International Tourist Arrivals by Region of Residence, 1997–2007 (Persons)

Economy of Destination	1997	1998	1999	2000	2001	2002	2003	2004	2005	2006	2007
East Asia	4,568,837	4,583,160	5,195,972	5,752,871	6,064,117	6,531,546	6,166,460	7,034,024	6,692,982	7,942,143	7,981,205
ASEAN	1,767,316	1,765,488	1,941,415	2,114,355	2,385,528	2,614,627	2,646,003	2,926,259	3,099,569	3,556,395	3,755,554
Brunei Darussalam	6,938	12,569	9,277	12,762	13,912	13,755	17,244	13,905	15,124	12,662	12,430
Cambodia	–	–	–	43,104	54,399	79,219	73,868	98,551	112,477	125,336	108,776
Indonesia	89,110	69,474	132,216	145,066	153,458	164,994	167,414	201,303	186,687	218,167	233,919
Lao PDR	28,301	49,738	71,722	74,832	86,357	94,052	104,468	116,357	208,097	282,239	521,062
Malaysia	1,046,029	918,071	991,060	1,054,469	1,159,630	1,296,109	1,338,624	1,388,981	1,341,535	1,578,632	1,551,959
Myanmar	–	–	–	47,164	42,903	42,266	37,180	45,963	56,466	67,054	75,183
Philippines	76,727	78,181	87,326	106,724	129,818	142,940	143,015	173,218	188,404	202,305	198,873
Singapore	492,089	586,113	604,867	655,767	664,980	683,296	629,103	732,180	795,322	818,162	799,100
Viet Nam	28,122	51,342	44,947	56,959	80,071	97,996	135,087	155,801	195,457	251,838	254,252
China, People's Republic of	439,795	571,061	775,626	704,080	694,886	763,139	624,214	779,070	761,904	1,033,305	1,003,141
Hong Kong, China	472,325	517,966	429,944	487,151	523,465	526,138	649,920	656,941	438,519	463,339	448,057
Japan	965,454	986,264	1,064,539	1,197,931	1,168,548	1,222,270	1,014,513	1,182,067	1,181,913	1,293,313	1,248,700
Korea, Republic of	411,087	202,841	338,039	447,798	552,977	716,778	694,340	909,789	815,862	1,101,525	1,075,516
Taipei,China	448,280	457,360	557,629	707,305	724,769	673,652	521,941	556,341	375,299	472,851	427,033
Others	64,580	82,180	88,780	11,759	13,944	14,942	15,529	23,557	19,916	21,415	23,204
South Asia	229,571	258,815	280,422	339,413	333,248	390,745	390,335	468,316	518,878	605,236	685,574
Bangladesh	20,911	22,061	25,300	29,708	32,941	41,145	57,651	59,413	46,187	44,081	47,999
India	135,121	147,579	163,980	202,868	206,132	253,110	230,316	300,163	352,766	429,732	506,237
Nepal	14,141	14,725	16,681	19,603	19,009	23,001	22,397	23,512	24,545	23,205	20,538
Pakistan	35,151	37,232	39,054	49,148	35,737	29,902	30,894	37,633	41,002	45,122	47,761
Sri Lanka	18,981	29,725	26,612	29,586	29,147	32,441	38,309	34,226	39,348	47,448	44,239

continued on next page

Table A8.14 (continued)

Economy of Destination	1997	1998	1999	2000	2001	2002	2003	2004	2005	2006	2007
Others	5,266	7,493	8,795	8,500	10,282	11,146	10,768	13,369	15,030	15,648	18,800
Europe	1,585,915	1,888,673	1,990,449	2,168,996	2,304,640	2,450,878	2,256,160	2,616,347	2,686,567	3,321,795	3,689,770
The Americas	388,190	448,761	514,595	584,967	604,041	640,143	576,589	692,827	739,707	825,118	817,564
Oceania	271,442	348,346	350,555	381,464	427,673	423,501	343,914	466,907	501,882	627,246	731,283
Middle East	126,427	165,078	175,106	200,523	237,268	272,805	203,878	289,571	304,047	405,856	453,891
Africa	50,963	72,097	73,233	80,389	90,963	89,449	67,117	82,711	72,873	94,408	104,941
Total	7,221,345	7,764,930	8,580,332	9,508,623	10,061,950	10,799,067	10,004,453	11,650,703	11,516,936	13,821,802	14,464,228

ASEAN = Association of Southeast Asian Nations, Lao PDR = Lao People's Democratic Republic, – = no data available.

Source: Immigration Bureau.

Table A8.15 International Tourist Arrivals by Country of Residence, 1997–2007 (%)

Economy of Destination	1997	1998	1999	2000	2001	2002	2003	2004	2005	2006	2007
East Asia	**63.27**	**59.02**	**60.56**	**60.50**	**60.27**	**60.48**	**61.64**	**60.37**	**58.11**	**57.46**	**55.18**
ASEAN	24.47	22.74	22.63	22.24	23.71	24.21	26.45	25.12	26.91	25.73	25.96
Brunei Darussalam	0.10	0.16	0.11	0.13	0.14	0.13	0.17	0.12	0.13	0.09	0.09
Cambodia	–	–	–	0.45	0.54	0.73	0.74	0.85	0.98	0.91	0.75
Indonesia	1.23	0.89	1.54	1.53	1.53	1.53	1.67	1.73	1.62	1.58	1.62
Lao PDR	0.39	0.64	0.84	0.79	0.86	0.87	1.04	1.00	1.81	2.04	3.60
Malaysia	14.49	11.82	11.55	11.09	11.52	12.00	13.38	11.92	11.65	11.42	10.73
Myanmar	–	–	–	0.50	0.43	0.39	0.37	0.39	0.49	0.49	0.52
Philippines	1.06	1.01	1.02	1.12	1.29	1.32	1.43	1.49	1.64	1.46	1.37
Singapore	6.81	7.55	7.05	6.90	6.61	6.33	6.29	6.28	6.91	5.92	5.52
Viet Nam	0.39	0.66	0.52	0.60	0.80	0.91	1.35	1.34	1.70	1.82	1.76
China, People's Republic of	6.09	7.35	9.04	7.40	6.91	7.07	6.24	6.69	6.62	7.48	6.94
Hong Kong, China	6.54	6.67	5.01	5.12	5.20	4.87	6.50	5.64	3.81	3.35	3.10
Japan	13.37	12.70	12.41	12.60	11.61	11.32	10.14	10.15	10.26	9.36	8.63
Korea, Republic of	5.69	2.61	3.94	4.71	5.50	6.64	6.94	7.81	7.08	7.97	7.44
Taipei,China	6.21	5.89	6.50	7.44	7.20	6.24	5.22	4.78	3.26	3.42	2.95
Others	0.89	1.06	1.03	0.12	0.14	0.14	0.16	0.20	0.17	0.15	0.16
South Asia	**3.18**	**3.33**	**3.27**	**3.57**	**3.31**	**3.62**	**3.90**	**4.02**	**4.51**	**4.38**	**4.74**
Bangladesh	0.29	0.28	0.29	0.31	0.33	0.38	0.58	0.51	0.40	0.32	0.33
India	1.87	1.90	1.91	2.13	2.05	2.34	2.30	2.58	3.06	3.11	3.50

continued on next page

Table A8.15 (continued)

Economy of Destination	1997	1998	1999	2000	2001	2002	2003	2004	2005	2006	2007
Nepal	0.20	0.19	0.19	0.21	0.19	0.21	0.22	0.20	0.21	0.17	0.14
Pakistan	0.49	0.48	0.46	0.52	0.36	0.28	0.31	0.32	0.36	0.33	0.33
Sri Lanka	0.26	0.38	0.31	0.31	0.29	0.30	0.38	0.29	0.34	0.34	0.31
Others	0.07	0.10	0.10	0.09	0.10	0.10	0.11	0.11	0.13	0.11	0.13
Europe	**21.96**	**24.32**	**23.20**	**22.81**	**22.90**	**22.70**	**22.55**	**22.46**	**23.33**	**24.03**	**25.51**
The Americas	**5.38**	**5.78**	**6.00**	**6.15**	**6.00**	**5.93**	**5.76**	**5.95**	**6.42**	**5.97**	**5.65**
Oceania	**3.76**	**4.49**	**4.09**	**4.01**	**4.25**	**3.92**	**3.44**	**4.01**	**4.36**	**4.54**	**5.06**
Middle East	**1.75**	**2.13**	**2.04**	**2.11**	**2.36**	**2.53**	**2.04**	**2.49**	**2.64**	**2.94**	**3.14**
Africa	**0.71**	**0.93**	**0.85**	**0.85**	**0.90**	**0.83**	**0.67**	**0.71**	**0.63**	**0.68**	**0.73**
Total	**100.0**	**100.0**	**100.0**	**100.0**	**100.0**	**100.0**	**100.0**	**100.0**	**100.0**	**100.0**	**100.0**

ASEAN = Association of Southeast Asian Nations, Lao PDR = Lao People's Democratic Republic, – = no data available, % = percent.

Source: Immigration Bureau.

Table A8.16 Outgoing Thai Nationals by Country of Destination, 1997–2007 (Persons)

Economy of Destination	1997	1998	1999	2000	2001	2002	2003	2004	2005	2006	2007
East Asia	**1,272,846**	**1,161,179**	**1,360,424**	**1,568,469**	**1,672,049**	**1,890,945**	**1,774,181**	**2,265,068**	**2,562,844**	**2,843,598**	**3,368,321**
ASEAN	664,353	712,795	785,342	932,179	1,043,580	1,181,176	1,191,560	1,404,726	1,561,642	1,770,514	2,232,200
Brunei Darussalam	26,269	26,106	15,926	12,600	11,472	11,357	11,424	11,331	9,645	9,584	9,822
Cambodia	14,137	11,259	16,985	22,175	24,171	24,099	17,505	22,301	24,077	31,244	35,796
Indonesia	20,886	8,551	7,795	15,731	16,704	18,277	17,361	22,449	21,059	21,491	28,814
Lao PDR	51,180	53,818	62,640	67,251	63,774	74,991	82,776	106,880	271,988	390,991	600,044
Malaysia	376,036	403,248	445,552	540,278	627,798	740,570	788,204	863,665	831,338	897,203	1,135,336
Myanmar	19,133	17,718	19,362	19,820	16,605	16,885	20,708	31,808	23,357	27,297	33,048
Philippines	13,332	10,854	11,625	12,201	10,710	12,077	12,158	13,593	16,650	16,708	18,971
Singapore	211,114	194,490	225,431	234,482	245,499	243,828	205,600	287,597	316,754	297,050	267,695
Viet Nam	16,716	15,728	16,373	21,851	26,857	39,092	35,824	45,102	46,774	78,946	102,674
China, People's Republic of	91,492	69,919	120,819	135,517	165,222	223,859	155,682	285,893	363,156	380,345	410,623
Hong Kong, China	201,368	130,731	178,030	195,678	192,959	202,515	149,449	238,566	253,737	257,715	222,383
Japan	86,831	67,529	76,776	88,900	88,050	99,395	111,434	143,152	168,456	192,475	234,137
Korea, Republic of	21,344	27,505	35,605	61,465	44,973	54,027	55,075	68,402	84,804	85,116	105,742
Taipei,China	116,500	118,173	121,589	134,880	131,267	123,918	104,446	107,749	114,400	126,438	121,727
Others	6,508	5,550	5,916	5,640	5,998	6,055	6,535	16,580	16,649	30,995	41,509
South Asia	**25,720**	**22,496**	**23,470**	**28,356**	**27,880**	**28,884**	**40,960**	**50,548**	**55,818**	**66,119**	**83,072**
Bangladesh	1,828	2,076	2,032	2,739	3,145	3,843	4,349	4,469	4,728	5,042	6,366
India	15,026	12,756	12,942	15,646	15,570	16,171	22,567	29,835	37,976	42,488	56,718
Nepal	2,358	2,060	2,694	3,731	3,761	2,554	5,315	5,992	3,578	4,006	4,889
Pakistan	1,541	1,733	1,619	2,378	1,752	1,489	1,754	2,162	2,768	2,987	3,275

continued on next page

Table A8.16 (continued)

Economy of Destination	1997	1998	1999	2000	2001	2002	2003	2004	2005	2006	2007
Sri Lanka	4,759	3,697	3,771	3,476	3,130	4,257	6,355	7,114	5,971	7,508	5,744
Others	208	174	412	386	522	570	620	976	797	4,088	6,080
Europe	155,661	102,312	132,664	158,598	161,215	178,408	185,329	222,912	249,205	280,708	317,699
The Americas	59,303	35,803	45,557	48,457	42,073	35,259	32,229	36,392	45,695	43,242	63,479
Oceania	63,462	38,055	55,882	63,714	68,801	73,581	69,505	71,402	71,189	74,007	90,460
Middle East	57,524	32,002	33,015	35,846	35,027	36,170	44,531	60,174	59,273	69,659	87,164
Africa	3,079	1,998	3,722	5,488	3,573	6,392	4,974	2,445	2,525	4,296	7,518
Total	1,637,595	1,393,845	1,654,734	1,908,928	2,010,618	2,249,639	2,151,709	2,708,941	3,046,549	3,381,629	4,017,713

ASEAN = Association of Southeast Asian Nations, Lao PDR = Lao People's Democratic Republic.

Source: Immigration Bureau.

Table A8.17 Outgoing Thai Nationals by Country of Destination, 1997–2007 (%)

Economy of Destination	1997	1998	1999	2000	2001	2002	2003	2004	2005	2006	2007
East Asia	**77.73**	**83.31**	**82.21**	**82.16**	**83.16**	**84.06**	**82.45**	**83.61**	**84.12**	**84.09**	**83.84**
ASEAN	40.57	51.14	47.46	48.83	51.90	52.51	55.38	51.86	51.26	52.36	55.56
Brunei Darussalam	1.60	1.87	0.96	0.66	0.57	0.50	0.53	0.42	0.32	0.28	0.24
Cambodia	0.86	0.81	1.03	1.16	1.20	1.07	0.81	0.82	0.79	0.92	0.89
Indonesia	1.28	0.61	0.47	0.82	0.83	0.81	0.81	0.83	0.69	0.64	0.72
Lao PDR	3.13	3.86	3.79	3.52	3.17	3.33	3.85	3.95	8.93	11.56	14.93
Malaysia	22.96	28.93	26.93	28.30	31.22	32.92	36.63	31.88	27.29	26.53	28.26
Myanmar	1.17	1.27	1.17	1.04	0.83	0.75	0.96	1.17	0.77	0.81	0.82
Philippines	0.81	0.78	0.70	0.64	0.53	0.54	0.57	0.50	0.55	0.49	0.47
Singapore	12.89	13.95	13.62	12.28	12.21	10.84	9.56	10.62	10.40	8.78	6.66
Viet Nam	1.02	1.13	0.99	1.14	1.34	1.74	1.66	1.66	1.54	2.33	2.56
China, People's Rep. of	5.59	5.02	7.30	7.10	8.22	9.95	7.24	10.55	11.92	11.25	10.22
Hong Kong, China	12.30	9.38	10.76	10.25	9.60	9.00	6.95	8.81	8.33	7.62	5.54
Japan	5.30	4.84	4.64	4.66	4.38	4.42	5.18	5.28	5.53	5.69	5.83
Korea, Rep. of	1.30	1.97	2.15	3.22	2.24	2.40	2.56	2.53	2.78	2.52	2.63
Taipei,China	7.11	8.48	7.35	7.07	6.53	5.51	4.85	3.98	3.76	3.74	3.03
Others	0.40	0.40	0.36	0.30	0.30	0.27	0.30	0.61	0.55	0.92	1.03
South Asia	**1.57**	**1.61**	**1.42**	**1.49**	**1.39**	**1.28**	**1.90**	**1.87**	**1.83**	**1.96**	**2.07**
Bangladesh	0.11	0.15	0.12	0.14	0.16	0.17	0.20	0.16	0.16	0.15	0.16
India	0.92	0.92	0.78	0.82	0.77	0.72	1.05	1.10	1.25	1.26	1.41

continued on next page

Table A8.17 (continued)

Economy of Destination	1997	1998	1999	2000	2001	2002	2003	2004	2005	2006	2007
Nepal	0.14	0.15	0.16	0.20	0.19	0.11	0.25	0.22	0.12	0.12	0.12
Pakistan	0.09	0.12	0.10	0.12	0.09	0.07	0.08	0.08	0.09	0.09	0.08
Sri Lanka	0.29	0.27	0.23	0.18	0.16	0.19	0.30	0.26	0.20	0.22	0.14
Others	0.01	0.01	0.02	0.02	0.03	0.03	0.03	0.04	0.03	0.12	0.15
Europe	**9.51**	**7.34**	**8.02**	**8.31**	**8.02**	**7.93**	**8.61**	**8.23**	**8.18**	**8.30**	**7.91**
The Americas	**3.62**	**2.57**	**2.75**	**2.54**	**2.09**	**1.57**	**1.50**	**1.34**	**1.50**	**1.28**	**1.58**
Oceania	**3.88**	**2.73**	**3.38**	**3.34**	**3.42**	**3.27**	**3.23**	**2.64**	**2.34**	**2.19**	**2.25**
Middle East	**3.51**	**2.30**	**2.00**	**1.88**	**1.74**	**1.61**	**2.07**	**2.22**	**1.95**	**2.06**	**2.17**
Africa	**0.19**	**0.14**	**0.22**	**0.29**	**0.18**	**0.28**	**0.23**	**0.09**	**0.08**	**0.13**	**0.19**
Total	**100.0**	**100.0**	**100.0**	**100.0**	**100.0**	**100.0**	**100.0**	**100.0**	**100.0**	**100.0**	**100.0**

ASEAN = Association of Southeast Asian Nations, Lao PDR = Lao People's Democratic Republic, Rep. = Republic, % = percent.

Source: Immigration Bureau.

Singapore

Ramkishen Rajan and Shandre Mugan Thangavelu

Introduction: Economic Structure and External Orientation

Singapore's rapid economic development from a modest trading post under British colonial rule into a modern, prosperous, self-confident, and sovereign nation is one of the more notable success stories in growth and development during the second half of the 20th century. The Singapore economy has experienced one of the highest growth rates in the world over the past three decades, its gross domestic product (GDP) growing an annual average 7.6% during 1970–2005. The growth has in turn propelled Singapore's average real per capita income from $512 in 1965 to its current level of over $26,982 by 2005, which is one of the highest in the world (Figure 9.1).

However, long-term averages hide the fact that the Singapore economy has been fairly vulnerable to external shocks over the last 5 years. Specifically, following a sharp downturn in the global electronics industry and the sluggish regional and global growth, Singapore experienced an acute

Figure 9.1 GDP Growth for Singapore Economy, 1970–2005 (2000 market prices)

GDP = gross domestic product, % = percent.

Source: Singapore Department of Statistics.

economic contraction in 2001, its worst in 30 years. Its impact on rising rates of redundancies, bankruptcies, financial and asset markets, consumer and business sentiment, and the like, have been deep and widespread. The depth of the recession was largely due to the confluence of a number of negative factors, including the events of 11 September 2001, the bird flu and severe acute respiratory syndrome outbreaks, the December 2004 tsunami, war in the Middle East, shocks to the price of oil, and the dot-com bubble crash. All of these incidents illustrated, once again, the acute vulnerability of the city-state to external shocks. Indeed, the Singapore economy has appeared relatively fragile and much more at risk to boom-bust cycles since the Asian financial crisis of 1997/98.[1] It is only in the last few years that the economy has regained its robustness. The Singapore economy expanded at a strong pace of 8.7% in 2004 and 6.4% in 2005. The growth momentum is also expected to keep pace in 2006 and is forecasted to do so in 2007 as well (Table 9.1).

Sectoral Growth

At a sectoral level, construction has remained a drag on the economy. The economic rebound in recent years has largely been driven by the nonconstruction manufacturing and services sectors. The manufacturing sector grew at an average pace of 8.5% between 2002 and 2005, while the services output growth averaged 5%. Within services, the wholesale and retail trade has been growing at double-digit rates. The hotels and restaurants, financial services, and transport and communications have all rebounded in the last few years, driving services sector growth (Table 9.2). The service sector has consistently accounted for over 60% of Singapore's gross value-added, while the manufacturing sector has accounted for about 25%. The Government has a conscious policy of ensuring that both manufacturing and services continue to form the twin engines of economic growth.

---

[1] Singapore was one of the few economies in East Asia to have staved off outright contraction that year despite the city-state's intensive trade and financial links with the other crisis-hit economies. This was due to a combination of strong fundamentals of the economy and prompt devaluation of the Singapore dollar (unlike the rigidity of the Hong Kong dollar, for instance). Somewhat less certain was the impact of the set of cost measures including a 10% reduction in the employers' contribution to the Central Provident Fund (a mandatory pension fund, voluntary wage reductions), cuts in nominal wages, government-controlled rentals for commercial and industrial properties and utility charges for electricity and telecommunications (Rajan et al 2002). While these interim recommendations of the Committee on Singapore's Competitiveness (CSC) were meant to have positive supply-side effects, they may have had negative demand-side effects in the short run.

Table 9.1 Key Macroeconomic Indicators, 1999–2005

	1999	2000	2001	2002	2003	2004	2005
Real GDP (% change, 2000 prices)	7.2	10.0	(2.3)	4.0	2.9	8.7	6.4
Manufacturing	13.6	15.3	(12.8)	8.4	3.0	13.9	9.3
Services	6.0	9.0	1.9	4.0	3.3	7.6	6.0
Construction	(8.8)	(1.7)	(1.2)	(14.0)	(9.0)	(6.1)	(1.1)
Share of gross value-added (%)							
Manufacturing	23.1	26.8	23.7	25.8	26.3	27.7	27.3
Services	63.6	61.9	64.5	63.5	63.4	63.0	63.8
Construction	7.9	6.3	6.1	5.4	5.0	4.3	3.7
Others	5.1	5.0	5.7	5.3	5.3	5.0	5.2
Employment share (%)							
Manufacturing	21.0	20.8	18.8	18.2	17.9	17.3	21.4
Services	71.1	65.5	74.2	75.0	75.6	76.3	69.6
Construction	6.9	13.1	6.1	5.9	5.6	5.5	8.1
Others	1.0	0.6	0.9	0.9	0.9	0.9	0.9
Unemployment rate (%, average)	3.5	3.1	3.3	3.6	4.0	3.4	3.1

GDP = gross domestic product, % = percent, ( ) = negative value.

Services sector includes: wholesale and retail trade, hotels and restaurants, transport and communication, financial services, business services, other services.

Source: Thangavelu and Toh (2005).

Employment and Income Distribution

As would be expected, employment growth has lagged behind economic recovery, with unemployment peaking at 4% in 2003. However, the strong output growth since then has been complemented by robust employment growth in 2004 and 2005 (Table 9.3). The overall unemployment rate has consequently declined to 3.1% in 2005. Notwithstanding this decline in cyclical unemployment, the structural adjustment of the economy to higher value-added activities appears to have contributed to slower trend growth in employment and a consequent rise in structural unemployment. The economy also relies heavily on foreign workers to augment its labor force and to plug gaps in human capital requirements.

The structural changes in the economy have also created a challenge in terms of a widening income gap. The income of the lower 20th percentile appears to have stagnated, while that of the top 10th percentile has risen markedly. As with many other countries that have embraced globalization, this widening income gap presents some important challenges that need to be addressed by policy makers (Figure 9.2).

Table 9.2 Key Economic Indicators by Sector, % change (2000 market prices)

	2002	2003	2004	2005
Goods producing industries	3.9	1.1	10.5	7.7
Manufacturing	8.4	3.0	13.9	9.3
Construction	(14.0)	(9.0)	(6.1)	(1.1)
Services producing industries	4.0	3.3	7.6	6.0
Wholesale and retail trade	18.2	10.6	15.6	10.5
Hotels and restaurants	(2.4)	(8.7)	11.5	4.6
Transport and communications	6.3	(0.7)	8.5	4.5
Financial services	(3.4)	7.6	5.4	6.5
Business services	3.9	(1.0)	2.8	4.9
Total	**4.0**	**2.9**	**8.7**	**6.4**

( ) = negative value, % = percent.

Source: Singapore Department of Statistics.

Table 9.3 Labor Market, 2002–2005

Item	2002	2003	2004	2005
Labor force ('000), as of June	2,321	2,312	2,342	2,367
Employed persons ('000), as of year-end	2,148	2,135	2,207	2,320
Unemployment rate (%, average)	3.6	4.0	3.4	3.1
Changes in employment (number)	(22,900)	(12,900)	71,400	113,300

( ) = decrease, % = percent.

Sources: Singapore Department of Statistics and Ministry of Manpower.

Unit Labor and Business Costs

Table 9.4 summarizes recent trends in unit labor cost for the Singapore economy. There appears to be a declining trend between 2002 and 2005. Labor costs form the highest proportion of overall business cost. Consequently, there is a similar declining trend in the unit business cost index of manufacturing. However, the cost of services has been rising, as have and government rates and fees, implying the unit business costs have not been declining as sharply as unit labor costs.

Free Trade Agreements

The cornerstone of Singapore's economic strategy has been its openness to international trade and investment flows. Advances in information and

Figure 9.2 Gross Monthly Income of Full-Time Employed Residents, 1994–2004

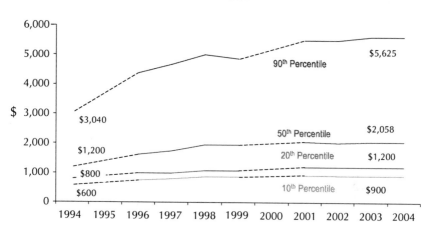

$ = Singapore dollar.

Source: Report of the Ministerial Committee on Low-Wage Workers.

communications technology (ICT) have significantly shrunk economic distances between nations and markets, possibly reducing the demand for some conventional roles that Singapore has played in serving as an entrepôt, a location for overseas headquarters, and other hub and ancillary services. This, along with the fact that Singapore is probably the most open economy in the world with few natural resources to speak of, implies a need for the city-state to be particularly aware of and responsive to the powerful forces that are transforming markets and ways of doing business, so as to remain ahead of the game. This is especially so as the competition for investments, export markets, and skilled labor intensifies (more economies are embracing free trade and investment policies) and some of Singapore's hub roles are now being duplicated in lower-cost regional destinations.

In an effort to ensure sustained growth of Singapore's exports, the city-state has attempted to aggressively source free trade agreements (FTAs) with a number of countries in Asia and elsewhere. FTAs are not an entirely new component of Singapore's commercial trade strategy, which in turn is the cornerstone of the city-state's larger international economic policy. While being among the most ardent of supporters of the global trading system, Singapore has actively pursued a second track to liberalization via the regional route in the 1980s and 1990s. Regionalism has hitherto involved both the Southeast Asian region via the 10-member Association of Southeast Asian Nations (ASEAN) grouping and the

Table 9.4 Indices of Unit Labor and Unit Business Costs, 2000 base year

	2002	2003	2004	2005
Unit Labor Cost Index of Overall Economy	102.6	100.8	96.9	95.4
Unit Business Cost Index of Manufacturing	102.5	100.9	97.9	97.7
Unit Labor Cost	106.6	102.5	95.0	92.2
Services Cost	99.4	99.9	100.4	102.4
Government Rates and Fees	89.4	86.5	95.1	96.2

Source: Singapore Department of Statistics.

larger Asia and Pacific region via the 21-member Asia-Pacific Economic Cooperation (APEC) grouping. However, indications are that the recent Asian financial crisis has impeded commitment by some of the ASEAN members to trade liberalization, while APEC has become rather unwieldy and appears ill-equipped to handle substantive trade and investment liberalization issues effectively. Accordingly, Singapore's policy makers have underscored the need to explore alternative liberalization paths. Sourcing of trade pacts on a bilateral basis has become an integral part of Singapore's new commercial trade strategy (Rajan and Sen 2002, Thangavelu and Toh 2005).

As of November 2006, apart from the ASEAN Free Trade Area (AFTA), Singapore had signed trade agreements with Australia, European Free Trade Association (EFTA), India, Japan, Jordan, Republic of Korea, New Zealand, Panama, Trans-Pacific Strategic Economic Partnership (Brunei, New Zealand, Chile, and Singapore), and the United States (US). Singapore is also negotiating bilateral agreements with Bahrain, Canada, People's Republic of China (PRC), Egypt, Kuwait, Mexico, Pakistan, Peru, Qatar, Sri Lanka, and the United Arab Emirates. On a regional basis, Singapore through ASEAN is negotiating agreements with ASEAN's full-dialogue partners: Australia, PRC, India, Japan, Republic of Korea, and New Zealand.

Singapore's choice of partners as part of its trade strategy of bilateralism may be broadly divided into two groups. The first group, which includes Japan and the US, is comprised of major established trading partners, constituting roughly one third of the city-state's total merchandise trade. These economic giants are also major investors in the city-state as they are in Southeast Asia at large. Bilateral trade accords with these two economies are best seen as a formalization of the de facto extensive and deep links that already exist. Entering into broad-ranging trade agreements with them is not only a means by which Singapore might gain greater market access (with Japan in particular); it is also a way to avoid the possible imposition of protectionist measures in the future (with regard to the US in particular), as well as managing future trade tensions, including establishing orderly dispute settlement mechanisms. Being among the first few countries to establish trade accords with these two and other economically significant economies also ensures that Singapore is not discriminated against ex post in the event that its trade competitors form such pacts with third countries. The second group of countries with which Singapore is attempting to formalize or has formalized trade accords—including Australia, the EFTA countries, India, and New Zealand—individually do not account for more than 3% of either Singapore's total exports, domestic exports, or total imports. The aim here is to seek out new markets, sources, and opportunities for investment.

This chapter offers a brief overview of Singapore's foreign direct investment (FDI) regime and FDI patterns. It addresses the emerging trade patterns of the Singapore economy and outlines relevant trade policies; discusses recent initiatives undertaken by the city-state pertaining to trade and investment-related infrastructure; and considers Singapore's trade policies and issues relating to the services sector focusing on the city-state's multilateral and bilateral commitments. As will be apparent, deepening economic relations with India has dominated the story of Singapore's growing economic engagement with South Asia. Accordingly, this chapter also considers the specific case of Singapore's bilateral economic relations with India, which have been blossoming in recent times and provide a good case study of intensifying East and South Asia economic links in general. The final section highlights some policy challenges and implications for the Singapore economy going forward.

Foreign Direct Investment—Policies, Trends, and Patterns

Foreign Direct Investment Regime

The Government of Singapore has a conscious policy of actively encouraging FDI inflows. The Economic Development Board (EDB) was established in 1961 as a one-stop agency to lead Singapore's industrialization drive by encouraging export-oriented FDI into Singapore. To this end, the EDB has worked very closely with various ministries and other government bodies to facilitate FDI. While the initial emphasis of the EDB was on labor-intensive manufacturing, over the years the focus has shifted to higher-value-added areas and skill-intensive manufacturing activities as well as knowledge-based professional service-sector activities such as financial, information and communications technology, and offshore services. Businesses are also encouraged to establish research and development (R&D) facilities in the city-state as well as to use the country as an international or regional head-quarters. The emphasis of Singapore's FDI promotion has always been on developing clusters. Thus, the EDB helped develop chemical, electronics, and engineering clusters, all of which became key economic engines for Singapore. More recently emphasis has been on product development, bio-medical research, educational, and health care services. Table 9.5 presents a summary of Singapore's main incentives to attract FDI.

Singapore does not impose any restrictions on foreign ownership in manufacturing, but does maintain restrictions on key strategic sectors such as arms and ammunition (for national security reasons) and certain services sectors. However, since the late 1990s, the Government has been liberalizing the services sector by relaxing foreign ownership limits. For instance, in financial services, the 40% limit on foreign ownership of local banks was lifted in 1999. The 70% limit on foreign ownership was removed in the Stock Exchange of Singapore (SES) and foreign ownership restrictions were completely removed in telecommunication services in 2002. However, the Government still maintains ownership restrictions in specific professional services such as in air transport, law, and media (newspaper publishing). Overall, the Government of Singapore neither screens FDI inflows nor maintains policies on performance requirements, and it has fairly liberal investment regulations. Singapore largely complies with the World Trade Organization's (WTO) Trade-Related Investment Measures (TRIMS) obligations. Singapore has signed Investment Guarantee Agreements (IGAs) with its ASEAN members and a number of other countries. These agreements offer mutual protection of nationals or companies of either country against war and noncommercial risks of expropriation and nationalization. In addition, the city-state has signed a number of trade pacts, most of which offer some form of investor protection. In any event, the Government of Singapore has not expropriated foreign investments in the past.

Trends and Patterns of Foreign Direct Investment to and from Singapore

Table 9.6 outlines the sources of Singapore's FDI between 1997 and 2003 by country. With regard to FDI inflows, European Union (EU), Japan, and US are the key sources of investment. FDIs from Europe have increased strongly from 35% in the period 1997–1999 to nearly 40% in the period 2000–2003. The US share has remained fairly stable at 15–16%, while Japan's share has declined from 17% to less than 14%. Table 9.7 provides the sources of FDI inflows to Singapore by region. Interestingly, Europe has

Table 9.5 Summary of Main Incentives to Attract Foreign Investments

Scheme	Eligibility	Incentives
Approved foreign loan scheme	Minimum loan of S$200,000 from a foreign lender to purchase of productive equipment.	Complete or partial exemption from withholding tax on interest payable to the lender.
Approved royalties incentive	Payment of royalties to a foreign partner.	Complete or partial exemption from withholding tax on royalties.
Development and expansion incentive	Companies undertaking new projects or expanding existing projects that provide significant economic gains to Singapore.	Concessional tax rate of 5%–15% for qualifying income streams.
Double deduction for R&D expenditure	Manufacturing and services firms engaged in R&D.	Double deduction for qualifying R&D expenses against income.
Investment allowance incentive	Proposed investment to be made within a qualifying period of not more than 5 years.	Exemption on a specified proportion of expenditure of new fixed investment in productive investment.
International headquarters	Companies providing management and other approved headquarters-related services to subsidiary, associated companies in other countries.	Concessional tax rate on income from providing qualifying headquarters services to approved network companies.
Pioneer status	New manufacturing and service investments introducing skills substantially more advanced than the average industry level.	Exemption from corporate income tax on qualifying profits for up to 10 years.
Regional headquarters	Companies providing management and other approved headquarters-related services to subsidiary, associated companies on a regional scale.	Concessional tax rate of 15% on income from providing qualifying headquarters services to approved companies for 3 years.

continued on next page

Table 9.5 (continued)

Scheme	Eligibility	Incentives
R&D and intellectual property management hub scheme	Companies engaged in R&D and/or intellectual property management activities from Singapore.	Exemption for a period of 5 financial years on foreign-sourced royalties or foreign-sourced interest remitted to Singapore to be spent on R&D.
Tax concessions on royalty income from approved inventions and innovations	Royalty income arising from an approved invention or approved innovations.	Royalty income will be taxed (at 10%) on 10% of gross royalty or net royalty income (after deductions), whichever is lower.
Technopreneur investment incentive	Companies which invest in qualifying Singapore-based technopreneurial start-up activity.	An investor in an approved company can deduct losses incurred from selling shares in the approved company against his or her own taxable income.
Venture capital fund incentive	Venture funds with activities in Singapore.	Complete or partial corporate tax exemption, for a set period, on income from divestment of shares, foreign dividend and foreign interest income.
Writing-down allowance for acquisition of know-how	Companies engaged in intellectual property management activities in Singapore.	Allows amortization of acquisition costs over 5 years for tax purpose.
Writing-down allowance for cost sharing agreement	Companies that have signed cost-sharing agreement to cost-sharing the expenses on R&D.	Allows amortization over 1–5 years of cost-sharing payments to R&D, which could otherwise not to be deductible.

R&D = research and development, S$ = Singapore dollars.

Source: Economic Development Board, Singapore.

overtaken Asia as the largest group of investors, accounting for 45% of total FDIs in 2004, up from 29% in 1995. North America's share (Canada and the US) has declined slightly from 20% to 17%. Within Europe, Netherlands, Switzerland, and United Kingdom (UK) constitute the bulk of FDI inflows to Singapore. Investments from Australia and New Zealand have declined in relative terms from 4% in 1995 to 1% in 2004. Interestingly, "others," a category that includes countries from the Middle East, has grown from 13% in 1995 to around 16–17%.

Table 9.6 Direction of FDI Inflows into Singapore, 1997–2003, %

Country	1997–1999	2000–2003
United States	15.0	16.6
Europe	35.5	40.0
Netherlands	10.0	13.5
Switzerland	9.0	7.2
United Kingdom	9.2	8.8
Malaysia	4.0	2.7
Japan	17.0	13.8
Australia	2.2	1.3
Latin America	14.6	16.3
Others	11.7	9.3

FDI = foreign direct investment, % = percent.

Source: *Singapore Statistical Yearbook*, Department of Statistics, Singapore.

Table 9.7 Sources of FDI Inflows to Singapore by Region, 1995, 2000, and 2004, %

Country/Region	1995	2000	2004
Europe	29	38	45
Asia	34	24	21
US and Canada	20	19	17
Australia and New Zealand	4	2	1
Others	13	17	16

FDI = foreign direct investment, US = United States, % = percent.

Source: Foreign Equity Investment in Singapore, various issues, Department of Statistics, Singapore.

It is noteworthy that Asia's share has slumped from 34% in 1995 to 21% by 2004. While this is largely a reflection of the decline in Japan's FDI share as noted above, it would be useful to examine the breakdown of FDI inflows to Singapore from Asia (Table 9.8). Interestingly Japan's share of Asia's FDI into Singapore has remained fairly stable since 1995 at around 60%. The other two traditional Asian investors in Singapore are Malaysia and Hong Kong, China. Both these economies were responsible for 25% of Asian FDI flows to Singapore in 1995 but their shares declined to 16% in 2004. In contrast, FDIs from Taipei,China have risen from 3.3% in 1995 to 10.5% by 2004, causing it to overtake Hong Kong, China; and Malaysia as sources of FDI inflows. Indonesia, Republic of Korea, Thailand, and Philippines follow as the next largest investors in 2004, each contributing 2–3% of total FDI to Singapore. Anecdotal evidence suggests that Indian firms have begun

Table 9.8 Source of Asia's FDI Inflows in Singapore by Country in 1995, 2000, and 2004, %

Country	1995	2000	2004
Brunei Darussalam	0.7	0.5	0.5
Indonesia	2.8	3.7	2.9
Malaysia	12.4	10.9	8.1
Philippines	1.3	2.3	1.6
Thailand	2.8	1.5	1.7
Viet Nam	0.0	0.0	0.0
China, People's Republic of	1.2	2.0	0.4
Hong Kong, China	13.8	12.7	7.9
Japan	59.8	55.7	58.2
Korea, Republic of	0.8	2.2	2.5
Taipei,China	3.3	7.5	10.5
Other Asia	1.2	1.0	5.7

FDI = foreign direct investment, % = percent.

Source: Foreign Equity Investment in Singapore, various issues, Department of Statistics, Singapore.

to establish headquarters in Singapore as a platform to East Asia. This is reflected in the rising share of Other Asia from 1.2% in 1995 to 5.7% by 2004 (see page 512 for detail elaboration on Singapore–India ties).

Table 9.9 breaks down FDI into Singapore by industry. Around 35% of FDI inflows to Singapore have gone to the manufacturing sector and the rest into the services sector. Within services, financial and insurance, commerce, and business services account for the bulk of FDI inflows.

Table 9.10 provides a more detailed breakdown of the FDI inflows into Singapore by regional blocs of countries and economic sectors. The overall FDI flows indicate that the major developed economies of Japan, EU, and US have been reducing their investments in Singapore. Japan and Europe have slashed their overall investment in Singapore by half from 1999 to 2003, and a similar trend is observed with the emerging economies of ASEAN. FDI flows by key economic sector indicate that manufacturing and financial sectors are the key recipients of investments from Japan, EU, and US. Although Japan and EU reduced their investments in manufacturing in 2003, this was somewhat balanced by higher investments from the US. Japan has increased its investment in the financial sector in 2003 as compared to 1999. There was also a surge in investment in real estate in 2003 from developed and emerging economies.

As noted, since the early 1990s, Singapore has also been heavily investing both in the region and beyond, with the country's major government holding

Table 9.9 FDI Inflow to Singapore by Industry, 1997–2003, %

Industry	1997–1999	2000–2003
Manufacturing	34.0	36.0
Commerce	15.2	14.8
Transport and communication	3.7	4.5
Financial and insurance	36.6	37.0
Real estate	3.4	3.0
Business services	3.6	4.1
Others	3.5	0.6

Source: *Singapore Statistical Yearbook*, Department of Statistics, Singapore.

company (Temasek) and other government-linked companies (GLCs) leading these outward ventures. Table 9.11 details distribution of Singapore's FDI outflows across the world. The share of FDIs to the US has remained stable at around 5%. The EU has been the key destination, accounting for 13% of Singapore's outflows between 1997 and 1999 and just over 9% between 2000 and 2003. Singapore has also invested aggressively in Malaysia and Hong Kong, China, both of which made up 20% of the city-state's outward investments in the period 1997–1999 and 16% in the period 2000–2003. The PRC has also been an important destination for Singapore investments (15% in 1997–1999 and 13% in 2000–2003). Beyond Asia, EU, and US, one third of Singapore's investments went to Latin America, the Middle East, and other areas in 1997–1999, with this share increasing to two fifths in the period 2000–2003. This suggests that Singapore's investments have been fairly well diversified and are becoming more so over the years, although Asia still dominates on a stock basis (United Nations Conference on Trade and Development [UNCTAD] 2005).

Table 9.12 reveals the sectoral shares of FDI outflows from Singapore. Half of Singapore's outward investments have been related to finance and insurance, a reflection of the aggressive outward orientation of Singapore's financial institutions since the late 1990s. This sector appears to be gaining in importance as countries in the region and elsewhere continue to liberalize their financial sectors. About 20% of investments from Singapore have been to the manufacturing sector, although this share declined from 25% in 1997–1999 to 20% in the period 2000–2003.

The outbound FDIs from Singapore are clearly intended to take advantage of convergence in the economic growth in the region. Another motive is to facilitate the kind of regional integration that would bring about stronger economic development, thereby complementing the growth of the PRC and India. Singapore's economy has been using cross-border sourcing as part of its development and growth strategy since the 1970s in the form of the

Table 9.10 FDI Flows to Singapore by Economic Sector and Regional Bloc, $ Mn

Economic Sector	Japan	US	EU	Korea, Rep. of	Hong Kong, China	Taipei, China	PRC	Total	ASEAN
1999									
Agriculture, fishery, and forestry	0	0	0	0	2	0	0	2	(38)
Mining and quarrying	0	0	0	0	0	0	0	0	0
Manufacturing	230	517	3,432	3	(41)	3	(7)	(42)	(11)
Construction	(42)	(2)	16	(76)	(6)	(3)	12	(73)	0
Trade/Commerce	945	450	381	246	31	9	17	303	(19)
Financial and intermediate services	88	1,502	2,697	17	189	51	23	280	107
Real estate	2	22	(50)	2	(35)	23	19	10	476
Services	84	620	410	35	38	17	(1)	89	37
Others	6	188	55	12	12	13	(72)	(36)	79
Total	**1,313**	**3,296**	**6,939**	**238**	**191**	**113**	**(10)**	**531**	**632**
2000									
Agriculture, fishery, and forestry	0	0	0	0	0	(1)	1	0	3
Mining and quarrying	–	0	0	–	–	–	–	–	0
Manufacturing	168	778	1,267	3	20	13	0	36	13
Construction	(20)	(41)	64	(31)	(6)	0	(3)	(39)	4
Trade/Commerce	193	479	545	(33)	102	(4)	(3)	63	(24)
Financial and intermediate services	346	903	1,572	14	63	149	(41)	185	49
Real estate	25	27	113	7	(35)	3	27	1	327
Services	34	214	(60)	(4)	(2)	1	8	3	28
Others	(2)	75	(54)	34	12	31	(2)	76	21
Total	**749**	**2,434**	**3,449**	**(10)**	**156**	**193**	**(13)**	**326**	**421**

ASEAN = Association of Southeast Asian Nations, EU = European Union, FDI = foreign direct investment, PRC = People's Republic of China, US = United States, $ Mn = millions of US dollars, – = no data available, ( ) = negative value.

Source: ASEAN Secretariat, *ASEAN Statistical Yearbook*, 2004.

"flying geese" with East Asian countries, FTAs in the late 1990s, and with the "growth triangle" or "subregional economic zones" (Toh 2006). The recent announcement of closer economic partnerships (CEPs)—such as forming the Indonesia–Malaysia–Singapore growth triangle (IMS-GT)—is a prime example of a policy to encourage cross-border sourcing. This is an interesting economic strategy of consolidating Singapore economy as part of the regional and global value chain. In 1995, Malaysia was the key

**Table 9.11 Direction of FDI Flows from Singapore,
1997–2003, %**

Country	1997–1999	2000–2003
United States	5.4	5.8
Europe	13.3	9.4
Netherlands	2.5	1.0
Switzerland	0.5	0.3
United Kingdom	3.9	4.9
Malaysia	9.4	8.3
Japan	1.3	2.4
Australia	2.5	2.4
Latin America	13.3	24.7
China, People's Republic of	15.5	13.2
Hong Kong, China	10.5	8.2
Thailand	3.5	3.0
Taipei,China	2.9	2.4
Korea, Republic of	2.0	1.8
India	0.6	1.1
Others	19.8	16.6

FDI = foreign direct investment, % = percent.

Source: *Singapore Statistical Yearbook*, Department of Statistics,
Singapore.

investor in the growth area; in 1999, Indonesia took on that role, while
Singapore was the prime investor in 2003. Electronics and chemicals are
the main sectors of investment for all three countries. As labor- and capital-intensive multinational activities hollow out Singapore's economy, the
IMS-GT allows firms to take advantage of abundant labor and material
resources in Indonesia and also integrate with the global network through
their higher value-added operations in Singapore. In 2003, radio, televi-
sion, and communication equipment formed the largest area for FDI in the
IMS-GT area. (Appendix Table A9.1 for details).

Singapore's Trade Performance and Patterns with Emphasis on East and South Asia

Commodity Composition

Given Singapore's lack of natural resources, it is highly dependent on
exports as well as imports for its growth (Table 9.13). Since its independence

Table 9.12 FDI Outflows from Singapore by Industry, 1997–2003, %

Industry	1997–1999	2000–2003
Manufacturing	24.9	20.2
Commerce	8.2	7.0
Transport and communication	6.0	8.0
Financial and insurance	48.2	55.0
Real estate	7.4	5.2
Business services	2.7	1.2
Others	2.6	3.4

FDI = foreign direct investment, % = percent.

Source: *Singapore Statistical Yearbook*, Department of Statistics, Singapore.

Table 9.13 External Trade at Current Prices, % share

	1979–1989	1999	2002	2005
Total	**10.3**	**8.1**	**1.5**	**13.8**
Imports	9.7	10.8	0.3	13.6
Exports	10.9	5.7	2.7	14.0
Domestic Exports	**11.7**	**9.8**	**0.8**	**15.1**
Oil	3.9	12.4	(3.9)	41.5
Non-oil	16.4	9.5	10.6	8.2
Re-exports	9.6	0.2	8.0	12.7

( ) = negative value, % = percent.

Source: *Economic Survey of Singapore*, Ministry of Trade and Industry, various issues.

in 1965, the Singapore economy relied heavily on the entrepôt trade of goods, thereby building its trade networks globally. As seen from Table 9.13, re-exports have constituted at least 45% of total exports in recent times.

Figure 9.3 reveals that three fifths of Singapore's total exports are concentrated in transport and machinery exports (Standard International Trade Classification [SITC] 7).[2] However, the composition of exports in the SITC 7 category has been changing since the Asian financial crisis of 1997/98. It appears from Table 9.14 that the share of exports of biomedical and pharmaceutical products has increased over the years, rising from 6%

---

[2] See United Nations Statistics Division for information on Standard International Trade Classification (SITC).

Figure 9.3 Singapore Total Export Composition, % of total exports

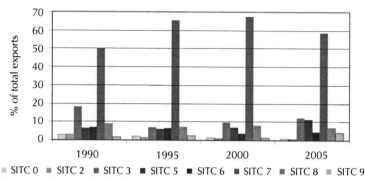

SITC = Standard Industrial Trade Classification, % = percent.

Source: *Economic Survey of Singapore*, Ministry of Trade and Industry, various issues.

in 1994 to 12% in 2005. Merchandise exports constitute around 60% of Singapore's total exports, with services making up the rest. This proportion has remained constant over the last few years. Within services transportation, travel, and other services (including education) constituted about 35% of total service exports in 2005, down from 50% in 1994.

The share of imports of transport and machinery products (SITC 7) has been in the range of 50–60% of the city-state's total imports (Figure 9.4). The high share of intermediate inputs (70–75% of total imports) indicates that the economy's production structure is fragmented and integrated with the global production value chain. Merchandise imports constitute around 70–75% of Singapore's total imports, with services making up the rest (Table 9.15). This proportion has remained constant in the last few years. Within services transportation, travel, and other services (including education) have constituted about three fifths of total service imports. This share has remained fairly stable.

Country Composition of Merchandise Trade[3]

Figure 9.5 reveals that the share of Asian merchandise exports from Singapore has been steadily increasing from around 50% in 1990 to 75% by 2005. While ASEAN remains the main market for Singapore, accounting for nearly 25% of total exports, its share has declined from 30% in 1995. Malaysia is the dominant export destination within ASEAN, absorbing 19.2% of the total exports before the 1997/98 crisis. Thereafter, the export share to Malaysia fell to around 13.2% in 2005. The export share to

---

[3]   Given the lack of data on services trade at a bilateral level, this section is inevitably limited to merchandise trade.

Table 9.14 Product Composition of Singapore's Exports, 1994–2005, % share

Item	1994	1999	2003	2005
Export of goods (values S$ Mn)	145,079	196,004	281,699	386,919
Electrical and electronic components, and machinery	45.6	55.3	50.8	58.8
Manufactured goods	6.0	4.3	3.7	4.6
Chemicals and pharmaceuticals	5.7	8.0	11.8	11.4
Fuels and petroleum products	9.5	7.9	11.1	15.0
Textiles and clothing	1.4	2.0	1.0	1.0
Transport equipment	18.3	11.0	10.3	1.6
Food, beverages, crude materials	4.4	3.3	1.9	2.2
Miscellaneous manufactures	9.1	8.2	9.4	5.4
Export of services (values S$ Mn)	55,474	40,158	63,157	85,435
Transportation	53.2	40.5	38.4	34.9
Travel	19.8	19.3	13.0	11.1
Financial and insurance	0.7	5.9	8.7	9.4
Other services	26.3	34.3	39.9	44.4

S$ Mn = millions of Singapore dollars, % = percent.

Sources: Ministry of Trade and Industry, *Economic Survey of Singapore*, various issues; *Yearbook of Statistics*, Singapore, various issues.

Thailand also fell from around 5.8% in 1995 to 4.1% in 2005. In contrast, the export shares of Indonesia increased from 2% in 1995 to nearly 4.1% in 2005.[4] The PRC and India are becoming important trading partners for Singapore as exports to both countries have been growing over 20% for the last 2 years (Figure 9.6). The share of exports to the PRC increased from 2.3% in 1995 to nearly 8.6% in 2005, while India's share increased from 1.6% in 1995 to nearly 2.6% in the same period.

Table 9.16 highlights the share of Singapore's merchandise exports to various Asian economies. In 2005, machinery and transport equipment (SITC 7) dominated Singapore's exports to most Asian economies, except for Indonesia and Viet Nam where mineral fuels (SITC 3) dominated. Singapore also exported chemical products (SITC 5) to the rest of Asia.

Figure 9.7 reveals that the share of Asian merchandise imports to Singapore has been steadily increasing from around 55% in 1990 to 65%

---

[4]   Indonesia data must be treated with caution because Singapore does not officially declare bilateral trade with Indonesia.

Figure 9.4 Singapore Total Import Composition, % of total imports

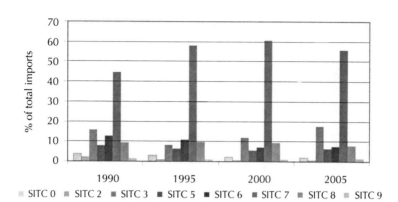

SITC = Standard International Trade Classification, % = percent.

Source: *Economic Survey of Singapore*, Ministry of Trade and Industry, various issues.

Table 9.15 Product Composition of Singapore's Merchandise Imports, 1994–2005, % share

Item	1994	1999	2003	2005
Import of goods (values S$ Mn)	146,679	176,845	230,203	323,743
Electrical and electronic components, and machinery	33.6	41.9	41.7	34.9
Manufactured goods	10.6	8.0	6.8	7.5
Chemicals and pharmaceuticals	6.5	6.0	6.7	6.2
Fuels and petroleum products	8.8	9.1	13.6	17.8
Textiles and clothing	2.0	1.1	1.0	0.3
Transport equipment	22.8	18.3	17.4	20.9
Food, beverages, crude materials	5.1	4.0	1.2	2.8
Miscellaneous manufactures	10.6	11.6	11.6	9.6
Import of services (values S$ Mn)	34,210	31998	69,187	90,349
Transportation	25.8	33.3	33.5	36.6
Travel	17.4	24.6	20.1	18.1
Financial and insurance	3.9	4.9	5.8	5.6
Other services	52.9	37.2	40.6	39.7

S$ Mn = millions of Singapore dollars, % = percent.

Sources: Ministry of Trade and Industry, *Economic Survey of Singapore*, various issues; *Yearbook of Statistics*, Singapore, various issues.

Figure 9.5 Country Share of Singapore's Exports, 1990–2005, %

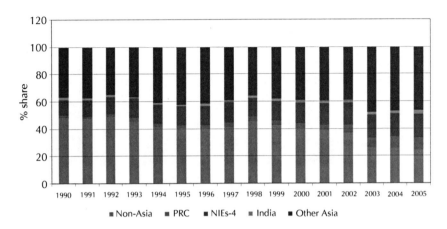

NIEs-4 = newly industrialized economies of Hong Kong, China; Republic of Korea; Singapore; and Taipei,China; PRC = People's Republic of China; % = percent.

Source: Asian Development Bank.

by 2005. The import shares for Singapore's key trading countries in Asia are given in Table 9.17. Singapore's neighbor, Malaysia, has been a major source of imports, constituting about 14–15% of Singapore's total exports. Notably, Singapore's reliance on the PRC for its imports has increased from 3.3% of total imports in 1995 to 10.3% in 2005. The import share with India has also risen, albeit more slowly, from 0.7% in 1995 to over 2% in 2005. Figure 9.8 reveals that Singapore's imports have grown fastest from South Asia in recent years, suggesting further integration between the city-state and South Asia, particularly India. This data only refers to merchandise trade. It is likely that Singapore's services trade with India has been rising fairly markedly.

Appendix Tables A9.6 and A9.7 summarize the top five exports of Singapore to the various Asian economies and show the share of exports by commodities (SITC classification) and by countries in Asia. Singapore's dynamic trade links with the Asian countries is apparent by three key export products: machinery and transport equipment (SITC 7), mineral fuel (SITC 3), and chemicals (SITC 5). The high share of trade in machines, transport equipment, and chemicals reflects the links between the production structures of Singapore with the regional production network. The export share to the PRC in machinery and transport equipment (SITC 7) rose from 40% in 1995 to nearly 65% in 2005, while the export share in chemicals (SITC 5) to the PRC hovered around 15% in 1995–2005. In contrast, the export share of mineral fuels (SITC 3) and basic manufactures (SITC 6) has declined drastically over the years.

Figure 9.6 Annual Growth of Singapore's Merchandise Exports to Asia, 1991–2005

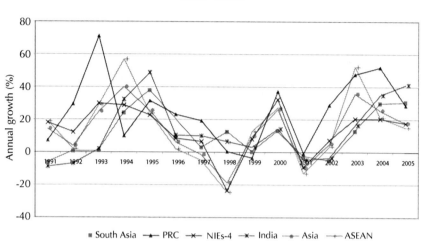

ASEAN = Association of Southeast Asian Nations; NIEs-4 = newly industrialized economies of Hong Kong, China; Republic of Korea; Singapore; and Taipei,China; PRC = People's Republic of China; % = percent.

Source: Asian Development Bank.

Table 9.16 Singapore's Export Markets in Asia: Share of Total Exports, 1995–2005, %

Export Market	1995	2000	2005
China, People's Republic of	2.33	3.90	8.60
Hong Kong, China	8.57	7.86	9.37
Indonesia[a]	2.00	2.75	4.12
Japan	7.8	7.5	5.8
Malaysia	19.18	18.16	13.23
Philippines	1.63	2.45	1.82
Korea, Republic of	2.74	3.57	3.51
Thailand	5.77	4.26	4.09
Viet Nam	1.51	1.52	1.93
Bangladesh	0.50	0.57	0.30
India	1.59	2.02	2.57
Pakistan	0.26	0.27	0.28
Sri Lanka	0.32	0.33	0.30

% = percent.

[a] Indonesia's exports to Singapore are treated as Singapore imports from Indonesia.

Source: United Nations Commodity Trade Statistics Online.

Figure 9.7 Country Share of Singapore's Imports, 1990–2005, %

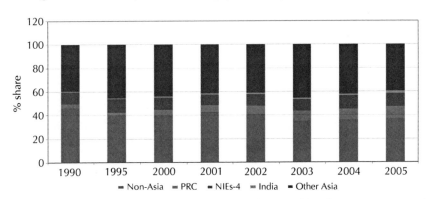

NIEs-4 = newly industrialized economies of Hong Kong, China; Republic of Korea; Singapore; and Taipei,China; PRC = People's Republic of China, % = percent.

Source: Asian Development Bank.

As with the PRC, Singapore's exports to South Asia are mostly machines, transport equipment, and chemicals. The export share in machinery and transport equipment to India accounts for nearly 50% of exports to that country. The export share of SITC 7 to Bangladesh increased from 19% in 1995 to over 49% in 2005. A similar trend is apparent for Pakistan, where the share increased from 36% in 1995 to 50% in 2005.

The export shares of SITC 5 and SITC 7 to the Republic of Korea and Hong Kong, China are also quite strong and indicate growing production links between these countries and Singapore. The export share of SITC 7 to Malaysia, Philippines, and Thailand is more than 50% of the total exports to these countries. Indonesia is the only exception in ASEAN, where the share of Singapore's exports in SITC 7 declined from 25% in 1995 to only 10% in 2005. In contrast, the share of exports of SITC 3 (mineral fuels) increased from 34% in 1995 to 69% in 2005. Among the emerging ASEAN countries, Viet Nam is becoming an important export destination, particularly in SITC 3, SITC 5, and SITC 7, where exports have increased significantly over the years.

The relatively high import share of SITC 7 (machinery and transport equipment) from Asian countries, indicate the prevalence of intraindustry trade with Singapore.[5] Bangladesh, Pakistan, Sri Lanka, and Viet Nam are important sources of imports by Singapore of agricultural food products and live animals. Although, Indonesia, Thailand, Viet Nam, and South Asian countries provide mineral fuels for Singapore's manufacturing. Singapore's linkages to the production chain in Asia are reflected by the import share of SITC 7 to ASEAN countries. The import share of machinery

---

[5]   Appendix Table A9.8 highlights the import shares by commodities and countries.

Table 9.17 Singapore's Import Sources in Asia: Share of Total Imports, 1995–2005, %

Import Source	1995	2000	2005
China, People's Republic of	3.25	5.29	10.26
Hong Kong, China	3.30	2.61	2.10
Indonesia[a]	3.03	4.88	3.92
Japan	21.1	17.2	11.0
Malaysia	15.48	16.97	13.66
Philippines	0.88	2.50	2.32
Korea, Republic of	4.34	3.58	4.30
Thailand	5.16	4.31	3.76
Viet Nam	0.36	0.61	0.91
Bangladesh	0.02	0.06	0.05
India	0.74	0.80	2.04
Pakistan	0.05	0.05	0.02
Sri Lanka	0.04	0.04	0.03

% = percent.

[a] Indonesia's imports from Singapore are treated as Singapore exports to Indonesia.

Source: United Nations Commodity Trade Statistics Online.

Figure 9.8 Annual Growth of Singapore's Merchandise Imports from Asia, 1991–2005, %

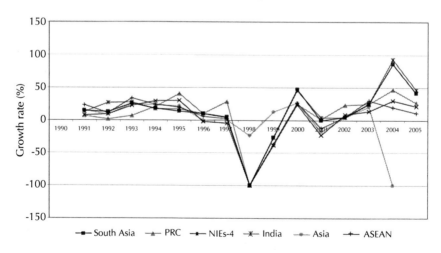

ASEAN = Association of Southeast Asian Nations; NIEs-4 = newly industrialized economies of Hong Kong, China; Republic of Korea; Singapore; and Taipei,China; PRC = People's Republic of China; % = percent.

Source: Asian Development Bank.

and transport equipment is more than 60% of the total imports from Indonesia, Malaysia, Philippines, and Thailand in 2005. These countries are important conduits for the integration of the value chain in Southeast Asia. Singapore is also strongly linked to the East Asian economies of the Republic of Korea and Hong Kong, China with shares of SITC 7 imports of nearly 65% and 78%, respectively. It is also interesting to observe that the share of imports of machinery and transport equipment from the PRC rose from 40% in 1995 to nearly 70% in 2005.

Trade and Investment-Related Infrastructure and Policies

Import Protection and Export Promotion

Singapore has embraced a policy of free trade and has imposed very few border measures. Most of the measures imposed at the border are for health, security, and environmental reasons. Singapore imposes negligible tariffs, with only six tariff lines subject to specific rates of duty (WTO 2004). The exception is the import of rice, which faces import licensing because the Government wishes to maintain a good supply for food security. The other charges that are imposed on imports are a goods and services tax (GST) of 5%, which applies to most imports, and an excise tax on alcohol, motor vehicles, petroleum, and tobacco products.

While customs clearance for most goods is automatic, with minimal administrative delays (Section 9.2), certain imports such as fresh and processed food products are required to be registered with customs as well as the Agri-Food and Veterinary Authority (AVA). The Government also provides exemption from import duty and GST for goods that are re-exported within 3 months of import. Imports that are used as intermediate inputs in production are eligible for exemption from custom duties and excise tax. In addition, nontariff restrictions such as quantity or quota restrictions are imposed on certain products for environmental, health, and security reasons. There are quantitative restrictions on chewing gum (except for oral and medicinal chewing gums), certain cosmetics, imports of used motor vehicles more than 3 years old, telecommunications equipment such as military communication equipment, and other items. The details of the tariff barriers imposed by the Government of Singapore are given in Appendix Table A9.2; nontariff barriers (NTBs) are given in Appendix Table A9.3.

Singapore does not apply any export levies or taxes. However, all exporters registered under the Companies Act or Business Registration Act are required to be registered with customs electronically (see Customs Clearance on page 505). All traders exporting strategic goods such as arms, chemicals, biological materials, and nuclear-related products are required to seek approval from customs by applying for valid permits prior to export. Permits are also required for exports of certain products subject to quotas, such as textiles and clothing to certain markets; safety and health documents are also required for agricultural products. Export restrictions are maintained mainly for health and security reasons that involve animals, animal products, fish and fish products, arms and explosives, and chemical and radioactive products.

The Government of Singapore provides extensive tax concessions and exemptions to companies engaged in international trade through a government statutory board called International Enterprise (IE) Singapore. Under the Global Trader Program (GTP), approved companies are granted a concessionary tax rate of 10% on international trading activities. In the International Shipping Enterprise Incentive scheme (AIS), approved international shipping companies are given tax exemptions for 10 years on income from qualifying shipping operations (Table 9.18). IE Singapore also provides incentives for local companies to venture overseas and to establish strong regional and global trade links through the Overseas Investment Incentive Scheme and Regionalization Finance Scheme.

Trade Enhancing Infrastructure and Infrastructure Policy

Air Transport

The average growth of the transport and communications sector in Singapore averaged around 4.5% annually from 1999 to 2005. The air transport sector has been the key sector of growth of the economy since independence, and development of major domestic corporations such as Singapore Airlines (SIA), Singapore Airport Terminal Services (SATS), SIA Engineering, SIA Cargo, and Changi Airport are the key drivers of the aviation hub in Singapore. SIA is the national carrier and a publicly listed company majority-owned (57%) by Temasek.

Singapore's aviation policy is based on free and open competition to provide an extensive framework for air services to Singapore. Singapore has air service agreements with more than 90 countries and several open skies agreement with major countries allowing for unrestricted direct passenger services between these countries and Singapore (WTO 2004). Changi Airport, which was opened in 1981, has scheduled flights to 152 destinations in 51 countries and served over 29 million passengers in 2002. Singapore falls within the top 10 largest airfreight airports in the world, its annual 1,855,000-ton (t) throughput surpassing Dubai, London, and New York (Arnold 2007). Given Singapore's status as the regional aviation hub, large multination freight services companies such as DHL, FedEx, and UPS maintain their headquarters in Singapore.

Table 9.18 Incentives to Promote Trade in Singapore

Scheme	Eligibility	Incentive
Global Trader Program	International companies involved in international trade, procurement, marketing, and distribution of qualifying commodities and products.	Concessionary tax rates on international trading activities in approved commodities and products.
Approved International Shipping Enterprise Incentive (AIS)	International shipping companies with worldwide networks.	Tax exemptions for 10 years on income from qualifying shipping operations.
Approved Cyber Trader Program (ACT)	Companies conducting international business through internet.	Concessionary tax rate of 10% of qualifying offshore income on qualifying products.
Double Tax Deduction for Market Development (DTD)	All Singapore-registered companies with main purpose of promoting trade in goods and services.	Deduction against taxable income of twice the eligible expenses incurred in approved activities as covered under Section 14B of the Income Tax Act.
Double deduction for overseas investment development expenditure	Manufacturing and services companies.	Double deduction for qualifying expenditure incurred in approved feasibility studies and maintenance of overseas project offices against income.
Overseas Investment Incentive	All Singapore-registered companies.	Deferred income tax payments from profitable operations in Singapore for 2 years if approved overseas investment incurs operating losses during the first 3 years of investment.
Regionalization Finance Scheme	Singapore-registered company with 51% local equity and fixed productive asset of not more than S$30 million. If the company is involved in the services sector, it must employ not more than 200 employees.	Fixed-cost financing program to assist local enterprises to globalize their operations. Fixed-rate loans are available under the scheme for acquiring fixed asset for overseas projects.

S$ = Singapore dollars.

Source: World Trade Organization (2004).

Singapore has been actively strengthening its position as the regional aviation hub. The Civil Aviation Authority of Singapore (CAAS) announced that it was setting up the Air Hub Development Fund (AHDF), which will provide rebates and incentives worth more than Singapore dollars (S$)210 million to develop Singapore as the aviation hub. Currently, the Government has completed the first terminal at Changi Airport for the development and operation of budget airlines in the region. In addition to the three terminals at Changi Airport, the Government is building a fourth terminal to handle the 64 million passengers per year that are expected to transit through Changi Airport in the next 10 years. The regional aviation hub status is further boosted by the opening of the Airport Logistics Park in 2003, which is operated by GLC Jurong Town Corporation (JTC) and CASS.

Maritime Transport

Given the strategic location of Singapore in Asia, maritime transport plays an important role in promoting trade and services in the economy. Maritime transport contributes nearly 3% of GDP; Singapore was the world's busiest port in terms of shipping tonnage with nearly 986.4 million gross ton and having 135,386 vessels calling at the port in 2003. In 2003, the port handled nearly 18.4 million 20-foot equivalent units (TEUs) of container traffic (WTO 2004).

Singapore operates a very liberal and highly competitive environment and does not have a freight rate filling system. Shipping companies may determine their own freight rates and there are no restrictions on foreign participation in shipping. To promote the maritime cluster in Singapore, the Maritime and Port Authority of Singapore (MPA) announced an S$80 million Maritime Cluster Fund (MCF) in 2002. The fund will be used to upgrade and train manpower and to help shipping companies reduce their operating costs in Singapore.[6]

Customs Clearance

Singapore Customs maintains electronic infrastructure that reduces transaction costs in permit applications and seamlessly allow greater flow of goods and services across the borders. All importers and exporters are required to apply for a central registration number from Singapore Customs, allowing customs to electronically interface with the relevant parties through an electronic system known as TradeNet. The central registration number allows importers and exporters to submit all required trade permits electronically, which allows a single application to be cleared by both Customs

---

[6] See Maritime Cluster Fund at http://www.mpa.gov.sg/homepage/mcf-programs.html.

and the relevant government agencies. Payment of duties, GST, and other fees are directly deducted from the trader's bank account, which reduces transaction costs. Traders report their warehouse inventory through a system called Warehouse Inventory Submission Electronically via Internet (WISE) for dutiable goods and Petrolink for petroleum products. Together with the EDB and Infocomm Development Authority, Singapore Customs will also launch TradeXchange, which offers an integrated electronic system of "workflow, submissions and enquiries to the Sea Ports, Airports, Maritime Authorities, Customs and Controlling Agencies."

Singapore also offers free trade zones (FTZ), licensed warehouses, and export processing zones (EPZs). FTZs facilitate entrepôt trade in dutiable goods, allowing traders to repackage, sort, recondition, and store their goods (except for liquors and cigarettes). In licensed warehouses, traders may store liquor, tobacco products, motor vehicles, and other goods that are subject to GST. Under the Land Transport Authority's EPZ scheme, for example, traders may keep their deregistered vehicles pending export for up to 12 months.

Infrastructure to Facilitate Labor Mobility

Singapore has among the world's fastest clearance times for migrant workers. Thanks to the Immigration Automated Clearance System (IACS), which uses biometrics and smart card technologies, frequent travelers may enjoy speedy immigration clearance through automated lanes at checkpoints. Because Singapore participates in the APEC Business Travel Card (ABTC) scheme, which facilitates business travel between APEC countries, ABTC cardholders may also pass through designated ABTC lanes.

Infrastructure to Facilitate Foreign Direct Investment

In its effort to cut red tape, the Online Application System for Integrated Services (OASIS), has been developed. OASIS spans more than 30 government agencies, through its Online Business Licensing Service (OBLS), and offers on average an 8-day business license processing time. The Ministry of Trade and Industry's Pro-Enterprise Panel also actively solicits feedback to remove rules and regulations that hamper businesses. Action Community for Entrepreneurship (ACE), a collaborative program between the private and government sectors, also facilitates debates on business rules and regulations.

Singapore offers a good environment for high-technology and information technology (IT) corporations. Singapore has strong intellectual property rights (IPR) protection. To resolve disputes in new frontiers such as e-commerce, Singapore Subordinate Courts offer alternative dispute resolution. To promote healthy competition among firms in the market, the newly established Competition Commission of Singapore administers and enforces the Competition Act.

Singapore also supports R&D-related businesses. Singapore Science Park provides the infrastructure in its three science parks. The Agency for Science, Technology and Research (A*Star)—through projects known as Fusionopolis (information and media industries) and Biopolis (biomedical sciences industry)—fosters scientific research in Singapore.

Other Government E-Services

The Government of Singapore offers various e-services to facilitate paper-work. Singapore Customs, for example, allows applications for registration, permits, and licenses to be submitted electronically. At the Immigration and Checkpoints Authority, applicants can extend Social Visit Passes and apply for visa or student passes online. Through the Inland Revenue Authority of Singapore's myTax Portal, taxpayers may file and pay their taxes online.

Services Trade Policies and Issues

Singapore accounts for nearly 2% of total global trade in services and ranks within the top 20 service-exporting countries in the world. The export com-position of services trade in Singapore is noted in Table 9.14. Transport ser-vices account for nearly 40% of Singapore's total export of services during 1994–2005. However, the share of the transport services is declining over the years, falling to nearly 35% in 2005 from 53% in 1994. The financial services is emerging as a strong sector for services export, rising to nearly 9.4% in 2005 from 1% in 1994 of total export in services.

Given financial sector liberalization in 1999 that removed the barriers for foreign banks to set up fully licensed banks in Singapore, the financial sector is expected to grow. The key focus of the liberalization is to position Singapore as a leading international financial center by attracting more global banks and more foreign investment in the services sector. The other important sector that has also been subjected to liberalization is the tele-communication sector. In 2000, the Government lifted foreign ownership limits in the telecommunication sector and allowed greater competition in telecommunications services. Temasek, the major shareholder of SingTel, announced a reduction of its shareholding from 67% to 5% in 2004.

Under the General Agreement on Trade in Services (GATS), Singapore has made commitments in services related to business, communications, construction, finance, transport, and tourism. Under its Schedule of Com-mitments, market access for natural persons is unbound, except for the temporary movement of intracorporate transfers of personnel up to 3 years, extending for another 2 years. Foreigners registering their companies in Singapore are subjected to commercial presence restrictions. However, most favored nation (MFN) exemptions apply for the following: preferences for workers from traditional source of supply, investment guarantees against unforeseen contingencies (such as war) only for signatories of Investment Guarantee Agreement with Singapore, and tax relief for income derived from a Commonwealth country (WTO 2004). Further exemptions are given for several services sectors that include legal services, broadcasting, maritime transport, insurance, banking and other financial services. Table 9.19 outlines Singapore's general approach to trade in services and its multilateral commitments in the services sector.

Bilateral trade accords, particularly the recent ones, also encompass liberalization of services trade and other behind the border impediments to trade and investment flows. They include trade and investment facilitation measures such as investment protection, harmonization and mutual recognition of standards and certification, protection of intellectual property rights, opening of government procurement markets, streamlining and harmonization of customs procedures, and the development of dispute settlement procedures (Table 9.20). Simultaneously, to the extent that contracting parties to a trade accord agree to move beyond their respective commitments under the WTO, there may be a demonstration effect that motivates future rounds of broader multilateral negotiations under the auspices of the WTO (Rajan and Sen 2002).

Singapore's trade pacts go beyond the GATS commitments to include financial services, business and professional services, telecommunications, education, and environmental services. For instance, trade in services is the main component of US–Singapore FTA, where there is substantial market access to the services sectors subject to a negative list that deals with sensitive government institutions and policy.[7] Examples of sectors where commitments that go beyond those made under the GATS include legal services (only for Australia and the US); business services; courier services (except in the FTAs with India and the Republic of Korea); maritime freight transport and other related services; basis telecommunications (no ownership restriction for facilities based services) in most FTAs; retailing services in all FTAs, although limits attached vary; air transport services (for selected FTA); and financial services (e.g., removal of foreign equity limits on insurance).

The FTAs with Australia and the US also contain provisions stating that anticompetitive practices would be addressed through legislation.

---

[7] A positive-list approach has been pursued with the European Free Trade Agreement, India, Japan, and New Zealand, and a negative-list approach has been pursued with Australia and the Republic of Korea.

Table 9.19 Singapore's Approach to Trade in Services in 2004

Section	Current Entry Requirements
Foreign investment or right of establishment (including joint venture requirements)	Commercial presence is generally unrestricted. Subject to notification and the following residency requirement, all forms of commercial presence are allowed in Singapore: - Business: One manager who is either a Singapore citizen, Singapore permanent resident, or Singapore Employment Pass holder ("locally resident"). Note: Employment Passes are essentially permits allowing foreigners to work in Singapore. - Branch: Two agents who are locally resident. - Local company: One director who is locally resident.
Temporary entry and stay of service providers and intracorporate transferees	Managers, executives, and specialists employed by foreign corporations (at least 1 year preceding the application for entry) may freely be transferred into local offices or affiliates in Singapore. They will be granted entry for a 2-year period, which may be extended for up to 3 additional years. Entry is subject to the usual immigration requirements. In the services areas listed below, there are no restrictions on trade other than horizontal measures (commercial presence and entry of natural persons) as outlined above: veterinary; dental; library; interior design, excluding architecture; software implementation; data processing; database; information technology consultancy; advertising; market research and public opinion polling; management consulting; public relations consultancy; biotechnology; those incidental to agriculture, hunting and forestry, fishing and mining; building cleaning; translation and interpretation; motion picture and video tape production, distribution, and projection; sound recording; general construction work for buildings; installation and assembly work; building completion and finishing work; hotel and restaurant. Cross-border supplies in terms of market access that are unbound due to lack of technical feasibility: travel agencies and tour operations; tourist guide services; economic and behavioral research; industrial research; freight transportation less cabotage; shipping brokerage and agency.
Foreign exchange controls	Singapore lifted all controls on foreign exchange in 1978.

Source: http://www.apec-iap.org

This is expected to apply to all activities including the private sector and GLCs in all sectors, unless there are exclusions and exemptions for reasons of public policy and interest. Singapore has also actively engaged in efforts to improve corporate governance through the voluntary Code of Corporate Governance for all listed companies. Specifically, a Council on

Table 9.20 Elements of Selected FTAs Negotiated by Singapore

Agreement / Sector	ANZSCEP	JSEPA	ESFTA	SAFTA	USSFTA
	Agreement with New Zealand for Closer Economic Partnership, since January 2001.	Agreement with Japan for a New-Age Economic Partnership, since November 2002.	Agreement with EFTA states, since January 2003.	Agreement with Australia, since July 2003.	Agreement with US since, January 2004.
Goods	Elimination of customs duties.	Elimination of tariffs based on a positive list. For the rest, tariff elimination is phased over a 3.5–8 year period.	Elimination of duties on industrial goods, and liberalization of duties on agricultural goods based on positive list; duties on processed agricultural and fish products to be liberalized based on positive lists with each EFTA state.	Elimination of customs duties.	Elimination of tariffs based on a positive list. For most exports to the US, immediate tariff elimination, and a transition period of 3–10 years for others.
Services	Based on a positive list; goal of free trade in services by 2010. Preferential treatment extended to non-parties engaged in "substantive business operations" in either of the parties.	Based on a positive list; preferential treatment also extended to non-parties engaged in "substantive business operations" in either of the parties.	Based on a positive list and to be reviewed with the goal of eliminating substantially all remaining restrictions in services covered at the end of 10 years.	Based on a negative list; preferential treatment extended to non-parties engaged in "substantive business operations" in either of the parties.	Based on a negative list, with exceptions to market access and national treatment listed in annexes.
	Singapore's commitments beyond GATS include professional, telecommunications, financial, business, and transport services.				
Contingency measures	No right to take safeguard measures against each others' imports; antidumping provisions are stricter than those applied under GATT Article VI.	May take emergency measures against each others' imports only during the 10-year transition period; antidumping measures to be in accordance with GATT Article VI.	May take emergency measures against each others' imports but not antidumping measures.	No right to take safeguard measures against each others' imports; anti-dumping rules are stricter than those applied under GATT Article VI.	Safeguard measures may be taken during the 10-year transition period; anti-dumping measures may be taken in accordance with GATT Article VI.

continued on next page

Table 9.20 (continued)

Agreement / Sector	ANZSCEP	JSEPA	ESFTA	SAFTA	USSFTA
	Agreement with New Zealand for Closer Economic Partnership, since January 2001.	Agreement with Japan for a New-Age Economic Partnership, since November 2002.	Agreement with EFTA states, since January 2003.	Agreement with Australia, since July 2003.	Agreement with US since, January 2004.
Intellectual property rights	WTO TRIPS Agreement provisions to apply.	WTO TRIPS Agreement provisions to apply. Cooperation on IPR matters, including through a joint committee.	WTO TRIPS Agreement provisions to apply.	WTO TRIPS Agreement provisions to apply. Cooperation inter alia on enforcement and education.	Singapore to accede to international conventions (i.e., WIPO Copyright Treaty).
Competition	Implement APEC Principles to Enhance Competition and Regulatory Reform. Mutual consultation on new competition measures.	Cooperation on controlling anticompetitive practices including the exchange of information on such practices.	Cooperation through consultations on eliminating anticompetitive business practices.	Mutual consultation and review to address anticompetitive practices.	Singapore to enact generic competition legislation by 2005, ensuring that government-linked corporations do not engage in agreements that restrain competition.
Investment	Provisions apply to all goods and those services listed in the parties' schedules.	Provisions apply to all goods and those services listed in the parties' schedules. Performance requirements are prohibited.	Provisions on investment do not apply to measures affecting trade in services and to investors investing in services (subject to a review after 10 years).	Provisions apply to all goods and services (except where reservations have been listed by the parties).	Negative list for goods and services except those scheduled, and detailed investor-state dispute settlement provisions. Performance requirements are prohibited.
Government procurement	Single market for procurement valued at over SDR50,000.	Provisions of the WTO GPA apply. Procurement threshold of SDR100,000.	Provisions of the WTO GPA apply.	Single market between the two parties.	Preferences up to S$102,710 for goods and services for ministries (S$910,000 for statutory boards), and S$11,376,000 for construction services.
Others					Provisions on labor and environment.

APEC = Asia-Pacific Economic Cooperation, EFTA = European Free Trade Association, FTA = free trade agreement, GATS = General Agreement on Trade in Services, GATT = General Agreement on Tariffs and Trade, GPA = Agreement for Government Procurement, IPR = intellectual property rights, SDR = Special Drawing Rights, TRIPS = Trade-Related Aspects of Intellectual Property Rights, US = United States, WIPO = World Intellectual Property Organization, WTO = World Trade Organization, S$ = Singapore dollar.

Source: WTO Secretariat, based on the texts of Singapore's bilateral free trade agreements. Ministry of Trade and Industry, Singapore: http://app.fta.gov.sg/

Corporate Disclosure and Governance was established in 2002 to prescribe and strengthen existing accounting standards, disclosure practices, and reporting standards in Singapore.

Because of FTAs with Australia, EU, New Zealand, and US, there have been significant changes in the framework of IPRs in Singapore. For example, Singapore extends copyright protection to the life of the author plus 70 years, measures against the circumvention of technologies that protect copyright works, imposes protection of well-known marks, and an extension of the patent term for pharmaceuticals because of the delays in marketing approval (WTO-plus TPE Singapore 2004). Further, Singapore has acceded to some international agreements regarding copyrights and marks (e.g., Madrid Protocol on 31 October 2000, Patent Cooperation Treaty, Trademark Law Treaty, UPOV [International Union for the Protection of New Varieties of Plants] convention in 1991, World Intellectual Property Organization [WIPO] Copyright in 1991 and 1996, and Phonograms Treaty in 1996) that were due to be effective by the beginning of 2005. Overall, bilateral FTAs are creating greater access to local markets and also helping harmonize the domestic regulatory framework across countries.

Growing Economic Relations with India—A Case Study in Deepening Integration Between South Asia and East Asia

Given India's needs for massive financial resources for development, and Singapore's desire to expand its external wing, one would have expected significant synergies between the two countries. This is particularly so in view of the close geographical proximity between the two countries (particularly South India and Singapore). However, it was only since the mid-1990s that Singapore started viewing India as a serious investment destination. Unlike companies from Japan or the Republic of Korea, Singapore-owned companies are rarely manufacturing powerhouses. Nonetheless, Singaporean companies have significant financial resources and expertise in infrastructural development such as townships, industrial parks, real estate, urban planning, airports and seaports.[8]

Singapore is particularly strong in the logistics sector, an area of comparative weakness for India. There are thus many collaborative ventures between Singapore and various states in India. For instance, the Port of Singapore Authority (PSA) has been involved in the development and management of the Tuticorin Port in Tamil Nadu and the Pipavav port in Gujarat, while Singapore's initial large-scale investment was in the multi-

---

[8] This section is based on Asher and Sen (2005).

million dollar IT Park in Bangalore in 1994 (by Singapore-based Ascendas). Singapore's investments in India encompass banking, infrastructure, pharmaceuticals, and telecommunications. The Government of Singapore's holding company, the Government of Singapore Investment Corporation (GIC), has emerged as a major foreign institutional investor in India, thus providing a greater deal of equity capital to many Indian businesses.

Many Indian companies are increasingly viewing Singapore as a good secondary base for operations to service overseas clients (in the event that services in India are disrupted as a result of conflict or natural disasters). Many Indian companies, such as Bilcare, eSys, Satyam, Tata Consultancy Services, and VSNL, have already established key regional operations in Singapore, and many more are likely to do so in the near future.

While Indian companies are finding it difficult to gain outsourcing contracts from Japanese and Korean firms because of the language and cultural differences, there is a belief that Singapore-owned and -based companies may be more willing and able to outsource to India on a larger scale.[9] At a strategic and political level, as noted, Singapore has been instrumental in helping India become more accepted into the broader East Asian community of nations. Aggregate trade between India and Singapore has been steadily growing since 1999, reaching $4.6 billion in 2003 and doubling the 1999 level by 2005 (Tables 9.21–9.23). Specifically, over the last 5 years, India's imports from Singapore have increased by 26.4%; during the same period, India's exports to Singapore have doubled.[10] In fact, in recent years, Singapore's trade with India has outpaced its growth with other Asian neighbors (Figure 9.9).

The growing closeness in ties between India and Singapore is apparent from the establishment of a bilateral Comprehensive Economic Cooperation Agreement (CECA) on 29 June 2005; the agreement came into force from 1 August 2005. The India–Singapore CECA consists of an FTA, a bilateral agreement on investment, an improved double taxation avoidance agreement, and a cooperation pact in areas like education, science, air services, media, e-commerce, intellectual property, and flow of human resources (Table 9.22).

The agreement aims to catalyze the growing flows of trade, investment, and people and intends to develop a long-term economic and strategic partnership between the two countries. Both countries have offered tariff concessions on a number of products. Given that Singapore has essentially

---

[9] Thus far, many of these companies have preferred outsourcing to other countries in the Association of Southeast Asian Nations (ASEAN), such as Malaysia or the Philippines. Other companies have chosen to automate many frontline services.

[10] Singapore's exports to India consist of re-exports, which constitute slightly over 50% of Singapore's exports to India.

Table 9.21 India's Bilateral Trade with Singapore, 1999–2003, $ Bn

Year	India's Exports to Singapore	India's Imports from Singapore	India's Imports from Singapore Less Entrepôt Trade	Total Bilateral Trade
1999	0.74	2.50	0.61	3.23
2000	1.06	2.74	0.48	3.81
2001	1.13	2.76	0.50	3.90
2002	1.18	2.67	0.40	3.85
2003	1.48	3.16	0.22	4.64

$ Bn = billions of US dollars.

Source: Federation of Indian Chambers of Commerce and Industry.

zero external tariffs, the bulk of the adjustment has fallen on India.[11] One of India's tariff concessions on goods refers to 506 products that have been identified in the early harvest list and are free of duties from 1 August 2005 (i.e., electronics, instrumentation, pharmaceuticals, and publishing). For a list of 4,609 products, a phased elimination is in place by 1 April 2009.[12] Some 6,551 products are on a negative list, meaning that they will not be liberalized and will continue to receive the MFN rates on their imports. India's concessions cover about 80% of Singapore's present exports to India.

Given the importance of the services sector to India and Singapore, the CECA has also focused on removing quantitative restrictions (and guaranteeing market access) on many professional services, education, distribution, financial, transportation, telecommunication, environmental, tourism, construction, and related engineering services. Most notable is the agreement on financial services, whereby India allows three Singapore banks to set up wholly owned subsidiaries in the country subject to meeting the Reserve Bank of India's (RBI) prudential norms. Singapore's three main local banks—DBS, OCBC, and UOB—are to be offered national treatment on par with Indian banks when it comes to branching, operating venues, and prudential requirements. Singaporean banks have also been permitted to acquire private Indian banks under the existing foreign investment policy framework, although they will have to comply with the overall restrictions imposed on foreign banks, and they cannot exceed 15% of total banking sector assets. Conversely, Indian banks and financial institutions have been granted preferential access into the Singapore market. Indian

---

[11] Singapore has negligible tariffs on all but six items and it has agreed to bind all its tariff lines at zero customs duty.

[12] Half of the products on this list will be on a fast-track scheme whereby their tariffs will be halved quickly.

**Figure 9.9 Singapore's Trade Growth with Asian Economies,
1990–2005, %**

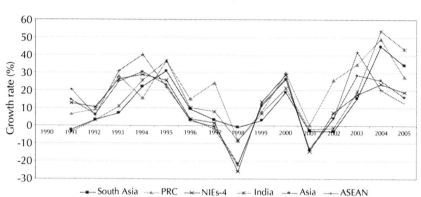

ASEAN = Association of Southeast Asian Nations; NIEs-4 = newly industrialized economies of Hong Kong, China; Republic of Korea; Singapore; and Taipei,China; PRC = People's Republic of China, % = percent.

Source: Asian Development Bank.

banks that satisfy Singapore's admission criteria will be given wholesale banking licenses and up to three bank licenses with qualifying full bank (QFB) privileges. This allows Indian banks in Singapore to undertake electronic fund transfers and establishing automated teller machines and clearances. In addition, Indian insurers and capital market intermediaries will have open access to Singapore.

Another notable aspect of the India–Singapore CECA pertains to the movement of natural persons (Mode 4). Specifically, both countries are to ease restrictions for temporary entry under four categories of persons: (i) business visitors, (ii) short-term service suppliers, (iii) professionals, and (iv) intracorporate transferees.

Given that Singapore accounts for almost half of India's trade with ASEAN, and that the CECA is the first comprehensive agreement that India has signed, it is understandable that the agreement is viewed in some quarters as a template for India's future dealings with East Asia. Particular attention has focused on India's willingness to liberalize its financial sector.

However, an important caveat should be kept in mind with regard to this sectoral liberalization. Concerns have been expressed in some quarters that India has not been able to obtain maximum reciprocal benefits from the agreement. Specifically, while Singapore has three main local banks that have all been given access to the large Indian market and Singapore has reciprocated by extending full licenses to three Indian banks, Singapore offered unlimited access to all US banks to Singapore. Table 9.23 summa-

Table 9.22 Key Features of India–Singapore Comprehensive Economic Cooperation Agreement

Sections	Provisions
Rules of origin	Local value-added rule of 40% and a change in tariff classification at the 4-digit level. Specific considerations for a list of products that is exempt from the general rule given unique production pattern of Singapore.
Standards and technical regulations, sanitary and phytosanitary measures	Key sectors that are included in this framework are electrical and electronics and telecommunication equipments.
Services sectors	Liberalization of various services sectors beyond commitments to the WTO.
	Asset management: Mutual funds and collective investment schemes could be listed on the stock exchange by registered fund managers in their respective countries.
	Telecommunication services: India will increase its limit from 25% to 49% for basic, cellular, and long-distance services and 74% for internet and infrastructure services. Singapore companies will be given access to public infrastructure to offer their services.
Movement of natural persons	Easier access for movement of natural persons. Intracorporate transferees (i.e., managers, executives, and specialist within organizations) will be permitted to stay and work in India and Singapore for an initial period of up to 2 years or the period of the contract, whichever is less. The period could be extended up to 3 years and total term not exceeding 8 years.
Education	University linkages: National University of Singapore (NUS)–Indian Institute of Technology Bombay (IIT–B) tie-up

WTO = World Trade Organization.

Source: Ministry of Trade and Industry, Singapore: http://app.fta.gov.sg/

rizes the commitments Singapore has offered to the US compared to those offered to India. There is pressure on the Government to ensure that, at the minimum, in future trade agreements India receives the same level of concessions offered to others.[13] Given the limited agricultural sector in Singapore, this issue has not been a point of contention; however, it could become a problem if India negotiates agreements with East Asian countries such as Japan that protect their agricultural sectors. Nonetheless, from Singapore's perspective, the CECA does not only promote trade in services and investment, but it also allows for certain deregulation of the Indian economy. It commits India to an open, liberal trade policy with Singapore, and thereby

---

[13] It might be unfair to focus on a single issue, but the important issue in such agreements is the idea of issue-linkage. For instance, India may have received somewhat less favorable terms on the financial services side but it has received concessions desired on cross-border labor mobility.

Table 9.23 Singapore's Financial Sector Commitments to India and the US

Type of Service	Commitments to US	Commitments to India
Qualified full-banking licenses	No restriction and free access to locations	Restricted to three licenses
Insurance (life and nonlife)	Free presence with National Treatment	Commercial presence under Mode 3 (i.e., need to establish branches)
Foreign exchange dealings	No approval needed	Require prior approval from local authorities
Investment advisory	National treatment for cross-border services	Curbs under Modes 1, 2, 3
Insurance brokers	Mode 3 presence not required	Placed under Mode 3 with commercial presence

US = United States.

Source: Srinath (2005).

locking-in to similar treatments to future bilateral negotiations with other countries in ASEAN.

Policy Implications

Singapore is among the most open and pro-business economies in the world. Singaporean policy makers' attention has always been on facilitating economic integration with the rest of the world, not simply a specific region or subregion. Indeed, it is notable that Singapore has signed a number of trade pacts with many Asian and non-Asian economies. While Singapore's overall exports to Asia have risen significantly (as discussed previously), this is arguably more an effect of rapid economic growth in the PRC and India, as well as general revitalization in East Asia since the Asian financial crisis of 1997/98.

Unlike small landlocked Asian economies such as Nepal, which depend heavily on their direct neighbors, Singapore is truly dependent on the global economy. What Singapore policy makers have therefore done is actively promote cross-border investment, and remove almost all barriers to trade. Measures to this end have included paperless trading, removal of visa restrictions for short-term business and leisure travelers, and increased transparency and certainty in regulations and procedures. Singapore has also actively participated in regional and international trade and investment forums and has simultaneously been vigorously seeking out bilateral trade pacts with many countries so as to integrate itself as much as possible with the global economy.

Despite progress in promoting and facilitating trade and investment, some challenges remain for Singapore.

One, it is commonly noted that since Singapore has one of the most liberal trade and investment regimes in the world, the scope for trade diversion (i.e., replacement of lower cost suppliers from nonmember countries) from Singapore's vantage point is quite small. Nonetheless, it would be wrong to conclude that there are no ill effects whatsoever. An important issue of concern is the extent to which various bilateral, subregional, and transnational arrangements might contradict each other, and if and how such contradictions will be overcome. However, the proliferation of a number of overlapping trade agreements raises many technical problems with regard to the implementation of special provisions or rules of origin (ROOs), which are meant to prevent goods being re-exported from and/or circumvented through the lower tariff country to the higher tariff one (i.e., trade deflection).

Even with a single FTA, a concern is that ROO with a particular country—for example, the US—may induce Singapore exporters to source their inputs from the US than some other developing country in Asia (such as the Republic of Korea, for instance). In other words, the US exports its external tariffs to Singapore. ROOs also give rise to significant costs due to the need for administrative surveillance and implementation. In practice, ROOs are particularly complex as they have to take into account tariffs on imported intermediate goods used in products produced within the FTA. The bookkeeping and related costs escalate sharply as production becomes more integrated internationally and countries get involved with an increasing Asian "noodle bowl" of separate but overlapping FTAs. For instance, under AFTA, imported products must be wholly produced in an ASEAN country or must have at least a cumulative basis of 40% of the finished product with ASEAN content. In the US–Singapore FTA, products must be wholly produced in the US, or for electronic products produced by Singapore or the US, value-added content must range from 30% to 60% of the free-on-board price of the final product. For certain chemical or petroleum products, a specified production process must have occurred in the US or Singapore to be considered for different tariff classification of the final product (see Appendix Table A9.10 for full details).

Concerted efforts must be taken by the policy makers to harmonize its ROOs in the various trade pacts it has signed and will continue to sign in the future. Given that the Singapore has been at the forefront of the FTA phenomenon, its policy makers will need to play a proactive role in establishing a set of multilateral ROOs and seeing it through to global acceptance and implementation.

Two, although both manufacturing and services are the twin engines for economic growth, increasingly, the services sector will play an important role in output and employment creation. As noted, several key factors are already in place for improving the efficiency and productive performance of the economy. Further improvements in and the successful implementation of the competition policy could greatly improve efficiency, competition, and economic openness. Particular attention needs to be paid to the further restructuring and liberalization of various infrastructure-related services, including telecommunications, energy, and finance. In this respect, the future role of GLCs in economic and global integration must be clearly defined in terms of their activities in the economy and greater corporate transparency. The introduction of the competition law that will apply to all private and GLCs is important in ensuring efficient markets, transparency, and competition.

Three, given that Singapore has taken a strong position in the bilateral FTAs that go beyond WTO provisions, the full benefits of such an undertaking could only be attained if ASEAN countries see the potential benefits of the WTO-plus bilateral FTAs in services. Since the services sector will be crucial for the next phase of growth, a common framework for a cohesive and coordinated ASEAN to engage bilateral agreements with major trading partners should be developed. Within ASEAN, the focus should be on enhancing the pace of integration of some sectors like tourism and air transport. Singapore can lead the way in this regard, given its comparative advantage in many services and its experience thus far with services liberalization. However, the extent of liberalization in ASEAN countries tends to be quite diverse. Indonesia, Malaysia, the Philippines, and Thailand have adopted a more defensive approach since the Asian financial crisis of 1997/98. ASEAN countries should be more proactive in negotiating on key sensitive sectors to reduce barriers to trade in services.

Singapore's FTAs appear to have energized other countries in ASEAN to adopt more proactive trade policies, and instilled a sense of urgency in liberalizing trade and investment policies. The response from ASEAN, especially Malaysia and Thailand, have been to seek their own FTAs to match the record number of FTAs signed by Singapore. The focus on creating trade has also revitalized the regional economies to promote deeper integration through ASEAN. In 2006, the ASEAN Secretariat announced that ASEAN member countries are well on their way toward establishing AFTA, with tariff elimination in the ASEAN-6 (Brunei Darussalam, Indonesia, Malaysia, Philippines, Singapore, and Thailand) and Cambodia, Lao People's Democratic Republic (Lao PDR), Myanmar, and Viet Nam, bringing down the tariff rates to the 0–5% range. The current emphasis of AFTA is on trade facilitation, liberalization of services, and opening up of the investment regimes in ASEAN. Clearly, the integration of the ASEAN market is an important factor in increasing the attractiveness of Southeast Asia as a destination for FDI. ASEAN integration is necessitated by intraregional production networks and the interest that investors have in ensuring larger market scale, especially against the background of the rise of the PRC and India. Multinational corporations continue to seek competitive and diversified locations for their production activities in East Asia. To capture a larger share of the opportunities that foreign investors create, a priority for Southeast Asian governments is to regain the momentum of national and regional regulatory and institutional reform that is the foundation of a strong investment environment.

Four, even more emphasis needs to be placed on IPR protection. For instance, the adoption and recognition of global standards on IPR will have significant impact on innovation and therefore on FDI in Singapore.

Five, while the Singapore International Arbitration Centre has entered into a joint venture with the American Arbitration Association to open a new arbitration center in Singapore—the International Centre for Dispute Resolution Singapore—further efforts are needed to ensure a more sophisticated and integrated dispute resolution complex to facilitate business transaction.

Six, the industrial strategy for moving to higher-value-added activities has, until recently, focused on multinational and GLCs. In this process, small and medium-sized enterprises (SMEs) have been critically marginalized. The development of SMEs will be crucial for the Singapore economy's next phase of growth and for Singapore to reap the full potential benefits of FTAs. With the disinvestment of GLCs and with the introduction of the competition policy noted previously, there should be greater scope for SMEs to compete in markets that have so far been dominated by GLCs. This should create greater entrepreneurial activities within the domestic economy. It bears keeping in mind that in a knowledge-based economy, entrepreneurship is crucial to dynamism and innovation.

Seven, another important area of development is in human capital. In the new global economy, the quality of human resources is key to success. Given that 34% of Singapore's labor force has a secondary education or below, it is imperative that the workforce should be retrained for the new growth areas in manufacturing and services. The aim of the Workers Development Agency (WDA) is to enhance the productivity and employability of the workers through training, retraining, and retaining workers in the labor market. Greater flexibility in the institutions to ensure rapid and flexible response to external shocks and imbalances will be very crucial for a small, open economy. The Government of Singapore has flexible labor market policy and introduced wage reform recently. This is to ensure greater flexibility and competitiveness in the wage system.

Eight, given the importance of foreign labor to supplement domestic labor and the continued dependence on business and tourism flows, continued effort needs to be placed on ensuring hassle-free immigration and customs procedures. Mutual recognition of foreign degrees, especially from selected institutes in South Asia, can facilitate Singapore's desire to remain attractive to global talent.

Nine, apart from the need to further strengthen the anticompetitive agreements, decisions and practices noted above, there is a need to ensure greater transparency in government tendering procedures so as to ensure openness, fairness, and efficiency in business operations and procedures.[14]

Ten, given Singapore's geographical location, multicultural environment, economic openness, and strategic position in regional trade, logistics, IT, business, and financial services, Singapore is uniquely placed to facilitate greater engagement between South and East Asia. Indeed, Singapore has played an important complementary role to India's Look East policy, hence facilitating India's integration fairly rapidly with the rest of East Asia. Singapore should continue to work toward integrating South and East Asia more closely via actively promoting the East Asian Summit (EAS) and promoting more open membership in APEC to include India and other South Asian economies. The city-state should also consider expanding its FTAs to include more South Asian economies in addition to India through bilateral pacts and/or three-way agreements. Given Singapore's strengths in logistics, including development of industrial parks and townships, Singapore can, along with Japan and the Republic of Korea, play a major role in the industrial development of India and the rest of South Asia and in turn help the Indian subcontinent to integrate even more closely with the rest of East Asia.

References

Arnold, J. 2007. The Role of Logistics Infrastructure and Trade Facilitation in Asian Trade. In *Pan-Asian Integration: Linking East and South Asia*, edited by J. F. Francois, P. B. Rana, and G. Wignaraja. Basingstoke: Palgrave Macmillan.

Asher, M. G., and R. Sen. 2005. India-East Asia Integration: A Win-Win for Asia. *Economic and Political Weekly* 40 (36): 3932–3941.

Audretsch, D. B. 2003. Entrepreneurship, Innovation and Globalization: Does Singapore Need a New Policy Approach? In *Sustaining Competitiveness in the New Global Economy: A Case Study of Singapore*, edited by R. S. Rajan. Cheltenham: Edward Elgar.

---

[14] GeBIZ is Singapore's one stop e-procurement system where those interested can find all procurement opportunities. Potential suppliers can register as a GeBIZ Trading Partner.

Baldwin, R. E. 2006. Multilateralising Regionalism: Spaghetti Bowls as Building Blocs on the Path to Global Free Trade. *The World Economy* 29(11): 1451–1518.

Bansal, R. 2004. The Monday Interview: Goh Chok Tong. *Financial Express.* July 12.

Bhaskaran, M. 2003. Structural Challenges Facing the Singapore Economy. In *Sustaining Competitiveness in the New Global Economy: A Case Study of Singapore*, edited by R. S. Rajan. Cheltenham: Edward Elgar.

Chia, S. Y. 1992. Foreign Direct Investment in ASEAN Economies. *Asian Development Review* 5: 60–102.

Das, S. B., and R. Sen. 2005. Singapore-India CECA: Rationale, Overview and Implications. In Investors Guide to India-Singapore Comprehensive Economic Cooperation Agreement, edited by M. Pillay. Singapore: Reed Elsevier.

Federation of Indian Chambers of Commerce and Industry (FICCI). 2005. FICCII Survey on India Thailand FTA – Emerging Issues, June. Available: www.ficci.com/ficci/surveys/The_India_Thailand_FTA-Report.pdf.

Ho, K. W., A. T. Koh, and S. Thangavelu. 2002. Enhancing Technopreneurship: Issues and Challenges. In *Singapore's Economy in the 21ˢᵗ Century: Issues and Strategies*, edited by A. T. Koh, K. L. Lim, W. T. Hui, and B. Rao. Singapore: McGraw Hill.

Hu, A., and J. Shin. 2002. Climbing the Technology Ladder: Challenges Facing Singapore in a Globalized World. In *Singapore's Economy in the 21ˢᵗ Century: Issues and Strategies*, edited by A. T. Koh, K. L. Lim, W. T. Hui, and B. Rao. Singapore: McGraw Hill.

International Monetary Fund (IMF). 2000. Singapore: Selected Issues. *Staff Country Report* No.00/83, Washington, DC: IMF.

Joint Study Group. 2003. Report on India–Singapore Comprehensive Economic Cooperation Agreement, April.

Lee, B. Y. 2002. Challenges of the New Economy. *Singapore.* September. Available: www.mfa.gov.sg/washington/sep2002.pdf

Lall, S. 2000. Export Performance, Technological Upgrading and Foreign Direct Investment Strategies in the Asian Newly Industrializing Economies: With Special Reference to Singapore. *Desarollo Productivo ECLAC Series No. 88.* Santiago, Chile: Economic Commission for Latin America and the Caribbean (ECLAC). October.

Ministry of Trade and Industry. 2005. India–Singapore Comprehensive Economic Cooperation Agreement (CECA). Information Kit, 29 June. Available: www.fta.gov.sg/

Rajan, R. S. 2003. Introduction and Overview: Sustaining Competitiveness in the New Global Economy. In *Sustaining Competitiveness in the*

New Global Economy: A Case Study of Singapore, edited by R. S. Rajan. Cheltenham: Edward Elgar.

———. 2004. Measures to Attract Foreign Direct Investment: Investment Promotion, Incentives. *Economic and Political Weekly* 39 (3): 12–16. January.

Rajan, R. S., and R. Sen. 2005. Singapore's New Commercial Trade Strategy: The Pros and Cons of Bilateralism. In *Singapore Perspectives 2002*, edited by L. L. Chang. Singapore: Times Academic Press.

———. The New Wave of Free Trade Agreements in Asia: With Particular Reference to ASEAN, China and India. *Asian Economic Cooperation and Integration: Progress, Prospects and Challenges*. Manila: ADB.

Rajan, R., R. Sen, and R. Siregar. 2002. Hong Kong, Singapore and the East Asian Crisis: How Important were Trade Spillovers? *The World Economy* 25(4): 503–37.

Roy, M., J. Marchetti, and H. Lim. 2006. Services Liberalization in New Generation of Preferential Trade Agreements: How Much Further than the GATS? Mimeo (September).

Sen, R., M. G. Asher, and R. S. Rajan. 2004. ASEAN-India Economic Relations: Current Trends and Future Prospects. *Economic and Political Weekly* 34: 3297–3309.

Srinath, S. 2005. Little Credit for Financial Services. *Business Line*, August 3.

Thanadsillapakul, L. 2006. The Investment Regime in ASEAN Countries. *Thailand Law Source*, December. Available: http://asialaw.tripod.com/articles/lawaninvestment.html

Thangavelu, S. M., and M. H. Toh. 2005. Bilateral "WTO-Plus" Free Trade Agreements: The WTO Trade Policy Review of Singapore 2004. *The World Economy* 28(9): 1211–1228.

Toh, M. H. 2006. Singapore's Perspectives on the Proliferation of RTAs in East Asia and Beyond. *Global Economic Review* 35: 259–284.

United Nations Conference on Trade and Development (UNCTAD). 2005. Case Study on Outward Foreign Direct Investment by Singaporean Firms: Enterprise Competitiveness and Development. November.

World Bank. 2005. *Doing Business in 2005 - Removing Obstacles to Growth*. Washington, DC: Oxford University Press for the World Bank.

World Trade Organization. 2004. Trade Policy Review: Singapore. Available: www.wto.org/English/tratop_e/tpr_e/tp229_e.htm

Yeung, H. 2000. Global Cities and Developmental States: Understanding Singapore's Global Reach. Mimeo. March.

Appendix Tables

Table A9.1 Singapore's Approach to Investment in 2004

Section	Current Investment Measures Applied
General Policy Framework	Singapore is committed to achieving a free and open investment regime, and the Government actively promotes foreign investment. The Economic Development Board (EDB), the agency that focuses on investment promotion, helps to provide information pertaining to investment.
	Businesses in Singapore need to register with the Accounting and Corporate Regulatory Authority, which was formed when the previous Registry of Companies and Businesses merged with the Public Accountants Board.
	With exceptions for national security and certain industries, no restrictions are placed on foreign ownership of businesses in Singapore. A few products require Government approval under the Control of Manufacture Act (COMA), although these regulations apply to both foreign and local investors. To date, items that require Government approval for manufacturing include beer and stout, cigars, drawn steel products, cigarettes, matches, and chewing gum (other than medicinal or oral-dental gum).
	To improve the protection of intellectual property rights and enhance the regulatory system for the manufacture of optical discs, the manufacture of optical discs is now legislated under the Manufacture of Optical Discs Act (MODA). A license is required for the manufacture of optical discs under MODA with effect from July 2004. Compact discs, compact discs with read-only memory (CD-ROMs), video compact discs (VCDs), digital video discs (DVDs), and digital video discs with read-only memory (DVD-ROMs), as well as master discs and stampers used in the production of optical discs are regulated under MODA rather than COMA. Laws, regulations, administrative guidelines, and policies are in place and continue to improve. If there are changes, public announcements are made and ample time provided for implementation.
	To enable a framework conducive to business growth and bilateral investments, Singapore has free trade agreements (FTAs) with ASEAN, Australia, European Free Trade Association, Japan, Jordan, New Zealand, and the United States (US).
Transparency	Singapore has a regulatory investment environment based on clarity, fair competition, and sound business practices. There are minimal investment regulations. The Asia-Pacific Economic Cooperation (APEC) Leaders' Transparency Standards on Investment apply, as described below.
	1. Singapore's investment laws, regulations, procedures, and administrative rulings for general application ("investment measures") are promptly published or made available online to enable interested persons and other economies to become acquainted with them. Investment measures apply to all investors, irrespective of nationality.

continued on next page

Table A9.1 (continued)

Section	Current Investment Measures Applied
2.	The Government of Singapore promotes feedback and consultation with relevant bodies and the public. The Government publishes in advance any investment measures proposed for adoption and provides a reasonable opportunity for public comment. There is a Government online consultation portal where public agencies post consultation papers to seek feedback and ideas.
3.	Upon request from an interested person or another economy, the Government of Singapore endeavors to promptly provide information and respond to questions pertaining to any actual or proposed investment measures. Suitable contact points including the EDB are in place to facilitate communications with the requesting party.
4.	Singapore has in place appropriate domestic procedures to enable prompt review and correction of final administrative actions, other than those taken for sensitive prudential reasons, regarding investment matters covered by the transparency standards. The system provides:
	(a) for tribunals or panels that are impartial and independent of any office or authority entrusted with administrative enforcement and have no substantial interest in the outcome of the investment matter;
	(b) parties to any proceeding with a reasonable opportunity to present their respective positions;
	(c) parties to any proceeding with a decision based on the evidence and submissions of record or, where required by domestic law, the record complied by the administrative authority; and
	(d) assurance subject to appeal or further review under domestic law, that such decisions will be implemented by, and govern the practice of, the offices or authorities regarding the administrative action at issue.
5.	There is no need for screening, evaluation, or scoring of projects for approval in Singapore. The COMA sets out the list of products that require approval and registration for manufacture. The list is applicable to all investors irrespective of nationality.
6.	The procedures for registering and licensing investment are kept clear and simple. Explanation of steps regarding application and registration and criteria for licensing—including information on standards, technical regulations, and conformity requirements—are published and made available online in Singapore. A central online business license service has started operating and will be further developed.
7.	No prior authorization of investment is required in Singapore and hence no procedures for this purpose exist. The Government has reviewed the procedures for business registration and license application to ensure that they are simple and transparent.
8.	Singapore, through the EDB, makes available to investors all rules and other appropriate information relating to investment promotion programs. These are also published under the Economic Expansion Incentives (Relief from Income Tax) Act available online.

continued on next page

Table A9.1 (continued)

Section	Current Investment Measures Applied
	9. Free-trade agreements negotiated contain investor–state dispute settlement mechanism and transparency provisions.
	10. Singapore participates fully in APEC-wide efforts to update the *APEC Investment Guidebook*.
Nondiscrimination	Singapore provides most-favored nation (MFN) treatment. All foreign investors are allowed to maintain 100% foreign equity and are free to make their own decisions on markets, technology licensing, and other investment areas. The Government actively encourages foreign investment and generally treats foreign capital the same as local capital. Generally there are no restrictions on the types of businesses that may be set up in Singapore, and there are no limitations on foreign companies' access to sources of finance. Singapore extends national treatment economy-wide.
Expropriation and compensation	The provision for expropriation and compensation is usually included in bilateral investment guarantee agreements (IGAs). There have been no disputes brought to court for expropriation of or compensation for foreign investment in Singapore.
Protection from strife and similar events	Singapore has bilateral IGAs with other economies to promote and protect investment coming into and going out of Singapore. In general, under the agreements, investments by nationals or companies of both contracting parties in each other's economy are protected for an initial period of usually 15 years against war and noncommercial risks like expropriation and nationalization. In the event of noncommercial risks, Singapore will compensate such foreign investors in a manner no less favorable than that which the latter party accords to investors of any third economy. There are similar provisions in Singapore's FTAs. To date, Singapore has signed IGAs with ASEAN; Bahrain; Bangladesh; the Belgo-Luxembourg Economic Union; Belarus; Bulgaria; Cambodia; Canada; People's Republic of China (PRC); Czech Republic; Egypt; France; Germany; Hungary; Mauritius; Mongolia; the Lao People's Democratic Republic; Latvia; Netherlands; Pakistan; Peru; Poland; Riau Archipelago; Slovenia; Sri Lanka; Switzerland; Taipei,China; United Kingdom; US; Viet Nam; Uzbekistan; and Zimbabwe. Besides bilateral IGAs, the Multilateral Investment Guarantee Agency (MIGA), which Singapore joined in 1998, provides guarantees at the multilateral level against certain noncommercial risks for eligible investors.
Transfers of capital related to investments	There are no restrictions on the repatriation or transfer of profits, capital gains, or dividends arising from investments. The free transfer of funds related to investment are included under bilateral IGAs and FTAs. As part of its globalization strategy, Singapore encourages its companies to invest abroad.
Performance requirements	There are no laws or policies stating performance requirements, local content requirements, or technology transfer requirements which are inconsistent with the World Trade Organization's (WTO) Trade-Related Investment Measures (TRIMs). All contracts are treated as commercial dealings.

continued on next page

Table A9.1 (continued)

Section	Current Investment Measures Applied
Entry and stay of personnel	Singapore welcomes foreign talent. Business or social visit passes are required for the temporary entry and sojourn of key foreign technical and managerial personnel for the purpose of engaging in activities connected with foreign investment. Foreign personnel require work passes to engage in employment. The three tiers of work passes are: (i) P passes for those who hold administrative, professional, or managerial jobs, or who are working as entrepreneurs, investors, or specialists; (ii) Q1 passes for skilled workers and technicians; and (iii) S passes for middle-tier skilled workers. Entry visas are required for holders of travel documents issued by the governments of Afghanistan; Algeria; Bangladesh; PRC; Egypt; Hong Kong, China (documents of identity); India; Iran; Iraq; Jordan; Lebanon; Libya; Morocco; Myanmar; Commonwealth of Independent States; Pakistan; Saudi Arabia; Somalia; Sudan; Syria; Tunisia; and Yemen.
Settlement of disputes	In its bilateral IGAs and FTAs, Singapore allows for prompt settlement of investment-related disputes through consultations, negotiations, and—in case of failure—arbitration. Singapore has institutionalized and internationalized arbitration. This has been achieved through (i) ratification of the International Convention on the Settlement of Investment Disputes between States and Nationals of other States and the Convention on the Recognition and Enforcement of Foreign Arbitral Awards (the New York Convention), and (ii) the creation of the Singapore International Arbitration Centre. Singapore enacted the Arbitration (International Investment Disputes) Act in 1968 to implement the Convention and the International Arbitration Act in 1994 to provide the framework for international arbitration. The latter was based on a model law adopted by the United Nations General Assembly (the United Nations Commission for International Trade Law [UNCITRAL]). The New York Convention makes more effective the international recognition of arbitration agreements and foreign arbitral awards, as well as the enforcement of arbitration awards.
Intellectual property	Singapore's intellectual property rights laws are in line with WTO requirements. Singapore has been a member of the World Intellectual Property Organization (WIPO) since 1990. Singapore has its own patent law, the Patents Act 1994 and the Patent Rules 1995, and has acceded to several international intellectual property treaties, including the Paris Convention, the Budapest Treaty, the Patent Cooperation Treaty, the Berne Convention, the Nice Agreement, and the Madrid Protocol. Accession allows patents and trade marks filed in Singapore to be examined worldwide. Copyright protection is provided under the Copyright Act without the need for registration or application. The Government has provided relatively good protection for intellectual property with enforcement and raids on counterfeit goods stepped up. To improve the protection of intellectual property rights and enhance the regulatory system for the manufacture of optical discs, a license is required for the manufacture of optical discs under the MODA.

continued on next page

Table A9.1 (continued)

Section	Current Investment Measures Applied
Avoidance of double taxation	Singapore has signed bilateral agreements to avoid double taxation with 52 economies. These are Australia; Austria; Bangladesh; Bahrain; Belgium; Bulgaria; Canada; PRC; Cyprus; Czech Republic; Denmark; Egypt; Finland; France; Germany; Hungary; India; Indonesia; Israel; Italy; Japan; Republic of Korea; Kuwait; Latvia; Lithuania; Luxembourg; Malaysia; Mauritius; Mexico; Mongolia; Myanmar; Netherlands; New Zealand; Norway; Oman; Pakistan; Papua New Guinea; Philippines; Poland; Portugal; Romania; Russia; South Africa; Sri Lanka; Sweden; Switzerland; Taipei,China; Thailand; Turkey; United Arab Emirates; the United Kingdom; and Viet Nam. The agreements generally allow tax credit for the foreign tax paid on the remitted amount up to the amount of Singapore tax payable on the same income.
Competition policy and regulatory reform	There are no antitrust or other laws to regulate competition in Singapore. All industries and services are developed to enhance national competitiveness. The Government is privatizing its services to stay ahead of competition. A new competition law is being developed to prevent companies from engaging in anticompetitive behavior. The public has been consulted, and the Competition Bill has been tabled in Parliament. A new statutory board would enforce the competition law.
Business facilitating measures to improve the domestic business environment	Besides quality physical infrastructure including one-stop-shop facilities for greater efficiency, legal, financial, accounting, taxation, corporate governance, and labor sourcing system capabilities are in place, serving well the domestic business environment and adding to Singapore's attractiveness for investment. The civil service has in place a Zero-In-Process (ZIP) program to provide swifter and more integrated service to the public. The BizFile program of the Accounting and Corporate Regulatory Authority enables business to set up shop in Singapore with a quicker and cheaper start. The E-government Action Plan I launched in June 2000 moved about 1,600 public services online as of July 2003, resulting in cost savings. Arising from the Economic Review Committee's call to minimize Government rules and regulations, the work of the Pro-Enterprise Panel (a joint public– and private-sector committee set up in 2000 to promote a more pro-business environment) and the Rules Review Panel resulted in the removal or relaxation of several rules and regulations. The International Accounting Standards was adopted as Singapore's accounting standard from January 2003. All Singapore-listed companies (except those with market capitalization of S$20 million and below, which were given 1 year's deferment) have to report financial accounts on a quarterly basis.

ASEAN = Association of Southeast Asian Nations, S$ = Singapore dollar.

Source: www.apec-iap.org

Table A9.2 Singapore's Current Tariff Arrangements

Section	Current Tariff Arrangement
Bound tariffs	Singapore has bound 5,636 (94%) of the total 5,981 tariff lines at rates of 6.5% and below. This excludes the 55 tariff lines for alcohol and tobacco products that have been bound at applied specific rates of duty. This is also based on 2002 HS Nomenclature.
Applied tariffs	Singapore has fully implemented the tariff elements of the sectoral proposals under the Early Voluntary Sectoral Liberalization (EVSL) initiative on the basis of the product coverage and end rates endorsed by Trade Ministers in June 1998. Customs and excise duties are only levied on four broad categories of goods: (i) intoxicating liquors, (ii) tobacco products, (iii) motor vehicles, and (iv) petroleum products. Of the tariff lines in these categories, only four lines of alcoholic products—beer, stout, medicated samsoo, and other samsoo—attract both customs and excise duties. There are 82 other tariff lines that attract excise duty. The complete list of dutiable goods and contact details are available at www.customs.gov.sg.
Tariff quotas	Singapore does not impose tariff quotas on any products.
Tariff preferences	Under ASEAN's Common Effective Preferential Tariff Scheme, (www.aseansec.org/economic/afta/afta_ag2.htm), with effect from 1 January 2001, Singapore offers duty-free access on all 6,036 tariff lines (HS 9-digit level, 2002) in the "inclusion list". Singapore also offers duty-free access for all 6,036 tariff lines (2002) to its various preferential trade partners.
Transparency of tariff regime	Six chapters, with 16 tariff headings of Singapore's tariff schedule (effective from 1 January 2002), are available for viewing in the Asia-Pacific Economic Cooperation forum's tariff database (www.apectariff.org/).

ASEAN = Association of Southeast Asian Nations, HS = harmonized system of commodity trade classification.

Source: www.apec-iap.org

Table A9.3 Singapore's Current Nontariff Measures Applied

Section	Current Nontariff Measures Applied
Quantitative import restrictions and prohibitions	• Chewing gum (excluding oral-dental and medicinal chewing gums) • Cigarette and table lighters in the shape of pistols or revolvers • Rough diamonds from Liberia and other countries that have not participated in the Kimberley Process • Round logs and timber products originating in Liberia • Firecrackers • Medicines/drugs containing amidopyrine, noramidopyrine, amygdalin, danthron, pangamic acid, and suprofen • Tobacco products that do not comply with stipulated nicotine and tar limits • Cosmetics containing prohibited substances and/or additives above the stipulated limits • Confectioneries, food products, toys, or other articles that are designed to resemble tobacco products or are sold in a package designed to resemble tobacco products • Articles of asbestos • Used motor vehicles more than 3 years old • Rhinoceros horn (parts and products) • Ivory for commercial consignments and tiger products • Plants of rubber, cocoa, coconut, and palm oil from Central and South America, as well as West and Central Africa • Controlled telecommunications equipment such as scanning receivers, military communication equipment, and automatic call diverters
Quantitative export restrictions and prohibitions	Under the Regulation of Imports and Exports Act, 1996, Singapore prohibits exports of certain products, for example arms and related materials, to certain countries, such as Iraq, Rwanda, and Sierra Leone. Some of the products prohibited for export include certain ozone-depleting substances, ivory and derivatives of tiger and rhinoceros horn, and scheduled chemicals under the Chemical Weapons Convention (CWC).
Import levies	None
Export levies	Singapore does not impose any levies on the export of goods.
Discretionary import licensing	• Artificial sweetening agents, food containing artificial sweetening agents, and irradiated food • Specific plants, plant products, and other materials (insects, microorganisms, and soil) • Endangered species

continued on next page

Table A9.3 (continued)

Section	Current Nontariff Measures Applied
Automatic import licensing	• Fruit or jackpot machines • Hazardous substances (poisons) • Radioactive materials and irradiating apparatus • Medicines, poisons, drugs, PRC proprietary medicines, and Category 1 cosmetic products • Controlled telecommunication equipment (other than those specified under the prohibited import list) • Rice • Poppy seeds (kaskas) • Precursor chemicals • Arms and explosives • Scheduled chemicals under the CWC–National Authority • Fresh fruits and vegetables; plants and plant produce; meat and meat products; animals, birds, eggs, and biologics; veterinary medicaments; animal feed; endangered species; imports, exports, or transshipments of fish other than ornamental fish; skimmed milk powder (colored for animal feed) • Amusement machines, coin or disc-operated, including pin-tables, shooting galleries, and cinematography machines • Mastering equipment and replication equipment for CDs, CD-ROMs, VCDs, DVDs, and DVD-ROMs • Publications, gramophone records, paintings, and prints • Films, videotapes, and video discs • Cellulose nitrates; machetes; axes; SOS shrill alarms; handcuffs; Christmas crackers; articles of clothing intended as protection against attack, including bulletproof vests; steel helmets; toy guns, including pistols and revolvers • Certain ozone-depleting substances (imports for re-export)
Discretionary export licensing	• Arms, ammunition, implements of war, and atomic energy materials and equipment • Articles of clothing for protection against attack (i.e., steel helmets, toy guns, and handcuffs) • Controlled drugs (e.g., morphine, pethidine, and other therapeutic products) under the Single Convention on Narcotics Drugs and psychotropic substances (e.g., diazepam, midozalam, and phentermine) under the Convention on Psychotropic Substances • Animals, birds, plants, and wildlife under the Convention on International Trade in Endangered Species (CITES)

continued on next page

Table A9.3 (continued)

Section	Current Nontariff Measures Applied
Voluntary export restraints	Under the World Trade Organization's (WTO) Agreement on Textiles and Clothing (ATC), Singapore maintains three bilateral export restraints with Canada, European Union (EU), and United States (US).
Export subsidies	Singapore's Double Tax Deduction (DTD) Scheme conforms to the WTO Agreement on Subsidies and Countervailing Measures.
Minimum import prices	Singapore does not impose any minimum import prices.

Other nontariff measures maintained	Technical Standards and Requirements
	• With effect from 1 January 2001, all petrol and diesel-driven vehicles, before they can be registered for use in Singapore, are required to comply with the exhaust emission standards as specified in the European Directive:
	  (i) 96/69/EC for passenger cars and light duty vehicles with maximum laden weight (MLW) of 3,500 kilograms (kg) or less, and
	  (ii) 91/542/EEC Stage II for heavy-duty vehicles with MLW of more than 3,500 kg.
	• Importers of bottled natural mineral, drinking, and spring water are required to submit to the Food Control Division of the Agri-Food and Veterinary Authority of Singapore an original health certificate issued by the country of origin for every incoming consignment. The document should show the source where the water is obtained and certify that the natural mineral, drinking, or spring water is genuine.
	• Importers of soy sauce, oyster sauce, beancurd sheets/sticks, porcelain foodwares, flour, starch, nuts, corn, irradiated food, mineral water, whisky/brandy, preserved fruits and vegetables, agar agar, or Eastern Europe foodstuffs are required to contact the Food Control Division of the Agri-Food and Veterinary Authority of Singapore or fax the import permit for inspection/sampling.
	• Importers of brandy and whisky are required to submit documentary evidence furnished by the place of origin confirming that the products have been aged in wood for a period of at least 3 years.
	• Electronic, electrical, and gas consumer products designated as controlled items are required to be registered with the Standards, Productivity and Innovation Board (SPRING Singapore) based on a type-test report with supporting documents. These products would be required to have a safety mark on them or their packaging. Regular and random market surveillance is conducted to ensure that only registered goods with the safety mark are supplied in the local market. These products include: components of liquefied petroleum gas (LPG) systems, gas cookers, electric cooking ranges, electric irons, microwave ovens, televisions, video cassette recorders, electric fans, electric kettles, immersion water heaters, refrigerators, rice cookers, room air conditioners, vacuum cleaners, washing machines, and hi-fi equipment.

continued on next page

Table A9.3 (continued)

Section	Current Nontariff Measures Applied
	• Under the Weights and Measures Regulations, any person in the business of repairing or manufacturing weighing or measuring instruments used for trade must have a valid license issued by SPRING Singapore. All new or repaired weighing or measuring instruments for trade use must be verified, sealed, and stamped by the Weights and Measures Office of SPRING Singapore as prescribed under the Weights and Measures Regulations.

Labeling and Packaging Requirements
• Meat and poultry must have a label containing the description of the product, name, and designation number of the slaughterhouse and/or processing establishment, date of slaughter and/or processing, batch number, net weight, and country of origin.
• Products with nutritional claims are required to have nutritional information panels on product labels.
• Date-marking is required for perishable and selected "high-risk" products.
• Labeling requirements exist for paints containing red lead oxide in which the lead content is more than 0.06% by weight or for paints containing other lead components in which the lead content is more than 0.25% by weight.
• Labeling requirements exist for medicines (including PRC proprietary medicines), poisons, and cosmetic products under the relevant legislation.
• Tobacco products are required to display stipulated health warning labels.

Antidumping, Countervailing, and Safeguard Measures
• Singapore currently does not impose any antidumping or countervailing duty.
• Singapore does not have any safeguard legislation.

Excise Duties
Excise duties are charged on four categories of products:
• Motor vehicles (excluding goods vehicles): 12% of open market value (OMV) for motorcycles and scooters; 20% of OMV for other passenger motor vehicles
• Petroleum products: specific rates
• Premium petrol (leaded): S$7.10/dekaliter (daL)
• Premium petrol (unleaded): S$4.40/daL

continued on next page

Table A9.3 (continued)

Section	Current Nontariff Measures Applied
	• Regular petrol (leaded): S$6.30/daL • Regular petrol (unleaded): S$3.70/daL • Other petrol (leaded): S$6.80/daL • Other petrol (unleaded): S$4.10/daL • Intoxicating liquors: specific rates S$0.80–70/liter of alcohol • Tobacco products: specific rates S$151–293/kg. For cigarettes, the duty imposed will be S$0.293 for the first gram or part thereof of each stick of cigarette and an additional S$0.293 for each additional gram or part thereof for each cigarette. Singapore charges a flat 5% tax on most goods and services irrespective of whether domestically produced or imported, with the exception of the grant, assignment, or surrender of any interest in, or right over, any residential properties, and financial services as listed on the Fourth Schedule to the Goods and Services Tax (GST) Act.

S$ = Singapore dollar.

Source: www.apec-iap.org

Table A9.4 Approved Manufacturing Investment Projects in Indonesia–Malaysia–Singapore Growth Triangle, by Industry Classification, 1995 and 1999, $ Mn

		1995					1999				
		Indonesia		Malaysia	Singapore	Total	Indonesia		Malaysia	Singapore	Total
SSIC		Sumatra	Batam	Johor			Sumatra	Batam	Johor		
15	Food products and beverages	35.46	–	19.53	65.28	120.27	238.62	1.0	11.53	149.56	399.7
16	Tobacco products	–	–	–	–	–	–	–	–	–	–
17	Textiles	1	–	16.17	2.33	19.5	–	–	10.71	–	10.71
18	Wearing apparel; dressing and dyeing fur	3.91	–	2.5	–	6.41	5.75	2.45	3.15	–	8.9
19	Tanning and dressing of leather; etc.	–	–	3.11	0.28	3.4	–	–	–	–	–
20	Wood, wood products, and cork, except furniture; etc.	8.39	–	52.93	–	61.32	2.37	0.3	0.12	–	2.49
21	Paper and paper products	–	–	17.93	13.06	30.98	0.85	0.85	250.92	1.47	253.25
22	Publishing, printing, and reproduction of recorded media	12.95	12.95	1.68	93.51	108.14	–	–	12.36	44.6	56.96
23	Coke, refined petroleum products, etc.	–	–	546.53	837.26	1,383.79	3,002.07	3,000.00	–	3.54	3,005.61
24	Chemicals and chemical products	4.5	4.5	248.02	1,117.78	1,370.31	0.9	0.5	29.12	1,557.23	1,587.25
25	Rubber and plastics products	18.79	17.79	25.88	38.67	83.34	4.77	4.77	8.19	49.91	62.87
26	Other nonmetallic mineral products	11.4	–	99.51	30.42	141.33	1	–	16.74	23.36	41.11

continued on next page

Table A9.4 (continued)

	1995					1999				
	Indonesia		Malaysia			Indonesia		Malaysia		
SSIC	Sumatra	Batam	Johor	Singapore	Total	Sumatra	Batam	Johor	Singapore	Total
27 Basic metals	–	–	21.73	45.02	66.75	0.87	0.87	6.11	8.5	15.47
28 Fabricated metal products, except machinery and equipment	44.73	44.73	24.13	196.54	265.4	4.75	2.25	6.97	176.76	188.48
29 Machinery and equipment, n.e.c.	2.52	2.02	56.54	233.52	292.59	4.72	4.72	30.47	287.2	322.38
30 Office, accounting, and computing machinery	5.08	5.08	–	–	5.08	2.17	2.17	–	–	2.17
31 Electrical machinery and apparatus n.e.c.	4.85	4.85	16.35	79.46	100.67	3.54	3.54	3.52	66.49	73.55
32 Radio, television, and communications equipment and apparatus	58.4	52.97	97.16	1,800.49	1,956.06	75.51	60.08	149.83	1,941.42	2,166.75
33 Medical, precision, and optical instruments	–	–	–	34.93	34.93	–	–	–	219.88	219.88
34 Motor vehicles, trailers, and semi-trailers	–	–	5.19	–	5.19	–	–	–	–	–
35 Other transport equipment	7.55	7.55	19.87	209.24	236.67	3.6	3.6	2.34	187.2	193.14
36 Furniture; manufacturing n.e.c.	–	–	16.26	7.55	23.81	1.09	–	6.23	24.72	32.04
37 Recycling	–	–	–	–	–	–	–	–	–	–
Others	–	–	1.24	–	1.24	–	–	–	–	–
Total	219.53	152.44	1,292.26	4,805.36	6,317.15	3,352.56	3,087.10	548.31	4,741.83	8,642.70
Foreign portion			3,424.42	4,936.20				3,691.50	7,592.37	

ASEAN = Association of Southeast Asian Nations, n.e.c. = not elsewhere classified, SSIC = Singapore Standard Industrial Classification, – = no data available, $ Mn = millions of US dollars.

Source: ASEAN Secretariat. ASEAN FDI Database, 2004.

Table A9.5 Approved Manufacturing Investment Projects in Indonesia–Malaysia–Singapore Growth Triangle by Industry Classification, 2003, $ Mn

	SSIC	Indonesia		Malaysia	Singapore	Total
		Sumatra	Batam	Johor		
15	Food products and beverages	143.21	–	62.47	–	**205.68**
16	Tobacco products	–	–	–	–	**–**
17	Textiles	2.20	2.20	2.82	–	**5.02**
18	Wearing apparel; dressing and dyeing of fur	–	–	0.61	–	**0.61**
19	Tanning and dressing of leather; luggage, etc.	0.29	0.15	1.46	–	**1.75**
20	Wood, wood products, and cork, except furniture; etc.	77.41	0.51	46.84	–	**124.26**
21	Paper and paper products	781.48	0.58	16.87	–	**798.35**
22	Publishing, printing, and reproduction of recorded media	–	–	–	–	**–**
23	Coke, refined petroleum products, etc.	–	–	–	–	
24	Chemicals and chemical products	10.03	2.00	14.22	2,070.60	**2,094.85**
25	Rubber and plastic products	9.23	6.73	46.14	211.20	**266.57**
26	Other nonmetallic mineral products	–	–	3.81	–	**3.81**
27	Basic metals	86.89	62.58	–	–	**86.89**
28	Fabricated metal products, except machinery and equipment	–	–	84.83	57.40	**142.23**
29	Machinery and equipment, n.e.c.	5.00	–	13.45	277.40	**295.85**
30	Office, accounting, and computing machinery	–	–	–	–	**–**

continued on next page

Table A9.5 (continued)

SSIC		Indonesia		Malaysia	Singapore	Total
		Sumatra	Batam	Johor		
31	Electrical machinery and apparatus, n.e.c.	1.0	–	4.91	–	5.91
32	Radio, television, and communication equipment and apparatus	–	–	31.97	4,224.10	4,256.07
33	Medical, precision, and optical instruments, etc.	2.46	2.46	3.96	–	6.42
34	Motor vehicles, trailers, and semi-trailers	1.10	1.10	–	–	1.10
35	Other transport equipment	0.38	0.38	3.61	–	3.99
36	Furniture; manufacturing, n.e.c.	3.75	1.40	5.69	670.20	679.64
37	Recycling	–	–	–	–	–
	Others	–	0.84	–	0.84	–
	Total	1,124.43	80.08	344.51	7,510.90	8,979.84
	Foreign portion			6,270.80	7,739.74	

ASEAN = Association of Southeast Asian Nations, n.e.c. = not elsewhere classified, SSIC = Singapore Standard Industrial Classification, – = no data available, $ Mn = millions of US dollars.

Source: ASEAN Secretariat. ASEAN FDI Database, 2004.

Table A9.6 Direction of Singapore's Exports, 1991–2005

Country/Region	$ Mn			% Share			% Growth rates		
	1991	1998	2005	1991	1998	2005	1991–1998	1998–2005	1991–2005
Asia	32,565	60,675	157,162	55.2	55.2	68.4	9.3	14.6	11.9
Bahrain	33	32	171	0.1	0.0	0.1	(0.5)	27.1	12.5
Bangladesh	363	675	695	0.6	0.6	0.3	9.3	0.4	4.8
Brunei Darussalam	553	615	496	0.9	0.6	0.2	1.5	(3.0)	(0.8)
Cambodia	–	296	303	–	0.3	0.1	–	0.3	–
China, People's Republic of	859	4,064	19,757	1.5	3.7	8.6	24.9	25.3	25.1
Hong Kong, China	4,252	9,221	21,522	7.2	8.4	9.4	11.7	12.9	12.3
India	1,000	2,436	5,893	1.7	2.2	2.6	13.6	13.5	13.5
Indonesia	–	–	22,103	–	–	9.6	–	–	–
Iran	147	91	494	0.3	0.1	0.2	(6.6)	27.3	9.0
Japan	5,114	7,231	12,532	8.7	6.6	5.5	5.1	8.2	6.6
Korea, Republic of	1,394	2,566	8,052	2.4	2.3	3.5	9.1	17.7	13.3
Kuwait	50	65	102	0.1	0.1	0.0	3.6	6.7	5.1
Lao PDR	–	20	40	–	0.0	0.0	–	10.4	–
Malaysia	8,818	16,746	30,385	15.0	15.2	13.2	9.6	8.9	9.2
Pakistan	262	313	646	0.4	0.3	0.3	2.6	10.9	6.7
Philippines	680	2,462	4,184	1.2	2.2	1.8	20.2	7.9	13.9
Saudi Arabia	453	382	425	0.8	0.3	0.2	(2.4)	1.5	(0.5)
Sri Lanka	231	524	681	0.4	0.5	0.3	12.4	3.8	8.0

continued on next page

Table A9.6 (continued)

Country/Region	$ Mn			% Share			% Growth rates		
	1991	1998	2005	1991	1998	2005	1991–1998	1998–2005	1991–2005
Thailand	3,704	4,209	9,402	6.3	3.8	4.1	1.8	12.2	6.9
United Arab Emirates	599	1,025	3,695	1.0	0.9	1.6	8.0	20.1	13.9
Viet Nam	–	1,514	4,421	–	1.4	1.9	–	16.5	–
America	13,307	24,383	29,044	22.6	22.2	12.6	9.0	2.5	5.7
Brazil	110	293	849	0.2	0.3	0.4	15.0	16.4	15.7
Canada	451	563	517	0.8	0.5	0.2	3.2	(1.2)	1.0
United States	11,654	21,868	23,871	19.8	19.9	10.4	9.4	1.3	5.3
Europe	9,835	19,597	29,104	16.7	17.8	12.7	10.4	5.8	8.1
European Union	8,555	17,417	26,418	14.5	15.8	11.5	10.7	6.1	8.4
France	689	2,257	3,625	1.2	2.1	1.6	18.5	7.0	12.6
Germany	2,467	3,328	6,306	4.2	3	2.7	4.4	9.6	6.9
Italy	557	515	593	0.9	0.5	0.3	(1.1)	2.0	0.4
Netherlands	1,516	3,787	5,480	2.6	3.4	2.4	14.0	5.4	9.6
Sweden	178	113	127	0.3	0.1	0.1	(6.3)	1.6	(2.4)
United Kingdom	1,784	3,730	6,318	3.0	3.4	2.8	11.1	7.8	9.5
Switzerland	447	1,128	668	0.8	1	0.3	14.1	(7.2)	2.9
Oceania	1,968	3,809	11,819	3.3	3.5	5.1	9.9	17.6	13.7
Australia	1,456	3,155	8,432	2.5	2.9	3.7	11.7	15.1	13.4
New Zealand	189	368	1,163	0.3	0.3	0.5	10.0	17.9	13.9
Africa	1,276	1,439	2,522	2.2	1.3	1.1	1.7	8.3	5.0
Total	58,953	109,905	229,652	100.0	100.0	100.0	9.3	11.1	10.2

Lao PDR = Lao People's Democratic Republic, – = not available, % = percent, ( ) = negative value, $ Mn = millions of US dollars.

Source: United Nations Commodity Trade Statistics Database; authors' calculation.

Table A9.7 Singapore Exports by SITC 1-Digit Category as a Percentage of Total Exports, 1995–2005, %

Country	Year	SITC Category									
		0	1	2	3	4	5	6	7	8	9
China, People's Republic of	1995	1.53	1.63	2.79	18.27	1.52	13.07	13.19	40.07	3.63	4.31
	2000	0.71	0.18	1.99	13.31	0.08	14.66	4.56	57.57	6.13	0.81
	2005	0.50	0.45	1.21	7.76	0.02	14.97	2.56	65.45	5.91	1.16
Hong Kong, China	1995	1.75	2.26	0.79	18.46	0.43	6.08	4.31	57.04	7.89	0.99
	2000	1.07	0.82	0.42	21.86	0.04	6.21	3.41	58.71	5.99	1.46
	2005	0.60	0.17	0.29	24.76	0.01	5.26	2.12	60.50	4.28	2.01
Indonesia	1995	0.97	0.13	5.60	34.33	0.95	21.18	5.95	25.39	5.49	0.01
	2000	1.06	0.02	2.05	45.53	0.22	19.72	9.12	19.99	2.29	0.00
	2005	1.59	0.08	1.11	69.07	0.11	12.16	4.31	10.35	1.22	0.00
Malaysia	1995	2.35	0.39	1.17	5.70	0.09	6.58	12.30	64.35	6.18	0.89
	2000	1.13	0.34	0.74	9.41	0.04	5.59	6.50	69.79	5.52	0.93
	2005	0.96	0.56	0.63	14.29	0.06	7.26	6.28	63.36	5.36	1.23

continued on next page

Table A9.7 (continued)

Country	Year	SITC Category									
		0	1	2	3	4	5	6	7	8	9
Philippines	1995	2.96	4.17	1.07	6.42	0.56	15.77	8.17	50.50	6.50	3.86
	2000	1.86	5.82	0.37	9.09	0.21	10.67	3.44	60.19	6.73	1.61
	2005	2.39	2.28	0.19	19.53	0.15	10.66	3.58	51.88	6.43	2.92
Korea, Republic of	1995	1.14	6.88	1.58	7.99	0.19	11.98	6.12	55.59	7.36	1.17
	2000	0.57	0.64	0.39	4.19	0.13	9.43	4.04	73.70	6.34	0.56
	2005	0.48	0.18	0.26	1.13	0.01	10.21	3.16	76.38	6.51	1.68
Thailand	1995	1.54	0.18	0.86	12.57	0.36	11.34	8.06	58.40	4.65	2.05
	2000	1.06	0.46	0.81	3.05	0.11	13.52	5.51	66.25	7.92	1.31
	2005	1.20	0.69	0.47	5.22	0.06	18.13	5.76	56.62	9.86	1.99
Viet Nam	1995	1.93	12.51	0.65	34.68	0.78	9.84	9.51	25.12	4.09	0.89
	2000	0.73	7.90	0.52	43.73	0.05	9.82	5.59	25.15	5.83	0.68
	2005	0.83	4.17	0.48	50.45	0.10	10.88	5.35	22.98	3.49	1.26

continued on next page

Table A9.7 (continued)

Country	Year	SITC Category									
		0	1	2	3	4	5	6	7	8	9
Bangladesh	1995	2.48	0.75	2.28	41.32	1.04	8.57	17.66	19.27	5.68	0.97
	2000	1.36	0.64	0.71	35.39	0.81	12.15	10.71	29.95	8.15	0.12
	2005	3.19	0.49	4.27	6.13	0.17	18.39	8.25	49.13	8.42	1.55
India	1995	1.02	1.18	5.34	12.38	0.37	9.77	13.71	43.65	8.33	4.27
	2000	0.95	0.66	2.49	11.13	0.20	13.57	8.41	50.16	10.99	1.44
	2005	0.33	0.29	1.58	12.64	0.07	14.63	6.25	51.68	9.81	2.73
Pakistan	1995	3.82	0.47	6.91	0.41	0.97	26.87	13.73	36.09	8.28	2.46
	2000	3.78	0.16	2.03	2.01	0.50	21.86	9.81	48.88	10.73	0.23
	2005	1.25	0.25	0.86	3.07	0.28	25.73	8.14	50.28	9.45	0.70
Sri Lanka	1995	2.38	0.92	4.35	4.09	1.74	16.62	27.48	29.48	9.66	3.29
	2000	1.49	1.98	1.64	11.55	1.82	14.33	12.72	39.47	7.80	7.20
	2005	2.20	1.47	1.97	17.81	0.88	13.83	9.09	39.58	6.22	6.95

Standard International Trade Classification (SITC): 0 – Food and live animals; 1 – Beverages and Tobacco; 2 – Crude materials; 3 – Mineral fuel; 4 – Animal and vegetable oils, fats; 5 – Chemical; 6 – Basic manufactures; 7 – Machinery and transport equipment; 8 – Miscellaneous manufactured goods; 9 – Goods not classified, % = percent.

Source: United Nations Commodity Trade Statistics Online.

Table A9.8 Singapore Imports by SITC 1-Digit Category as a Percentage of Total Imports, 1995–2005, %

Country	Year	SITC Category									
		0	1	2	3	4	5	6	7	8	9
China, People's Republic of	1995	8.05	3.23	1.96	5.36	0.06	4.01	25.53	39.99	11.54	0.29
	2000	3.25	0.63	0.64	8.09	0.04	2.91	11.42	60.96	11.86	0.20
	2005	1.55	0.42	0.31	6.51	0.07	2.53	8.87	69.27	10.13	0.34
Hong Kong, China	1995	1.23	1.57	0.28	0.21	0.01	1.88	7.94	62.31	23.18	1.38
	2000	1.19	0.09	0.23	0.37	0.01	2.53	6.65	63.20	24.85	0.88
	2005	0.59	0.75	0.51	0.01	0.00	2.06	6.10	68.71	20.83	0.45
Indonesia[a]	1995	8.47	0.28	8.82	16.61	0.37	1.89	18.88	29.83	13.92	0.91
	2000	5.50	0.18	2.47	11.96	1.21	3.35	14.30	49.21	8.12	3.71
	2005	4.18	0.75	3.03	10.49	2.27	3.40	17.44	53.01	4.41	1.02
Malaysia	1995	4.40	0.18	3.04	4.78	2.44	1.84	7.58	64.01	11.56	0.18
	2000	2.78	0.52	2.04	3.39	0.79	2.53	6.06	71.93	9.80	0.15
	2005	2.65	0.41	0.94	9.01	0.83	3.32	5.67	67.81	9.11	0.25

continued on next page

Table A9.8 (continued)

Country	Year	SITC Category									
		0	1	2	3	4	5	6	7	8	9
Philippines	1995	2.96	0.03	1.40	1.47	0.69	0.73	5.64	79.36	3.26	4.44
	2000	0.52	0.13	0.35	1.64	0.00	0.34	1.10	93.74	1.74	0.44
	2005	0.53	0.22	0.85	7.40	0.00	0.36	0.92	87.41	2.18	0.12
Korea, Republic of	1995	0.68	0.02	0.26	0.89	0.00	2.48	10.95	80.97	3.54	0.19
	2000	0.60	0.02	0.87	6.59	0.01	2.74	9.80	75.45	3.32	0.60
	2005	0.24	0.07	0.20	6.73	0.01	3.88	7.27	78.97	2.04	0.60
Thailand	1995	4.66	0.22	1.74	1.15	0.05	1.18	6.31	80.94	3.61	0.13
	2000	5.04	0.20	1.27	10.83	0.01	2.74	6.05	70.60	3.17	0.09
	2005	3.64	0.20	1.58	19.96	0.06	5.51	6.52	58.08	4.00	0.46
Viet Nam	1995	33.19	0.05	9.88	40.45	0.08	2.03	2.75	5.20	6.11	0.26
	2000	13.27	0.53	1.95	67.91	0.00	0.78	2.33	5.86	7.11	0.24
	2005	3.91	0.67	0.45	80.07	0.00	0.73	2.43	5.52	5.92	0.29
Bangladesh	1995	21.48	0.00	0.04	25.31	0.00	0.87	14.03	8.13	28.87	1.29
	2000	2.61	0.10	0.03	5.99	0.01	0.58	2.94	8.05	78.52	1.17
	2005	1.99	0.46	0.07	37.29	0.01	0.44	2.23	5.57	50.63	1.31

continued on next page

Table A9.8 (continued)

Country	Year	SITC Category									
		0	1	2	3	4	5	6	7	8	9
India	1995	10.21	0.16	4.38	1.84	0.30	9.14	37.80	24.09	11.81	0.27
	2000	5.86	0.50	2.63	9.81	0.05	11.91	29.98	26.90	11.85	0.51
	2005	1.79	0.24	1.42	26.55	0.03	6.93	49.89	6.90	5.93	0.32
Pakistan	1995	11.48	0.00	2.18	0.00	0.00	2.50	66.58	2.89	12.64	1.74
	2000	10.33	0.03	0.65	35.29	0.00	4.95	35.01	2.15	11.48	0.12
	2005	15.48	1.41	1.45	17.66	0.00	15.45	25.66	5.12	16.87	0.91
Sri Lanka	1995	24.47	0.14	6.74	8.67	0.10	2.08	10.04	31.01	15.55	1.20
	2000	24.04	0.30	1.09	25.84	0.15	2.61	10.59	25.39	8.82	1.18
	2005	18.43	3.39	1.52	0.00	0.00	6.16	11.83	45.53	12.53	0.60

[a] Indonesia's exports to Singapore are treated as Singapore imports from Indonesia.

Standard International Trade Classification (SITC): 0 – Food and live animals; 1 – Beverages and Tobacco; 2 – Crude materials; 3 – Mineral fuels; 4 – Animal and vegetable oils, fats; 5 – Chemical; 6 – Basic manufactures; 7 – Machinery and transport equipment; 8 – Miscellaneous manufactured goods; 9 – Goods not classified, % = percent.

Source: United Nations Commodity Trade Statistics Online.

Table A9.9 Singapore's Approach to Customs Procedures in 2004

Section	Current Activities/Measures
Greater public availability of information	Singapore's Customs Act and its subsidiary legislation, as well as the Regulation of Imports and Exports Act and its subsidiary legislation, are available on the internet and for sale to the public. Information on administrative regulations and procedures are also made available via brochures, circulars, helplists, guidebooks, call center, and the Customs' TradeNet™ and Strategic Goods Control websites.
	Information on customs procedures can be found at www.customs.gov.sg. Information on the TradeNet™ system can be found at www.tradenet.gov.sg. Information on strategic goods control system can be found at www.stgc. gov.sg.
	Singapore has in place an advance ruling system. Singapore Customs has a unit that attends to requests for advance rulings regarding classification of goods, rules of origin, etc. Advance rulings are made available on a list of frequently asked questions, circulars, and helplists on its website.
	Singapore has in place an open system for appeals. Businesses can approach Singapore Customs directly in writing, in person, or over the telephone for appeals to decisions or for clarification or redress. They can also appeal decisions on procedures at regular dialogue sessions or write to the Ministry of Finance for assistance and advice.
	Inquiry contact points to the various branches of Singapore Customs are provided on its website. The updating of information, disseminated through various channels, on customs procedures is an ongoing process.
Paperless trading	Singapore utilizes information technology extensively in its customs and trade operations.
	Currently, nearly 100% of all customs and trade declarations are submitted electronically through the TradeNet™ system, which complies with the United Nations' EDIFACT standards. When the declaration is approved by Customs, duties and goods and services tax (GST) assessed on the declaration will be electronically deducted via Inter-Bank GIRO.
	A paperless system has also been implemented for the clearance of containerized cargo at all checkpoints.

continued on next page

Table A9.9 (continued)

Section	Current Activities/Measures
Provision of temporary importation facilities	Singapore provides various facilities for temporary importation. Singapore has been a contracting party to the Convention on the ATA Carnet for the Temporary Admission of Goods (ATA Convention) since 1983. Goods, except tobacco products and liquors, can be imported under the Temporary Import Scheme for repairs, trade exhibitions, displays, and other approved purposes without payment of duty and/or GST. Bona fide trade samples can also be imported without payment of duty and/or GST. Since 2002, Singapore Customs has also accepted insurance bonds, in addition to bank guarantees, as a form of security for temporarily imported goods.
Implementation of clear appeals provisions	Singapore has in place an open system for appeals. Businesses can approach Singapore Customs directly in writing, in person, or over the telephone to appeal decisions or seek clarification or redress. They can also appeal decisions on procedures at regular dialogue sessions or write to the Ministry of Finance for assistance and advice.
Alignment with WTO valuation agreement	Singapore implemented the WTO Customs Valuation Agreement on 17 October 1997, 3 years ahead of schedule.
Adoption of Kyoto convention	Singapore is in the process of studying the Revised Kyoto Convention with a view of aligning customs procedures and practices with the convention's provisions.
Implementation of Harmonized System convention	Singapore has been using the Harmonized System (HS) for the classification of goods since 1 January 1989. Singapore implemented the 1996 version of the HS on 1 January 1996 and the HS 2002 amendments on 1 January 2002. Singapore implemented the ASEAN Harmonized Tariff Nomenclature (AHTN) on 1 January 2003. The Harmonized Codes are standardized at the 8-digit level for use by all ASEAN countries. The purpose of the AHTN is to promote consistency, predictability and uniform interpretation in the classification of goods, and to facilitate trade among the 10 ASEAN countries.
Implementation of an advance classification ruling system	Singapore has in place an advance classification ruling system. Singapore Customs has a classification section that attends to inquiries on the classification of goods. Classification certificates are issued upon request.
Implementation of the TRIPs agreement	Singapore's intellectual property protection regime pertaining to border enforcement is compliant with the TRIPS Agreement.
Development of a compendium of harmonized trade data elements	Singapore is studying the WCO Data Model sets against its own data requirements for customs and trade documentation. Singapore is also in the process of reviewing the structure and integrating certain aspects of the TradeNet™ system to remove excessive fields to facilitate trade declarations.

continued on next page

Table A9.9 (continued)

Section	Current Activities/Measures
Adoption of systematic risk management techniques	Singapore has implemented risk management techniques in cargo and passenger clearance operations.
	Radiographic inspection systems have also been deployed at the port areas since 2003 to allow containers to be inspected quickly and to improve the detection capability of border enforcement agencies.
Implementation of WCO guidelines on express consignment clearance	Singapore has an efficient electronic system known as the Advance Clearance for Courier and Express Shipments (ACCESS) for the clearance of express consignments.
Integrity	Singapore has put in place stringent standards to ensure a high level of integrity among its officers.
	Singapore Customs officers and border enforcement officers are briefed on integrity matters upon joining the civil service. Officers are also required to submit mandatory declarations of investments, assets, and indebtedness annually. Singapore Customs is also subjected to internal and external audit checks.
	The Prevention of Corruption Act is also in place and enforced by the Corrupt Practices Investigation Bureau.
Customs–business partnership	This CAP was established in February 2002. Singapore has in place official liaison channels with businesses and trade associations in the form of outreach sessions, trade consultations, regular dialogue sessions, and the Customs Advisory Committee, among others, to foster a better working relationship. A better working relationship would result in (i) obtaining feedback to improve the Government's requirements and procedures; and (ii) enhancing communication and cooperation between Singapore Customs and the business sector.
	Singapore has contributed four programs—ACCESS, dialogue sessions with trade, a Customs Advisory Committee, and the Customs Documentation Course—to the Compendium on Best Practices on Customs-Business Partnership compiled by Hong Kong Customs.

ASEAN = Association of Southeast Asian Nations, CAP = Collective Action Plan, EDIFACT = Electronic Data Interchange for Administration, Commerce, and Transport, TRIPS = Trade-Related Aspects of Intellectual Property Rights, WCO = World Customs Organization, WTO = World Trade Organization.

Source: www.apec-iap.org

Table A9.10 Singapore's Approach to Implementation of WTO Obligations

Section	Current Implementation Status of WTO Obligations
World Trade Organization (WTO) Agreement Annex 1A (Goods)	Singapore has already implemented its Uruguay Round tariff binding commitments, which bind 70% of tariff lines at rates of 10% and below by 1 January 1996.
	Singapore has brought its antidumping act (1996) and regulations (1997) into conformity with the WTO Agreement on Implementation of Article VI of the General Agreement on Tariffs and Trade and fulfilled the various notification requirements under the Agreement.
	Singapore has brought its countervailing duty act (1996) and regulations (1997) into conformity with the WTO Agreement on Subsidies and Countervailing Measures. Singapore also phased out its export subsidies or brought them into conformity with the Agreement by 1999, 3 years ahead of the committed timeframe.
	Singapore maintains stringent standards on agricultural and food safety while recognizing foreign national standards and testing carried out by competent foreign authorities in accordance with internationally accepted protocols.
	Singapore implemented the WTO Customs Valuation Agreement for assessing customs duty on imported goods on 17 October 1997. Singapore's Customs (Valuation) (Import Duty) Regulations conform to this Agreement.
	Singapore does not maintain any trade-related investment measures that do not conform with the Agreement on Trade-Related Investment Measures.
WTO Agreement, Annex 1B (Services)	Singapore has implemented its commitments under the General Agreement on Trade in Services.
WTO Agreement, Annex 1C (IPR)	Singapore implemented TRIPS on 1 January 1999, a year ahead of schedule.
WTO Multilateral Agreements	Singapore was one of the signatories to the WTO Ministerial Declaration on Trade in Information Technology Products, which was agreed at the close of the first WTO Ministerial Conference on 13 December 1996 in Singapore. The Information Technology Agreement (ITA) was implemented over four stages from 1997 to 2000. Singapore has implemented its ITA tariff binding commitments, in which all bindings are at zero rates of duty.

continued on next page

Table A9.10 (continued)

Section	Current Implementation Status of WTO Obligations
Rules of Origin (ROOs)	Singapore's ROOs are simple, liberal, and in compliance with the above disciplines. Singapore has notified the WTO of its existing ROOs. Essentially, there are no ROOs specifically applied to normal imports into Singapore. There are ROOs applicable to imports entering Singapore under the ASEAN comprehensive preferential tariff schemes. For normal exports to qualify as Singaporean in origin, they must either: (i) be wholly obtained in Singapore, or (ii) possess local content of at least 25% of the ex-factory price of the product if it is manufactured with imported materials. Products which undergo minimal processing are not conferred originating status. Applications for the Singapore Certificate of Origin (COO) can be made through Singapore Customs (http://www.tradenet.gov.sg) and six authorized organizations. Singapore has been actively participating in the harmonization work program being conducted under WTO and the World Customs Organization.

ASEAN = Association of Southeast Asian Nations, IPR = intellectual property rights, TRIPS = Trade-Related Aspects of Intellectual Property Rights.

Source: www.apec-iap.org

Index

Lightning Source UK Ltd.
Milton Keynes UK
27 November 2010

163526UK00002B/66/P